Toyota Yaris

Service and Repair Manual

R M Jex

Models covered *(4265 - 272)*

Hatchback, including special/limited editions
1.0 litre (998cc) & 1.3 litre (1299cc) petrol

Does NOT cover T-Sport, Free-Tronic/MMT clutchless transmission or Diesel models
Does NOT cover features specific to Verso models

ABCDE
FGHIJ
KLMNO
PQRST

A book in the **Haynes Service and Repair Manual Series**

ISBN **1 84425 265 5**

British Library Cataloguing in Publication Data
A catalogue record for this book is available from the British Library.

Printed in the USA

Haynes Publishing
Sparkford, Yeovil, Somerset BA22 7JJ, England

Haynes North America, Inc
861 Lawrence Drive, Newbury Park, California 91320, USA

Editions Haynes
4, Rue de l'Abreuvoir
92415 COURBEVOIE CEDEX, France

Haynes Publishing Nordiska AB
Box 1504, 751 45 UPPSALA, Sweden

Contents

LIVING WITH YOUR TOYOTA YARIS

Roadside repairs

Weekly checks

MAINTENANCE

Routine maintenance and servicing

Contents

REPAIRS AND OVERHAUL

Advanced driving

Many people see the words 'advanced driving' and believe that it won't interest them or that it is a style of driving beyond their own abilities. Nothing could be further from the truth. Advanced driving is straightforward safe, sensible driving - the sort of driving we should all do every time we get behind the wheel.

An average of 10 people are killed every day on UK roads and 870 more are injured, some seriously. Lives are ruined daily, usually because somebody did something stupid. Something like 95% of all accidents are due to human error, mostly driver failure. Sometimes we make genuine mistakes - everyone does. Sometimes we have lapses of concentration. Sometimes we deliberately take risks.

For many people, the process of 'learning to drive' doesn't go much further than learning how to pass the driving test because of a common belief that good drivers are made by 'experience'.

Learning to drive by 'experience' teaches three driving skills:

- ☐ Quick reactions. (Whoops, that was close!)
- ☐ Good handling skills. (Horn, swerve, brake, horn).
- ☐ Reliance on vehicle technology. (Great stuff this ABS, stop in no distance even in the wet...)

Drivers whose skills are 'experience based' generally have a lot of near misses and the odd accident. The results can be seen every day in our courts and our hospital casualty departments.

Advanced drivers have learnt to control the risks by controlling the position and speed of their vehicle. They avoid accidents and near misses, even if the drivers around them make mistakes.

The key skills of advanced driving are **concentration,** effective all-round **observation, anticipation** and **planning.** When **good vehicle handling** is added to these skills, all driving situations can be approached and negotiated in a safe, methodical way, leaving nothing to chance.

Concentration means applying your mind to safe driving, completely excluding anything that's not relevant. Driving is usually the most dangerous activity that most of us undertake in our daily routines. It deserves our full attention.

Observation means not just looking, but seeing and seeking out the information found in the driving environment.

Anticipation means asking yourself what is happening, what you can reasonably expect to happen and what could happen unexpectedly. (One of the commonest words used in compiling accident reports is 'suddenly'.)

Planning is the link between seeing something and taking the appropriate action. For many drivers, planning is the missing link.

If you want to become a safer and more skilful driver and you want to enjoy your driving more, contact the Institute of Advanced Motorists at www.iam.org.uk, phone 0208 996 9600, or write to IAM House, 510 Chiswick High Road, London W4 5RG for an information pack.

Working on your car can be dangerous. This page shows just some of the potential risks and hazards, with the aim of creating a safety-conscious attitude.

General hazards

Scalding

- Don't remove the radiator or expansion tank cap while the engine is hot.
- Engine oil, automatic transmission fluid or power steering fluid may also be dangerously hot if the engine has recently been running.

Burning

- Beware of burns from the exhaust system and from any part of the engine. Brake discs and drums can also be extremely hot immediately after use.

Crushing

- When working under or near a raised vehicle, always supplement the jack with axle stands, or use drive-on ramps. ***Never venture under a car which is only supported by a jack.***

- Take care if loosening or tightening high-torque nuts when the vehicle is on stands. Initial loosening and final tightening should be done with the wheels on the ground.

Fire

- Fuel is highly flammable; fuel vapour is explosive.
- Don't let fuel spill onto a hot engine.
- Do not smoke or allow naked lights (including pilot lights) anywhere near a vehicle being worked on. Also beware of creating sparks (electrically or by use of tools).
- Fuel vapour is heavier than air, so don't work on the fuel system with the vehicle over an inspection pit.
- Another cause of fire is an electrical overload or short-circuit. Take care when repairing or modifying the vehicle wiring.
- Keep a fire extinguisher handy, of a type suitable for use on fuel and electrical fires.

Electric shock

- Ignition HT voltage can be dangerous, especially to people with heart problems or a pacemaker. Don't work on or near the ignition system with the engine running or the ignition switched on.
- Mains voltage is also dangerous. Make sure that any mains-operated equipment is correctly earthed. Mains power points should be protected by a residual current device (RCD) circuit breaker.

Fume or gas intoxication

- Exhaust fumes are poisonous; they often contain carbon monoxide, which is rapidly fatal if inhaled. Never run the engine in a confined space such as a garage with the doors shut.

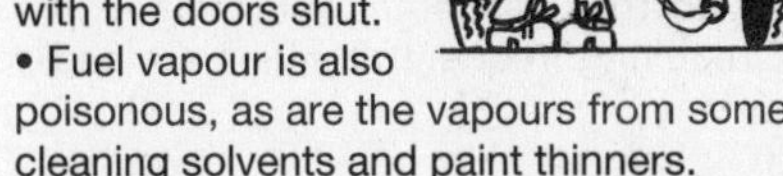

- Fuel vapour is also poisonous, as are the vapours from some cleaning solvents and paint thinners.

Poisonous or irritant substances

- Avoid skin contact with battery acid and with any fuel, fluid or lubricant, especially antifreeze, brake hydraulic fluid and Diesel fuel. Don't syphon them by mouth. If such a substance is swallowed or gets into the eyes, seek medical advice.
- Prolonged contact with used engine oil can cause skin cancer. Wear gloves or use a barrier cream if necessary. Change out of oil-soaked clothes and do not keep oily rags in your pocket.
- Air conditioning refrigerant forms a poisonous gas if exposed to a naked flame (including a cigarette). It can also cause skin burns on contact.

Asbestos

- Asbestos dust can cause cancer if inhaled or swallowed. Asbestos may be found in gaskets and in brake and clutch linings. When dealing with such components it is safest to assume that they contain asbestos.

Special hazards

Hydrofluoric acid

- This extremely corrosive acid is formed when certain types of synthetic rubber, found in some O-rings, oil seals, fuel hoses etc, are exposed to temperatures above 400°C. The rubber changes into a charred or sticky substance containing the acid. *Once formed, the acid remains dangerous for years. If it gets onto the skin, it may be necessary to amputate the limb concerned.*
- When dealing with a vehicle which has suffered a fire, or with components salvaged from such a vehicle, wear protective gloves and discard them after use.

The battery

- Batteries contain sulphuric acid, which attacks clothing, eyes and skin. Take care when topping-up or carrying the battery.
- The hydrogen gas given off by the battery is highly explosive. Never cause a spark or allow a naked light nearby. Be careful when connecting and disconnecting battery chargers or jump leads.

Air bags

- Air bags can cause injury if they go off accidentally. Take care when removing the steering wheel and/or facia. Special storage instructions may apply.

Diesel injection equipment

- Diesel injection pumps supply fuel at very high pressure. Take care when working on the fuel injectors and fuel pipes.

Warning: Never expose the hands, face or any other part of the body to injector spray; the fuel can penetrate the skin with potentially fatal results.

Remember...

DO

- Do use eye protection when using power tools, and when working under the vehicle.
- Do wear gloves or use barrier cream to protect your hands when necessary.
- Do get someone to check periodically that all is well when working alone on the vehicle.
- Do keep loose clothing and long hair well out of the way of moving mechanical parts.
- Do remove rings, wristwatch etc, before working on the vehicle – especially the electrical system.
- Do ensure that any lifting or jacking equipment has a safe working load rating adequate for the job.

DON'T

- Don't attempt to lift a heavy component which may be beyond your capability – get assistance.
- Don't rush to finish a job, or take unverified short cuts.
- Don't use ill-fitting tools which may slip and cause injury.
- Don't leave tools or parts lying around where someone can trip over them. Mop up oil and fuel spills at once.
- Don't allow children or pets to play in or near a vehicle being worked on.

The Toyota Yaris was introduced into the UK in March 1999, as the successor to the long-running Starlet. A completely 'clean-sheet' design, with no carry-over of parts from other models, the Yaris represents a true next-generation small car. Though shorter than its class rivals, passenger space is maximised through ingenious use of space, hinted at externally by the tall body, long wheelbase and minimal overhangs. The uniquely-styled facia, with its central instrument pod, also offers plenty of storage space.

Complementing the small yet spacious body are small-capacity (1.0 and 1.3 litre) engines which, thanks to multi-point injection, four valves per cylinder and variable valve timing, manage to offer the performance of larger units. The engines are mounted transversely at the front of the car.

As befits a modern supermini, the Yaris offers high levels of passenger safety, with an impact-absorbing bodyshell and highly-rigid cabin, driver's airbag and seat belt tensioners. Most of the latest models also have passenger and side airbags as standard, and the Yaris has recently been awarded a four-star Euro NCAP safety rating.

Three- and five-door Hatchback models are available, as well as a Verso 'estate' (not fully covered by this manual). From approximately 2001, the UK began receiving imports of Yaris models assembled in Toyota's French plant – generally speaking, these differ only in detail to those made in Japan. The range received a facelift in May 2003, with minor revisions to the headlights, bumpers and interior trim, as well as some safety-related improvements.

All models have front-wheel-drive, with a five-speed manual transmission (or an optional four-speed automatic on 1.3 litre models). The front suspension is of conventional MacPherson strut type, incorporating lower arms, and an anti-roll bar; at the rear, a semi-independent beam axle is combined with compact under-floor springs to provide a more spacious load area.

The Yaris has a high equipment level, even at the lower end of the model range. The latest models all feature a driver's airbag, anti-lock brakes, trip computer, engine immobiliser, adjustable rear seat, radio/cassette and power steering – central locking, electric windows and air conditioning are among the equipment fitted higher up the range.

For the home mechanic, the Yaris is a straightforward car to maintain and repair, since design features have been incorporated to reduce the actual cost of ownership to a minimum, and most of the items requiring frequent attention are easily accessible.

Your Toyota Yaris manual

The aim of this manual is to help you get the best value from your car. It can do so in several ways. It can help you decide what work must be done (even should you choose to get it done by a garage). It will also provide information on routine maintenance and servicing, and give a logical course of action and diagnosis when random faults occur. However, it is hoped that you will use the manual by tackling the work yourself. On simpler jobs it may even be quicker than booking the car into a garage and going there twice, to leave and collect it. Perhaps most important, a lot of money can be saved by avoiding the costs a garage must charge to cover its labour and overheads.

The manual has drawings and descriptions to show the function of the various components so that their layout can be understood. Tasks are described and photographed in a clear step-by-step sequence.

References to the 'left' and 'right' of the car are in the sense of a person in the driver's seat, facing forwards.

Acknowledgements

Thanks are due to Draper tools Limited, who provided some of the workshop tools, and to all those people at Sparkford who helped in the production of this manual.

We take great pride in the accuracy of information given in this manual, but car manufacturers make alterations and design changes during the production run of a particular car of which they do not inform us. No liability can be accepted by the authors or publishers for loss, damage or injury caused by any errors in, or omissions from, the information given.

The following pages are intended to help in dealing with common roadside emergencies and breakdowns. You will find more detailed fault finding information at the back of the manual, and repair information in the main chapters.

If your car won't start and the starter motor doesn't turn

- ☐ Open the bonnet and make sure that the battery terminals are clean and tight.
- ☐ Switch on the headlights and try to start the engine. If the headlights go very dim when you're trying to start, the battery is probably flat. Try jump starting (see next page) using another car.

If your car won't start even though the starter motor turns as normal

- ☐ Is there fuel in the tank?
- ☐ Has the engine immobiliser been deactivated? This should happen automatically, on inserting the ignition key. However, if a new key has been obtained (other than from a Toyota dealer), it may not contain the transponder chip necessary to deactivate the system.
- ☐ If it's a model with automatic transmission, the footbrake must be applied.
- ☐ Is there moisture on electrical components under the bonnet? Switch off the ignition, then wipe off any obvious dampness with a dry cloth. Spray a water-repellent aerosol product (WD-40 or equivalent) on ignition and fuel system electrical connectors like those shown in the photos. Pay special attention to the ignition coil wiring connectors.

A Check the condition and security of the battery connections.

B With the ignition off, check that the wiring connectors are securely connected to the four ignition coils.

C Check that the camshaft position sensor wiring plug is securely connected.

Check that electrical connections are secure (with the ignition switched off) and spray them with a water-dispersant spray like WD-40 if you suspect a problem due to damp.

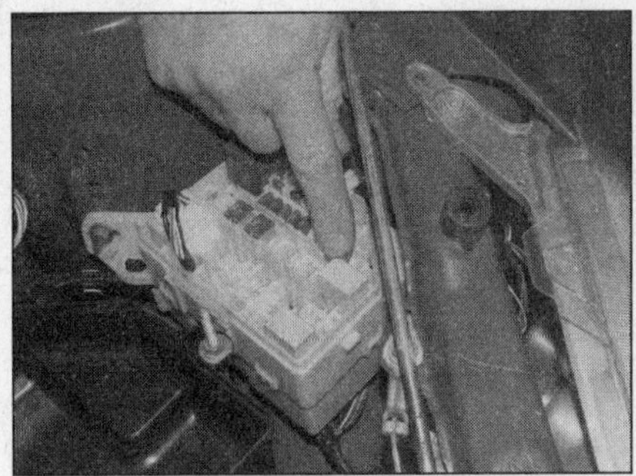

D With the ignition off, check the fuses and relays in the engine compartment fusebox.

Jump starting

When jump-starting a car using a booster battery, observe the following precautions:

- ✔ Before connecting the booster battery, make sure that the ignition is switched off.
- ✔ Ensure that all electrical equipment (lights, heater, wipers, etc) is switched off.
- ✔ Take note of any special precautions printed on the battery case.
- ✔ Make sure that the booster battery is the same voltage as the discharged one in the vehicle.
- ✔ If the battery is being jump-started from the battery in another vehicle, the two vehicles MUST NOT TOUCH each other.
- ✔ Make sure that the transmission is in neutral (or PARK, in the case of automatic transmission).

HAYNES HiNT

Jump starting will get you out of trouble, but you must correct whatever made the battery go flat in the first place. There are three possibilities:

1 The battery has been drained by repeated attempts to start, or by leaving the lights on.

2 The charging system is not working properly (alternator drivebelt slack or broken, alternator wiring fault or alternator itself faulty).

3 The battery itself is at fault (electrolyte low, or battery worn out).

1 Unclip the plastic cover from the jump-start terminal (+) on the top of the inlet manifold, and connect the red jump lead to the terminal.

2 Connect the other end of the red lead to the positive (+) terminal of the booster battery.

3 Connect one end of the black jump lead to the negative (-) terminal of the booster battery.

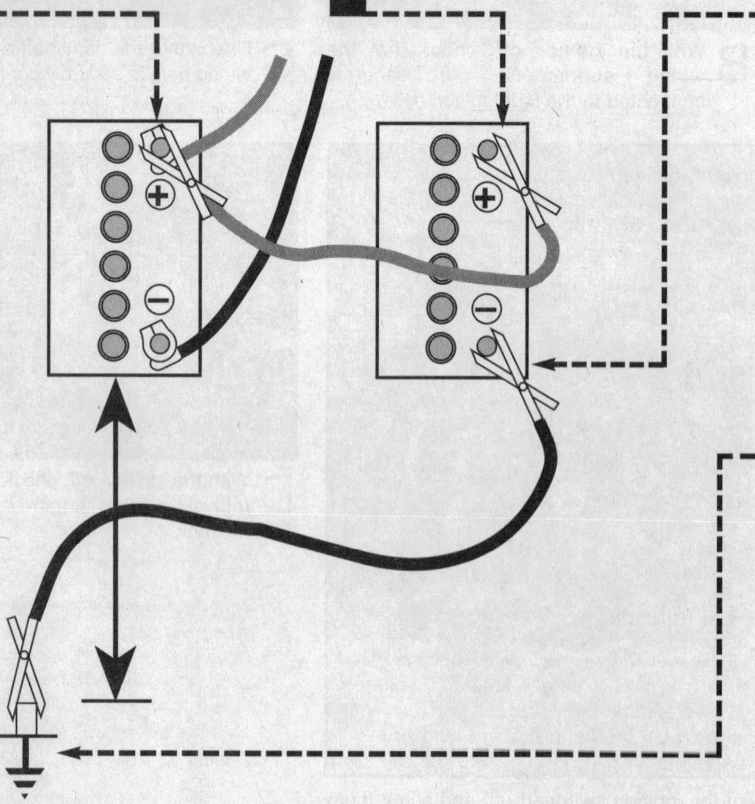

4 Connect the other end of the black jump lead to jump start negative terminal located on the right-hand suspension turret in the engine compartment.

5 Make sure that the jump leads will not come into contact with the cooling fan drivebelts or other moving parts on the engine.

6 Start the engine, then with the engine running at fast idle speed, disconnect the jump leads in the reverse order of connection, ie, negative (black) lead first. Securely refit the plastic cover to the jump start positive terminal.

Wheel changing

Warning: Do not change a wheel in a situation where you risk being hit by another vehicle. On busy roads, try to stop in a lay-by or a gateway. Be wary of passing traffic while changing the wheel – it is easy to become distracted by the job in hand.

Preparation

- ☐ When a puncture occurs, stop as soon as it is safe to do so.
- ☐ Park on firm level ground, if possible, and well out of the way of other traffic.
- ☐ Use hazard warning lights if necessary.
- ☐ If you have one, use a warning triangle to alert other drivers of your presence.
- ☐ Apply the handbrake, and engage first or reverse gear (or P on automatic transmission).
- ☐ Chock the wheel diagonally opposite the one being removed – a couple of large stones will do for this.
- ☐ If the ground is soft, use a flat piece of wood to spread the load under the jack.

Changing the wheel

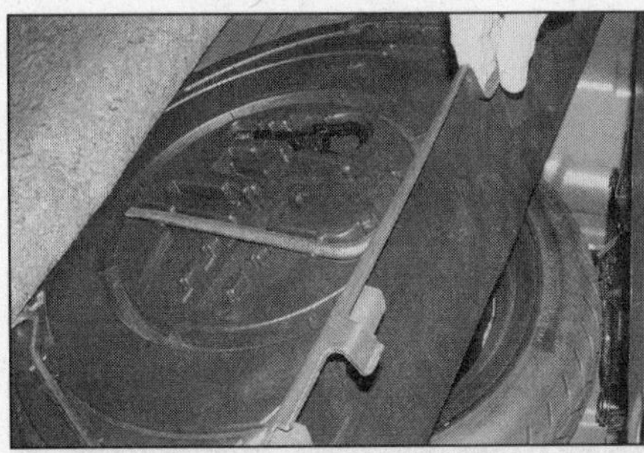

1 The spare wheel and tools are located in the luggage compartment, under the boot carpet. Fold back the carpet, then lift out the tool tray, which contains the jack handle, wheelbrace (and towing eye).

2 Unscrew the spare wheel retainer anti-clockwise, then lift out the spare wheel. The vehicle jack is stored next to the spare wheel, at the rear of the wheel recess.

3 Prise off the wheel trim (where applicable) from the punctured wheel, using the end of the wheelbrace. Use the wheelbrace to loosen each wheel nut by half a turn. On models with alloy wheels, one of the wheel nuts may be of the locking type – use the 'key' tool (a special socket usually provided in the glovebox) with the wheelbrace to undo this.

4 Locate the jack head below the jacking point nearest the wheel to be changed. The jacking points are between two small indentations in the sill lower edge. Only use the jack on firm, level ground. Ensure that the slot in the jack head engages with the sill flange at the jacking point.

5 Turn the jack handle clockwise until the wheel is raised clear of the ground. Remove the nuts and lift the punctured wheel clear.

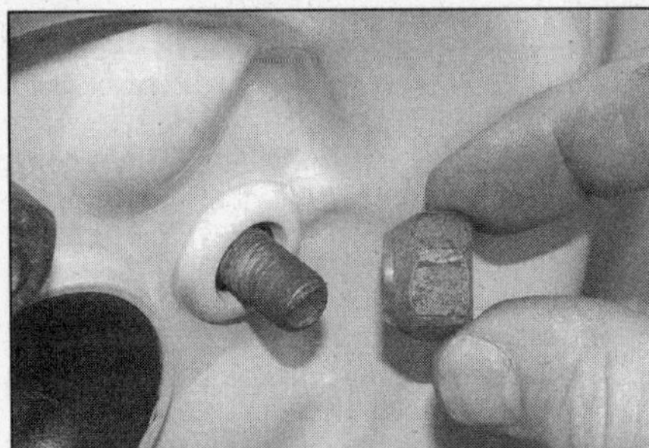

6 Fit the spare wheel. Refit the wheel nuts, tapered end inwards, and tighten moderately with the wheelbrace.

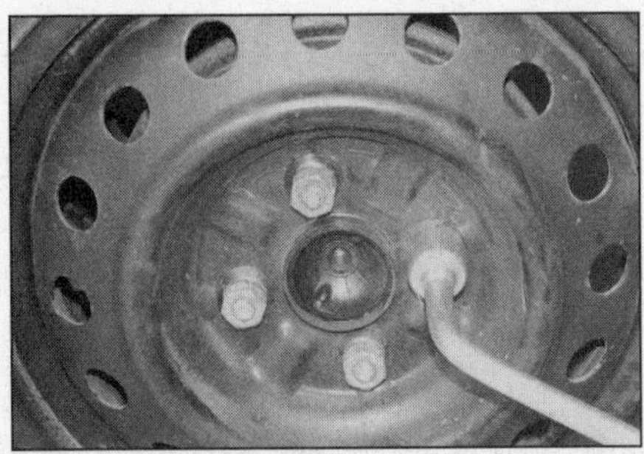

7 Lower the car to the ground, then finally tighten the wheel nuts in a diagonal sequence. Refit the wheel trim (where applicable). Ideally, the wheel nuts should be slackened and retightened to the specified torque at the earliest opportunity.

Finally...

- ☐ Remove the wheel chocks.
- ☐ Stow the jack and tools in the correct locations in the car.
- ☐ Check the tyre pressure on the wheel just fitted. If it is low, or if you don't have a pressure gauge with you, drive slowly to the nearest garage and inflate the tyre to the right pressure.
- ☐ The space-saver spare wheel is for temporary use only. Drive with extra care – limit yourself to a maximum of 50 mph, and to the shortest possible journeys, while it is fitted.
- ☐ Have the damaged tyre or wheel repaired as soon as possible.

Identifying leaks

Puddles on the garage floor or drive, or obvious wetness under the bonnet or underneath the car, suggest a leak that needs investigating. It can sometimes be difficult to decide where the leak is coming from, especially if the engine bay is very dirty already. Leaking oil or fluid can also be blown rearwards by the passage of air under the car, giving a false impression of where the problem lies.

Warning: Most automotive oils and fluids are poisonous. Wash them off skin, and change out of contaminated clothing, without delay.

The smell of a fluid leaking from the car may provide a clue to what's leaking. Some fluids are distinctively coloured.
It may help to clean the car carefully and to park it over some clean paper overnight as an aid to locating the source of the leak.
Remember that some leaks may only occur while the engine is running.

Sump oil

Engine oil may leak from the drain plug...

Oil from filter

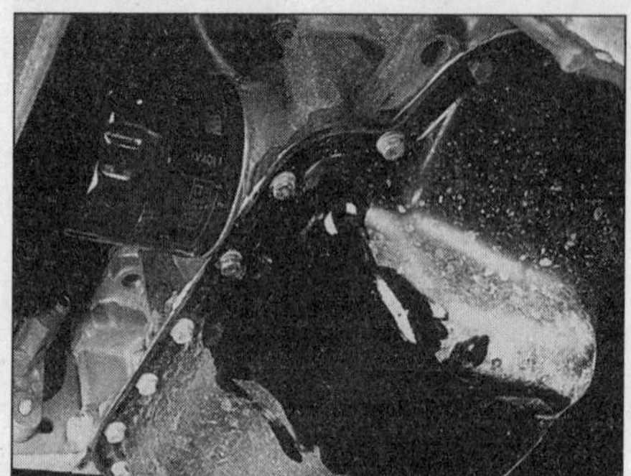

...or from the base of the oil filter.

Gearbox oil

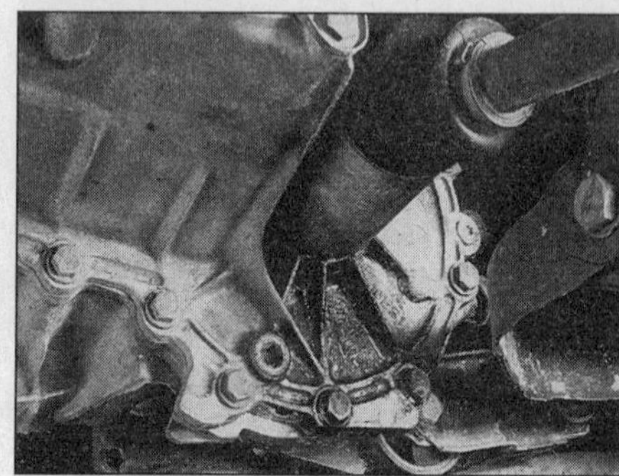

Gearbox oil can leak from the seals at the inboard ends of the driveshafts.

Antifreeze

Leaking antifreeze often leaves a crystalline deposit like this.

Brake fluid

A leak occurring at a wheel is almost certainly brake fluid.

Power steering fluid

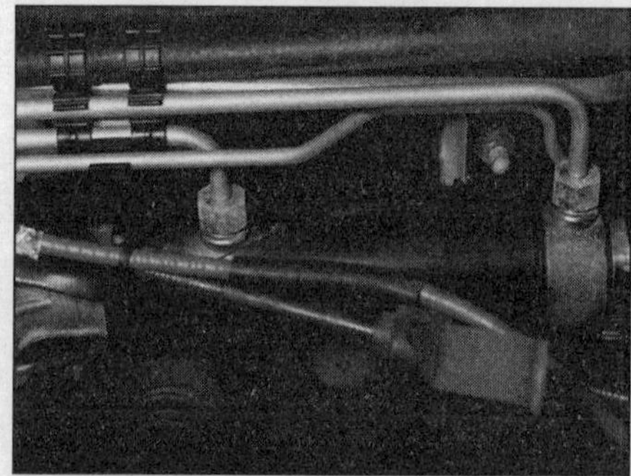

Power steering fluid may leak from the pipe connectors on the steering rack.

Towing

When all else fails, you may find yourself having to get a tow home – or of course you may be helping somebody else. Long-distance recovery should only be done by a garage or breakdown service. For shorter distances, DIY towing using another car is easy enough, but observe the following points:

☐ Use a proper tow-rope – they are not expensive. The vehicle being towed must display an ON TOW sign in its rear window.

☐ Always turn the ignition key to the 'on' position when the vehicle is being towed, so that the steering lock is released, and that the direction indicator and brake lights will work.

☐ Before being towed, release the handbrake and select neutral on the transmission.

☐ On models with automatic transmission, if possible, the car should be towed with its front wheels raised clear of the ground, or transmission damage may occur.

☐ Note that greater-than-usual pedal pressure will be required to operate the brakes, since the vacuum servo unit is only operational with the engine running.

☐ On models with power steering, greater-than-usual steering effort may also be required.

☐ The driver of the car being towed must keep the tow-rope taut at all times to avoid snatching.

☐ Make sure that both drivers know the route before setting off.

☐ Only drive at moderate speeds and keep the distance towed to a minimum. Drive smoothly and allow plenty of time for slowing down at junctions.

☐ A front towing eye is located with the jack and wheelbrace in the luggage compartment (see *Wheel changing*). The rear lashing eye (not designed for towing) is a conventional loop under the rear bumper. To fit the front towing eye, prise out the cover on the right-hand side of the front bumper, and remove it. Screw the towing eye in as far as it will go. Tighten the towing eye with the wheelbrace.

Introduction

There are some very simple checks which need only take a few minutes to carry out, but which could save you a lot of inconvenience and expense.

These *Weekly checks* require no great skill or special tools, and the small amount of time they take to perform could prove to be very well spent, for example;

☐ Keeping an eye on tyre condition and pressures, will not only help to stop them wearing out prematurely, but could also save your life.

☐ Many breakdowns are caused by electrical problems. Battery-related faults are particularly common, and a quick check on a regular basis will often prevent the majority of these.

☐ If your car develops a brake fluid leak, the first time you might know about it is when your brakes don't work properly. Checking the level regularly will give advance warning of this kind of problem.

☐ If the oil or coolant levels run low, the cost of repairing any engine damage will be far greater than fixing the leak, for example.

Underbonnet check points

◀ 1.0 litre engine

A *Engine oil level dipstick*
B *Engine oil filler cap*
C *Coolant reservoir (expansion tank)*
D *Brake and clutch fluid reservoir*
E *Power steering fluid reservoir*
F *Washer fluid reservoir*
G *Battery*

◀ 1.3 litre engine (typical)

A *Engine oil level dipstick*
B *Engine oil filler cap*
C *Coolant reservoir (expansion tank)*
D *Brake and clutch fluid reservoir*
E *Power steering fluid reservoir*
F *Washer fluid reservoir*
G *Battery*

Engine oil level

Before you start

✔ Make sure that your car is on level ground.

✔ Check the oil level before the car is driven, or at least 5 minutes after the engine has been switched off.

If the oil is checked immediately after driving the car, some of the oil will remain in the upper engine components, resulting in an inaccurate reading on the dipstick.

The correct oil

Modern engines place great demands on their oil. It is very important that the correct oil for your car is used (see *Lubricants and fluids*).

Car Care

● If you have to add oil frequently, you should check whether you have any oil leaks. Place some clean paper under the car overnight, and check for stains in the morning. If there are no leaks, the engine may be burning oil (see *Fault finding*).

● Always maintain the level between the upper and lower dipstick marks (see photo 3). If the level is too low, severe engine damage may occur. Oil seal failure may result if the engine is overfilled by adding too much oil.

1 The dipstick is located in a tube at the front of the engine on all engines (see *Underbonnet check points* on page 0•11 for exact location). Withdraw the dipstick.

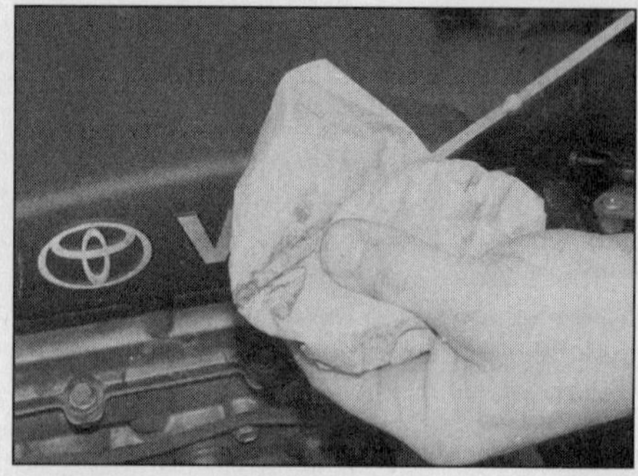

2 Using a clean rag or paper towel, wipe all the oil from the dipstick. Insert the clean dipstick into the tube as far as it will go, then withdraw it again.

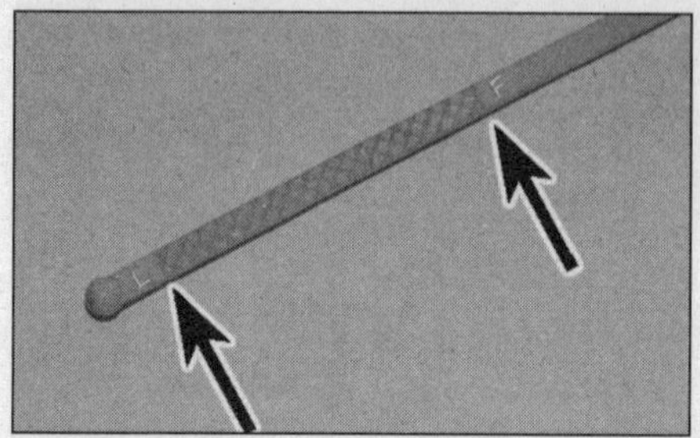

3 Note the oil level on the end of the dipstick, which should be within the 'hatched' area, between the upper (F) mark and the lower (L) mark. If the engine is very hot, the oil level may appear to be above the upper mark, owing to thermal expansion. Approximately 0.5 to 1.0 litre of oil will raise the level from the lower to the upper mark.

4 Oil is added through the filler cap. Unscrew the filler cap, then top-up the level. A funnel may help to reduce spillage. Add the oil slowly, checking the level on the dipstick often. Don't overfill.

Coolant level

Warning: DO NOT attempt to remove the expansion tank pressure cap when the engine is hot, as there is a very great risk of scalding. Do not leave open containers of coolant about, as it is poisonous.

Car care

● With a sealed-type cooling system, adding coolant should not be necessary on a regular basis. If frequent topping-up is required, it is likely there is a leak. Check the radiator, all hoses and joint faces for signs of staining or wetness, and rectify as necessary.

● It is important that antifreeze is used in the cooling system all year round, not just during the winter months. Don't top-up with water alone, as the antifreeze will become too diluted.

1 The coolant level varies with the temperature of the engine. The see-through expansion tank (located behind the radiator) has F (full) and L (low) level markings (which are hard to see, except from behind). When cold, the level should be between the two marks. When the engine is hot, the level may rise slightly above the F mark.

2 If topping-up is necessary, wait until the engine is **cold**, then remove the cap on the expansion tank.

3 Add a mixture of water and antifreeze to the expansion tank, until the coolant is up to the F mark. Use antifreeze of the same type (and colour) as that which is already in the system. Refit the cap securely.

Brake and clutch* fluid level

** The brake fluid reservoir also supplies fluid to the clutch master cylinder.*

Warning: Brake fluid can harm your eyes and damage painted surfaces, so use extreme caution when handling and pouring it.

- ***Do not use fluid that has been standing open for some time, as it absorbs moisture from the air, which can cause a dangerous loss of braking effectiveness.***

Safety first!

- If the reservoir requires repeated topping-up, this is an indication of a fluid leak somewhere in the brake or clutch system, which should be investigated immediately.
- The fluid level in the reservoir will drop slightly as the brake pads wear down, but the fluid level must never be allowed to drop below the MIN mark.
- If a leak is suspected, the car should not be driven until the braking system has been checked. Never take any risks where brakes are concerned.

1 The MAX and MIN marks are indicated on the side of the reservoir, which is located right at the back of the engine compartment, on the driver's side. The fluid level must be kept between these two marks.

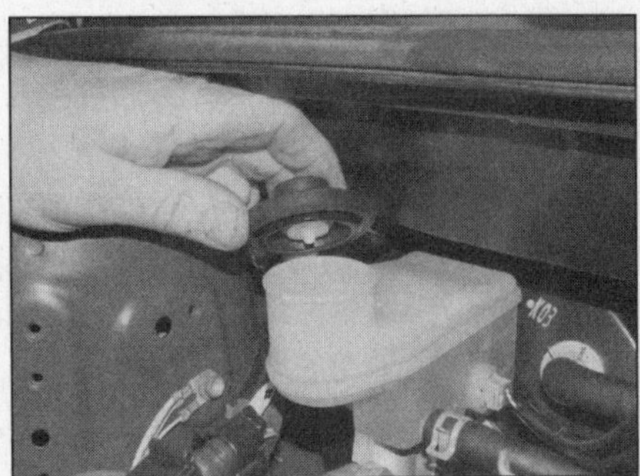

2 If topping-up is necessary, first wipe the area around the filler cap with a clean rag, then unscrew the cap. When adding fluid, it's a good idea to inspect the reservoir. The fluid should be changed if it appears to be dark, or if dirt is visible.

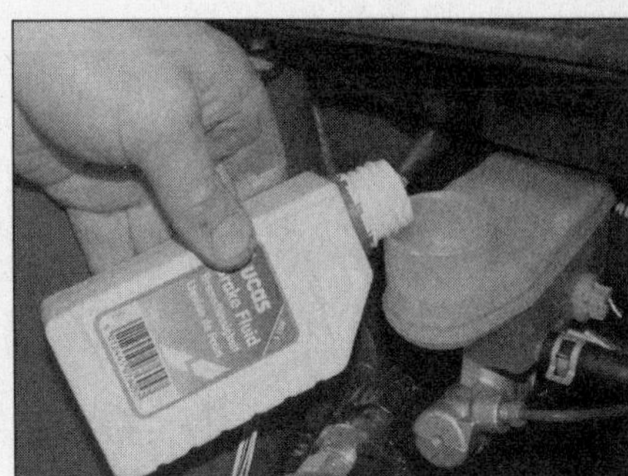

3 Carefully add fluid, avoiding spilling it on surrounding paintwork. Use only the specified hydraulic fluid; mixing different types of fluid can cause damage to the system and/or a loss of braking effectiveness. After filling to the correct level, refit the cap securely. Wipe off any spilt fluid.

Screen washer fluid level

Screenwash additives not only keep the windscreen clean during foul weather, they also prevent the washer system freezing in cold weather – which is when you are likely to need it most. Don't top-up using plain water as the screenwash will become too diluted, and will freeze during cold weather.

Warning: On no account use coolant antifreeze in the washer system – this could discolour or damage paintwork.

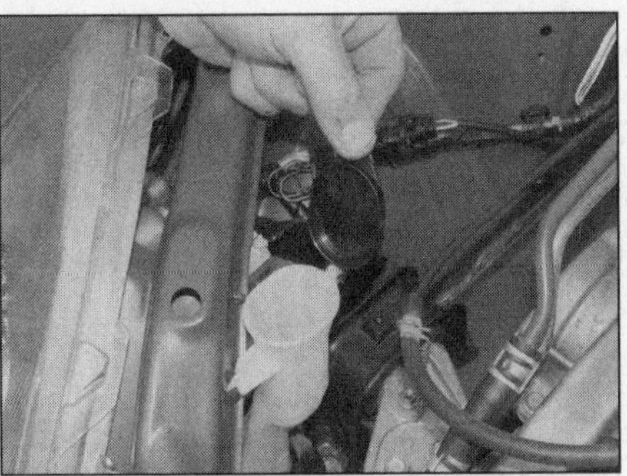

1 The windscreen/tailgate washer fluid reservoir filler neck is located on the driver's side of the engine compartment, behind the headlight. If topping-up is necessary, open the cap.

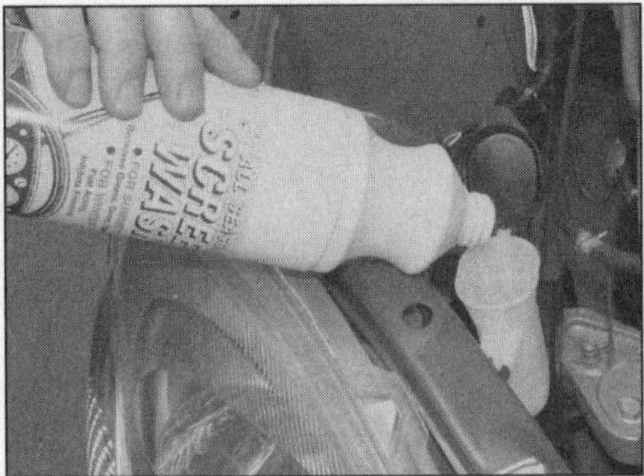

2 When topping-up the reservoir, a screenwash additive should be added in the quantities recommended on the bottle.

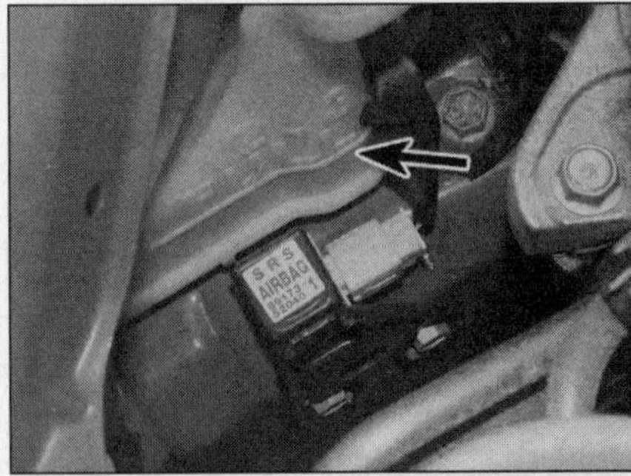

3 Though there's no harm in filling the bottle right up, there is a FULL level mark provided.

Power steering fluid level

Before you start

● The level should be checked either when the engine is cold (before the car is driven), or for greater accuracy, when the engine is hot (after a run of more than 5 miles).

● Note that models with manual or electric power steering do not use hydraulic fluid.

Safety first!

● The need for frequent topping-up indicates a leak, which should be investigated immediately.

1 The power steering fluid reservoir is located at the front of the engine compartment, next to the washer filler neck – on some models, however, it may be at the rear, next to the brake/clutch fluid reservoir. The fluid level should be checked with the engine stopped. Unscrew the filler cap, which incorporates a dipstick on the underside. Wipe the dipstick using a clean cloth.

2 Replace the filler cap loosely without screwing it down, so that the dipstick is inserted into the reservoir. Withdraw the dipstick/cap, and check the level on the dipstick. Two fluid level ranges are provided on the dipstick – depending on whether the fluid is hot or cold, the level should be in the HOT or COLD areas.

3 If topping-up is necessary, wipe the surrounding area so that dirt does not enter the reservoir. Top-up the fluid level to the top of the relevant area on the dipstick, using the specified type of fluid (do not overfill the reservoir), then refit and tighten the filler cap.

Wiper blades

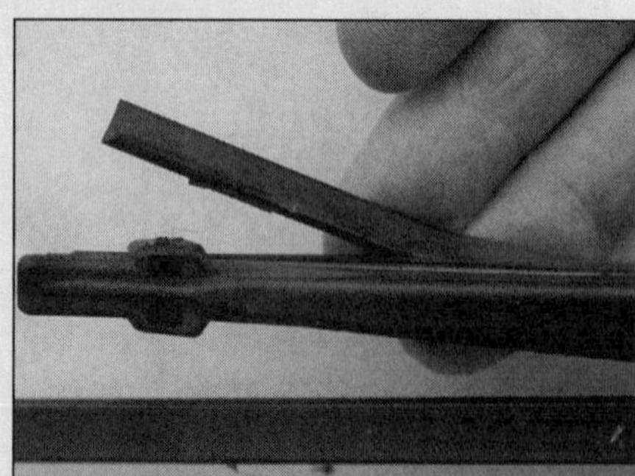

1 Check the condition of the wiper blades; if they are cracked or show any signs of deterioration, or if the glass swept area is smeared, renew them. For maximum clarity of vision, wiper blades should be renewed annually, as a matter of course.

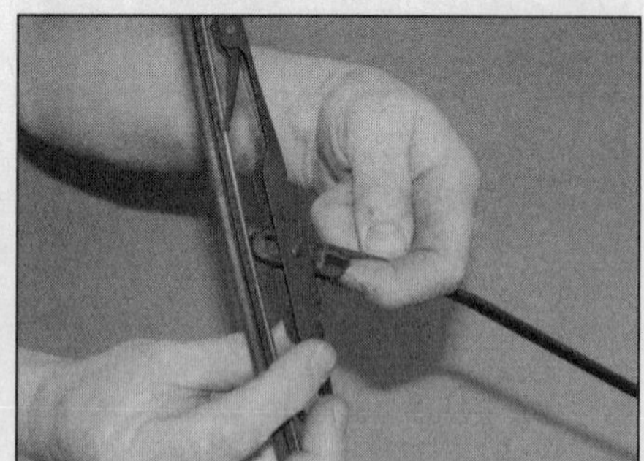

2 To remove a windscreen wiper blade, pull the arm fully away from the screen until it locks. Swivel the blade through 90°, then depress the locking clip at the base of the mounting block, and slide the blade out of the hooked end of the arm.

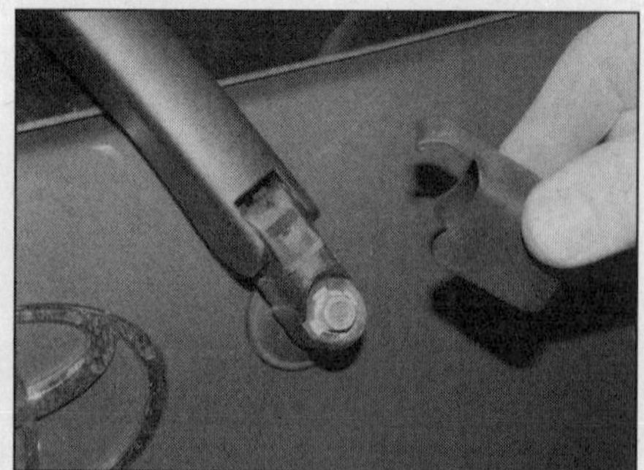

3 Don't forget to check the tailgate wiper blade as well. The blade and wiper arm appear to be one unit, so renewal would require a new wiper arm assembly. The wiper arm can be removed as described in Chapter 12 (but check with a Toyota dealer on parts availability first).

Tyre condition and pressure

It is very important that tyres are in good condition, and at the correct pressure - having a tyre failure at any speed is highly dangerous. Tyre wear is influenced by driving style - harsh braking and acceleration, or fast cornering, will all produce more rapid tyre wear. As a general rule, the front tyres wear out faster than the rears. Interchanging the tyres from front to rear ("rotating" the tyres) may result in more even wear. However, if this is completely effective, you may have the expense of replacing all four tyres at once!

Remove any nails or stones embedded in the tread before they penetrate the tyre to cause deflation. If removal of a nail does reveal that the tyre has been punctured, refit the nail so that its point of penetration is marked. Then immediately change the wheel, and have the tyre repaired by a tyre dealer.

Regularly check the tyres for damage in the form of cuts or bulges, especially in the sidewalls. Periodically remove the wheels, and clean any dirt or mud from the inside and outside surfaces. Examine the wheel rims for signs of rusting, corrosion or other damage. Light alloy wheels are easily damaged by "kerbing" whilst parking; steel wheels may also become dented or buckled. A new wheel is very often the only way to overcome severe damage.

New tyres should be balanced when they are fitted, but it may become necessary to re-balance them as they wear, or if the balance weights fitted to the wheel rim should fall off. Unbalanced tyres will wear more quickly, as will the steering and suspension components. Wheel imbalance is normally signified by vibration, particularly at a certain speed (typically around 50 mph). If this vibration is felt only through the steering, then it is likely that just the front wheels need balancing. If, however, the vibration is felt through the whole car, the rear wheels could be out of balance. Wheel balancing should be carried out by a tyre dealer or garage.

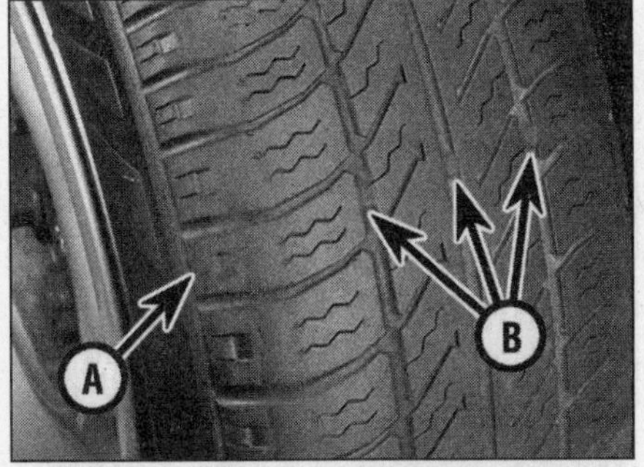

1 ***Tread Depth - visual check***
The original tyres have tread wear safety bands (B), which will appear when the tread depth reaches approximately 1.6 mm. The band positions are indicated by a triangular mark on the tyre sidewall (A).

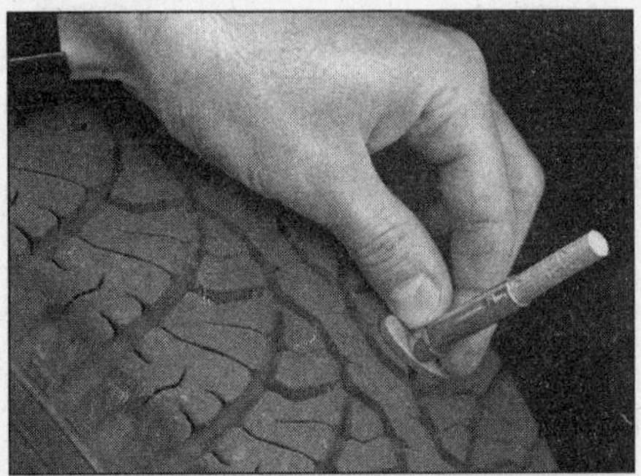

2 ***Tread Depth - manual check***
Alternatively, tread wear can be monitored with a simple, inexpensive device known as a tread depth indicator gauge.

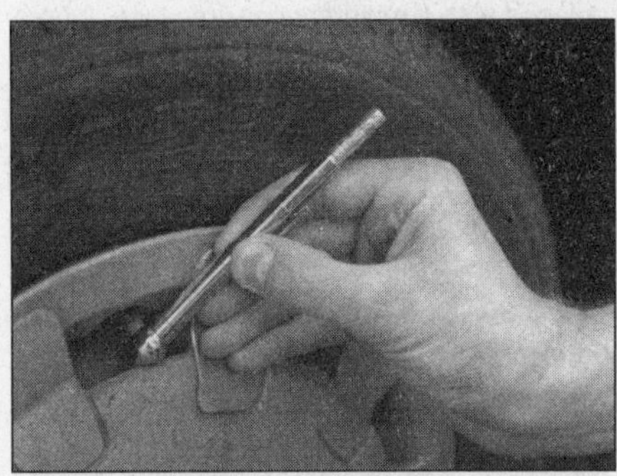

3 ***Tyre Pressure Check***
Check the tyre pressures regularly with the tyres cold. Do not adjust the tyre pressures immediately after the vehicle has been used, or an inaccurate setting will result.

Tyre tread wear patterns

Shoulder Wear

Underinflation (wear on both sides)
Under-inflation will cause overheating of the tyre, because the tyre will flex too much, and the tread will not sit correctly on the road surface. This will cause a loss of grip and excessive wear, not to mention the danger of sudden tyre failure due to heat build-up.
Check and adjust pressures
Incorrect wheel camber (wear on one side)
Repair or renew suspension parts
Hard cornering
Reduce speed!

Centre Wear

Overinflation
Over-inflation will cause rapid wear of the centre part of the tyre tread, coupled with reduced grip, harsher ride, and the danger of shock damage occurring in the tyre casing.
Check and adjust pressures

If you sometimes have to inflate your car's tyres to the higher pressures specified for maximum load or sustained high speed, don't forget to reduce the pressures to normal afterwards.

Uneven Wear

Front tyres may wear unevenly as a result of wheel misalignment. Most tyre dealers and garages can check and adjust the wheel alignment (or "tracking") for a modest charge.
Incorrect camber or castor
Repair or renew suspension parts
Malfunctioning suspension
Repair or renew suspension parts
Unbalanced wheel
Balance tyres
Incorrect toe setting
Adjust front wheel alignment
Note: *The feathered edge of the tread which typifies toe wear is best checked by feel.*

Battery

Caution: Before carrying out any work on the battery, read the precautions given in 'Safety first!' at the start of this manual.

✔ Make sure that the battery tray is in good condition, and that the clamp is tight. Corrosion on the tray, retaining clamp and the battery itself can be removed with a solution of water and baking soda. Thoroughly rinse all cleaned areas with water. Any metal parts damaged by corrosion should be covered with a zinc-based primer, then painted.

✔ Periodically (approximately every three months), check the charge condition of the battery as described in Chapter 5A.

✔ If the original Toyota battery has been replaced with a maintenance-free type, ignore the advice about topping-up the water (this will usually be impossible in any case, with such a battery).

✔ If the battery is flat, and you need to jump start your car, see *Roadside repairs*.

HAYNES HiNT

Battery corrosion can be kept to a minimum by applying a layer of petroleum jelly to the clamps and terminals after they are reconnected.

1 The battery is located on the passenger side of the engine compartment. The exterior of the battery should be inspected periodically for damage such as a cracked case or cover.

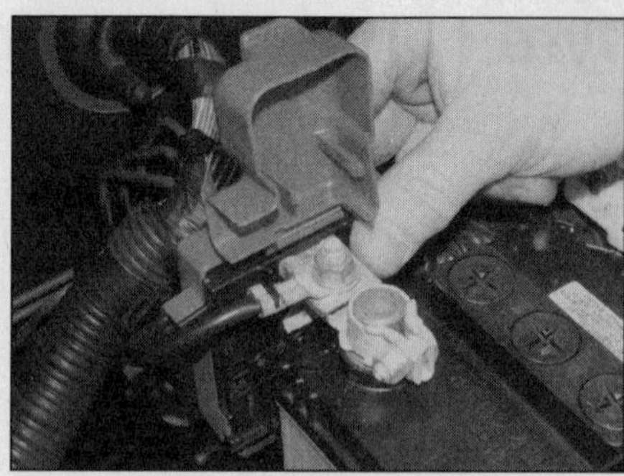

2 Check the tightness of the battery cable clamps to ensure good electrical connections. You should not be able to move them. Also check each cable for cracks and frayed conductors. If corrosion (white, fluffy deposits) is evident, remove the cables from the battery terminals, clean them with a small wire brush, then refit them.

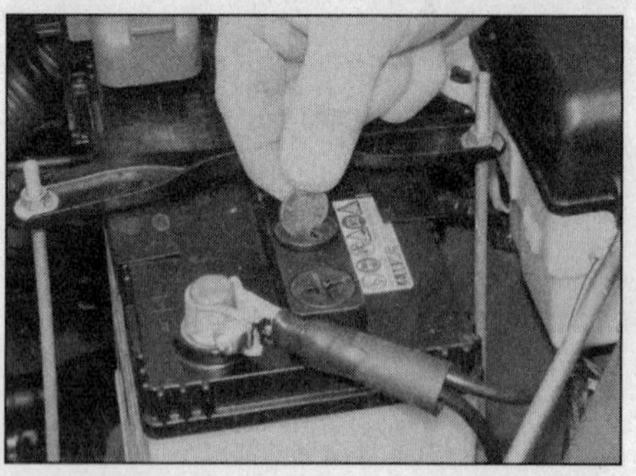

3 The original Toyota battery is unusual nowadays in that it requires periodic water level checking and topping-up. The water level in each of the six cells can be seen through the translucent side of the battery, which also has upper and lower level markings. If topping-up is required, use a coin to unscrew the cell caps . . .

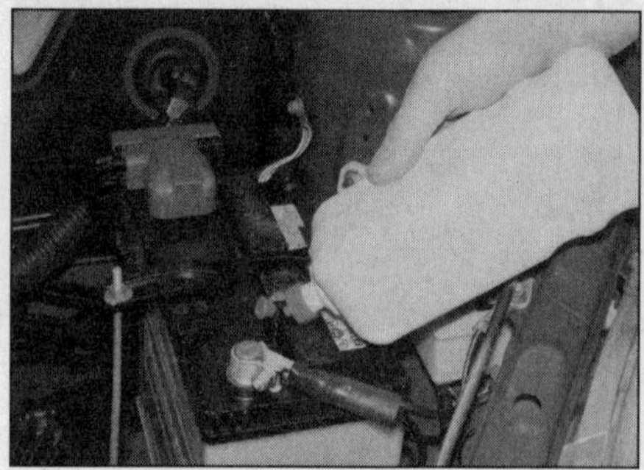

4 . . . then add distilled water a little at a time until the level reaches the upper marking on the side of the battery. Remember at all times that there's powerful acid in the battery – wipe up any spills and wash your hands afterwards (wearing gloves is a wise precaution). Refit the cell caps securely on completion.

Electrical systems

✔ Check all external lights and the horn. Refer to the appropriate Sections of Chapter 12 for details if any of the circuits are found to be inoperative.

✔ Visually check all accessible wiring connectors, harnesses and retaining clips for security, and for signs of chafing or damage.

If you need to check your brake lights and indicators unaided, back up to a wall or garage door and operate the lights. The reflected light should show if they are working properly.

1 If a single indicator light, brake light or headlight has failed, it is likely that a bulb has blown and will need to be renewed. Refer to Chapter 12 for details. If both brake lights have failed, it is possible that the brake light switch operated by the brake pedal has failed. Refer to Chapter 9 for details.

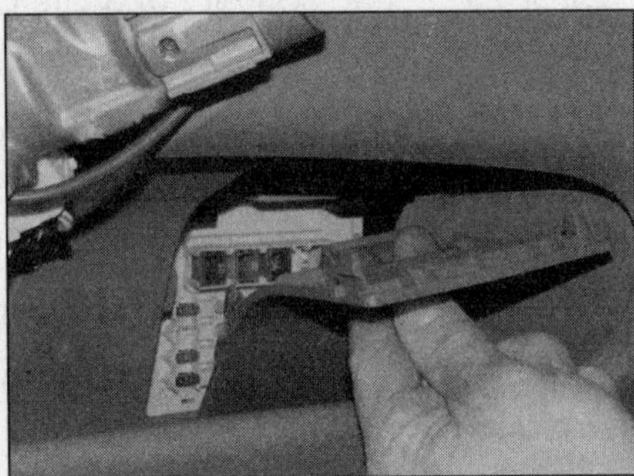

2 If more than one indicator light or headlight has failed, it is likely that either a fuse has blown, or that there is a fault in the circuit (see Chapter 12). The main fuses are mounted behind a panel in the driver's lower storage compartment. Unclip the panel and release it from the facia.

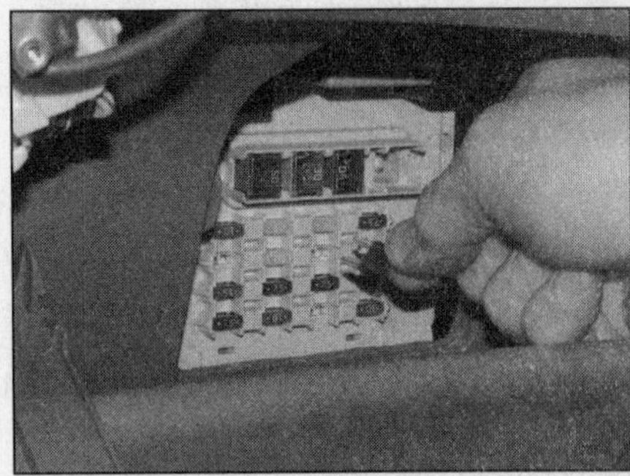

3 To renew a blown fuse, remove it using the plastic tweezer tool provided (where applicable). Fit a new fuse of the same rating, available from car accessory shops. It is important that you find the reason that the fuse blew (see *Electrical fault finding* in Chapter 12).

Lubricants and fluids

Engine	Engine oil, SAE 5W-30 or 10W-30, to specification API SJ or SL
Cooling system	Ethylene glycol-based antifreeze suitable for use in mixed-metal engines – Toyota Long Life Coolant (red) or Super Long Life Coolant (pink)*
Manual transmission	Gear oil, SAE 75W-90, to specification API GL-4 or GL-5
Automatic transmission	Automatic transmission fluid (ATF) – Type T-IV or equivalent (refer to Toyota dealer if necessary)
Brake and clutch systems	Hydraulic fluid to DOT 3 or DOT 4
Power steering (hydraulic type)	Automatic transmission fluid (ATF) – Dexron II or III

** Do not mix the two types of coolant listed with each other, nor top-up with any other type of coolant. Alternative types of coolant may only be used once the system has been drained and completely flushed, as described in Chapter 1.*

Choosing your engine oil

Engines need oil, not only to lubricate moving parts and minimise wear, but also to maximise power output and to improve fuel economy.

HOW ENGINE OIL WORKS

• *Beating friction*

Without oil, the moving surfaces inside your engine will rub together, heat up and melt, quickly causing the engine to seize. Engine oil creates a film which separates these moving parts, preventing wear and heat build-up.

• *Cooling hot-spots*

Temperatures inside the engine can exceed 1000° C. The engine oil circulates and acts as a coolant, transferring heat from the hot-spots to the sump.

• *Cleaning the engine internally*

Good quality engine oils clean the inside of your engine, collecting and dispersing combustion deposits and controlling them until they are trapped by the oil filter or flushed out at oil change.

OIL CARE - FOLLOW THE CODE

To handle and dispose of used engine oil safely, always:

- ***Avoid skin contact with used engine oil. Repeated or prolonged contact can be harmful.***
- ***Dispose of used oil and empty packs in a responsible manner in an authorised disposal site. Call 0800 663366 to find the one nearest to you. Never tip oil down drains or onto the ground.***

Tyre pressures

Note: *Pressures given here are a guide only, and apply to original-equipment tyres – the recommended pressures may vary if any other make or type of tyre is fitted; check with the car handbook, or the tyre manufacturer or supplier for latest recommendations. A tyre pressure label is fitted inside the glovebox.*

	Front	Rear
Normal load (up to 2 people)		
Except 185/55 R 15 tyres	2.3 bar (33 psi)	2.1 bar (30 psi)
185/55 R 15 tyres	2.1 bar (30 psi)	2.0 bar (29 psi)
Full load (more than 2 people)		
All tyre sizes	2.3 bar (33 psi)	2.2 bar (32 psi)
Space-saver spare tyre		
All load conditions, front or rear	4.2 bar (61 psi)	

Chapter 1
Routine maintenance & servicing

Contents

Degrees of difficulty

Easy, suitable for novice with little experience 

Fairly easy, suitable for beginner with some experience 

Fairly difficult, suitable for competent DIY mechanic 

Difficult, suitable for experienced DIY mechanic 

Very difficult, suitable for expert DIY or professional 

Servicing specifications

Lubricants and fluids	Refer to *Weekly checks*

Capacities

Engine oil (including oil filter)	
All models	3.2 litres
Cooling system (approximate)	
All models	4.7 litres
Manual transmission	
1.0 litre engine models	1.4 litres
1.3 litre engine models	1.9 litres
Automatic transmission	
From dry	5.5 litres
Drain and refill	2.1 litres
Fuel tank	
All models	45.0 litres

Cooling system

Antifreeze mixture:	
50% antifreeze	Protection down to -37°C

Note: *Refer to antifreeze manufacturer for latest recommendations.*

Auxiliary drivebelt

Deflection (tension check):	
Models with manual steering*:	
New belt	4.5 to 5.5 mm
Used belt	6.0 to 6.5 mm
Models with electric power steering*:	
New belt	4.5 to 5.5 mm
Used belt	6.0 to 6.5 mm
Models with hydraulic power steering*:	
New belt	8.5 to 10.5 mm
Used belt	11.5 to 12.5 mm

***Note**: *Models with hydraulic power steering will have a fluid reservoir – refer to 'Weekly checks'.*

Ignition system

Spark plugs:	
1.0 litre engine models:	
Up to June 2001:	**Gap***
NGK BKR5EYA or Denso K16R-U	0.8 mm
July 2001 onwards:	
Bosch FR7KCU	0.9 to 1.0 mm
Denso K20R-U11	1.0 to 1.1 mm
1.3 litre 2SZ-FE engine models:	
Denso K16R-U	0.8 mm
1.3 litre 2NZ-FE engine models:	
NGK BKR5EYA11 or Denso K16R-U11	1.1 mm

** The spark plug gap quoted is that recommended by Toyota for their specified plugs listed above. If spark plugs of any other type are to be fitted, refer to their manufacturer's recommendations.*

Note: *Refer to Chapter 2A for engine code information.*

Brakes

Friction material minimum thickness:	
Front brake pads	1.0 mm
Rear brake shoes	1.0 mm

Tyre pressures

See end of *Weekly checks* on page 0•18

Torque wrench settings	Nm	lbf ft
Alternator adjuster lockbolt	19	14
Alternator pivot bolt:		
1.0 litre and 1.3 litre 2SZ-FE engines	44	32
1.3 litre 2NZ-FE engine	54	40
Automatic transmission:		
Fluid drain plug	17	13
Fluid pan bolts	10	7
Fluid strainer bolts	10	7
Engine block coolant drain plug*:		
1.0 litre and 1.3 litre 2SZ-FE engines	30	22
1.3 litre 2NZ-FE engine	35	26
Engine mounting:		
Right-hand mounting centre nut	52	38
Right-hand mounting upper section	45	33
Engine oil drain plug:		
1.0 litre and 1.3 litre 2SZ-FE engines	30	22
1.3 litre 2NZ-FE engine	38	28
Manual transmission:		
Drain plug	39	29
Filler/level plug	39	29
Roadwheel nuts	103	76
Seat belt mounting bolts	41	30
Spark plugs	18	13

** Use thread-locking fluid.*

Note: *Refer to Chapter 2A for engine code information.*

Underbonnet view of a 1.0 litre engine model

1 *Brake/clutch fluid reservoir*
2 *Power steering pressure switch*
3 *Engine right-hand mounting*
4 *Washer fluid reservoir*
5 *Engine oil filler cap*
6 *Air cleaner housing*
7 *Canister purge valve*
8 *Charcoal canister*
9 *Heater hose*
10 *Gearchange cables*
11 *Engine compartment fusebox*
12 *Battery negative terminal*
13 *Air inlet duct*
14 *Coolant expansion tank*
15 *Radiator top hose*
16 *Horn*
17 *Radiator pressure cap*
18 *Bonnet lock*
19 *Exhaust manifold*
20 *Clutch bleed screw*
21 *Engine oil dipstick*
22 *Ignition coil*
23 *Power steering fluid reservoir*
24 *Accelerator cable*

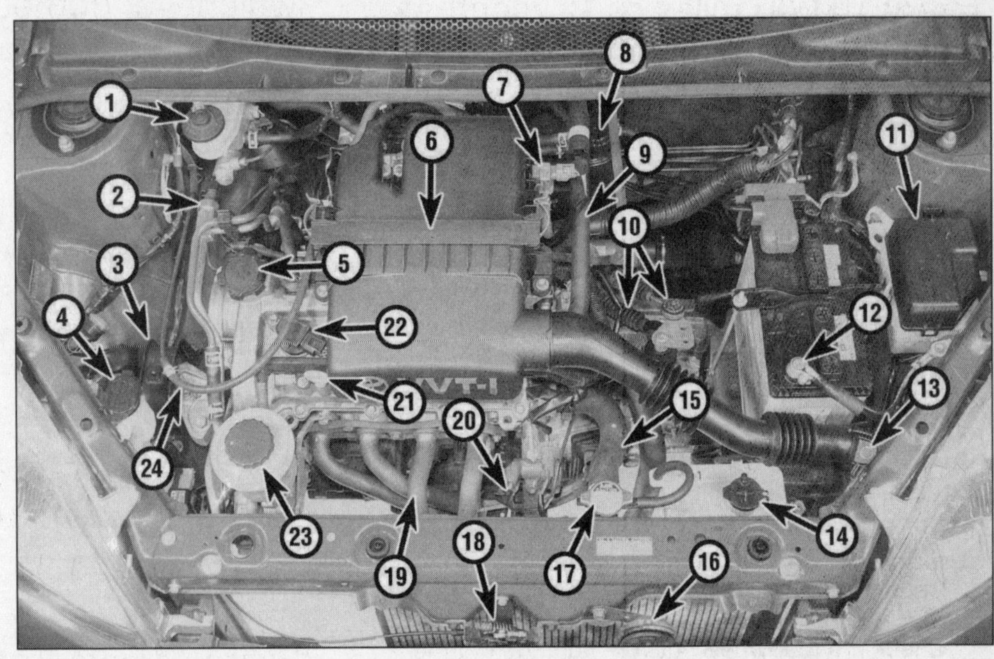

The maintenance intervals in this manual are provided with the assumption that you, not the dealer, will be carrying out the work. These are the minimum maintenance intervals recommended by us for cars driven daily. If you wish to keep your car in peak condition at all times, you may wish to perform some of these procedures more often. We encourage frequent maintenance, because it enhances the efficiency, performance and resale value of your car.

If the car is driven in dusty areas, used to tow a trailer, or driven frequently at slow speeds (idling in traffic) or on short journeys, more frequent maintenance intervals are recommended.

When the car is new, it should be serviced by a factory-authorised dealer service department, in order to preserve the factory warranty.

Every 250 miles or weekly

- ☐ Refer to *Weekly checks*

Every 5000 miles or 6 months, whichever comes first

- ☐ Renew the engine oil and filter (Section 3)

Note: *Toyota recommend that the engine oil and filter are changed every 10 000 miles or 12 months. However, oil and filter changes are good for the engine, and we recommend that the oil and filter are renewed more frequently, especially if the car is used mainly for short journeys.*

Every 10 000 miles or 12 months, whichever comes first

- ☐ Check the pollen filter (Section 4)
- ☐ Check all components, pipes and hoses for fluid leaks (Section 5)
- ☐ Check the exhaust system (Section 6)
- ☐ Check the condition and tension of the auxiliary drivebelt (Section 7)
- ☐ Check and if necessary adjust the handbrake (Section 8)
- ☐ Check and if necessary adjust the clutch and brake pedals (Section 9)
- ☐ Check the condition and operation of the seat belts (Section 10)
- ☐ Lubricate all hinges and locks (Section 11)
- ☐ Check the front brake pads and discs for wear (Section 12)
- ☐ Check the steering and suspension components for condition and security (Section 13)
- ☐ Check the condition of the driveshaft gaiters (Section 14)
- ☐ Check the roadwheel nuts are tightened to the specified torque (Section 15)
- ☐ Check the automatic transmission fluid level (Section 16)
- ☐ Carry out a road test (Section 17)

Every 20 000 miles or 2 years, whichever comes first

- ☐ Renew the spark plugs (Section 18)
- ☐ Renew the air filter element (Section 19)
- ☐ Check the rear brake shoes and drums for wear (Section 20)
- ☐ Check the charcoal canister (Section 21)
- ☐ Renew the automatic transmission fluid (Section 22)

Every 40 000 miles or 4 years, whichever comes first

- ☐ Check the manual transmission oil level (Section 23)
- ☐ Renew the auxiliary drivebelt (Section 24)

Every 60 000 miles or 6 years, whichever comes first

- ☐ Check the valve clearances (Section 25)

Every 2 years, regardless of mileage

- ☐ Renew the brake fluid (Section 26)

Every 4 years, regardless of mileage

- ☐ Renew the coolant* (Section 27)

Note: *If the system is filled with pink Super Long Life Coolant the renewal interval is 10 years.*

Underbonnet view of a 1.3 litre (2NZ-FE) engine model

1 *Brake/clutch fluid reservoir*
2 *Brake servo vacuum hose*
3 *Power steering fluid reservoir*
4 *Engine oil filler cap*
5 *Fuel supply hose*
6 *Canister purge valve*
7 *Air cleaner housing*
8 *Engine compartment fusebox*
9 *Battery negative terminal*
10 *Accelerator cable*
11 *Air conditioning sight glass*
12 *Coolant expansion tank*
13 *Automatic transmission fluid dipstick*
14 *Radiator hose*
15 *Radiator pressure cap*
16 *Engine oil dipstick*
17 *Inlet manifold*
18 *Alternator*
19 *Washer fluid reservoir*
20 *Engine right-hand mounting*

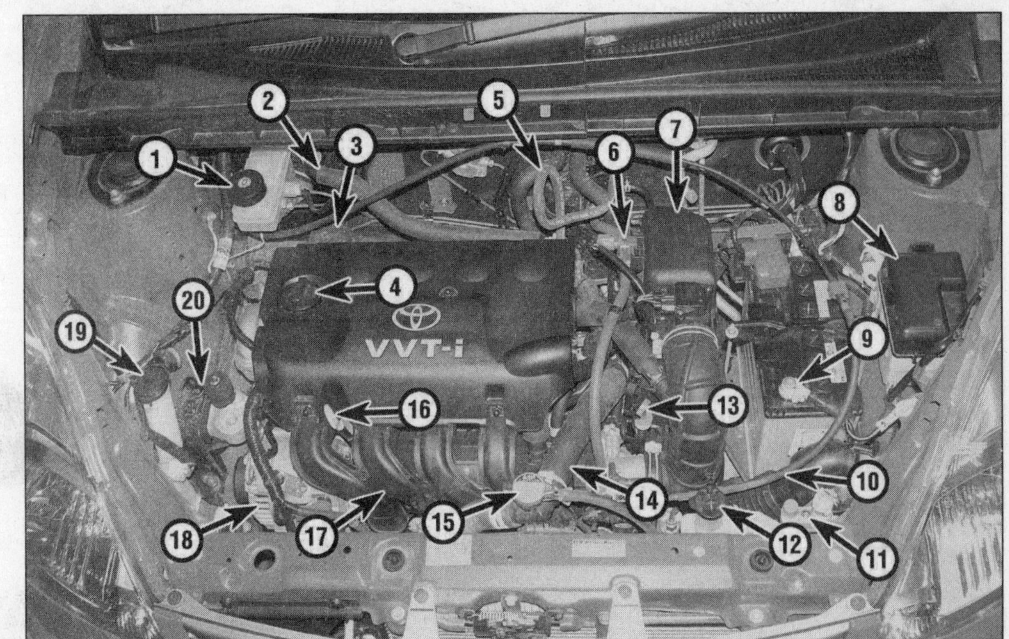

Front underbody view

1 *Front brake caliper*
2 *Auxiliary drivebelt*
3 *Engine oil drain plug*
4 *Driveshaft*
5 *Catalytic converter*
6 *Oxygen sensor*
7 *Radiator cooling fan motor*
8 *Left-hand mounting*
9 *Transmission oil drain plug*
10 *Front suspension lower arm*
11 *Track rod*
12 *Subframe reinforcement bar*
13 *Subframe*
14 *Exhaust front mounting*
15 *Gearchange cables*
16 *Radiator bottom hose*
17 *Radiator drain tap*

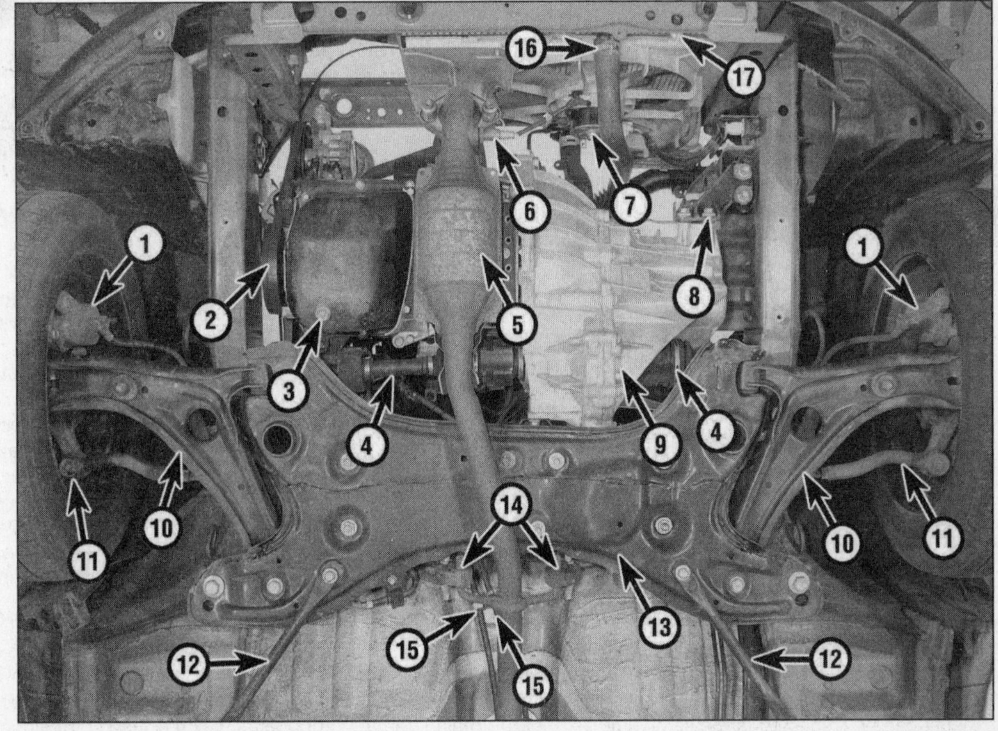

Rear underbody view

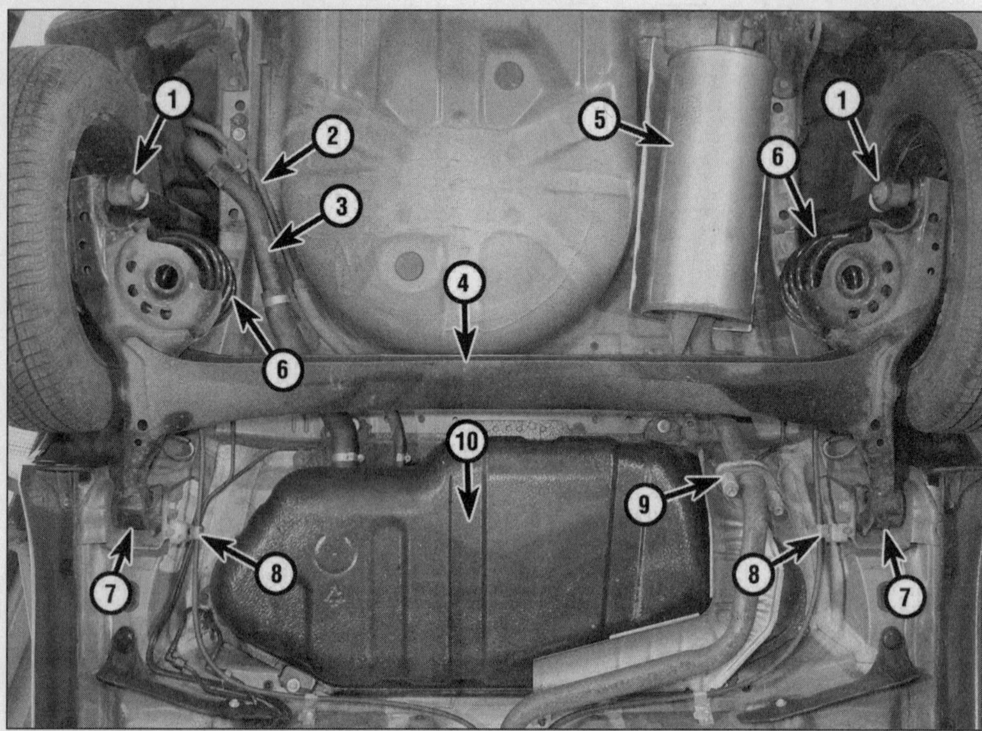

1 Rear shock absorber mounting
2 Fuel tank vent hose
3 Fuel filler hose
4 Rear axle
5 Exhaust rear silencer
6 Rear spring
7 Rear axle pivot/mounting
8 Handbrake cable
9 Exhaust joint
10 Fuel tank

1 General information

1 This Chapter is designed to help the home mechanic maintain his/her car for safety, economy, long life and peak performance.

2 The Chapter contains a master maintenance schedule, followed by Sections dealing specifically with each task in the schedule. Visual checks, adjustments, component renewal and other helpful items are included. Refer to the accompanying illustrations of the engine compartment and the underside of the car for the locations of the various components.

3 Servicing your car in accordance with the mileage/time maintenance schedule and the following Sections will provide a planned maintenance programme, which should result in a long and reliable service life. This is a comprehensive plan, so maintaining some items but not others at the specified service intervals, will not produce the same results.

4 As you service your car, you will discover that many of the procedures can – and should – be grouped together, because of the particular procedure being performed, or because of the proximity of two otherwise-unrelated components to one another. For example, if the car is raised for any reason, the exhaust can be inspected at the same time as the suspension and steering components.

5 The first step in this maintenance programme is to prepare yourself before the actual work begins. Read through all the Sections relevant to the work to be carried out, then make a list and gather all the parts and tools required. If a problem is encountered, seek advice from a parts specialist, or a dealer service department.

2 Regular maintenance

1 If, from the time the car is new, the routine maintenance schedule is followed closely, and frequent checks are made of fluid levels and high-wear items, as suggested throughout this manual, the engine will be kept in relatively good running condition, and the need for additional work will be minimised.

2 It is possible that there will be times when the engine is running poorly due to the lack of regular maintenance. This is even more likely if a used car, which has not received regular and frequent maintenance checks, is purchased. In such cases, additional work may need to be carried out, outside of the regular maintenance intervals.

3 If engine wear is suspected, a compression test (refer to Chapter 2A) will provide valuable information regarding the overall performance of the main internal components. Such a test can be used as a basis to decide on the extent of the work to be carried out. If, for example, a compression test indicates serious internal engine wear, conventional maintenance as described in this Chapter will not greatly improve the performance of the engine, and may prove a waste of time and money, unless extensive overhaul work is carried out first.

4 The following series of operations are those most often required to improve the performance of a generally poor-running engine:

Primary operations

a) Clean, inspect and test the battery (refer to 'Weekly checks').
b) Check all the engine-related fluids (refer to 'Weekly checks').
c) Check the condition and tension of the auxiliary drivebelt (Section 7).
d) Renew the spark plugs (Section 18).
e) Check the condition of the air filter, and renew if necessary (Section 19).
f) Check the condition of all hoses, and check for fluid leaks (Section 5).

5 If the above operations do not prove fully effective, carry out the following secondary operations:

Secondary operations

All items listed under *Primary operations*, plus the following:

a) Check the charging system (Chapter 5A).
b) Check the ignition system (Chapter 5B).
c) Check the fuel system (Chapter 4A).

Every 5000 miles or 6 months

3 Engine oil and filter renewal

1 Frequent oil and filter changes are the most important preventative maintenance procedures which can be undertaken by the DIY owner. As engine oil ages, it becomes diluted and contaminated, which leads to premature engine wear.

2 Before starting this procedure, gather together all the necessary tools and materials. Also make sure that you have plenty of clean rags and newspapers handy, to mop up any spills. Ideally, the engine oil should be warm, as it will drain more easily, and more built-up sludge will be removed with it. Take care not to touch the exhaust or any other hot parts of the engine when working under the car. To avoid any possibility of scalding, and to protect yourself from possible skin irritants and other harmful contaminants in used engine oils, it is advisable to wear gloves when carrying out this work.

3 Firmly apply the handbrake, then jack up the front of the car and support it on axle stands (see *Jacking and vehicle support*). Remove the engine lower covers from under the car – this is not essential, but it improves access to the oil filter. The covers are secured by a number of different fasteners (note their locations as they are removed), along the base of the bumper and up inside the wheel arch **(see illustrations)**.

4 Remove the oil filler cap, and pull out the dipstick **(see illustrations)**.

5 Using a spanner, or preferably a socket and bar, slacken the drain plug about half a turn **(see illustrations)**. Position the draining container under the drain plug, then remove the plug completely.

Keep the drain plug pressed into the sump while unscrewing it by hand last couple of turns. As the plug releases, move it away sharply so the stream of oil issuing from the sump runs into the container, not up your sleeve.

6 Allow some time for the oil to drain, noting that it may be necessary to reposition the container as the oil flow slows to a trickle **(see illustration)**.

3.3a The engine lower cover panels are secured along the front of the car . . .

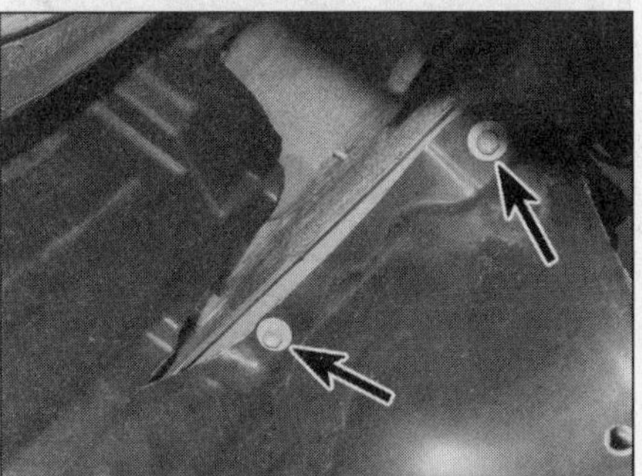

3.3b . . . and up inside the wheel arch

3.3c Remove the fasteners and lower the panels from the car

3.4a Remove the oil filler cap . . .

3.4b . . . and pull out the dipstick

3.5a Slackening the sump drain plug – 1.0 litre engine

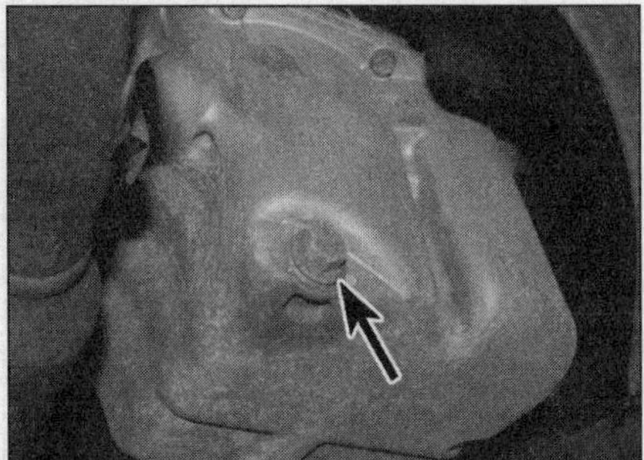

3.5b Sump drain plug – 1.3 litre 2SZ-FE engine

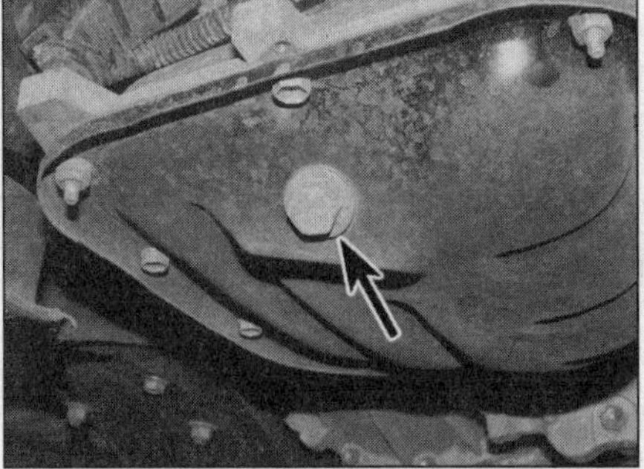

3.5c Sump drain plug – 1.3 litre 2NZ-FE engine

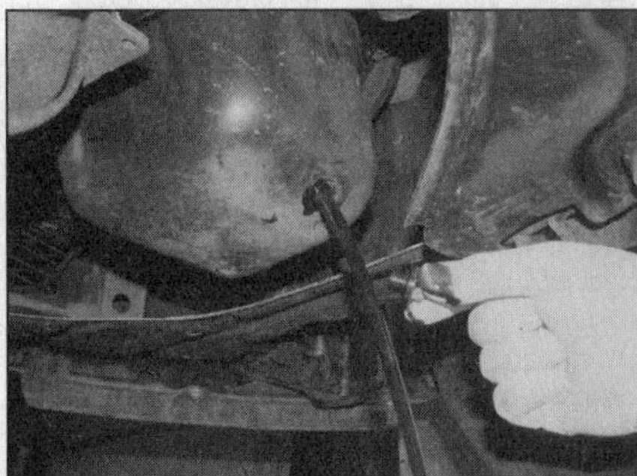

3.6 Try not to drop the drain plug when removing it

3.8a Oil filter on the 1.0 litre engine

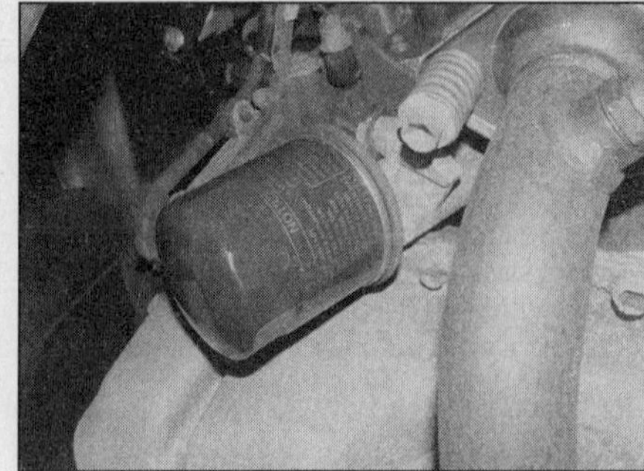
3.8b Oil filter on the 1.3 litre 2SZ-FE engine

3.8c Oil filter on the 1.3 litre 2NZ-FE engine

3.9 Loosening the oil filter using a claw-type removal tool

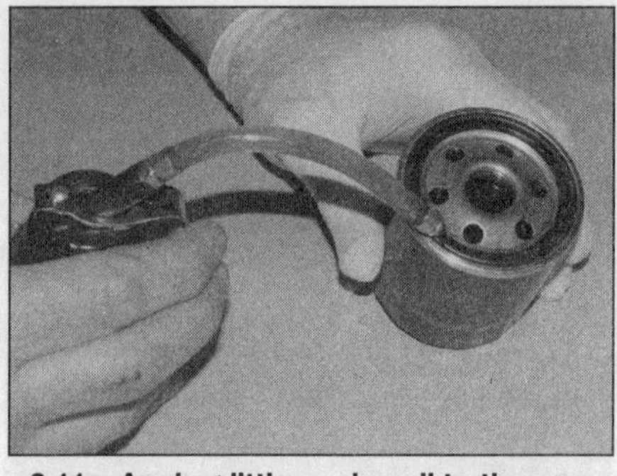
3.11a Apply a little engine oil to the new filter's sealing ring . . .

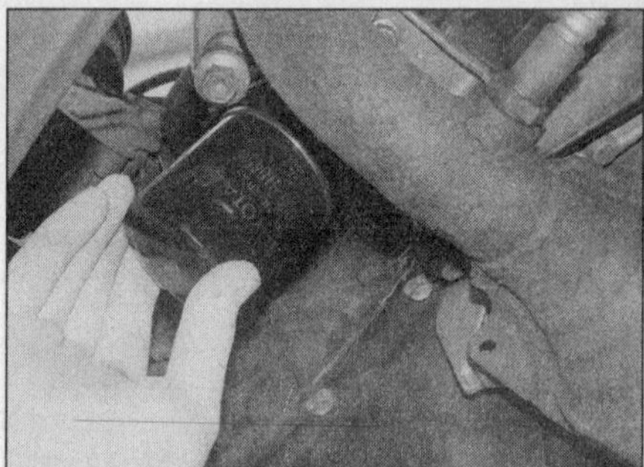
3.11b . . . then screw it firmly into place by hand only

7 After all the oil has drained, wipe the drain plug with a clean rag. Examine the condition of the drain plug seal/washer, and renew it if it shows signs of damage which may prevent an oil-tight seal. Clean the area around the drain plug opening, then refit the plug and tighten it securely.

8 Move the container into position under the oil filter, which is located on the front of the cylinder block **(see illustrations)**. Where applicable, take care not to burn yourself on the exhaust if the engine is still hot.

9 Use an oil filter removal tool to slacken the filter initially, then unscrew it by hand the rest of the way **(see illustration)**. Empty the oil from the old filter into the container.

10 Use a clean rag to remove all oil, dirt and sludge from the filter sealing area on the engine.

11 Apply a light coating of clean engine oil to the sealing ring on the new filter, then screw the filter into position on the engine **(see illustrations)**. Tighten the filter firmly by hand only – **do not** use any tools.

12 Remove the old oil and all tools from under the car, then lower the car to the ground.

13 Fill the engine through the filler hole, using the correct grade and type of oil (refer to *Weekly checks* for oil specifications) **(see illustrations)**. Pour in half the specified quantity of oil first, then wait a few minutes for the oil to drain into the sump. Continue to add oil, a small quantity at a time, until the level is up to the lower mark on the dipstick. Adding approximately a further 0.5 to 1.0 litre will bring the level up to the upper mark on the dipstick.

14 Start the engine and run it for a few minutes, while checking for leaks around the oil filter seal and the sump drain plug. Note that there may be a delay of a few seconds before the oil pressure warning light goes out when the engine is first started, as the oil circulates through the new oil filter and the engine oil galleries before the pressure builds-up.

15 Stop the engine, and wait a few minutes for the oil to settle in the sump once more. With the new oil circulated and the filter now completely full, recheck the level on the dipstick, and add more oil as necessary.

16 Dispose of the used engine oil safely, with reference to *General repair procedures*.

3.13a Remove the oil filler cap . . .

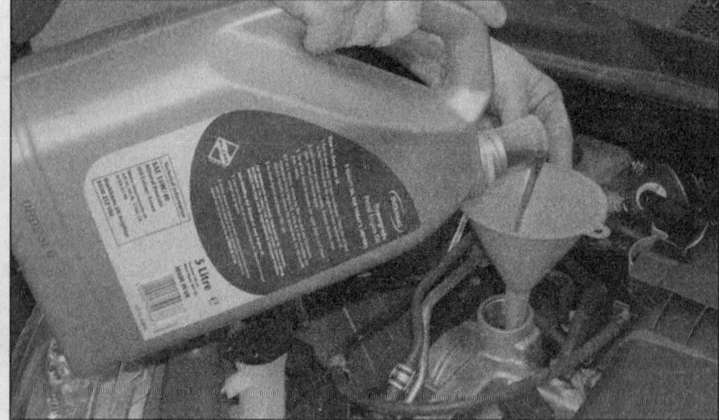
3.13b . . . then fill the engine using the correct grade and quantity of oil

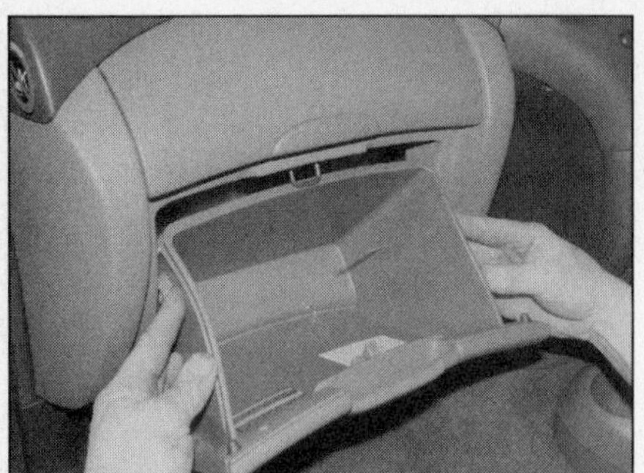
4.1a Open the main glovebox, then press in the sides . . .

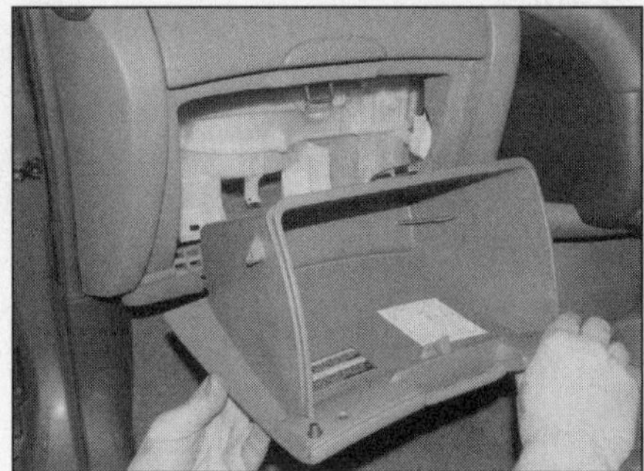
4.1b . . . and pull it out at the base to remove it

4.2a Release the catches at either side . . .

Every 10 000 miles or 12 months

4 Pollen filter check

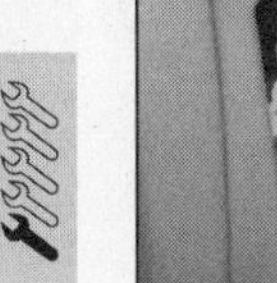

1 Open the main glovebox, then press in the sides and pull it out to release it at the base **(see illustrations)**.

2 Release the catches at either side of the filter housing, and slide the housing out of the facia **(see illustrations)**.

3 The filter element is held in the housing by two clips either side – release the clips and lift out the element, noting which way up it is fitted **(see illustration)**.

4 Check the condition of the element – if it is excessively dirty or otherwise contaminated, airflow into the car will be seriously reduced, and a new element should be fitted.

5 Fit the new element (or refit the old one, as applicable), observing any markings indicating its fitted direction, then slide the housing back into the facia, and ensure the catches engage.

6 Refit the glovebox to complete.

5 Hose and fluid leak check

Coolant

Warning: Refer to the safety information given in 'Safety first!' and Chapter 3 before disturbing any of the cooling system components.

1 Carefully check the radiator and heater coolant hoses along their entire length. Renew any hose which is cracked, swollen or which shows signs of deterioration. Cracks will show up better if the hose is squeezed. Pay close attention to the clips that secure the hoses to the cooling system components. Hose clips that have been overtightened can pinch and puncture hoses, resulting in cooling system leaks.

4.2b . . . then slide the filter carrier out

4.3 Unclip the filter element and remove it

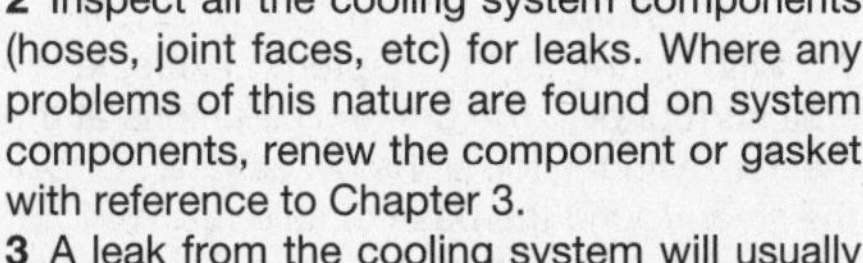

2 Inspect all the cooling system components (hoses, joint faces, etc) for leaks. Where any problems of this nature are found on system components, renew the component or gasket with reference to Chapter 3.

3 A leak from the cooling system will usually show up as white or rust-coloured deposits, on the area surrounding the leak **(see Haynes Hint)**.

Fuel

Warning: Refer to the safety information given in 'Safety first!' and Chapter 4A before disturbing any of the fuel system components.

4 Check all fuel lines at their connections to the pulsation damper (1.0 litre models) and the fuel rail.

A leak in the cooling system will usually show up as white- or rust-coloured deposits on the area adjoining the leak

5 Examine each fuel hose/pipe along its length for splits or cracks. Check for signs of leakage, which could be anything from a damp hose to an area of bodywork adjacent to the hose which seems especially clean (from being 'washed' by leaking fuel).

6 To identify fuel leaks between the fuel tank and the engine bay, the car should raised and securely supported on axle stands. Inspect the fuel tank and filler neck for punctures, cracks and other damage. The connection between the filler neck and tank is especially critical. Sometimes a rubber filler neck or connecting hose will leak due to loose retaining clamps or deteriorated rubber.

7 Carefully check all rubber hoses and metal fuel lines leading away from the fuel tank **(see illustration)**. Check for loose connections, deteriorated hoses, kinked lines, and other damage. Pay particular attention to the vent pipes and hoses, which often loop up around the filler neck and can become blocked or

5.7 Check the fuel tank hoses for leaks

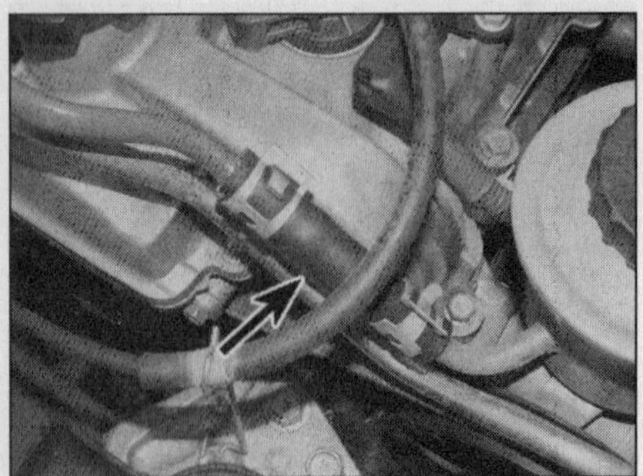
5.9 Check the power steering fluid hoses

5.15a Check the brake flexible hoses at the front . . .

5.15b . . . and at the rear (remove the rear wheels for best access)

kinked, making tank filling difficult. Follow the fuel supply line to the front of the car, carefully inspecting it all the way for signs of damage or corrosion. Renew damaged sections as necessary.

Engine oil

8 Inspect the area around the camshaft cover, timing chain cover, cylinder head, oil filter and sump joint faces. Bear in mind that, over a period of time, some very slight seepage from these areas is to be expected – what you are really looking for is any indication of a serious leak caused by gasket failure. Engine oil seeping from the base of the timing chain cover or the transmission bellhousing may be an indication of crankshaft or input shaft oil seal failure. Should a leak be found, renew the failed gasket or oil seal by referring to the appropriate Chapters in this manual.

Power-assisted steering fluid

Note: *This check does not apply to models with manual or electric power steering.*

9 Examine the hose running between the fluid reservoir and the power steering pump, and the return hose running from the steering rack to the fluid reservoir **(see illustration)**. Also examine the high-pressure supply hose between the pump and the steering rack.

10 Pay particular attention to crimped unions, and the area surrounding the hoses that are secured with spring clips.

Air conditioning refrigerant

Warning: Refer to the safety information given in 'Safety first!' and Chapter 3, regarding the dangers of disturbing any of the air conditioning system components.

11 The air conditioning system is filled with a liquid refrigerant, which is retained under high pressure. If the air conditioning system is opened and depressurised without the aid of specialised equipment, the refrigerant will immediately turn into gas and escape into the atmosphere. If the liquid comes into contact with your skin, it can cause severe frostbite. In addition, the refrigerant contains substances which are environmentally damaging; for this reason, it should not be allowed to escape into the atmosphere.

12 Any suspected air conditioning system leaks should be immediately referred to a Toyota dealer or air conditioning specialist. Leakage will be shown up as a steady drop in the level of refrigerant in the system.

13 Note that water may drip from the condenser drain pipe, underneath the car, immediately after the air conditioning system has been in use. This is normal, and should not be cause for concern.

Brake (and clutch) fluid

Warning: Refer to the safety information given in 'Safety first!' and Chapter 9, regarding the dangers of handling brake fluid.

14 With reference to Chapter 9, examine the area surrounding the brake pipe unions at the master cylinder for signs of leakage. Check the area around the base of fluid reservoir, for signs of leakage caused by seal failure. Also examine the brake pipe unions at the ABS hydraulic unit, where applicable.

15 Inspect the braking system rubber hoses fitted to each front caliper, and above each rear spring **(see illustrations)**. Look for perished, swollen or hardened rubber, and any signs of cracking, especially at the metal end fittings. If there's any doubt as to the condition of any hose, renew it as described in Chapter 9.

16 If fluid loss is evident, but the leak cannot be pinpointed in the engine bay, the brake calipers and underbody brake lines and should be carefully checked with the car raised and supported on axle stands. Leakage of fluid from the braking system is serious fault that must be rectified immediately.

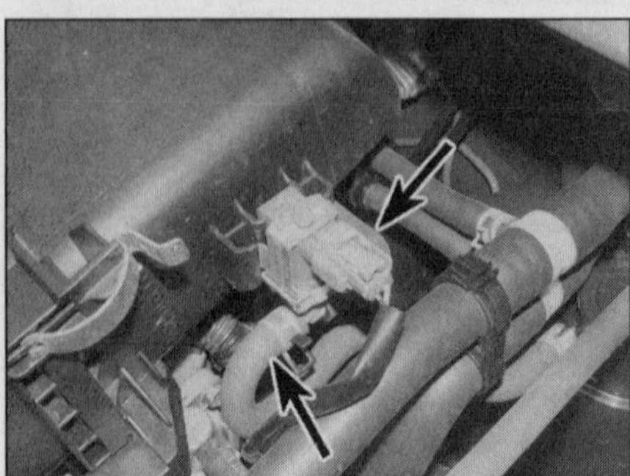
5.21 Emission control component hoses should be checked for signs of damage

17 Refer to Chapter 6 and check for leakage around the hydraulic fluid line connections to the clutch master cylinder at the bulkhead, and to the clutch slave cylinder on the transmission.

18 Brake/clutch hydraulic fluid is a toxic substance with a watery consistency. New fluid is almost colourless, but it becomes darker with age and use.

Unidentified fluid leaks

19 If there are signs that a fluid of some description is leaking from the car, but you cannot identify the type of fluid or its exact origin, park the car overnight and slide a large piece of card underneath it. Providing that the card is positioned in roughly in the right location, even the smallest leak will show up on the card. Not only will this help you to pinpoint the exact location of the leak, it should be easier to identify the fluid from its colour. Bear in mind, though, that the leak may only be occurring when the engine is running!

Vacuum hoses

20 Although the braking system is hydraulically-operated, the brake servo unit amplifies the effort you apply at the brake pedal, by making use of the vacuum available in the inlet manifold (see Chapter 9). Vacuum is ported to the servo by means of a large-bore hose. Any leaks that develop in this hose will reduce the effectiveness of the braking system, and may affect engine running.

21 In addition, many of the underbonnet components, particularly the emission control components, are driven by vacuum via narrow-bore hoses **(see illustration)**. A leak in a vacuum hose means that air is being drawn into the hose (rather than escaping from it) and this makes leakage very difficult to detect.

22 However, if an initial examination of the hoses shows perishing and cracks (especially at the hose ends), or any signs that the hose has become hardened, renewal of that section of hose is advisable.

23 One method for detecting leaks is to use an old length of vacuum hose as a kind of stethoscope – hold one end close to (but not

6.2a Check the condition of all exhaust mountings . . .

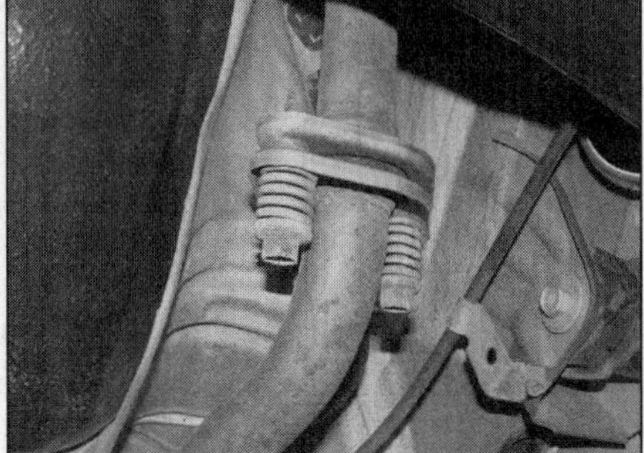

6.2b . . . and for signs of leaks, especially at the front and rear joints

in) your ear and use the other end to probe the area around the suspected leak. When the end of the hose is directly over a vacuum leak, a hissing sound will be heard clearly through the hose. Care must be taken to avoid contacting hot or moving components, as the engine must be running, when testing in this manner. Renew any vacuum hoses that are found to be defective.

6 Exhaust system check

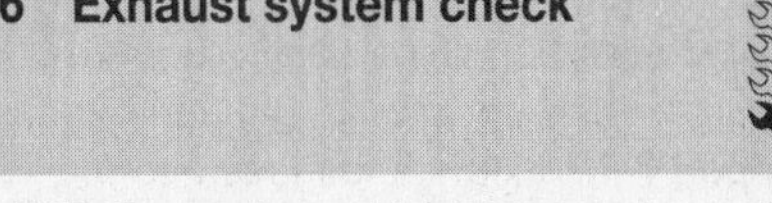

1 With the engine cold (at least an hour after the car has been driven), check the complete exhaust system from the engine to the end of the tailpipe. The exhaust system is most easily checked with the car raised on a hoist, or suitably supported on axle stands, so that the exhaust components are readily visible and accessible.

2 Check the exhaust pipes and connections for evidence of leaks, severe corrosion and damage. Make sure that all brackets and mountings are in good condition, and that all relevant nuts and bolts are tight **(see illustrations)**.

3 Leakage at any of the joints or in other parts of the system will usually show up as a black sooty stain in the vicinity of the leak. To confirm the presence of a leak, with the engine running, briefly block the exhaust tailpipe with a large pad of rag – take care to avoid burning from the hot pipe or hot gases. If the system is sound, there should be a noticeable build-up of pressure – if not, the increased noise should make it possible to pinpoint the source of the leak.

4 Rattles and other noises can often be traced to the exhaust system, especially the brackets and mountings. Try to move the pipes and silencers. If the components are able to come into contact with the body or suspension parts, secure the system with new mountings. Otherwise separate the joints (if possible) and twist the pipes as necessary to provide additional clearance.

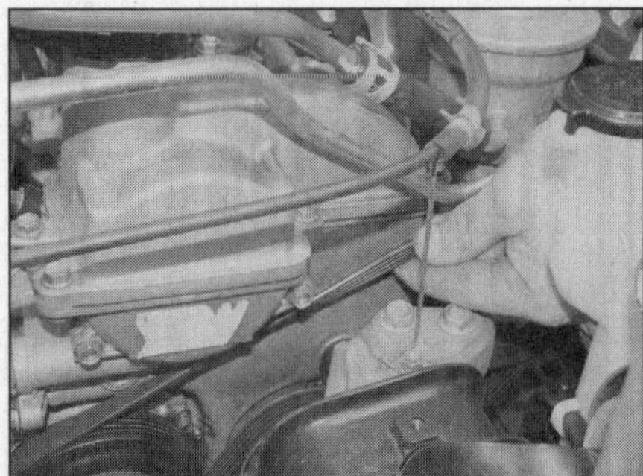

7.4 Twist the drivebelt to check its condition

7 Auxiliary drivebelt check

General

1 A single auxiliary drivebelt is fitted at the right-hand side of the engine. The length of the drivebelt varies according to whether (hydraulic) power steering or air conditioning is fitted. A manual tensioner is fitted, so the drivebelt tension should be checked at regular intervals (and particularly after fitting a new drivebelt).

Checking

2 Due to their function and material makeup, drivebelts are prone to failure after a long period of time, and should therefore be inspected regularly.

3 Since the drivebelt is located very close to the right-hand side of the engine compartment, it is possible to gain better access by jacking up the right-hand front wheel (see *Jacking and vehicle support*) and removing the engine right-hand lower cover panel.

4 With the engine stopped, inspect the full length of the drivebelt for cracks and separation of the belt plies. It will be necessary to turn the engine (using a spanner or socket and bar on the crankshaft pulley bolt) in order to move the belt from the pulleys so that the belt can be inspected thoroughly. Twist the belt between the pulleys so that both sides can be viewed **(see illustration)**. Also check for fraying, and glazing which gives the belt a shiny appearance. Check the pulleys for nicks, cracks, distortion and corrosion.

5 Small cracks in the belt ribs are not usually serious, but look closely to see whether the crack has extended into the belt plies. If the belt is in any way suspect, or is known to have seen long service, renew it as described in Section 24.

6 Check the drivebelt tension by pressing on the belt at a point midway on the longest run between two pulleys. Compare the deflection noted with the figures quoted in the Specifications at the start of this Chapter. If the drivebelt appears excessively taut or slack, refer to Section 24 and adjust the belt tension.

7 If the belt appears not to be too slack, but has actually been slipping in service, check the belt for any sign of external contamination (eg, by oil or water). If found, cure the source of the leak before fitting a new belt as described in Section 24.

8 Handbrake check and adjustment

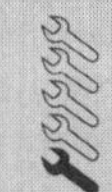

Checking

1 The handbrake should be fully applied (and capable of holding the car on a slope) after six to nine clicks of the ratchet. The operating cables will stretch over time, and adjustment will be needed.

2 Aside from providing equal braking effort to both rear wheels, for the purposes of the MoT inspection, the handbrake lever must be securely mounted, and the ratchet mechanism should release only by means of the lever's button – if the ratchet releases (for example) when the lever is knocked sideways, the lever assembly should be removed for checking as described in Chapter 9.

Adjustment

3 Remove the centre console as described in Chapter 11.

4 Loosen the handbrake locknut, so that the adjuster nut below it is free to turn.

5 If the handbrake lever has been removed, or new cables have been fitted, the mechanism must first be settled as follows. Apply the handbrake by four notches, then tighten the adjustment nut until all the slack has been taken up (when the nut starts to feel tight). Apply and release the handbrake firmly ten times, then loosen the adjuster nut to the end of its thread. Finally, depress the footbrake firmly fifteen times.

6 Release the handbrake, and (if new cables have been fitted) check that the cable end is located properly on the lever.

7 Tighten the adjuster nut by a quarter-turn at a time, then recheck the operation of the handbrake. The handbrake should be fully applied at six to nine notches – do not over-adjust, or the handbrake may not release fully.

8 To fully check that the handbrake has been

11.1 Lubricate the door check straps and locks

correctly adjusted, jack up the rear of the car, and support it on axle stands (see *Jacking and vehicle support*).

9 With the handbrake released, turn the rear wheels, and check for signs that the handbrake may be dragging. If drag is felt on either wheel, loosen off the adjuster nut at least two full turns, and try adjusting again.

10 Apply the handbrake by one notch at a time, and check that the rear wheels start to lock up within one or two clicks of each other. Failure to achieve this suggests a problem of some kind with the rear shoes – remove the drums as described in Chapter 9 and inspect. Uneven operation could also be due to a seized handbrake cable or linkage (refer to Chapter 9, Section 20).

11 When handbrake operation is satisfactory, tighten the locknut up to the adjuster nut – use a second spanner to hold the adjuster nut still. Lower the car to the ground.

12 Check the operation of the handbrake several times before returning the car to normal service.

9 Clutch and brake pedal adjustment check

Clutch pedal

1 The Yaris is equipped with a hydraulic clutch so, for the most part, wear in the clutch friction disc is automatically compensated for. If the clutch is working satisfactorily, further checking is not strictly necessary.

2 Poor clutch operation may indicate the need for bleeding the hydraulic system as described in Chapter 6. Otherwise, the pedal travel and stroke may be checked and adjusted as described in Chapter 6, Section 6.

Brake pedal

3 As with all modern cars, the braking system on the Yaris is self-adjusting. Provided the brake pedal feels satisfactory (and the brakes work effectively), the chances are that the pedal does not need adjusting.

4 Excessive brake pedal travel may indicate that the brakes need bleeding as described in Chapter 9. Otherwise, if the pedal seems set too low, the free play is excessive, or if the

12.2 The thickness of the brake pads can be seen through the caliper window

history of the car is unknown, the brake pedal can be checked and adjusted as described in Chapter 9, Section 9.

10 Seat belt check

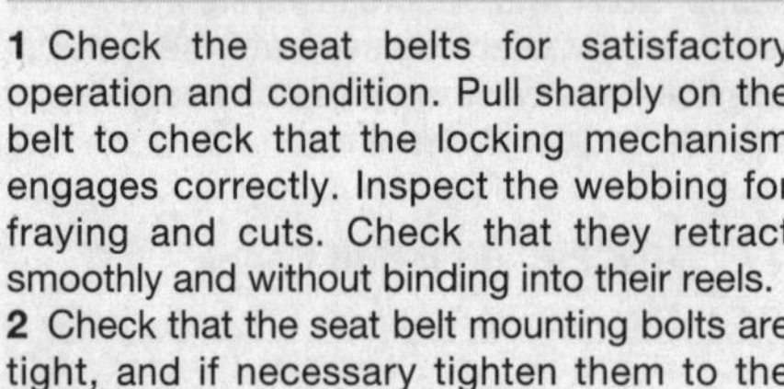

1 Check the seat belts for satisfactory operation and condition. Pull sharply on the belt to check that the locking mechanism engages correctly. Inspect the webbing for fraying and cuts. Check that they retract smoothly and without binding into their reels.

2 Check that the seat belt mounting bolts are tight, and if necessary tighten them to the specified torque wrench setting.

11 Hinge and lock lubrication

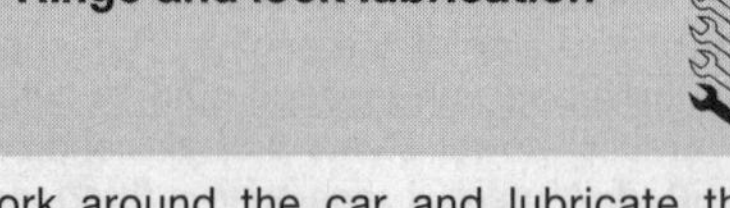

1 Work around the car and lubricate the hinges of the bonnet, doors and tailgate with light oil **(see illustration)**.

2 Lightly lubricate the bonnet release mechanism with a smear of grease.

3 Check carefully the security and operation of all hinges, latches and locks, adjusting them where required. Check the operation of the central locking system, where applicable.

4 Check the condition and operation of the tailgate struts, renewing them if either is leaking or no longer able to support the tailgate securely when raised.

13.2 Check the condition of the balljoint rubber gaiters

12 Front brake pad and disc wear check

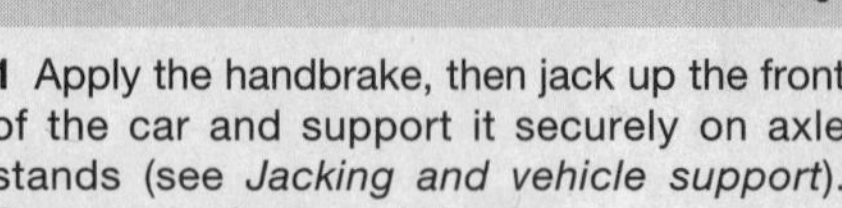

1 Apply the handbrake, then jack up the front of the car and support it securely on axle stands (see *Jacking and vehicle support*). Remove the front roadwheels.

2 The brake pad thickness, and the condition of the disc, can be assessed roughly with just the wheels removed **(see illustration)**. For a comprehensive check, the brake pads should be removed and cleaned. The operation of the caliper can then also be checked, and the condition of the brake disc itself can be fully examined on both sides. Refer to Chapter 9 for further information.

3 On completion, refit the roadwheels and lower the car to the ground.

13 Steering and suspension check

Front suspension and steering

1 Raise the front of the car, and securely support it on axle stands (see *Jacking and vehicle support*).

2 Visually inspect the balljoint dust covers and the steering rack-and-pinion gaiters for splits, chafing or deterioration **(see illustration)**. Any wear of these components will cause loss of lubricant, together with dirt and water entry, resulting in rapid deterioration of the balljoints or steering gear.

3 Check the (hydraulic) power steering fluid hoses for chafing or deterioration, and the pipe and hose unions for fluid leaks. Also check for signs of fluid leakage under pressure from the steering gear rubber gaiters, which would indicate failed fluid seals within the steering gear.

4 Grasp the roadwheel at the 12 o'clock and 6 o'clock positions, and try to rock it **(see illustration)**. Very slight free play may be felt, but if the movement is appreciable, further investigation is necessary to determine the source. Continue rocking the wheel while an assistant depresses the footbrake. If the

13.4 Check for wear in the hub bearings by grasping the wheel and trying to rock it

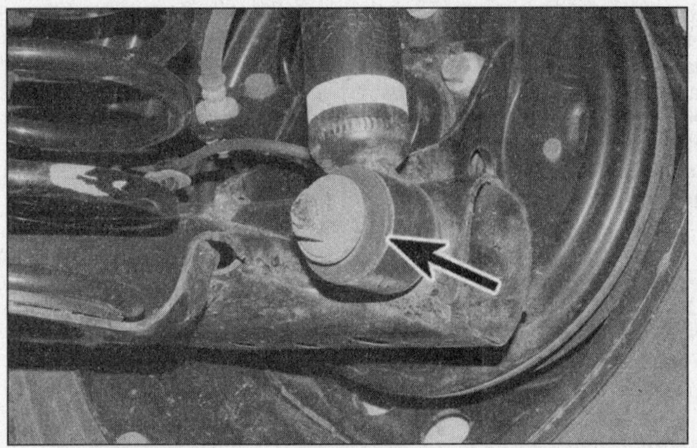

13.9 Check for signs of wear in the shock absorber lower mountings

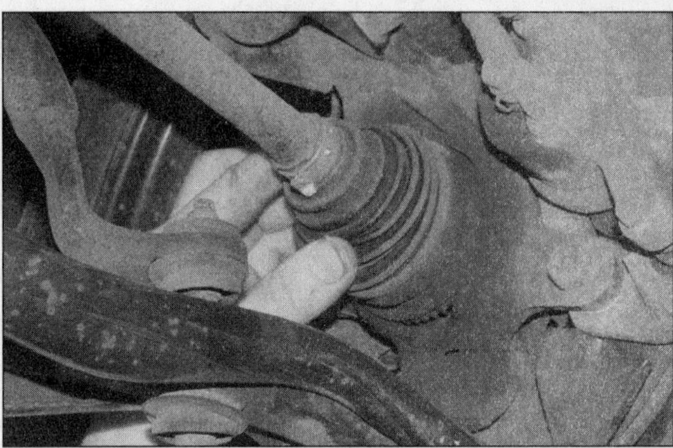

14.1 Check for splits in the driveshaft gaiters

movement is now eliminated or significantly reduced, it is likely that the hub bearings are at fault. If the free play is still evident with the footbrake depressed, then there is wear in the suspension joints or mountings.

5 Now grasp the wheel at the 9 o'clock and 3 o'clock positions, and try to rock it as before. Any movement felt now may again be caused by wear in the hub bearings or the steering track rod balljoints. If the outer balljoint is worn, the visual movement will be obvious. If the inner joint is suspect, it can be felt by placing a hand over the rack-and-pinion rubber gaiter and gripping the track rod. If the wheel is now rocked, movement will be felt at the inner joint if wear has taken place.

6 Using a large screwdriver or flat bar, check for wear in the suspension mounting bushes by levering between the relevant suspension component and its attachment point. Some movement is to be expected, as the mountings are made of rubber, but excessive wear should be obvious. Also check the condition of any visible rubber bushes, looking for splits, cracks or contamination of the rubber.

7 With the car standing on its wheels, have an assistant turn the steering wheel back-and-forth, about an eighth of a turn each way. There should be very little, if any, lost movement between the steering wheel and roadwheels. If this is not the case, closely observe the joints and mountings previously described. In addition, check the steering column universal joints for wear, and also check the rack-and-pinion steering gear itself.

Rear suspension

8 Chock the front wheels, then jack up the rear of the car and support securely on axle stands (see *Jacking and vehicle support*).

9 Working as described previously for the front suspension, check the rear hub bearings, the suspension bushes and the shock absorber mountings for wear **(see illustration)**.

Shock absorber

10 Check for any signs of fluid leakage around the shock absorber body, or from the rubber gaiter around the piston rod. Should any fluid be noticed, the shock absorber is defective internally, and should be renewed. **Note:** *Shock absorbers should always be renewed in pairs on the same axle.*

11 The efficiency of the shock absorber may be checked by bouncing the car at each corner. Generally speaking, the body will return to its normal position and stop after being depressed. If it rises and returns on a rebound, the shock absorber is probably suspect. Also examine the shock absorber upper and lower mountings for any signs of wear.

14 Driveshaft gaiter check

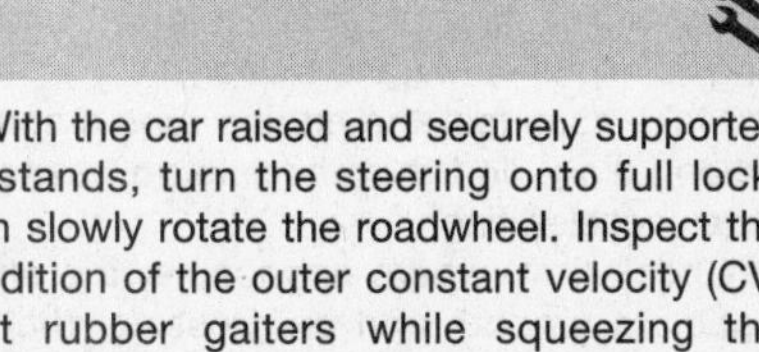

1 With the car raised and securely supported on stands, turn the steering onto full lock, then slowly rotate the roadwheel. Inspect the condition of the outer constant velocity (CV) joint rubber gaiters while squeezing the gaiters to open out the folds **(see illustration)**. Check for signs of cracking, splits or deterioration of the rubber which may allow the grease to escape and lead to water and grit entry into the joint. Also check the security and condition of the retaining clips. Repeat these checks on the inner CV joints. If any damage or deterioration is found, the gaiters should be renewed as described in Chapter 8.

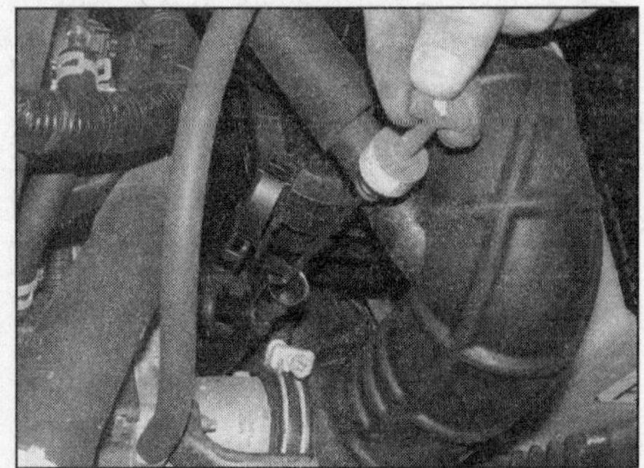

16.4 Unclip and withdraw the fluid level dipstick (which had an orange handle on our car)

2 At the same time, check the general condition of the CV joints themselves by first holding the driveshaft and attempting to rotate the wheel. Repeat this check by holding the inner joint and attempting to rotate the driveshaft. Any appreciable movement indicates wear in the joints, wear in the driveshaft splines, or a loose driveshaft retaining nut.

15 Roadwheel nut tightness check

1 Remove the wheel trims or alloy wheel centre covers, and slacken the roadwheel nuts slightly.

2 Tighten the nuts to the specified torque, using a torque wrench.

16 Automatic transmission fluid level check

1 The level of the automatic transmission fluid should be carefully maintained. Low fluid level can lead to slipping or loss of drive, while overfilling can cause foaming, loss of fluid and transmission damage.

2 The transmission fluid level should be checked when the fluid is hot (around 80°C), ie, when the car has just been driven for about 30 minutes.

3 Park the car on level ground, apply the handbrake, and start the engine. With the engine idling and the brake pedal depressed, move the selector lever through all gear positions, holding the lever in each gear for about 3 seconds before moving to the next. On completion, return the lever to the P position.

4 Wait two minutes then, with the engine still idling, release the clip and remove the dipstick from its tube, which is located at the front of the transmission **(see illustration)**. Note the

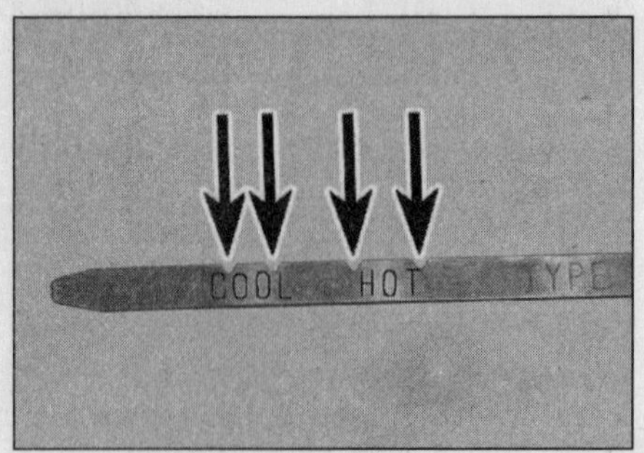

16.6 The fluid dipstick has two sets of level marks, for use when the fluid is hot (HOT) or cold (COOL)

condition and colour of the fluid on the dipstick.

5 Wipe the fluid from the dipstick with a clean rag, and re-insert it into the filler tube until the cap seats.

6 Pull the dipstick out again, and note the fluid level. The level should be between the lower and upper marks, on the upper section of the dipstick (marked HOT) **(see illustration)**.

7 If the level is on the lower mark, stop the engine, and add the specified automatic transmission fluid through the dipstick tube, using a clean funnel if necessary. Cleanliness is of great importance; it is vitally important not to introduce dirt into the transmission when topping-up.

8 Add the fluid a little at a time, and keep checking the level as previously described until it is correct. The difference between the lower and upper marks on the dipstick is less than 0.5 litres. The transmission must not be overfilled – this will result in increased operating temperatures and fluid leaks. If overfilling occurs, the excess should be drained off (refer to Section 22).

9 If the car has not been driven and the engine and transmission are cold, carry out the procedures in paragraphs 3 to 6, but use the lower section of the dipstick marked COLD (or COOL).

10 The need for regular topping-up of the transmission fluid indicates a leak, which should be found and rectified without delay.

11 The condition of the fluid should also be checked along with the level. If the fluid at the end of the dipstick is black or a dark reddish-brown colour, or if it has a burned smell, the fluid should be changed. If you are in doubt about the condition of the fluid, purchase some new fluid, and compare the two for colour and smell. Fluid renewal is described in Section 22.

17 Road test

Instruments and electrical equipment

1 Check the operation of all instruments and electrical equipment.

2 Make sure that all instruments read correctly, and switch on all electrical equipment in turn, to check that it functions properly.

Steering and suspension

3 Check for any abnormalities in the steering, suspension, handling or road 'feel'.

4 Drive the car, and check that there are no unusual vibrations or noises.

5 Check that the steering feels positive, with no excessive 'sloppiness', or roughness, and check for any suspension noises when cornering and driving over bumps.

Drivetrain

6 Check the performance of the engine, clutch, transmission and driveshafts.

7 Listen for any unusual noises from the engine, clutch and transmission.

8 Make sure that the engine runs smoothly when idling, and that there is no hesitation when accelerating.

9 Check that, where applicable, the clutch action is smooth and progressive, that the drive is taken up smoothly, and that the pedal travel is not excessive. Also listen for any noises when the clutch pedal is depressed.

10 Check that all gears can be engaged smoothly without noise, and that the gear lever action is smooth and not abnormally vague or 'notchy'.

11 Listen for a metallic clicking sound from the front of the car, as the car is driven slowly in a circle with the steering on full-lock. Carry out this check in both directions. If a clicking noise is heard, this indicates wear in a driveshaft joint (see Chapter 8).

Braking system

12 Make sure that the car does not pull to one side when braking, and that the wheels do not lock when braking hard.

13 Check that there is no vibration through the steering when braking.

14 Check that the handbrake operates correctly, without excessive movement of the lever, and that it holds the car stationary on a slope.

15 Test the operation of the brake servo unit as follows. Depress the footbrake four or five times to exhaust the vacuum, then start the engine. As the engine starts, there should be a noticeable 'give' in the brake pedal as vacuum builds up. Allow the engine to run for at least two minutes, and then switch it off. If the brake pedal is now depressed again, it should be possible to detect a hiss from the servo as the pedal is depressed. After about four or five applications, no further hissing should be heard, and the pedal should feel considerably harder.

Exhaust system

16 Listen carefully for any unusual noises from the system, which might indicate that it has started blowing, or that the mountings may be deteriorated, allowing the system to hit the underside of the car.

17 If any noises are detected, inspect the system with the car raised and supported on axle stands (see *Jacking and vehicle support*). Leaks are often accompanied by sooty stains, and are most common at the joints, and at welded sections, where pipes enter silencer boxes. Check the condition of the rubber mountings – if they are cracked or perished, fit new ones.

Every 20 000 miles or 2 years

18 Spark plug renewal

1 The correct functioning of the spark plugs is vital for the correct running and efficiency of the engine. It is essential that the plugs fitted are appropriate for the engine; suitable types are specified at the beginning of this Chapter, on the Vehicle Emissions Control Information (VECI) label located on the underside of the bonnet (only on models sold in some areas) or in the Owner's Handbook. If the correct type is used and the engine is in good condition, the spark plugs should not need attention between scheduled intervals. Spark plug cleaning is rarely necessary, and should not be attempted unless specialised equipment is available, as damage can easily be caused to the firing ends.

2 Remove the four ignition coils as described in Chapter 5B. The Yaris has a direct ignition system (DIS) featuring one ignition coil per spark plug, mounted directly over the plug, with no HT leads.

3 The spark plugs are quite deeply recessed in the top of the engine, and a 16 mm spark plug socket and extension bar will be needed to reach them. It is not advisable to use an ordinary deep socket for this job, since the plug may tend to fall out of the socket once it has been unscrewed, and will then have to be retrieved from the recess using thin-nosed pliers (fitting the new plugs will also be a problem, of course).

4 It is advisable (if possible) to remove any dirt from the spark plug recesses using a clean brush, vacuum cleaner or compressed air before removing the plugs, to prevent dirt dropping into the cylinders. However, the deep recesses on the Yaris engine make this an almost-impossible task – just be aware of the danger of anything falling into the spark

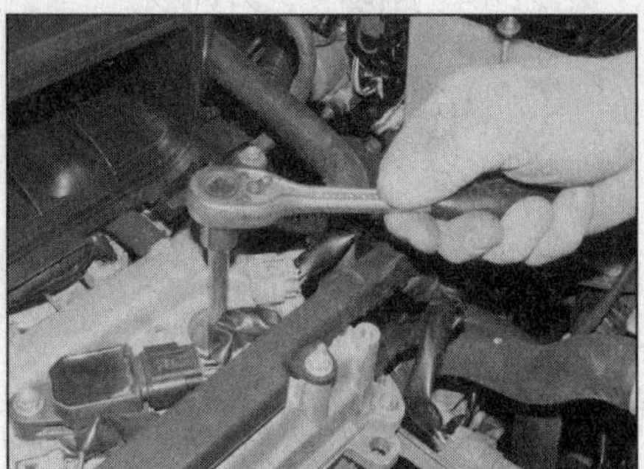

18.5a Using a spark plug socket and extension . . .

18.5b . . . unscrew and remove the spark plugs

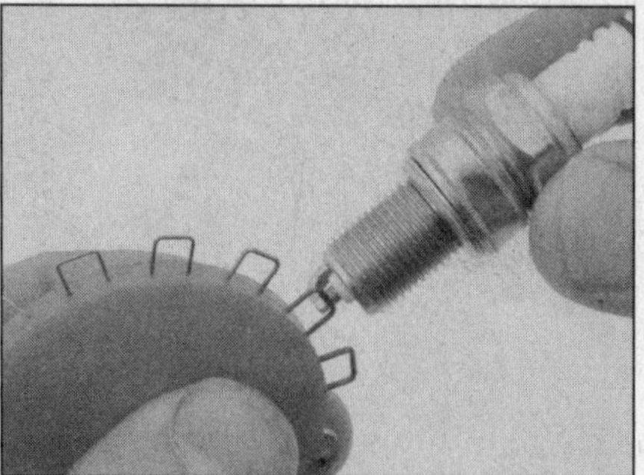

18.10a Using a wire-type gauge when checking the gap

plug holes when the plugs are removed, and take all possible precautions.

5 Lower the socket and extension into the recesses carefully – if the socket is misaligned and forced in, the ceramic insulator may be broken off. Unscrew each plug in turn, then carefully withdraw it from the recess so that it does not fall out of the socket **(see illustrations)**. As each plug is removed, examine it as follows.

6 Examination of the spark plugs will give a good indication of the condition of the engine. If the insulator nose of the spark plug is clean and white, with no deposits, this is indicative of a weak mixture or too hot a plug (a hot plug transfers heat away from the electrode slowly, a cold plug transfers heat away quickly).

7 If the tip and insulator nose are covered with hard black-looking deposits, then this is indicative that the mixture is too rich. Should the plug be black and oily, then it is likely that the engine is fairly worn, as well as the mixture being too rich.

8 If the insulator nose is covered with light tan to greyish-brown deposits, then the mixture is correct and it is likely that the engine is in good condition.

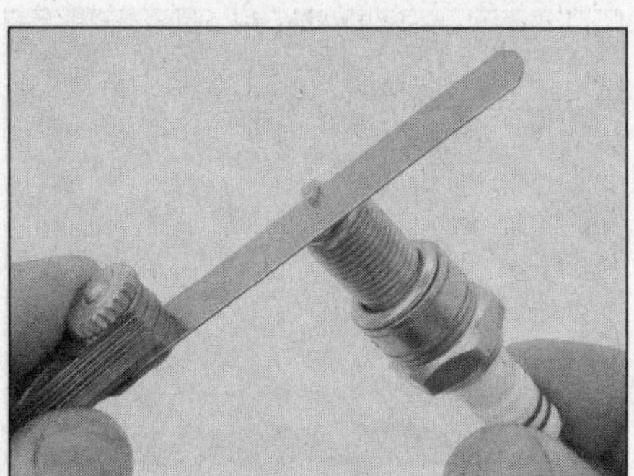

18.10b Measuring a spark plug gap with a feeler blade

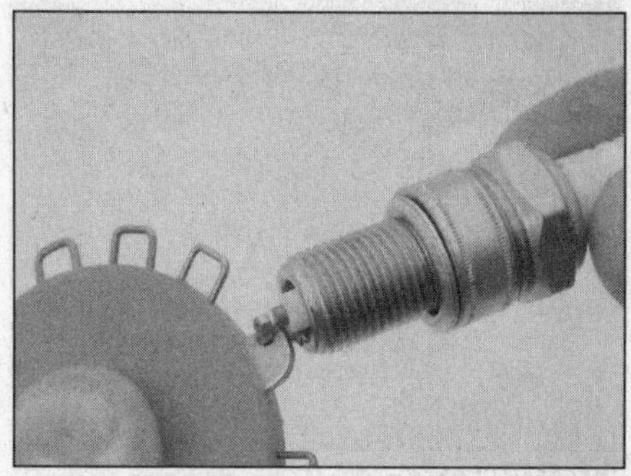

18.10c To change the gap, bend the outer electrode only

HAYNES HiNT

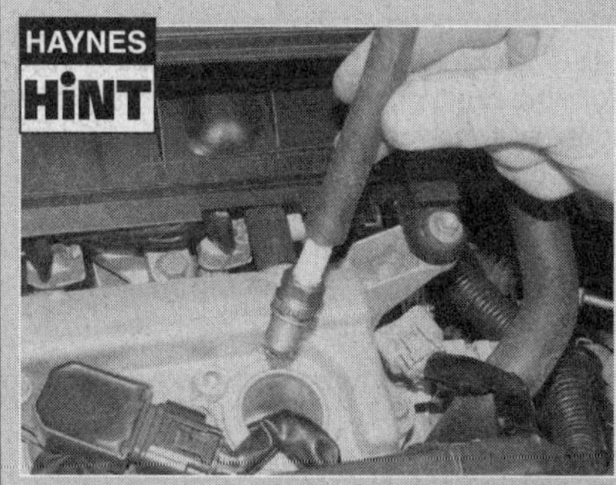

It's often difficult to insert spark plugs into their holes without cross-threading them. To avoid this possibility, fit a short length of rubber or plastic hose over the end of the spark plug. The flexible hose acts as a universal joint, to help align the plug with the plug hole. Should the plug begin to cross thread, the hose will slip on the spark plug, preventing thread damage to the aluminium cylinder head

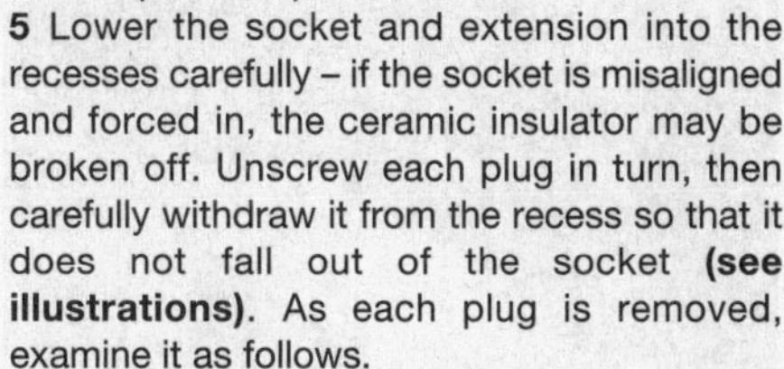

9 The spark plug electrode gap is of considerable importance as, if it is too large or too small, the size of the spark and its efficiency will be seriously impaired. The gap should be set to the value given in the Specifications at the beginning of this Chapter. Note, however, that modern spark plugs sometimes feature more than one earth electrode – generally, plugs of this type are set at the factory, and their gaps should not be adjusted.

10 To set the gap (on a single earth electrode plug), measure it with a feeler blade and then bend open, or closed, the outer plug electrode until the correct gap is achieved. The centre electrode should never be bent, as this may crack the insulator and cause plug failure, if nothing worse. If using feeler blades, the gap is correct when the appropriate-size blade is a firm sliding fit **(see illustrations)**.

18.13 If available, tighten the spark plugs using a torque wrench

11 Special spark plug electrode gap adjusting tools are available from most motor accessory shops, or from some spark plug manufacturers.

12 Before fitting the spark plugs, check that the threaded connector sleeves are tight, and that the plug exterior surfaces and threads are clean **(see Haynes Hint)**.

13 Remove the rubber/plastic hose (if used), and tighten the plug to the specified torque using the spark plug socket and a torque wrench **(see illustration)**. Refit the remaining spark plugs in the same manner.

14 Refit the ignition coils as described in Chapter 5B, and the air cleaner/inlet duct as described in Chapter 4A.

19 Air filter element renewal

1.0 litre and 1.3 litre 2SZ-FE engine models

1 The air cleaner is located on top of the engine.

2 Release the spring clip either side of the air cleaner, and pull the front half of the unit away (the air inlet hose will remain attached, but this

19.2 Release the two spring clips . . .

19.3 . . . then pull the front half of the air cleaner forwards, and remove the element

19.7a Loosen the clamp screw . . .

19.7b . . . and pull off the air cleaner duct

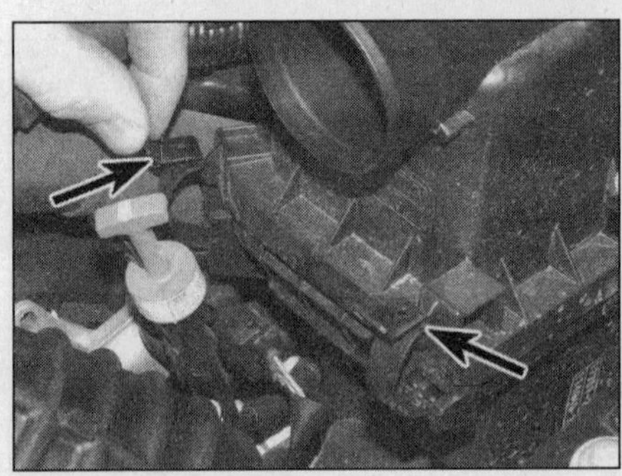

19.8 Release the two clips at the front of the air cleaner

19.9 Lift the air cleaner upper section, and remove the filter element

does not hinder renewal of the element) **(see illustration)**.

3 Noting how it is fitted, withdraw the air filter element from the body **(see illustration)**.

4 If the inside of the air cleaner body is dirty, either vacuum it out, or carefully wipe it out using a damp cloth. It is important not to allow dust or debris to enter the engine as a result of this cleaning.

5 Fit the new element, observing any markings indicating correct orientation, then refit the front part of the air cleaner and secure with the two spring clips.

1.3 litre 2NZ-FE engine models

6 The air cleaner is located to one side of the engine.

7 Loosen the clamp screw on the air duct at the front of the air cleaner, and pull off the duct **(see illustrations)**.

8 Although there are many pipes and plugs attached to the air cleaner body, to renew the element all that's required is to release the two spring clips at the front of the housing, then lift the top cover and unhook it at the rear **(see illustration)**.

9 Noting how it is fitted, withdraw the air filter element from the air cleaner body **(see illustration)**.

10 If the inside of the air cleaner body is dirty, either vacuum it out, or carefully wipe it out using a damp cloth. It is important not to allow dust or debris to enter the engine as a result of this cleaning. If necessary, to do a more thorough job, release the large clip securing the air inlet duct at the front of the top cover, and move the cover to one side.

11 Fit the new element, observing any markings indicating correct orientation, then refit the air cleaner top cover and secure with the two spring clips. Refit the air inlet duct, and tighten the clip securely, to prevent air leaks.

20 Rear brake shoe and drum wear check

Remove the rear brake drums, and check the brake shoes for signs of wear or contamination. At the same time, also inspect the wheel cylinders for signs of leakage, and the brake drum for signs of wear. Refer to the relevant Sections of Chapter 9 for further information.

21 Charcoal canister check

The charcoal canister is mounted on the engine compartment bulkhead, and collects vapours from the fuel tank for burning in the engine (rather than have them escape into the atmosphere). The canister and its pipework should be periodically checked for damage, especially if any fuel smells have been noted. A full check of the system can only be carried out by a Toyota dealer, but this should not normally be necessary.

22 Automatic transmission fluid renewal

1 Raise and securely support the front of the car (see *Jacking and vehicle support*).

2 Remove the engine left-hand lower cover panel from under the car.

3 Remove the drain plug at the rear of the fluid pan on the base of the transmission, and allow the contents of the transmission to drain into a suitable container **(see illustration)**. Refit the drain plug, using a new washer, and tighten it to the specified torque.

Caution: If the car has just been run, the transmission fluid may be very hot – protect your hands to avoid scalding.

4 This is all that is required for a routine fluid change, though it should be noted that a

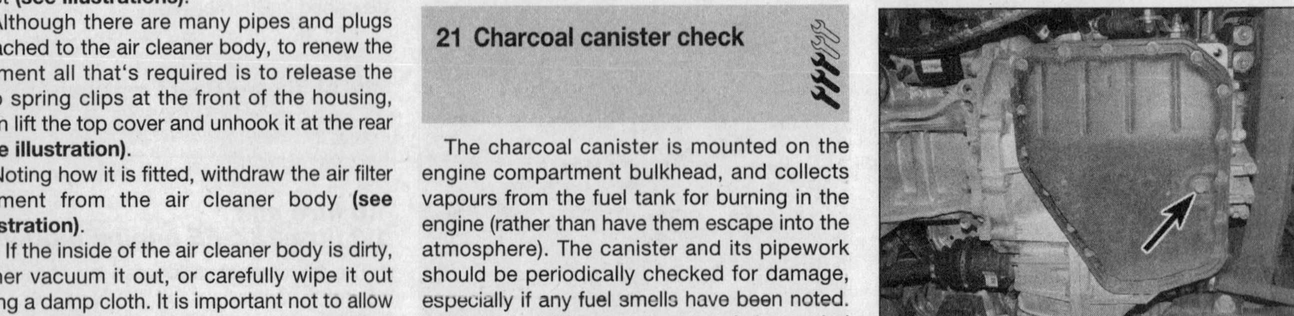

22.3 Automatic transmission fluid drain plug

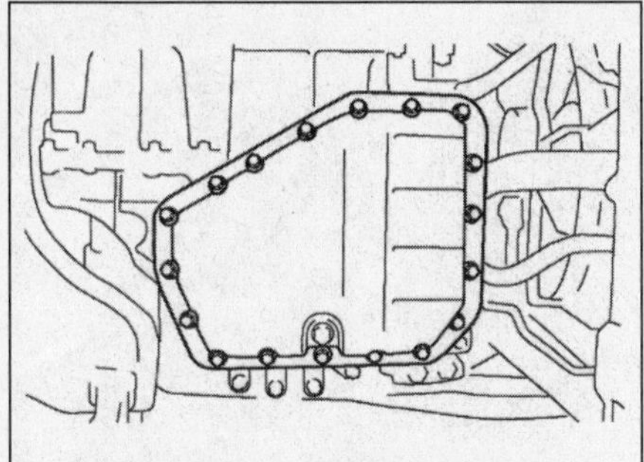

22.5 Remove the fluid pan bolts

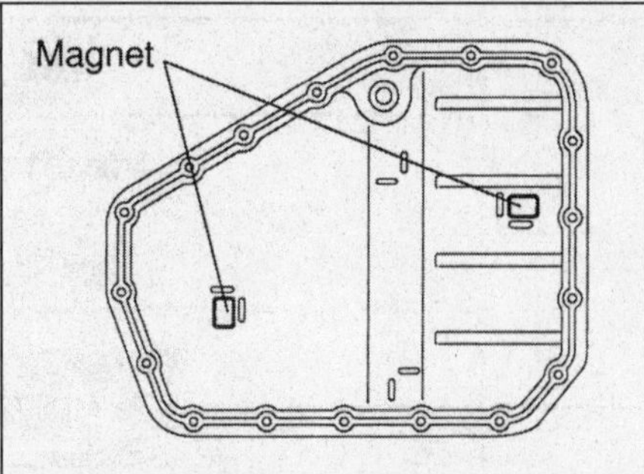

22.6 Remove and clean the two magnets from the fluid pan

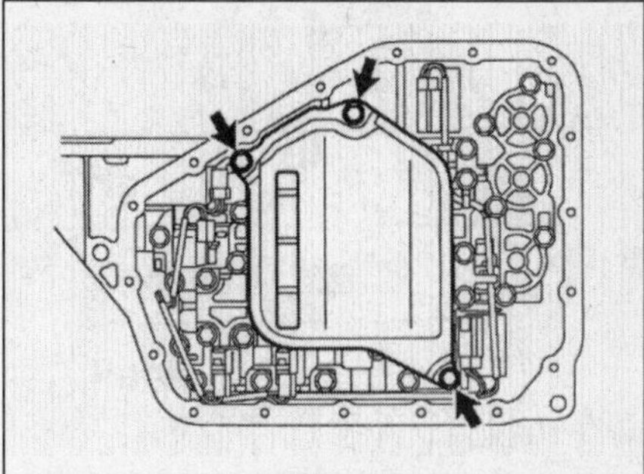

22.7 Remove the three fluid strainer bolts

significant amount of fluid will still remain in the transmission. If the fluid drained appears contaminated, or the history of the car is unknown, a more thorough draining procedure is recommended.

5 Remove the eighteen (or nineteen) bolts securing the fluid pan to the base of the transmission, then, anticipating some further fluid spillage, lower the pan and recover the gasket **(see illustration)**.

6 Remove and clean the two magnets fitted into the fluid pan, then fit them back in place **(see illustration)**.

7 The fluid strainer is secured by three bolts to the base of the transmission. Remove the bolts and lower out the strainer, noting that it contains more fluid **(see illustration)**.

8 If the strainer requires cleaning, seek the advice of a Toyota dealer or automatic transmission specialist. Any solvent used must itself be cleaned off (or allowed to dry) before the strainer is refitted – any solvent remaining would contaminate the fresh fluid. For safety, flush the strainer through with fresh fluid after cleaning, before refitting to the transmission.

9 Refit the strainer and fluid using new gaskets, and tighten the bolts to the specified torque.

10 Refit the engine lower cover panel, then lower the car to the ground.

11 Remove the transmission dipstick. Slowly add the 'drain and refill' quantity of fresh automatic transmission fluid of the specified type, via the transmission dipstick tube. Use a clean funnel if necessary – it is vitally important that no foreign matter enters the transmission. Once the specified quantity of fluid has been added, allow a few minutes for the fluid level to stabilise.

12 With the car parked on level ground, apply the handbrake, and start the engine. With the engine idling and the brake pedal depressed, move the selector lever through all gear positions, holding the lever in each gear for about 3 seconds before moving to the next. On completion, return the lever to the P position.

13 Wait two minutes then, with the engine still idling, remove the dipstick from its tube.

14 Wipe the fluid from the dipstick with a clean rag, and re-insert it into the filler tube until the cap seats.

15 Pull the dipstick out again, and note the fluid level. The level should be between the MIN and MAX marks, on the lower section of the dipstick (marked COLD).

16 If the level is on the MIN mark, stop the engine, and add a little more transmission fluid through the dipstick tube.

17 Add the fluid a little at a time, and keep checking the level as previously described until it is correct. Note that the fluid level check is most accurate when the fluid is hot – once the level is at least above the MIN mark on the COLD section of the dipstick, take the car for a run, then recheck the level using the HOT scale.

18 Dispose of the old fluid safely (see *General repair procedures*).

Every 40 000 miles or 4 years

23 Manual transmission oil level check

1 Position the car over an inspection pit, on car ramps, or jack it up (see *Jacking and vehicle support*), but make sure that it is level.

2 Remove the engine lower cover panels from under the car (see Section 3).

3 Remove all traces of dirt, then unscrew the filler/level plug from the front face of the transmission – where applicable, this is the lower of the two bolts **(see illustration)**. This will probably be very tight – use a good-quality spanner or socket to unscrew it, and take care to avoid personal injury. A new washer should be fitted to the filler/level plug when refitting.

4 The level must be level with, or less than 5 mm below, the bottom edge of the filler/level plug hole. If necessary, use a cranked tool such as an Allen key to check the level, but nothing which might break off and fall into the transmission.

5 If necessary, top up the level with the specified grade of oil (see *Lubricants and fluids*) until the oil just starts to run out **(see illustration)**. Allow any excess oil to flow out until the level stabilises.

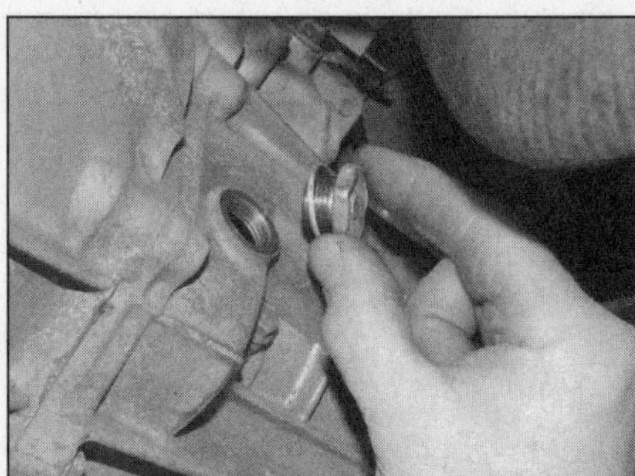

23.1 Unscrew and remove the transmission filler/level plug

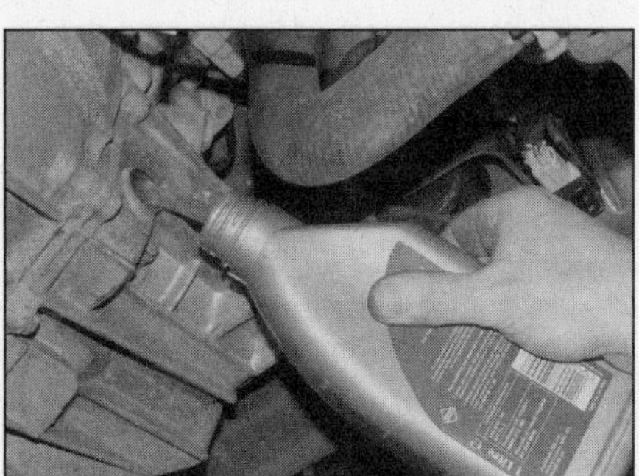

23.5 Top-up the oil level if necessary

When a transmission oil bottle is more than half-full, squeezing it will force the oil in from below – after that, the bottle will have to be manoeuvred in from above.

6 When the level is correct, clean and refit the filler/level plug (with a new washer), then tighten it to the specified torque.

7 Refit the lower cover panels, and lower the car to the ground.

8 Although not part of the manufacturer's routine maintenance schedule, it is a good

24.2a Loosen the alternator pivot bolt . . .

24.2b . . . and the lockbolt (A) for the adjuster bolt (B)

24.3 Remove the belt from the alternator pulley

idea to change the transmission oil after a high mileage has been completed, or perhaps periodically on a car which does a lot of stop-start driving. A drain plug is provided – see Chapter 7A for details.

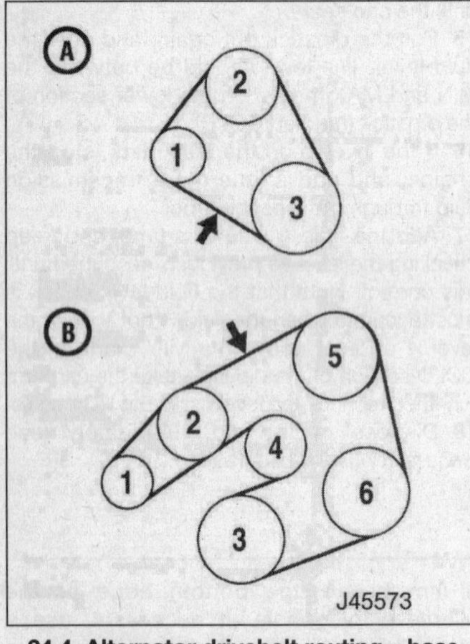

24.4 Alternator drivebelt routing – base models (A) and higher-spec models (B)

1 Alternator
2 Water pump
3 Crankshaft
4 Idler pulley
5 Power steering pump (or idler pulley)
6 Air conditioning compressor

24 Auxiliary drivebelt renewal and adjustment

Removal

1 Jack up the right-hand front wheel, and support the car using an axle stand (see *Jacking and vehicle support*). Remove the engine right-hand lower cover panel from under the car.

2 Loosen the alternator lower pivot bolt (at the base of the alternator), and the lockbolt for the adjuster bolt (at the top) **(see illustrations)**.

3 Unscrew the adjuster bolt and push the alternator forwards, to release the drivebelt tension enough to free the belt from the alternator pulley **(see illustration)**.

4 Noting how it is routed, remove the belt from all the pulleys **(see illustration)**. On models with manual steering, or with the later electric power steering system, it is now possible to remove the belt completely. If hydraulic power steering is fitted, the belt is trapped by the engine right-hand mounting, which has to be dismantled to remove the belt.

Models with hydraulic power steering

5 The weight of the engine must now be supported by one of the following alternative methods. Whichever one is chosen, there should be provision made for lifting the engine a little further once the mounting has been released, to pass the drivebelt through.

6 Either support the weight of the assembly from underneath, using a jack and a suitable piece of wood between the jack and the sump (to prevent damage), or from above by attaching a hoist to the engine. A third method is to use a suitable support bar, with end pieces which will engage in the water channel each side of the bonnet lid aperture; using an adjustable hook and chain connected to the engine, the weight of the engine and transmission can then be taken from the mountings.

7 Where applicable, first unclip the throttle cable from the wire support bracket (or unbolt the bracket itself from the top of the mounting) **(see illustration)**.

8 Remove the three (black) bolts securing the upper section of the engine mounting to the inner wing **(see illustration)**.

9 Working underneath, remove the nut from the engine mounting central stud **(see illustration)**.

10 Remove the two (silver) bolts securing the top section of the mounting to the engine

24.7 Unclip the throttle cable from the support bracket

24.8 Unscrew and remove the three mounting-to-wing bolts

24.9 Engine mounting nut seen from below

24.10 Lifting off the engine mounting upper section

24.11 Removing the auxiliary drivebelt

bracket, and lift the top section away **(see illustration)**.

11 Take off the old belt, and (if applicable) fit the new one loosely in its place as soon as possible **(see illustration)**. Refit the upper section of the mounting, and tighten its bolts and nut to the specified torque.

Refitting

12 Fitting the belt is a direct reversal of removal. Feed the belt onto as many pulleys as possible, ensuring that it is seated properly in the pulley grooves - leave the alternator pulley until last.

13 If necessary, loosen the adjuster bolt even more to allow a new (unstretched) belt to fit, then install the belt onto the alternator pulley, again making sure the belt seats in the grooves.

14 Tighten the adjuster bolt to take up the slack in the belt, but do not try to set the tension at this stage.

15 Using a spanner or socket on the crankshaft pulley bolt, turn the engine through a few turns in the normal direction of travel (clockwise) to settle the belt and ensure that it is running properly in all the pulley grooves.

Tensioning

16 If not already done, loosen the alternator lower pivot bolt (at the base of the alternator), and the lockbolt for the adjuster bolt (at the top).

17 Adjust the belt tension by turning the adjuster bolt in the appropriate direction in small steps at a time.

18 Check the drivebelt tension by pressing on the belt at a point midway on the longest run between two pulleys. Compare the deflection noted with the figures quoted in the Specifications at the start of this Chapter.

19 To ensure accuracy, each time the belt tension is adjusted, using a spanner or socket on the crankshaft pulley bolt, turn the engine through a few turns in the normal direction of travel (clockwise) to settle the belt.

20 Repeat the procedure in paragraphs 17 to 19 until the belt tension is satisfactory. On completion, tighten the adjuster lockbolt and the alternator lower pivot bolt to the specified torque. Lower the car to the ground, then run the engine to check for signs of slipping (noises from the belt).

21 If a new belt has been fitted, do not over-tension it to allow for the belt stretching - instead, recheck the tension after (say) a month or 1000 miles. It is quite normal for a new belt to require retensioning after its initial 'running-in' period.

Every 60 000 miles or 6 years

25 Valve clearance check and adjustment

According to Toyota, the first stage in valve clearance checking is to determine whether the engine is displaying any tappet noise (or whether any significant increase in noise level has been noted). The valve clearances on the Yaris are not adjusted in the conventional manner, and indeed, the need for adjustment is considered unusual. Adjustment will only be necessary to compensate for wear in the camshaft lobes or the tappets. Therefore, if the engine is running well, and is not noisy (rattly), the valve clearances may not even need checking, never mind adjusting.

Refer to Chapter 2A for checking and adjusting procedures.

Every 2 years, regardless of mileage

26 Brake fluid renewal

Warning: Brake hydraulic fluid can harm your eyes and damage painted surfaces, so use extreme caution when handling and pouring it. Do not use fluid that has been standing open for some time, as it absorbs moisture from the air. Excess moisture can cause a dangerous loss of braking effectiveness.

1 The procedure is similar to that for bleeding the hydraulic system as described in Chapter 9, except that allowance should be made for the old fluid to be expelled when bleeding each section of the circuit.

2 Working as described in Chapter 9, open the first bleed screw in the sequence, and pump the brake pedal gently until the level in the reservoir is approaching the MIN mark. Top-up to the MAX level with new fluid, and continue pumping until only new fluid remains in the reservoir, and new fluid can be seen emerging from the bleed screw. Tighten the screw, and top the reservoir level up to the MAX level line.

3 Work through all the remaining bleed screws in the sequence until new fluid can be seen at all of them. Be careful to keep the master cylinder reservoir topped-up above the MIN level at all times, or air may enter the system. If this happens, further bleeding will be required, to remove the air.

Old hydraulic fluid is invariably much darker in colour than the new, making it easy to distinguish the two.

4 When the operation is complete, check that all bleed screws are securely tightened, and that their dust caps are refitted. Wash off all traces of spilt fluid, and recheck the master cylinder reservoir fluid level.

5 Check the operation of the brakes before taking the car on the road.

Every 4 years, regardless of mileage

27 Coolant renewal and pressure cap check

Cooling system draining

Warning: Wait until the engine is cold before starting this procedure. Do not allow antifreeze to come in contact with your skin, or with the painted surfaces of the car. Rinse off spills immediately with plenty of water. Never leave antifreeze lying around in an open container, or in a puddle in the driveway or on the garage floor. Children and pets are attracted by its sweet smell, but antifreeze can be fatal if ingested.

1 With the engine completely cold, remove the expansion tank filler cap and the radiator cap. Turn the cap anti-clockwise, wait until any pressure remaining in the system is released, then unscrew it and lift it off.

2 Position a suitable container beneath the radiator drain plug, at the bottom left-hand corner of the radiator (left as seen from the driver's seat) **(see illustration)**.

3 Slacken the drain plug, and allow the coolant to drain into the container.

4 When the flow of coolant stops, refit and tighten the radiator drain plug, using a new O-ring seal.

5 If the coolant has been drained for a reason other than renewal, then provided it is clean and less than two years old, it can be re-used, though this is not recommended.

6 For complete draining, the coolant drain plug on the engine block should also be unscrewed. The plug is located at the transmission end of the engine block, on the front on 1.0 litre models, or at the back on the 1.3 litre (access to which is hampered by the exhaust manifold) **(see illustration)**.

7 Place a container under the engine, then slacken the drain plug and allow any coolant remaining in the block to drain. The plug actually has a stub fitting, which would allow a suitable diameter hose to be fitted if wished, making it easier to direct the flow of coolant **(see illustration)**.

8 While the coolant is draining, clean the threads of the drain plug – on refitting, apply a few drops of thread-locking fluid to the plug threads, and tighten the plug to the specified torque.

Cooling system flushing

9 If coolant renewal has been neglected, or if the antifreeze mixture has become diluted, then in time, the cooling system may gradually lose efficiency, as the coolant passages become restricted due to rust, scale deposits, and other sediment. The cooling system efficiency can be restored by flushing the system clean.

10 The radiator should be flushed independently of the engine, to avoid unnecessary contamination.

Radiator flushing

11 Disconnect the top and bottom hoses and any other relevant hoses from the radiator, with reference to Chapter 3.

12 Insert a garden hose into the radiator top inlet. Direct a flow of clean water through the radiator, and continue flushing until clean water emerges from the radiator bottom outlet.

13 If after a reasonable period, the water still does not run clear, the radiator can be flushed with a good proprietary cleaning agent. It is important that their manufacturer's instructions are followed carefully. If the contamination is particularly bad, insert the hose in the radiator bottom outlet, and reverse-flush the radiator.

Engine flushing

14 Remove the thermostat as described in Chapter 3 then, if the radiator top hose has been disconnected from the engine, temporarily reconnect the hose.

15 With the top and bottom hoses disconnected from the radiator, insert a garden hose into the radiator top hose. Direct a clean flow of water through the engine, and continue flushing until clean water emerges from the radiator bottom hose.

16 On completion of flushing, refit the thermostat and reconnect the hoses with reference to Chapter 3.

Antifreeze mixture

17 The antifreeze should always be renewed at the specified intervals. This is necessary not only to maintain the antifreeze properties, but also to prevent corrosion which would otherwise occur as the corrosion inhibitors become progressively less effective.

18 Always use an ethylene-glycol based antifreeze which is suitable for use in mixed-metal cooling systems. The quantity of antifreeze and levels of protection are given in the Specifications.

19 The antifreeze recommended by Toyota at the time of writing is their (pink) Super Long Life Coolant, which is said to have a 10-year, 100 000 mile life. Some models may be supplied with (red) Long Life Coolant, or conventional green coolant. Owners may still wish to change their antifreeze on a regular basis, especially if the type and quality in the system is unknown.

20 Note that neither type of Long Life Coolant should ever be mixed with any other type, especially if it is wished to preserve the 'long life' qualities (even the red and pink types should not be mixed).

21 Remember that a small amount of coolant will always be present in the system, even after draining. Therefore, if coolant of a different type is to be used, the engine and radiator should be thoroughly flushed with clean water as described previously in this Section.

22 Before adding antifreeze, check all hoses for condition and security.

23 After filling with antifreeze, a label should be attached to the expansion tank, stating the type and concentration of antifreeze used, and the date installed. Any subsequent topping-up should be made with the same type and concentration of antifreeze.

24 Do not use engine antifreeze in the windscreen/tailgate washer system, as it will cause damage to the paintwork. A screenwash additive should be added to the

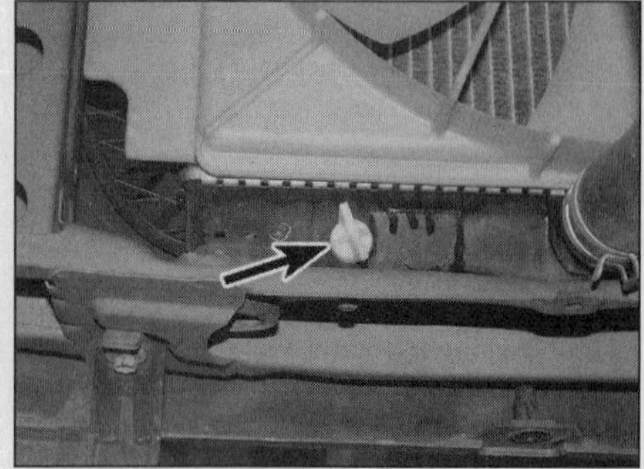

27.2 The radiator drain tap is on the left-hand side

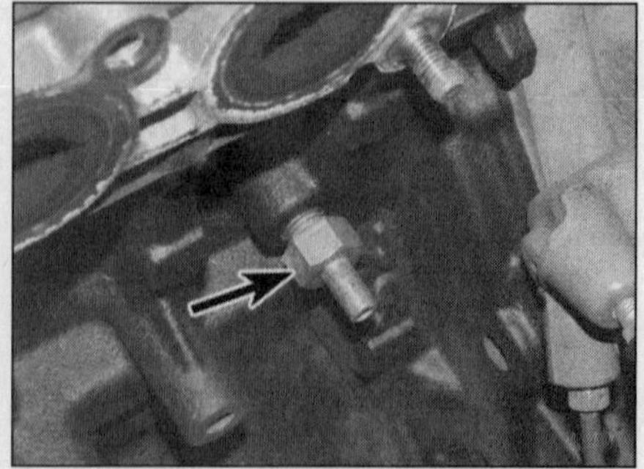

27.6 Engine block coolant drain plug – seen with the front manifold removed

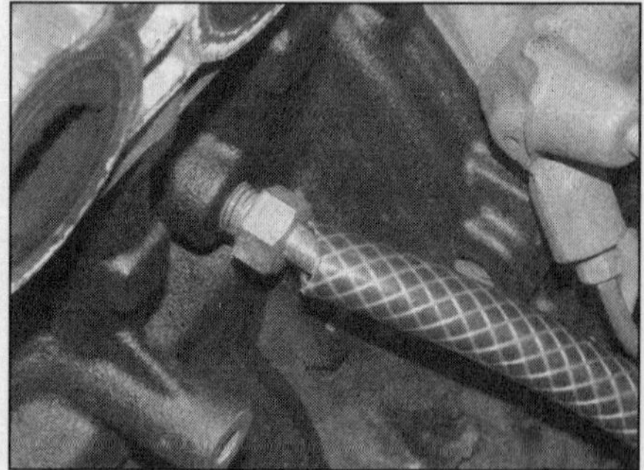

27.7 The block drain can be fitted with a hose

washer system in the quantities stated on the bottle.

Cooling system filling

25 Before attempting to fill the cooling system, make sure that all hoses and clips are in good condition, and that the clips are tight. Note that an antifreeze mixture must be used all year round, to prevent corrosion of the engine components.

26 Remove the radiator filler cap. If a funnel is available for filling the cooling system, use it to reduce the risk of spillage onto the paintwork under the bonnet.

27 Slowly fill the system until the level in the radiator stabilises. Similarly, remove the expansion tank cap, and top up the level. This process should take several minutes – gently squeeze the radiator hoses to help disperse any trapped air, and keep checking the level in both radiator and the expansion tank.

28 Start the engine, let it run for two minutes, then switch off. Be prepared to top-up the radiator (or expansion tank) as soon as the engine starts – the levels may drop quite quickly.

29 Leave the engine for a few minutes, then recheck the coolant levels in the radiator and expansion tank, and top-up if necessary. Fit the radiator and expansion tank caps once the levels have stabilised.

30 Start the engine once more, and run it at idle until the radiator top hose is fully warm (preferably, wait until the cooling fan cuts in). Keep an eye on the temperature display – if overheating is indicated at any time, switch the engine off immediately. **Note:** *Yaris models feature a temperature display warning light (or lights) – blue when the engine is cold (below 60°C) and red when hot (above 117°C).* Once the engine has warmed-up, switch it off, and allow it to cool. When the engine has cooled (preferably overnight), recheck the levels once more, and top-up if necessary.

Airlocks

31 If, after draining and refilling the system, symptoms of overheating are found which did not occur previously, then the fault is almost certainly due to trapped air at some point in the system, causing an airlock and restricting the flow of coolant; usually, the air is trapped because the system was refilled too quickly.

32 If an airlock is suspected, first try gently squeezing all visible coolant hoses. A coolant hose which is full of air feels quite different to one full of coolant when squeezed. After refilling the system, most airlocks will clear once the system has cooled, and been topped-up.

33 While the engine is running at operating temperature, switch on the heater and heater fan, and check for heat output. Provided there is sufficient coolant in the system, any lack of heat output could be due to an airlock in the system.

34 Airlocks can have more serious effects than simply reducing heater output – a severe airlock could reduce coolant flow around the engine. Check that the radiator top hose is hot when the engine is at operating temperature – a top hose which stays cold could be the result of an airlock (or a non-opening thermostat).

35 If the problem persists, stop the engine and allow it to cool down **completely**, before unscrewing the radiator and expansion tank caps, or loosening the hose clips and squeezing the hoses to bleed out the trapped air. In the worst case, the system will have to be at least partially drained (this time, the coolant can be saved for re-use) and flushed to clear the problem.

Radiator cap check

36 Clean the pressure cap, and inspect the seal inside the cap for damage or deterioration. If there is any sign of damage or deterioration to the seal, fit a new pressure cap.

Chapter 2 Part A:
Engine in-car repair procedures

Contents

Degrees of difficulty

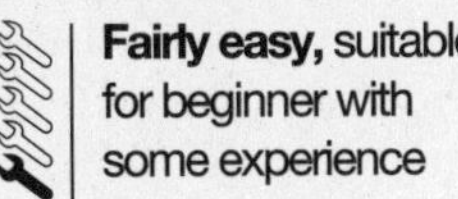

Easy, suitable for novice with little experience	**Fairly easy,** suitable for beginner with some experience	**Fairly difficult,** suitable for competent DIY mechanic	**Difficult,** suitable for experienced DIY mechanic	**Very difficult,** suitable for expert DIY or professional

Specifications

General

Engine type	Four-cylinder, in-line, twin overhead cam 16-valve, VVT-i (variable valve timing intelligent)
Engine code:	
1.0 litre engine	1SZ-FE
1.3 litre engine:	
Japanese-built models	2NZ-FE
French-built models	2SZ-FE
Capacity:	
1.0 litre engine	998 cc
1.3 litre engine	1299 cc
Bore:	
1.0 litre engine	69.0 mm
1.3 litre engine:	
2NZ-FE	75.0 mm
2SZ-FE	72.0 mm
Stroke:	
1.0 litre engine	66.7 mm
1.3 litre engine:	
2NZ-FE	73.5 mm
2SZ-FE	79.7 mm
Compression ratio:	
1.0 litre engine	10.0:1
1.3 litre engine	10.5:1
Firing order	1-3-4-2 (No 1 cylinder at timing chain end)
Direction of crankshaft rotation	Clockwise (seen from right-hand side of car)
Compression pressures:	
At engine cranking speed (400 rpm)	213 psi or more
Minimum pressure	163 psi
Maximum difference between cylinders	15 psi

Valves

Valve clearances (cold):	
1.0 litre and 1.3 litre 2SZ-FE engines:	
Checking:	
Inlet	0.145 to 0.235 mm
Exhaust	0.215 to 0.305 mm
Setting:	
Inlet	0.18 mm
Exhaust	0.25 mm
1.3 litre 2NZ-FE engine:	
Inlet	0.15 to 0.25 mm
Exhaust	0.25 to 0.35 mm
Tappet diameter:	
1.0 litre and 1.3 litre 2SZ-FE engines	27.975 to 27.985 mm
1.3 litre 2NZ-FE engine	30.966 to 30.976 mm
Valve length:	
1.0 litre and 1.3 litre 2SZ-FE engines:	
Inlet	88.15 mm (minimum 87.85 mm)
Exhaust	89.10 mm (minimum 88.80 mm)
1.3 litre 2NZ-FE engine:	
Inlet	89.25 mm (minimum 88.75 mm)
Exhaust	87.90 mm (minimum 87.40 mm)
Valve stem diameter	4.965 to 4.990 mm
Valve stem-to-guide clearance	0.010 to 0.065 mm
Valve spring free length:	
1.0 litre and 1.3 litre 2SZ-FE engines	55.38 mm
1.3 litre 2NZ-FE engine	45.1 mm

Timing chain/sprockets

Timing chain length wear limit (maximum):	
1.0 litre and 1.3 litre 2SZ-FE engines	122.6 mm per 16 links
1.3 litre 2NZ-FE engine	123.2 mm per 16 links
Camshaft sprocket diameter (minimum):	
1.0 litre and 1.3 litre 2SZ-FE engines	97.3 mm
1.3 litre 2NZ-FE engine	96.2 mm
Crankshaft sprocket diameter (minimum):	
1.0 litre and 1.3 litre 2SZ-FE engines	51.6 mm
1.3 litre 2NZ-FE engine	50.5 mm

Cylinder head

Maximum permissible gasket surface distortion	0.05 mm

Camshafts

Bearing journal diameter:	
1.0 litre and 1.3 litre 2SZ-FE engines:	
No 1 inlet	33.984 to 34.000 mm
Other inlet	22.979 to 22.995 mm
No 1 exhaust	25.979 to 25.995 mm
Other exhaust	22.979 to 22.995 mm
1.3 litre 2NZ-FE engine:	
No 1 bearing	34.449 to 34.465 mm
Others	22.949 to 22.965 mm
Endfloat:	
1.0 litre and 1.3 litre 2SZ-FE engines	0.10 to 0.24 mm
1.3 litre 2NZ-FE engine	0.04 to 0.11 mm

Cylinder block

Cylinder bore diameter:	
1.0 litre engine	69.000 to 69.012 mm
1.3 litre:	
2NZ-FE engine	75.000 to 75.013 mm
2SZ-FE engine	72.000 to 72.012 mm

Gudgeon pin

Diameter	17.999 to 18.002 mm

Connecting rods

Radial clearance	0.016 to 0.040 mm
Axial clearance	0.1 to 0.3 mm

Pistons and piston rings

Piston diameter:	
1.0 litre engine:	
Standard	68.960 to 68.972 mm
Oversize	69.460 to 69.472 mm
1.3 litre:	
2NZ-FE engine:	
Standard	74.945 to 74.955 mm
2SZ-FE engine:	
Standard	71.946 to 71.960 mm
Oversize	72.460 to 72.472 mm
Piston-to-cylinder bore clearance:	
1.0 litre and 1.3 litre 2SZ-FE engines	0.028 to 0.052 mm
1.3 litre 2NZ-FE engine	0.045 to 0.068 mm
Piston ring end gap – installed:	
1.0 litre engine:	
Top compression ring	0.25 to 0.35 mm
Second compression ring	0.35 to 0.45 mm
Oil control ring	0.15 to 0.40 mm
1.3 litre:	
2NZ-FE engine:	
Top compression ring	0.22 to 0.32 mm
Second compression ring	0.32 to 0.47 mm
Oil control ring	0.10 to 0.35 mm
2SZ-FE engine:	
Top compression ring	0.20 to 0.30 mm
Second compression ring	0.40 to 0.55 mm
Oil control ring	0.10 to 0.35 mm
Piston ring-to-groove clearance:	
1.0 litre and 1.3 litre 2SZ-FE engines:	
Top compression ring	0.030 mm to 0.070 mm
Second compression ring	0.020 mm to 0.060 mm
Oil control ring	0.070 mm to 0.150 mm
1.3 litre 2NZ-FE engine	0.030 mm to 0.070 mm

Crankshaft and bearings

Main bearing journal diameter:	
Standard	45.988 to 46.000 mm
Undersize	45.745 to 45.755 mm
Crankpin (big-end) bearing journal diameter:	
1.0 litre engine	34.992 to 35.000 mm
1.3 litre engine	39.992 to 40.000 mm
Crankshaft endfloat:	
1.0 litre and 1.3 litre 2SZ-FE engines	0.020 to 0.220 mm
1.3 litre 2NZ-FE engine	0.090 to 0.190 mm
Thrustwasher thickness:	
1.0 litre and 1.3 litre 2SZ-FE engines	1.940 to 1.990 mm
1.3 litre 2NZ-FE engine	2.430 to 2.480 mm

Lubrication

1.0 litre and 1.3 litre 2SZ-FE engines:	
Oil pressure:	
At idle speed	12 psi minimum
At 6000 rpm	58 to 78 psi
Oil pump clearances:	
Inner rotor tip clearance	0.08 to 0.15 mm
Outer rotor endfloat	0.03 to 0.08 mm
Outer rotor-to-body clearance	0.155 to 0.265 mm
1.3 litre 2NZ-FE engine:	
Oil pressure:	
At idle speed	4.3 psi minimum
At 6000 rpm	22 to 80 psi
Oil pump clearances:	
Inner rotor tip clearance	0.06 to 0.18 mm
Outer rotor side clearance	0.03 to 0.09 mm
Outer rotor-to-body clearance	0.250 to 0.325 mm

Torque wrench settings

	Nm	lbf ft
Big-end bearing cap bolts*:		
1.0 litre engine:		
Stage 1	22	16
Stage 2	Angle-tighten a further 90°	
1.3 litre engines:		
Stage 1	15	11
Stage 2	Angle-tighten a further 90°	
Camshaft bearing caps:		
No 1 cap on 1.3 litre 2NZ-FE engine	23	17
All other caps	13	10
Camshaft sprocket bolts:		
1.0 litre and 1.3 litre 2SZ-FE engines:		
Exhaust sprocket	9	7
Inlet camshaft sprocket/VVT-i controller	47	35
1.3 litre 2NZ-FE engine	64	47
Crankshaft oil seal retainer bolts:		
1.0 litre and 1.3 litre 2SZ-FE engines	9	7
Crankshaft pulley bolt:		
Except 1.3 litre 2SZ-FE engine	130	96
1.3 litre 2SZ-FE engine	150	111
Cylinder head cover nuts/bolts	9	7
Cylinder head bolts:		
1.0 litre engine:		
Stage 1	34	25
Stage 2	Angle-tighten a further 90°	
1.3 litre 2NZ-FE engine:		
Stage 1	30	22
Stage 2	Angle-tighten a further 90°	
Stage 3	Angle-tighten a further 90°	
1.3 litre 2SZ-FE engine:		
Stage 1	34	25
Stage 2	Angle-tighten a further 180°	
Downpipe to manifold	60	44
Driveplate bolts (automatic transmission)**:		
1.0 litre and 1.3 litre 2SZ-FE engines	78	58
1.3 litre 2NZ-FE engine	88	65
Engine lifting bracket bolt to cylinder head	20	15
Engine mountings:		
Left-hand mounting bolts	49	36
Rear mounting bracket-to-engine bolts	49	36
Rear mounting through-bolt	64	47
Rear mounting-to-subframe nuts/bolt	80	59
Right-hand mounting centre nut	52	38
Right-hand mounting to engine:		
1.0 litre engine	44	32
1.3 litre:		
2NZ-FE engine	55	41
2SZ-FE engine:		
Mounting bracket	42	31
Stay bar	18	13
Right-hand mounting upper section	45	33
Engine oil drain plug:		
1.0 litre engine	30	22
1.3 litre engine	38	28
Exhaust manifold	25	18
Flywheel bolts (manual transmission)**:		
1.0 litre engine:		
Stage 1	32	24
Stage 2	64	47
1.3 litre 2NZ-FE engine:		
Stage 1	49	36
Stage 2	Angle-tighten a further 90°	
1.3 litre 2SZ-FE engine:		
Stage 1	32	24
Stage 2	78	58
Idler pulley bolt	44	32

Torque wrench settings

	Nm	lbf ft
Inlet manifold:		
1.0 litre and 1.3 litre 2SZ-FE engines	19	14
1.3 litre 2NZ-FE engine	30	22
Knock sensor	39	29
Lower crankcase bolts (1.3 litre 2NZ-FE engine)	24	18
Main bearing cap bolts:		
1.0 litre and 1.3 litre 2SZ-FE engines:		
Stage 1	47	35
Stage 2	59	44
1.3 litre 2NZ-FE engine:		
Stage 1	22	16
Stage 2	Angle-tighten a further 90°	
Oil filter housing (1.3 litre 2SZ-FE engine)	18	13
Oil pick-up pipe nuts/bolt	8	6
Oil pressure relief valve	40	30
Oil pump mounting bolts	9	7
Sump bolts:		
Except 1.3 litre 2SZ-FE engine	9	7
1.3 litre 2SZ-FE engine:		
Large bolts (x3)	40	30
Small bolts (x9)	9	7
Nuts (x2)	11	8
Sump-to-transmission stiffener plate bolts	39	29
Thermostat housing nut/bolt	9	7
Timing chain cover:		
1.0 litre and 1.3 litre 2SZ-FE engines:		
Front upper bolt	18	13
Other bolts	9	7
1.3 litre 2NZ-FE engine:		
Three upper bolts and rear nut	24	18
Other bolts	11	8
Timing chain guides	8	6
Timing chain tensioner arm (rear guide pivot bolt)	19	14
Timing chain tensioner mounting bolt/nut	9	7
Transmission-to-engine bolts	64	47
VVT-i oil control valve bolt	8	6
Water bypass pipe nuts/bracket bolts:		
1.3 litre 2NZ-FE engine	9	7

** Use new bolts.*
*** Use thread-locking fluid.*

1 General information

How to use this Chapter

This Part of Chapter 2 is devoted to engine in-car repair procedures. All procedures concerning engine removal and refitting, and engine block/cylinder head overhaul, can be found in Chapter 2B.

Refer to '*Vehicle identification numbers*' in the Reference Section at the end of this manual for details of engine code locations.

Most of the operations included in this chapter are based on the assumption that the engine is still installed in the car. Therefore, if this information is being used during a complete engine overhaul, with the engine already removed, many of the steps included here will not apply.

Engine description

The engine is a twin overhead cam, water-cooled, four cylinder in-line unit, with Toyota's VVT-i variable valve timing system. The engine is an all-new design, mounted transversely at the front of the car together with the transmission to form a combined power unit.

The crankshaft is supported in five shell-type main bearings. The connecting rod big-end bearings are also split shell-type, and are attached to the pistons by floating-fit gudgeon pins. Each piston is fitted with two compression rings and one oil control ring.

Drive for the overhead camshafts is provided by a spring-tensioned 'silent' timing chain. The valves are operated by 'solid' tappets which are directly operated by the cam lobes; no adjustment shims are fitted, so the valve clearances are determined by the thickness of the tappets themselves. This reduces the weight of the valve components, and gives a virtually maintenance-free valve setup. The valves are each closed by a single valve spring, and operate in guides integral in the aluminium alloy cylinder head.

The variable valve timing system allows the inlet camshaft timing to be varied under the control of the engine management system, to boost both low-speed torque and top-end power, as well as reducing exhaust emissions. The cylindrical VVT-i controller is fitted directly to the end of the inlet camshaft, and is supplied with two pressurised oil feeds through passages in the camshaft itself. An oil control valve, operated by the engine management system, is fitted to the cylinder head, and this is used to supply the pressurised oil to the controller through the two oil feeds. The controller contains four vane chambers – depending on which of the two oil feeds is enabled by the control valve, the oil pressure will turn the inlet camshaft clockwise (advance) or anti-clockwise (retard) to adjust the valve timing as required. If pressure is removed from both feeds, this induces a timing 'hold' condition. Thus, the inlet valve timing is infinitely variable within a 60° range.

The oil pump is mounted externally on the crankcase, and is driven by the timing chain.

Engine codes

The 1.0 litre and 1.3 litre engines offered in the Yaris appear similar on paper, but there are some significant differences between them. This leads to some difficulty describing the engines in the procedures in this manual – it would be easier if the engines were totally different to each other.

The 1.0 litre engine is easiest, as it was unchanged throughout its production run. The 1.0 litre engine has a cast-iron cylinder block, with the exhaust manifold at the front.

There are two 1.3 litre engines fitted to the Yaris – the 2NZ-FE, and the 2SZ-FE, fitted to French-built models. The 2NZ-FE 1.3 engine has an aluminium alloy block, and a front-mounted plastic inlet manifold. The 2SZ-FE 1.3 engine is closely related to the 1.0 litre unit, having a cast-iron block, with the exhaust manifold on the front.

The position of the manifolds also dictates the position of the inlet and exhaust camshafts, type and position of the inlet manifold and throttle body, and so on.

Broadly speaking, then, the 'odd one out' in the engine range is the 2NZ-FE 1.3 litre unit, but even this, despite its 'reversed' cylinder head, is still very similar in many respects to the other two engines. Our main project car was a 1.0 litre model, so many of the photographs show the 1.0 litre, but the two 1.3 litre engines were also seen and photographed in our workshop.

Operations with engine in car

The following work can be carried out with the engine in the car:

- *a) Camshafts and tappets – removal, inspection and refitting.*
- *b) Cylinder head – removal and refitting.*
- *c) Crankshaft oil seals – renewal.*
- *d) Timing chain, sprockets and tensioner – removal, inspection and refitting.*
- *e) Oil pump – removal and refitting.*
- *f) Sump – removal and refitting.*
- *g) Connecting rods and pistons – removal and refitting*.*
- *h) Flywheel – removal, inspection and refitting.*
- *i) Engine/transmission mountings – inspection and renewal.*

** Although the operation marked with an asterisk can be carried out with the engine in the car after removal of the sump, it is better for the engine to be removed in the interests of cleanliness and improved access. For this reason, the procedure is described in Part B of this Chapter.*

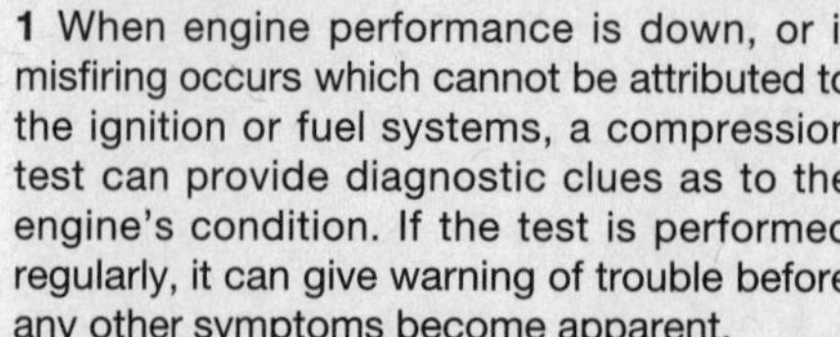

2 Compression test – description and interpretation

1 When engine performance is down, or if misfiring occurs which cannot be attributed to the ignition or fuel systems, a compression test can provide diagnostic clues as to the engine's condition. If the test is performed regularly, it can give warning of trouble before any other symptoms become apparent.

2 The engine must be fully warmed-up to operating temperature, the oil level must be correct and the battery must be fully-charged. The help of an assistant will also be required.

3 Refer to the wiring diagrams in Chapter 12 and remove the fuel pump fuse from the fusebox. Now start the engine and allow it to run until it stalls.

4 On 1.0 litre and 1.3 litre 2SZ-FE engines, remove the air cleaner as described in Chapter 4A. On the 1.3 litre engines, remove the four nuts/bolts securing the engine top cover, and take it off.

5 Disable the ignition system by disconnecting the multi-plugs from the four coils on top of the engine. Remove all the spark plugs with reference to Chapter 1.

6 Fit a compression tester to the No 1 cylinder spark plug hole – the type of tester which screws into the spark plug thread is preferable.

7 Arrange for an assistant to hold the accelerator pedal fully depressed to the floor, while at the same time cranking the engine over for several seconds on the starter motor. Observe the compression gauge reading. The compression will build-up fairly quickly in a healthy engine. Low compression on the first stroke, followed by gradually-increasing pressure on successive strokes, indicates worn piston rings. A low compression on the first stroke which does not rise on successive strokes, indicates leaking valves or a blown head gasket (a cracked cylinder head could also be the cause). Deposits on the underside of the valve heads can also cause low compression. Record the highest gauge reading obtained, then repeat the procedure for the remaining cylinders.

8 Compare the readings obtained with that specified at the start of this Chapter. The most important factor is that the compression pressures are uniform in all cylinders, and that is what this test is mainly concerned with.

9 Add some engine oil (about three squirts from a plunger type oil can) to each cylinder through the spark plug holes, and then repeat the test.

10 If the compression increases after the oil is added, the piston rings are probably worn. If the compression does not increase significantly, the leakage is occurring at the valves or the head gasket. Leakage past the valves may be caused by burned valve seats and/or faces, or warped, cracked or bent valves.

11 If two adjacent cylinders have equally low compressions, it is most likely that the head gasket has blown between them. The appearance of coolant in the combustion chambers or on the engine oil dipstick would verify this condition.

12 If one cylinder is about 20 percent lower than the other, and the engine has a slightly rough idle, a worn lobe on the camshaft could be the cause.

13 On completion of the checks, refit the spark plugs, then reconnect the coil multi-plugs. Refit the fuel pump fuse to the fusebox.

3 Top Dead Centre (TDC) for No 1 piston – locating

1 Top dead centre (TDC) is the highest point of the cylinder that each piston reaches as the crankshaft turns. Each piston reaches its TDC position at the end of its compression stroke, and then again at the end of its exhaust stroke. For the purpose of engine timing, TDC at the end of the compression stroke for No 1 piston is used. No 1 cylinder is at the crankshaft pulley/timing chain end of the engine. Proceed as follows.

2 Ensure that the ignition is switched off (take out the key). Remove the spark plugs as described in Chapter 1.

3 Turn the engine clockwise using a spanner or socket on the crankshaft pulley bolt. If necessary for improved access, apply the handbrake, then jack up the front of the car and support it on axle stands (see *Jacking and vehicle support*). Remove the plastic cover panel below the engine on the driver's side.

4 Turn the engine to the point where the notch in the outer edge of the crankshaft pulley aligns with the 0 notch in the timing plate above the pulley **(see illustration)**. To ensure that it is on its compression stroke, place a finger over the No 1 cylinder plug hole, and feel to ensure that air pressure exits from the cylinder as the piston reaches the top of its stroke.

5 For further confirmation, remove the cylinder head cover as described in Section 4.

6 If the engine is at TDC on the compression stroke, the marks on the camshaft sprockets

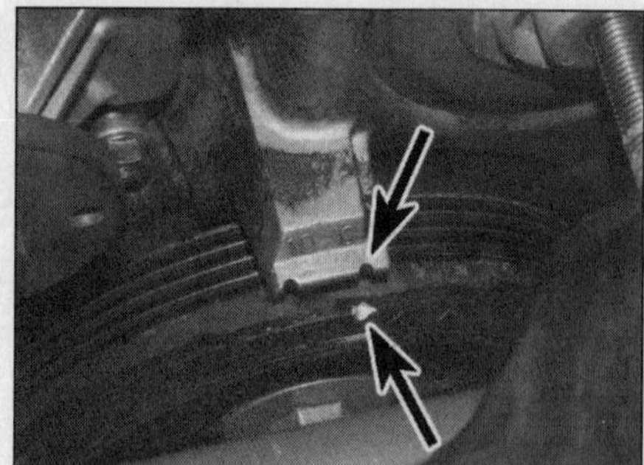

3.4 Crankshaft pulley timing mark aligned with timing cover plate

should be visible (under the timing chain) at the 12 o'clock position in both cases – if not, turn the crankshaft pulley through a full turn and realign the pulley mark with the 0 timing mark **(see illustration)**.

7 Once No 1 cylinder has been positioned at TDC on the compression stroke, TDC for any of the other cylinders can then be located by rotating the crankshaft clockwise (in its normal direction of rotation), 180° at a time, and following the firing order (see *Specifications*).

8 On completion, where applicable, refit the cylinder head cover and engine lower cover panel, then lower the car to the ground. Refit the spark plugs as described in Chapter 1.

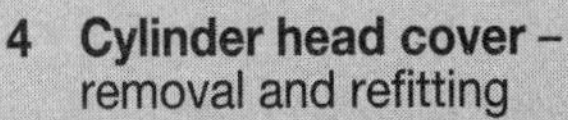

4 Cylinder head cover – removal and refitting

Removal

1 On 1.0 litre and 1.3 litre 2SZ-FE engines, remove the air cleaner as described in Chapter 4A. On 1.3 litre engines, remove the engine top cover, which is secured by four nuts/bolts **(see illustrations)**.

2 Remove the two nuts used to secure the wiring harness to the cylinder head cover, then disconnect the coil wiring plugs and move the harness clear **(see illustrations)**.

3 Unclip the injector wiring harness from the mounting brackets on the cylinder head cover **(see illustration)**. If required, these brackets can be unbolted and removed.

4 Pull off both the crankcase breather hoses from the cylinder head cover, noting their locations for refitting. 1.0 litre and 1.3 litre 2SZ-FE engines have the two hoses at the back of the cover, while both hoses on the 1.3 litre 2NZ-FE engine are at the transmission end **(see illustrations)**.

5 On 1.0 litre and 1.3 litre 2SZ-FE engines, it is helpful to disconnect the accelerator cable from the throttle body, as described in Chapter 4A.

6 Where necessary, pull out the dipstick, wipe it, and place it to one side **(see illustration)**.

3.6 At TDC, the timing dot on both camshaft sprockets should be at the top

4.1a Removing the engine top cover – 1.3 litre 2SZ-FE engine

4.1b Removing the top cover from the 1.3 litre 2NZ-FE engine

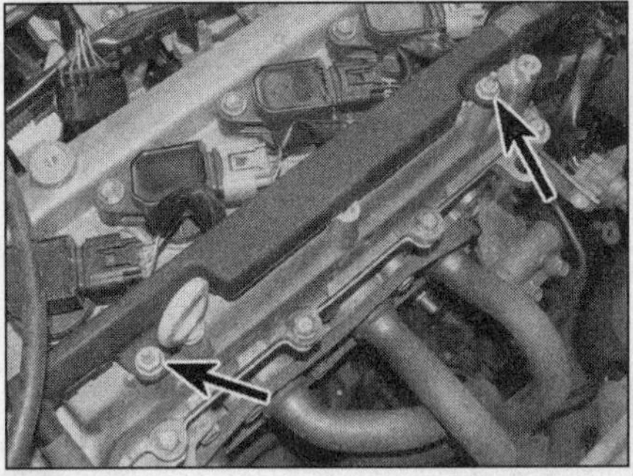

4.2a Unscrew the two mounting nuts . . .

4.2b . . . then disconnect the coil wiring plugs and remove the harness assembly

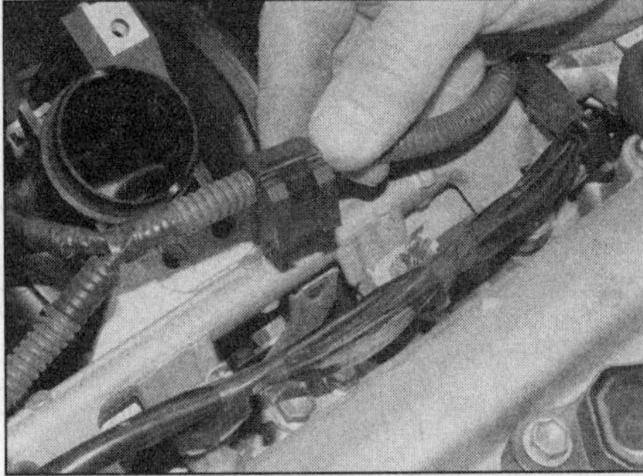

4.3 Unclip the injector wiring harness as necessary

4.4a Disconnect the crankcase breather hoses . . .

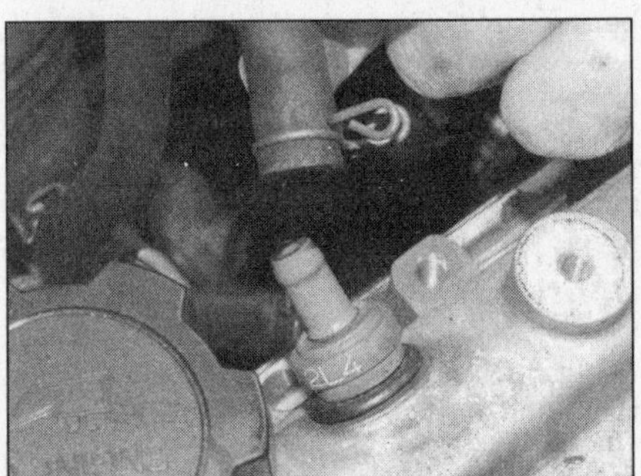

4.4b . . . from both ends of the cylinder head cover – 1.0 litre and 1.3 litre 2SZ-FE engines

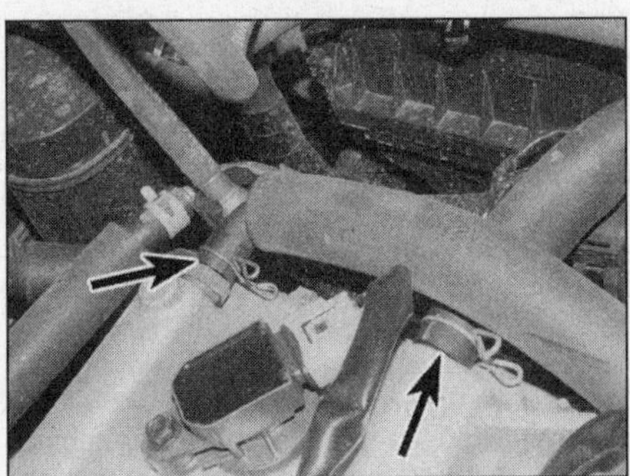

4.4c Breather hoses (arrowed) on the 1.3 litre 2NZ-FE engine

4.6 Pull out the dipstick

4.7a Unscrew the centre nuts . . .

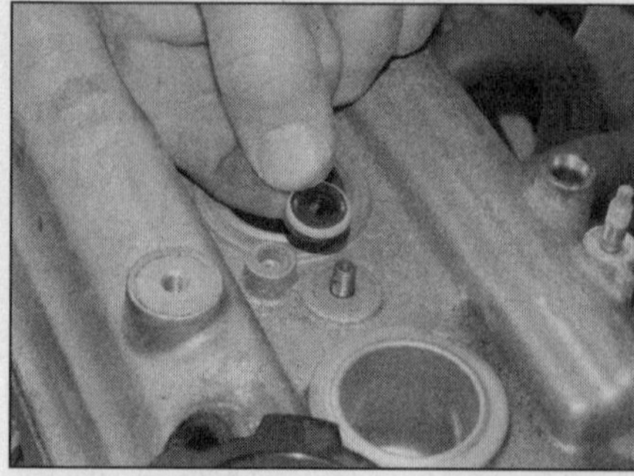
4.7b . . . and recover the washers beneath

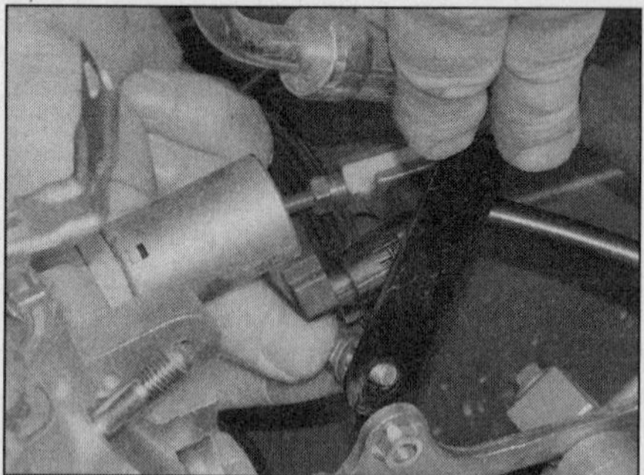
4.8a Where necessary, unbolt the power steering pipe support bracket . . .

4.8b . . . and hold the pipes aside as the cylinder head cover is removed

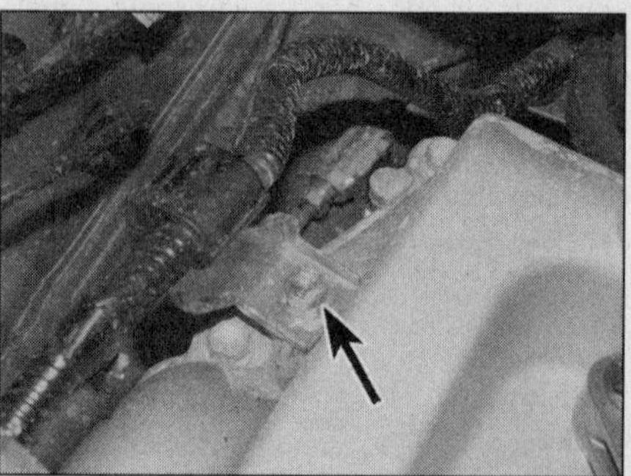
4.8c Some of the head cover bolts also secure wiring harness brackets

4.11 Fit the rubber gasket into the cover groove

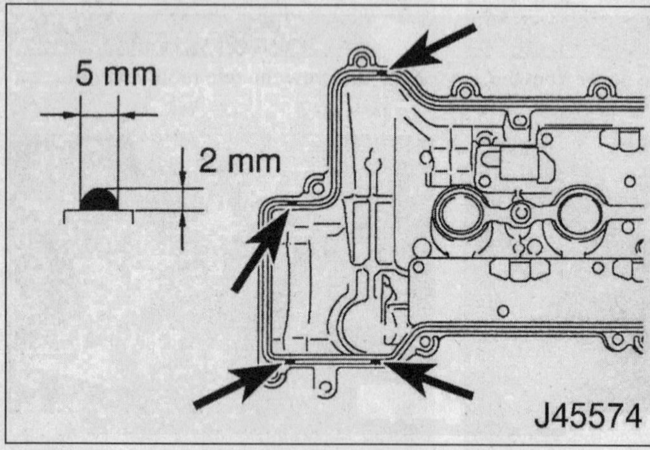

4.12a Apply sealant to the four areas shown – 1.0 litre and 1.3 litre 2SZ-FE engines

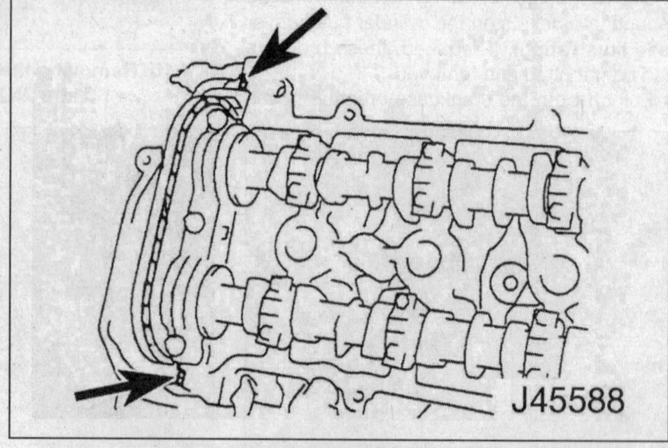

4.12b On the 1.3 litre 2NZ-FE engine, apply sealant to the two areas shown

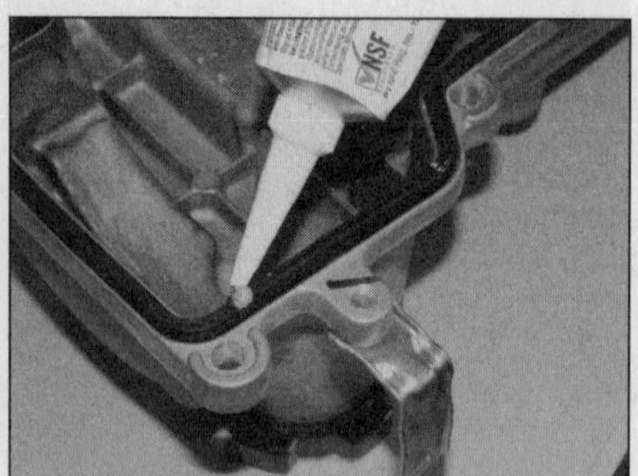
4.12c Only a spot of sealant is required at each point

7 Unscrew and remove the two nuts (recover the washers) fitted in the centre of the cylinder head cover **(see illustrations)**.

8 Work round the edge of the cylinder head cover, and remove a total of eleven securing bolts (seven bolts on 1.3 litre 2NZ-FE engines) – some bolts are used to secure wiring brackets. With all the bolts removed, carefully lift the cover clear of the cylinder head. On 1.0 litre and 1.3 litre 2SZ-FE engines at least, we found it necessary to unbolt the power steering pipe bracket behind the engine, and to pull the fluid pipes to one side, to allow the head cover to pass **(see illustrations)**.

9 Recover the rubber gasket, which may well be stuck to the engine at the timing chain end – unless the old one can be removed cleanly, a new gasket should be obtained for refitting.

10 With the gasket removed, clean all traces of old sealant from the top of the cylinder head, the cylinder head cover, and the old gasket itself (if it is to be re-used).

Refitting

11 Fit the new (or reclaimed) gasket to the cylinder head cover, making sure it is located fully in the cover groove **(see illustration)**.

12 Apply a spot of suitable RTV sealant (Toyota part number 08826-00080, Loctite 5699, or equivalent) to the points on the gasket as shown **(see illustrations)**.

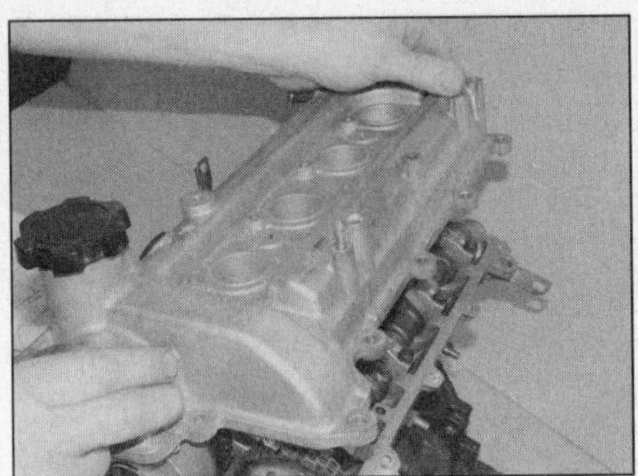

4.14 Line the cover up carefully when refitting

13 Once the sealant has been applied, the cover must be fitted within three minutes. The cover must also be fitted accurately for the sealant to be effective – place a few bolts loosely through the cover before lowering it into position, to help with the alignment.

14 Place the cover on top of the engine, making sure the gasket stays in place, and secure it with the bolts and two nuts **(see illustration)**. Tighten the bolts/nuts progressively and evenly in a diagonal sequence to the specified torque, then wipe away any excess sealant.

15 Further refitting is a reversal of removal. Allow sufficient time for the sealant to cure before starting the engine.

5 Timing chain and sprockets – removal, inspection and refitting

Removal

1 Drain the engine oil and remove the auxiliary drivebelt as described in Chapter 1. Before removing the drivebelt, loosen the water pump pulley bolts, but don't remove them yet.

2 Set the engine to TDC on No 1 cylinder as described in Section 3.

3 Remove the cylinder head cover as described in Section 4.

4 Remove the crankshaft pulley as described in Section 14.

5 On 1.0 litre and 1.3 litre 2SZ-FE engines, remove the sump as described in Section 10.

6 Where applicable, disconnect the wiring plug from the power steering pressure switch, at the back of the engine.

7 Unbolt and remove the (hydraulic) power steering pump, using the information in Chapter 10. The fluid pipes should not need to be disconnected – once the pump has been unbolted, it can be placed to one side, clear of the timing chain cover.

8 Disconnect the wiring plug from the crankshaft position sensor, and unbolt the sensor wiring brackets – move the wiring clear of the timing chain cover.

9 Unbolt and remove the auxiliary drivebelt idler pulleys as necessary **(see illustration)**. Depending on model and equipment, it will also be necessary to unbolt and remove the two idler pulley brackets.

10 Disconnect the wiring plug from the VVT-i oil control valve – this is on the rear of the head on 1.0 litre and 1.3 litre 2SZ-FE engines, and on the front for the 1.3 litre 2NZ-FE engine. Remove the single mounting bolt, and withdraw the oil control valve from the head **(see illustrations)**.

11 The engine must now be supported, as the right-hand mounting must be unbolted and removed. The best option is to use an engine crane or hoist, and support the engine from above. An engine support bar could be used, but might hamper access to the timing chain area. Though the sump has been removed, supporting the engine from below is also an option, providing a large block of wood is used between the jack head and across the crankcase surfaces. We made up a DIY support, using a stout piece of bar, drilled to accept two threaded rods, attached to the head front and rear **(see illustration)**.

12 Either unclip the throttle cable from the wire support bracket, or unbolt the bracket itself from the top of the mounting. Move the throttle cable aside.

13 Remove the three (black) bolts securing the upper section of the engine mounting to the inner wing.

14 Working underneath, remove the nut from the engine mounting central stud.

15 Remove the two bolts securing the top

5.9 Unbolt the auxiliary drivebelt pulleys

5.10a Disconnect the VVT-i oil control valve wiring plug . . .

5.10b . . . then unscrew the mounting bolt and remove the valve – 1.0 litre engine

5.10c Disconnect the VVT-i valve wiring plug . . .

5.11 DIY engine support bar in position

5.10d . . . then remove the bolt (arrowed) and withdraw the valve – 1.3 litre 2NZ-FE engine

5.15 Unbolt the upper section of the engine right-hand mounting

5.16 Unbolt the engine mounting bracket from the engine

5.17a Hold the water pump pulley using a screwdriver while the bolts are loosened

section of the mounting to the engine bracket, and lift the top section away **(see illustration)**.

16 Remove the engine mounting bracket from the engine – this is secured by two bolts and a nut, or four bolts (1.3 litre 2NZ-FE engine) **(see illustration)**. On 1.3 litre 2SZ-FE engines, also remove the two bolts securing the mounting stay bar.

17 Remove the bolts securing the water pump pulley (these are tight, and should have been loosened before the auxiliary drivebelt was removed – if not, try passing a screwdriver shaft between two of the bolts to hold it). Remove the pulley from the engine **(see illustrations)**.

18 On 1.3 litre 2NZ-FE engines, remove the water pump, which is secured by three bolts and two nuts. Recover the gasket – a new one must be used when refitting.

19 Remove the nine bolts (thirteen on 1.3 litre 2NZ-FE engines) and one nut securing the timing chain cover – note the positions of the bolts, as they are of different sizes **(see illustration)**. The shorter bolts appear to be used at the base of the cover.

20 The cover will probably have to be prised off, as sealant is used during fitting – take care not to mark the sealing surfaces. Alternatively, if a soft mallet is used, the cover can be tapped off at the front edge **(see illustration)**.

21 The cover will not come free, as it fits over two studs, and there is insufficient room between it and the inner wing for it to slide off them. To solve this problem, screw two nuts onto each stud, and unscrew them from the engine. The lower stud (for the drivebelt idler pulley) will itself not come right out when unscrewed, but can be withdrawn with the now-free timing cover **(see illustrations)**.

22 Once the cover is removed, remove the gasket/O-rings fitted to the inside, and discard – new ones should be used when refitting.

23 On 1.0 litre and 1.3 litre 2SZ-FE engines, slide off the crankshaft position sensor rotor (which looks like a thin sprocket with a tooth missing), noting how it is fitted **(see illustration)**.

24 Before removing the timing chain tensioner, rotate the lockplate downwards, then push the tensioner plunger into the body

5.17b Remove the water pump pulley

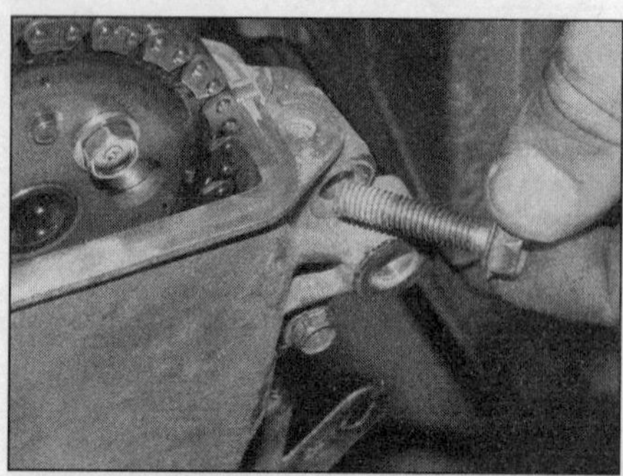
5.19 Remove the timing cover bolts – this is the largest on the 1.0 litre and 1.3 litre 2SZ-FE engines

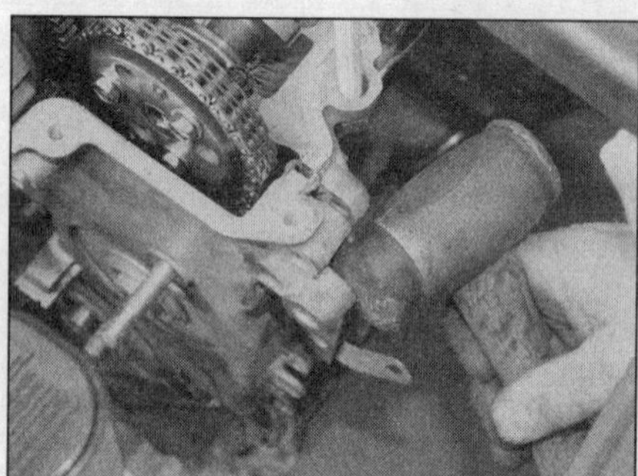
5.20 The cover is attached with sealant, and will have to be prised or tapped off

5.21a Unscrew the studs – only the upper one can be removed . . .

5.21b . . . while the lower one comes off with the cover

5.23 On 1.0 litre and 1.3 litre 2SZ-FE engines, remove the crankshaft position sensor rotor

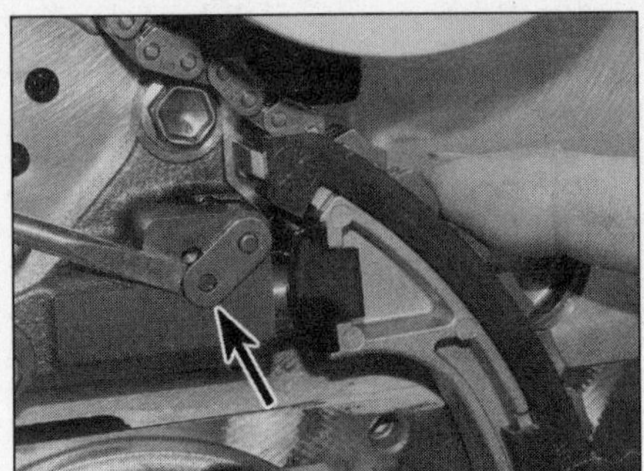

5.24a Turn the tensioner lockplate downwards to release the ratchet, and push the plunger in

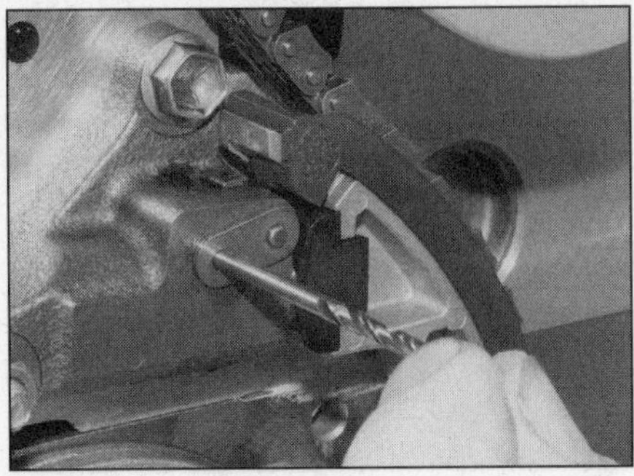

5.24b Insert a drill bit to lock the tensioner plunger

5.25a Unscrew the nut, then remove the bolt (arrowed) . . .

as far as possible (some oil will probably be lost from around the tensioner as this is done). Insert a 2 to 3 mm drill bit through the hole in the lockplate to hold it – some 'fiddling' may be required (turning the lockplate and moving the plunger) until the drill bit locks the plunger **(see illustrations)**.

25 Remove the nut and bolt securing the tensioner to the cylinder head, and remove it without disturbing the drill bit **(see illustrations)**.

26 Remove the lower pivot bolt, and take off the timing chain rear guide (which is operated on by the tensioner at the top) **(see illustration)**.

27 Remove the timing chain lower guide, which is secured by two bolts. If required, the chain front guide can be unbolted for inspection (this is necessary if the cylinder head is being removed later) **(see illustrations)**.

28 Before removing the timing chain, check for a mark on the crankshaft sprocket – this is used in relation to the two gold timing chain links when refitting. It may be useful to mark the sprocket with a dab of paint, in between the two gold links.

29 Unhook the timing chain, and remove it **(see illustration)**. The crankshaft sprocket just slides off the nose of the crankshaft, over the Woodruff key.

30 Where applicable, it is a good idea to unbolt and blow through the timing chain oil supply jet fitted above the oil pump sprocket.

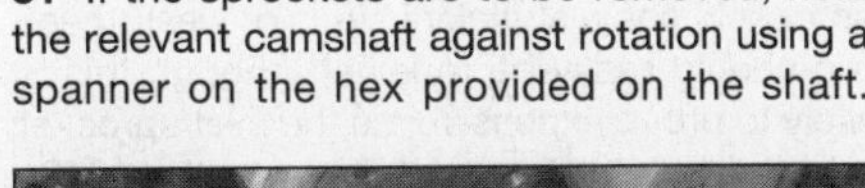

31 If the sprockets are to be removed, hold the relevant camshaft against rotation using a spanner on the hex provided on the shaft. Undo the bolts securing the inlet sprocket and VVT-i controller assembly, and the exhaust sprocket, and remove both from their

5.25b . . . and remove the timing chain tensioner with the drill bit

5.26a Remove the lower pivot bolt . . .

5.26b . . . and take off the timing chain rear guide

5.27a Remove the two bolts . . .

5.27b . . . and take off the timing chain lower guide

5.27c If required, the front guide can also be unbolted and removed

5.29 Removing the timing chain

5.31a Hold the inlet camshaft using the hex fitting . . .

5.31b . . . then unscrew the single bolt and remove the inlet sprocket/VVT-i controller

5.31c The 1.0 litre and 1.3 litre 2SZ-FE engine exhaust sprocket has three bolts, but is removed the same way

respective camshafts **(see illustrations)**. Do not attempt to separate the VVT-i controller from the inlet sprocket.

Inspection

32 Check the chain rear guide (the one operated by the tensioner) for wear. If the chain has worn a groove deeper then 0.5 mm in the guide, a new guide should be fitted. If the rear guide has worn, it is likely that the other guides will also require renewal.

33 Check the timing chain length and the sprocket diameters against the Specifications at the start of this Chapter. If the chain is known to have seen long service (over 100 000 miles), it's worth considering fitting a new one, if only for peace of mind. No renewal interval is specified by Toyota, and although a timing chain is more robust than the rubber 'cambelt' used on other engines, if the chain were to snap, the consequences for the engine would be equally serious. If the sprockets show sufficient signs of wear, these too should really be renewed (though this is likely to prove expensive, as the inlet sprocket is not available separately from the VVT-i controller).

34 Remove the drill bit from the chain tensioner to release the plunger. Turn the lockplate anti-clockwise, hold it in this position, and check that the plunger moves freely. Also check that the plunger locks when the lockplate is released. If a new timing chain or rear guide is being fitted, or if there is any doubt about the tensioner's condition, fit a new one as a matter of course. If the old tensioner is being refitted, compress the plunger and refit the drill bit to hold it.

35 While the timing chain cover is removed, it is recommended that the opportunity is taken to fit a new crankshaft oil seal. Prise or drive out the old seal, taking care not to damage the sealing surface in the timing cover. Lubricate the new seal with clean engine oil, then drive the seal in until flush with the edge of the cover, using a suitable tube or socket **(see illustrations)**.

Refitting

36 Liberally oil the end of the inlet camshaft, which should be positioned so that the locating peg is at the 12 o'clock position. Hold the VVT-i controller/inlet sprocket with the timing mark at the top, and fit it onto the locating peg on the end of the inlet camshaft. No particular force should be required – secure the controller with the bolt, hand-tight only at this stage **(see illustrations)**.

37 Hold the exhaust camshaft sprocket with the timing mark upwards, and locate it onto

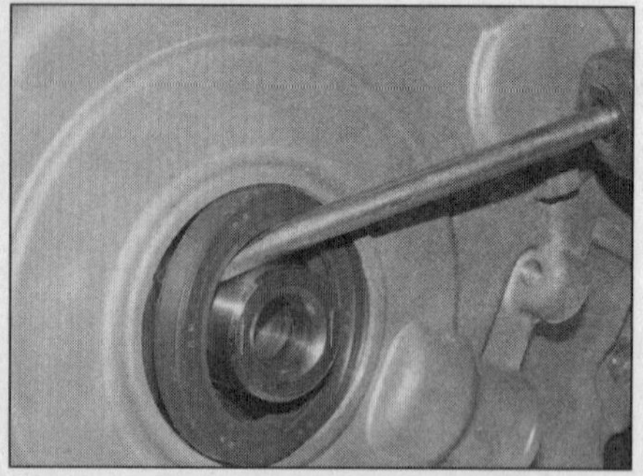
5.35a Prise out the old seal

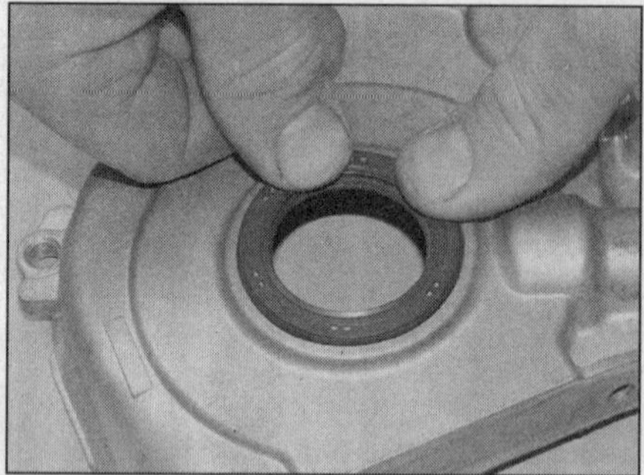
5.35b Start the new seal in using finger pressure . . .

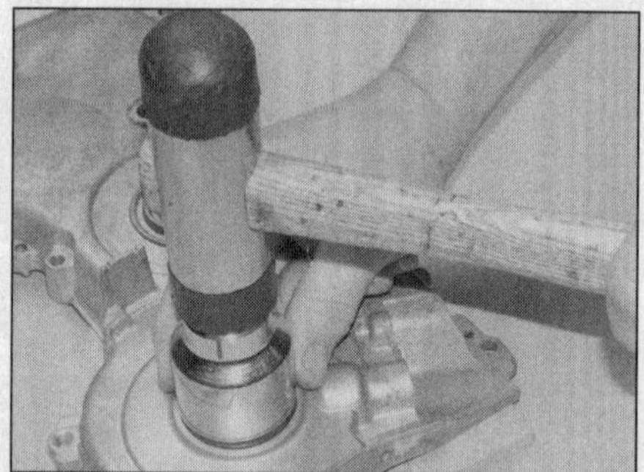
5.35c . . . tap it in square using a suitable socket . . .

5.35d . . . then if necessary tap it flush using a soft-headed mallet

5.36a Fit the inlet camshaft sprocket onto the locating peg . . .

5.36b . . . and secure with the bolt

5.37 Locate the exhaust sprocket on its peg

5.38 Tighten the sprocket bolts while holding the camshaft using a spanner

5.40 Slide the crankshaft sprocket into position . . .

the peg on the end of the camshaft (which should be at the 12 o'clock position) **(see illustration)**. Again, secure the sprocket with the three bolts (single bolt on 1.3 litre 2NZ-FE engines), hand-tight.

38 As for removal, hold the inlet and exhaust camshafts in turn using a spanner on the shaft's hex, and tighten the sprocket bolts to the specified torques **(see illustration)**. Note that the inlet and exhaust camshaft sprocket bolt torques may be different.

1.0 litre and 1.3 litre 2SZ-FE engines

39 Set the camshaft sprockets to the correct position for TDC on No 1 cylinder – ie, with the markings at 12 o'clock. Do not turn the camshafts excessively to achieve this, as there is a danger of the valves hitting the pistons.

40 Fit the crankshaft sprocket onto the crankshaft **(see illustration)**.

41 Refit the crankshaft's Woodruff key **(see illustration)**.

42 Offer up the timing chain. The adjacent pair of gold links should sit either side of the crankshaft sprocket timing mark, with the two single gold links lined up with the camshaft sprocket marks **(see illustrations)**. If this condition cannot be achieved, the crankshaft or camshaft sprockets need re-aligning slightly. The oil pump sprocket does not require any particular aligning when refitting the chain.

43 If removed, refit the timing chain front guide **(see illustration)**.

5.41 . . . followed by the Woodruff key

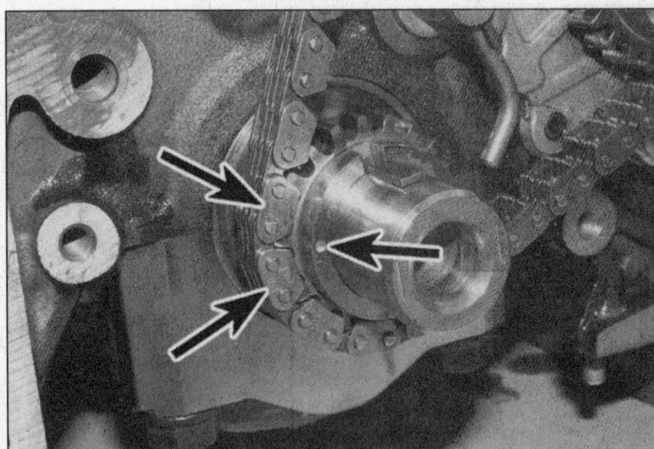

5.42a The two gold links should sit either side of the dot mark on the crankshaft sprocket

5.42b The two single gold links should align with the camshaft sprocket dot marks

5.43 Refit the timing chain front guide

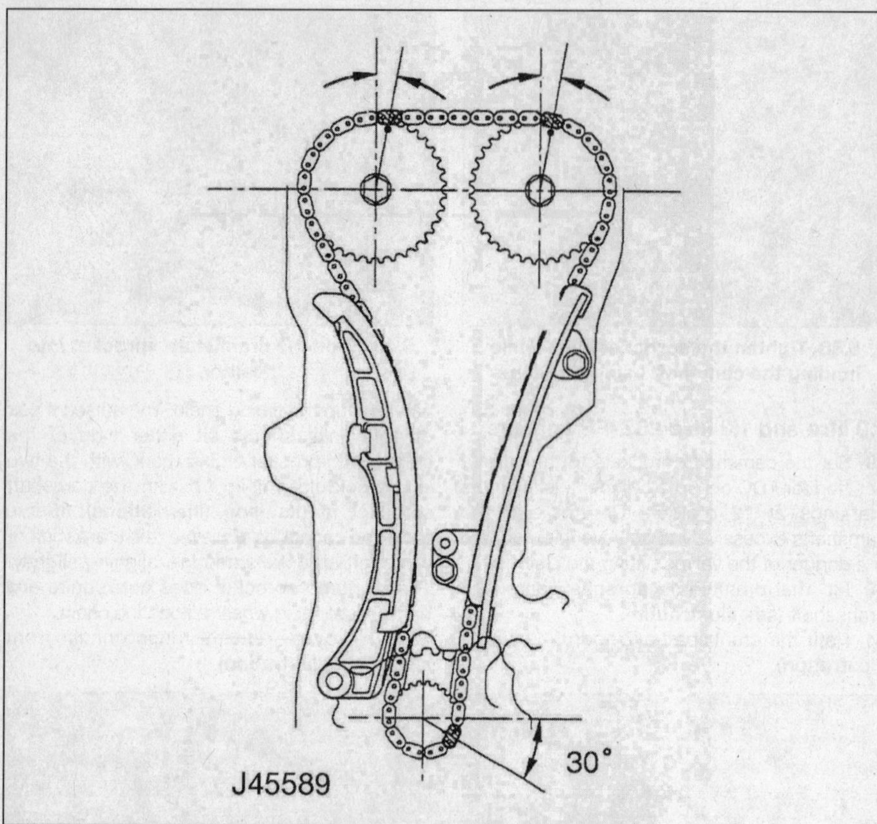

5.46 **Align the timing chain marks as shown – 1.3 litre 2NZ-FE engine**

5.53a Refit the timing chain lower guide . . .

5.53b . . . and the rear guide lower pivot bolt

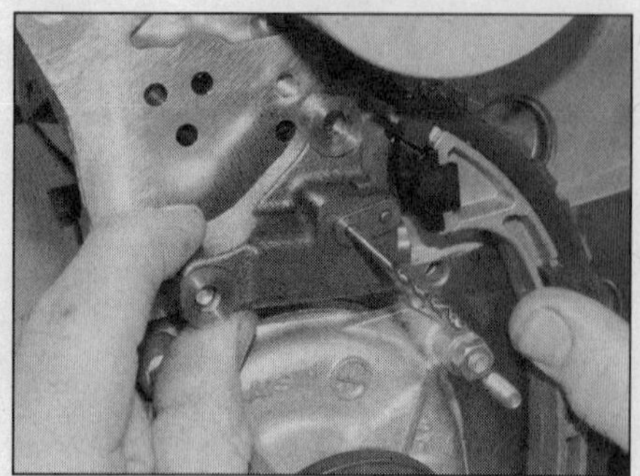

5.54 Refit the timing chain tensioner, then remove the drill bit

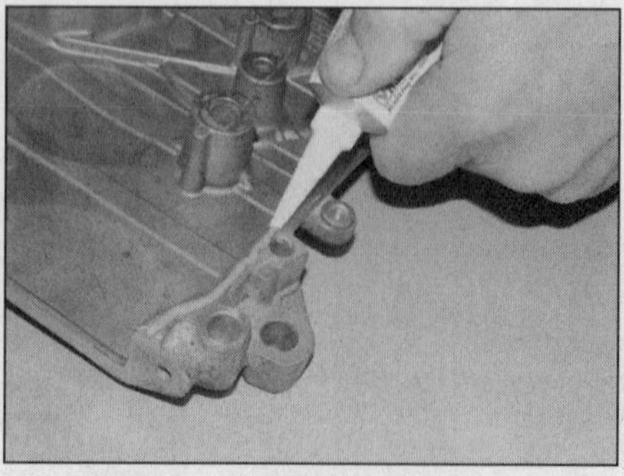

5.55 Refit the crankshaft position sensor plate – 1.0 litre and 1.3 litre 2SZ-FE engines

1.3 litre 2NZ-FE engine

44 According to Toyota, the chain should be fitted with the camshaft sprocket timing marks set at 20° ATDC (after top dead centre) – this despite the fact that there are no ATDC markings to line up with.

45 Refit the crankshaft sprocket over the Woodruff key, and turn the crankshaft forwards to between 40 and 140° ATDC.

46 Turn both camshaft sprockets forward (in the normal direction of rotation) to the 20° ATDC position indicated in the accompanying diagram **(see illustration)**.

47 Now turn the crankshaft sprocket backwards to the 20° ATDC position. At this point, the sprocket timing mark will be approximately 30° below horizontal (or about the 4 o'clock position).

48 If removed, refit the timing chain front guide.

49 Offer up the timing chain. The single gold/yellow link on each camshaft sprocket should align with the sprocket timing mark, with no slack in between the sprockets. It may be necessary to hold the exhaust (rear) camshaft, using a spanner on the shaft's hex fitting, against the pressure of the valve springs, to achieve alignment between the sprocket and chain marks.

50 Similarly, the single marked link at the base of the chain's run should align with the mark on the crankshaft sprocket.

51 It may be necessary to re-align the sprockets slightly to achieve a satisfactory fit, but do not turn the sprockets far with the chain removed, or valve-to-piston contact may occur.

52 Although **not** the procedure stated by Toyota, there would appear to be nothing wrong in fitting the chain with all three sprockets in the TDC position. This approach could perhaps be adopted if the 20° ATDC position method proves unsatisfactory. At all times, however, remember to only turn the sprockets as little as possible to achieve alignment, to avoid valve-to-piston contact.

All engines

53 Refit the timing chain lower guide, then the rear guide, tightening the bolts to the specified torque **(see illustrations)**.

54 Holding the rear guide out of the way, refit the timing chain tensioner, and tighten the nut and bolt to the specified torque **(see illustration)**. Release the tensioner by removing the drill bit, ensuring that the plunger engages with the timing chain rear guide. Allow the tensioner to take up the slack in the chain.

55 On 1.0 litre and 1.3 litre 2SZ-FE engines, refit the crankshaft position sensor plate over the crankshaft's Woodruff key, with the F marking facing outwards **(see illustration)**.

56 Clean any old sealant from the timing chain cover mating faces. Apply a 3 mm diameter bead of suitable flange sealant (Toyota part number 08826-00100, Loctite 5699, or equivalent) to the cover, with three further circles of sealant applied around the three central holes **(see illustration)**. Once

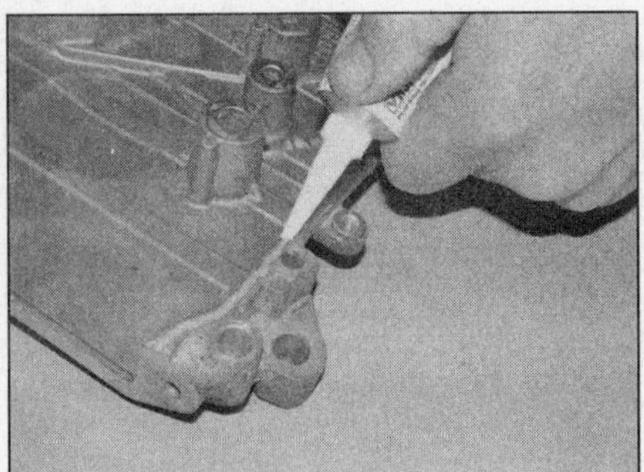

5.56 Apply a bead of sealant to the timing cover mating faces

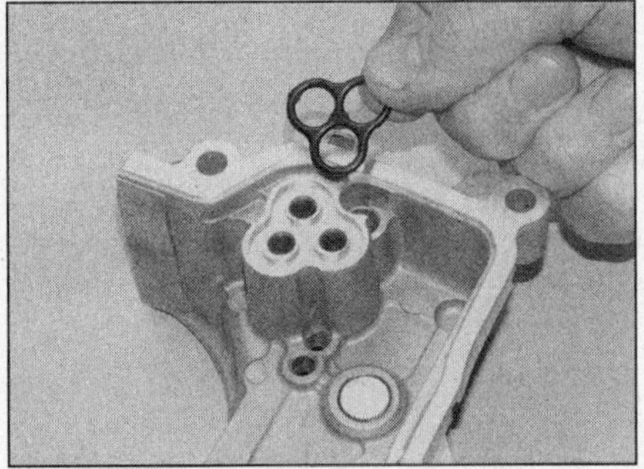

5.57 Fit a new timing cover gasket

5.58 Align the timing cover carefully, to avoid damaging the sealant

the sealant has been applied, the cover should be refitted within three minutes.

57 Fit a new timing chain cover gasket or O-rings, as applicable. On 1.0 litre and 1.3 litre 2SZ-FE engines, the small gasket at the top looks like three O-rings joined together **(see illustration)**. On the 1.3 litre 2NZ-FE engine, two O-rings are fitted between the timing cover and the lower crankcase.

58 Offer the cover into position, then refit the nut and bolts to their previously-noted positions **(see illustration)**.

59 Progressively tighten the bolts and single nut in several stages, to pull the cover evenly into place. Finally, tighten the nut and bolts to the specified torques.

60 The remainder of refitting is a reversal of removal, noting the following points:

a) *Before refitting the cylinder head cover, turn the engine two complete turns clockwise, and check that the crankshaft and camshaft timing marks come back into alignment as described in Section 3.*

b) *Tighten all fasteners to the specified torque.*

c) *Allow sufficient time for the sealant used on the timing chain and cylinder head covers, and on the sump, to cure before starting the engine.*

6 Timing chain tensioner – removal, inspection and refitting

Remove the timing chain cover using the information in Section 5. The tensioner can be removed as described in paragraphs 24 and 25, and inspected as described in paragraph 34.

7 Camshafts and tappets – removal, inspection and refitting

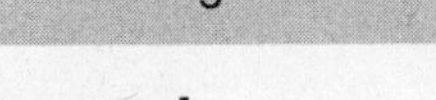

Removal

1 Remove the timing chain and sprockets as described in Section 5.

1.0 litre and 1.3 litre 2SZ-FE engines

2 Progressively loosen the four bolts, and remove the 'double' No 1 camshaft bearing cap (nearest the timing chain end) **(see illustration)**.

3 Before removing the remaining caps, turn the inlet (rear) camshaft, using a spanner on the hex halfway along the shaft, until the lobes for cylinders 3 and 4 are pointing downwards. Similarly, turn the exhaust (front) camshaft so the lobes for cylinders 2 and 4 are pointing downwards.

4 It's essential that the camshaft bearing caps are refitted to their original locations. Before loosening the caps, check that they're marked with a number, indicating their fitted position (No 1 is at the timing chain end, inlet and exhaust can be deduced from the manifolds) **(see illustration)**. If no numbers can be seen, make your own with paint or a dot-punch.

5 Loosen the inlet camshaft bearing cap bolts by a quarter-turn each at a time, in the following order – No 4, No 5, No 2 and No 3 – until they are all loose. Carefully remove the caps and the camshaft, and store them safely – tape the caps to the camshaft to keep them together **(see illustrations)**.

6 Similarly, progressively slacken the exhaust camshaft bearing caps in the following order – No 3, No 5, No 2 and No 4. Carefully remove

7.2 Unbolt and remove the 'double' No 1 camshaft bearing cap

7.4 This is the No 5 inlet camshaft bearing cap – marked I5, with an arrow pointing to the timing chain

7.5a Loosen the bearing cap bolts . . .

7.5b . . . then remove the caps . . .

7.5c . . . and lift out the camshaft

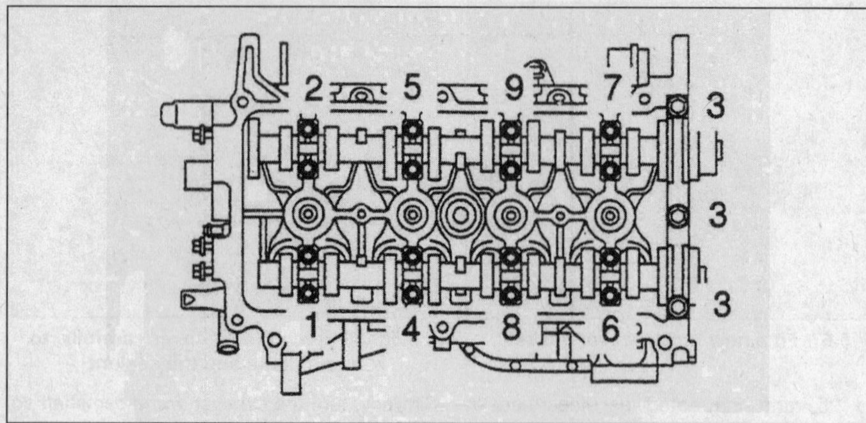

7.7 Camshaft bearing cap loosening sequence – 1.3 litre 2NZ-FE engine

the caps and the camshaft, and store them safely – tape the caps to the camshaft to keep them together.

1.3 litre 2NZ-FE engine

7 Working in sequence, progressively loosen the bearing cap bolts until all are loose **(see illustration)**. Carefully remove the caps and the camshafts, and store them safely – tape the caps to the camshaft to keep them together.

All engines

8 Before lifting out the tappets, it's best to have ready a box that's been divided up into sixteen sections, or failing that, a piece of card clearly marked, so the tappets can be arranged and kept in their fitted order. The tappets should not be marked in any way (other than perhaps by wrapping a piece of masking tape round, onto which a number can be written). Lift each tappet out, and store it so that it can be refitted in the same location **(see illustration)**.

Inspection

Note: *For complete dismantling of the cylinder head (removal of the valves, etc), refer to Part B of this Chapter.*

9 With the camshafts and tappets removed, check each for signs of obvious wear (scoring, pitting, etc) and for ovality, and renew if necessary.

10 Measure the outside diameter of each tappet – take measurements at the top and bottom of each tappet, then a second set at right-angles to the first; if any measurement is significantly different from the others, the tappet is tapered or oval (as applicable) and must be renewed. If the top surface of any tappet is worn, check the corresponding lobe on the camshaft.

7.8 Lift out the tappets (here using a magnetic pick-up tool) and store them in their fitted order

11 Visually examine the camshaft lobes for score marks, pitting, galling (wear due to rubbing) and evidence of overheating (blue, discoloured areas). Look for flaking away of the hardened surface layer of each lobe. Renew the camshaft if any of these conditions are apparent. Examine the condition of the bearing surfaces, both on the camshaft journals and in the cylinder head. If the head bearing surfaces are worn excessively, the cylinder head will need to be renewed.

Refitting

12 Oil the cylinder head tappets and bores, and carefully refit the tappets to their original positions in the cylinder head – some care will be required to enter the tappets squarely into their bores **(see illustration)**. Check that each tappet rotates freely.

13 Liberally oil the exhaust camshaft lobes and the camshaft bearings in the cylinder head **(see illustration)**.

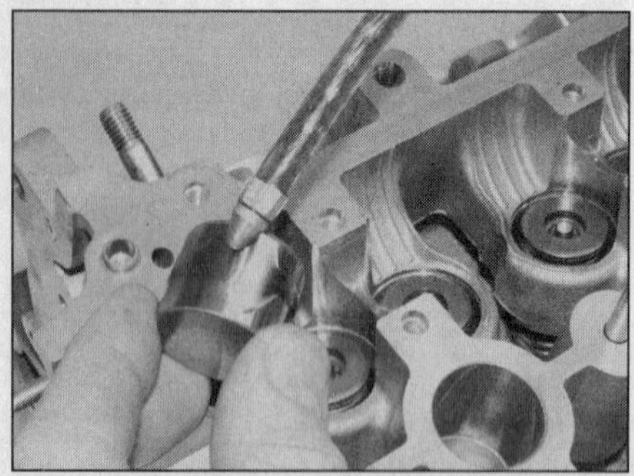

7.12 Oil the tappets and their bores before fitting

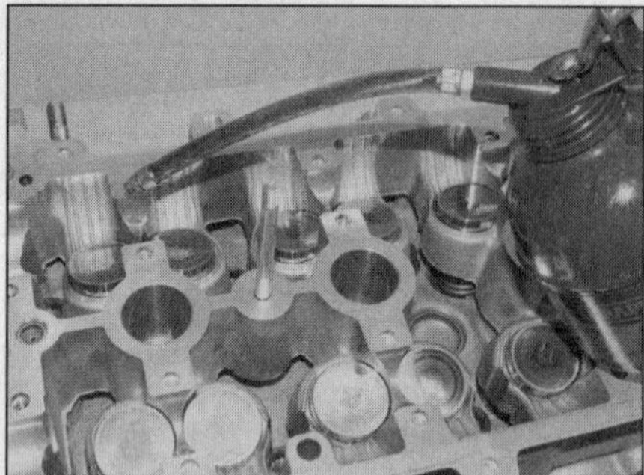

7.13 Oil the camshaft bearing surfaces and the camshaft lobes

1.0 litre and 1.3 litre 2SZ-FE engines

14 Place the camshaft onto the cylinder head with the camshaft lobes for cylinders 2 and 4 pointing downwards. Fit the No 3 and 5 bearing caps, and tighten their bolts by a quarter-turn at a time, to the specified torque **(see illustration)**. Fit the No 2 and 4 bearing caps, and again progressively tighten the remaining four bolts. On completion, the camshaft can be turned so that the sprocket locating peg is at the 12 o'clock position.

15 Similarly, lay the inlet camshaft in place on the cylinder head, with the lobes for cylinders 3 and 4 facing down. Fit the No 4 and 5 camshaft bearing caps, and tighten their bolts by a quarter-turn at a time, to the specified torque. Fit the No 2 and 3 bearing caps, and again progressively tighten the remaining four bolts. On completion, the camshaft can be turned so that the sprocket locating peg is at the 12 o'clock position.

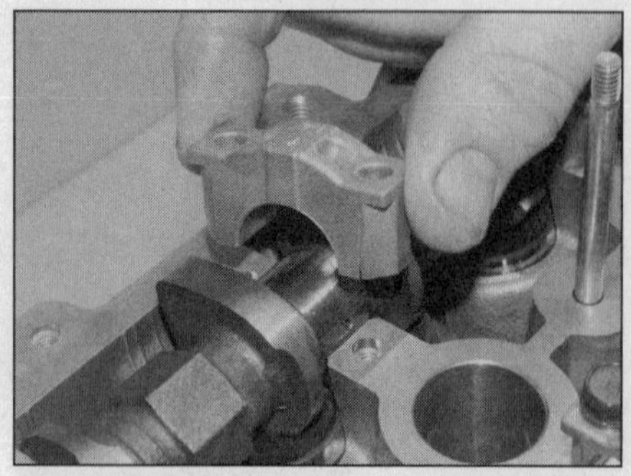

7.14 Fit the smaller bearing caps, and progressively tighten the bolts

7.16 Fit the 'double' No 1 bearing cap last

16 Fit the 'double' No 1 bearing cap in position **(see illustration)**. Starting with the centre bolts, tighten the four bolts by a quarter-turn at a time, to the specified torque.

1.3 litre 2NZ-FE engine

17 Place the camshafts in position, with the No 1 cam lobes facing upwards.

18 Refit the bearing caps with lightly-oiled bolts, and tighten the bolts progressively in sequence, to the specified torques **(see illustration)**. Note that the torque for the double No 1 cap bolts is higher than the rest.

All engines

19 Refit the timing chain and sprockets as described in Section 5.

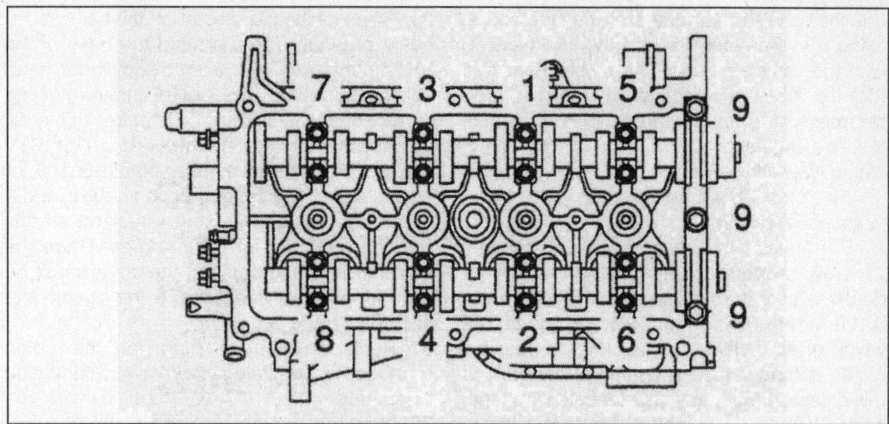

7.18 Camshaft bearing cap tightening sequence - 1.3 litre 2NZ-FE engine

8 Valve clearances - checking and adjustment

Note: *Because the tappets are not fitted with shims, valve clearance adjustment is carried out by fitting new tappets, which requires removing the camshafts.*

Checking

1 Remove the cylinder head cover as described in Section 4.

2 Set the engine to TDC on No 1 cylinder as described in Section 3.

3 With the engine in this position, check the clearances for No 1 and 2 cylinder inlet valves, and the exhaust valve clearances for cylinders 1 and 3.

4 Insert a feeler blade between the camshaft lobe and the tappet, and record the clearance found for all eight valves **(see illustration)**. If the clearances found are within the 'checking' specification (refer to the start of this Chapter), no adjustment will be required.

5 Turn the engine, using a spanner or socket on the crankshaft pulley bolt, through one complete turn. The crankshaft pulley mark should now be aligned with the 0 mark, but the camshaft sprocket timing marks should not be visible.

6 With the engine in this position, check the clearances for No 3 and 4 cylinder inlet valves, and the exhaust valve clearances for cylinders 2 and 4.

7 Insert a feeler blade between the camshaft lobe and the tappet, and record the clearance found for the remaining eight valves. If the clearances found are within specification (refer to the start of this Chapter), no adjustment will be required.

8 If no adjustment is needed, refit the cylinder head cover as described in Section 4.

Adjustment

Note: *The following procedure allows the camshafts to be removed without completely removing the timing chain, which is a time-consuming job. However, if difficulty is experienced with this procedure, removing the timing chain as described in Section 5 is the only alternative.*

9 Reset the engine to TDC on No 1 cylinder as described in Section 3.

10 Paint alignment marks on the timing chain, in line with the timing marks on the sprockets.

11 On 1.0 litre and 1.3 litre 2SZ-FE engines, remove the two bolts securing the half-circular cover around the base of the VVT-i controller - the cover is fitted using sealant, and may have to be prised off **(see illustration)**.

12 Unscrew the timing cover plug fitted below the rear camshaft - this gives access to the timing chain tensioner **(see illustration)**.

13 Using a pointed tool through the timing cover access hole, turn the chain tensioner lockplate downwards to release the plunger ratchet **(refer to illustration 5.24a)**.

14 At the same time, using a spanner on the hex halfway along the rear camshaft, have an assistant turn the shaft clockwise as far as possible, against the resistance of the timing chain tensioner.

15 Take a 2 or 3 mm drill bit, and try to insert it through the tensioner lockplate to hold the plunger in the retracted position **(refer to illustration 5.24b)**. If the drill bit will not go in first time, have your assistant move the rear camshaft back-and-forth slightly.

16 With the tension released from the timing chain, lift the chain off the exhaust camshaft sprocket. If the chain will not come off easily, turn the exhaust camshaft slightly.

17 Hold the inlet camshaft against rotation using the spanner on the hex halfway along the shaft, and undo the bolt securing the VVT-i controller. Slide the controller and inlet sprocket, complete with chain, off the end of the inlet camshaft.

18 Before lifting the timing chain off the inlet sprocket, have ready some wire or string to tie the chain up with - it must not be allowed to fall down (or even go slack), as it may disengage itself from the crankshaft sprocket, which would mean taking off the timing chain cover (Section 5). Lift off the timing chain, and secure it to the engine. Place the inlet sprocket and controller assembly to one side.

19 Remove the camshafts as described in Section 7. The exhaust sprocket can remain attached to its camshaft for this procedure.

20 Remove each tappet which requires adjustment in turn, and measure the thickness

8.4 Checking a valve clearance

8.11 Remove the half-circular cover from the VVT-i controller

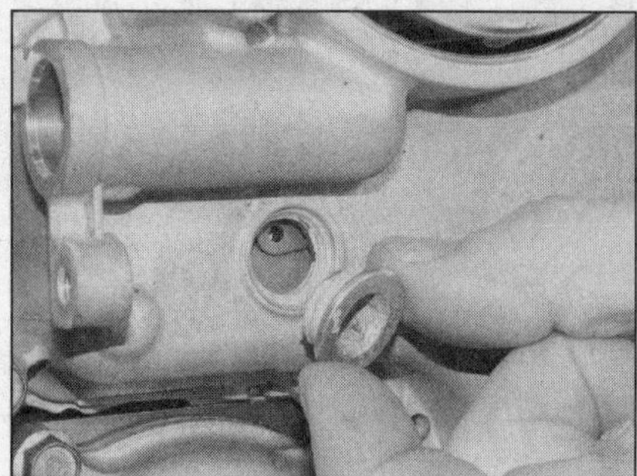

8.12 Unscrew the timing cover plug to access the tensioner lockplate

between the top surface and the inner boss, using a micrometer. Record the thickness (T) with the valve clearance previously measured (C) for use in calculating the required thickness of the new tappet (N). For example (1.0 litre engine):

Inlet: New (N) =
Thickness (T) + Clearance (C) – 0.18 mm.
Exhaust: New (N) =
Thickness (T) + Clearance (C) – 0.25 mm.

21 New tappets are available from Toyota dealers, in increments of 0.020 mm, from 5.120 mm to 5.680 mm. Select a new tappet which gives a clearance as close as possible to the setting values specified at the start of this Chapter. Mark any new tappets with tape, or store them (with any old tappets) in the correct fitted sequence.

22 Lubricate and fit the tappets, making sure they are all fitted to the correct locations. Check that they are free to turn.

23 Refit the camshafts as described in Section 7.

24 Keeping gentle tension on the chain at all times, refit it over the inlet sprocket, so that the mark made on the chain aligns with the sprocket timing mark. Slide the sprocket and controller assembly into place on the end of the camshaft, without applying any great force, and secure with the bolt, hand-tight.

25 Lift the timing chain over the exhaust camshaft sprocket, and fit it so that the chain mark aligns with the sprocket timing mark.

26 Hold the inlet camshaft against rotation using a spanner on the shaft's hex, and tighten the inlet sprocket bolt to the specified torque.

27 Turn the rear camshaft anti-clockwise slightly, to move any slack In the timing chain onto the rear side. Remove the drill bit from the chain tensioner, and allow the plunger to tension the chain.

28 Turn the engine through two complete turns, and check that the crankshaft and camshaft timing marks come back into alignment as described in Section 3. Recheck the valve clearances as described in paragraphs 3 to 7.

29 Clean all the old sealant off the half-circular cover originally fitted around the base of the VVT-i controller, and from the cylinder head sealing surfaces. The cover and its sealing surface on the head must be kept free of any oil.

30 Apply a 3 mm diameter bead of RTV sealant (Toyota part number 08826-00100, or equivalent) to the cover groove on the cylinder head – do not apply excess sealant, as this may find its way into the engine. Once the sealant has been applied, the cover must be refitted within 3 minutes. Fit the cover, and secure with the two bolts.

31 Refit the access plug for the chain tensioner to the timing chain cover, tightening it securely.

32 Turn the engine by hand through a few turns, and check that there is no excess sealant attached to the VVT-i controller.

33 On completion, refit the cylinder head cover as described in Section 4.

9 Cylinder head – removal and refitting

Removal

1 Drain the cooling system as described in Chapter 1.

2 Remove the nut or bolt securing the exhaust manifold to its stay/bracket – on 1.0 litre and 1.3 litre 2SZ-FE engines, this is located next to the oil filter, while on the 1.3 litre 2NZ-FE engine, this is at the rear of the engine. In either case, access is gained from below.

3 Remove the camshafts as described in Section 7 – this is necessary to gain access to the head bolts. Unless the head is being worked on further, the tappets can stay in place.

4 Remove the three bolts and two nuts from the exhaust manifold, and remove it from the cylinder head (on the 1.3 litre 2NZ-FE engine, take off the heat shield first – this is secured by four bolts). Recover the gasket – a new one should be used on reassembly.

5 Remove the injectors and inlet manifold as described in Chapter 4A. If not already done, also remove the air cleaner.

6 Disconnect the coolant hoses from the transmission end of the cylinder head, noting their positions for refitting **(see illustration)**.

7 Work around the cylinder head, and disconnect the wiring plugs, earth leads, wiring harness brackets, etc, as follows:

a) *Coolant temperature sensor, cooling fan switch and camshaft position sensor wiring plugs, at the transmission end of the cylinder head.*
b) *Earth lead and wiring harness bracket, also at the transmission end of the cylinder head.*
c) *VVT-i oil control valve, at the timing chain end.*
d) *Remove the wiring harness bracket at the front of the engine, next to the engine right-hand mounting.*
e) *On the 1.3 litre 2NZ-FE engine, unbolt the water bypass pipe bracket from the transmission end of the head.*

8 Support the engine securely from below before starting to loosen the cylinder head bolts (our DIY support bar located on the head itself, and had to be removed). Alternatively, partially refit the engine right-hand mounting, using only the two front bolts to secure the mounting bracket to the engine block **(see illustration)**.

9.6 Disconnect the coolant hoses from the end of the head

9.8a Refit the engine right-hand mounting bracket into the block only . . .

9.8b . . . then refit the mounting upper section to the bracket and wing

9.9a The head bolts have an unusual bi-hex fitting, which looks like a splined type

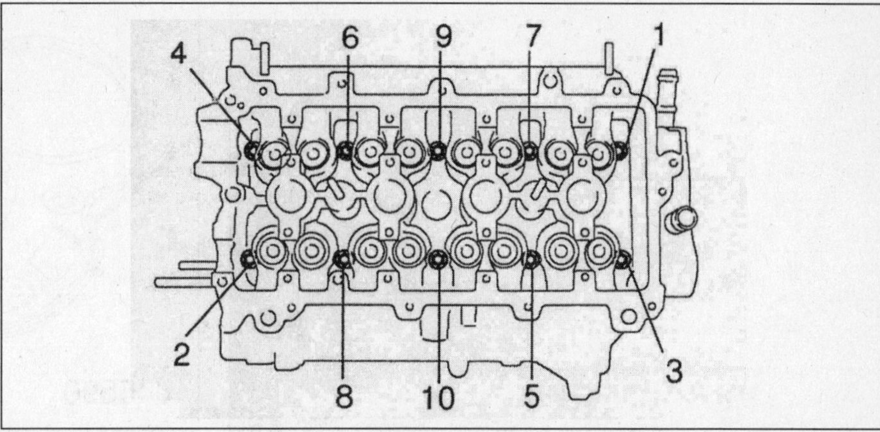

9.9b Cylinder head bolt loosening sequence

9 Loosen the cylinder head bolts by a quarter-turn at a time, in sequence. The head bolts on our car had a very unusual fitting – an 8 mm bi-hex. We managed to use an 8 mm 'single-hex' Allen bit to unscrew them – note that the bi-hex resembles a splined bolt, but a splined bit will not fit **(see illustrations)**. Soak out any oil from the bolt heads before starting.

10 Remove the ten bolts and washers – it is recommended that they are not re-used, and a complete new set be obtained for refitting **(see illustration)**. This is especially the case if the correct bit was not available to unscrew them, as the heads may become damaged.

11 Check round the head that there is nothing still attached, and nothing in the way which will hinder it being lifted away.

12 Carefully lift off the head, and place it on a clean surface – do not allow the lower face to be damaged, or even a new gasket will not seal properly **(see illustration)**. If the head is stuck, try rocking it backwards to free it, using a blunt lever (such as a wooden hammer handle) in the inlet and exhaust ports – space permitting. Once the gasket seal has been broken, the head should come off. Hitting the head is not advisable, as the alloy is easily damaged. Also note that the head is located on two dowels.

13 Recover the old head gasket, noting that it may be stuck in place with sealant at the timing chain end **(see illustration)**. Though it should not be re-used, it may be useful to hold onto it for now, to compare with the new one as verification.

14 If the head is to be dismantled for overhaul, remove the tappets as described in Section 7, then refer to Part B of this Chapter.

Preparation for refitting

15 The mating faces of the cylinder head and cylinder block/crankcase must be perfectly clean before refitting the head. Remove the two dowels (note their positions) and use a hard plastic or wood scraper to remove all traces of gasket and carbon; also clean the piston crowns.

16 Take particular care during the cleaning operations, as aluminium alloy is easily damaged. Also, make sure that the carbon is not allowed to enter the oil and water passages – this is particularly important for the lubrication system, as carbon could block the oil supply to the engine's components. Using adhesive tape and paper, seal the water, oil and bolt holes in the cylinder block/crankcase.

HAYNES HiNT ***To prevent carbon entering the gap between the pistons and bores, smear a little grease in the gap. After cleaning each piston, use a small brush to remove all traces of grease and carbon from the gap, then wipe away the remainder with a clean rag.***

17 Check the mating surfaces of the cylinder block/crankcase and the cylinder head for nicks, deep scratches and other damage. If slight, they may be removed carefully with a file, but if excessive, machining may be the only alternative to renewal.

18 If warpage of the cylinder head gasket surface is suspected, use a straight-edge to check it for distortion. Refer to Part B of this Chapter if necessary.

19 Check the condition of the old head bolts. If they came out easily, and are known not to have been disturbed before, then provided the threads show no sign of damage, they could be re-used. However, we recommend fitting a complete new set of bolts. Do not be tempted, either for convenience or saving money, to ignore this advice – if the bolts or their threads 'let go' when they're tightened, the bottom half of the engine could be reduced to scrap very quickly.

20 Although not essential, if a suitable tap-and-die set is available, it's worth running the correct-size tap down the bolt threads in the cylinder block. This will clean the threads of any debris, and go some way to restoring any damaged threads. Make absolutely sure the tap is the right size and thread pitch, and lightly oil the tap before starting.

21 If possible, clean out the bolt holes in the block using compressed air, to ensure no oil or water is present. Screwing a bolt into an oil- or water-filled hole can (in extreme cases) cause the block to fracture, due to the hydraulic pressure created.

9.10 Recover the washers below the head bolts

9.12 Lift the head off the locating dowels

9.13 Recover the old head gasket

9.23 Check that the locating dowels are refitted

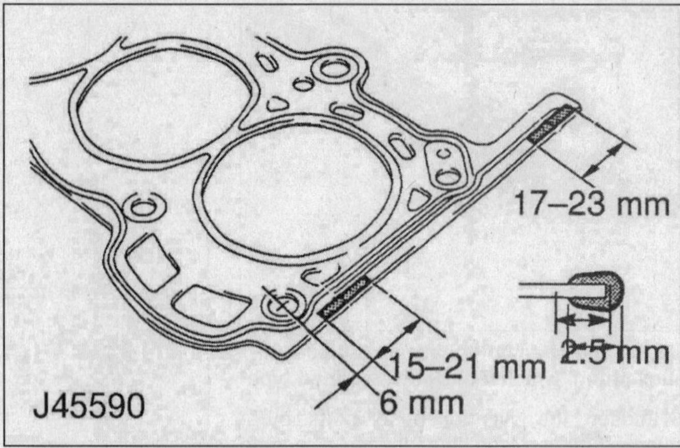

9.24a Apply sealant in the areas shown – 1.0 litre and 1.3 litre 2SZ-FE engine

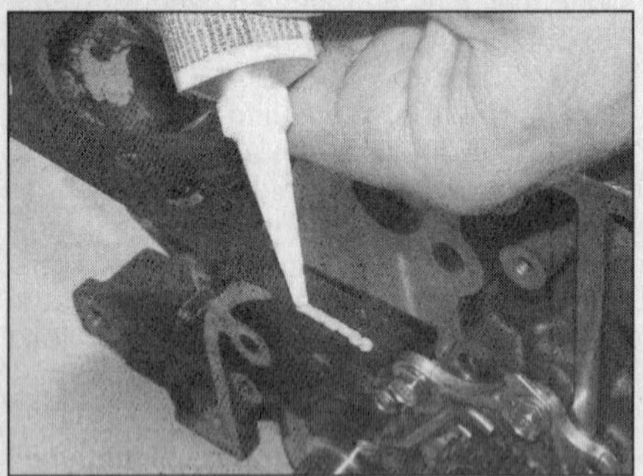

9.24b Apply the sealant to both sides of the gasket

9.25 Ensure that the gasket is fitted the right way up

9.27a Fit the washers . . .

Refitting

22 To avoid the possibility of valves hitting pistons when the camshafts are refitted and turned, it is advisable to turn the crankshaft a little, so that none of the pistons are at TDC. Make your own alignment marks on the crankshaft sprocket and block, so that the crankshaft TDC position can be easily reset before the timing chain is refitted.

23 Ensure the two locating dowels are refitted to their original positions on the block top surface **(see illustration)**.

24 On 1.0 litre and 1.3 litre 2SZ-FE engines, apply two small 2.5 mm diameter beads of RTV sealant to the timing chain end of the new gasket, as shown **(see illustrations)**. The Toyota part number for their sealant is 08826-00100, but we used Loctite 5699. Once the sealant has been applied, the gasket and cylinder head must be fitted within 5 minutes.

25 Check that the new cylinder head gasket is the same type as the original, and that any TOP marking is facing upwards, then locate it onto the top face of the cylinder block and over the dowels. Ensure that it is correctly aligned with the coolant passages and oilways **(see illustration)**.

26 It is helpful to have an assistant on hand as the head is offered into place, as various items may need to be held clear. Lower the head gently onto the block, making sure the gasket does not move, until it is located on the two dowels.

27 Fit the new bolts and washers. There is no harm in lightly oiling the bolt threads before fitting, though there is no requirement to do this by Toyota. Following the tightening sequence, tighten the head bolts to the specified Stage 1 torque **(see illustrations)**.

28 Now the head bolts should be tightened further, to their specified Stage 2 angle. It is

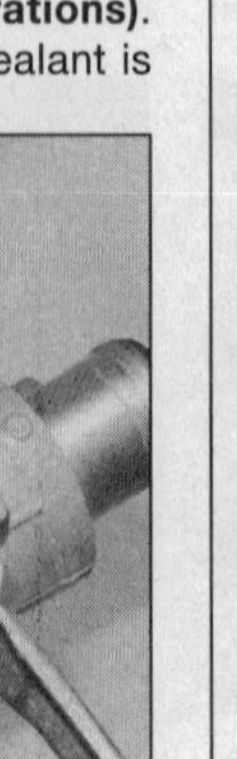

9.27b . . . and the new bolts

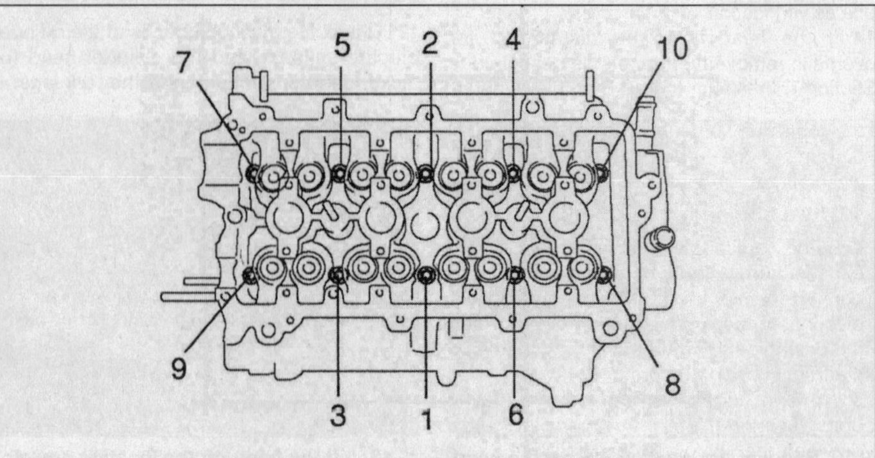

9.27c Cylinder head bolt tightening sequence

9.28 Angle-tightening the head bolts, using an angle gauge

strongly recommended that an angle gauge is used for this task **(see illustration)**. Again, follow the tightening sequence.

29 On 1.3 litre 2NZ-FE engine models only, the head bolts are tightened further, to a Stage 3 angle, using the same sequence for tightening as before.

30 The remainder of refitting is a reversal of removal, noting the following points:

a) Before refitting the cylinder head cover, turn the engine two complete turns clockwise, and check that the crankshaft and camshaft timing marks come back into alignment as described in Section 3.

b) Tighten all fasteners to the specified torque.

c) As applicable, allow sufficient time for the sealant used on the head gasket, timing chain and cylinder head covers, and on the sump, to cure before starting the engine.

d) When the engine is restarted, check for any sign of oil and/or coolant leakage from the various cylinder head joints.

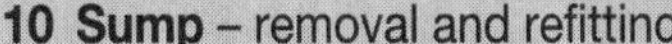

10 Sump – removal and refitting

Removal

1 Jack up the front of the car, and support it on axle stands (see *Jacking and vehicle support*). Remove the engine lower cover panels from under the car.

2 Drain the engine oil as described in Chapter 1. It makes sense to change the oil filter at the same time, but this is not essential.

3 Remove the engine oil dipstick, wipe it clean, and place it to one side.

1.0 litre engine

4 Refer to Chapter 4B and remove the exhaust front downpipe and catalytic converter. We found it was sufficient to disconnect the oxygen sensor wiring, unbolt the downpipe from the manifold, and unhook the front support rubbers.

5 Working under the car, remove the five bolts securing the stiffener plate fitted between the sump and transmission. Lower the plate, and remove it **(see illustrations)**.

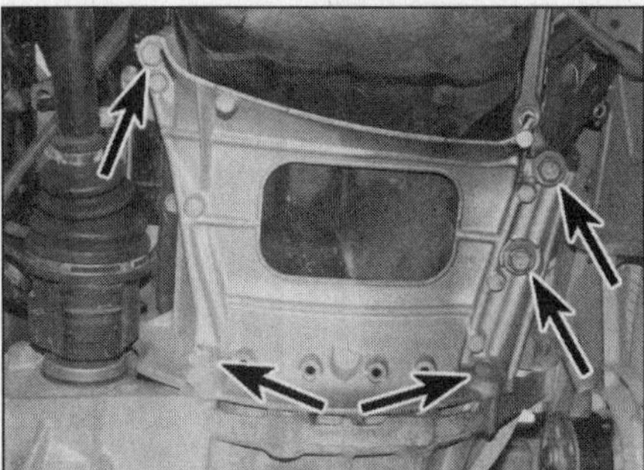
10.5a Unscrew and remove the five bolts . . .

10.5b . . . and take down the sump stiffener plate

6 Unscrew and remove the eleven bolts and three nuts used to secure the sump **(see illustration)**. Note that the two bolts at the timing chain end of the sump are shorter than the others.

1.3 litre 2SZ-FE engine

7 Refer to Chapter 4B and remove the exhaust front downpipe and catalytic converter. We found it was sufficient to disconnect the oxygen sensor wiring, unbolt the downpipe from the manifold, and unhook the front support rubbers.

8 Noting their locations, unscrew and remove the nine small bolts, two nuts, and three large bolts (transmission end) securing the sump.

1.3 litre 2NZ-FE engine

9 On automatic transmission models, remove the sump-to-transmission stiffener plate, which is secured by five bolts.

10 Unscrew and remove the nine bolts and two nuts used to secure the sump **(see illustration)**.

All engines

11 The sump is further secured in position with sealant, and some effort may be needed to prise it free.

12 Using a wide-bladed tool, carefully prise off the sump (if a screwdriver is used, take care not to deform the sealing edges of the pan) **(see illustration)**. If care is taken, the sump can be further 'assisted' off by removing the drain plug, then inserting a long-handled tool into the drain hole, and using this as a lever to pull the sump down. However, the sump is only made of thin material, and may be deformed if too much force is used (the threads for the drain plug may also be damaged using this method).

13 Keep the sump level as it is lowered, to prevent spillage of any remaining oil in it **(see illustration)**. Also be prepared for oil drips

10.6 Sump seen from below, showing retaining nuts and bolts – 1.0 litre engine

10.10 On the 1.3 litre 2NZ-FE engine, there are nine bolts and two nuts securing the sump

10.12 Prise off the sump using a wide-bladed tool

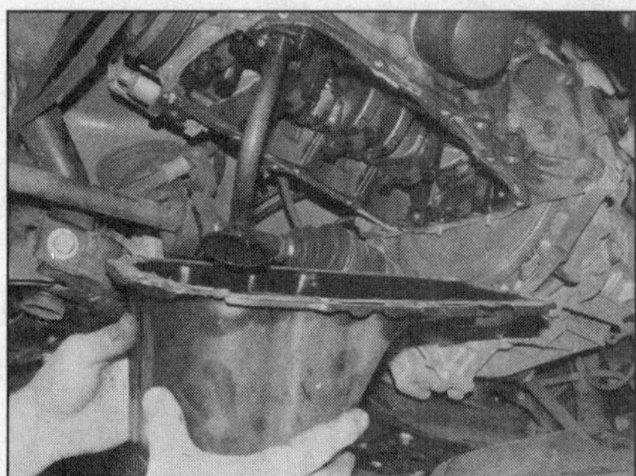
10.13 Once the sealant has been released, lower the sump

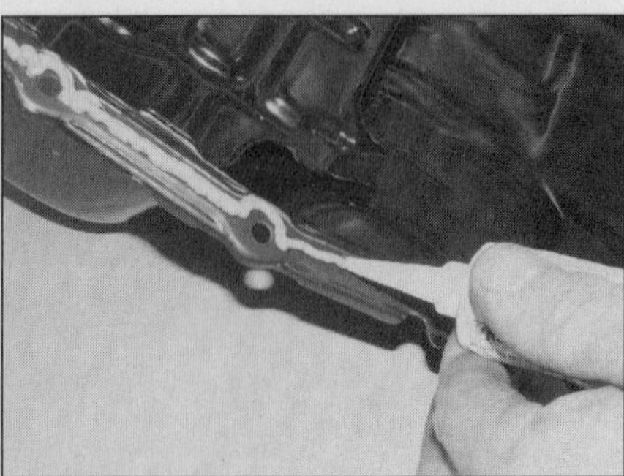
10.15 Apply a bead of sealant to the inside of the holes

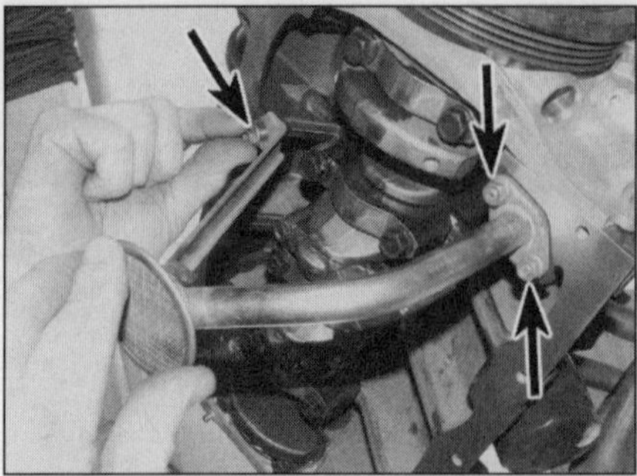
11.2 Unscrew the mounting bolt and two nuts, and remove the oil pick-up pipe

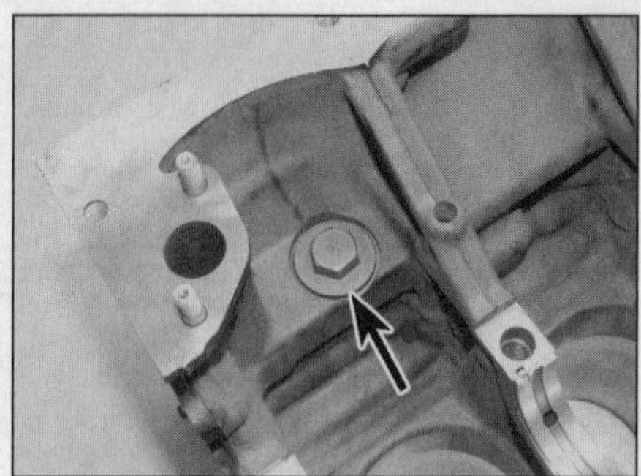
11.3a The oil pressure relief valve is screwed into the crankcase . . .

from the crankcase when the sump is removed.

14 Clean any sealant from the sump and engine mating faces – care must be taken not to damage the sealing surfaces. Wipe the mating faces with a suitable solvent, and allow to dry. While the sump is off, check that the oil pick-up strainer is clear, cleaning it if necessary.

Refitting

15 Apply a 2 to 3 mm diameter bead of RTV sealant (such as Toyota part number 08826-00080, Loctite 5699, or equivalent) to the sump sealing surface, to the inside of the bolt holes **(see illustration)**. Remember – any excess sealant may find its way into the engine, so use only enough to obtain a good seal. Once the sealant has been applied, the sump should then be fitted within 3 minutes.

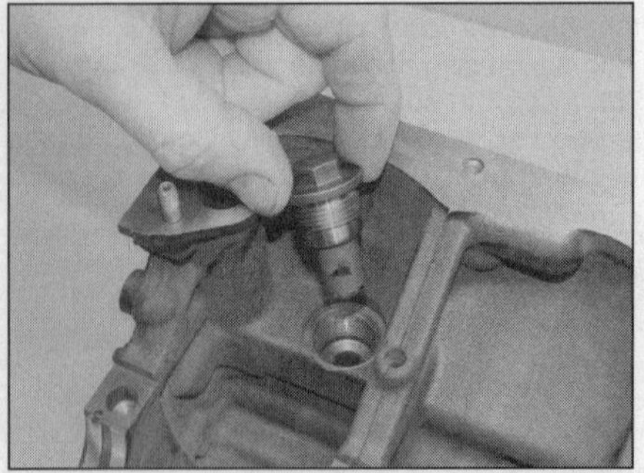
11.3b . . . and can be unscrewed for servicing

16 Offer the sump up to the engine, and locate it on the studs. Secure it hand-tight only at this stage, using all the nuts and bolts – on the 1.0 litre engine, note that the two bolts nearest the timing chain end (driver's side) of the engine are shorter than the others.

17 Progressively tighten the sump nuts/bolts to the specified torque, using a diagonal sequence, then go around and wipe away any excess sealant.

18 Check that the sump drain plug has been refitted and tightened securely – use a new sealing washer.

19 Where applicable, refit the sump-to-transmission stiffener plate, and tighten the bolts to the specified torque.

20 On 1.0 litre and 1.3 litre 2SZ-FE engines, refit the downpipe and catalytic converter as described in Chapter 4B.

21 On completion, lower the car to the ground. Allow time for the sealant to cure before refilling the engine with oil (and refitting the dipstick) as described in Chapter 1. Start the engine, and check for signs of leaks from the sump joint.

11 Oil pump – removal and refitting

Removal

1.0 litre and 1.3 litre 2SZ-FE engines

1 Remove the timing chain as described in Section 5.

2 Take off the two mounting nuts and single bolt, and remove the oil pick-up pipe from the bottom of the engine. Recover the gasket – a new one should be used when refitting **(see illustration)**.

3 Remove the oil pressure relief valve, which appears as a single bolt head next to the studs for the oil pick-up pipe just removed **(see illustration)**.

4 Unbolt the timing chain oil supply jet fitted above the oil pump sprocket **(see illustration)**.

5 Remove the three bolts securing the oil pump to the engine, and carefully withdraw it **(see illustration)**. Note that the oil pump driven (outer) rotor is not attached to the pump itself, and may fall off when the pump is removed – tilt the pump outwards at the top

11.4 Unbolt the timing chain oil supply jet

11.5 Unbolt and remove the oil pump

as it is removed to prevent this. The rotor has no 'front' or 'rear' side (can be fitted either way round).

1.3 litre 2NZ-FE engine

6 Remove the timing chain cover as described in Section 5.

7 The oil pump is fitted to the inside of the timing chain cover. Remove the two bolts and three screws, and withdraw the oil pump cover and gears **(see illustration)**. Note that the triangular marks on the driven and drive gears face the oil pump cover.

8 If required, unscrew the plug from the pressure relief valve, then withdraw the spring and valve.

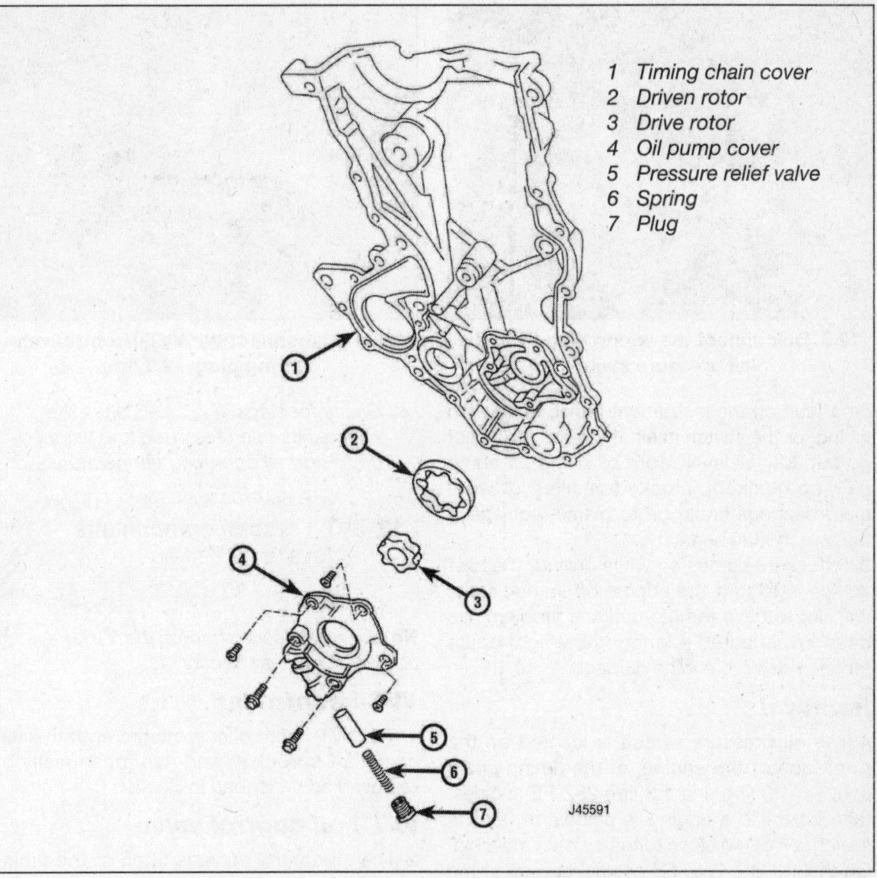

11.7 Oil pump details – 1.3 litre 2NZ-FE engine

Inspection

1.0 litre and 1.3 litre 2SZ-FE engines

9 Press the end of the pressure relief valve with a non-metal object (such as a wooden hammer handle), and check that it is not sticking.

10 Blow through the timing chain oil supply jet, and make sure it's not blocked. Similarly, rinse the oil pick-up pipe and strainer in solvent, and allow to dry.

11 Spin the oil pump drive gear, and check for any noise or roughness.

1.3 litre 2NZ-FE engine

12 Coat the relief valve with engine oil, and check that it falls into its hole in the pump under its own weight – if not, a new valve (or even a new pump) may be needed.

All engines

13 Check the oil pump inner and outer gear clearances, using feeler blades (and a straight-edge, in the case of the outer rotor endfloat) **(see illustrations)**. Compare the results with the specified values.

14 If any of the oil pump clearances are excessive, or if the pump displays any other signs of wear, a complete new pump should be fitted. If the engine is being completely overhauled, fitting a new pump (and perhaps an oil pressure relief valve) should almost be a matter of course.

Refitting

15 Liberally oil the pump rotors, and apply some oil to the pump location, before fitting. Check that the rotors are free of any dirt before fitting.

16 Offer the pump into position. Fit and tighten the mounting bolts/screws to the specified torque, then check that the drive gear turns smoothly.

17 Refit/reassemble the oil pressure relief valve, and tighten it (or its plug) to the specified torque.

18 On 1.0 litre engines, fit and tighten the timing chain oil supply jet bolt. Refit the oil pick-up pipe, together with a new gasket, and tighten the nuts and bolt to the specified torque **(see illustration)**.

19 Refit the timing chain (or cover) as described in Section 5.

12 Oil pressure switch – removal and refitting

1 The oil pressure switch is a vital early warning of low oil pressure. The switch operates the oil warning light on the instrument panel – the light should come on with the ignition, and go out almost immediately when the engine starts.

2 If the light does not come on, there could

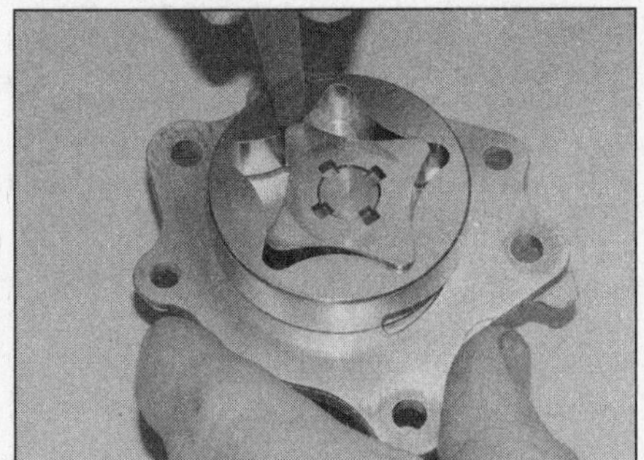

11.13a Checking the inner rotor tip clearance

11.13b Checking the outer rotor-to-body clearance

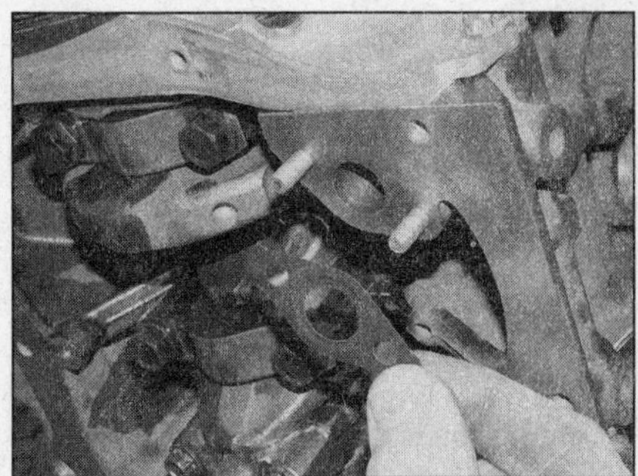

11.18 Use a new gasket when refitting the oil pick-up pipe

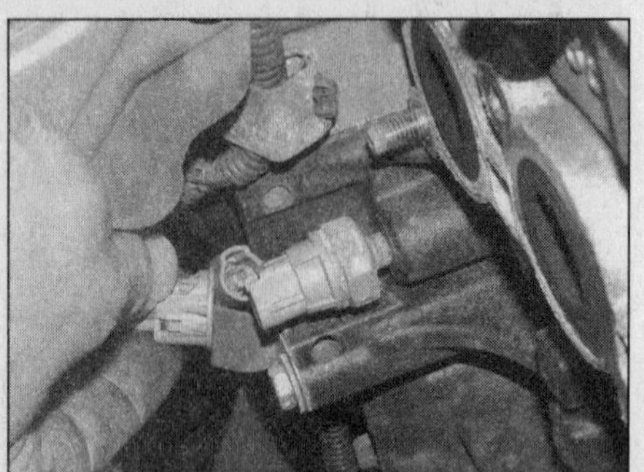

12.6 Disconnect the wiring plug from the oil pressure switch

be a fault on the instrument panel, the switch wiring, or the switch itself. If the light does not go out, low oil level, worn oil pump (or sump pick-up blocked), blocked oil filter, or worn main bearings could be to blame – or again, the switch may be faulty.

3 If the light comes on while driving, the best advice is to turn the engine off immediately, and not to drive the car until the problem has been investigated – ignoring the light could mean expensive engine damage.

Removal

4 The oil pressure switch is located on the front face of the engine, at the timing chain end. On 1.0 litre and 1.3 litre 2SZ-FE engines, take care if the engine is still warm, as the switch is located close to the exhaust manifold. On the 1.3 litre 2NZ-FE engine, access to the switch is hampered by the inlet manifold.

5 Access to the switch is easiest from below – raise the front of the car, and support it on axle stands (see *Jacking and vehicle support*).

6 Disconnect the wiring plug from the switch **(see illustration)**.

7 Unscrew the switch from the block, and remove it. There should only be a very slight loss of oil when this is done.

Inspection

8 Examine the switch for signs of cracking or splits. If the top part of the switch is loose, this is an early indication of impending failure.

9 Check that the wiring terminals at the switch are not loose, then trace the wire from the switch connector until it enters the main loom – any wiring defects will give rise to apparent oil pressure problems.

Refitting

10 Refitting is the reverse of the removal procedure, noting the following points:

a) Clean the switch threads, then apply a few drops of thread-locking fluid to them before fitting. Tighten the switch securely.

b) Reconnect the switch connector, making sure it clicks home properly. Ensure that the wiring is routed away from any hot or moving parts.

c) Lower the car to the ground, then check the engine oil level and top-up if necessary (see 'Weekly checks').

13.3a Disconnect the VVT-i control valve wiring plug – 1.0 litre

d) Check for signs of oil leaks once the engine has been restarted and warmed-up to normal operating temperature.

13 VVT-i system components – removal and refitting

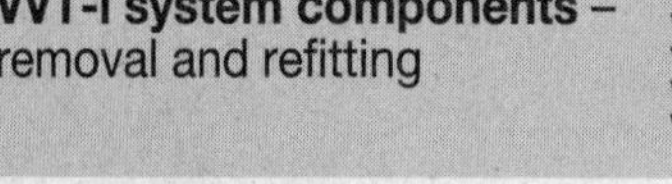

Note: *For a description of the VVT-i system operation, refer to Section 1.*

VVT-i controller

1 The VVT-i controller is integral with the inlet camshaft sprocket, and can most easily be removed as described in Section 8.

VVT-i oil control valve

2 The oil control valve is fitted at the timing chain end of the cylinder head – at the rear on 1.0 litre and 1.3 litre 2SZ-FE engines, or at the front on the 1.3 litre 2NZ-FE engine.

3 Disconnect the wiring plug from the valve **(see illustrations)**.

4 On the 1.3 litre 2NZ-FE engine, to improve access to the valve mounting bolt, unbolt and remove the alternator adjuster bracket.

5 Remove the valve mounting bolt, then carefully withdraw the valve from the head – anticipate a small amount of oil spillage as this is done **(see illustrations)**.

6 Recover the O-ring from the valve – a new one should be obtained for refitting.

7 Refitting is a reversal of removal, noting the following points:

a) Tighten the valve mounting bolt to the specified torque.

13.5a Unscrew the bolt . . .

13.3b On the 1.3 litre 2NZ-FE engine, the VVT-i valve is on the front

b) Check and if necessary top-up the oil level on completion (see 'Weekly checks').

c) On the 1.3 litre 2NZ-FE engines, if necessary, check and adjust the auxiliary drivebelt tension after refitting the alternator adjuster bracket.

d) Start the engine, and check for signs of oil leaks from the valve.

14 Crankshaft pulley – removal and refitting

Removal

1 Apply the handbrake, then jack up the front of the car and support it on axle stands (see *Jacking and vehicle support*). Remove the plastic cover panel below the engine on the driver's side.

2 If not already done, remove the auxiliary drivebelt as described in Chapter 1.

3 Undo the pulley centre retaining bolt using a socket and bar – make sure the car is securely supported, and that good-quality, close-fitting tools are used, as considerable force will be required.

4 The crankshaft pulley must be held stationary while its retaining bolt is slackened. The first, and easiest, method is to have an assistant sit in the car and engage a gear, then let the clutch pedal up and apply the footbrake hard. There will be considerable 'slack' to take up, but usually this method is sufficient to loosen the bolt.

5 To hold the pulley more directly, a home-

13.5b . . . and withdraw the valve from the head – note the O-ring

14.5 Loosen the crankshaft pulley bolt using a holding tool

14.7a Remove the pulley bolt . . .

14.7b . . . and take off the crankshaft pulley

made holding tool can be made from two thick, unequal-length, bolted-together strips of metal, with bolts fitted to the ends which can be engaged in the pulley spokes **(see illustration)**.

6 Alternatively, remove the starter motor as described in Chapter 5A, and jam the flywheel ring gear to prevent the engine turning.

7 Loosen and remove the pulley bolt, then take off the pulley **(see illustrations)**. The pulley should not be difficult to remove, but may require prising or tapping free.

8 Clean the threads, and examine the pulley bolt carefully once it has been removed. Toyota do not require that a new one is automatically fitted, but if there is any doubt about its condition, obtain a new one for refitting.

Refitting

9 Clean the inner side of the pulley, and slide it onto the crankshaft over the Woodruff key.

10 Fit the bolt, and tighten as far as possible until the pulley starts to turn.

11 Using the same method as for loosening to prevent the pulley turning while its bolt is tightened, tighten the pulley bolt to the specified torque.

12 On completion, refit the engine lower panel and lower the car to the ground.

15 Crankshaft oil seals – renewal

Right-hand oil seal

1 Remove the timing chain cover using the information in Section 5. Fitting a new oil seal to the cover is described in paragraph 35 of that Section. In theory a new seal could be fitted *in situ*, after the crankshaft pulley has been removed, but it is unlikely there would be sufficient room to work.

Left-hand oil seal

2 Remove the flywheel or driveplate as described in Section 16.

1.0 litre and 1.3 litre 2SZ-FE engines – Method 1

3 The oil seal is mounted in a separate carrier, which can be unbolted from the end of the engine. However, to do this also requires that the sump is removed, as described in Section 10. If preferred, the seal itself can be prised out, or pulled out after a self-tapping screw has been fitted **(see illustration)**.

4 Lightly lubricate the seal with oil or grease, and offer it into position.

5 Fitting the new seal can be achieved by tapping it in directly, or using a tube of similar diameter. We found that using the flywheel bolts and some packing washers, tightened evenly over the old seal, was enough to get the seal almost home (it should go in flush) **(see illustration)**.

1.0 litre and 1.3 litre 2SZ-FE engines – Method 2

6 Remove the sump as described in Section 10.

7 Undo the four bolts securing the oil seal carrier to the engine, then withdraw the seal carrier.

8 Support the seal carrier on two opposite edges, then tap out the old seal with a screwdriver or similar tool, taking care not to damage the seal carrier surfaces. Try not to destroy the old seal, as it may be useful for fitting the new one.

9 Lightly lubricate the seal with oil or grease, and offer it into position.

10 Work equally round the seal, tapping it squarely into the carrier until it is flush with the edge. Alternatively, sandwich the seal and the carrier between two pieces of wood, and press the seal in using a bench vice **(see illustration)**.

11 A thin layer of suitable sealant should be applied to the back of the seal carrier before fitting – the carrier has a groove which must be filled all round **(see illustration)**.

15.3 Fitting a self-tapping screw helps to pull the old seal out

15.5 Press the new seal in using the flywheel bolts and some packing washers

15.10 Using a vice and two pieces of wood to press in the new seal

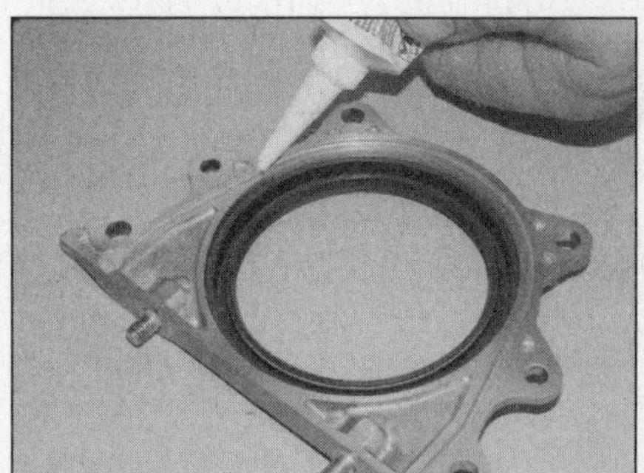
15.11 Apply flange sealant to the oil seal carrier groove

15.12 Offer the carrier over the end of the crankshaft

16.3 Home-made locking tool bolted in place to jam the flywheel ring gear

12 Apply a little more lubricant to the seal before carefully and squarely offering the carrier into place on the crankshaft **(see illustration)**.

13 Fit the four carrier mounting bolts, and tighten them to the specified torque.

14 Refit the sump as described in Section 10.

1.3 litre 2NZ-FE engine

15 Before removing the old seal, note its fitted depth, and which way round it is fitted, as a guide to fitting the new seal.

16 If necessary, use a sharp knife to trim away the oil seal lip. Using a screwdriver or other suitable instrument, prise out the oil seal. An alternative method is to drill two small holes in the oil seal, then screw in self-tapping screws and use grips to pull out the oil seal. If this method is used, make sure that all swarf is removed.

Sometimes, a seal can be loosened by pushing it in on one side - this tilts the seal outwards on the opposite side, and it can then be gripped with pliers and removed.

17 Lightly lubricate the new seal with oil or grease, and offer it into position.

18 Wrap a little tape over the end of the crankshaft, to protect the seal during fitting.

19 Carefully fit the seal onto the crankshaft, lips facing inwards, and slide it carefully up to the seat.

20 If a tube of the same diameter as the seal is available, this will help to ensure the seal is pressed squarely into place. Otherwise, the seal should be pressed in evenly using a blunt instrument.

21 Work equally round the seal, tapping it squarely into place until it is fitted to the same depth as the old one.

All engines

22 Refit the flywheel or driveplate as described in Section 16.

16 Flywheel/driveplate – removal, inspection and refitting

Removal

1 Remove the transmission as described in Chapter 7A or 7B (as applicable) then, on manual transmission models, remove the clutch as described in Chapter 6.

2 Paint an alignment mark between the engine and flywheel/driveplate before removal. Owing to the offset pattern of the bolt holes, the flywheel/driveplate can only be fitted in one position, but making a mark makes lining up the heavy component easier for refitting.

3 Jam a suitable tool into the ring gear to prevent the crankshaft from rotating as the bolts are removed **(see illustration)**. Take care – considerable effort will be needed to loosen the bolts, and any makeshift tools may slip.

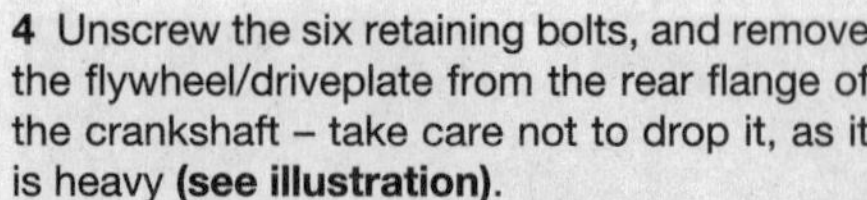

4 Unscrew the six retaining bolts, and remove the flywheel/driveplate from the rear flange of the crankshaft – take care not to drop it, as it is heavy **(see illustration)**.

5 Recover the adapter plate from the end face of the engine – it is retained by a single bolt, so should not be loose **(see illustration)**.

Inspection

6 If on removal, the flywheel/driveplate bolts are found to be in poor condition (damaged threads, etc) they must be renewed.

7 Inspect the starter ring gear for any broken or excessively-worn teeth. If evident, the ring gear must be renewed; this is a task best entrusted to a Toyota dealer or a competent garage. Alternatively, obtain a complete new flywheel or driveplate.

8 On manual transmission models, the clutch friction surface must be carefully inspected for grooving or hairline cracks (caused by overheating). If these conditions are evident, it may be possible to have the flywheel surface-ground, however this work must be carried out by an engine overhaul specialist. If surface-grinding is not possible, the flywheel must be renewed.

Refitting

9 Check that the mating faces of the flywheel/driveplate and crankshaft are clean before refitting. Apply a little thread-locking fluid to the bolt threads before they are screwed into position. Locate the flywheel onto the crankshaft so that the previously-made mark is aligned (where applicable), then insert the bolts. Hand-tighten them initially.

10 Prevent the crankshaft from turning as before for loosening, and tighten the bolts in a diagonal sequence to the specified torque **(see illustration)**. In the case of manual transmission models, all six bolts are tightened to the Stage 1 setting, then all six are tightened further to the Stage 2 torque. Use an angle gauge when tightening the bolts on 1.3 litre engines.

11 Where applicable, refit the clutch as described in Chapter 6.

12 Refit the transmission as described in Chapter 7A or 7B.

16.4 Unbolt and remove the flywheel

16.5 If required, the adapter plate can be unbolted and removed

16.10 Tighten the flywheel bolts to the specified torque

17.9a Unclip the accelerator cable . . .

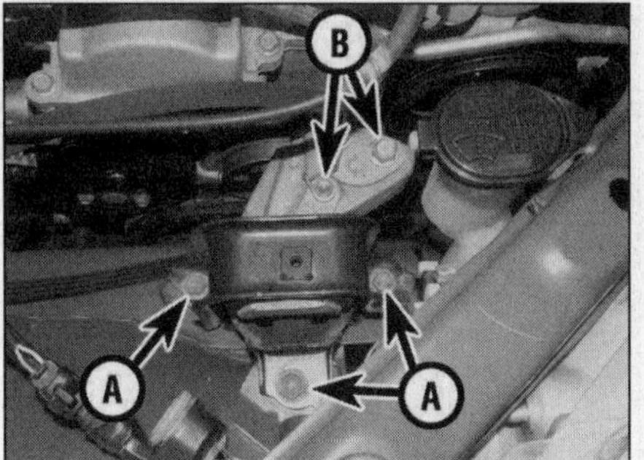

17.9b . . . then remove the three wing bolts (A) and two bracket bolts (B) . . .

17.9c . . . and the nut underneath . . .

17 Engine/transmission mountings – inspection and renewal

Inspection

1 The engine/transmission mountings seldom require attention, but broken or deteriorated mountings should be renewed immediately, or the added strain placed on the driveline components may cause damage or wear.

2 During the check, the engine/transmission must be raised slightly, to remove its weight from the mountings.

3 Apply the handbrake, then jack up the front of the car and support it on axle stands (see *Jacking and vehicle support*). Position a jack under the sump, with a large block of wood between the jack head and the sump, then carefully raise the engine just enough to take the weight off the mountings.

4 Check the mountings to see if the rubber is cracked, hardened or separated from the metal components. Sometimes, the rubber will split right down the centre.

5 Check for relative movement between each mounting's brackets and the engine or body (use a large screwdriver or lever to attempt to move the mountings). If movement is noted, lower the engine and check the mounting nuts and bolts for tightness.

Renewal

6 The engine mountings can be removed if the weight of the engine is supported by one of the following alternative methods.

7 Either support the weight of the assembly from underneath, using a jack and a suitable piece of wood between the jack and the sump (to prevent damage), or from above by attaching a hoist to the engine. A third method is to use a suitable support bar, with end pieces which will engage in the water channel each side of the bonnet lid aperture; using an adjustable hook and chain connected to the engine, the weight of the engine and transmission can then be taken from the mountings.

8 Once the weight of the engine and transmission is suitably supported, any of the mountings can be unbolted and removed. **Note:** *All references to left and right are as seen from the driver's seat.*

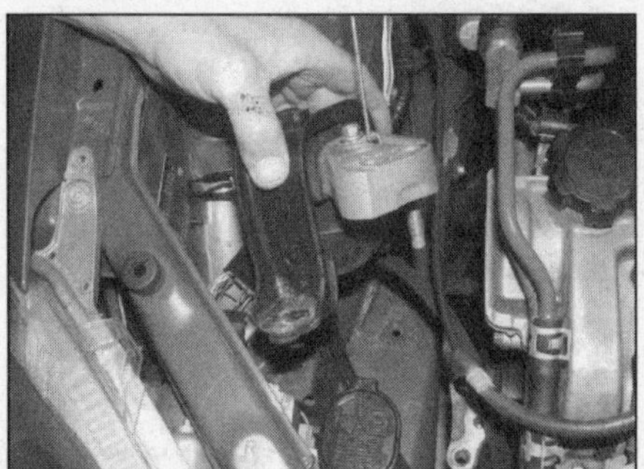
17.9d . . . and lift off the upper section

Right-hand mounting

9 To remove the right-hand mounting, first unclip the accelerator cable from the wire support bracket (or unbolt the bracket itself from the top of the mounting). Remove the three bolts securing the upper section of the engine mounting to the inner wing. Working underneath, remove the nut from the engine mounting central stud. Remove the two bolts securing the top section of the mounting to the engine bracket, and lift the top section away. If required, remove the nut and two further bolts (1.0 litre and 1.3 litre 2SZ-FE engine) or four bolts (1.3 litre 2NZ-FE engine) securing the engine mounting bracket to the engine, and remove the bracket **(see illustrations)**. The 1.3 litre 2SZ-FE engine has a stay bar, secured with two further bolts, which can also be removed.

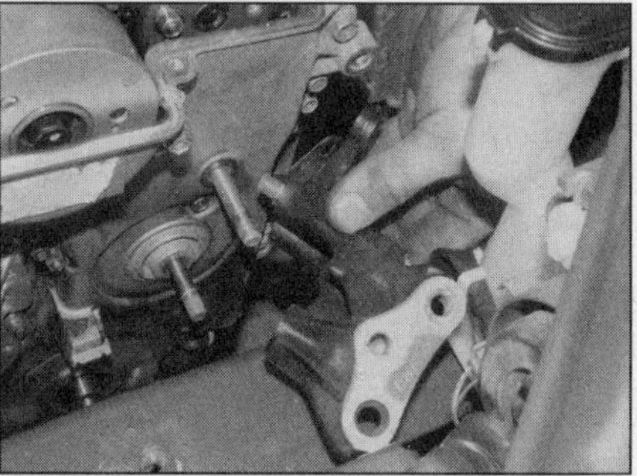
17.9e If required, the mounting bracket can be unbolted and removed

Left-hand mounting

10 To remove the left-hand (transmission) mounting, apply the handbrake, then jack up the front of the car and support it on axle stands (see *Jacking and vehicle support*). Working from below, remove the two bolts securing the mounting to the car body. If required, the mounting can also be unbolted from the front of the transmission, and removed completely **(see illustrations)**.

Rear mounting

11 To remove the engine rear mounting, apply the handbrake, then jack up the front of the car and support it on axle stands (see *Jacking and vehicle support*). Unscrew and pull out the through-bolt, and the mounting is free. The rubber section of the mounting can now be unbolted from the subframe (two nuts and one bolt, from below), and lifted out. If the mounting bracket attached to the engine is to

17.10a Left-hand mounting-to-body bolts (arrowed)

17.10b Mounting can be unbolted from transmission and removed

be removed, the engine can be swung forwards on its remaining mountings, and wedged using a suitable block of wood, to allow greater access. Unscrew the three bracket securing bolts, and remove the bracket **(see illustrations)**.

All mountings

12 Refitting of all mountings is a reversal of the removal procedure. Do not fully tighten the mounting nuts/bolts until all of the mountings are in position. Check that the mounting rubbers do not twist or distort as the mounting bolts and nuts are tightened to their specified torques.

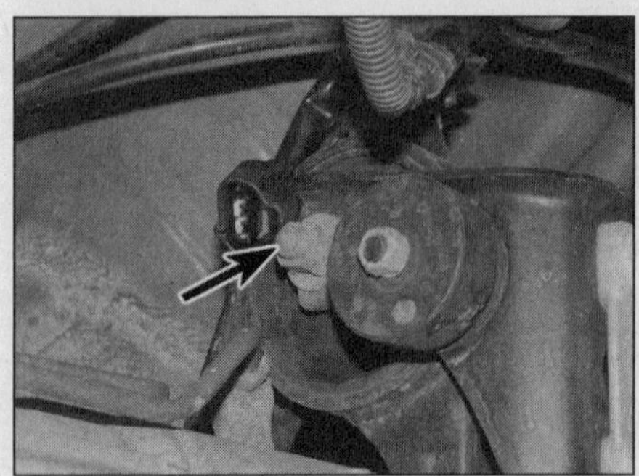

17.11a Remove the nut from the rear mounting through-bolt

17.11b The rear mounting can be removed completely

Chapter 2 Part B: Engine removal and overhaul procedures

Contents

Degrees of difficulty

Easy, suitable for novice with little experience 

Fairly easy, suitable for beginner with some experience 

Fairly difficult, suitable for competent DIY mechanic 

Difficult, suitable for experienced DIY mechanic 

Very difficult, suitable for expert DIY or professional

Specifications

Engine overhaul data and torque wrench settings

Refer to Specifications in Chapter 2A.

1 General information

Included in this part of Chapter 2 are the general overhaul procedures for the cylinder head, cylinder block/crankcase and internal engine components.

The information ranges from advice concerning preparation for an overhaul and the purchase of parts, to detailed step-by-step procedures covering removal, inspection, renovation and refitting of internal engine parts.

The following Sections have been compiled based on the assumption that the engine has been removed from the car. For information concerning in-car engine repair, as well as the removal and refitting of the external components necessary for the overhaul, refer to Part A, and to Section 5 of this Part.

2 Engine overhaul – general information

It is not always easy to determine when, or if, an engine should be completely overhauled, as a number of factors must be considered.

High mileage is not necessarily an indication that an overhaul is needed, while low mileage does not preclude the need for an overhaul. Frequency of servicing is probably the most important consideration. An engine which has had regular and frequent oil and filter changes, as well as other required maintenance, will most likely give many thousands of miles of reliable service. Conversely, a neglected engine may require an overhaul very early in its life.

Excessive oil consumption is an indication that piston rings, valve stem oil seals and/or valves and valve guides are in need of attention. Make sure that oil leaks are not responsible before deciding that the rings and/or guides are to blame. Perform a cylinder compression check to determine the extent of the work required.

Check the oil pressure with a gauge fitted in place of the oil pressure switch, and compare it with the value given in the Specifications. If it is extremely low, the main and big-end bearings and/or the oil pump are probably worn out.

Loss of power, rough running, knocking or metallic engine noises, excessive valve gear noise and high fuel consumption may also point to the need for an overhaul, especially if they are all present at the same time. If a complete tune-up does not remedy the situation, major mechanical work is the only solution.

An engine overhaul involves restoring the internal parts to the specifications of a new engine. During an overhaul, the pistons and rings are renewed, and the cylinder bores are reconditioned. New main bearings and connecting rod (big-end) bearings are generally fitted, and if necessary, the crankshaft may be reground to restore the journals. The valves are also serviced as well, since they are usually in less-than-perfect condition at this point. While the engine is being overhauled, other components, such as the starter and alternator, can be overhauled as well. The end result should be a like-new engine that will give many trouble-free miles. **Note:** *Critical cooling system components such as the hoses, drivebelts, thermostat and water pump MUST be renewed when an engine is overhauled. The radiator should be checked carefully, to ensure that it is not clogged or leaking. Also, it is a good idea to renew the oil pump whenever the engine is overhauled.*

Before beginning the engine overhaul, read through the entire procedure to familiarise yourself with the scope and requirements of the job. Overhauling an engine is not difficult if you follow all of the instructions carefully, have the necessary tools and equipment, and pay close attention to all specifications; however, it can be time-consuming. Plan on the car being tied up for a minimum of two weeks, especially if parts must be taken to an engineering works for repair or reconditioning. Check on the availability of parts, and make sure that any necessary special tools and equipment are obtained in advance. Most work can be done with typical hand tools, although a number of precision measuring tools are required for inspecting parts to determine if they must be renewed. Often the engineering works will handle the inspection of parts, and offer advice concerning reconditioning and renewal. **Note:** *Always wait until the engine has been completely dismantled, and all components, especially the engine block, have been inspected before deciding what service and repair operations must be performed by an engineering works. Since the condition of the block will be the major factor to consider when determining whether to overhaul the original engine or buy a reconditioned unit, do not purchase parts or have overhaul work done on other components until the block has been thoroughly inspected.* As a general rule, time is the primary cost of an overhaul, so it does not pay to fit worn or sub-standard parts.

As a final note, to ensure maximum life and minimum trouble from a reconditioned engine, everything must be assembled with care, and in a spotlessly-clean environment.

3 Engine removal – methods and precautions

If you have decided that an engine must be removed for overhaul or major repair work, several preliminary steps should be taken.

Locating a suitable place to work is extremely important. Adequate work space, along with storage space for the car, will be needed. If a garage is not available, at the very least a flat, level, clean work surface is required.

Cleaning the engine compartment and engine before beginning the removal procedure will help keep tools clean and organised.

The engine is removed complete with the transmission, by lowering it out of the car. The battery tray cannot be removed, and this hampers lifting out the engine/transmission, though we wouldn't rule out this method, provided sufficient angle can be achieved by raising the engine end first. If lowering the assembly, the car's body must be raised and supported securely, sufficiently high that the engine/transmission can be unbolted as a single unit and lowered to the ground.

Either way, an engine hoist or A-frame will be necessary. Make sure the equipment is rated in excess of the combined weight of the engine and transmission. Safety is of primary importance, considering the potential hazards involved in lifting the engine out of the car.

If the engine is being removed by a novice, an assistant should be available. Advice and aid from someone more experienced would also be helpful. There are many instances when one person cannot simultaneously perform all of the operations required when removing the engine from the car.

Plan the operation ahead of time. Arrange for, or obtain, all of the tools and equipment you will need, prior to beginning the job. Some of the equipment necessary to perform engine removal and installation safely and with relative ease are (in addition to an engine hoist) a heavy-duty trolley jack, complete sets of spanners and sockets as described at the end of this manual, wooden blocks, and plenty of rags and cleaning solvent for mopping-up spilled oil, coolant and fuel. If the hoist must be hired, make sure that you arrange for it in advance, and perform all of the operations possible without it beforehand. This will save you money and time.

Plan for the car to be out of use for quite a while. An engineering works will be required to perform some of the work which the do-it-yourselfer cannot accomplish without special equipment. These places often have a busy schedule, so it would be a good idea to consult them before removing the engine, in order to accurately estimate the amount of time required to rebuild or repair components that may need work.

Always be extremely careful when removing and refitting the engine. Serious injury can result from careless actions. Plan ahead, take your time, and you will find that a job of this nature, although major, can be accomplished successfully.

4 Engine – removal, separation and refitting

1 Depressurise the fuel system with reference to Chapter 4A.

2 Drain the cooling system as described in Chapter 1.

3 If the engine is being dismantled, drain the engine oil with reference to Chapter 1.

4 Remove the battery as described in Chapter 5A.

5 Remove the air cleaner and air inlet duct as described in Chapter 4A. Move the canister purge valve (clipped to the air cleaner) clear so that it will not hinder engine removal.

6 On 1.3 litre models, remove the engine top cover, which is secured by four nuts/bolts.

7 Disconnect the fuel line quick-release connection from the fuel rail, or unbolt the supply flange **(see illustration)**.

8 Disconnect the coolant hoses from the transmission end of the engine, noting their positions for refitting **(see illustrations)**. On the 1.3 litre 2NZ-FE engine, disconnect the

4.7 Unbolt the fuel supply flange from the fuel rail

4.8a Disconnect the heater hoses . . .

4.8b . . . and the larger radiator hoses from their stubs

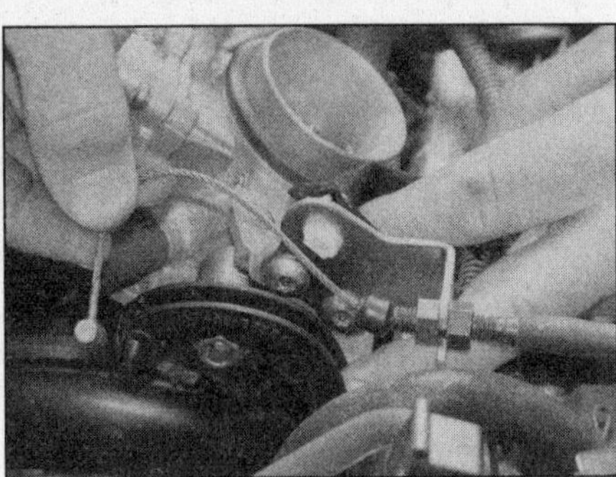
4.10 Unhook the throttle cable end fitting

4.11 Disconnect the ignition coil wiring plugs

4.12a Disconnect the wiring plug from the crankshaft position sensor . . .

radiator hose from the thermostat housing on the front of the engine.

9 Disconnect the brake servo vacuum pipe from the inlet manifold. Removing the engine is made a great deal easier by removing the inlet manifold as described in Chapter 4A, but this is not essential.

10 Loosen the adjuster nuts and detach the accelerator cable from the throttle body bracket. Disconnect the inner cable from the quadrant on the throttle body by pivoting the quadrant open, then releasing the end fitting **(see illustration)**. Release the cable from the securing clips on and around the engine.

11 Disconnect the wiring plugs from all four ignition coils, then unclip the coil wiring harness from the engine top cover, noting how it is routed **(see illustration)**.

12 Disconnect the wiring from the following components, and unclip (or unbolt) the harness locally from the engine **(see illustrations)**:

a) Alternator.
b) Starter motor.
c) Crankshaft position sensor (at the base of the timing chain cover).
d) Oil pressure switch (on the front of the engine).
e) Knock sensor (under the inlet manifold).
f) VVT-i oil control valve (at the timing chain end of the head).
g) Camshaft position sensor, coolant temperature sensor, and radio suppression condenser (all at the transmission end of the head).
h) Reversing light switch and vehicle speed sensor (at the front and rear of the transmission respectively).

13 On 1.0 litre and 1.3 litre 2SZ-FE engine models, disconnect the radiator cooling fan switch wiring plug **(see illustration)**.

14 As applicable, disconnect the earth leads at the transmission end of the engine, and from the transmission itself **(see illustration)**. Unclip the wiring harness from the transmission.

15 Disconnect the wiring plugs from the throttle body, noting their fitted positions.

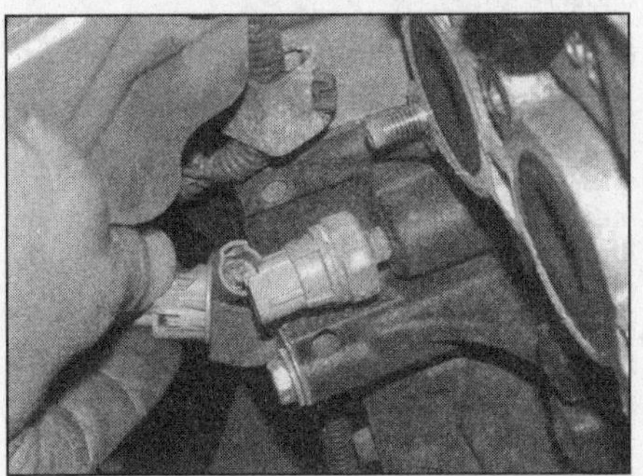
4.12b . . . oil pressure switch . . .

4.12c . . . VVT-i oil control valve . . .

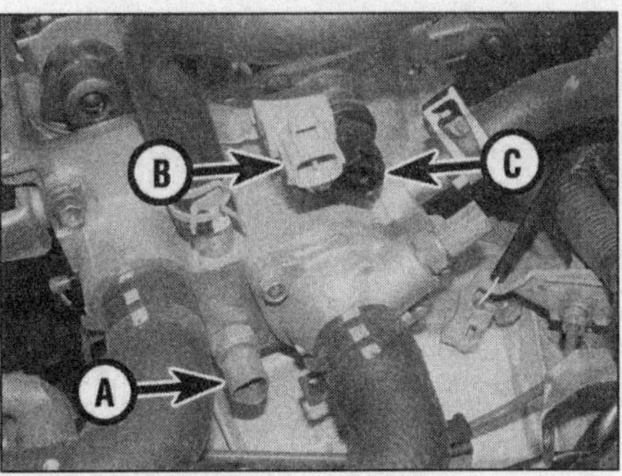

4.12d . . . coolant sensor (A), suppression condenser (B), and camshaft sensor (C) . . .

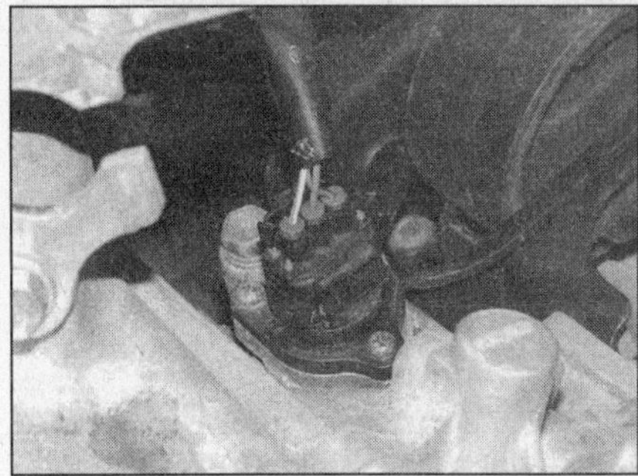
4.12e . . . the reversing light switch . . .

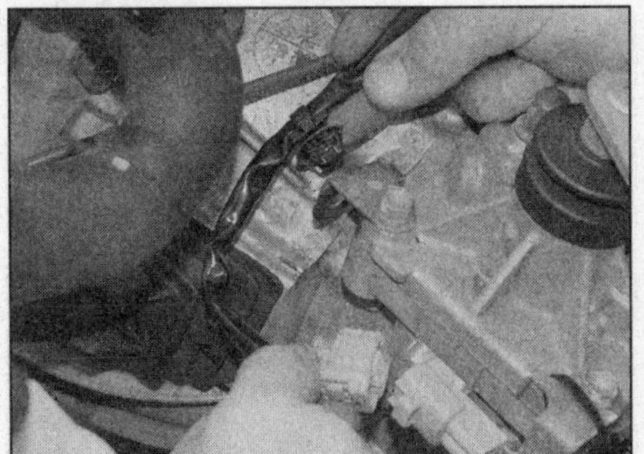
4.12f . . . and the vehicle speed sensor

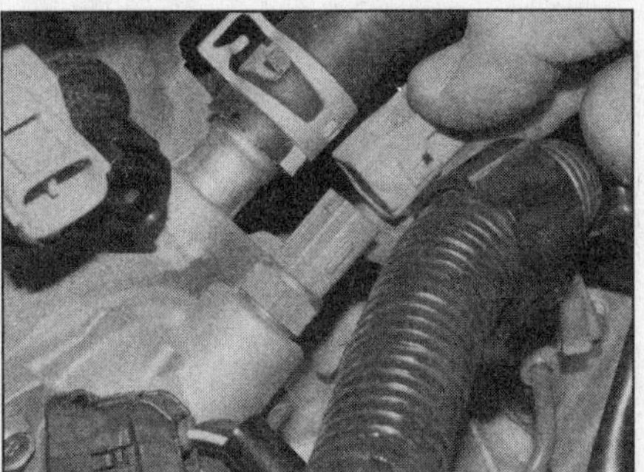
4.13 Disconnecting the radiator cooling fan switch wiring plug – 1.0 litre engine

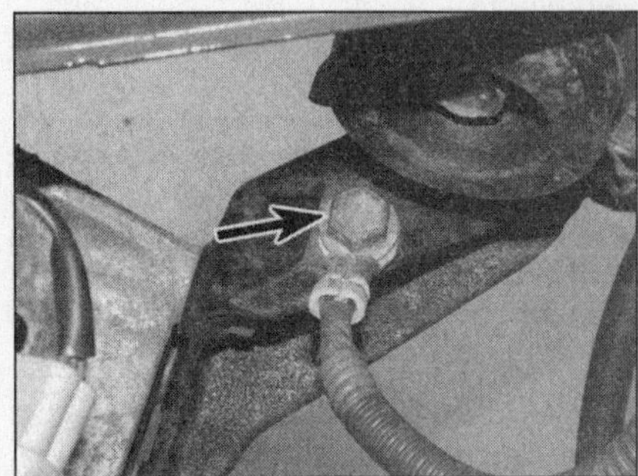
4.14 Unbolt the earth lead from the transmission mounting

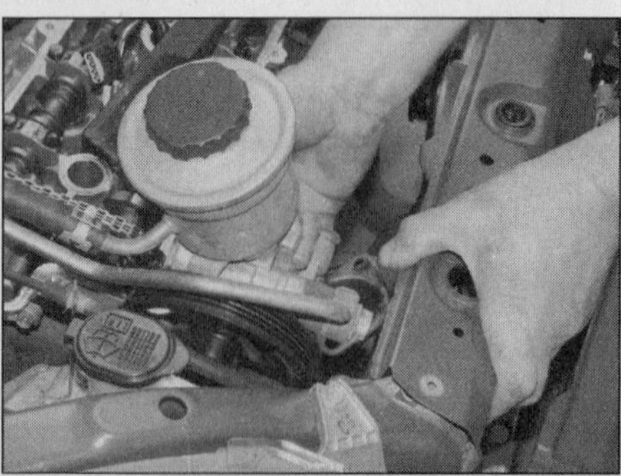
4.17a Unbolt the power steering pump . . .

4.17b . . . and secure it to one side

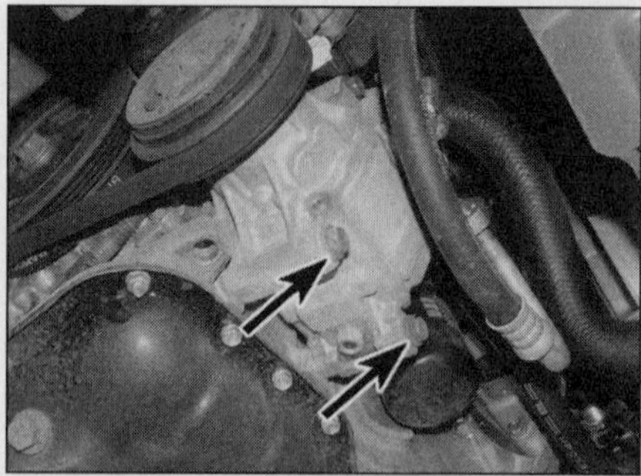
4.18a Two of the air conditioning compressor mounting bolts

Unplug the four injectors, and unclip the wiring harness from the top of the engine, noting how it is routed.

16 Remove the auxiliary drivebelt as described in Chapter 1.

17 Unbolt the (hydraulic) power steering pump (see Chapter 10 for details), then lift it off and secure it to one side, without disconnecting any fluid hoses **(see illustrations)**.

18 On models with air conditioning, unbolt the compressor (see Chapter 3 for details) and secure it to one side **without** disconnecting the refrigerant lines. Unbolt the refrigerant line support brackets as necessary **(see illustrations)**.

19 Jack up the front of the car, and support it on axle stands (see *Jacking and vehicle support*). Although not essential immediately, it would pay at this stage to raise the car sufficiently to allow the engine and transmission to be withdrawn from underneath.

Manual transmission models

20 Pull out the spring clips and recover the washers, then unhook the gearchange cable end fittings from the transmission shift/select mechanism, noting their positions **(see illustration)**. Move the cables clear of the transmission, taking care not to kink or bend them.

21 Again noting their positions, slide out the metal clips used to hold the gearchange cables to the support bracket on the transmission **(see illustration)**. Alternatively, the support bracket itself may be unbolted from the transmission housing, with the cables still attached.

22 Unclip and unbolt the clutch fluid pipe from the top of the transmission, then unbolt the clutch slave cylinder from the front. If care is taken not to bend the hydraulic pipe, the cylinder need not be disconnected, which saves bleeding the clutch later. If this method is chosen, wrap tape around the slave cylinder plunger to retain it while removed **(see illustrations)**.

Automatic transmission models

23 Remove the nut and washer, and detach the selector cable from the operating lever on the front of the transmission. Slide out the metal clip holding the selector cable to the

4.18b Unbolt the refrigerant line support brackets as necessary

4.20 Disconnect the gearchange cable end fittings . . .

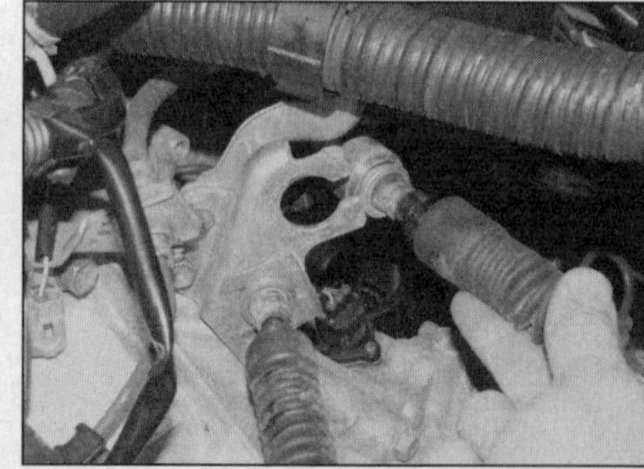
4.21 . . . and the gearchange cables themselves

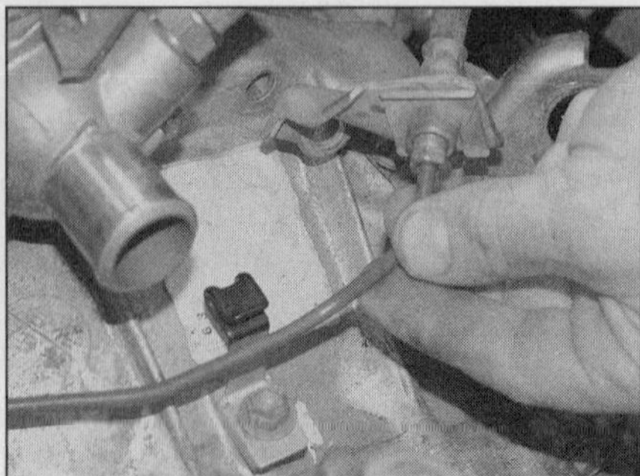
4.22a Unclip the clutch fluid pipe from the top of the transmission . . .

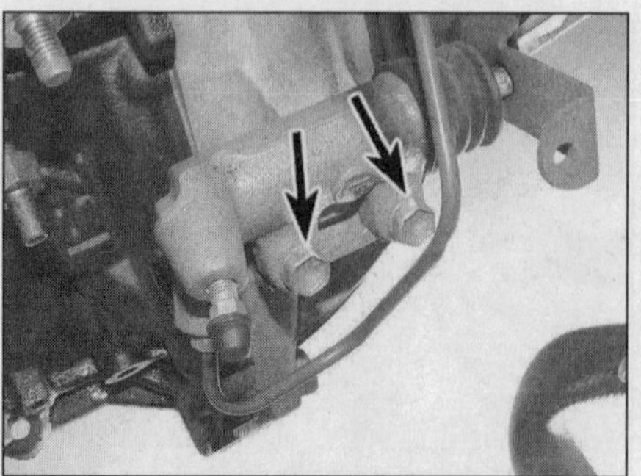
4.22b . . . then unbolt the clutch slave cylinder . . .

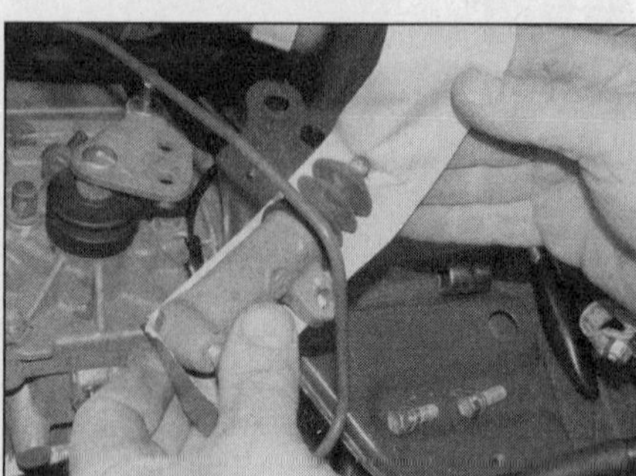
4.22c . . . and tape up the cylinder plunger

4.31 **Unclip any remaining wiring from the engine and transmission**

support bracket, and withdraw the cable. Lay it to one side, clear of the transmission, without bending it excessively.

24 Noting their positions for refitting, disconnect the wiring plugs from the following components on and around the transmission:

a) Direct clutch speed sensor (on top).
b) Neutral start switch (at the front).
c) Release the clamp and disconnect the solenoid wiring plug.
d) Oxygen sensor.

25 Unbolt the fluid dipstick/filler tube from the front of the transmission. Pull the tube out of its location, and recover the O-ring at the base – a new one should be used when refitting the tube.

26 Disconnect the two fluid hoses which run to the radiator – anticipate some fluid spillage as this is done. If possible, clamp the hoses prior to disconnection, and either plug or tape over them to prevent further fluid loss and dirt entry.

27 If the engine and automatic transmission are to be separated, remove the five bolts securing the sump-to-transmission stiffener plate, and lower out the plate for access to the torque converter mounting bolts. Loosen and remove the first of the torque converter mounting bolts, using a suitable tool to jam the driveplate ring gear. Using a spanner or socket on the crankshaft pulley bolt, turn the engine so that the remaining bolts can be removed. Note that one of the bolts is marked with grey paint – this bolt must be refitted first, so also note its location.

All models

28 The exhaust must at least be disconnected from the manifold to allow the engine to be lowered out – this is especially true on 1.0 litre and 1.3 litre 2SZ-FE engine models, as the exhaust system passes under the sump. To avoid disturbing too many joints, it is preferable to disconnect the oxygen sensor wiring, separate the manifold-to-downpipe joint, then to unhook the rubber mountings and lower the complete system to the floor (refer to Chapter 4B for details).

29 Remove both driveshafts as described in Chapter 8.

30 Separate the engine rear mounting by removing the through-bolt, referring to Chapter 2A if necessary. Once the rear mounting is disconnected, the engine will be free to swing on its remaining two mountings. To create more room for lowering, it is advisable to unbolt the rear mounting completely, and remove it.

31 Make a final check round the engine and transmission, to make sure nothing (apart from the left- and right-hand mountings) remains attached or in the way which will prevent it from being lowered out **(see illustration)**. Also make sure there is enough room under the front of the car for the engine/transmission to be lowered out and withdrawn.

Lowering the engine/transmission onto a large board, some strong card, or even an old piece of carpet, will not only protect it from damage, but will make it easier to drag out from under the car.

32 Securely attach the engine/transmission unit to a suitable engine crane or hoist, and raise it so that the weight is just taken off the two remaining engine mountings. It is helpful at this stage to have an assistant available, either to work the crane or to guide the engine out.

33 With the engine securely supported, working from below, remove the two transmission (left-hand) mounting bolts securing the mounting to the car body.

34 To remove the right-hand mounting, first unclip the throttle cable from the wire support bracket (or unbolt the bracket itself from the top of the mounting). Remove the three bolts securing the upper section of the engine mounting to the inner wing. Working underneath, remove the nut from the engine mounting central stud. Remove the two bolts securing the top section of the mounting to the engine bracket, and lift the top section away.

35 With the help of an assistant, carefully lower the assembly from the engine compartment, making sure it clears the surrounding components and bodywork. Be prepared to steady the engine when it touches down, to stop it toppling over **(see illustrations)**. Withdraw the assembly from under the car, and remove it to wherever it will be worked on.

Separation

36 To separate the transmission from the engine, first remove the starter motor with reference to Chapter 5A.

Manual transmission models

37 Progressively unscrew and remove the transmission-to-engine bolts.

38 With the help of an assistant, withdraw the transmission directly from the engine, making sure that its weight is not allowed to bear on the clutch friction disc.

Automatic transmission models

39 Refer to Chapter 7B, Section 2.

4.35a **With the engine released from its mountings, guide it downwards . . .**

4.35b **. . . until it reaches the floor**

Refitting

40 Refitting is a reversal of removal, noting the following additional points:

a) Make sure that all mating faces are clean, and use new gaskets where necessary.
b) Tighten all nuts and bolts to the specified torque setting, where given.
c) On manual transmission models, apply a smear of high-melting-point grease to the splines of the transmission input shaft. Do not apply too much, otherwise there is the possibility of the grease contaminating the clutch friction disc. On completion, bleed the clutch hydraulic system as described in Chapter 6.
d) Refit the automatic transmission using the information in Chapter 7B, Section 2.
e) Refit the driveshafts as described in Chapter 8.
f) Refit the exhaust system as described in Chapter 4B.
g) Replenish the transmission oil or fluid, and check the level with reference to Chapter 1.
h) Refill the cooling system as described in Chapter 1.

5 Engine overhaul – dismantling sequence

1 It is much easier to dismantle and work on the engine if it is mounted on a portable engine stand. These stands can often be hired from a tool hire shop. Before the engine is mounted on a stand, the flywheel should be removed from the engine, so that the engine stand bolts can be tightened into the end of the cylinder block.

2 If a stand is not available, it is possible to dismantle the engine with it blocked up on a sturdy workbench or on the floor. Be extra-careful not to tip or drop the engine when working without a stand.

3 If you're going to obtain a reconditioned ('recon') engine, all external components must be removed first, to be transferred to the new engine (just as they will if you are doing a complete engine overhaul yourself). **Note:** *When removing the external components from the engine, pay close attention to details that may be helpful or important during refitting. Note the fitted position of gaskets, seals, spacers, pins, washers, bolts and other small items. These external components include the following:*

a) Alternator, power steering pump, etc ('ancillaries').
b) Ignition coils and spark plugs.
c) Thermostat housing.
d) Fuel injection equipment.
e) Inlet and exhaust manifolds.
f) Oil filter.
g) Engine mountings and lifting brackets.
h) Coolant pipes and hoses.
i) Flywheel.

4 If you are obtaining a 'short' motor (which, when available, consists of the engine cylinder block, crankshaft, pistons and connecting rods all assembled), then the cylinder head, sump, oil pump, and timing belt (where applicable) will have to be removed also.

5 If you are planning a complete overhaul, the engine can be disassembled and the internal components removed in the following order:

a) Engine external components (including inlet and exhaust manifolds).
b) Timing sprockets and chain.
c) Cylinder head.
d) Flywheel.
e) Sump (and stiffener plate or lower crankcase, as applicable).
f) Oil pump.
g) Pistons and connecting rods.
h) Crankshaft and main bearings.

6 Before beginning the disassembly and overhaul procedures, make sure that you have all of the correct tools necessary. Refer to the reference section at the end of this manual for further information.

6 Cylinder head – dismantling

Note: *New and reconditioned cylinder heads are available from the manufacturers and from engine overhaul specialists. Due to the fact that some specialist tools are required for the dismantling and inspection procedures, and new components may not be readily available, it may be more practical and economical for the home mechanic to purchase a reconditioned head rather than dismantle, inspect and recondition the original head.*

1 Remove the cylinder head as described in Part A of this Chapter.

2 If not already done, remove all external brackets and elbows.

3 Again, if not already done, remove the tappets as described in Part A of this Chapter, being careful to store the components as described.

4 Using a valve spring compressor, compress each valve spring in turn until the split collets can be removed; compressors are now widely available from most good motor accessory shops. Release the compressor, and lift off the spring upper seat and spring.

5 If, when the valve spring compressor is screwed down, the spring upper seat refuses to free and expose the split collets, gently tap the top of the tool, directly over the upper seat, with a light hammer. This will free the seat.

6 Withdraw the valve through the combustion chamber. If it binds in the guide (won't pull through), push it back in, and de-burr the area around the collet groove with a fine file; take care not to mark the tappet bores.

7 Pull the valve stem seals from the valve guides using a pair of pliers. As the seals are removed, note whether they are of different colours for the inlet and exhaust valves – compare with the new parts, and note this for refitting.

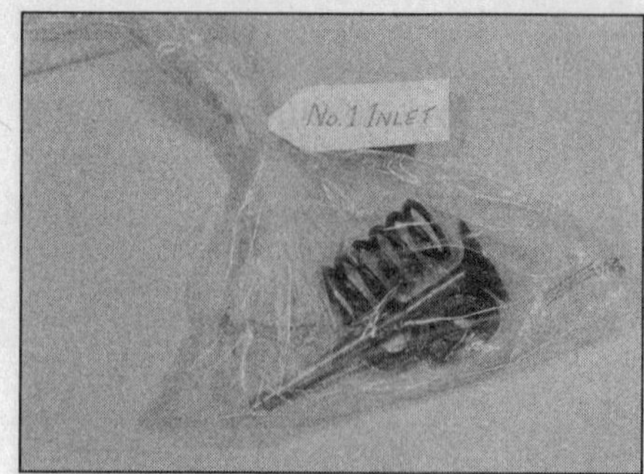

6.9 Keep all the valve components together in labelled containers

8 Remove the valve spring lower seats, and store them with their respective springs.

9 It is essential that the valves are kept together with their collets, spring seats and springs, and in their correct sequence (unless they are so badly worn that they are to be renewed). If they are going to be kept and used again, place them in a labelled polythene bag or similar small container **(see illustration)**. Note that No 1 valve is nearest to the timing chain end of the engine.

7 Cylinder head and valves – cleaning, inspection and renovation

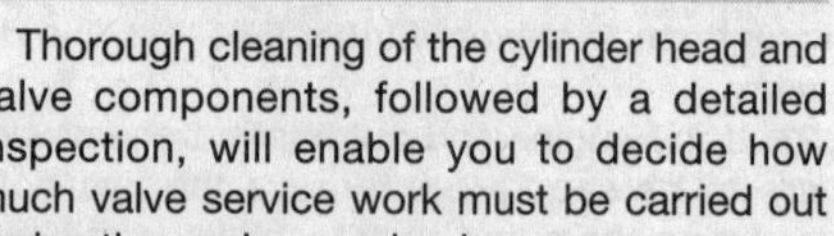

1 Thorough cleaning of the cylinder head and valve components, followed by a detailed inspection, will enable you to decide how much valve service work must be carried out during the engine overhaul.

Cleaning

2 Scrape away all traces of old gasket material and sealing compound from the cylinder head. Take care not to damage the cylinder head surfaces.

3 Scrape away the carbon from the combustion chambers and ports, then wash the cylinder head thoroughly with paraffin or a suitable solvent.

4 Scrape off any heavy carbon deposits that may have formed on the valves, then use a power-operated wire brush to remove deposits from the valve heads and stems.

5 If the head is extremely dirty, it should be steam-cleaned. On completion, make sure that all oil holes and oil galleries are cleaned.

Inspection and renovation

Note: *Be sure to perform all the following inspection procedures before concluding that the services of an engine overhaul specialist are required. Make a list of all items that require attention.*

Cylinder head

6 Inspect the head very carefully for cracks, evidence of coolant leakage and other

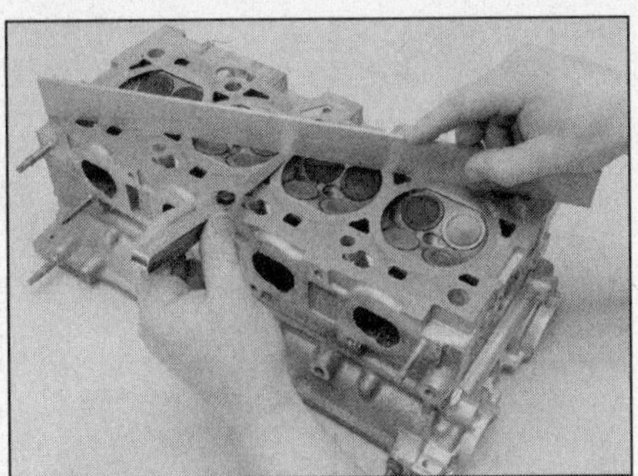
7.7 Check the head for warpage using a straight-edge and feeler blades

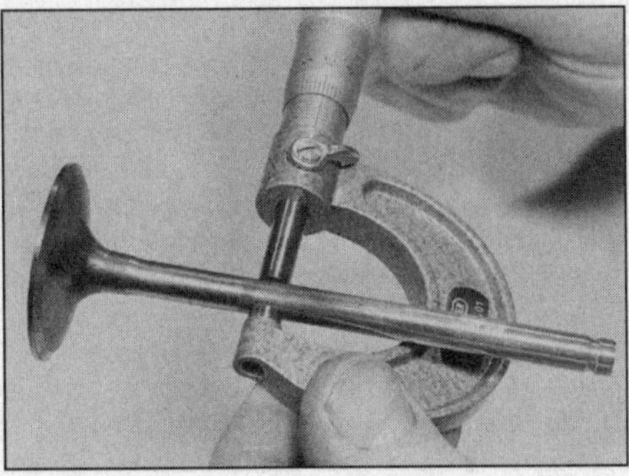
7.13 Measuring the diameter of a valve stem

7.16 Grinding-in a valve seat

damage. If cracks are found, a new cylinder head should be obtained.

7 Use a straight-edge and feeler blade to check that the cylinder head surface is not distorted **(see illustration)**. If the specified distortion limit is exceeded, machining of the gasket face is not recommended by the manufacturers, so the only course of action is to renew the cylinder head.

8 Examine the valve seats in each of the combustion chambers. If they are severely pitted, cracked or burned, then they will need to be renewed or recut by an engine overhaul specialist. If they are only slightly pitted, this can be removed by grinding the valve heads and seats together with coarse, then fine, grinding paste as described below.

9 If the valve guides are worn, indicated by a side-to-side motion of the valve in the guide, new guides must be fitted. If necessary, insert a new valve in the guides to determine if the wear is on the guide or valve. If new guides are to be fitted, the valves must be renewed as a matter of course. Valve guides may be renewed using a press and a suitable mandrel, however, the work is best carried out by an engine overhaul specialist, since if it is not done skilfully, there is a risk of damaging the cylinder head.

10 Check the tappet bores in the cylinder head for wear. If excessive wear is evident, the cylinder head must be renewed.

11 Examine the camshaft bearing surfaces in the cylinder head as described in Chapter 2A.

Valves

12 Examine the head of each valve for pitting, burning, cracks and general wear, and check the valve stem for scoring and wear ridges. Rotate the valve, and check for any obvious indication that it is bent. Look for pits and excessive wear on the end of each valve stem.

13 If the valve appears satisfactory at this stage, measure the valve stem diameter at several points using a micrometer **(see illustration)**. Any significant difference in the readings obtained indicates wear of the valve stem. Should any of these conditions be apparent, the valve(s) must be renewed.

14 If the valves are in satisfactory condition, or if new valves are being fitted, they should be ground (lapped) into their respective seats to ensure a smooth gas-tight seal.

15 Valve grinding is carried out as follows. Place the cylinder head upside-down on a bench, with a block of wood at each end to give clearance for the valve stems. Take care to protect the camshaft bearing surfaces.

16 Smear a trace of coarse carborundum paste on the seat face, and press a suction grinding tool onto the valve head. With a semi-rotary action, grind the valve head to its seat, lifting the valve occasionally to redistribute the grinding paste **(see illustration)**.

17 When a dull-matt even surface is produced on both the valve seat and the valve, wipe off the paste and repeat the process with fine carborundum paste. A light spring placed under the valve head will greatly ease this operation.

18 When a smooth unbroken ring of light grey matt finish is produced on both the valve and seat, the grinding operation is complete. Be sure to remove all traces of grinding paste, using paraffin or a suitable solvent, before reassembly of the cylinder head.

Valve components

19 Examine the valve springs for signs of damage and discoloration, and also measure their free length using vernier calipers or a steel rule, or by comparing the existing spring with a new component **(see illustration)**.

20 Stand each spring on a flat surface, and check it for squareness. If any of the springs are damaged, distorted or have lost their tension, obtain a complete new set of springs. It is normal to renew the springs as a matter of course during a major overhaul.

21 Inspect the tappets for scoring, pitting, and wear ridges. Renew any components as required – this may be necessary anyway once the valve clearances have been checked (see Chapter 2A). Note that some scuffing is to be expected, and is acceptable provided that the tappets are not scored.

Valve stem oil seals

22 The valve stem oil seals should be renewed as a matter of course.

8 Cylinder head – reassembly

1 If a new or reconditioned head is being fitted, the coolant hose stubs fitted at the transmission end of the head may need to be transferred over. In fact, due to the difficulty which may be experienced getting the old ones out, it may be simpler to obtain a new set of stubs from your Toyota dealer.

2 To fit the new stubs, apply a thin layer of suitable adhesive (Toyota part number 08833-00070, Three Bond 1324, or equivalent) to the bottom end of each stub. On 1.0 litre and 1.3 litre 2SZ-FE engines, the smaller heater hose stubs are pressed in to a depth of 15 mm, while the larger radiator hose stub goes in to 18 mm – the opposite applies to the 1.3 litre 2NZ-FE engine.

3 Mark a line on each stub, indicating the correct fitted depth. Press each stub in squarely – start it by hand if possible, then tap home using a hammer and block of wood.

4 Fit all sixteen valve spring lower seats into their original positions **(see illustration)**.

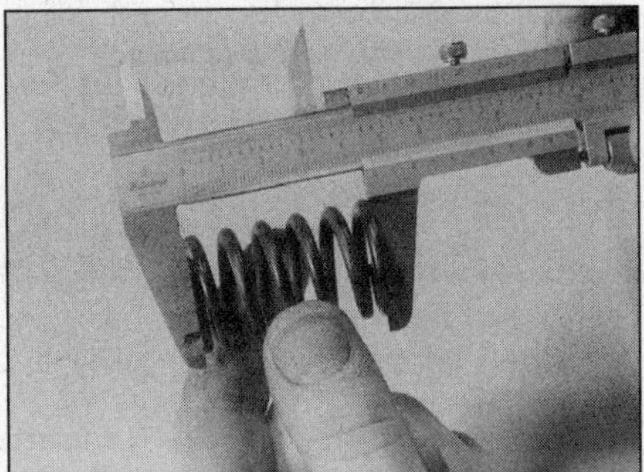
7.19 Checking the valve spring free length

8.4 Fit the valve spring lower seats

8.5a Fit the valve stem seals into a suitable socket . . .

8.5b . . . then press them fully onto the guide

8.7a Refit the valve springs . . .

8.7b . . . and the upper seats

8.8a Fit a valve spring compressor to compress the valve . . .

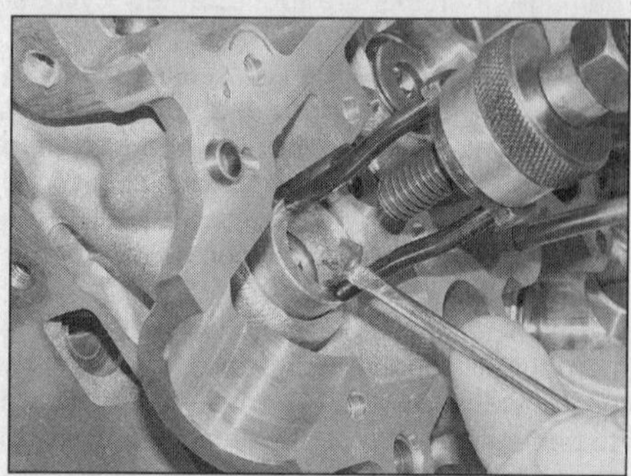
8.8b . . . then locate the collet halves into the valve stem grooves, using grease to 'stick' them in place

5 Lubricate the valve stem oil seals with clean engine oil, then fit them by pushing into position in the cylinder head using a suitable socket **(see illustrations)**. Ensure that the seals are fully engaged with the valve guide.

6 Lubricate the valve stems, then insert the valves into their original locations. If new valves are being fitted, insert them into the locations to which they have been ground. Take care not to damage the valve stem oil seal as each valve is fitted.

7 Fit the valve springs and upper seats in their original locations, where applicable **(see illustrations)**.

8 Compress the valve spring and locate the split collets in the recess in the valve stem **(see illustrations)**. Release the compressor, then repeat the procedure on the remaining valves.

9 With all the valves installed, place the cylinder head flat on the bench and, using a hammer and interposed block of wood, tap the end of each valve stem to settle the components.

10 The previously-removed components can now be refitted with reference to Section 6.

9 Timing chain components – general information

Refer to Part A, Section 5.

10 Piston/connecting rod assemblies – removal

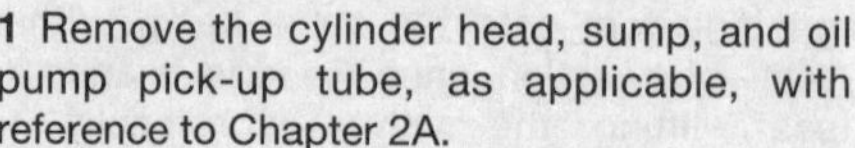

1 Remove the cylinder head, sump, and oil pump pick-up tube, as applicable, with reference to Chapter 2A.

2 Rotate the crankshaft so that No 1 big-end cap (timing chain end of the engine) is at the lowest point of its travel. If the big-end cap and rod are not already numbered, mark them with a marker pen. Mark both cap and rod to identify the cylinder they operate in.

3 Unscrew and remove the big-end bearing cap bolts, and withdraw the cap complete with shell bearing from the connecting rod. Make sure that the shell remains in the cap and if necessary identify it for position.

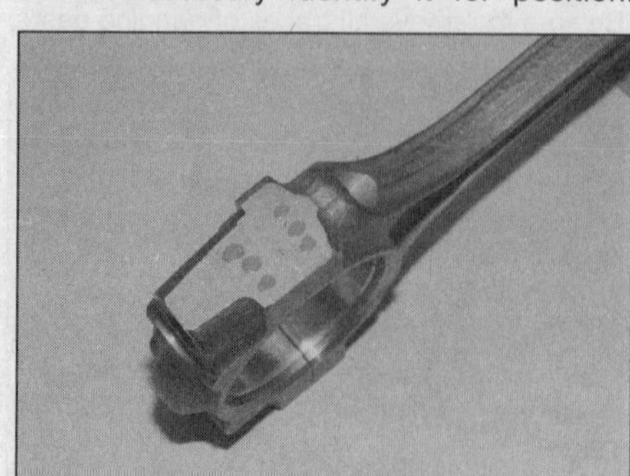
10.6 Mark the connecting rod and cap for position, and store together

Discard the bolts – they are 'stretch' type, and should not be re-used.

4 If only the bearing shells are being attended to, push the connecting rod up and off the crankpin, and remove the upper bearing shell. Keep the bearing shells and cap together in their correct sequence if they are to be refitted.

5 If the piston is being removed, push the connecting rod up and remove the piston and rod from the top of the bore. Note that if there is a pronounced wear ridge at the top of the bore, there is a risk of damaging the piston as the rings foul the ridge. However, it is reasonable to assume that a rebore and new pistons will be required in any case if the ridge is so pronounced.

6 Repeat the procedure for the remaining piston/connecting rod assemblies. Ensure that the caps and rods are marked before removal, as described previously, and keep all components in order **(see illustration)**.

11 Crankshaft – removal

1 Remove the timing chain, crankshaft sprocket, sump, oil pick-up tube, and flywheel.

2 On 1.0 litre and 1.3 litre 2SZ-FE engines, remove the crankshaft oil seal carrier.

3 On the 1.3 litre 2NZ-FE engine, the lower

11.5 Checking the crankshaft endfloat with a dial gauge

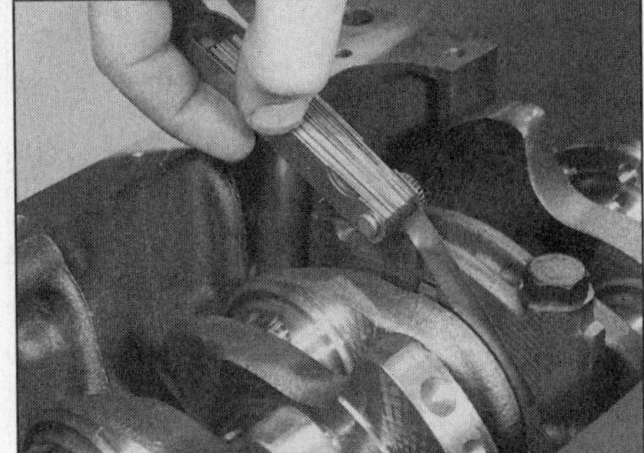

11.7 Crankshaft endfloat can also be checked with feeler blades

crankcase must be unbolted from the block. The lower crankcase is secured with thirteen bolts – loosen them progressively, and remove them. Note the positions of the bolts as they are removed, as they are of different lengths. Sealant is used in fitting the lower crankcase, and it will require prising to remove it – use the prise points provided, and take care not to damage the sealing surfaces. Recover the two O-ring seals.

4 The pistons/connecting rods must be free of the crankshaft journals, however it is not essential to remove them completely from the cylinder block.

5 Before the crankshaft is removed, check the endfloat. Mount a dial gauge with the probe in line with the crankshaft and just touching the crankshaft **(see illustration)**.

6 Push the crankshaft fully away from the gauge, and zero it. Next, lever the crankshaft towards the gauge as far as possible, and check the reading obtained. The distance that the crankshaft moved is its endfloat; if it is greater than specified, new thrustwashers will be required (see Chapter 2A Specifications).

7 If no dial gauge is available, feeler blades can be used. Gently lever or push the crankshaft in one direction, then insert feeler blades between the crankshaft web and the main bearing with the thrustwashers to determine the clearance **(see illustration)**.

8 Check that the main bearing caps have marks to indicate their respective fitted positions in the block. They may also have arrow marks pointing towards the timing end of the engine to indicate correct orientation.

9 Unscrew the retaining bolts, and remove the main bearing caps. If the caps are reluctant to separate from the block face, lightly tap them free using a plastic- or copper-faced hammer, or loosely refit the just-removed bolts and use them as 'levers'. If the bearing shells are likely to be used again, keep them with their bearing caps for safekeeping. However, unless the engine is known to be of low mileage, it is recommended that they be renewed.

10 Lift the crankshaft out from the crankcase, then extract the upper bearing shells, and the side thrustwashers from No 3 bearing. Keep them with their respective caps for correct repositioning if they are to be used again.

12 Cylinder block/crankcase and bores – cleaning and inspection

Cleaning

Caution: If cleaning the cylinder block with the crankshaft fitted, it is recommended that only the external surfaces are cleaned, as otherwise the internal oilways and channels may become contaminated, leading to premature wear of the crankshaft and main bearings.

1 For complete cleaning, the core plugs should be removed. Drill a small hole in them, then insert a self-tapping screw and pull out the plugs using pliers or a slide-hammer **(see illustration)**. Also remove all external components and senders (if not already done), noting their locations.

2 Scrape all traces of gasket or sealant from the cylinder block, taking care not to damage the head and sump mating faces.

3 If the block is extremely dirty, it should be steam-cleaned.

4 After the block has been steam-cleaned, clean all oil holes and oil galleries one more time. Flush all internal passages with warm water until the water runs clear, dry the block thoroughly and wipe all machined surfaces with a light rust-preventative oil. If you have access to compressed air, use it to speed up the drying process and to blow out all the oil holes and galleries.

Warning: Wear eye protection when using compressed air.

5 If the block is not very dirty, you can do an adequate cleaning job with hot soapy water and a stiff brush. Take plenty of time, and do a thorough job. Regardless of the cleaning method used, be sure to clean all oil holes and galleries very thoroughly, dry the block completely and coat all machined surfaces with light oil.

6 The threaded holes in the block must be clean to ensure accurate torque wrench readings during reassembly. Run the proper-size tap into each of the holes to remove rust, corrosion, thread sealant or sludge, and to restore damaged threads **(see illustration)**. If possible, use compressed air to clear the holes of debris produced by this operation. Now is a good time to clean the threads on the head bolts and the main bearing cap bolts as well.

7 Refit the main bearing caps, and tighten the bolts finger-tight.

8 After coating the mating surfaces of the new core plugs with suitable sealant, refit them in the cylinder block. Make sure that they are driven in straight and seated properly, or leakage could result. Special tools are available for this purpose, but a large socket, with an outside diameter that will just slip into the core plug, will work just as well **(see illustration)**.

9 If the engine is not going to be reassembled right away, cover it with a large plastic bag to keep it clean and prevent it rusting.

Inspection

10 Visually check the block for cracks, rust and corrosion. Look for stripped threads in

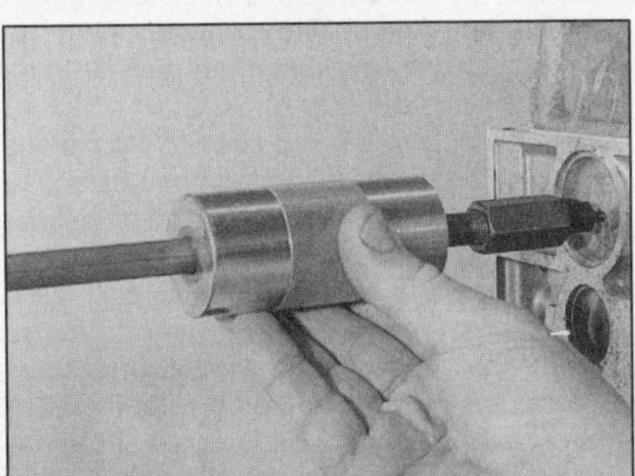

12.1 The core plugs should be removed with a puller – don't drive them inwards

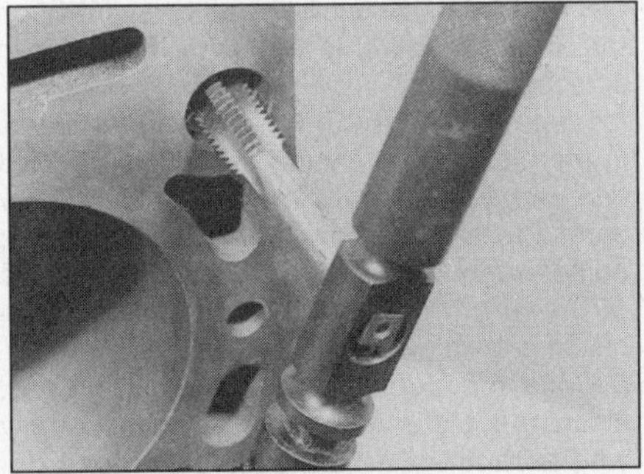

12.6 All the bolt holes in the block should be cleaned and restored with a tap

12.8 A large socket on an extension can be used to drive in new core plugs

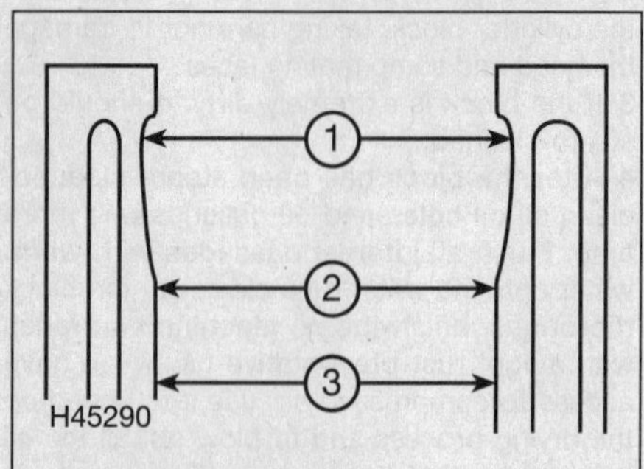

12.12 Measure the diameter of each cylinder under the wear ridge (1) at the centre (2) and the base (3)

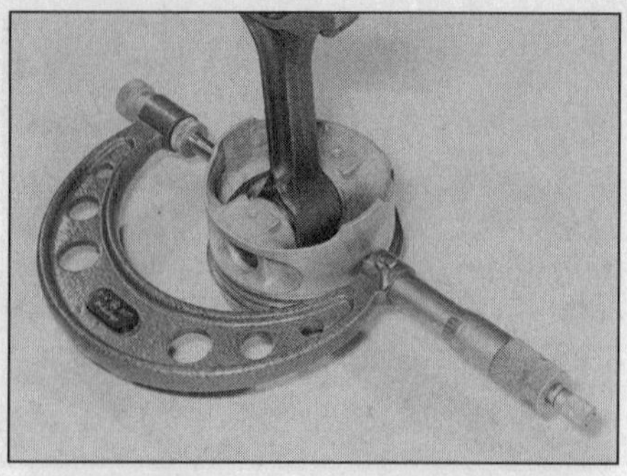
12.14 Measure the piston diameter at right-angles to the gudgeon pin axis, just above the base of the skirt

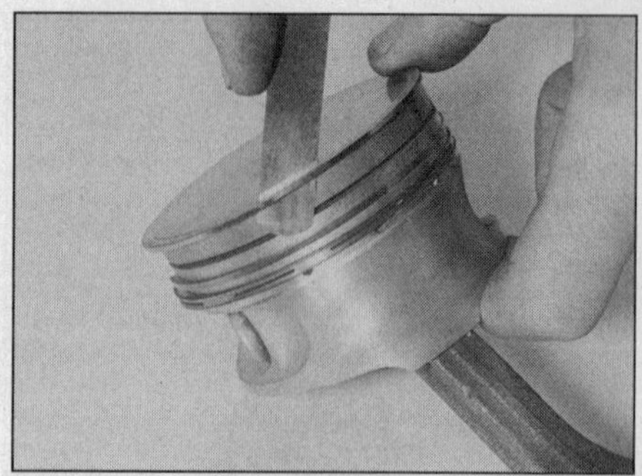
13.2 Using feeler blades to remove piston rings

the threaded holes. If there has been any history of internal water leakage, it may be worthwhile having an engine overhaul specialist check the block with special equipment. If defects are found, have the block repaired, if possible, or renewed.

11 Check the cylinder bores for scuffing and scoring. Normally, bore wear will be evident in the form of a wear ridge at the top of the bore. This ridge marks the limit of piston travel.

12 Measure the diameter of each cylinder at the top (just under the ridge area), centre and base of the cylinder bore, parallel to the crankshaft axis **(see illustration)**.

13 Next measure each cylinder's diameter at the same three locations across the crankshaft axis. If the difference between any of the measurements is greater than 0.20 mm, indicating that the cylinder is excessively out-of-round or tapered, then remedial action must be considered.

14 Repeat this procedure for the remaining cylinders, then measure the diameter of each piston at right-angles to the gudgeon pin axis, and compare the result with the information given in Chapter 2A Specifications **(see illustration)**. By comparing the piston diameters with the bore diameters, an idea can be obtained of the clearances.

15 If the cylinder walls are badly scuffed or scored, or if they are excessively out-of-round or tapered, have the cylinder block rebored (where possible) by an engine overhaul specialist. New pistons (oversize in the case of a rebore) will also be required.

16 If the cylinders are in reasonably good condition, then it may only be necessary to renew the piston rings.

17 If this is the case, the bores should be honed in order to allow the new rings to bed-in correctly and provide the best possible seal. The conventional type of hone has spring-loaded stones, and is used with a power drill. You will also need some paraffin or honing oil and rags. The hone should be moved up-and-down the cylinder to produce a crosshatch pattern, and plenty of honing oil should be used.

18 Ideally, the crosshatch lines should intersect at approximately a 60° angle. Do not take off more material than is necessary to produce the required finish. If new pistons are being fitted, the piston manufacturers may specify a finish with a different angle, so their instructions should be followed. Do not withdraw the hone from the cylinder while it is still being turned, but stop it first (keep the hone moving up-and-down the bore while it slows down).

19 After honing a cylinder, wipe out all traces of the honing oil. If equipment of this type is not available, or if you are not sure whether you are competent to undertake the task yourself, an engine overhaul specialist will carry out the work at a moderate cost.

20 Refit all external components and senders in their correct locations, as noted before removal.

13 Piston/connecting rod assemblies – inspection and reassembly

Inspection

1 Before the inspection process can begin, the piston/connecting rod assemblies must be cleaned, and the original piston rings removed from the pistons.

2 Carefully expand the old rings over the top of the pistons. The use of two or three old feeler blades will be helpful in preventing the rings dropping into empty grooves **(see illustration)**. Note that the oil control scraper ring is in three sections.

3 Scrape away all traces of carbon from the top of the piston. A hand-held wire brush or a piece of fine emery cloth can be used once the majority of the deposits have been scraped away.

4 Remove the carbon from the ring grooves in the piston by cleaning them using an old ring. Break the ring in half to do this. Be very careful to remove only the carbon deposits; do not remove any metal, or scratch the sides of the ring grooves. Protect your fingers – piston rings are sharp.

5 Once the deposits have been removed, clean the piston/connecting rod assembly with paraffin or a suitable solvent, and dry thoroughly. Make sure the oil return holes in the ring grooves are clear.

6 If the pistons and cylinder bores are not damaged or worn excessively, and if the cylinder block does not need to be rebored, the original pistons can be re-used. Normal piston wear appears as even vertical wear on the piston thrust surfaces, and slight looseness of the top ring in its groove. New piston rings, however, should always be used when the engine is reassembled.

7 Carefully inspect each piston for cracks around the skirt, at the gudgeon pin bosses, and at the piston ring lands (between the piston ring grooves).

8 Look for scoring and scuffing on the sides of the skirt, holes in the piston crown, and burned areas at the edge of the crown. If the skirt is scored or scuffed, the engine may have been suffering from overheating and/or abnormal combustion, which caused excessively-high operating temperatures. The cooling and lubricating systems should be checked thoroughly.

9 Scorch marks on the sides of the pistons show that blow-by has occurred and the rings are not sealing correctly. A hole in the piston crown is an indication that abnormal combustion (pre-ignition, knocking or detonation) has been occurring. If any of the above problems exist, the causes must be corrected, or the damage will occur again. Typically, the causes may include inlet air leaks, incorrect fuel/air mixture or incorrect ignition timing.

10 Corrosion of the piston, in the form of small pits, indicates that coolant is leaking into the combustion chamber and/or the crankcase. Again, the cause must be corrected, or the problem may persist in the rebuilt engine.

11 If new rings are being fitted to old pistons, measure the piston ring-to-groove clearance by placing a new piston ring in each ring groove and measuring the clearance with a feeler blade. Check the clearance at three or four places around each groove. Where no values are specified, if the measured clearance is excessive – say greater than 0.10 mm – new pistons will be required. If the new ring is excessively tight, the most likely cause is dirt remaining in the groove.

12 Check the piston-to-bore clearance by

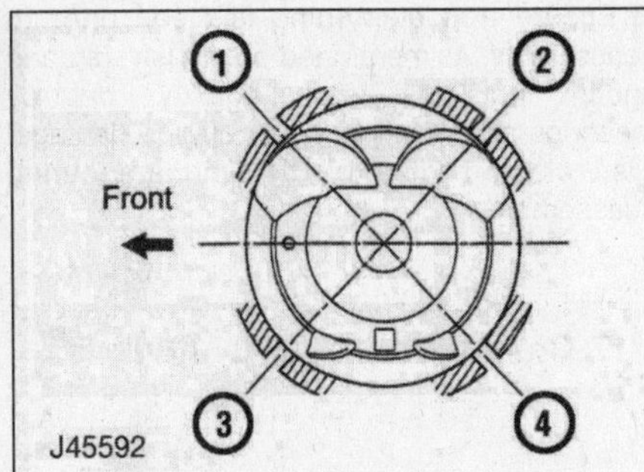

13.16 Piston ring end gap alignment

1 Top compression ring and oil control expander
2 Oil control lower side rail
3 Oil control upper side rail
4 Second compression ring

measuring the cylinder bore (see Section 12) and the piston diameter. Measure the piston across the skirt, at a 90° angle to the gudgeon pin, approximately half-way down the skirt. Subtract the piston diameter from the bore diameter to obtain the clearance. If this is greater than the figures given in the Specifications, the block will have to be rebored and new pistons and rings fitted.

13 Check the fit of the gudgeon pin by twisting the piston and connecting rod in opposite directions. Any noticeable play indicates excessive wear, which must be corrected. The gudgeon pins are secured by circlips, so the pistons and connecting rods can be separated without difficulty. Note the position of the piston relative to the rod before dismantling, and use new circlips on reassembly.

14 Before refitting the rings to the pistons, check their end gaps by inserting each of them in their cylinder bores. Use the piston to make sure that they are square. Using feeler blades, check that the gaps are within the tolerances given in the Specifications. Genuine rings are supplied pregapped; no attempt should be made to adjust the gaps by filing.

Reassembly

15 Install the new rings by fitting them over the top of the piston, starting with the oil control scraper ring sections. Use feeler blades in the same way as when removing the old rings. New rings generally have their top surfaces identified, and must be fitted the correct way round. Note that the first and second compression rings have different sections. Be careful when handling the compression rings; they will break if they are handled roughly or expanded too far.

16 With all the rings in position, space the two top ring gaps at 180° to each other (on opposite sides of the piston). The oil control ring top and bottom rails must be positioned at 90° to the first and second ring gaps – ie, so that none of the end gaps align directly above or below each other **(see illustration)**.

14.4 Measure the diameter of each crankshaft journal at several points, to detect taper and out-of-round conditions

14 Crankshaft – inspection

1 Clean the crankshaft and dry it with compressed air if available. Be sure to clean the oil holes with a cotton bud or similar probe.

Warning: Wear eye protection when using compressed air.

2 Check the main and big-end bearing journals for uneven wear, scoring, pitting and cracking.

3 If the crankshaft has been reground, check for burrs around the crankshaft oil holes (the holes are usually chamfered, so burrs should not be a problem unless regrinding has been carried out carelessly). Remove any burrs with a fine file or scraper, and thoroughly clean the oil holes as described previously.

4 Using a micrometer, measure the diameter of the main bearing and connecting rod journals, and compare the results with the Specifications (Chapter 2A). By measuring the diameter at a number of points around each journal's circumference, you will be able to determine whether or not the journal is out-of-round **(see illustration)**. Take the measurement at each end of the journal, near the webs, to determine if the journal is tapered. If any of the measurements vary by more than 0.02 mm, the crankshaft will have to be reground, and undersize bearings fitted.

5 Check the oil seal contact surfaces at each end of the crankshaft for wear and damage. If an excessive groove is evident in the surface of the crankshaft, consult an engine overhaul specialist who will be able to advise whether a repair is possible or if a new crankshaft is necessary.

6 Check the condition of the crankshaft position sensor rotor (which looks like a thin sprocket). On 1.0 litre and 1.3 litre 2SZ-FE engines, the rotor slides off (and should already have been removed), but on the 1.3 litre 2NZ-FE engine, the rotor is a press-fit on the crankshaft. Check that the rotor is not distorted or damaged – it should have one tooth missing, which is used as a reference by the crankshaft position sensor.

15 Main and big-end bearings – inspection

1 Even though the main and big-end bearings should be renewed during the engine overhaul, the old bearings should be retained for close examination, as they may reveal valuable information about the condition of the engine. The size of the bearing shells is stamped on the back metal, and this information should be given to the supplier of the new shells.

2 Bearing failure occurs because of lack of lubrication, the presence of dirt or other foreign particles, overloading the engine, and corrosion **(see illustration)**. Regardless of the cause of bearing failure, it must be corrected before the engine is reassembled, to prevent it from happening again.

3 When examining the bearings, remove them from the engine block, the main bearing caps, the connecting rods and the rod caps, and lay them out on a clean surface in the same general position as their location in the engine. This will enable you to match any bearing problems with the corresponding crankshaft journal.

4 Dirt and other foreign particles get into the engine in a variety of ways. Dirt may be left in the engine during assembly, or it may pass through filters or the crankcase ventilation system. It may get into the oil, and from there into the bearings. Metal chips from machining operations and normal engine wear are often present. Abrasives are sometimes left in engine components after reconditioning, especially when parts are not thoroughly cleaned using the proper cleaning methods.

5 Whatever the source, these foreign objects often end up embedded in the soft bearing material, and are easily recognised. Large

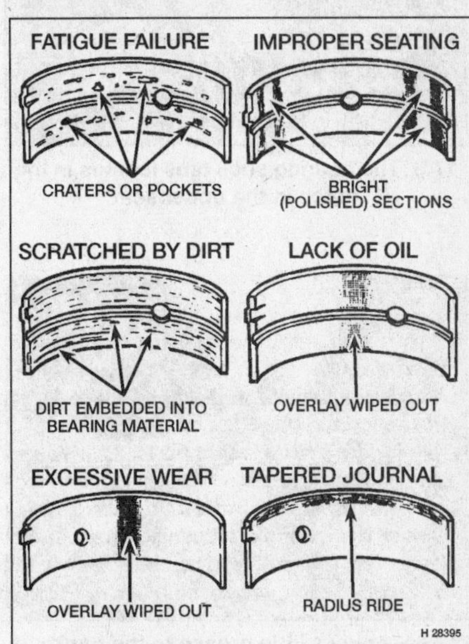

15.2 Typical bearing failures

particles will not embed in the bearing, and will score or gouge the bearing and journal. The best prevention for this cause of bearing failure is to clean all parts thoroughly, and keep everything spotlessly-clean during engine assembly. Frequent and regular engine oil and filter changes are also recommended.

6 Lack of lubrication (or lubrication breakdown) has a number of interrelated causes. Excessive heat (which thins the oil), overloading (which squeezes the oil from the bearing face) and oil leakage (from excessive bearing clearances, worn oil pump or high engine speeds) all contribute to lubrication breakdown. Blocked oil passages, which usually are the result of misaligned oil holes in a bearing shell, will also oil-starve a bearing and destroy it. When lack of lubrication is the cause of bearing failure, the bearing material is wiped or extruded from the steel backing of the bearing. Temperatures may increase to the point where the steel backing turns blue from overheating.

7 Driving habits can have a definite effect on bearing life. Full-throttle, low-speed operation (labouring the engine) puts very high loads on bearings, which tends to squeeze out the oil film. These loads cause the bearings to flex, which produces fine cracks in the bearing face (fatigue failure). Eventually, the bearing material will loosen in pieces and tear away from the steel backing. Short-trip driving leads to corrosion of bearings, because insufficient engine heat is produced to drive off the condensed water and corrosive gases. These products collect in the engine oil, forming acid and sludge. As the oil is carried to the engine bearings, the acid attacks and corrodes the bearing material.

8 Incorrect bearing installation during engine assembly will lead to bearing failure as well. Tight-fitting bearings leave insufficient bearing oil clearance, and will result in oil starvation. Dirt or foreign particles trapped behind a bearing shell result in high spots on the bearing which lead to failure.

9 *Do not* touch any shell's bearing surface with your fingers during reassembly; there is a risk of scratching the delicate surface, or of depositing particles of dirt on it.

10 As mentioned at the beginning of this Section, the bearing shells should be renewed as a matter of course during engine overhaul; to do otherwise is false economy.

17.3 The bearing shell tabs locates in the notch in the upper seat

16 Engine overhaul – reassembly sequence

1 Before reassembly begins, ensure that all new parts have been obtained and that all necessary tools are available. Read through the entire procedure to familiarise yourself with the work involved, and to ensure that all items necessary for reassembly of the engine are at hand. In addition to all normal tools and materials, flange sealant and thread-locking compound will be needed during engine reassembly. Do not use any kind of silicone-based sealant on any part of the fuel system or inlet manifold, and never use exhaust sealants upstream (on the engine side) of the catalytic converter.

2 In order to save time and avoid problems, engine reassembly can be carried out in the following order:

a) Crankshaft and main bearings.
b) Pistons and connecting rods.
c) Cylinder head.
d) Oil pump.
e) Timing sprockets and chain.
f) Sump.
g) Flywheel.
h) Engine external components (including inlet and exhaust manifolds).

3 Ensure that everything is clean prior to reassembly. As mentioned previously, dirt and metal particles can quickly destroy bearings and result in major engine damage. Use clean engine oil to lubricate during reassembly.

17 Crankshaft – refitting

Selection of new bearing shells

1 Have the crankshaft inspected and measured by a Toyota dealer or engine reconditioning specialist. They will be able to carry out any regrinding/repairs, and supply suitable main and big-end bearing shells.

Refitting

2 It is assumed at this point that the cylinder block/crankcase and crankshaft have been cleaned and repaired or reconditioned as necessary. Position the engine upside-down.

3 Wipe clean the main bearing shell seats in the crankcase and bearing caps, and clean the backs of the bearing shells. Insert the respective upper shells (dry) into position in the crankcase. Note that the upper shells have grooves and oil holes in them (the lower shells are plain). The shell oil holes must align with the oil supply holes in the crankcase. Where the old main bearings are being refitted, ensure that they are located in their original positions. Make sure that the tab on each bearing shell fits into the notch in the block or cap **(see illustration)**.

4 Place the crankshaft thrustwashers into position in the crankcase, either side of the centre (No 3) bearing, so that their oil grooves are facing outwards (away from the central web) **(see illustrations)**. Hold them in position with a little grease. Clean the bearing surfaces of the shells in the block, and the crankshaft main bearing journals with a clean, lint-free cloth.

5 Clean the bearing surfaces of the shells in the block, then apply a thin layer of clean engine oil to each shell **(see illustration)**.

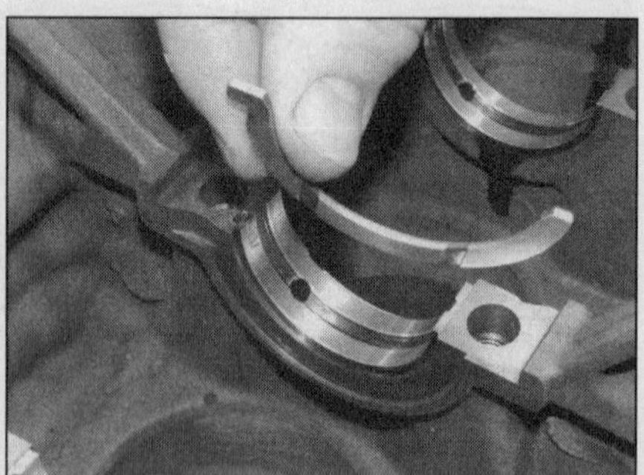

17.4a Apply a little grease to the backs of the thrustwashers before fitting . . .

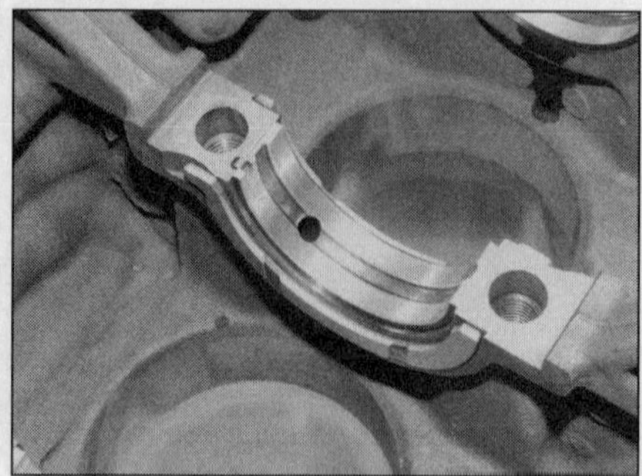

17.4b . . . and ensure they are fitted with the oil grooves facing outwards

17.5 Lubricate the bearing shells before fitting the crankshaft

17.6a Carefully lower the crankshaft into position

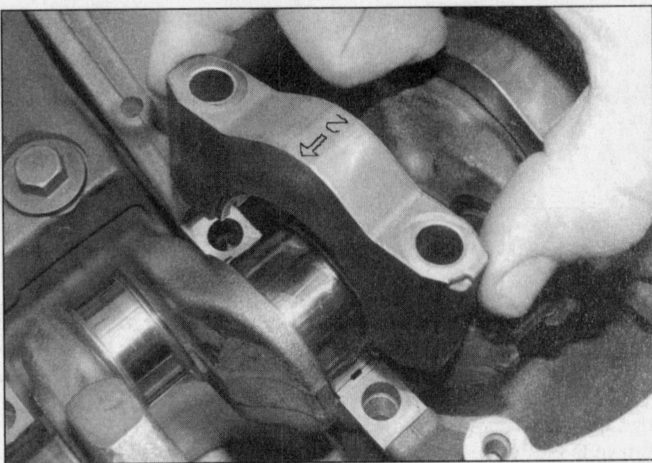
17.6b Fit the main bearing caps with the arrow marks facing the timing chain end

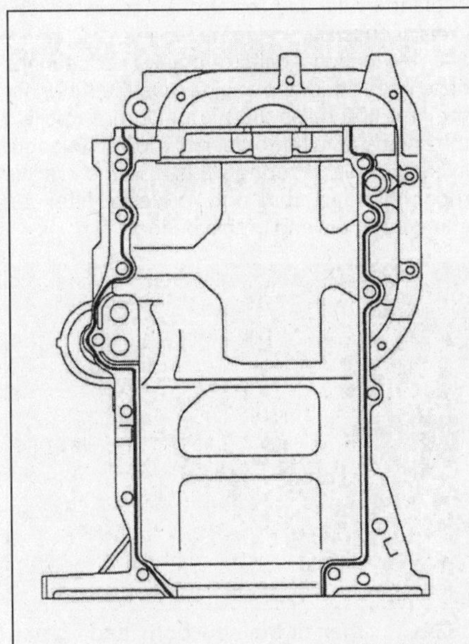
17.12a Apply a 2 to 3 mm bead of sealant to the lower crankcase

Lubricate the thrustwasher bearing surfaces as well.

6 Make sure the crankshaft journals are clean, then lay the crankshaft back in place in the block. Clean the bearing surfaces of the shells in the caps, then lubricate them with oil. Install the caps in their respective positions, with the arrows pointing to the timing chain end of the engine **(see illustrations)**.

7 Working in a diagonal sequence from the centre main bearing outwards (and ensuring that each cap is tightened down squarely and evenly onto the block), tighten the main bearing cap bolts to the specified Stage 1 torque wrench setting.

8 With all the main bearing bolts tightened to the Stage 1 setting, go round again in the same sequence and tighten them further to the Stage 2 torque.

9 Rotate the crankshaft a number of times by hand, to check for any obvious binding.

10 Check the crankshaft endfloat (refer to Section 11).

11 Fit new crankshaft oil seals as described in Chapter 2A (as applicable).

12 Refit the components removed in Section 13. On the 1.3 litre 2NZ-FE engine, apply a 2 to 3 mm bead of sealant (such as Toyota part number 08826-00080) to the lower crankcase as shown. Fit the lower crankcase, refitting the bolts to their original locations, and tighten them progressively to the specified torque, in sequence **(see illustrations)**.

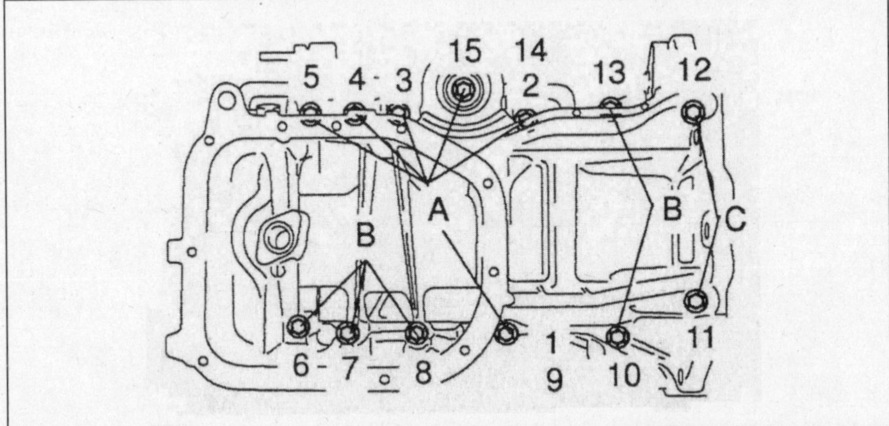

17.12b Lower crankcase bolt tightening sequence – 1.3 litre engines

18 Pistons/connecting rods – refitting

1 Clean the backs of the big-end bearing shells, and the recesses in the connecting rods and big-end caps. If new shells are being fitted, ensure that all traces of the protective grease are cleaned off using paraffin. Wipe the shells and connecting rods dry with a lint-free cloth.

2 Lubricate No 1 piston and piston rings, and check that the ring gaps are spaced as described in Section 13.

3 Fit the connecting rod bearing shells in place, making sure the shell's locating tab engages correctly **(see illustration)**.

4 Fit a ring compressor to No 1 piston, then insert the piston and connecting rod into No 1

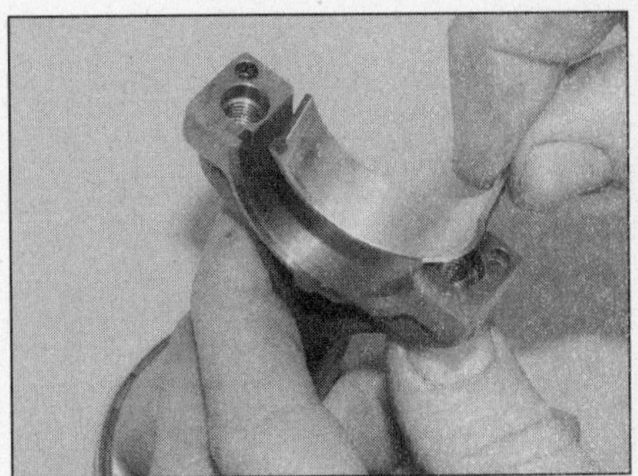
18.3 Fit the connecting rod bearing shell, ensuring the tab seats correctly

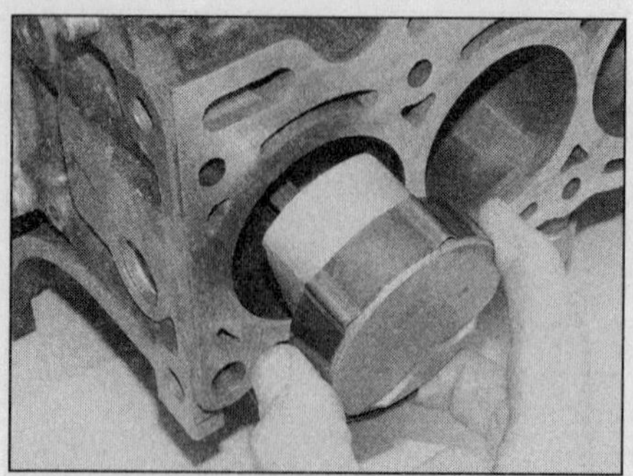
18.4a Fit a ring compressor, and offer in the piston . . .

18.4b . . . then tap the piston through the compressor using a hammer handle

18.4c Dot on the piston crown should face the timing chain end

cylinder. Make sure that the dot on the piston crown is facing the timing end of the engine. With No 1 crankpin at its lowest point, drive the piston carefully into the cylinder with the wooden handle of a hammer, at the same time guiding the connecting rod onto the crankpin **(see illustrations)**.

5 Press the big-end bearing shells into the connecting rod caps, aligning each shell with its locating groove.

6 Liberally lubricate the crankpin journals and big-end bearing shells. Refit the bearing caps, which have dowels to ensure correct positioning. Tighten the new bearing cap bolts to the specified torque and angles, and turn the crankshaft each time to make sure that it is free before moving on to the next assembly **(see illustrations)**.

19 Engine – initial start-up after overhaul

1 With the engine refitted in the car, double-check the engine oil and coolant levels (see *Weekly checks*). Make a final check that everything has been reconnected, and that there are no tools or rags left in the engine compartment.

2 With the ignition and fuel injection systems disabled by disconnecting the ignition coil wiring plugs (Chapter 5B) and removing the fuel pump fuse (Chapter 4A or Chapter 12 wiring diagrams), crank the engine on the starter motor until the oil pressure light goes out.

3 Reconnect the ignition coils, and refit the fuel pump fuse.

4 Start the engine, noting that this may take a little longer than usual.

5 While the engine is idling, check for fuel, water and oil leaks. Check the (hydraulic) power steering pipe/hose unions for leakage. Do not be alarmed if there are some odd smells and smoke from parts getting hot and burning off oil deposits.

6 Keep the engine idling until hot water is felt circulating through the top hose, then switch it off.

7 After a few minutes, recheck the oil and coolant levels, and top-up as necessary (see *Weekly checks*).

8 If new pistons, rings or crankshaft bearings have been fitted, the engine must be run-in for the first 500 miles (800 km). Do not operate the engine at full-throttle, nor allow it to labour in any gear during this period. It is recommended that the oil and filter be changed at the end of this period.

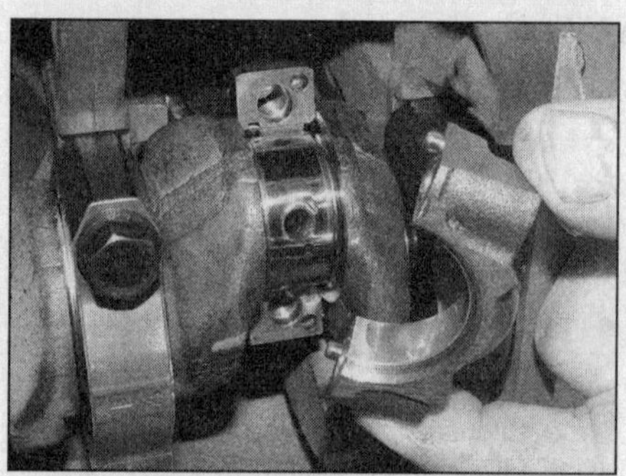
18.6a Oil and refit the connecting rod bearing caps . . .

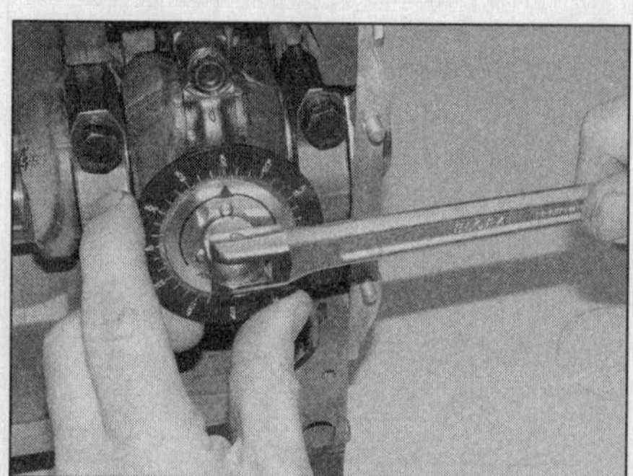
18.6b . . . then fit the new bolts and tighten as specified

Chapter 3
Cooling, heating and air conditioning systems

Contents

Degrees of difficulty

Easy, suitable for novice with little experience 	**Fairly easy,** suitable for beginner with some experience 	**Fairly difficult,** suitable for competent DIY mechanic 	**Difficult,** suitable for experienced DIY mechanic 	**Very difficult,** suitable for expert DIY or professional

Specifications

General

Thermostat opening temperature	78 to 82 °C
Radiator cap relief valve opening pressure	13.5 to 17.8 psi

Torque wrench settings

	Nm	lbf ft
Air conditioning compressor mounting bolts	25	18
Coolant drain plug (on engine block)	13	10
Coolant temperature sensor	20	15
Cooling fan switch	34	25
Thermostat housing nut/bolt	9	7
Water pump mounting nuts/bolts	10	7
Water pump pulley bolts	13	10

1 General information and precautions

General information

The cooling system is of pressurised type, comprising a pump driven by the auxiliary drivebelt, an aluminium crossflow radiator, electric cooling fan, and a thermostat. The system functions as follows. Cold coolant from the radiator passes through the hose to the water pump, where it is pumped around the cylinder block and head passages. After cooling the cylinder bores, combustion surfaces and valve seats, the coolant reaches the underside of the thermostat, which is initially closed. The coolant passes through the heater, and is returned via the cylinder block to the water pump.

When the engine is cold, the thermostat is shut, and the coolant circulates only through the cylinder block, cylinder head and heater. However, at high engine speeds with the thermostat shut, the excess coolant pressure opens a spring-loaded valve in the thermostat housing, and the supply to the heater matrix is temporarily cut – this ensures an adequate flow of coolant under these conditions.

When the coolant reaches a predetermined temperature, the thermostat opens and the coolant passes through to the radiator. As the coolant circulates through the radiator, it is cooled by the inrush of air when the car is in forward motion. Airflow is supplemented by the action of the electric cooling fan when necessary. Once the coolant has passed through the radiator, and has cooled, the cycle is repeated.

The electric cooling fan, mounted on the rear of the radiator, is controlled by a thermostatic switch. At a predetermined coolant temperature, the switch actuates the fan, via the engine ECU. On models with air conditioning, a three-speed cooling fan is fitted; which of the three speeds is used is dependent on the coolant temperature switch, and on whether the air conditioning system is in use.

The coolant temperature is signalled to the engine ECU, and to the temperature display on the instrument panel, by another sensor fitted to the coolant elbow at the transmission end of the cylinder head.

An expansion tank is fitted to allow for the expansion of the coolant when hot. The expansion tank is connected to the top of the radiator.

Refer to Section 10 for information on the air conditioning system.

Precautions

Warning: Do not attempt to remove the radiator filler cap, or disturb any part of the cooling system, while the engine is hot; there is a high risk of scalding. If the radiator filler cap must be removed before the engine and radiator have fully cooled (even though this is not recommended) the pressure in the cooling system must first be relieved. Cover the cap with a thick layer of cloth, to avoid scalding, and slowly unscrew the filler cap until a hissing sound can be heard. When

2.3a Slide the spring clips up the hose, then pull the hose free

2.3b On larger spring clips, a screw-type clip can sometimes be used to slacken them

the hissing has stopped, indicating that the pressure has reduced, slowly unscrew the filler cap until it can be removed; if more hissing sounds are heard, wait until they have stopped before unscrewing the cap completely. At all times, keep well away from the filler cap opening.

Warning: Do not allow antifreeze to come into contact with skin, or with the painted surfaces of the car. Rinse off spills immediately, with plenty of water. Never leave antifreeze lying around in an open container, or in a puddle on the driveway or garage floor. Children and pets are attracted by its sweet smell, but antifreeze can be fatal if ingested.

Warning: If the engine is hot, the electric cooling fan may start rotating even if the engine is not running; be careful to keep hands, hair and loose clothing well clear when working in the engine compartment.

Warning: Refer to Section 10 for precautions to be observed when working on models equipped with air conditioning.

2 Cooling system hoses – disconnection and renewal

Note: *Refer to the warnings given in Section 1 of this Chapter before proceeding. Do not attempt to disconnect any hose while the system is still hot.*

1 If the checks described in the relevant part of Chapter 1 reveal a faulty hose, it must be renewed as follows.

2 First drain the cooling system (see Chapter 1). If the coolant is not due for renewal, it may be re-used if it is collected in a clean container.

3 Before disconnecting a hose, first note its routing in the engine compartment, and whether it is secured by any clips or ties. Use a pair of pliers to release the spring clamps (or a screwdriver to slacken screw-type clamps) then move them along the hose, clear of the relevant inlet/outlet union. Carefully work the hose free **(see illustrations)**.

4 Note that the coolant unions are fragile (some are made of plastic); do not use excessive force when attempting to remove the hoses. If a hose proves to be difficult to remove, try to release it by rotating the hose ends before attempting to free it – if this fails, try gently prising up the end of the hose with a small screwdriver to 'break' the seal.

If all else fails, cut the coolant hose with a sharp knife, then slit it so that it can be peeled off in two pieces. Although this may prove expensive if the hose is otherwise undamaged, it is preferable to buying a new radiator.

5 When fitting a hose, first slide the clamps onto the hose, then work the hose into position. If spring-type clamps were originally fitted, it is a good idea to use screw-type clamps when refitting the hose (if only to make removal easier, next time). If the hose is stiff, use a little soapy water (washing-up liquid is ideal) as a lubricant, or soften the hose by soaking it in hot water.

6 Work the hose into position, checking that it is correctly routed and secured. Slide each clamp along the hose until it passes over the flared end of the relevant inlet/outlet union, before tightening the clamps securely.

7 Refill the cooling system with reference to Chapter 1.

8 Check thoroughly for leaks as soon as possible after disturbing any part of the cooling system.

3 Radiator – removal, inspection and refitting

Note: *If leakage is the reason for removing the radiator, bear in mind that minor leaks can often be cured using a radiator sealant with the radiator in situ.*

Removal

1 Drain the cooling system as described in Chapter 1.

2 Apply the handbrake, then jack up the front of the car and support securely on axle stands (see *Jacking and vehicle support*).

3 Remove the two engine lower cover panels from under the car.

4 Disconnect the cooling fan wiring plug, and unclip the wiring harness as necessary **(see illustrations)**. On 1.3 litre 2NZ-FE engine models, disconnect the cooling fan switch from the side of the radiator.

5 Bearing in mind the advice given in Section 2, disconnect the upper and lower hoses from the radiator **(see illustrations)**.

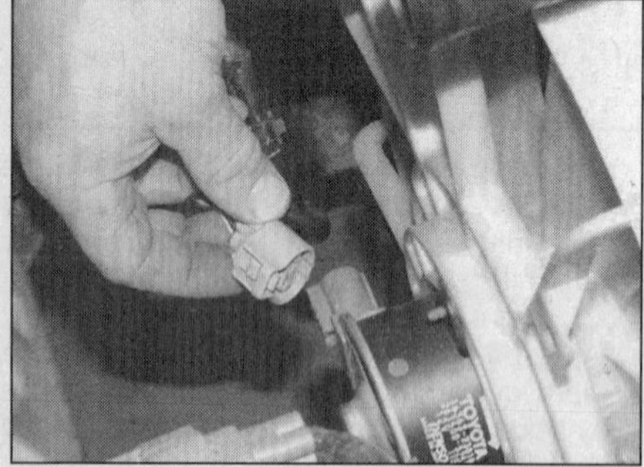
3.4a Disconnect the cooling fan motor wiring plug . . .

3.4b . . . and unclip the wiring harness

3.5a Release the spring clips . . .

3.5b . . . and disconnect the radiator hoses

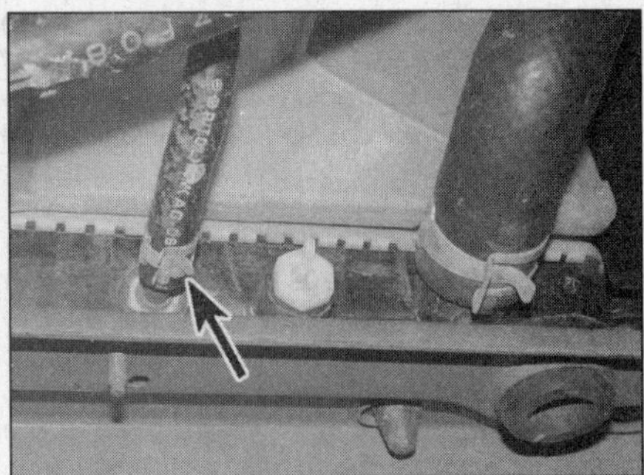

3.6 One of the transmission fluid cooler hoses at the base of the radiator

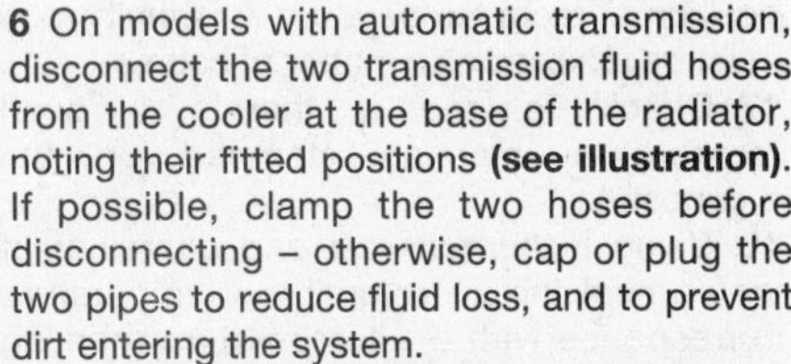

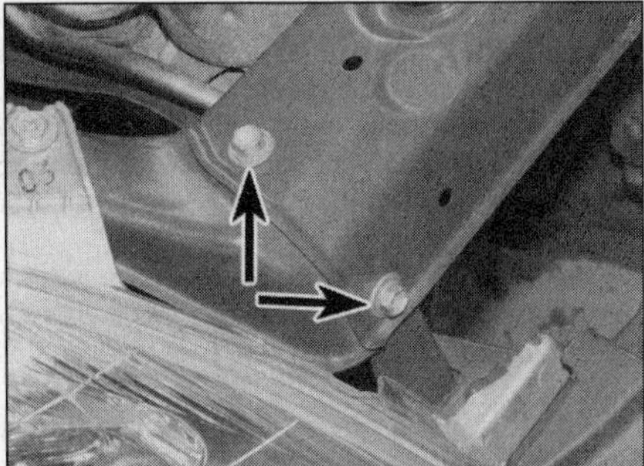

3.7a Remove the front panel (lock carrier) bolts . . .

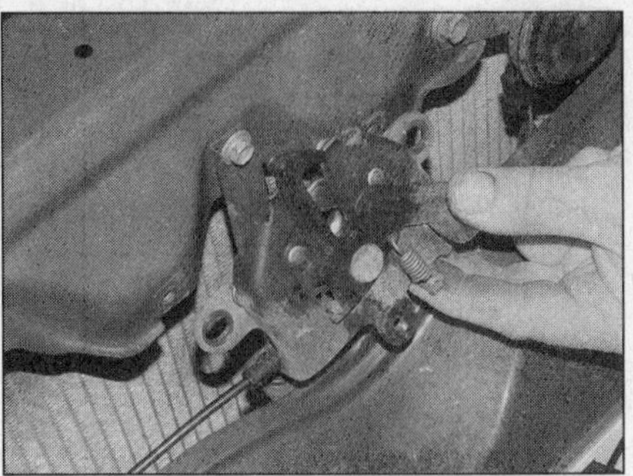

3.7b . . . including the ones for the bonnet lock, which can be moved aside

6 On models with automatic transmission, disconnect the two transmission fluid hoses from the cooler at the base of the radiator, noting their fitted positions **(see illustration)**. If possible, clamp the two hoses before disconnecting – otherwise, cap or plug the two pipes to reduce fluid loss, and to prevent dirt entering the system.

7 To remove the radiator, the front panel (lock carrier) must be unbolted and lifted away. Models with air conditioning fitted have a total of nine bolts to remove, while those without it have seven – in both cases, two of the bolts are for the bonnet lock, which should be moved clear without disconnecting the cable **(see illustrations)**. On 1.3 litre 2NZ-FE engine models, unbolt the coolant filler neck from the rear of the panel.

8 Lift the front panel off, noting that the two upper mounting rubbers may come with it – make sure they are retained for refitting. Disconnect the wiring plug from the horn as the panel is removed **(see illustrations)**.

9 Lift the radiator out, taking care not to damage the cooling fan (or the air conditioning condenser, where applicable). Recover the two lower mounting rubbers **(see illustrations)**.

10 Remove the two screws, and unclip the side cover from the radiator **(see illustration)**.

11 If required, the cooling fan and shroud can be removed, after unscrewing the three mounting bolts **(see illustration)**. To remove the motor, undo the fan's central nut and remove the fan – the motor is then secured by three bolts.

Inspection

12 If the radiator has been removed due to suspected blockage, reverse-flush it as described in Chapter 1. Clean dirt and debris from the radiator fins, using an air line (in which case, wear eye protection) or a soft brush. Be careful, as the fins are easily damaged, and are sharp.

13 If necessary, a radiator specialist can perform a 'flow test' on the radiator, to establish whether an internal blockage exists.

14 A leaking radiator must be referred to a specialist for permanent repair. Do not attempt to weld or solder a leaking radiator, as damage may result.

Refitting

15 Refitting is a reversal of removal, bearing in mind the following points:

a) Ensure that all hoses are correctly reconnected, and their retaining clips securely fitted (or tightened).

3.8a Lift off the front panel . . .

3.8b . . . and disconnect the horn wiring plug

3.9a Lift out the radiator . . .

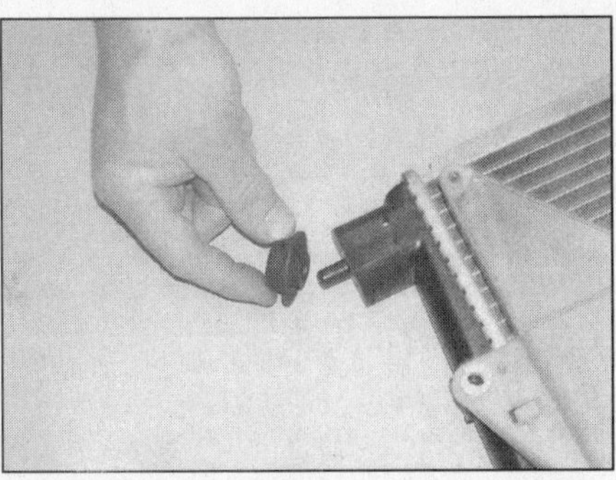

3.9b . . . and recover the lower mounting rubbers

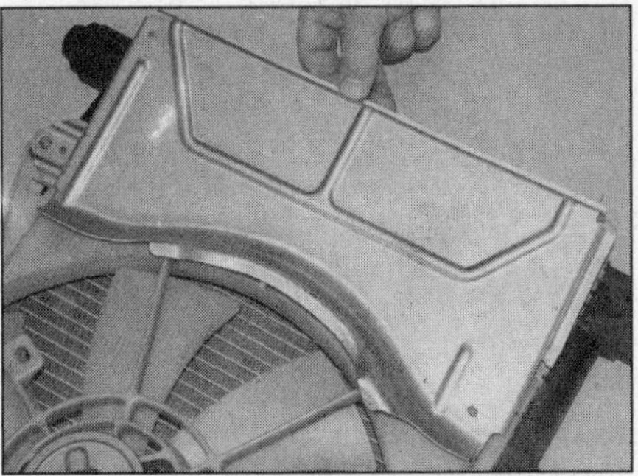

3.10 Unclip the side cover from the radiator

3.11 One of the three cooling fan shroud mounting bolts

b) *Reconnect the radiator fan wiring, and ensure the harness is routed clear of the fan blades or hot components.*
c) *On completion, refill the cooling system as described in Chapter 1.*
d) *On models with automatic transmission, check and top-up the fluid level if necessary, as described in Chapter 1.*

4 Thermostat – removal, testing and refitting

1 As the thermostat ages, it will become slower to react to changes in water temperature ('lazy'). Ultimately, the unit may stick in the open or closed position, and this causes problems. A thermostat which is stuck open will result in a very slow warm-up; a thermostat which is stuck shut will lead to rapid overheating.

2 Before assuming the thermostat is to blame for a cooling system problem, check the coolant level. If the system is draining due to a leak, or has not been properly filled, there may be an airlock in the system (refer to the coolant renewal procedure in Chapter 1).

3 If the engine seems to be taking a long time to warm-up (based on heater output), the thermostat could be stuck open. Don't necessarily believe the temperature gauge reading – some gauges never seem to register very high in normal driving.

4 A lengthy warm-up period might suggest that the thermostat is missing – it may have been removed or inadvertently omitted by a previous owner or mechanic. Don't drive the car without a thermostat – the engine management system's ECU will then stay in warm-up mode for longer than necessary, causing emissions and fuel economy to suffer.

5 If the engine runs hot, use your hand to check the temperature of the radiator top hose. If the hose isn't hot, but the engine clearly is, the thermostat is probably stuck closed, preventing the coolant inside the engine from escaping to the radiator – renew the thermostat. Again, this problem may also be due to an airlock (refer to the coolant renewal procedure in Chapter 1).

6 If the radiator top hose is hot, it means that the coolant is flowing (at least as far as the radiator) and the thermostat is open. Consult the *Fault diagnosis* section at the end of this manual to assist in tracing possible cooling system faults, but a lack of heater output would now definitely suggest an airlock or a blockage.

7 To gain a rough idea of whether the thermostat is working properly when the engine is warming up, without dismantling the system, proceed as follows.

8 With the engine completely cold, start the engine and let it idle, while checking the temperature of the radiator top hose. Periodically check the temperature indicated on the instrument panel – if overheating is indicated, switch the engine off immediately. **Note:** *Yaris models feature a temperature display warning light (or lights) – blue when the engine is cold (below 60°C) and red when hot (above 117°C).*

9 The top hose should feel cold for some time as the engine warms-up, and should then get warm quite quickly as the thermostat opens.

10 The above is not a precise or definitive test of thermostat operation, but if the system does not perform as described, remove and test the thermostat as described below.

Removal

11 Allow the engine to cool completely, then drain the coolant as described in Chapter 1.

12 On 1.0 litre and 1.3 litre 2SZ-FE engines, to improve access to the thermostat housing, which is located at the transmission end of the engine, remove the air cleaner inlet duct as described in Chapter 4A. Disconnect the wiring plug from the cooling fan switch.

13 On the 1.3 litre 2NZ-FE engine, the thermostat housing is at the front of the engine, under the inlet manifold. It may be easier to access the housing from below, in which case jack up the front of the car, and support it on axle stands (see *Jacking and vehicle support*). Disconnect the wiring harness clip from the thermostat housing

14 Disconnect the large-diameter radiator hose from the thermostat housing, then remove the mounting nuts (or nut and bolt), and take off the thermostat cover **(see illustrations)**.

15 Pull out the thermostat and recover the O-ring seal – the seal should not be re-used **(see illustration)**.

Testing

Note: *Frankly, if there is any question about the operation of the thermostat, it's best to renew it – they are not expensive items. Testing involves heating in, or over, an open pan of boiling water, which carries with it the risk of scalding. A thermostat which has seen more than five years' service may well be past its best already.*

16 If the thermostat remains in the open position at room temperature, it is faulty, and must be renewed as a matter of course.

17 Check to see if there's a open temperature marking stamped on the thermostat.

18 Using a thermometer and container of water, heat the water until the temperature corresponds with the temperature marking stamped on the thermostat. If no marking is found, start the test with the water hot, and heat slowly until it boils.

19 Suspend the (closed) thermostat on a length of string in the water, and check that maximum opening occurs within two minutes, or before the water boils.

20 Remove the thermostat and allow it to cool down; check that it closes fully.

21 If the thermostat does not open and close as described, or if it sticks in either position, it must be renewed.

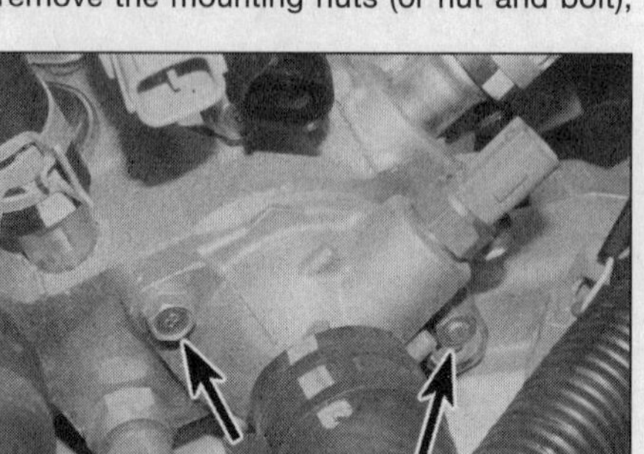

4.14a Thermostat housing mounting nut and bolt

4.14b Release the hose clip, then pull off the radiator hose . . .

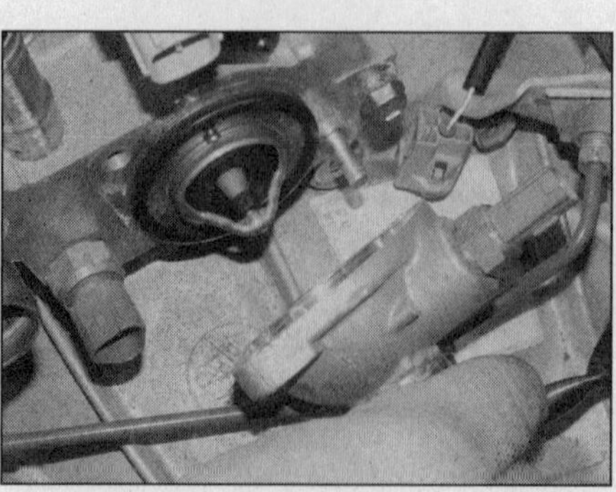

4.14c . . . and remove the thermostat housing

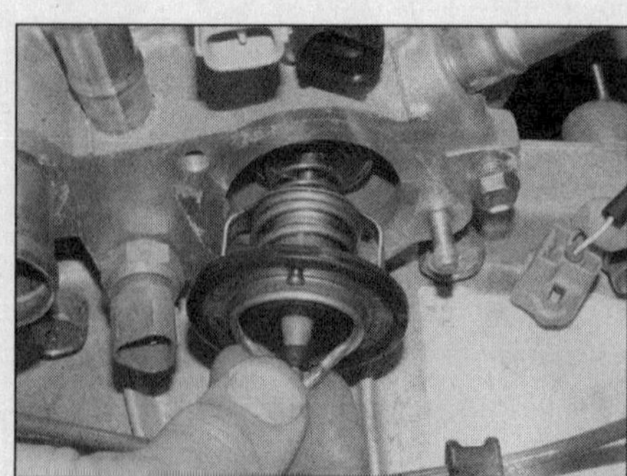

4.15 Pull the thermostat out, and recover the O-ring

4.22a The thermostat housing arrowhead mark, and air bleed valve hole

4.22b The thermostat air bleed valve should be at the top

4.22c Use a new rubber seal when refitting the thermostat

Refitting

22 Refitting is a reversal of removal, noting the following points:

a) *The thermostat housing has an arrowhead marking on top. If the thermostat has a 'jiggle pin' (air bleed valve) fitted, this too should be at the top when refitting **(see illustrations)**.*

b) *Use a new O-ring, and tighten the cover nut/bolt to the specified torque **(see illustration)**.*

c) *On completion, refill the cooling system as described in Chapter 1.*

5 Radiator cooling fan – testing, removal and refitting

Testing

1 On all models, the cooling fan is controlled by the engine management ECU, using signals provided by the cooling fan switch.

2 To check the fan switch circuit, with the engine cold, disconnect the cooling fan switch wiring plug, then switch on the ignition. The cooling fan should operate.

3 The fan motor can be checked by connecting the fan motor directly to a 12 volt power supply. Disconnect the motor wiring plug, and apply 12 volts across the motor terminals.

4 If the fan fails to operate, the fan motor is almost certainly at fault.

5 If the motor works with battery voltage applied, but fails to cut in once the engine is hot, check the following:

a) *Cooling fan switch and coolant temperature sensor (Section 6).*

b) *Cooling fan relay and engine main relay (engine compartment fusebox – see Chapter 12).*

c) *Fuses (check all relevant fuses in both boxes – see Chapter 12).*

d) *Check the condition of all wiring and connectors.*

6 Testing of the fan motor control circuit must be entrusted to a Toyota dealer, who will have the necessary specialist diagnostic equipment to test the system – do not attempt to test the system using conventional test equipment, as the ECU may be damaged.

Removal

7 Drain the cooling system as described in Chapter 1. Since only the radiator top hose and expansion tank hose need to be disconnected, the system need only be partially drained – alternatively, have ready a container to catch the coolant as the two hoses are disconnected.

8 Disconnect the cooling fan wiring plug, and unclip the wiring harness as necessary. Also disconnect the wiring plug from the horn.

9 Bearing in mind the advice given in Section 2 and in paragraph 7, disconnect the upper hose, and the expansion tank hose, from the radiator.

10 Remove the two upper clips, and lift out the side cover from in front of the radiator.

11 Now the upper support panel (lock carrier) must be unbolted and lifted away. Models with air conditioning fitted have a total of nine bolts to remove, while those without it have seven – in both cases, two of the bolts are for the bonnet lock, which should be moved clear without disconnecting the cable. On 1.3 litre 2NZ-FE engine models, unbolt the coolant filler neck from the rear of the panel.

12 Lift the upper support panel off, noting that the two radiator upper mounting rubbers may come with it – make sure they are retained for refitting.

13 Remove the three mounting bolts (two above, one centrally below) for the cooling fan shroud, and lift the shroud/fan assembly out. On models with air conditioning, if access to the bolts is not possible, remove the radiator assembly as described in Section 3.

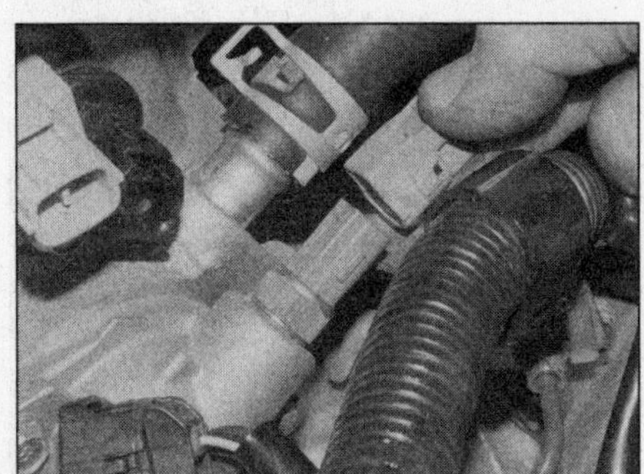

6.4 Disconnect the plug from the cooling fan switch – 1.0 litre engine

14 To remove the motor, undo the fan's central nut and remove the fan – the motor is then secured by three bolts.

Refitting

15 Refitting is a reversal of removal. Reconnect the radiator fan wiring securely, and ensure the harness is routed clear of the fan blades or hot components.

6 Cooling system switches and sensors – removal and refitting

Warning: Do not attempt to remove any switch or sensor while the cooling system is hot and/or pressurised, as there is a great risk of scalding.

1 Allow the engine to cool, then slowly remove the cap from the coolant expansion tank to de-pressurise the cooling system. To avoid any chance of coolant spillage, the system can be drained as described in Chapter 1, but this is not essential if a new sensor is being fitted, and can quickly be substituted for the old one. Otherwise, if the system is not drained and the sensor will be left out for some time, a plug of some kind should be inserted to reduce coolant loss.

Cooling fan switch

2 On 1.0 litre and 1.3 litre 2SZ-FE engines, the switch is screwed into the top of the thermostat cover, at the transmission end of the engine. If necessary, to improve access, remove the air cleaner inlet duct as described in Chapter 4A.

3 On models with the 1.3 litre 2NZ-FE engine, the switch is more conventionally located in the radiator.

4 Disconnect the switch wiring plug, then unscrew the switch and remove it **(see illustration)**. Where applicable, recover the O-ring seal – a new one should be used when refitting.

5 Refitting is a reversal of removal. Ideally, the switch should be tightened to the specified torque, but the shape of the switch (and lack of access to it) mean using a torque wrench may be difficult – use the figure quoted as a guide to tightening by hand if necessary.

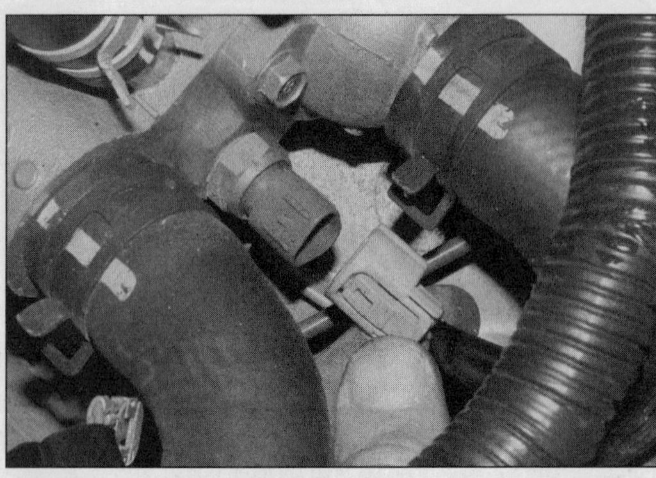

6.7 Disconnect the coolant temperature switch – 1.0 litre engine

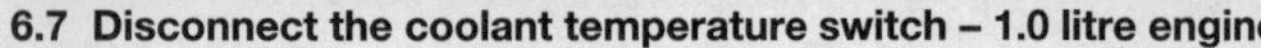

7.3 Use a screwdriver to hold the pulley while each bolt is loosened

6 Either refill or top-up the cooling system as described in Chapter 1 or *Weekly checks*.

Coolant temperature sensor

Note: *Yaris models feature a temperature display warning light (or lights) – blue when the engine is cold (below 60°C) and red when hot (above 117°C).*

7 The switch is screwed horizontally into the coolant elbow at the transmission end of the cylinder head – on 1.0 litre models, do not confuse it with the larger cooling fan switch, which is mounted more vertically **(see illustration)**.

8 Disconnect the sensor wiring plug, then unscrew the sensor and remove it. Where applicable, recover the O-ring seal – a new one should be used when refitting.

9 Refitting is a reversal of removal. Ideally, the sensor should be tightened to the specified torque, but the shape of the sensor (and lack of access to it) mean using a torque wrench may be difficult – use the figure quoted as a guide to tightening by hand if necessary.

10 Either refill or top-up the cooling system as described in Chapter 1 or *Weekly checks*.

7 Water pump – removal and refitting

Removal

1 Drain the cooling system as described in Chapter 1.

2 Raise the front of the car, and support it on axle stands (see *Jacking and vehicle support*). Remove the driver's-side engine lower cover.

3 Before removing the auxiliary drivebelt, loosen the water pump pulley bolts. These bolts are tight – try passing a screwdriver shaft between two of the bolts to hold the pulley while the remaining bolt is loosened, and repeat until all three are loose **(see illustration)**.

4 Remove the auxiliary drivebelt as described in Chapter 1.

5 Unscrew the securing bolts, and remove the water pump pulley **(see illustration)**.

6 Unscrew the three bolts and two nuts, and withdraw the water pump. Be prepared for a substantial amount of water spillage as the pump is removed, even if the system has been drained. Recover the gasket – a new one will be needed for reassembly **(see illustrations)**.

Inspection

7 If the pump has been removed for reasons other than to fit a new one, inspect it as follows.

8 Check around the drain hole on the pump body for signs of coolant leakage (typically, white or rust-coloured deposits). Even a slight leak is a sign of impending failure, and the pump should be renewed.

9 Spin the pump impeller, and listen for a noisy bearing. A rough scraping sound indicates that the pump is not worth refitting, and a new one should be obtained.

Refitting

10 Commence refitting by thoroughly cleaning the mating faces of the water pump and the cylinder block.

11 Refit the water pump, using a new gasket,

7.5 Remove the loosened bolts, and take off the water pump pulley

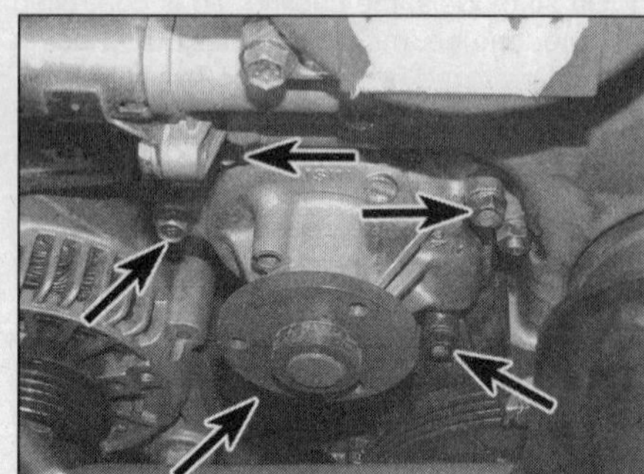

7.6a Unscrew the water pump nuts and bolts . . .

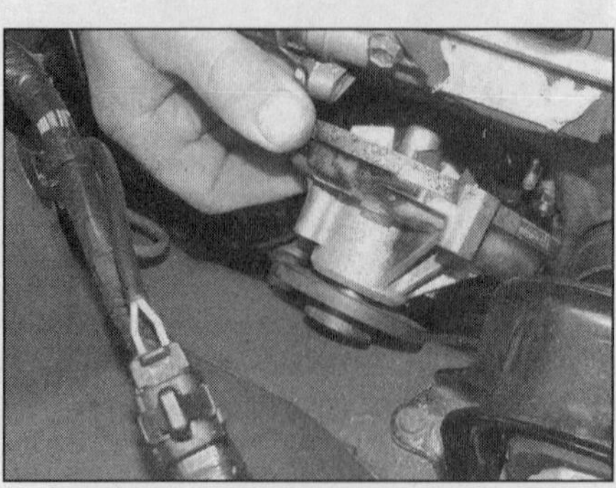

7.6b . . . then withdraw the pump . . .

7.6c . . . and recover the gasket

7.11a Fit a new gasket . . .

7.11b . . . then refit the water pump . . .

7.11c . . . and tighten the three bolts and two nuts

and tighten the securing nuts and bolts to the specified torque **(see illustrations)**.

12 Further refitting is a reversal of removal, bearing in mind the following points:

a) Tighten all fixings to the specified torque (where given). Delay fully tightening the water pump pulley bolts until the drivebelt has been fitted.

b) Refit the auxiliary drivebelt as described in Chapter 1.

c) On completion, refill the cooling system as described in Chapter 1.

8 Heating and ventilation system – general information

The heater/ventilation system consists of a four-speed blower motor (housed behind the facia), face-level vents in the centre and at each end of the facia, and air ducts to the front footwells.

The control unit is located in the facia, and the controls operate flap valves, to deflect and mix the air flowing through the various parts of the heater/ventilation system. The flap valves are contained in the air distribution housing, which acts as a central distribution unit, passing air to the various ducts and vents.

Cold air enters the system through the grille at the rear of the engine compartment, and is filtered by a fine-mesh filter mounted above the glovebox, to remove particles like dust and pollen before they enter the cabin.

The air (boosted by the four-speed blower fan if required) then flows through the various ducts, according to the settings of the controls. Stale air is expelled through ducts at the rear of the car. If warm air is required, the cold air is passed through the heater matrix, which is heated by the engine coolant.

A recirculation control enables the outside air supply to be closed off, while the air inside the car is recirculated. This can be useful to prevent unpleasant odours entering from outside the car, but should only be used briefly, as the recirculated air inside the car will soon deteriorate.

9 Heater/ventilation system components – removal and refitting

Heater/ventilation control panel

Removal

1 If the heater control cables are going to be disconnected, set the heater controls fully to the left, as follows:

a) Recirculation slider control to 'recirc' position.

b) Air distribution control to 'face/head' position.

c) Temperature control to 'fully cool' position.

2 Carefully pull the knobs from the controls **(see illustration)**. If pliers are needed, cover the jaws using card or tape.

3 Remove the screw behind each outer control **(see illustration)**.

4 Taking great care not to scratch the panels, prise off the control panel, which is secured by six clips around its edge **(see illustration)**. We found the panel would come off without using tools, which is preferable, as it reduces the risk of marking the panel.

5 When the panel is free, disconnect the wiring plugs from behind, noting their locations, and remove it **(see illustration)**.

6 To remove the rear panel, release the securing tangs at either side, then pull it forwards **(see illustration)**. On models with air

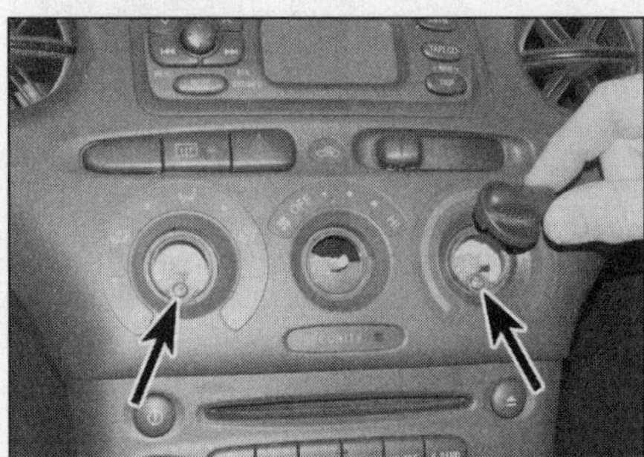
9.2 Pull the knobs off all the controls, for access to the two screws

9.3 Remove the screws . . .

9.4 . . . then unclip the panel from the facia

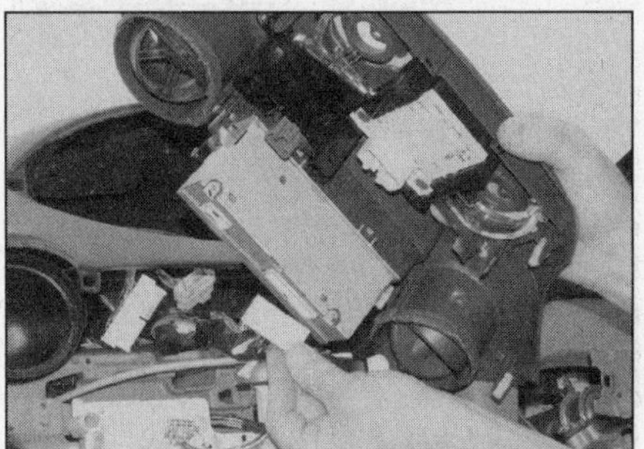
9.5 Disconnect the wiring plugs from the back of the heater control panel

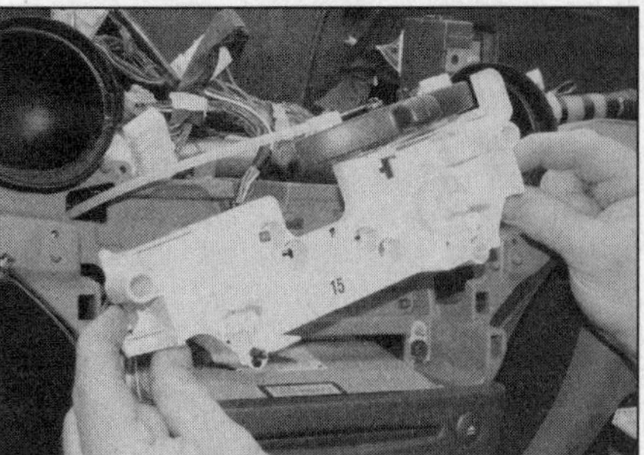
9.6 Release the catches either side, and pull out the panel rear section

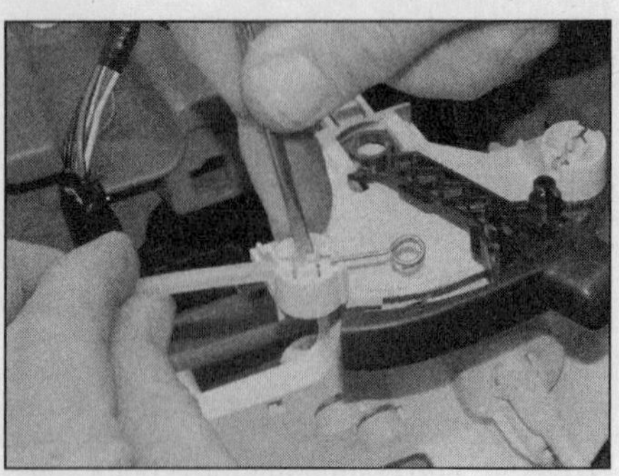
9.7a Use a small screwdriver to open the cable clamps . . .

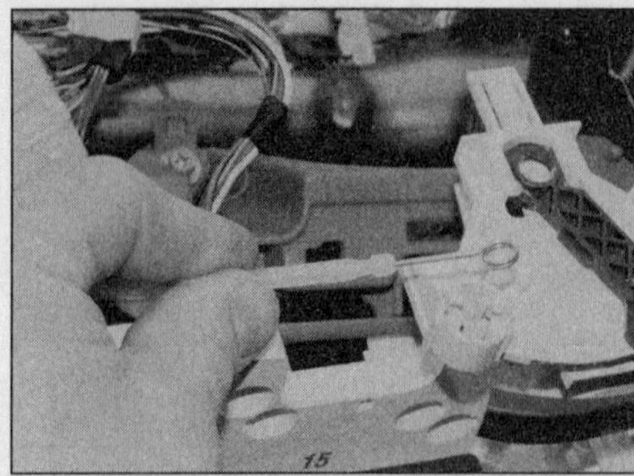
9.7b . . . then unhook the end fitting and detach the cable

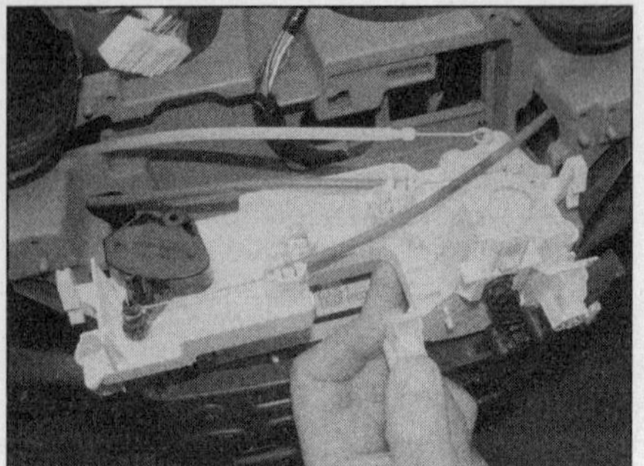
9.7c Note how the air distribution and temperature cables are routed

9.7d Once all cables have been detached, the panel can be removed

conditioning, disconnect the wiring plug at the rear.

7 Note the fitted positions of all three cables. Starting with the recirculation control cable (white), use a small screwdriver to open the cable clamps, then unhook the cable end fitting. Note how the other two cables are clipped to the panel, then remove them the same way. The heater control panel is now free to be removed, leaving the cables behind **(see illustrations)**.

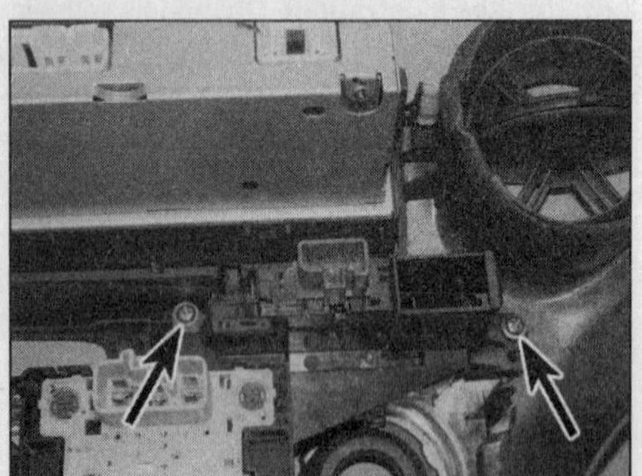
9.13a Remove the two screws at the top of the switch panel . . .

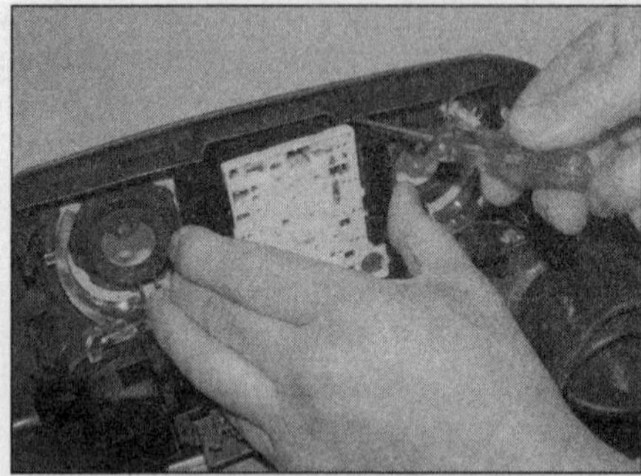
9.13b . . . then release the tabs at the base . . .

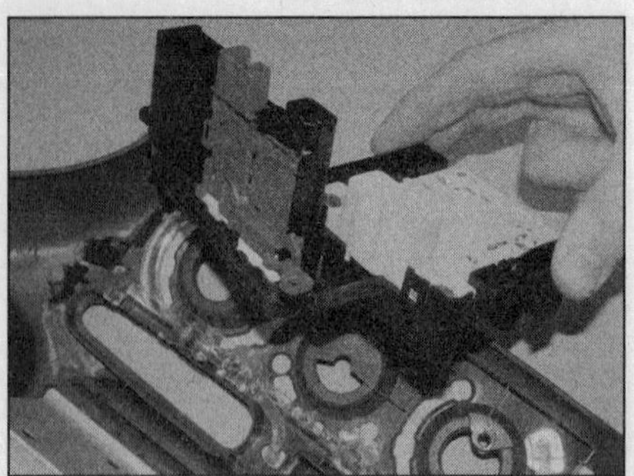
9.13c . . . and the panel can be withdrawn

9.18 Unclip the cable from the flap lever on the heater unit

8 For reference, the heater control cables are colour-coded as follows:

a) Recirculation control – White.
b) Air distribution control – Blue.
c) Temperature control – Grey.

Refitting

9 Make sure the heater controls are still set to the same positions as described in paragraph 1 – temporarily refit the control knobs to check if necessary.

10 Without disturbing the position of the control lever, hook the first cable end fitting on, and secure the outer cable with the clamp. Repeat for the other two cables.

11 Further refitting is a reversal of removal.

Heater blower motor switch

Removal

12 Remove the heater control panel as described earlier in this Section.

13 The heater switch panel and blower switch assembly can be removed by first taking out the two screws securing it to the rear of the main panel. Carefully prise the switch panel at the base to release the tabs, and the panel will come free **(see illustrations)**. Check with a Toyota dealer whether the blower switch is available separately, but it does appear to be possible to prise it from the panel.

Refitting

14 Refitting is a reversal of removal.

Recirculation control cable

Removal

15 Remove the heater control panel as described earlier in this Section.

16 To improve access, remove the upper section of the facia panel as described in Chapter 11.

17 Trace the cable from the rear of the heater control panel across to the upper left-hand side of the heater unit, noting its routing. Release the cable from any clips or ties.

18 Unclip the cable outer at the control lever on the heater unit, then slide the end fitting off sideways **(see illustration)**. Do not disturb the position of the control lever, if possible.

Refitting

19 Refitting is a reversal of removal. Ensure that the cable is routed as before, and that the heater unit control lever is the same position as when the cable was disconnected. Hook on the end fitting, then clip in the cable outer exactly as before. Check its operation before refitting the panel.

Air distribution cable

Removal

20 Remove the heater control panel as described earlier in this Section.

21 Access to the cable may be possible from under the facia, but ultimately, it may be necessary to remove the lower section of the facia panel as described in Chapter 11.

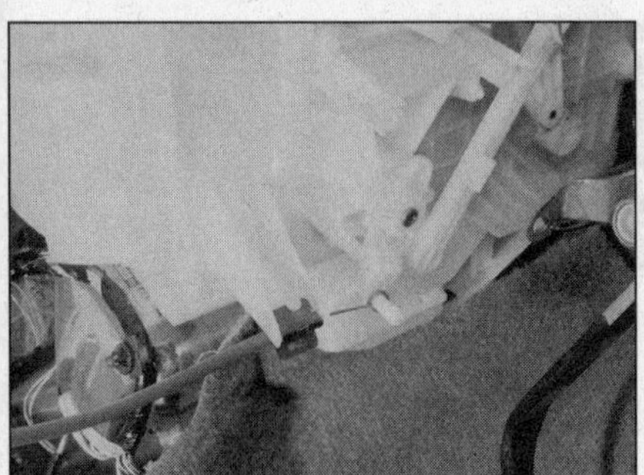

9.23 Unclip the cable from the right-hand side of the unit

9.28 The temperature control cable is on top of the heater unit

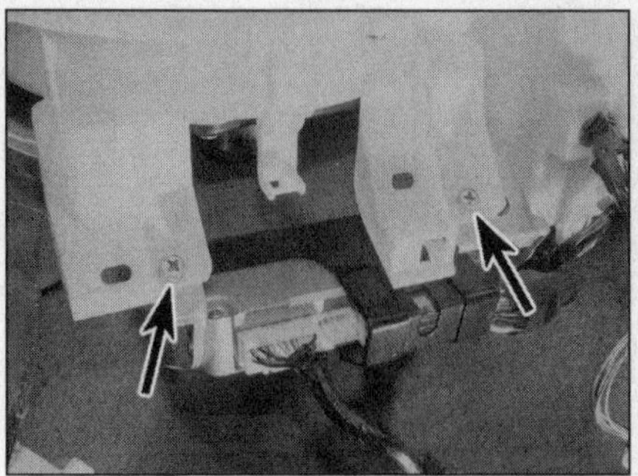

9.31a Remove the ECU mounting screws . . .

22 Trace the cable from the rear of the heater control panel across to the right-hand side of the heater unit, noting its routing. Release the cable from any clips or ties.

23 Unclip the cable outer at the control lever on the heater unit, then slide the end fitting off sideways **(see illustration)**. Do not disturb the position of the control lever, if possible.

Refitting

24 Refitting is a reversal of removal. Ensure that the cable is routed as before, and that the heater unit control lever is the same position as when the cable was disconnected. Hook on the end fitting, then clip in the cable outer exactly as before. Check its operation before refitting the panel by temporarily refitting the control knob.

Temperature control cable

Removal

25 Remove the heater control panel as described earlier in this Section.

26 To improve access, remove the upper section of the facia panel as described in Chapter 11.

27 Trace the cable from the rear of the heater control panel back to the centre of the heater unit, just above the matrix, noting its routing. Release the cable from any clips or ties.

28 Unclip the cable outer at the control lever on top of the heater unit, then slide the end fitting off **(see illustration)**. Do not disturb the position of the control lever, if possible.

Refitting

29 Refitting is a reversal of removal. Ensure that the cable is routed as before, and that the heater unit control lever is the same position as when the cable was disconnected. Hook on the end fitting, then clip in the cable outer exactly as before. Check its operation before refitting the panel, by temporarily refitting the control knob.

Heater blower motor

Removal

30 Open the glovebox door, then carefully press the door in at both sides and pull the door out of the facia.

31 Remove the two screws at the front, which secure the engine ECU. Slide the ECU out of its rear retaining bracket, and lower it out without disconnecting the wiring **(see illustrations)**.

32 Unscrew and remove the retaining bracket for the ECU **(see illustration)**.

33 Remove the three screws, and lower the motor out from under the facia **(see illustrations)**.

34 Disconnect the wiring from the blower motor, and remove it completely **(see illustration)**.

Refitting

35 Refitting is a reversal of removal.

Heater blower motor resistor

Removal

36 Proceed as described for removing the blower motor, in paragraphs 30 and 31.

37 Disconnect the wiring plug from the resistor

9.31b . . . then release the unit from its rear bracket, and lower it out

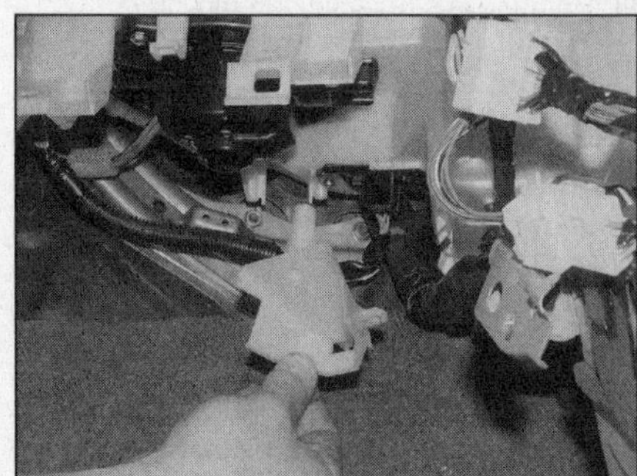

9.32 Remove the ECU retaining bracket

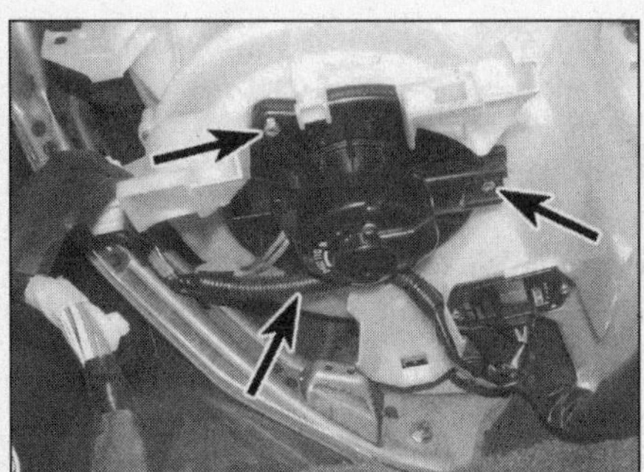

9.33a Remove the three mounting screws on the base of the motor . . .

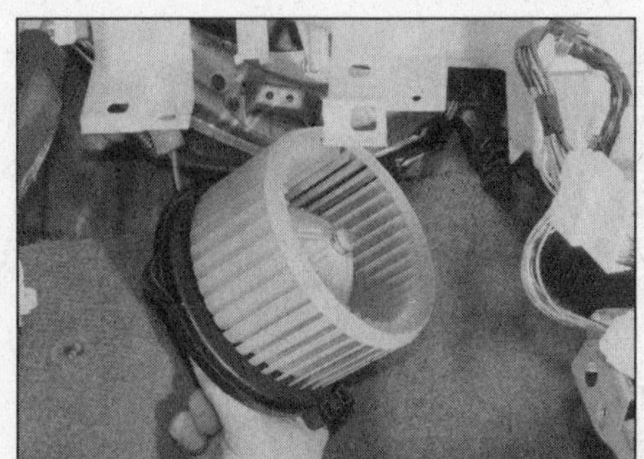

9.33b . . . and lower the unit out

9.34 Disconnect the wiring plug, and remove the motor completely

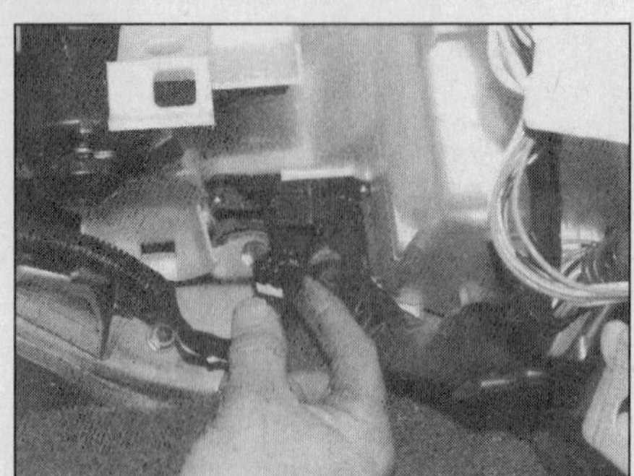
9.37a Disconnect the resistor unit wiring plug . . .

9.37b . . . then remove the two mounting screws and lower the unit out

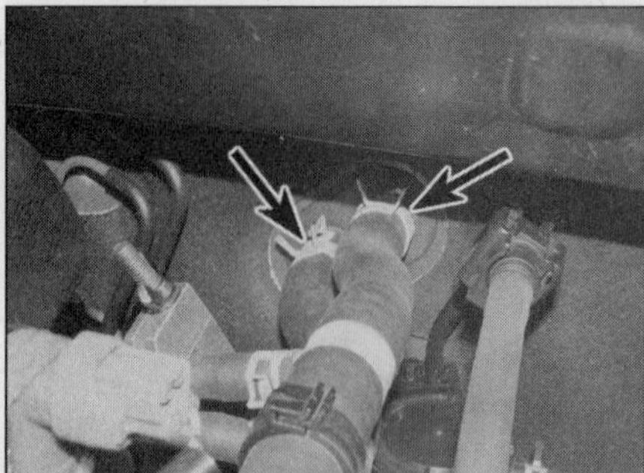
9.41 Release the spring clips and disconnect the heater hoses at the bulkhead

9.44a Prise out the clip in the centre . . .

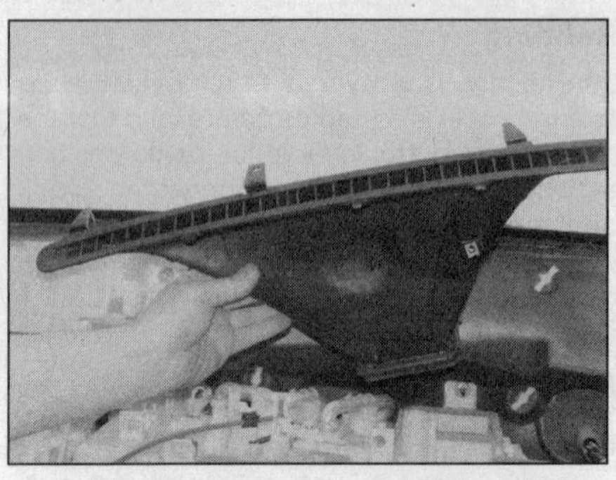
9.44b . . . then unclip and lift out the windscreen demister duct

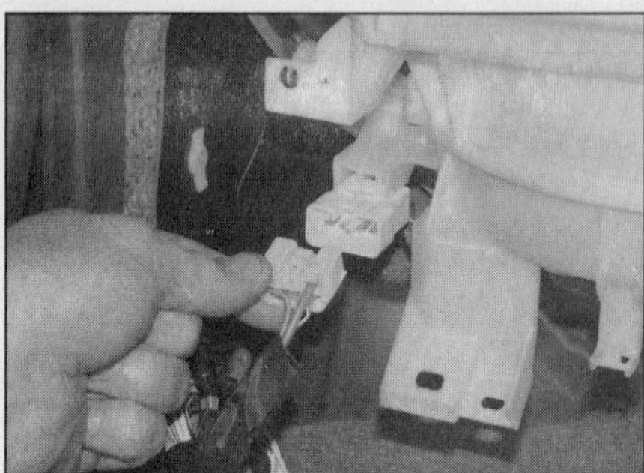
9.45 Unplug the wiring connector from the front of the heater unit

unit, then remove the two mounting screws and lower the unit out **(see illustrations)**.

Refitting

38 Refitting is a reversal of removal.

Heater matrix

Warning: On models with air conditioning, the system must be discharged before starting this procedure. The heater assembly must be moved back inside the car to allow the matrix's rigid pipes to clear the bulkhead, and this means detaching the air conditioning pipes where they pass through the bulkhead as well. Discharging the air conditioning system must be carried out by a specialist, or by a Toyota dealer.

Removal

39 Drain the cooling system as described in Chapter 1.

40 Have the air conditioning system professionally discharged, on models so equipped.

41 At the rear of the engine compartment, release the spring-type hose clips and disconnect the two coolant hoses which pass through the bulkhead to the heater **(see illustration)**. On models with air conditioning, there will be two additional pipes passing through the bulkhead, with a single bolt securing their retaining plate – once the bolt is removed, the plate can be released, and the pipes disconnected. **Do not** disturb the refrigerant pipes unless the system has been discharged first (see Section 10) – for maximum personal safety, have these pipes disconnected by the engineer who discharges the system for you, and ensure the system is kept switched off afterwards.

42 Remove the upper and lower sections of the facia panel as described in Chapter 11, including removal of the facia crossmember.

43 On models so equipped, the air conditioning unit is removed prior to taking out the main heater unit, as follows. Disconnect the wiring plugs, then release the wiring from any clips or ties. Remove two bolts, two nuts, and two screws, and carefully withdraw the air conditioning unit from the heater unit.

44 Remove the three clips on top, and lift out the windscreen demister duct from the top of the heater unit **(see illustrations)**.

45 Disconnect the wiring plug from the front of the heater unit **(see illustration)**.

46 Release the clips securing the carpet either side of the base of the heater unit **(see illustration)**.

47 The heater unit is secured by two nuts either side at the top, two central bolts, one nut on the passenger side, and two more underneath. Remove the nuts and bolts then, with the help of an assistant, ease the heater unit away from the bulkhead and into the car **(see illustrations)**.

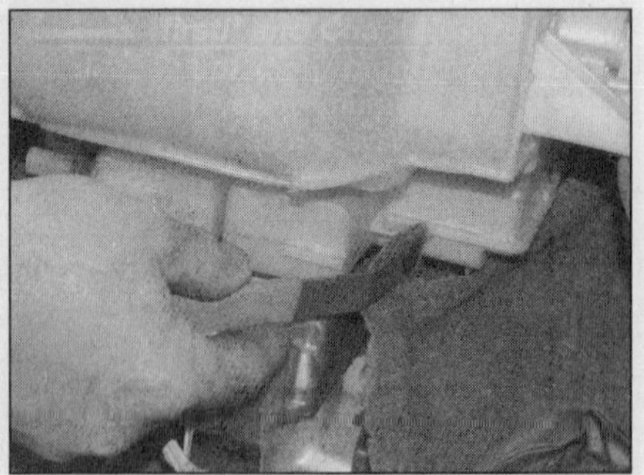
9.46 Detach the carpet at the base of the heater

9.47a Heater unit mountings – nut at the left-hand side . . .

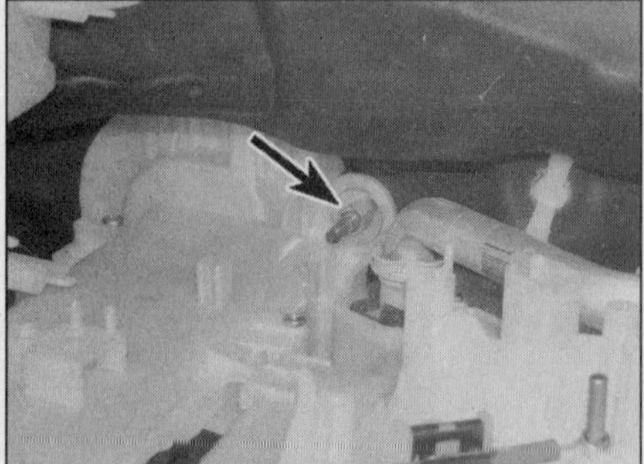
9.47b . . . one nut top left . . .

9.47c . . . two bolts in the centre . . .

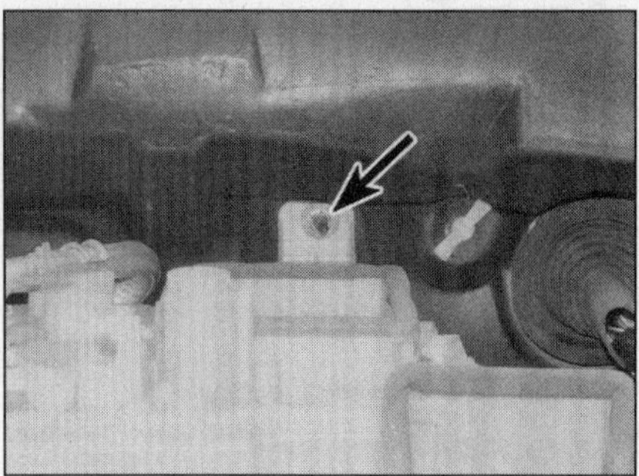
9.47d . . . another nut top right . . .

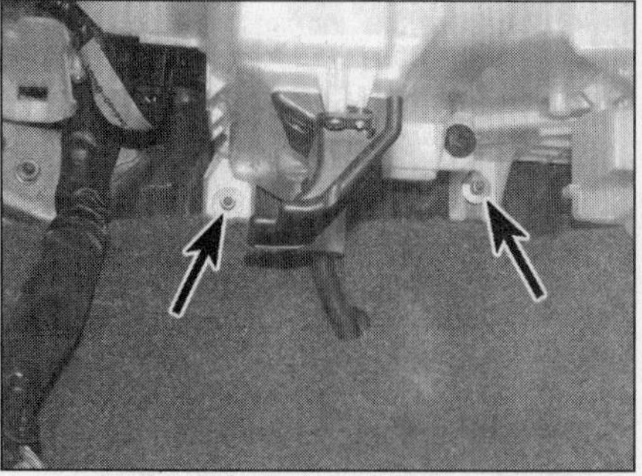
9.47e . . . and two nuts underneath

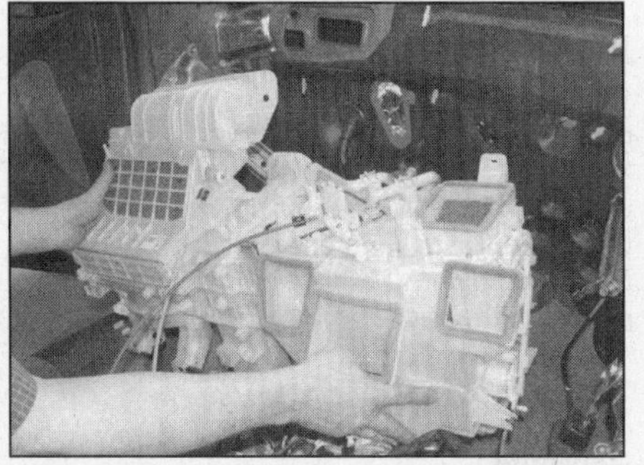
9.47f Withdraw the heater unit into the car

Keep the unit tilted backwards slightly, to avoid coolant spilling onto the carpet. Plug the heater matrix pipes as soon as possible (or drain the coolant into a suitable container).

48 Remove the two screws and the two pipe clamps, then carefully slide the heater matrix out from the top of the heater unit **(see illustrations)**.

Refitting

49 Refitting is a reversal of removal, noting the following points:

a) Check the condition of the rubber grommet(s) where the pipes pass through the bulkhead – if necessary, fit new when refitting.

b) On completion, fill and bleed the cooling system as described in Chapter 1.

c) On models with air conditioning, have the refrigerant pipes reconnected (using new O-ring seals) and the system recharged by a specialist or a Toyota dealer.

Heater unit

Warning: On models with air conditioning, read the precautions given in Section 10, and have the system discharged by a Toyota dealer or an air conditioning specialist. Do not carry out the following work unless the system had been discharged.

50 Removal and refitting of the heater assembly are as previously described in this Section for the heater matrix.

Facia vents

Removal

51 The facia end vents can only be accessed after the upper facia panel has been removed, as described in Chapter 11. The centre vents are removed with the heater control panel as described in paragraphs 2 to 5, but the vents themselves do not appear to separate from the panel.

52 Each end vent is secured by two screws – remove the screws, and withdraw the vent.

Refitting

53 Refitting is a reversal of removal. Refit the facia panel as described in Chapter 11.

10 Air conditioning system – general information and precautions

General information

1 Air conditioning is available on certain models. It enables the temperature of incoming air to be lowered, and also dehumidifies the air, which makes for rapid demisting and increased comfort.

2 The cooling side of the system works in the same way as a domestic refrigerator. Refrigerant gas is drawn into a belt-driven compressor, and passes into a condenser mounted in front of the radiator, where it loses heat and becomes liquid. The liquid passes through an expansion valve to an evaporator, where it changes from liquid under high pressure to gas under low pressure. This change is accompanied by a drop in temperature, which cools the evaporator. The refrigerant returns to the compressor, and the cycle begins again.

3 Air blown through the evaporator passes to the heater assembly, where it is mixed with hot air blown through the heater matrix, to achieve the desired temperature in the passenger compartment.

4 The heating side of the system works in the same way as on models without air conditioning (see Section 8).

5 The operation of the system is controlled electronically. A thermistor mounted below the passenger airbag monitors the cabin temperature, which allows the system to maintain the value set on the control – for removal and refitting, see Section 11. Any problems with the system should be referred to a Toyota dealer or an air conditioning specialist in the first instance.

Precautions

Warning: The air conditioning system is under high pressure. Do not loosen any fittings or remove any components until after the system has been discharged. Air conditioning refrigerant should be properly discharged at a dealer service department or an automotive air conditioning repair facility capable of handling R134a refrigerant. Always wear eye protection when disconnecting air conditioning system fittings.

6 When an air conditioning system is fitted, it is necessary to observe the following special precautions whenever dealing with any part of the system, its associated components, and any items which necessitate disconnection of the system:

9.48a Remove the screws and take off the pipe clamps . . .

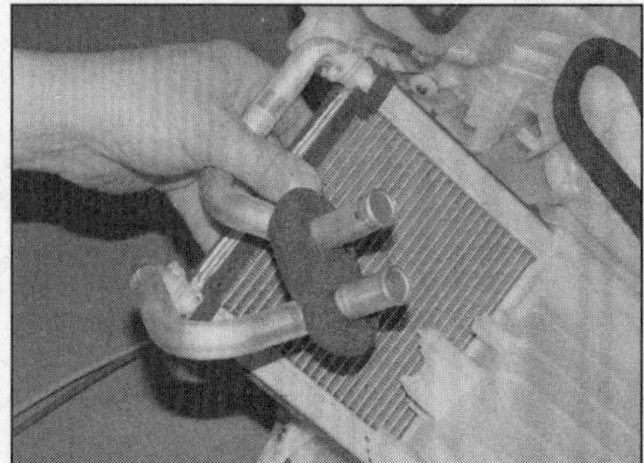
9.48b . . . then slide the heater matrix upwards out of the heater unit

a) *While the refrigerant used – R134a – is less damaging to the environment than the previously-used R12, it is still a very dangerous substance. It must not be allowed into contact with the skin or eyes, or there is a risk of frostbite. It must also not be discharged in an enclosed space – while it is not toxic, there is a risk of suffocation. The refrigerant is heavier than air, and so must never be discharged over a pit.*
b) *The refrigerant must not be allowed to come in contact with a naked flame, otherwise a poisonous gas will be created – under certain circumstances, this can form an explosive mixture with air. For similar reasons, smoking in the presence of refrigerant is highly dangerous, particularly if the vapour is inhaled through a lighted cigarette.*
c) *Never discharge the system to the atmosphere – R134a is not an ozone-depleting ChloroFluoroCarbon (CFC) like R12, but is instead a hydrofluorocarbon, which causes environmental damage by contributing to the 'greenhouse effect' if released into the atmosphere.*
d) *R134a refrigerant must not be mixed with R12; the system uses different seals (now green-coloured, previously black) and has different fittings requiring different tools, so that there is no chance of the two types of refrigerant becoming mixed accidentally.*
e) *If for any reason the system must be disconnected, entrust this task to your Toyota dealer or a refrigeration engineer.*
f) *It is essential that the system be professionally discharged prior to using any form of heat – welding, soldering, brazing, etc – in the vicinity of the system, before having the car oven-dried at a temperature exceeding 70°C after repainting, and before disconnecting any part of the system.*

11 Air conditioning system components – removal and refitting

Warning: Read the precautions given in Section 10, and have the system discharged by a Toyota dealer or an air conditioning specialist. Do not carry out the following work unless the system has been discharged (where necessary).

Air inlet control motor

Removal

1 Remove the passenger airbag as described in Chapter 12.

2 Working through the airbag aperture in the facia, at the back, disconnect the transformer wiring plug, then remove the single screw and remove the transformer with its mounting bracket.

3 Disconnect the control motor wiring plug, then remove the three mounting screws and take out the motor.

Refitting

4 Refitting is a reversal of removal.

Thermistor

Removal

5 Remove the passenger airbag as described in Chapter 12.

6 The thermistor is located below the wiring plug for the air inlet control motor. Disconnect the thermistor wiring plug and release the harness clips. Using a small screwdriver, prise the thermistor housing up from its location. The thermistor itself can be removed from the housing by prising apart the retaining tangs at its base.

Refitting

7 Refitting is a reversal of removal.

Compressor

Note: *If the compressor is being removed as part of another procedure, it may not be necessary to have the system discharged. Usually, the compressor can be unbolted and tied to one side without the need to disturb the refrigerant lines.*

Removal

8 Remove the auxiliary drivebelt as described in Chapter 1.

9 Jack up the front of the car, and support it on axle stands (see *Jacking and vehicle support*). Remove the driver's-side engine lower cover panel from under the car.

10 Disconnect the compressor wiring plug, and release the wiring from the securing clip.

11 With the system discharged, disconnect the refrigerant lines from the compressor. Discard the O-ring seals – new ones must be used when refitting.

12 Support the compressor, then remove the three mounting bolts, and lower the compressor out of the engine bay **(see illustration)**.

Refitting

13 Refitting is a reversal of removal, noting the following points:
a) *Use new O-rings, coated with refrigerant oil, when reconnecting the refrigerant lines.*
b) *Tighten the compressor mounting bolts to the specified torque.*
c) *Have the system professionally recharged and tested on completion.*

11.12 Two of the air conditioning compressor mounting bolts

Evaporator

14 The evaporator is fitted inside its own housing on the side of the heater unit. Removal and refitting of the heater unit is described in Section 9. Thereafter, removing the evaporator involves unscrewing three bolts, removing the housing top cover, and lifting out the evaporator.

Condenser

Removal

15 Apply the handbrake, then jack up the front of the car and support securely on axle stands (see *Jacking and vehicle support*).

16 With the system discharged, disconnect the refrigerant lines from the condenser. Discard the O-rings – new ones must be used when refitting.

17 Remove the three bolts securing the bonnet lock, and the centre brace bolt behind the lock. Move the lock clear of the radiator support panel (lock carrier), without disconnecting the release cable.

18 Remove the two clips at the top securing the radiator side cover panel, and lift out the panel.

19 Disconnect the wiring plug from the horn, and remove the bolt from the earth lead at one side of the support panel.

20 Remove the remaining six bolts securing the radiator support panel, then lift the panel away. Recover the radiator upper rubber mountings if they are loose.

21 Carefully lift out the condenser, taking care not to catch the fins on any surrounding components.

Refitting

22 Refitting is a reversal of removal, noting the following points:
a) *Use new O-rings, coated with refrigerant oil, when reconnecting the refrigerant lines.*
b) *Have the system professionally recharged and tested on completion.*

Chapter 4 Part A:
Fuel system

Contents

Degrees of difficulty

Easy, suitable for novice with little experience

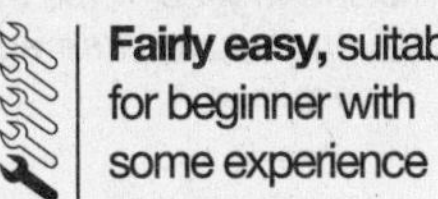

Fairly easy, suitable for beginner with some experience

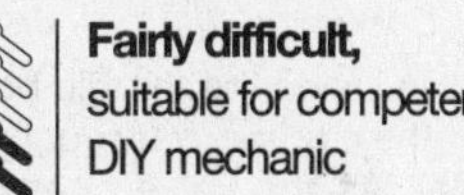

Fairly difficult, suitable for competent DIY mechanic

Difficult, suitable for experienced DIY mechanic

Very difficult, suitable for expert DIY or professional

Specifications

General

System type	Toyota L-type sequential multi-port fuel injection
Fuel octane requirement	95 RON unleaded
Fuel system pressure:	
Regulated pressure at idle	44 to 50 psi
Hold pressure (after 5 minutes)	21 psi minimum
Idle speed (ECU-controlled):	
Manual transmission models	650 ± 50 rpm
Automatic transmission models	700 ± 50 rpm

Sensor resistances

Camshaft or crankshaft position sensor:	
Cold	985 to 1600 ohms
Hot	1265 to 1890 ohms

Torque wrench settings

	Nm	lbf ft
Fuel rail flange bolts:		
1.0 litre and 1.3 litre 2SZ-FE engines	8	6
Fuel rail mounting bolts	20	15
Fuel tank mounting bolts	20	15
Inlet manifold nuts/bolts:		
1.0 litre and 1.3 litre 2SZ-FE engines	19	14
1.3 litre 2NZ-FE engine models	30	22
Throttle body mountings:		
1.0 litre and 1.3 litre 2SZ-FE engines:		
Rear bolt	8	6
Two front bolts	21	15
1.3 litre 2NZ-FE engine models (nuts/bolt)	30	22
Throttle body mounting bracket bolts	21	15

1 General information and precautions

General information

The fuel system consists of a fuel tank (mounted under the floor, beneath the rear seats), fuel hoses, an electric fuel pump mounted in the fuel tank, and a sequential electronic fuel injection system controlled by an engine management electronic control unit (ECU).

The electric fuel pump supplies fuel under pressure to the fuel rail, which distributes fuel to the injectors. A pressure regulator fitted to the pump itself controls the system pressure at the pump end, while a pulsation damper is fitted to the fuel line where it enters the fuel rail. With this system there is no fuel return line, reducing evaporative emissions caused by warmer fuel returning to the fuel tank. From the fuel rail, fuel is injected into the inlet ports, just above the inlet valves, by four fuel injectors. The fuel rail is mounted to the cylinder head, just above the plastic inlet manifold.

The amount of fuel supplied by the injectors is precisely controlled by the ECU. The ECU uses the signals from the crankshaft position sensor and the camshaft position sensor, to trigger each injector separately in cylinder firing order (sequential injection), with benefits in terms of better fuel economy and leaner exhaust emissions.

The ECU is the heart of the entire engine management system, controlling the fuel injection, ignition and emissions control systems. The ECU receives information from various sensors which is then computed and compared with preset values stored in its memory, to determine the required period of injection.

Information on crankshaft position and engine speed is generated by a crankshaft position sensor. The inductive head of the sensor runs just inboard of the crankshaft pulley, and scans the teeth on a special sensor plate fitted behind the pulley. As the crankshaft rotates, the sensor transmits a pulse to the ECU every time a tooth passes it. The teeth are 10° apart, and there are two missing teeth together on the sensor plate – the ECU recognises the absence of a pulse from the crankshaft position sensor at this point to establish a reference mark for crankshaft position. Similarly, the time interval between absent pulses is used to determine engine speed. This information is then fed to the ECU for further processing.

The camshaft position sensor is located at the transmission end of the cylinder head, and functions similarly to the crankshaft position sensor. In this case, however, there are three lugs, 90° apart, fitted to a plate on the end of the inlet camshaft. The missing fourth lug provides a sensor signal which is used by the ECU to calculate the correct fuel and ignition timing, and is also used to control the variable valve timing system (VVT-i).

Engine temperature information is supplied by the coolant temperature sensor (see Chapter 3). The sensor is an NTC (Negative Temperature Coefficient) thermistor – that is, a semi-conductor whose electrical resistance decreases as its temperature increases. The sensor provides the ECU with a constantly-varying (analogue) voltage signal, corresponding to the temperature of the engine coolant. This is used to refine the calculations made by the ECU, when determining the correct amount of fuel required to achieve the ideal air/fuel mixture ratio.

Inlet air temperature and density information for air/fuel mixture ratio calculations is provided by a hot-wire type airflow meter. Air passing through the meter cools an electrically-heated wire filament – the amount of cooling is proportional to the air mass flow rate. The cooling has the effect of altering the electrical resistance of the filament, and this in turn alters the signal voltage produced by the meter and sent to the ECU. As the air mass flow rate is measured directly, there is no requirement for an inlet air temperature sensor or a manifold absolute pressure sensor.

The throttle valve inside the throttle body is controlled by the driver, through the accelerator pedal. As the valve opens, the amount of air that can pass through the system increases. As the throttle valve opens further, the airflow meter signal alters, and the ECU opens each injector for a longer duration, to increase the amount of fuel delivered to the inlet ports.

A throttle position sensor is mounted on the end of the throttle valve spindle, to provide the ECU with a constantly-varying (analogue) voltage signal corresponding to the throttle opening. This allows the ECU to register the driver's input when determining the amount of fuel required by the engine. An idle speed control valve allows the ECU to adjust the idle speed as necessary, to aid driveability, and to provide an anti-stall function determined by engine temperature, and the load caused by engine-driven accessories

Roadspeed is monitored by the vehicle speed sensor. This component is a Hall-effect generator, mounted on top of the transmission, in place of the old speedometer drive. It supplies the ECU with a series of pulses corresponding to the car's roadspeed, enabling the ECU to control features such as the fuel shut-off on overrun.

An oxygen sensor in the exhaust system provides the ECU with constant feedback – 'closed-loop' control – which enables it to adjust the mixture to provide the best possible operating conditions for the catalytic converter. A further sensor is fitted, downstream of the converter, to monitor the converter's operation, and this provides an even finer degree of emission control.

Both the idle speed and mixture are under the control of the ECU, and cannot be adjusted.

Precautions

Warning: Many of the procedures in this Chapter require the removal of fuel lines and connections, which may result in some fuel spillage. Before carrying out any operation on the fuel system, refer to the precautions given in 'Safety first!' at the beginning of this manual, and follow them implicitly. Petrol is a highly-dangerous and volatile liquid, and the precautions necessary when handling it cannot be overstressed.

Note 1: *Residual pressure will remain in the fuel lines long after the car was last used. When disconnecting any fuel line, first depressurise the fuel system as described in Section 2.*

Note 2*: Before disconnecting any of the fuel injection system sensor wiring plugs, ensure at least that the ignition is switched off (ideally, disconnect the battery). If this is not done, it could result in a fault code being logged in the system memory, and may even cause damage to the component concerned.*

2 Fuel system – depressurisation

Warning: The following procedure will merely relieve the pressure in the fuel system – remember that fuel will still be present in the system components, and take precautions accordingly before disconnecting any of them.

Note: *Refer to the warning note in Section 1 before proceeding.*

1 The fuel system referred to in this Chapter is defined as the fuel tank and tank-mounted fuel pump/fuel gauge sender unit, fuel pressure regulator, the fuel filter, the fuel injectors, and the metal pipes and flexible hoses of the fuel lines between these components. All these contain fuel, which will be under pressure while the engine is running and/or while the ignition is switched on.

2 The pressure will remain for some time after the ignition has been switched off, and must be relieved before any of these components is disturbed for servicing work.

3 The simplest depressurisation method is to disconnect the fuel pump electrical supply by removing the fuel pump fuse. Make sure the ignition is switched off, then remove fuse number 6 (marked 'EFI') in the

2.3 Removing the fuel pump (EFI) fuse from the engine compartment fusebox

5.1 Unbolt the air cleaner inlet duct from the inner wing

engine compartment fusebox **(see illustration)**.

4 Start the engine; allow the engine to idle until it stops through lack of fuel. Turn the engine over once or twice on the starter to ensure that all pressure is released, then switch off the ignition; do not forget to refit the fuse when work is complete.

5 Note that, once the fuel system has been depressurised and drained (even partially), it will take significantly longer to restart the engine – perhaps several seconds of cranking – before the system is refilled and pressure restored.

3 Unleaded petrol – general information and usage

All petrol models are designed to run on fuel with a minimum octane rating of 95 (RON). All models have a catalytic converter, and so must be run on unleaded fuel **only**. Under no circumstances should leaded fuel (UK '4-star' or LRP) be used, as this will damage the converter.

Super unleaded petrol (98 octane) can also be used in all models if wished, though there is no advantage in doing so.

4 Fuel lines and fittings – general information

Note: *Refer to the warning note in Section 1 before proceeding.*

Quick-release couplings

1 Quick-release couplings are employed at many of the unions in the fuel feed and return lines.

2 Before disconnecting any fuel system component, relieve the residual pressure in the system (see Section 2), and equalise tank pressure by removing the fuel filler cap.

Warning: This procedure will merely relieve the increased pressure necessary for the engine to run – remember that fuel will still be present in the system components, and take precautions accordingly before disconnecting any of them.

3 Unclip the plastic collar fitted around the connector, then twist the end fitting in the direction of the arrow (usually anti-clockwise) and pull off the fitting. Use rag to soak up any spilt fuel. Where the unions are colour-coded, the pipes cannot be confused. Where both unions are the same colour, note carefully which pipe is connected to which, and ensure that they are correctly reconnected on refitting.

4 To reconnect one of these couplings, line them up, press them firmly together, and twist the fitting clockwise to secure. Clip on the plastic collar to finish. Switch the ignition on and off five times to pressurise the system, and check for any sign of fuel leakage around the disturbed coupling before attempting to start the engine.

Checking fuel lines

5 Checking procedures for the fuel lines are included in Chapter 1.

Component renewal

6 If any damaged sections are to be renewed, use original-equipment hoses or pipes, constructed from exactly the same material as the section being renewed. Do not install substitutes constructed from inferior or inappropriate material; this could cause a fuel leak or a fire.

7 Before detaching or disconnecting any part of the fuel system, note the routing of all hoses and pipes, and the orientation of all clamps and clips. New sections must be installed in exactly the same manner.

8 Before disconnecting any part of the fuel system, be sure to relieve the fuel system pressure (see Section 2), and equalise tank pressure by removing the fuel filler cap. Also disconnect the battery negative (earth) lead – see *Disconnecting the battery*. Cover the fitting being disconnected with a rag, to absorb any fuel that may spray out.

5 Air cleaner assembly – removal and refitting

Removal

1.0 litre and 1.3 litre 2SZ-FE engines

1 Release the air cleaner inlet duct by removing the single bolt which attaches it to the inner wing **(see illustration)**.

2 Disconnect the wiring plug from the airflow meter (on the driver's side of the throttle body) **(see illustration)**.

3 Lift the canister purge valve out of its moulded holder on the side of the air cleaner housing **(see illustration)**. Move the valve to

5.2 Disconnect the airflow meter wiring plug

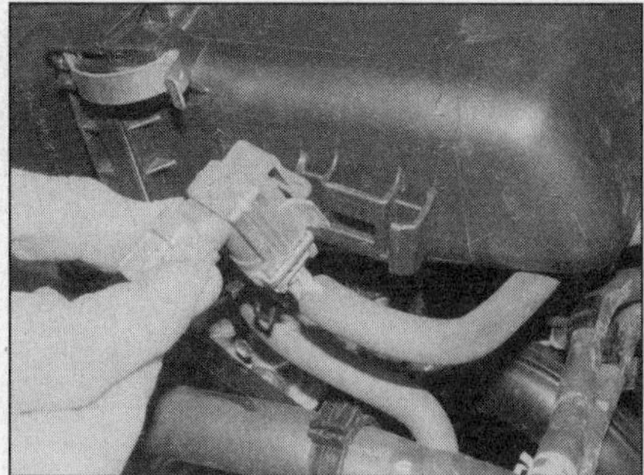
5.3 Lift the canister purge valve off its holder, and move it aside

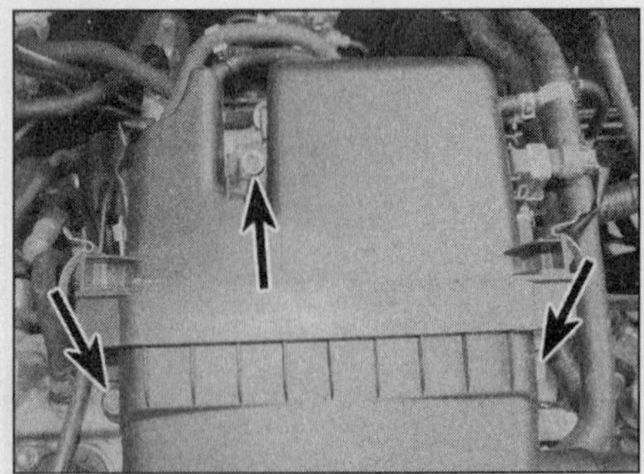
5.4a Remove the three mounting bolts . . .

5.4b . . . and lift off the air cleaner

5.4c Air cleaner mounting bolt – 1.3 litre 2SZ-FE engine

one side, without disconnecting the wiring or hoses. If it is necessary to remove the valve, which is part of the evaporative emissions system, refer to Chapter 4B.

4 Remove the three bolts securing the air cleaner to the top of the engine, and remove the air cleaner with the airflow meter **(see illustrations)**.

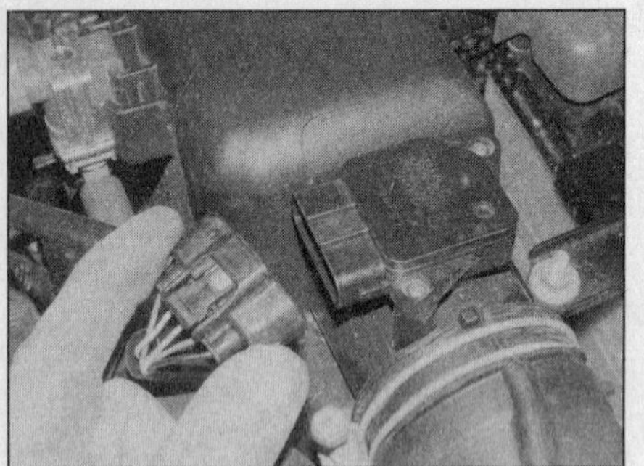
5.6 Disconnect the airflow meter wiring plug

5.7 Lift out the canister purge valve from the side of the air cleaner

5.8 Loosen both hose clips and remove the air inlet duct

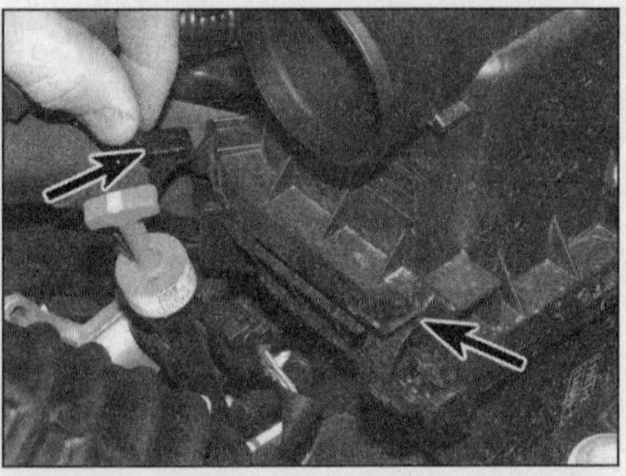
5.9a Release the two spring clips at the front . . .

1.3 litre 2NZ-FE engine

5 Release the spring clip and detach the crankcase breather hose from the air cleaner.

6 Disconnect the wiring plug from the airflow meter **(see illustration)**.

7 Unclip the canister purge valve from the side of the air cleaner top cover, and move the valve assembly to one side, without disconnecting the pipes **(see illustration)**.

8 Loosen the large hose clips securing the air inlet duct which leads to the throttle body, and remove the duct **(see illustration)**.

9 Release the two spring clips at the front of the air cleaner top cover, and lift the top half of the air cleaner away, complete with the airflow meter. Lift out the air filter element, noting how it is fitted **(see illustrations)**.

10 The lower half of the air cleaner is secured by three bolts inside the housing, and a further bolt secures the intake duct to the inner wing. Remove the bolts and lift out the air cleaner **(see illustrations)**.

Refitting

11 Refitting is a reversal of removal. Make sure the air cleaner duct is securely refitted, to prevent air leaks.

6 Accelerator cable – removal, refitting and adjustment

Removal

1 To improve access, move the driver's seat fully to the rear, and remove the lower trim panel fitted over the foot pedals.

5.9b . . . then lift off the upper section and remove the filter element

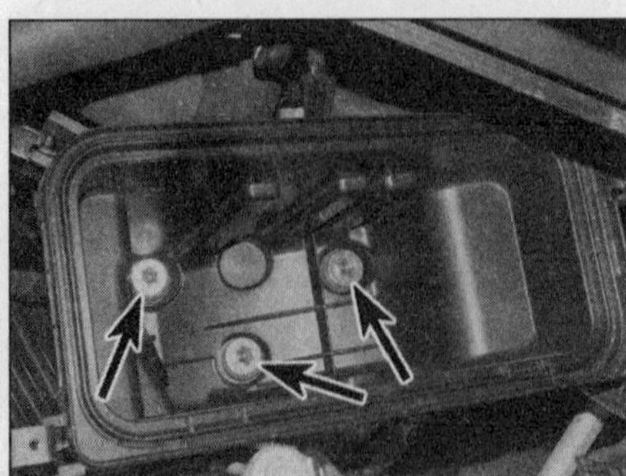
5.10a Remove the three bolts in the base, and the one on the inner wing . . .

5.10b . . . and lift out the lower section of the air cleaner

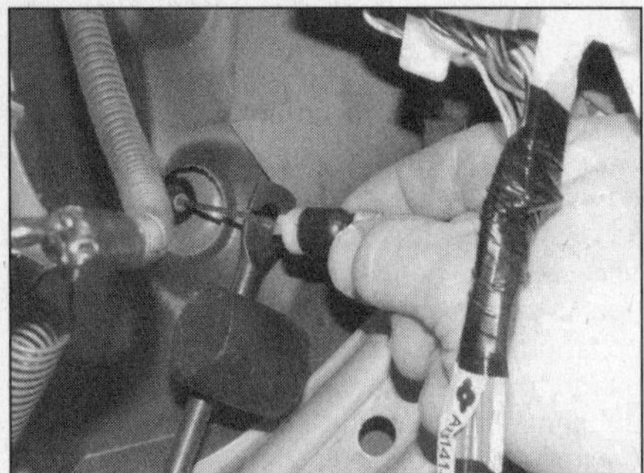
6.2 Unhook the cable end fitting from the top of the pedal

6.4 Unhook the cable end fitting from the throttle quadrant

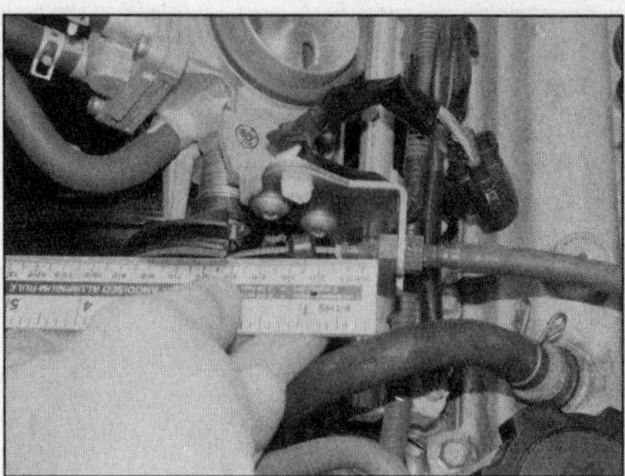
6.5a Measuring the exposed thread on the cable adjuster

2 Disconnect the inner cable from the top of the pedal by releasing the end fitting and sliding the cable out sideways **(see illustration)**.

3 Remove the air cleaner as described in Section 5.

4 Disconnect the inner cable from the quadrant on the throttle body by pivoting the quadrant open, then releasing the end fitting **(see illustration)**.

5 At the throttle body, loosen the adjuster nuts and detach the outer cable from the adjuster/support bracket. If the same cable is being refitted, it may be worth measuring the amount of exposed thread on the cable adjuster, so it can be reset to its original setting **(see illustrations)**.

6 Release the cable from the clips in the engine compartment, and withdraw it from the bulkhead.

Refitting

7 Refitting is a reversal of removal, ensuring that the cable is routed as before, and secured by all the clips. When the cable is reconnected at each end, adjust the cable as follows.

Adjustment

8 Refit the outer cable to the support bracket, and tighten the nuts by hand.

9 Check that the throttle quadrant moves smoothly and easily from the fully-closed to the fully-open position and back again as the assistant depresses and releases the accelerator pedal.

10 If there is excess slack in the cable when the accelerator is released, use the adjuster nuts to take up the slack **(see illustration)**. The cable should not however be too tight, otherwise the cable will hold the throttle open when the pedal is released. Adjust as necessary, checking the action of the pedal each time, as described in paragraph 9. On completion, tighten the nuts securely.

11 Take the car for a short road test to confirm correct operation, especially at idle. Remember that a feature of some modern engine management systems is to hold the engine speed above idle, even with the accelerator fully released, until the car comes to a complete stop – this is not a symptom of cable over-adjustment.

7 Accelerator pedal – removal and refitting

Removal

1 Detach the accelerator cable from the pedal (see Section 6), then unscrew the two mounting nuts and remove the pedal assembly from the bulkhead studs **(see illustration)**.

Refitting

2 Refit in the reverse order of removal. On completion, check the action of the pedal to ensure that the throttle has full unrestricted movement, and fully returns when released.

3 Check and if necessary adjust the accelerator cable as described in Section 6.

8 Fuel pump/fuel pressure – checking

Note: *Refer to the warning note in Section 1 before proceeding.*

Fuel pump

1 Switch on the ignition, and listen for the fuel pump (the sound of an electric motor running, audible from beneath the rear seats). Assuming there is sufficient fuel in the tank, the pump should start and run for approximately one or two seconds, then stop, each time the ignition is switched on.

2 If the pump does not run at all, check the fuse, relay and wiring (refer to the wiring diagrams in Chapter 12).

Fuel pressure

3 A fuel pressure gauge will be required for this check, and should be connected in the fuel line at the fuel inlet connection at the rear of the engine compartment, in accordance with the gauge maker's instructions.

4 Start the engine and allow it to idle. Note the gauge reading as soon as the pressure stabilises, and compare it with the regulated fuel pressure figure listed in the Specifications.

a) If the pressure is high, renew the fuel pressure regulator.

b) If the pressure is low, this also suggests a fuel pressure regulator problem. However, low voltage to the fuel pump, a faulty fuel

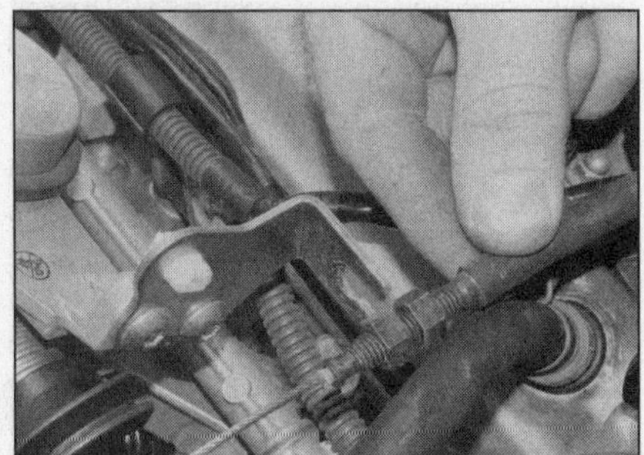
6.5b Loosen the adjuster nuts and remove the cable from the bracket

6.10 Accelerator cable adjuster nuts

7.1 Accelerator pedal mounting nuts

9.7a Fuel filler and breather hoses

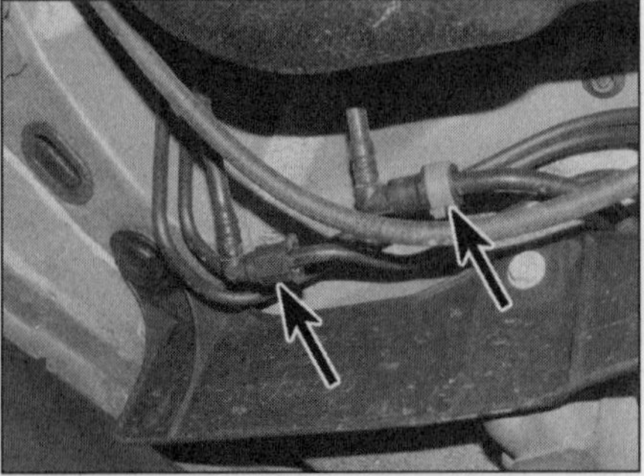

9.7b The fuel supply and vapour pipes have quick-release fittings

pump, or a blocked fuel pump filter (or other blockage in the fuel line) could be the cause.

5 Switch off the engine. Verify that a significant pressure remains for five minutes after the engine is turned off.

6 Carefully disconnect the fuel pressure gauge, depressurising the system first as described in Section 2. Be sure to cover the fitting with a rag before slackening it. Mop-up any spilt petrol.

7 Run the engine, and check that there are no fuel leaks.

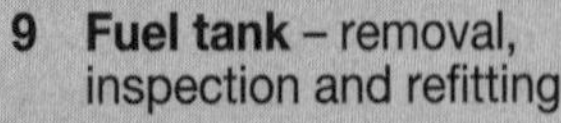

9 Fuel tank – removal, inspection and refitting

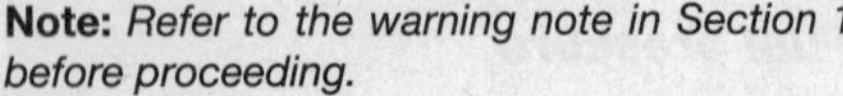

Note: *Refer to the warning note in Section 1 before proceeding.*

Removal

1 Run the fuel level as low as possible prior to removing the tank. There is no drain plug fitted (and syphoning may prove difficult) but it may be possible to drain the tank by removing the fuel filler pipe from the base of the tank, and letting the fuel drain into a suitable container.

2 Relieve the residual pressure in the fuel system (see Section 2), and equalise tank pressure by removing the fuel filler cap.

3 Disconnect the battery negative (earth) lead (see *Disconnecting the battery*).

4 Referring to Section 10, disconnect the wiring plug and pipes from the top of the fuel pump/gauge sender unit.

5 Chock the front wheels, then jack up the rear of the car and support it on axle stands (see *Jacking and vehicle support*). Remove the rear roadwheels.

6 Remove the two fasteners securing the tank lower heat shield (noting that it may also be necessary to unbolt a handbrake cable support bracket from it) and remove the shield.

7 If not already done, disconnect the filler pipe and breather hoses from the base of the tank, and the fuel supply/vapour pipes at the front **(see illustrations)**. Be prepared for fuel spillage when the filler pipe is disconnected, and for further spillage from the union on the tank (if it is not covered or plugged).

8 Check round the tank as far as possible to ensure that no pipes or wires are still connected which would prevent it from being lowered.

9 Have either an assistant or a trolley jack with a block of wood support the tank, then work round the tank seam, loosening the four mounting bolts **(see illustrations)**. When the tank is free, lower it to the ground (keeping it level, to reduce the chance of fuel spillage) and remove it from under the car.

Inspection

10 Whilst removed, the fuel tank can be inspected for damage or deterioration. Removal of the fuel pump/fuel gauge sender unit (see Section 10) will allow a partial inspection of the interior. If the tank is contaminated with sediment or water, swill it out with clean fuel. Do not under any circumstances undertake any repairs on a leaking or damaged fuel tank; this work must be carried out by a professional who has experience in this critical and potentially-dangerous work.

11 Whilst the fuel tank is removed from the car, it should be placed in a safe area where sparks or open flames cannot ignite the fumes coming out of the tank. Be especially careful inside garages where a natural-gas type appliance is located, because the pilot light could cause an explosion.

12 Check the condition of the filler pipe and renew it if necessary.

Refitting

13 Refitting is a reversal of the removal procedure, noting the following points:

a) *Ensure that all pipe and wiring connections are securely fitted.*

b) *Tighten the tank retaining bolts to the specified torque.*

c) *If evidence of contamination was found, do not return any previously-drained fuel to the tank unless it is carefully filtered first.*

10 Fuel pump/fuel gauge sender unit – removal and refitting

Note: *Refer to the warning note in Section 1 before proceeding.*

Removal

1 A combined fuel pump and fuel gauge sender unit is located in the top face of the fuel tank. An access cover is provided below the rear seat, meaning that the tank does not have to be removed.

2 Disconnect the battery negative (earth) lead (see *Disconnecting the battery*).

3 Fold the rear seat fully forwards, or remove the rear seat as described in Chapter 11.

4 Lift up the carpet, and prise up the access cover, which is stuck down with a bead of mastic **(see illustration)**.

5 Disconnect the wiring plug from the top of the pump/sender unit, using a small

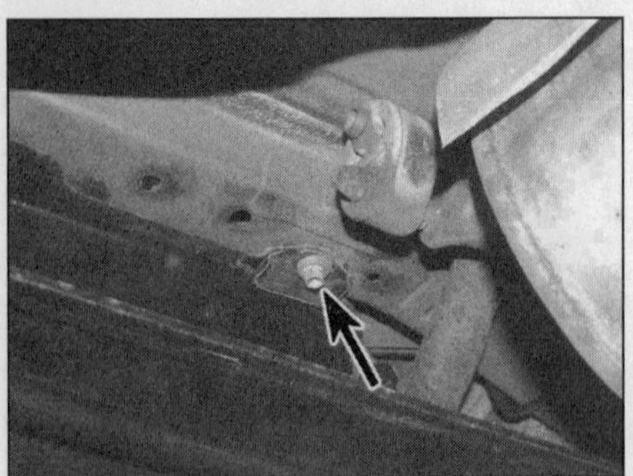

9.9a Fuel tank mounting bolt in front of the exhaust silencer . . .

9.9b . . . and next to the fuel pipe fittings

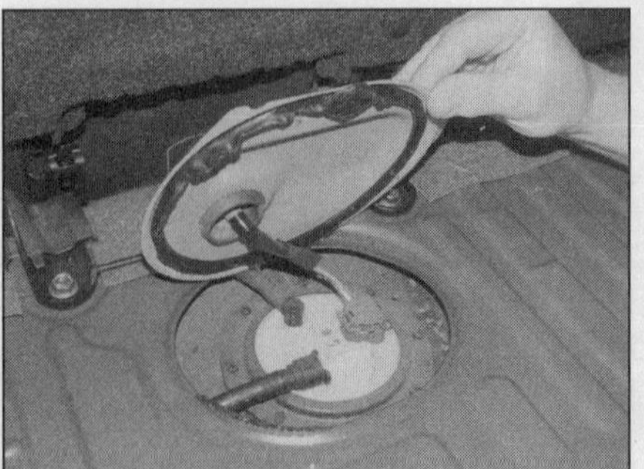

10.4 Prise up the fuel pump access cover below the rear seat

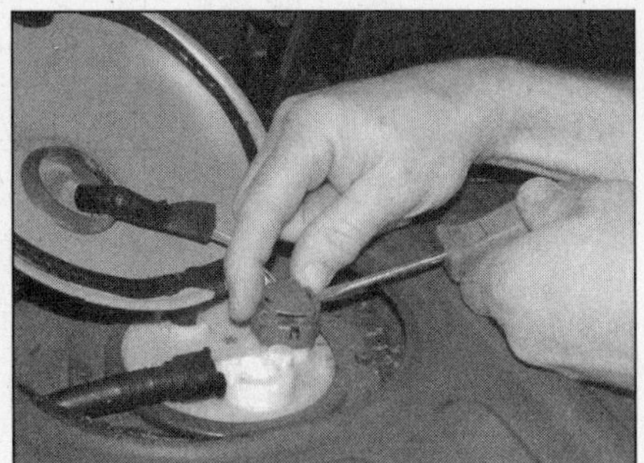
10.5 Disconnect the wiring plug with the help of a screwdriver

10.6a Slide out the retaining clip . . .

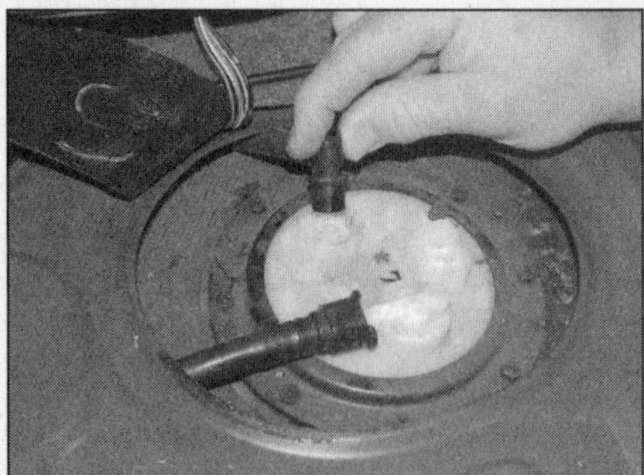
10.6b . . . and pull up to disconnect the fuel supply pipe

screwdriver to release the clip **(see illustration)**.

6 Slide out the retaining clip, and disconnect the fuel supply pipe from the top of the unit **(see illustrations)**. Anticipate a small amount of fuel spillage as this is done. Tape over the open union on top of the unit, and wrap more tape (or a plastic bag) over the disconnected supply pipe, to prevent dirt getting in.

7 The evaporative emissions connector has a quick-release fitting – squeeze the tabs together and pull it off **(see illustration)**.

8 Unscrew and remove the eight small bolts which secure the mounting plate, and lift the plate off **(see illustrations)**.

9 Lift out the fuel pump/sender unit, taking care not to damage the pump filter, nor to bend the sender unit float arm (which can get caught up on the tank lip as the unit is removed) **(see illustration)**. Allow any remaining fuel to drain into the tank before finally lifting it clear.

Fuel pump

10 To remove the fuel pump from the combined unit, first carefully release the plastic tabs which secure the two halves of the unit, using a small screwdriver. Separate the upper and lower sections **(see illustrations)**.

11 Disconnect the fuel pump wiring plug **(see illustration)**.

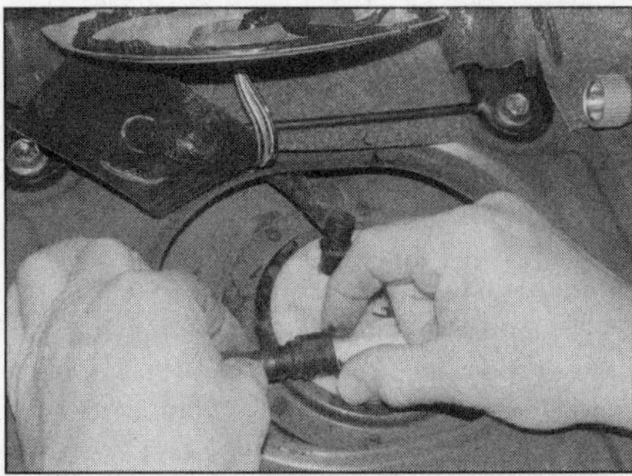
10.7 Squeeze the tabs on the EVAP hose connector, and pull it off

10.8a Unscrew the eight bolts . . .

10.8b . . . and lift out the fuel pump mounting plate

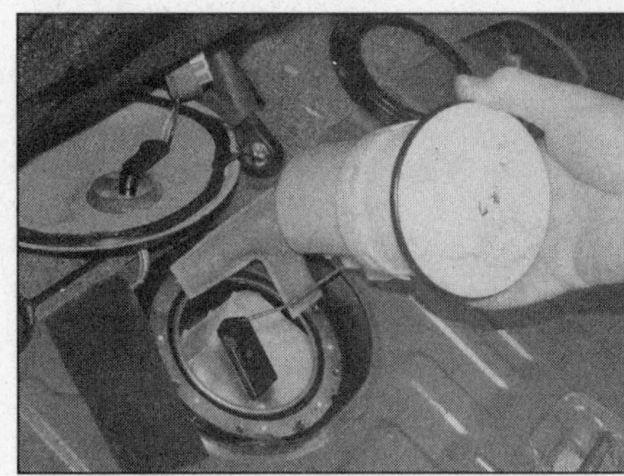
10.9 Lift out the fuel pump/sender unit, and let the excess fuel drain

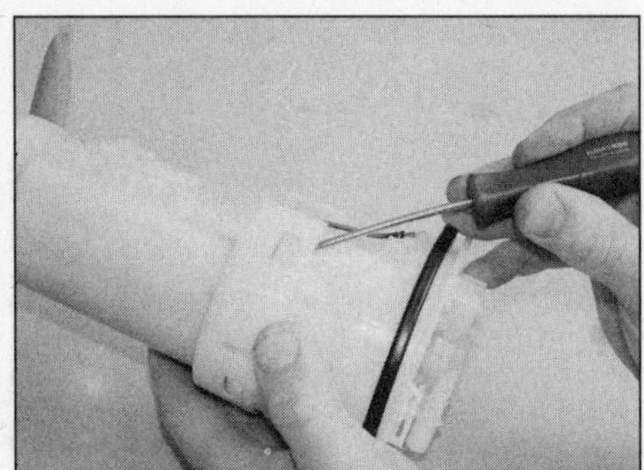
10.10a Use a screwdriver to release the plastic retaining tabs . . .

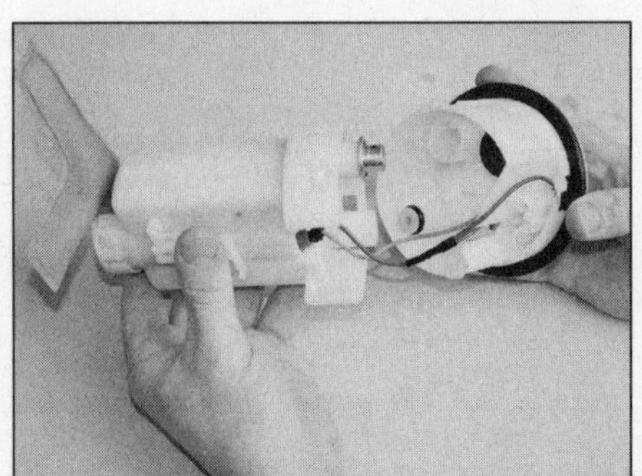
10.10b . . . and separate the upper and lower sections of the unit

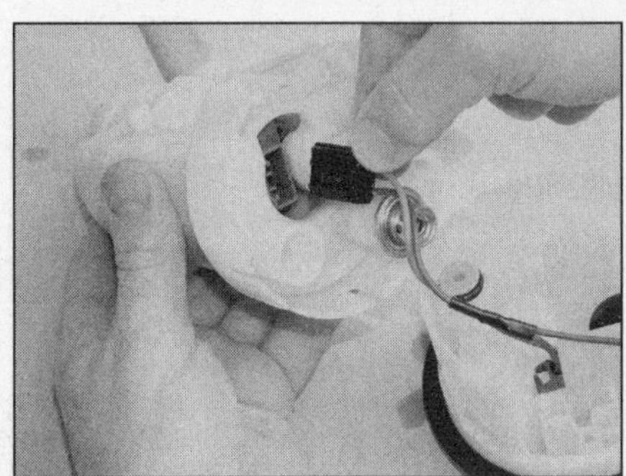
10.11 Disconnect the fuel pump wiring plug

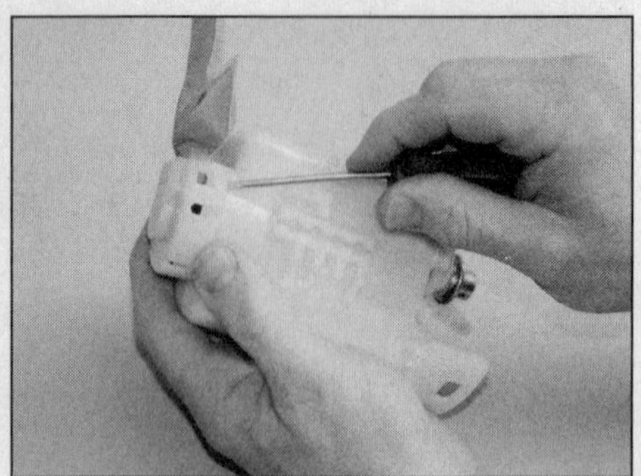
10.12a Use a screwdriver to release the lower cover retaining tabs . . .

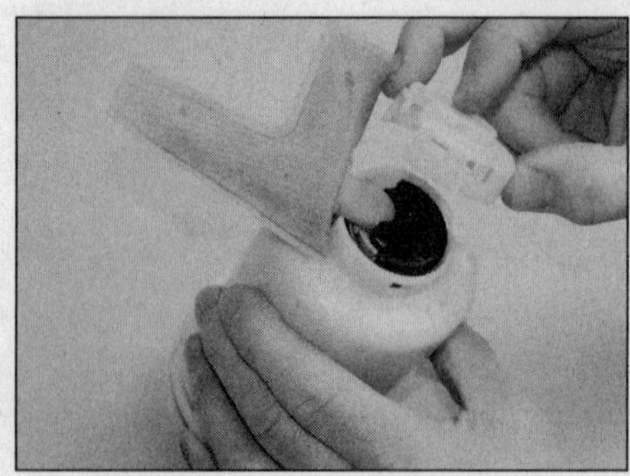
10.12b . . . and remove the cover

10.13 Lift out the pump lower spacer

12 Use a screwdriver to unclip the fuel pump lower cover, and remove it **(see illustrations)**.
13 Lift out the fuel pump lower spacer, noting how it is fitted **(see illustration)**.
14 The pump is a push-fit in the base, and can be slid out by pressing down on the wiring plug socket on top, using fingers only **(see illustration)**.
15 Refitting is a reversal of removal.

Fuel pressure regulator

16 Separate the upper and lower sections of the unit, and disconnect the fuel pump wiring plug, as described in paragraphs 10 and 11.
17 The fuel pressure regulator is pressed into the lower section. Prise it up using a small screwdriver, and remove it **(see illustration)**.
18 Refitting is a reversal of removal. Use a new O-ring if necessary.

Sender unit

19 Disconnect the sender unit wiring plug from the side of the main unit **(see illustration)**.
20 Pull out the retaining clip, noting how it is fitted **(see illustration)**.
21 When removing the sender unit from the side of the assembly, note its fitted location **(see illustration)**. It can only fit one way, but if care is not taken, it appears it will fit in several positions, which can cause confusion when refitting.
22 Refitting is a reversal of removal.

Refitting

23 Refitting the pump/sender unit is a reversal of removal, noting the following points **(see illustration)**:

a) Check the condition of the fuel filter, and clean it if necessary.
b) Check the condition of the rubber seal, and fit a new one if necessary.
c) Tighten the mounting plate bolts securely.
d) Once the unit has been refitted and the pipes connected, reconnect the battery and switch on the ignition. Check for correct pump operation, and for any sign of leaks from the supply pipe before refitting the access cover.

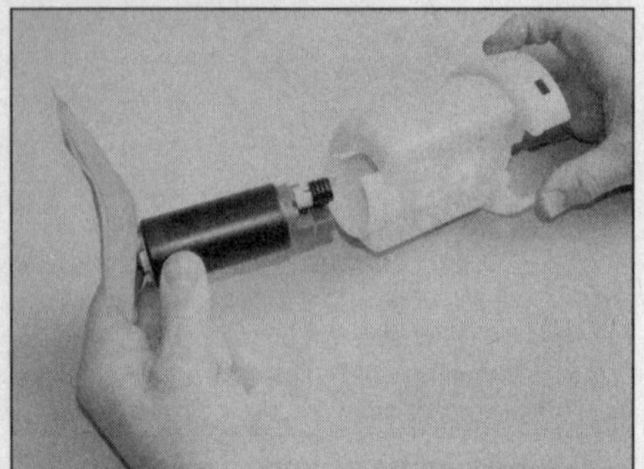
10.14 The fuel pump can be pushed out from the top

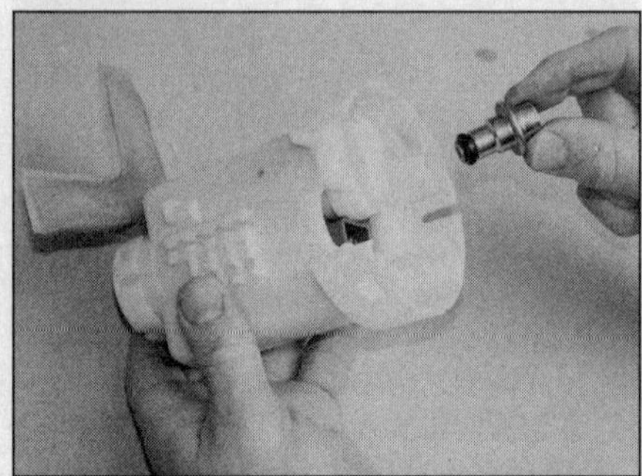
10.17 Prise out the fuel pressure regulator, and remove it

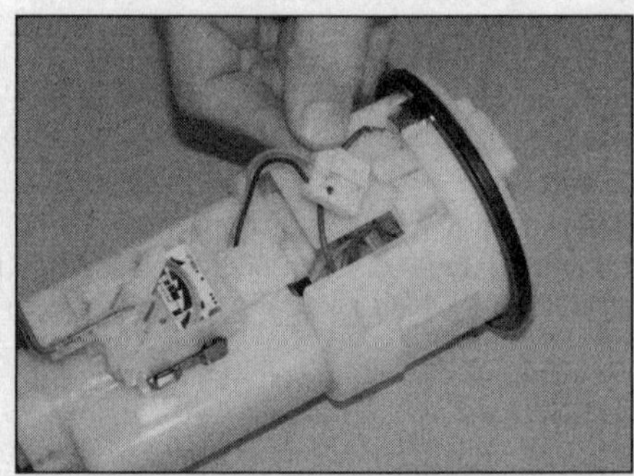
10.19 Disconnect the sender unit wiring plug

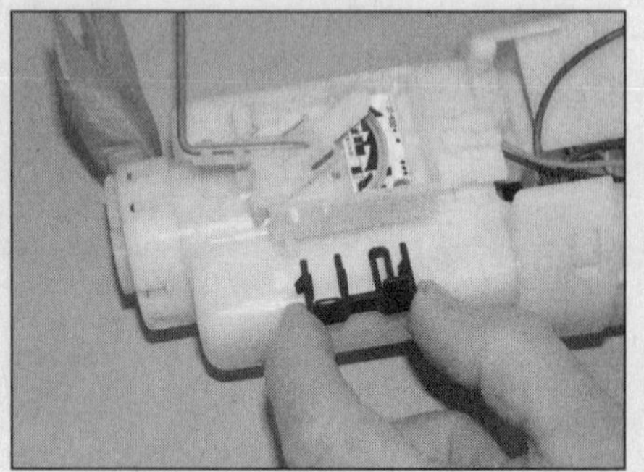
10.20 Pull out the plastic clip which secures the sender unit

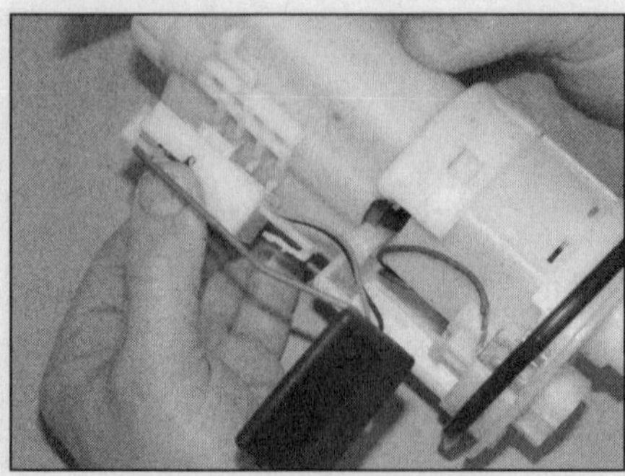
10.21 Note how the sender unit locates to the side of the main assembly

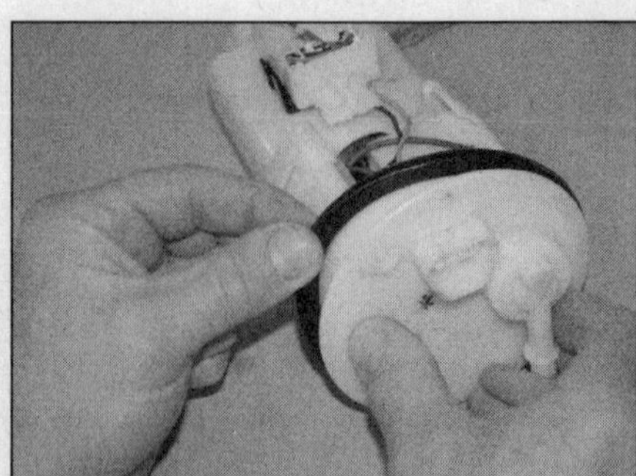
10.23 Check the condition of the rubber seal when refitting

11 Fuel injection system – checking

Note: *Refer to the warning note in Section 1 before proceeding.*

1 If a fault appears in the fuel injection system, first ensure that all the system wiring connectors are securely connected and free of corrosion – also refer to paragraphs 6 to 9 below. Then ensure that the fault is not due to poor maintenance; ie, check that the air cleaner filter element is clean, the spark plugs are in good condition and correctly gapped, the cylinder compression pressures are correct, the ignition system wiring is in good condition and securely connected, and the engine breather hoses are clear and undamaged, referring to Chapter 1, Chapter 2A and Chapter 5B.

2 If these checks fail to reveal the cause of the problem, the car should be taken to a suitably-equipped Toyota dealer for testing. A diagnostic connector is fitted below the steering column, into which dedicated electronic test equipment can be plugged. The test equipment is capable of 'interrogating' the engine management system ECU (ECU) electronically and accessing its internal fault log (reading fault codes).

3 Fault codes can only be extracted from the ECU using a dedicated fault code reader. A Toyota dealer will obviously have such a reader, but they are also available from other suppliers. It is unlikely to be cost-effective for the private owner to purchase a fault code reader, but a well-equipped local garage or auto-electrical specialist will have one.

4 Using this equipment, faults can be pinpointed quickly and simply, even if their occurrence is intermittent. Testing all the system components individually in an attempt to locate the fault by elimination is a time-consuming operation that is unlikely to be fruitful (particularly if the fault occurs dynamically), and carries a high risk of damage to the ECU's internal components.

5 Experienced home mechanics equipped with an accurate tachometer and a carefully-calibrated exhaust gas analyser may be able to check the exhaust gas CO content and the engine idle speed; if these are found to be out of specification, then the car must be taken to a suitably-equipped Toyota dealer for assessment. Neither the air/fuel mixture (exhaust gas CO content) nor the engine idle speed are manually adjustable; incorrect test results indicate the need for maintenance (possibly, injector cleaning) or a fault within the fuel injection system.

Limited Operation Strategy

6 Certain faults, such as failure of one of the engine management system sensors, will cause the system will revert to a backup (or 'limp-home') mode, often referred to as 'Limited Operation Strategy' (LOS). This is intended to be a 'get-you-home' facility only – the engine management warning light will come on when this mode is in operation.

7 In this mode, the signal from the defective sensor is substituted with a fixed value (it would normally vary), which may lead to loss of power, poor idling, and generally-poor running, especially when the engine is cold.

8 However, the engine may in fact run quite well in this situation, and the only clue (other than the warning light) would be that the exhaust CO emissions (for example) will be higher than they should be.

9 Bear in mind that, even if the defective sensor is correctly identified and renewed, the engine will not return to normal running until the fault code is erased, taking the system out of LOS. This also applies even if the cause of the fault was a loose connection or damaged piece of wire – until the fault code is erased, the system will continue in LOS.

12.2 Disconnecting the airflow meter wiring plug – 1.3 litre 2NZ-FE engines

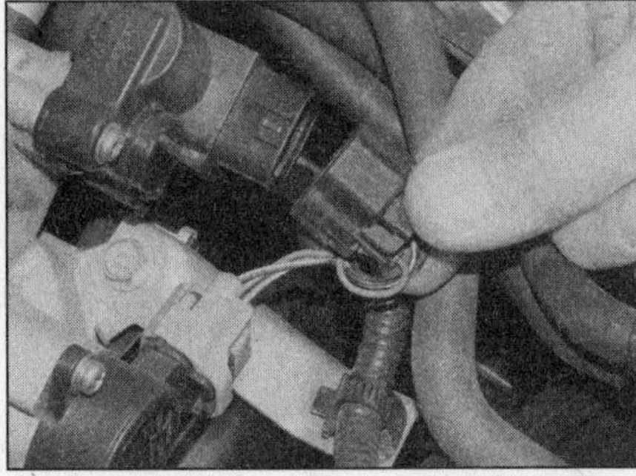

12.8a Disconnect the idle speed control valve. . .

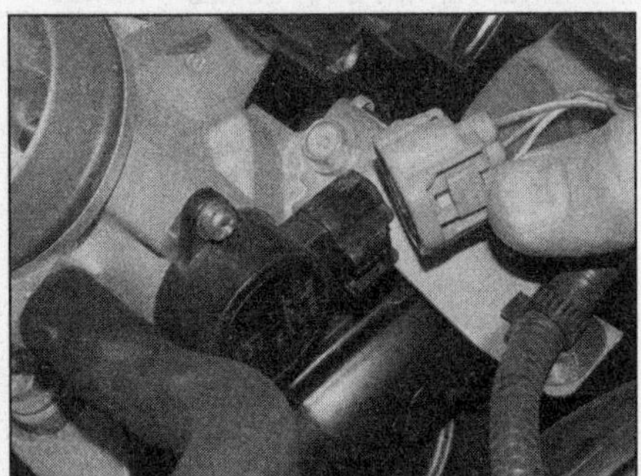

12.8b . . . and the throttle position sensor – 1.0 litre engine

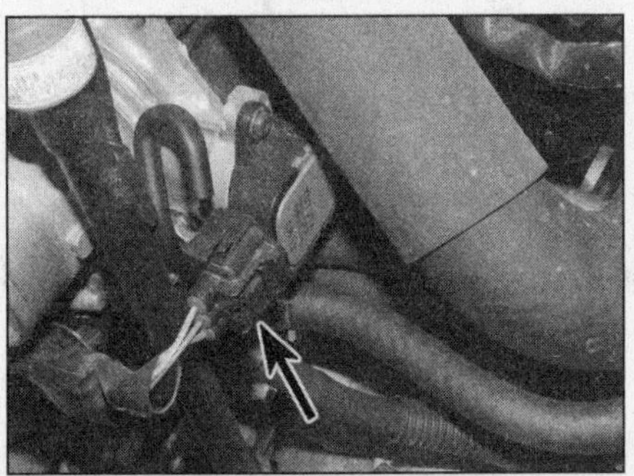

12.8c Throttle position sensor wiring plug – 1.3 litre 2NZ-FE engine

12 Fuel injection system components – removal and refitting

Note: *Refer to the precautions in Section 1 before proceeding.*

Airflow meter

1 On 1.0 litre and 1.3 litre 2SZ-FE engine models, remove the air cleaner as described in Section 5.

2 On 1.3 litre 2NZ-FE engine models, the meter is mounted right on top of the air cleaner – just disconnect the wiring plug **(see illustration)**.

3 Remove the two mounting screws, then carefully withdraw the airflow meter from the air cleaner. Recover the O-ring – a new one should be used for refitting, otherwise air leaks will cause various problems.

4 Refitting is a reversal of removal. Use a new O-ring, and tighten the mounting screws securely.

Throttle body

5 Remove the air cleaner and air inlet duct as described in Section 5.

6 Detach the accelerator cable from the throttle body as described in Section 6.

7 The throttle body receives a supply of coolant via two pipes on the idle speed control valve at the rear/base – because of this, the cooling system should be drained as described in Chapter 1 before removing the throttle body. However, the amount of coolant lost will be quite small if the system is not drained, and it may be sufficient to disconnect the pipes and point their ends upwards to avoid much loss. If the pipes can be clamped prior to disconnection, this is better still.

8 Disconnect the wiring plugs from the throttle position sensor and the idle speed control valve **(see illustrations)**.

12.9a Disconnect the crankcase breather . . .

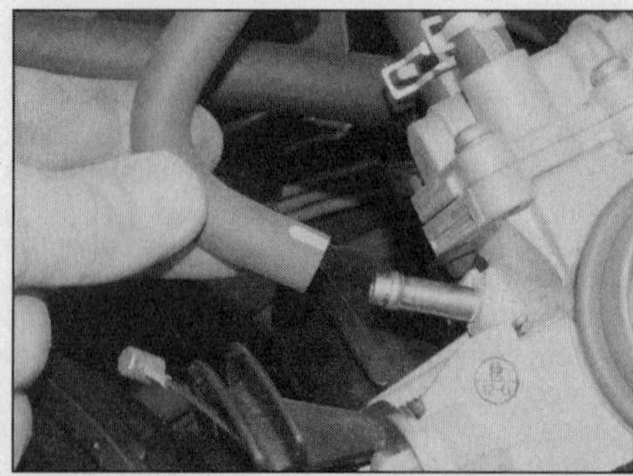
12.9b . . . and EVAP hoses (1.0 litre engine)

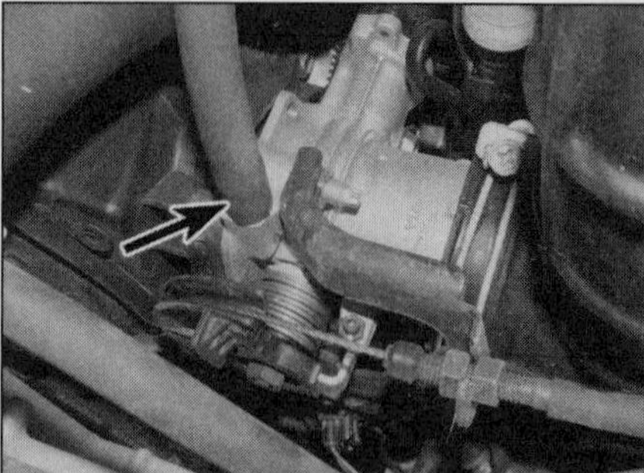
12.9c 1.3 litre 2NZ-FE engine throttle body – breather hose arrowed

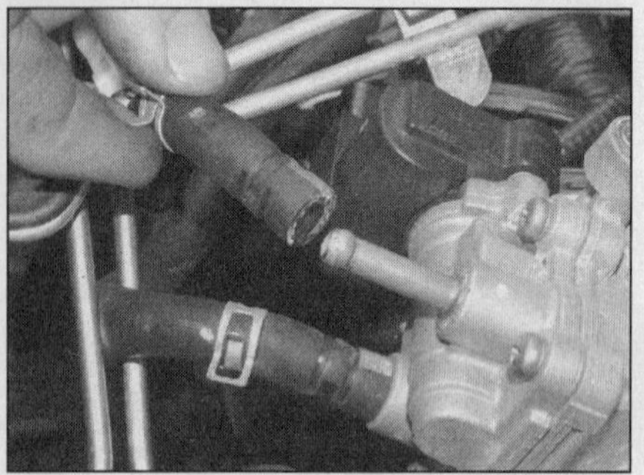
12.10 Clamp the coolant hoses, then disconnect them from the idle speed control valve

12.11a Remove the throttle body mounting bolts . . .

12.11b . . . and lift off the throttle body

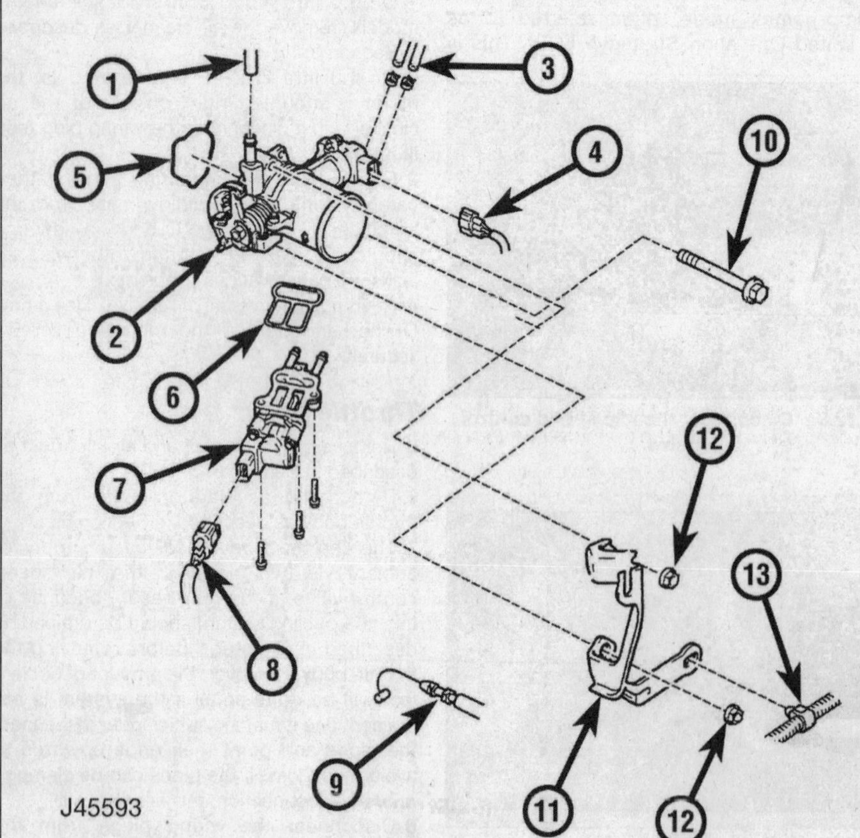

9 Noting their positions for refitting, disconnect the following **(see illustrations)**:

a) Crankcase breather hose.

b) EVAP hose (where fitted).

10 Finally, disconnect the two coolant hoses from the rear of the throttle body, noting the advice in paragraph 7 **(see illustration)**.

11 On 1.0 litre and 1.3 litre 2SZ-FE engine models, remove the three mounting bolts, and lift off the throttle body **(see illustrations)**. Note that the two front bolts screw into a mounting bracket – when refitting, these are tightened more than the third (rear) bolt, which screws into the plastic inlet manifold.

12 On 1.3 litre 2NZ-FE models, unclip the wiring harness from the accelerator cable bracket. Undo the two nuts and one bolt

12.12 Throttle body details – 1.3 litre 2NZ-FE engine

1 Breather hose
2 Throttle body
3 Idle speed control valve coolant hoses
4 Throttle position sensor wiring plug
5 Throttle body gasket
6 Idle speed control valve gasket
7 Idle speed control valve
8 Idle speed control valve wiring plug
9 Accelerator cable
10 Throttle body mounting bolt
11 Accelerator cable bracket
12 Bracket/throttle body mounting nut
13 Wiring harness

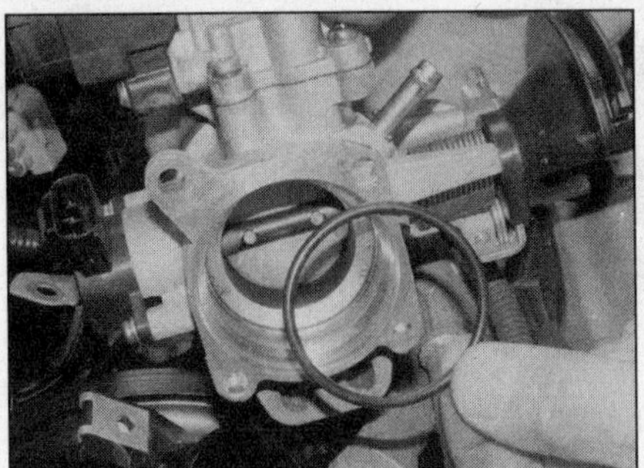

12.13 Recover the throttle body O-ring

12.14a Remove the two mounting bolts . . .

12.14b . . . and take off the throttle body mounting bracket

securing the throttle body, then withdraw it over the studs and off the inlet manifold, together with the accelerator cable bracket **(see illustration)**.

13 Recover the seal or O-ring from the base of the throttle body – a new one must be obtained for refitting **(see illustration)**. Any air leak from the base of the throttle body, caused by re-using the old seal, will cause all sorts of running problems.

14 On 1.0 litre and 1.3 litre 2SZ-FE engine models, if required, the throttle body mounting bracket can also be removed. Remove the two mounting bracket bolts, and lift the bracket off the back of the engine **(see illustration)**.

15 Refitting is a reversal of removal, noting the following points:

a) Use a new throttle body seal or O-ring, and fit it to the inlet manifold using only a little water or methylated spirit to 'lubricate' it if necessary.

b) If the mounting bracket was removed (paragraph 14), fit the bracket bolts and the two throttle body front bolts first, but only by a few threads. Fit and tighten the throttle body rear bolt to the specified torque, then the mounting bracket bolts, and finally, the two throttle body front bolts.

c) Reconnect the wiring plugs and hoses correctly and securely.

d) On completion, check and if necessary top-up the cooling system as described in 'Weekly checks'.

Fuel rail and injectors

16 Relieve the residual pressure in the fuel system (see Section 2), and equalise tank pressure by removing the fuel filler cap.

Warning: This procedure will merely relieve the increased pressure necessary for the engine to run – remember that fuel will still be present in the system components, and take precautions accordingly before disconnecting any of them.

17 Disconnect the battery negative (earth) lead (see *Disconnecting the battery*).

1.0 litre and 1.3 litre 2SZ-FE engines

18 Remove the air cleaner as described in Section 5.

19 Unclip the injector wiring harness from the brackets on the back of the cylinder head cover **(see illustration)**.

20 Pull off the breather hose from the left-hand side of the throttle body (left as seen from the driver's seat).

21 Place some rags underneath the transmission end of the fuel rail, at the flanged joint. Loosen and remove the two flange bolts, and separate the joint – there will be some spillage of fuel as this is done **(see illustration)**. Move the pipe to one side, clear of the fuel rail, and wrap a plastic bag around the open joint face and the pulsation damper, to prevent dirt getting in.

1.3 litre 2NZ-FE engine

22 Remove the cylinder head cover as described in Chapter 2A.

23 Trace the fuel line back from the fuel rail at the front of the cylinder head, and disconnect it at the quick-release connector **(see illustration)**. Although the system should have been depressurised (paragraph 16), be prepared for fuel spillage as this is done.

24 Remove the fuel pipe bracket securing bolt from the transmission end of the cylinder head.

All engines

25 Disconnect the four wiring plugs from the fuel injectors – though it should not be possible to mix them up when refitting, it may pay to label them as they are disconnected **(see illustration)**.

26 Loosen the two fuel rail securing bolts completely, but do not remove them from the

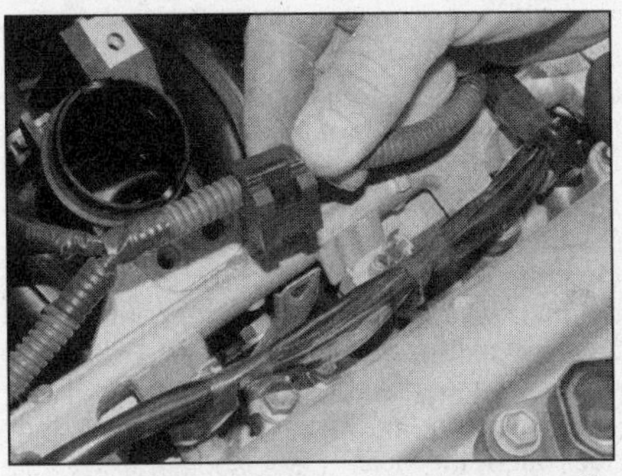

12.19 Pull the injector wiring harness off the cylinder head cover brackets

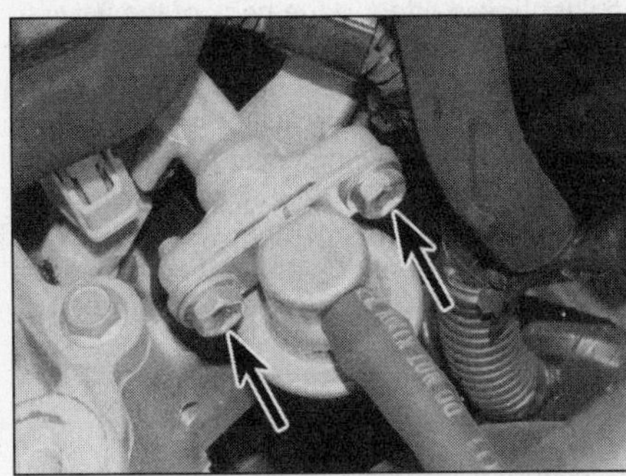

12.21 If the fuel rail is being removed completely, unbolt the fuel supply flange

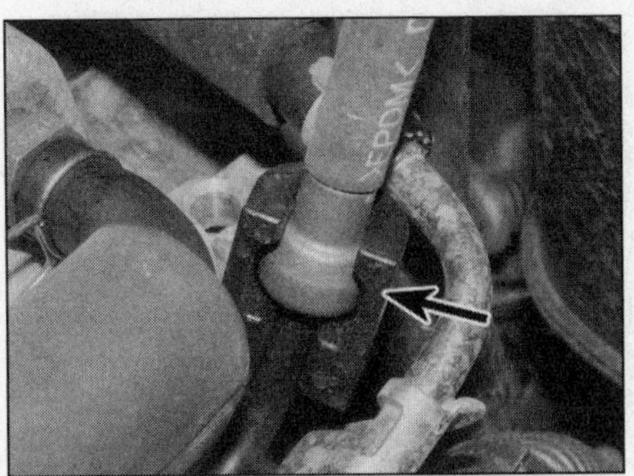

12.23 Disconnect the quick-release fitting by pulling it out of the clip and separating

12.25 Disconnect the injector wiring plugs

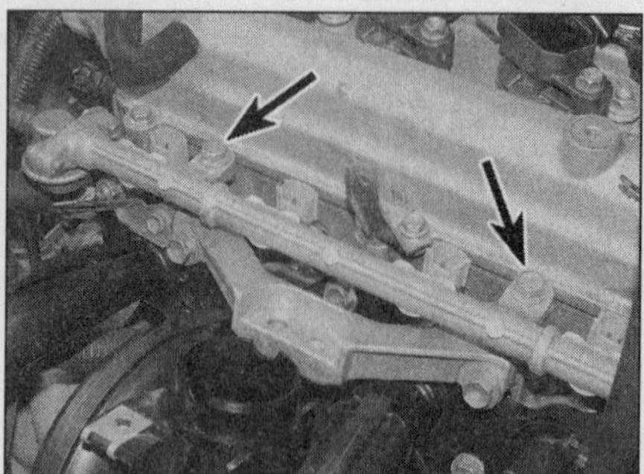

12.26a Fuel rail mounting bolts – 1.0 litre engine

12.26b Fuel rail mounting bolts 1.3 litre 2NZ-FE engine

12.27 Pull the fuel rail upwards to release the injector O-rings

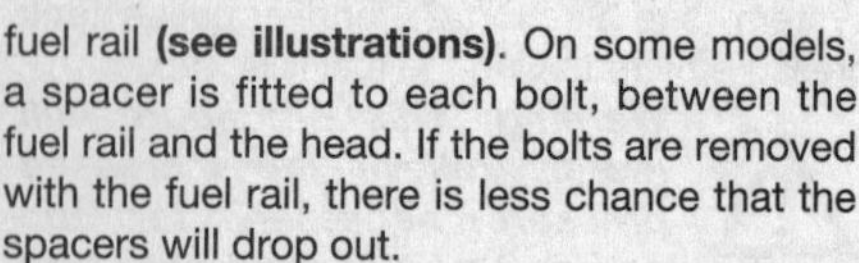

fuel rail **(see illustrations)**. On some models, a spacer is fitted to each bolt, between the fuel rail and the head. If the bolts are removed with the fuel rail, there is less chance that the spacers will drop out.

27 Carefully pull the fuel rail upwards to release the injectors – there will be some resistance from the injector O-ring seals **(see illustration)**. If necessary, recover the fuel rail bolt spacers from the head.

28 Recover the injector lower seals, noting which way up they are fitted – new ones must be used when refitting **(see illustration)**.

29 Carefully pull the injectors from the fuel rail, using a twisting motion to free them. Recover the small O-ring from the top of each injector – these also should be renewed when they are disturbed **(see illustration)**.

30 Refitting is the reverse of the removal procedure, noting the following points:

a) *Fit new injector O-rings and seals, and lubricate them with clean engine oil to aid refitting. Turn the injectors so that the wiring plug sockets will face forwards when the fuel rail is refitted.*

b) *Fit the mounting bolts through the rail, with the spacers below, and push the injectors into place. Before tightening the bolts to the specified torque, check that the injectors are free to rotate – if not, this points to incorrect fitting of the O-rings.*

c) *Ensure that the hoses and wiring are routed correctly, and secured on reconnection by any clips or ties provided.*

d) *On completion, switch the ignition on to activate the fuel pump and pressurise the system, without cranking the engine. Check for signs of fuel leaks around all disturbed unions and joints before attempting to start the engine.*

Fuel pressure regulator

31 The pressure regulator is combined with the fuel pump, which is fitted to the fuel tank. Refer to Section 10.

Idle speed control valve

1.0 litre and 1.3 litre 2SZ-FE engines

32 Remove the air cleaner as described in Section 5.

33 Refer to paragraph 7 regarding the coolant hoses fitted to the back of the valve – if care is taken, the cooling system need not be drained prior to removal. Disconnect the hoses, noting their locations for refitting.

34 Disconnect the wiring plug from the valve.

35 Remove the four mounting screws, then withdraw the valve from the back of the throttle body – anticipate a further small amount of coolant loss as this is done **(see illustration)**. Recover the gasket – a new one should be used when refitting.

1.3 litre 2NZ-FE engine

36 Remove the throttle body as described previously in this Section.

37 Disconnect the wiring plug from the valve.

38 Remove the three mounting bolts, then withdraw the valve from the base of the throttle body **(refer to illustration 12.12)**. Recover the gasket – a new one should be used when refitting.

All models

39 Refitting is a reversal of removal, noting the following points:

a) *Use a new gasket, and tighten the mounting bolts securely.*

b) *On 1.3 litre 2NZ-FE engine models, refit the throttle body as described previously in this Section.*

c) *On completion, check and if necessary top-up the cooling system as described in 'Weekly checks'.*

ECU

Note: *The ECU is fragile. Take care not to drop it, or subject it to any other kind of impact. Do not subject it to extremes of temperature, or allow it to get wet.*

40 Disconnect the battery negative lead, and place the lead away from the terminal (see *Disconnecting the battery*). It is essential that the battery is disconnected before separating the ECU wiring plug, or the ECU itself could be damaged.

41 Open the glovebox door, then carefully press the door in at both sides and pull the door out of the facia.

42 Remove the two ECU mounting bolts at the top, then pull the unit out slightly to

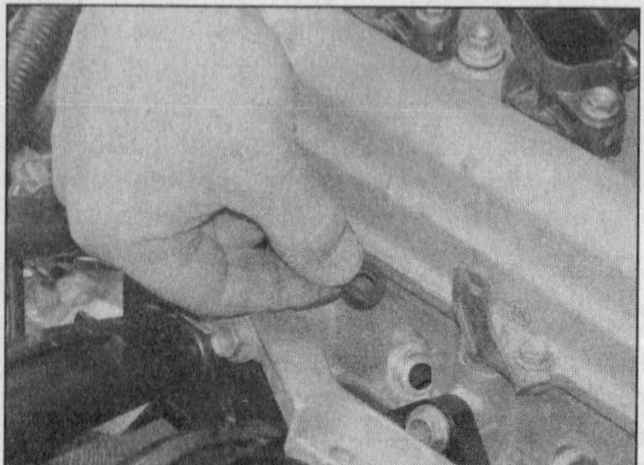

12.28 Recover the injector lower seals from the cylinder head

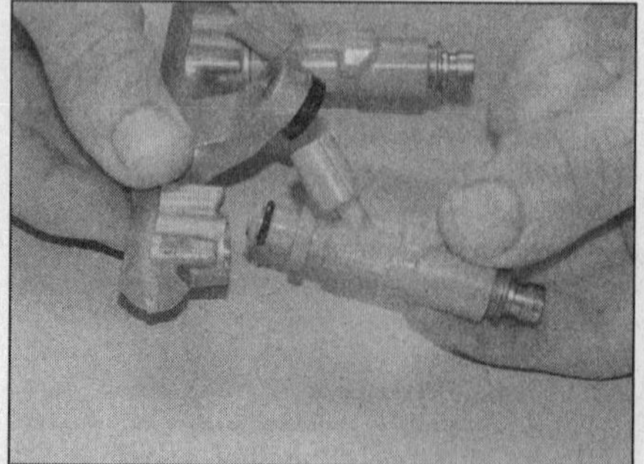

12.29 Twist the injectors from the fuel rail, and recover the upper injector

12.35 Idle speed control valve mounting screws

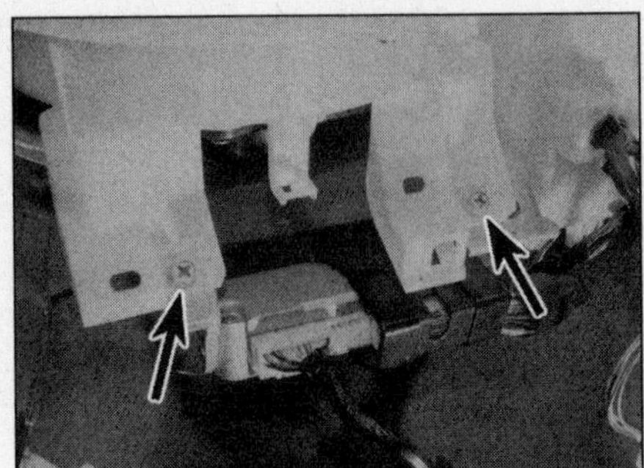
12.42 With the glovebox removed, the ECU mounting screws can be seen

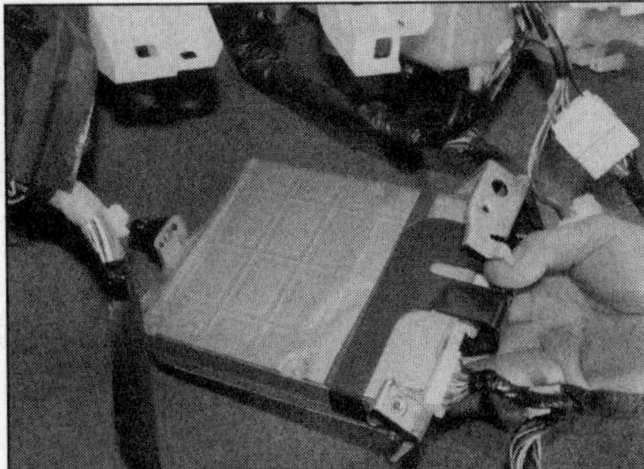
12.43a Remove the screws, then release the ECU tab at the rear

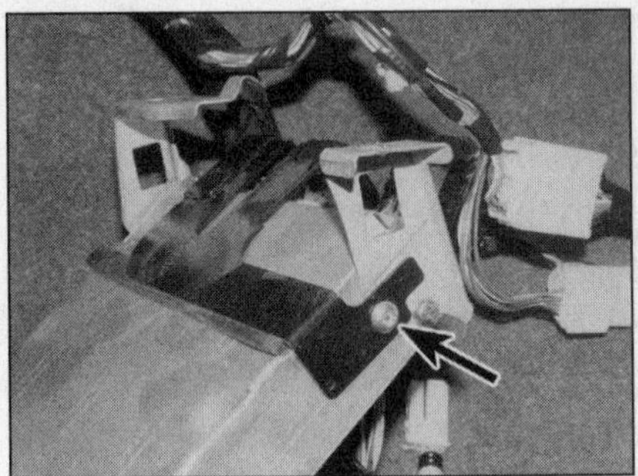
12.43b Take out the side screws to remove the unit from its bracket

disengage the rear mounting tab **(see illustration)**.

43 Disconnect the wiring plugs from the ECU, and remove it – refer to the note at the start of this section. If required, the ECU can be removed from its mounting bracket after taking out the screws either side **(see illustrations)**.

Crankshaft position sensor

44 The sensor is located at the base of the timing chain cover, next to the crankshaft pulley. Apply the handbrake, then jack up the front of the car and support it on axle stands (see *Jacking and vehicle support*). Remove the engine right-hand lower cover from under the car.

45 Unbolt and remove the sensor wiring harness mounting bracket from the front of the engine.

46 With the ignition switched off, disconnect the sensor wiring plug (slide back the plug locking catch, where applicable), then unscrew the mounting bolt and withdraw the sensor **(see illustrations)**.

47 The sensor resistance is quoted in the Specifications at the start of this Chapter – check by connecting a multimeter, set to the resistance function, across the sensor's plug terminals. A zero or infinity reading suggests the sensor is faulty.

48 Refitting is a reversal of removal. Ensure that the sensor is clean when refitting, and tighten the bolt securely.

Camshaft position sensor

49 The sensor is located at the transmission end of the cylinder head. Access to the sensor is hampered by the large number of coolant hoses nearby – for this reason, only try to remove the sensor when the engine is cold.

50 On 1.0 litre and 1.3 litre 2SZ-FE engines, access to the sensor will be (slightly) improved by removing the air cleaner inlet duct as described in Section 5.

51 On 1.3 litre 2NZ-FE engines, remove the engine top cover, which is secured by four nuts. Access will also be improved by removing the air cleaner top cover as described in Section 5.

52 With the ignition switched off, disconnect the wiring plug from the camshaft position sensor **(see illustration)**.

53 Unscrew the mounting bolt and withdraw the sensor from the cylinder head.

54 The sensor resistance is quoted in the Specifications at the start of this Chapter – check by connecting a multimeter, set to the resistance function, across the sensor's plug terminals. A zero or infinity reading suggests the sensor is faulty.

55 Refitting is a reversal of removal. Ensure that the sensor is clean when refitting, and tighten the bolt securely.

Coolant temperature sensor

56 See Chapter 3, Section 6. Only the coolant temperature sensor has any real bearing on the fuel system – the cooling fan switch, though under ECU control, is not relevant.

Throttle position sensor

57 The sensor is located on the throttle body. According to Toyota, the sensor is not available separately from the throttle body, and is not intended to be removed (though this does appear to be possible). If a problem with the sensor is suspected, have your findings confirmed by a Toyota dealer or other specialist, as a complete new throttle body may have to be fitted.

Oxygen sensor

58 Refer to Chapter 4B.

Vehicle speed sensor

Manual transmission models

59 The sensor is mounted on top of the transmission, at the rear.

12.46a Disconnect the crankshaft sensor . . .

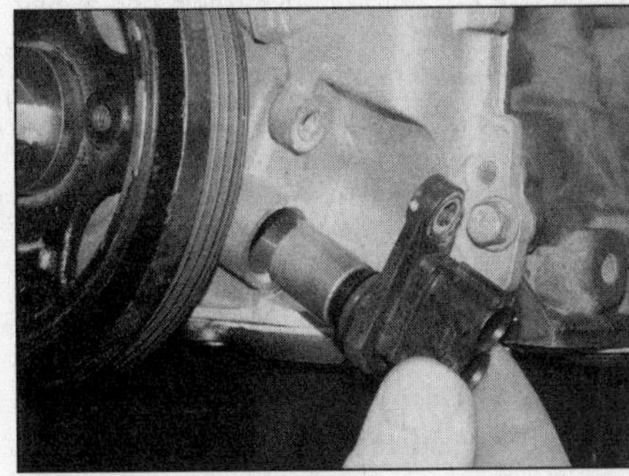
12.46b . . . then unbolt and remove it – 1.0 litre engine

12.46c Crankshaft position sensor – 1.3 litre 2NZ-FE engine (mounting bolt arrowed)

12.52 Disconnect the camshaft position sensor wiring plug

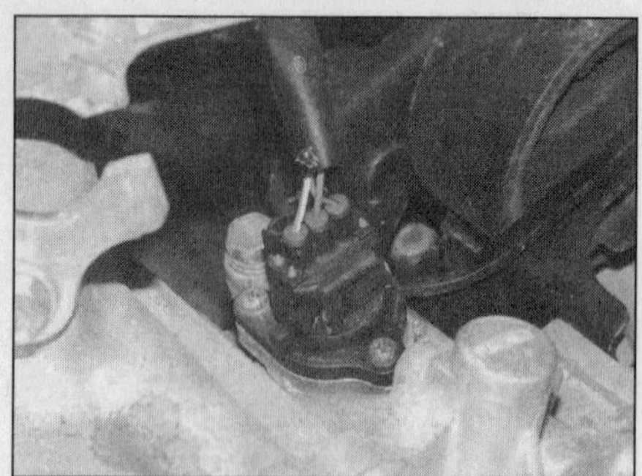

12.60 Disconnect the vehicle speed sensor wiring plug

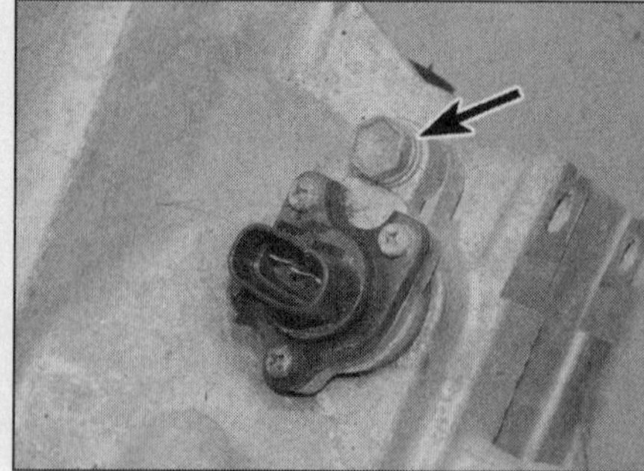

12.61 Remove the sensor mounting bolt, then withdraw it from the transmission

12.65a Power steering pressure switch – 1.0 litre engine

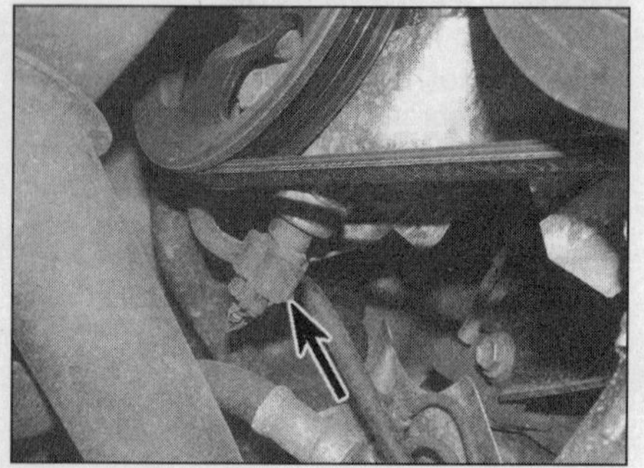

12.65b Power steering pressure switch – 1.3 litre 2NZ-FE engine

60 With the ignition switched off, disconnect the sensor wiring plug **(see illustration)**.

61 Remove the sensor mounting bolt, and lift the sensor out of the transmission (there may be some resistance, as the sensor has an O-ring seal) **(see illustration)**. Recover the O-ring – a new one should be used when refitting.

62 Using a small screwdriver, prise out the clip fitted below the sensor mounting flange, which secures the sensor to its driven gear.

63 Refitting is a reversal of removal. Fit a new O-ring, and tighten the mounting bolt securely.

Knock sensor

64 Refer to Chapter 5B.

12.68 Disconnect the switch wiring plug, then unscrew and remove it

Power steering pressure switch

65 On models with hydraulic power steering, a switch is fitted in the high-pressure fluid line to monitor the power steering fluid pressure **(see illustrations)**.

66 When the fluid pressure is high (such as when the steering is turned to full lock), this places extra load on the power steering pump, which in turn loads the engine.

67 At low engine speeds, this sudden loading might cause the engine to stall, but when the ECU receives a signal from the pressure switch, it raises the idle speed and prevents stalling.

68 To remove the switch, disconnect the wiring plug, then unscrew it from the power steering pipe (support the pipe if necessary, so that the twisting force does not damage the pipe) **(see illustration)**. Anticipate some loss of power steering fluid when the switch is removed, and take steps to prevent dirt from entering the system.

69 Refitting is a reversal of removal. Tighten the switch securely, then run the engine for a few minutes. Stop the engine, and top-up the power steering fluid level if necessary (see *Weekly checks*).

13 Inlet manifold – removal and refitting

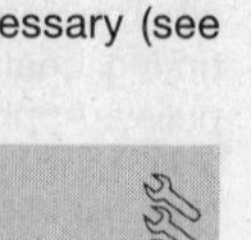

Note: *Refer to the warning note in Section 1 before proceeding. Note that the inlet manifold is made of plastic – do not strike it, nor use any great force when removing it.*

Removal

1.0 litre and 1.3 litre 2SZ-FE engines

1 Remove the throttle body and its mounting bracket as described in Section 12.

2 Noting their locations, disconnect the breather hose and the brake servo vacuum hose from the ports on the inlet manifold **(see illustrations)**.

13.2a Breather hose (A) and brake servo vacuum hose (B) connections on the inlet manifold – 1.0 litre engine

13.2b Release the spring clips, and pull off the hoses

13.3a Inlet manifold retaining nuts and bolts

13.3b Remove the inlet manifold from the engine

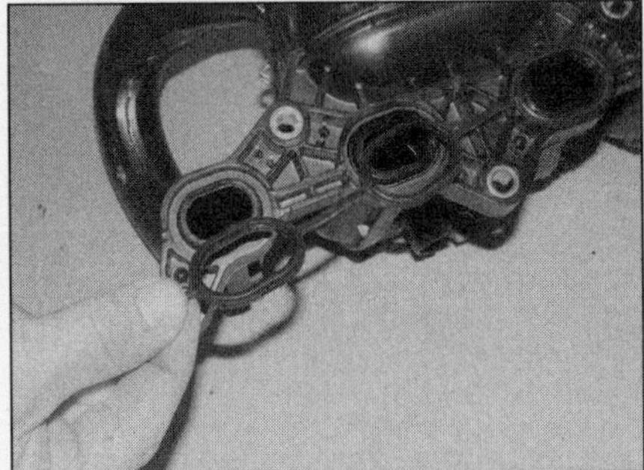

13.4 The inlet manifold gasket is a one-piece rubber type

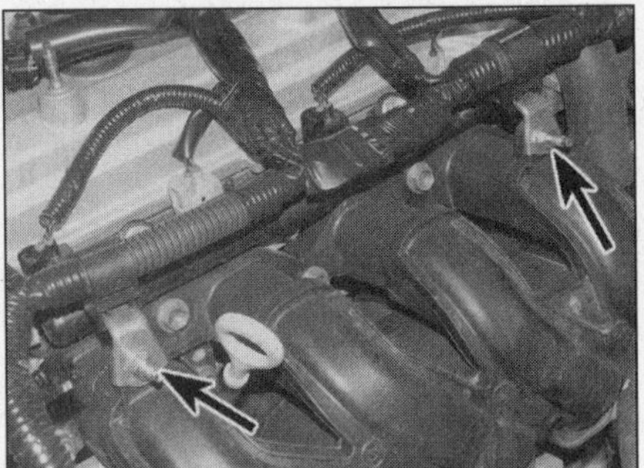

13.8a Remove the two nuts securing the wiring harness along the top . . .

13.8b . . . and unclip the wiring harness from the side of the manifold

13.9 Disconnect the breather and brake servo hoses from the manifold

3 Remove the three central bolts and two end nuts, and withdraw the manifold from the cylinder head **(see illustrations)**.

4 Recover the one-piece gasket – a new one should be used when refitting **(see illustration)**.

1.3 litre 2NZ-FE engine

5 Drain the cooling system as described in Chapter 1.

6 Remove the throttle body as described in Section 12.

7 Pull out the engine oil dipstick, and place it to one side.

8 Remove the nuts which secure the two wiring harness brackets to the manifold, and lift the harness clear. Unclip the wiring harness which runs down the side of the manifold next to the alternator **(see illustrations)**.

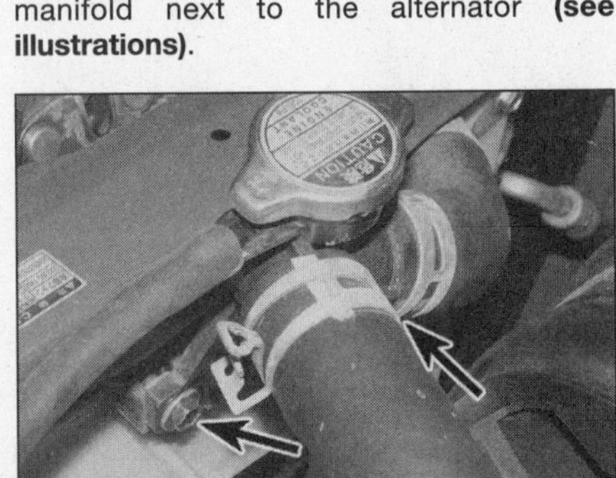

13.10 Unbolt and remove the coolant filler neck (two bolts)

9 Noting their locations, disconnect the breather hose and the brake servo vacuum hose from the ports on the inlet manifold **(see illustration)**.

10 Noting their locations, disconnect the hoses from the coolant filler neck mounted on the engine front panel. Unbolt the filler neck and remove it **(see illustration)**.

11 Remove the three central bolts and two end nuts, and withdraw the manifold from the cylinder head **(see illustration)**.

12 Recover the one-piece gasket – a new one should be used when refitting.

Refitting

13 Refitting is a reversal of removal, noting the following points:

a) Ensure that the mating faces are clean, and use a new manifold gasket.

b) Tighten the inlet manifold nuts and bolts to the specified torque.

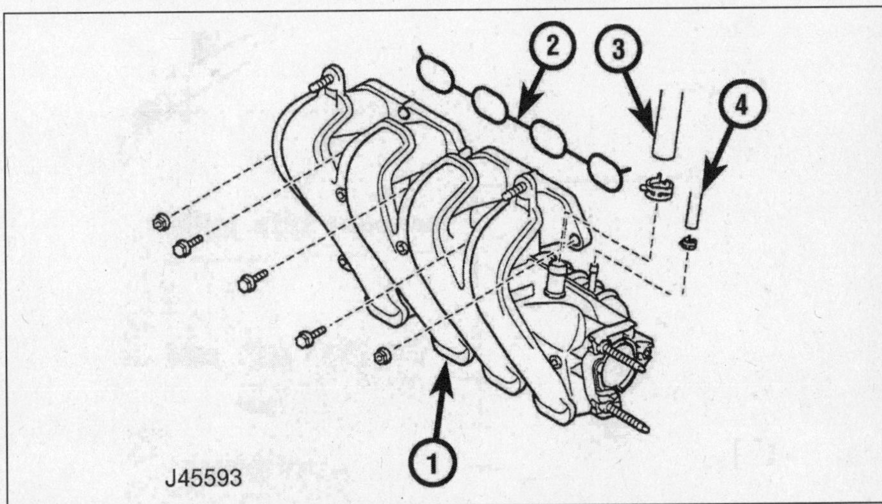

13.11 Inlet manifold details – 1.3 litre 2NZ-FE engine

1 Inlet manifold
2 Gasket
3 Crankcase breather hose
4 Brake servo vacuum hose

Notes

Chapter 4 Part B:
Emission control & exhaust systems

Contents

Degrees of difficulty

Easy, suitable for novice with little experience 	**Fairly easy,** suitable for beginner with some experience 	**Fairly difficult,** suitable for competent DIY mechanic 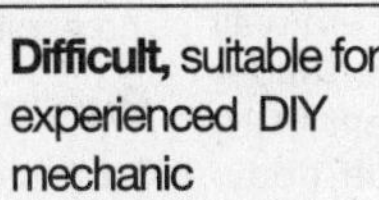	**Difficult,** suitable for experienced DIY mechanic 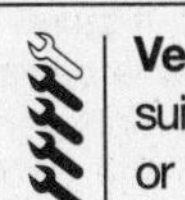	**Very difficult,** suitable for expert DIY or professional

Specifications

Torque wrench settings	**Nm**	**lbf ft**
Exhaust centre section-to-rear silencer bolts	45	33
Exhaust manifold nuts/bolts	25	18
Exhaust manifold support bracket:		
Mounting bolt	25	18
Mounting nut	18	13
Exhaust manifold-to-front downpipe bolts:		
Except 1.3 litre 2SZ-FE engine	60	44
1.3 litre 2SZ-FE engine	44	32
Oxygen (lambda) sensors	44	32

1 General information

Emission control systems

All models are designed to use unleaded petrol, and are controlled by engine management systems that are programmed to give the best compromise between driveability, fuel consumption and exhaust emission production. In addition, a number of systems are fitted that help to minimise other harmful emissions. A crankcase emission control system is fitted, which reduces the release of pollutants from the engine's lubrication system, and a catalytic converter is fitted which reduces exhaust gas pollutant. An evaporative loss emission control system is fitted which reduces the release of gaseous hydrocarbons from the fuel tank.

Crankcase emission control

To reduce the emission of unburned hydrocarbons from the crankcase into the atmosphere, the engine is sealed and the blow-by gases and oil vapour are drawn from inside the crankcase into the inlet tract to be burned by the engine during normal combustion.

Under conditions of high manifold depression, the gases will be sucked positively out of the crankcase. Under conditions of low manifold depression, the gases are forced out of the crankcase by the (relatively) higher crankcase pressure. If the engine is worn, the raised crankcase pressure (due to increased blow-by) will cause some of the flow to return under all manifold conditions.

Exhaust emission control

To minimise the amount of pollutants which escape into the atmosphere, all models are fitted with a three-way catalytic converter in the exhaust system. The fuelling system is of the closed-loop type, in which an oxygen (lambda) sensor in the exhaust system provides the engine management system ECU with constant feedback, enabling the ECU to adjust the air/fuel mixture to optimise combustion.

Most models have two oxygen sensors – one before the catalytic converter and one after. This enables more efficient monitoring of the exhaust gas, allowing a faster response time. The overall efficiency of the converters can also be checked.

The oxygen sensor has a built-in heating element, controlled by the ECU through the oxygen sensor relay, to quickly bring the sensor's tip to its optimum operating temperature. The sensor's tip is sensitive to oxygen, and sends a voltage signal to the ECU that varies according on the amount of oxygen in the exhaust gas. If the inlet air/fuel mixture is too rich, the exhaust gases are low in oxygen so the sensor sends a low-voltage signal, the voltage rising as the mixture weakens and the amount of oxygen rises in the exhaust gases. Peak conversion efficiency of all major pollutants occurs if the inlet air/fuel mixture is maintained at the chemically-correct ratio for the complete combustion of petrol of 14.7 parts (by weight) of air to 1 part of fuel (the stoichiometric ratio). The sensor output voltage alters in a large step at this point, the ECU using the signal change as a reference point and correcting the inlet air/fuel mixture accordingly by altering the fuel injector pulse width.

Evaporative emission control

To minimise the escape of unburned hydrocarbons into the atmosphere, an evaporative loss emission control system is fitted to all models. The fuel tank filler cap is

2.7 Disconnect the hoses from the top of the canister

sealed, and a charcoal canister is mounted at the rear of the engine compartment to collect the petrol vapours released from the fuel contained in the fuel tank. It stores them until they can be drawn from the canister (under the control of the engine management ECU) via the purge valve into the throttle body, where they are then burned by the engine during normal combustion.

To ensure that the engine runs correctly when it is cold and/or idling, and to protect the catalytic converter from the effects of an over-rich mixture, the purge control valve is not opened by the ECU until the engine has warmed up, and the engine is under load; the valve solenoid is then modulated on and off to allow the stored vapour to pass into the throttle body.

Exhaust systems

The exhaust system comprises the exhaust manifold, centre section (including the downpipe, catalytic converter, oxygen sensors and centre silencer), and the rear silencer.

The system is supported by various metal brackets screwed to the vehicle floor, with rubber vibration dampers fitted to suppress noise.

2 Evaporative loss emission control system – information and component renewal

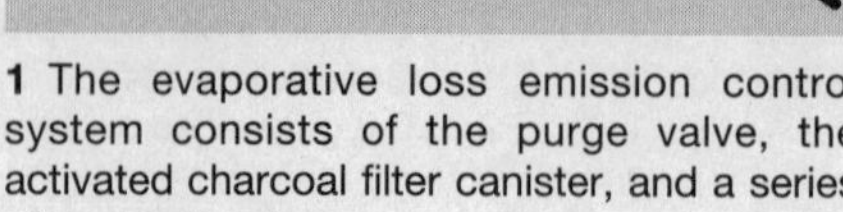

1 The evaporative loss emission control system consists of the purge valve, the activated charcoal filter canister, and a series of connecting hoses.

2 The purge valve is clipped to the side of the air cleaner, while the canister is mounted on the engine compartment bulkhead.

Purge valve

3 Ensure that the ignition is switched off, then unplug the wiring harness from the purge valve at the connector.

4 Pull the hoses off the purge valve ports. Make a note of their orientation or, preferably, mark them to aid refitting later.

5 Slide the purge valve upwards out of its holder on the side of the air cleaner, and remove it from the engine bay.

6 Refitting is a reversal of removal.

Charcoal canister

7 Disconnect the hoses from the top of the canister, noting their locations for refitting **(see illustration)**.

8 Pull the canister upwards and remove it from the engine compartment.

9 Refitting is a reversal of removal.

3 Crankcase emission system – general information

1 The crankcase emission control system consists of a series of hoses that connect the crankcase vent to the cylinder head cover vent and the throttle body.

2 The system requires no attention other than to check at regular intervals that the hose(s) are free of blockages and undamaged.

4 Oxygen sensors – removal and refitting

Note: *The oxygen sensors are delicate and will not work if dropped or knocked, if their power supply is disrupted, or if any cleaning materials are used on them.*

Removal

1 Jack up the front of the car, and support it on axle stands (see *Jacking and vehicle support*).

2 Trace the wiring back from the oxygen sensor to the connector and disconnect the wiring **(see illustrations)**.

3 Unscrew and remove the sensor from its location – an open-ended spanner will be needed, as the sensor wiring means a normal socket cannot be fitted **(see illustrations)**.

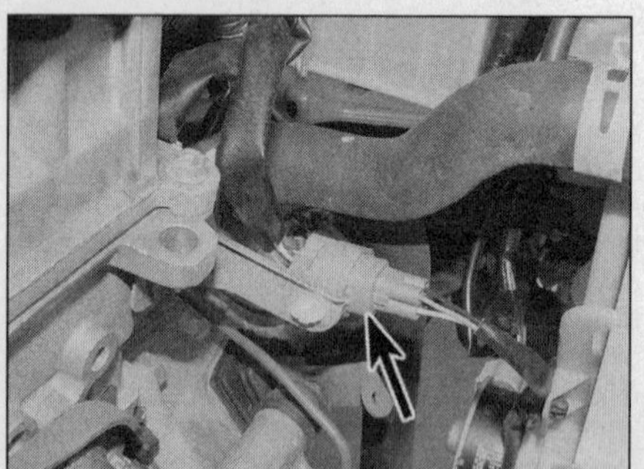

4.2a Models with the 1.0 litre engine have one sensor plug . . .

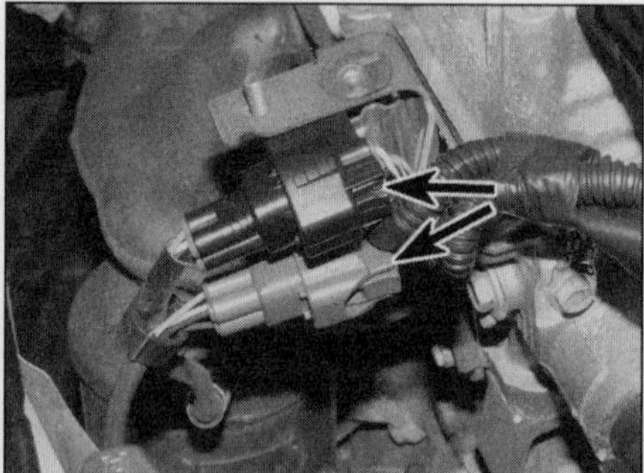

4.2b . . . while the 1.3 litre 2SZ-FE engine has two, at the front of the engine

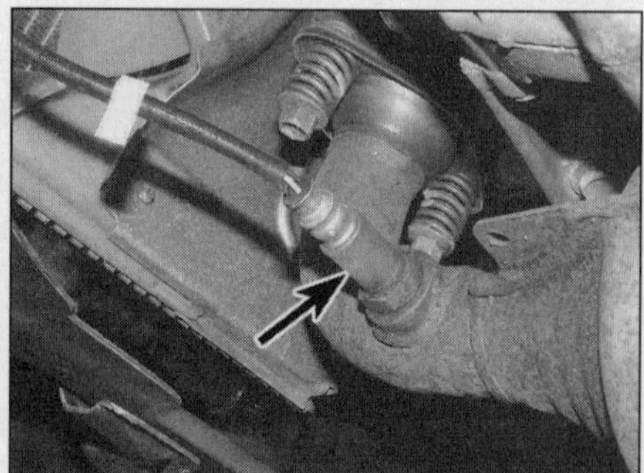

4.3a Front oxygen sensor (arrowed) – 1.0 litre engine

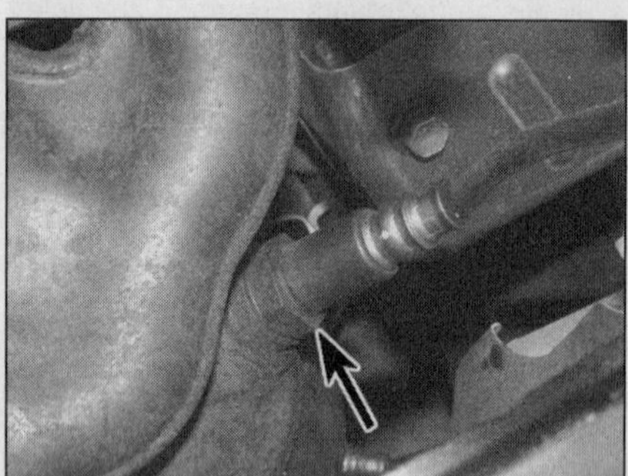

4.3b On the 1.3 litre 2SZ-FE engine, the front sensor is into the manifold

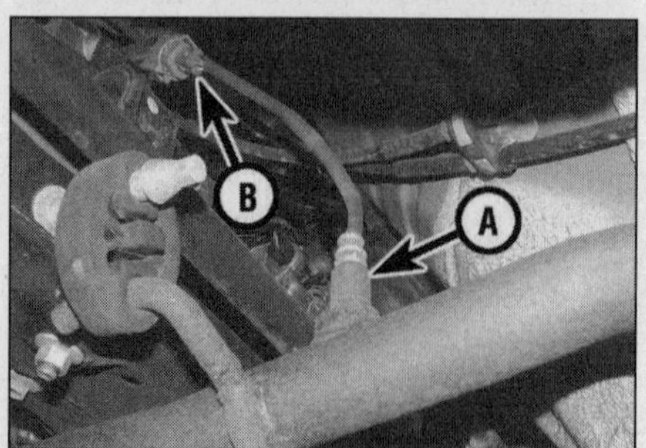

4.3c The rear oxygen sensor (A) is on top of the pipe – also visible is the sensor wiring plug (B)

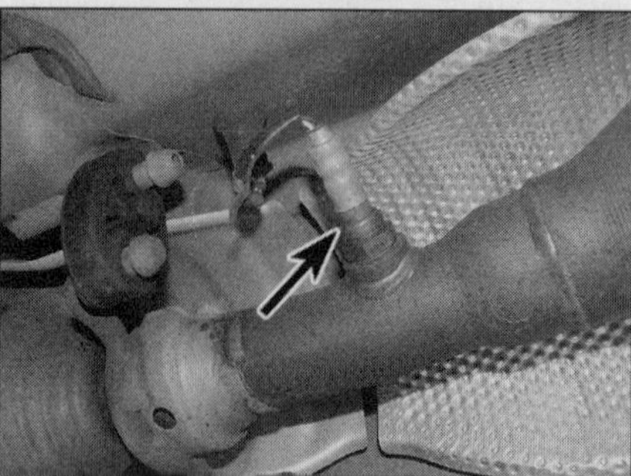

4.3d The rear sensor may also appear on the side of the pipe

5.2 Remove the nut and bolt from the manifold support bracket – 1.0 litre engine

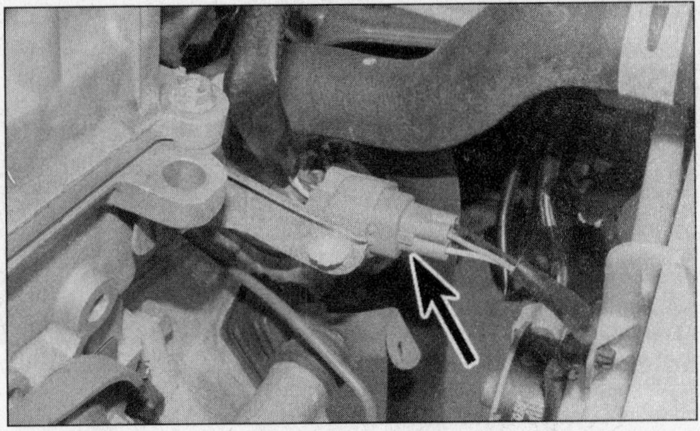

5.3 Disconnect the oxygen sensor wiring plug – 1.0 litre engine

Refitting

4 Refitting is a reversal of removal, noting the following points:

a) Clean the threads of the sensor and the threads in the exhaust manifold.

b) Ideally, the sensor should be tightened to the specified torque. However, unless a slotted socket is available, this will not be possible – use the figure quoted as a guide to hand-tightening using a spanner.

c) Reconnect the wiring, making sure that it is in no danger of contacting the exhaust or other moving parts.

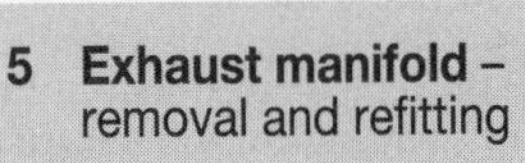

5 Exhaust manifold – removal and refitting

Warning: Allow ample time for the exhaust system to cool before starting work.

Removal

1 Jack up the front of the car, and support it on axle stands (see *Jacking and vehicle support*).

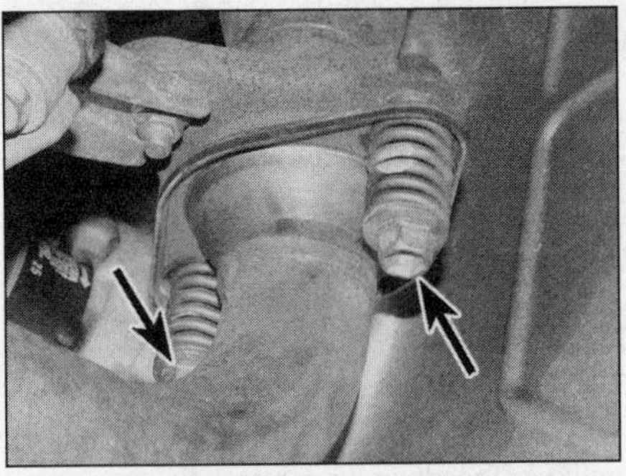

5.4a Remove the exhaust manifold-to-downpipe bolts . . .

5.4b . . . then separate the downpipe and lower it

2 Remove the nut and bolt (1.0 litre and 1.3 litre 2SZ-FE engines) or three bolts (1.3 litre 2NZ-FE engine) securing the manifold lower support bracket to the engine, and remove the bracket **(see illustration)**.

3 Trace the oxygen sensor wiring up to the connector plug(s), and disconnect it **(see illustration)**.

4 Remove the two bolts securing the manifold to the downpipe, and recover the springs. Lower the front part of the exhaust down (unhook the rubber mountings as necessary), and support the exhaust on an axle stand. Recover the 'metal O-ring' gasket from the joint – a new one should be used when refitting **(see illustrations)**.

5 On 1.3 litre 2NZ-FE engine models, remove the four bolts securing the heat shield on top of the manifold, and lift it off **(see illustration)**.

6 Unscrew and remove the three bolts and two nuts used to secure the manifold to the cylinder head **(see illustration)**. Use a wire brush and plenty of penetrating oil first if they appear to be rusty.

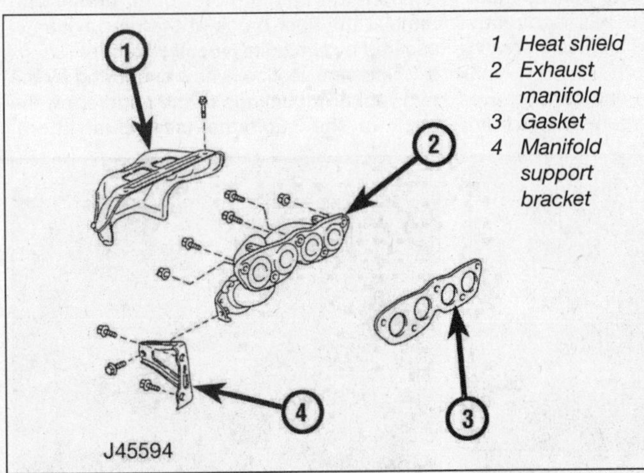

5.5 Exhaust manifold details – 1.3 litre 2NZ-FE engine

5.6 The exhaust manifold is secured by a nut either end, and three bolts

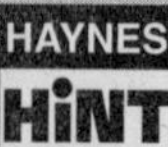

If a nut appears to be sticking, do not try to force it; tighten the nut back half a turn, apply some more penetrating oil to the stud threads, wait several seconds for it to soak in, then gradually unscrew the nut by one turn. Repeat this process until the nut is free.

7 Carefully withdraw the manifold from the cylinder head studs **(see illustration)**.

8 Recover the manifold gasket – a new one must be used when refitting **(see illustration)**. Examine the condition of the manifold mounting studs/nuts and bolts, and obtain new ones for refitting if necessary.

5.7 Removing the exhaust manifold

5.8 Recover the old gasket, and get a new one for refitting

Refitting

9 Refitting is a reversal of the removal procedure, noting the following points:

a) *Always fit new gaskets to the manifold-to-downpipe and manifold-to-head joints* ***(see illustrations)****.*
b) *It is recommended that new nuts are used as a matter of course – even if the old ones came off without difficulty, they may not stand being retightened. New components will be much easier to remove in future, should this be necessary.*
c) *If the old studs and bolts are re-used, clean the threads thoroughly to remove all traces of rust.*
d) *Tighten all fittings to the specified torque.*

5.9a Fit a new manifold-to-head gasket . . .

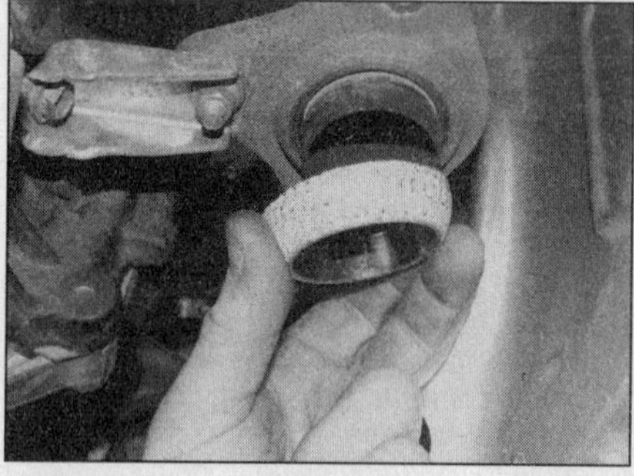

5.9b . . . and a new manifold-to-downpipe gasket

6 Exhaust system – component renewal

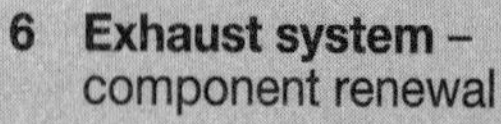

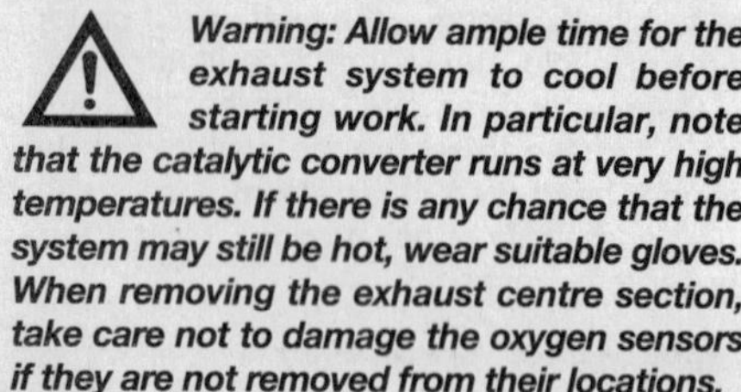

Warning: Allow ample time for the exhaust system to cool before starting work. In particular, note that the catalytic converter runs at very high temperatures. If there is any chance that the system may still be hot, wear suitable gloves. When removing the exhaust centre section, take care not to damage the oxygen sensors if they are not removed from their locations.

Removal

1 The original Toyota system fitted in the factory is in two sections. The centre section includes the downpipe, catalytic converter and centre silencer, and can be removed complete. The rear silencer can be removed and renewed separately.

2 To remove part of the system, first jack up the front or rear of the car and support it on axle stands (see *Jacking and vehicle support*). Alternatively, position the car over an inspection pit or on car ramps.

Centre section

3 Trace the wiring back from the front oxygen sensor, and disconnect the wiring connector. Unclip the wiring from any clips or brackets, noting how it is routed for refitting.

4 The wiring plug for the rear sensor must also be disconnected, and this is directly above and in front of the sensor itself – reach up under the car.

5 If a new exhaust section and catalyst are being fitted, unscrew the oxygen sensors from the old pipe, and fit them to the new section, using the information in Section 4.

6 Remove the two bolts at the front securing the manifold to the downpipe, and recover the springs. Lower the front part of the exhaust down, and support the exhaust on an axle stand. Recover the 'metal O-ring' gasket from the joint – a new one should be used when refitting.

7 Similarly, at the rear, remove the two bolts (and springs) securing the centre section rear flange to the rear silencer **(see illustration)**. Tap the flange if necessary, to separate it. Recover the 'metal O-ring' gasket from the joint – a new one should be used when refitting.

8 To create a little more room, unbolt and remove the floor brace at the rear, which is secured by two bolts **(see illustration)**.

9 The centre section is now supported by the two rubber mountings in the middle, on the back of the subframe **(see illustration)**.

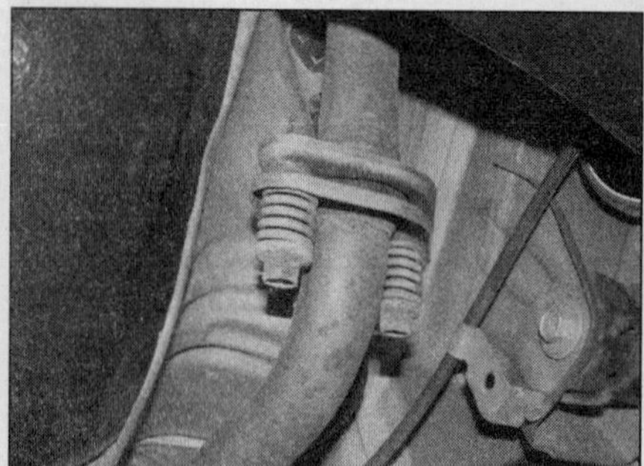

6.7 Exhaust rear silencer-to-centre section joint

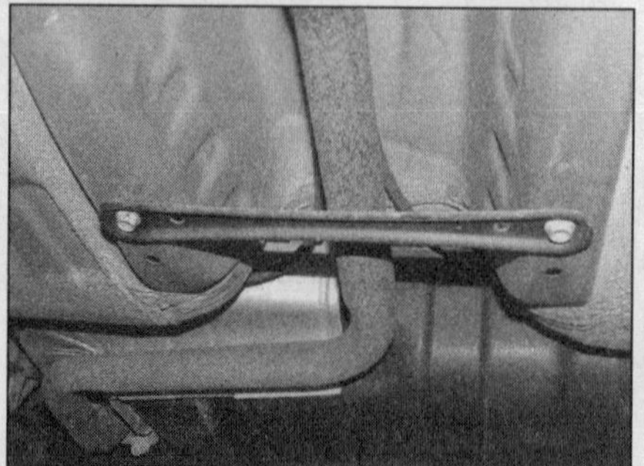

6.8 Remove the rear floor brace to allow the centre section to be lowered

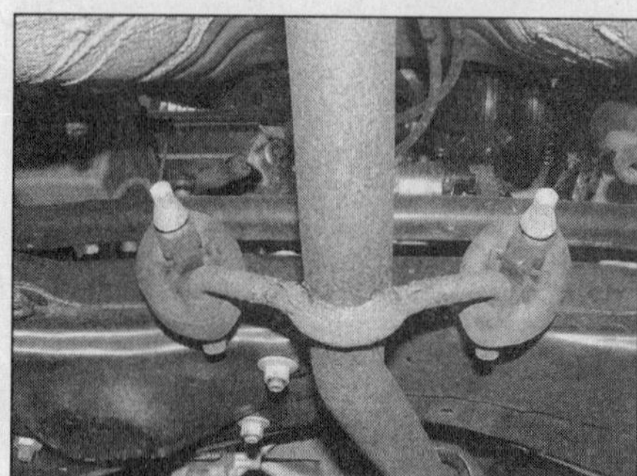

6.9 Exhaust centre section rubber mountings

6.11a Rear silencer front rubber mounting

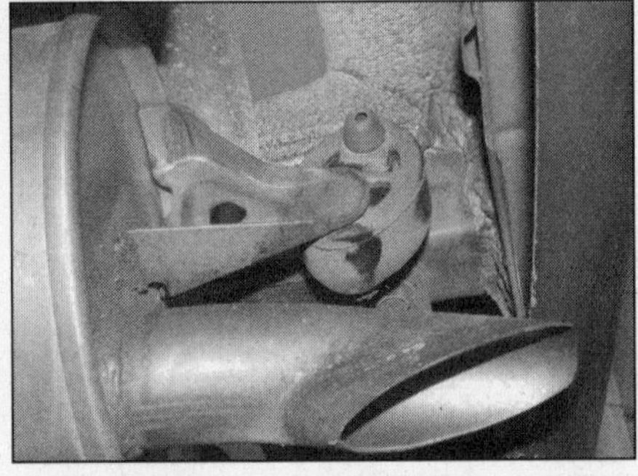
6.11b Rear silencer rear rubber mounting

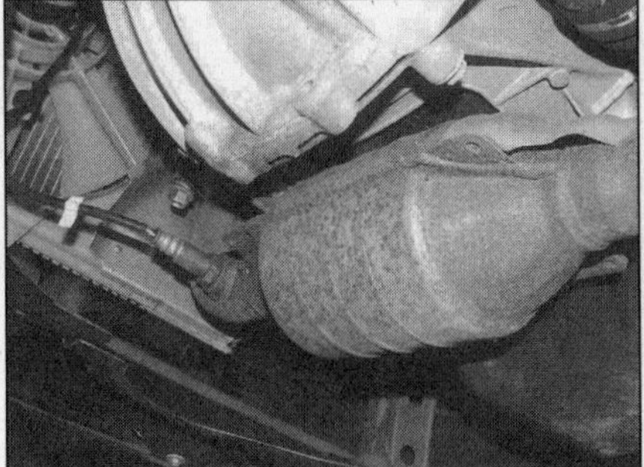
7.1 Catalytic converter – seen from below

Carefully unhook the rubbers, and lower the section to the floor.

Rear silencer

10 Remove the two bolts (and springs) securing the centre section rear flange to the rear silencer. Tap the flange if necessary, to separate it. Recover the 'metal O-ring' gasket from the joint – a new one should be used when refitting.

11 Unhook the rear silencer from the rubber mountings at the front and rear, and remove it from under the car **(see illustrations)**.

Refitting

12 Each section is refitted by a reversal of the removal sequence, noting the following points:

a) *Ensure that all traces of corrosion have been removed from the flanges or pipe ends, and renew all necessary gaskets.*
b) *If the flange bolts and springs are in poor condition, obtain new ones for refitting. Exhaust 'fitting kits' are now widely available from car accessory shops, which contain all the necessary parts (often including new gaskets).*
c) *Inspect the rubber mountings for signs of damage or deterioration, and renew as necessary.*
d) *If using exhaust assembly paste, make sure this is only applied to joints downstream of the catalyst.*
e) *Ensure that all rubber mountings are correctly located, and that there is adequate clearance between the exhaust system and vehicle underbody. Providing good-quality parts are fitted, the bolted flange joints should mean the exhaust alignment is preserved.*

7 Catalytic converter – general information and precautions

General information

1 The catalytic converter reduces harmful exhaust emissions by chemically converting the more poisonous gases to ones which (in theory at least) are less harmful. The chemical reaction is known as an 'oxidising' reaction, or one where oxygen is 'added' **(see illustration)**.

2 Inside the converter is a honeycomb structure, made of ceramic material and coated with the precious metals palladium, platinum and rhodium (the 'catalyst' which promotes the chemical reaction). The chemical reaction generates heat, which itself promotes the reaction – therefore, once the car has been driven several miles, the body of the converter will be very hot.

3 The ceramic structure contained within the converter is understandably fragile, and will not withstand rough treatment. Since the converter runs at a high temperature, driving through deep standing water (in flood conditions, for example) is to be avoided, since the thermal stresses imposed when plunging the hot converter into cold water may well cause the ceramic internals to fracture, resulting in a 'blocked' converter – a common cause of failure. A converter which has been damaged in this way can be checked by shaking it (do not strike it) – if a rattling noise is heard, this indicates probable failure.

Precautions

4 The catalytic converter is a reliable and simple device which needs no maintenance in itself, but there are some facts of which an owner should be aware if the converter is to function properly for its full service life:

a) *DO NOT use leaded petrol (or lead-replacement petrol, LRP) in a car equipped with a catalytic converter – the lead (or other additives) will coat the precious metals, reducing their converting efficiency and will eventually destroy the converter.*
b) *Always keep the ignition and fuel systems well-maintained in accordance with the manufacturer's schedule (see Chapter 1).*
c) *If the engine develops a misfire, do not drive the car at all (or at least as little as possible) until the fault is cured.*
d) *DO NOT push- or tow-start the car – this will soak the catalytic converter in unburned fuel, causing it to overheat when the engine does start.*
e) *DO NOT switch off the ignition at high engine speeds – ie, do not 'blip' the throttle immediately before switching off the engine.*
f) *DO NOT use fuel or engine oil additives – these may contain substances harmful to the catalytic converter.*
g) *DO NOT continue to use the car if the engine burns oil to the extent of leaving a visible trail of blue smoke.*
h) *Remember that the catalytic converter operates at very high temperatures. DO NOT, therefore, park the car in dry undergrowth, over long grass or piles of dead leaves after a long run.*
i) *As mentioned above, driving through deep water should be avoided if possible. The sudden cooling effect may fracture the ceramic honeycomb, damaging it beyond repair.*
j) *Remember that the catalytic converter is FRAGILE – do not strike it with tools during servicing work, and take care handling it when removing it from the car for any reason.*
k) *In some cases, a sulphurous smell (like that of rotten eggs) may be noticed from the exhaust. This is common to many catalytic converter-equipped cars, and has more to do with the sulphur content of the brand of fuel being used than the converter itself.*
l) *If a substantial loss of power is experienced, remember that this could be due to the converter being blocked. This can occur simply as a result of high mileage, but may be due to the ceramic element having fractured and collapsed internally (see paragraph 3). A new converter is the only cure in this instance.*
m) *The catalytic converter, used on a well-maintained and well-driven car, should last at least 100 000 miles – if the converter is no longer effective, it must be renewed.*

Chapter 5 Part A:
Starting and charging systems

Contents

Degrees of difficulty

Easy, suitable for novice with little experience 

Fairly easy, suitable for beginner with some experience 

Fairly difficult, suitable for competent DIY mechanic 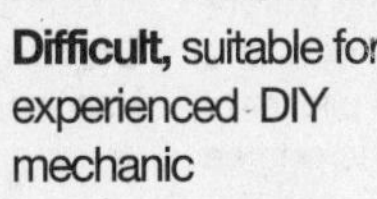

Difficult, suitable for experienced DIY mechanic

Very difficult, suitable for expert DIY or professional

Specifications

System type	12 volt, negative earth

Battery

Type	Lead-acid, low-maintenance or 'maintenance-free'
Charge condition:	
Poor	11.5 volts
Normal	12.0 volts
Good	12.5 volts

Alternator

Output (typical)	70, 80 or 90 amps
Regulated voltage	12.9 to 14.9 volts
Brush length (minimum)	1.5 mm

Starter motor

Rating:	
1.0 litre models:	
Up to June 2001	0.7 kW or 1.0 kW
June 2001 onwards	0.8 kW or 1.2 kW
1.3 litre models	0.8 kW or 1.0 kW
Brush length (minimum):	
1.0 litre models:	
Up to June 2001:	
0.7 kW type	6.0 mm
1.0 kW type	9.0 mm
July 2001 onwards:	
0.8 kW type	13.0 mm
1.2 kW type	9.0 mm
1.3 litre models	9.0 mm

Torque wrench settings	Nm	lbf ft
Alternator adjuster lockbolt	19	14
Alternator pivot bolt:		
1.0 litre models	44	32
1.3 litre models	54	40
Starter motor mounting bolts	39	29

1 General information, precautions and battery disconnection

General information

The engine electrical system consists mainly of the charging and starting systems. Because of their engine-related functions, these components are covered separately from the body electrical devices such as the lights, instruments, etc (which are covered in Chapter 12). Information on the ignition system is covered in Part B of this Chapter.

The electrical system is of 12 volt negative earth type.

The battery is of the low-maintenance or 'maintenance-free' (sealed for life) type and is charged by the alternator, which is belt-driven from the crankshaft pulley.

The starter motor is of the pre-engaged type incorporating an integral solenoid. On starting, the solenoid moves the drive pinion into engagement with the flywheel ring gear before the starter motor is energised. Once the engine has started, a one-way clutch prevents the motor armature being driven by the engine until the pinion disengages from the flywheel.

Precautions

It is necessary to take extra care when working on the electrical system to avoid damage to semi-conductor devices (diodes and transistors), and to avoid the risk of personal injury. In addition to the precautions given in *Safety first!* at the beginning of this manual, observe the following when working on the system:

- *Always remove rings, watches, etc, before working on the electrical system.* Even with the battery disconnected, capacitive discharge could occur if a component's live terminal is earthed through a metal object. This could cause a shock or nasty burn.
- *Do not reverse the battery connections.* Components such as the alternator, electronic control units, or any other components having semi-conductor circuitry could be irreparably damaged.
- If the engine is being started using jump leads and a slave battery, connect the batteries *positive-to-positive* and *negative-to-negative* (see *Jump starting*). This also applies when connecting a battery charger.
- Never disconnect the battery terminals, the alternator, any electrical wiring or any test instruments when the engine is running.
- Do not allow the engine to turn the alternator when the alternator is not connected.
- Never 'test' for alternator output by 'flashing' the output lead to earth.
- Never use an ohmmeter of the type incorporating a hand-cranked generator for circuit or continuity testing.
- Always ensure that the battery negative lead is disconnected when working on the electrical system.
- Before using electric-arc welding equipment on the car, disconnect the battery, alternator and components such as the fuel injection/ignition electronic control unit to protect them from the risk of damage.

Battery disconnection

Refer to the precautions listed in *Disconnecting the battery*, in the Reference section of this manual.

2 Electrical fault finding – general information

Refer to Chapter 12.

3 Battery – testing and charging

Testing

Standard and low-maintenance battery

1 If the car covers a small annual mileage, it is worthwhile checking the specific gravity of the electrolyte every three months to determine the state of charge of the battery. Use a hydrometer to make the check and compare the results with the following table. Note that the specific gravity readings assume an electrolyte temperature of 15°C (60°F); for every 10°C (18°F) below 15°C (60°F) subtract 0.007. For every 10°C (18°F) above 15°C (60°F) add 0.007.

	Ambient temperature	
	Above 25°C	**Below 25°C**
Fully-charged	*1.210 to 1.230*	*1.270 to 1.290*
70% charged	*1.170 to 1.190*	*1.230 to 1.250*
Discharged	*1.050 to 1.070*	*1.110 to 1.130*

2 If the battery condition is suspect, first check the specific gravity of electrolyte in each cell. A variation of 0.040 or more between any cells indicates loss of electrolyte or deterioration of the internal plates.

3 If the specific gravity variation is 0.040 or more, the battery should be renewed. If the cell variation is satisfactory but the battery is discharged, it should be charged as described later in this Section.

Maintenance-free battery

4 In cases where a 'sealed for life' maintenance-free battery is fitted, topping-up and testing of the electrolyte in each cell is not possible. The condition of the battery can therefore only be tested using a battery condition indicator or a voltmeter.

All battery types

5 If testing the battery using a voltmeter, connect the voltmeter across the battery and compare the result with those given in the Specifications under 'charge condition'. The test is only accurate if the battery has not been subjected to any kind of charge for the previous six hours. If this is not the case, switch on the headlights for 30 seconds, then wait four to five minutes before testing the battery after switching off the headlights. All other electrical circuits must be switched off, so check that the doors and tailgate are fully shut when making the test.

6 If the voltage reading is less than 12.0 volts, then the battery is discharged.

7 If the battery is to be charged, remove it from the car (Section 4) and charge it as described later in this Section.

Charging

Note: *The following is intended as a guide only. Always refer to the manufacturer's recommendations (often printed on a label attached to the battery), and always disconnect both terminal leads before charging a battery.*

Standard and low-maintenance battery

8 Charge the battery at a rate of 3.5 to 4 amps and continue to charge the battery at this rate until no further rise in specific gravity is noted over a four hour period.

9 Alternatively, a trickle charger charging at the rate of 1.5 amps can safely be used overnight.

10 Specially rapid 'boost' charges which are claimed to restore the power of the battery in 1 to 2 hours are not recommended, as they can cause serious damage to the battery plates through overheating.

11 While charging the battery, note that the temperature of the electrolyte should never exceed 37.8°C (100°F).

Maintenance-free battery

12 This battery type takes considerably longer to fully recharge than the standard type, the time taken being dependent on the extent of discharge, but it can take anything up to three days.

13 A constant voltage type charger is required, to be set, when connected, to 13.9 to 14.9 volts with a charger current below 25 amps. Using this method, the battery should be usable within three hours, giving a voltage reading of 12.5 volts, but this is for a partially-discharged battery and, as mentioned, full charging can take considerably longer.

14 If the battery is to be charged from a fully-discharged state (condition reading less than 12.2 volts), have it recharged by your Toyota dealer or local automotive electrician, as the charge rate is higher and constant supervision during charging is necessary.

4 Battery – removal and refitting

Note: *Refer to the warnings given in 'Safety first!' and in Section 1 of this Chapter before starting work.*

4.2 Loosen the clamp nut, and disconnect the negative lead . . .

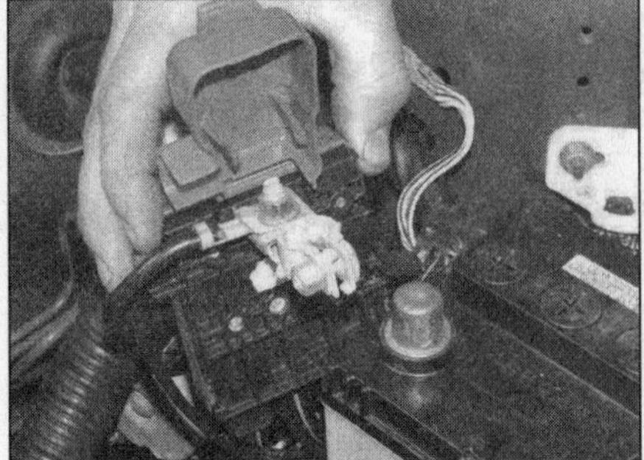
4.3 . . . followed by the positive lead

4.4a Loosen the clamp bar nuts, then unhook the rods . . .

Battery

Removal

1 The battery is located on the left-hand side of the engine compartment, on a platform above the transmission.

2 Loosen the clamp nut, then detach the earth lead from the battery negative (earth) terminal post **(see illustration)**. This is the terminal to disconnect before working on, or disconnecting, any electrical component on the car. Position the lead away from the battery.

3 Pivot up the plastic cover from the positive terminal, then loosen the positive lead clamp nut. Detach the positive lead from the terminal, and position it away from the battery **(see illustration)**.

4 Undo the two nuts securing the battery top clamp bar, unhook it from the tray at either side, and lift it off. On some models, the clamp bar nuts may also secure the accelerator cable support bracket **(see illustrations)**.

5 Lift out the battery, keeping it as level as possible. Take care, as the battery is heavy. If required, the plastic tray under the battery can also be removed **(see illustrations)**.

Refitting

6 Refitting is a reversal of removal. Reconnect the battery negative lead last. Make sure the battery terminals and clamps are clean before refitting, and that the clamp nuts are tightened securely.

Battery tray

7 A plastic tray is fitted under the battery, but the battery tray proper is welded in place, and cannot easily be removed.

5 Charging system – testing

Note: *Refer to the warnings given in 'Safety first!' and in Section 1 of this Chapter before starting work.*

1 If the charge warning light fails to illuminate when the ignition is switched on, first check the alternator wiring connections for security. If the light still fails to illuminate, check the continuity of the warning light feed wire from the alternator to the instrument panel. If all is satisfactory, the alternator is at fault and should be renewed or taken to an auto-electrician for testing and repair.

2 If the ignition warning light illuminates when the engine is running, stop the engine and check that the drivebelt is intact and correctly tensioned (see Chapter 1) and that the alternator connections are secure. If all is so far satisfactory, have the alternator checked by an auto-electrician for testing and repair.

3 If the alternator output is suspect even though the warning light functions correctly, the regulated voltage may be checked as follows.

4 Connect a voltmeter across the battery terminals and start the engine.

5 Increase the engine speed until the voltmeter reading remains steady; the reading should be approximately 12 to 13 volts, and no more than 14 volts.

4.4b . . . and lift the clamp bar off

4.4c The clamp bar nuts may also secure an accelerator cable support bracket

6 Switch on as many electrical accessories (eg, the headlights, heated rear window and heater blower) as possible, and check that the alternator maintains the regulated voltage at around 13 to 14 volts.

7 If the regulated voltage is not as stated, the fault may be due to worn brushes, weak brush springs, a faulty voltage regulator, a faulty diode, a severed phase winding or worn or damaged slip-rings. The alternator should be renewed or taken to an auto-electrician for testing and repair.

6 Alternator drivebelt – removal, refitting and tensioning

Refer to the procedure given for the auxiliary drivebelt in Chapter 1.

4.5a Lift out the battery . . .

4.5b . . . and take out the plastic tray

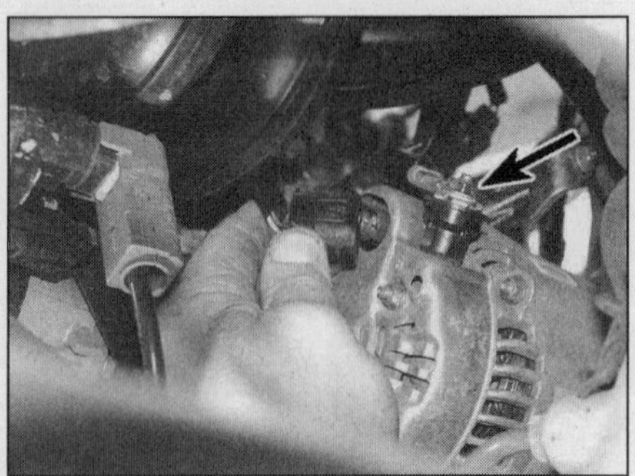

7.4a Disconnecting the main wiring plug – battery supply cable also arrowed (seen from below)

7.5a Remove the adjuster lockbolt . . .

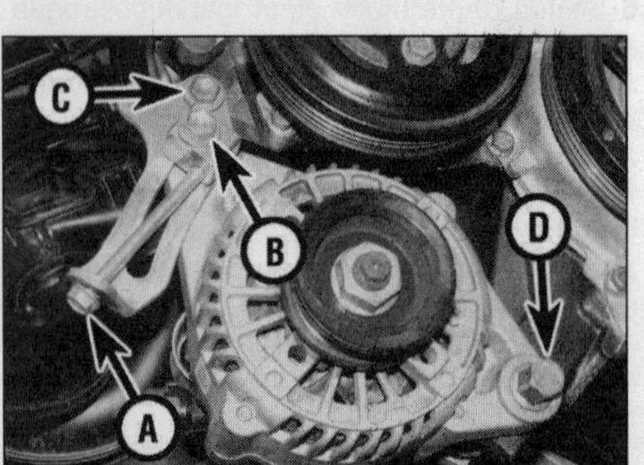

7.5c Alternator (1.0 litre engine) seen with engine removed

A Adjuster bolt
B Adjuster lockbolt
C Adjuster plate-to-engine bolt
D Lower pivot bolt

7.4b Battery supply cable (arrowed) – 1.3 litre 2NZ-FE engine (wiring plug is underneath)

7.5b . . . and the lower pivot bolt

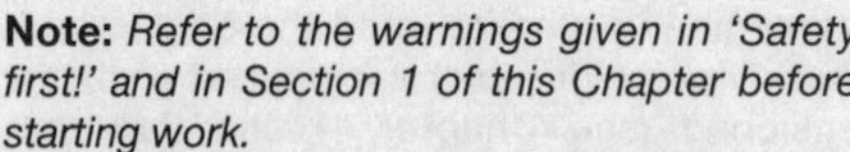

7 Alternator – removal and refitting

Note: *Refer to the warnings given in 'Safety first!' and in Section 1 of this Chapter before starting work.*

1 Loosen the clamp nut, then detach the earth lead from the battery negative (earth) terminal post. Position the lead well away from the battery.

Removal

2 Remove the auxiliary drivebelt as described in Chapter 1.

3 If not already done, jack up the front of the car, and support it on axle stands (see *Jacking and vehicle support*).

4 Disconnect the main wiring plug, then lift up the cover and undo the nut securing the battery supply cable. Recover any washers fitted, then lift off the supply cable and place it to one side **(see illustrations)**.

5 Support the alternator, then remove the upper adjuster lockbolt and lower pivot bolt, and remove the alternator from its mounting lugs on the engine **(see illustrations)**.

6 Manoeuvre the alternator out of the engine compartment. On the 1.0 litre or 1.3 litre 2SZ-FE engines, one way to do this is from below, which means unhooking the exhaust system from the two mounting rubbers on the rear of the subframe **(see illustration)**. The 1.3 litre 2NZ-FE engine is far easier in this respect, as the alternator just lifts out.

7 It is worth noting that, on the 1.0 litre or 1.3 litre 2SZ-FE engines, when the inlet manifold is removed as described in Chapter 4A, access to the alternator is excellent **(see illustration)**.

Refitting

8 Refitting is a reversal of removal, noting the following points:

a) Only fit the pivot and lockbolts hand-tight to begin with.

b) Ensure that the wiring is reconnected correctly, and that the retaining nuts are tight.

c) Refit and tension the auxiliary drivebelt as described in Chapter 1.

8 Alternator – testing and overhaul

If the alternator is thought to be suspect, it should be removed from the car and taken to an auto-electrician for testing. Most auto-electricians will be able to supply and fit brushes at a reasonable cost. However, check on the cost of repairs before proceeding, as it may prove more economical to obtain a new or exchange alternator.

7.5d Alternator upper adjuster bolt – 1.3 litre 2NZ-FE engine

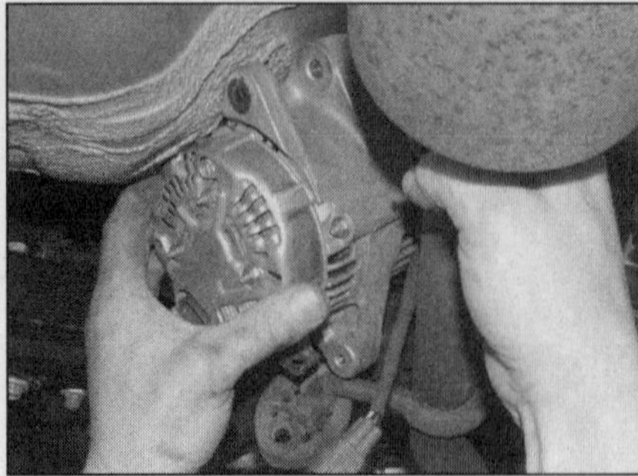

7.6 Removing the alternator from underneath, with the exhaust held aside

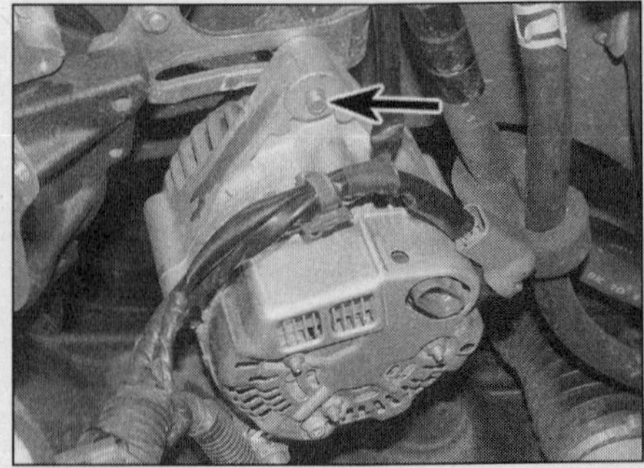

7.7 Alternator seen with the inlet manifold removed (1.0 litre engine) – adjuster lockbolt arrowed

10.3a Unclip the cover cap . . .

10.3b . . . then unscrew the nut and remove the wiring plug

10.3c Disconnect the lower wiring plug

9 Starting system – testing

Note: *Refer to the precautions given in 'Safety first!' and in Section 1 of this Chapter before starting work.*

1 If the starter motor fails to operate when the ignition key is turned to the appropriate position, the following possible causes may be to blame:

a) The battery is faulty.
b) The electrical connections between the switch, solenoid, battery and starter motor are somewhere failing to pass the necessary current from the battery through the starter to earth.
c) The solenoid is faulty.
d) The starter motor is mechanically or electrically defective.

2 To check the battery, switch on the headlights. If they dim after a few seconds, this indicates that the battery is discharged – recharge (see Section 3) or renew the battery. If the headlights glow brightly, operate the ignition switch and observe the lights. If they dim, then this indicates that current is reaching the starter motor, therefore the fault must lie in the starter motor. If the lights continue to glow brightly (and no clicking sound can be heard from the starter motor solenoid), this indicates that there is a fault in the circuit or solenoid – see following paragraphs. If the starter motor turns slowly when operated, but the battery is in good condition, then this indicates that either the starter motor is faulty, or there is considerable resistance somewhere in the circuit.

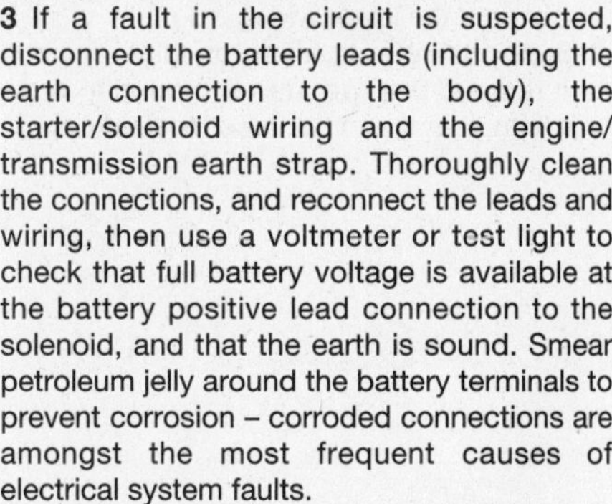

3 If a fault in the circuit is suspected, disconnect the battery leads (including the earth connection to the body), the starter/solenoid wiring and the engine/transmission earth strap. Thoroughly clean the connections, and reconnect the leads and wiring, then use a voltmeter or test light to check that full battery voltage is available at the battery positive lead connection to the solenoid, and that the earth is sound. Smear petroleum jelly around the battery terminals to prevent corrosion – corroded connections are amongst the most frequent causes of electrical system faults.

4 If the battery and all connections are in good condition, check the circuit by disconnecting the wire from the solenoid terminal. Connect a voltmeter or test light between the wire end and a good earth (such as the battery negative terminal), and check that the wire is live when the ignition switch is turned to the 'start' position. If it is, then the circuit is sound – if not, the circuit wiring can be checked as described in Chapter 12.

5 The solenoid contacts can be checked by connecting a voltmeter or test light between the battery positive feed connection on the starter side of the solenoid, and earth. When the ignition switch is turned to the 'start' position, there should be a reading or lighted bulb, as applicable. If there is no reading or lighted bulb, the solenoid is faulty and should be renewed.

6 If the circuit and solenoid are proved sound, the fault must lie in the starter motor. In this event, it may be possible to have the starter motor overhauled by a specialist, but check on the cost of spares before proceeding, as it may prove more economical to obtain a new or exchange motor.

10 Starter motor – removal and refitting

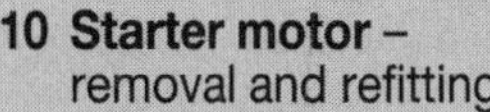

Note: *Refer to the warnings given in 'Safety first!' and in Section 1 of this Chapter before starting work.*

Removal

1 Loosen the clamp nut, then detach the earth lead from the battery negative (earth) terminal. Position the lead away from the battery.

2 Apply the handbrake, then jack up the front of the car and support on axle stands (see *Jacking and vehicle support*). Remove the engine left-hand lower cover for access to the starter from below.

1.0 litre and 1.3 litre 2SZ-FE engines

3 Working beneath the rear of the engine, unscrew the top nut and disconnect the wiring assembly from the starter motor. Also disconnect the lower wiring plug **(see illustrations)**.

4 Support the starter motor, then unscrew and remove the two starter mounting bolts from the transmission bellhousing, and withdraw the motor. Note that one of the bolts is also used to secure a bracket for the clutch fluid pipe **(see illustrations)**.

10.4a Remove the starter motor upper mounting bolt . . .

10.4b . . . and the lower mounting bolt . . .

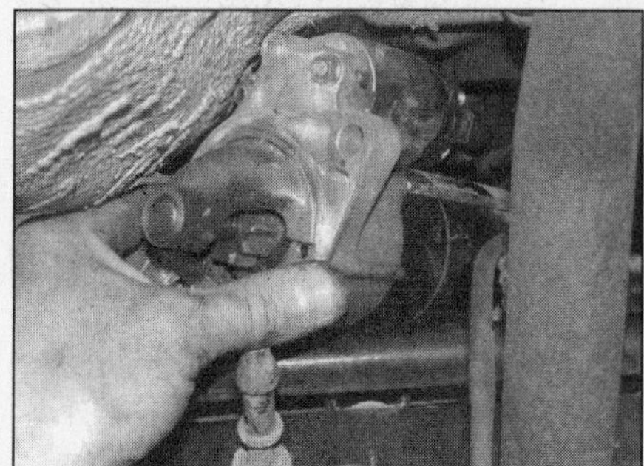

10.4c . . . and remove the starter motor from underneath

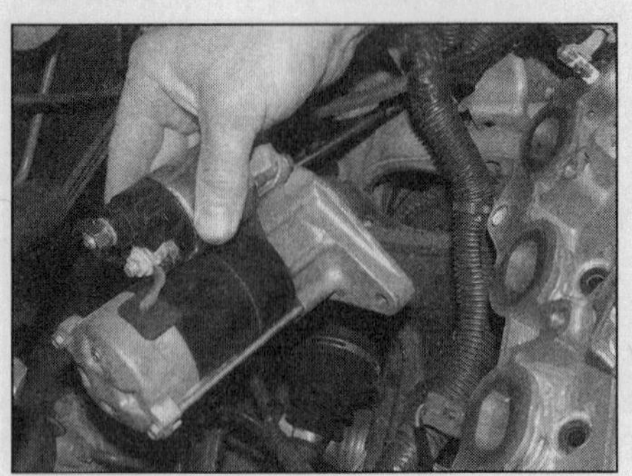
10.5 Removing the starter motor (seen with the inlet manifold removed – 1.0 litre engine)

5 Note that access to the starter motor is excellent when the inlet manifold is removed as described in Chapter 4A (see illustration).

1.3 litre 2NZ-FE engine

6 Working beneath the front of the car, unscrew the top nut and disconnect the wiring assembly from the starter motor. Also disconnect the lower wiring plug.

10.7 Starter motor lower mounting bolt – 1.3 litre 2NZ-FE engine

7 Support the starter motor, then unscrew and remove the two starter mounting bolts, and withdraw the motor (see illustration).

Refitting

8 Refitting is a reversal of removal, but tighten the mounting bolts to the specified torque.

11 Starter motor – testing and overhaul

If the starter motor is thought to be suspect, it should be removed from the car and taken to an auto-electrician for testing. Most auto-electricians will be able to supply and fit brushes at a reasonable cost. However, check on the cost of repairs before proceeding as it may prove more economical to obtain a new or exchange motor.

Chapter 5 Part B:
Ignition system

Contents

Degrees of difficulty

Easy, suitable for novice with little experience 	**Fairly easy,** suitable for beginner with some experience 	**Fairly difficult,** suitable for competent DIY mechanic 	**Difficult,** suitable for experienced DIY mechanic 	**Very difficult,** suitable for expert DIY or professional

Specifications

General

System type	Direct ignition system (DIS) with one ignition coil per cylinder, controlled by the engine ECU
Firing order	1-3-4-2
Location of No 1 cylinder	Timing chain end
Ignition timing (ECU-controlled)	8 to 12° BTDC @ idle

Ignition system data

Ignition timing	Controlled by the engine ECU
Ignition coil resistances (typical):	
Primary windings	0.4 to 0.6 ohms
Secondary windings	10 500 to 16 500 ohms

Torque wrench settings

Torque wrench settings	Nm	lbf ft
Ignition coil mounting bolts	8	6
Knock sensor	39	29
Spark plugs	18	13

1 General information and precautions

General information

The ignition system is integrated with the fuel injection system to form a combined engine management system under the control of the engine ECU (see Chapter 4A for further information). The main ignition system components include the ignition switch, the battery, the crankshaft speed/position sensor, the camshaft position sensor, the knock sensor, the four ignition coils, and the spark plugs.

A Direct Ignition System (DIS) is fitted, where the main functions of a conventional distributor are performed by a computerised module within the engine ECU. Based on the inputs from the crankshaft and camshaft position sensors (besides all the input on engine load, temperature, etc, from the fuel system sensors), the engine ECU is able to calculate precisely the best ignition timing for any given situation. The ECU sends out the trigger to each coil in the firing order, and the coils, which are fitted directly to their individual spark plugs, ignite the fuel/air mixture in the cylinders. Having one coil per cylinder gives an even greater control refinement, as the timing can be altered rapidly to suit changing conditions. Unlike the distributorless ignition systems seen on many modern cars, there is no 'wasted spark' with the coil-on-plug direct system, which theoretically means extended spark plug life. Greater potential reliability is also derived from having no ignition HT leads.

The information contained in this Chapter concentrates on the ignition-related components of the engine management system. Information covering the fuel, exhaust and emission control components can be found in the applicable Parts of Chapter 4.

Precautions

The following precautions must be observed, to prevent damage to the ignition system components and to reduce risk of personal injury:

a) Do not keep the ignition on for more than 10 seconds if the engine will not start.
b) Ensure that the ignition is switched off before disconnecting any of the ignition wiring.
c) Ensure that the ignition is switched off before connecting or disconnecting any ignition test equipment, such as a timing light.
d) Do not earth the coil primary or secondary circuits.

Warning: Voltages produced by an electronic ignition system are considerably higher than those produced by conventional ignition systems. Extreme care must be taken when working on the system with the ignition switched on. Persons with surgically-implanted cardiac pacemaker devices should keep well clear of the ignition circuits, components and test equipment.

2 Ignition system – testing

Note: *Don't overlook the possibility of a problem with the immobiliser system on a non-starting engine (see Chapter 12). Genuine Toyota keys will contain the necessary transponder chip, but ones supplied from other sources may not.*

1 If the engine either will not turn over at all, or only turns very slowly, check the battery and starter motor as described in Chapter 5A.

2 Check each coil's primary and secondary winding resistance as described in Section 3; renew the coil if faulty, but be careful to check carefully the wiring connections themselves before doing so, to ensure that the fault is not due to dirty or poorly-fastened connectors.

3 If the engine runs but has an irregular misfire, check the wiring plugs on the ignition coils, ensuring that all connections are clean and securely fastened. Also ensure that there is no damage to the wiring harness leading to each coil. It's not unknown for a coil to break down under load, especially in hot conditions. Check the spark plugs (by substitution, if necessary).

4 The most likely cause of total failure would be a problem with the crankshaft sensor (the camshaft sensor would perhaps be a close second). Check the condition of the wiring, and that the wiring plugs are clean and secure, as a first step. These components are both relatively easy to renew, but first weigh up their cost compared with having the car checked by a Toyota dealer or other specialist – the fault may lie elsewhere.

5 If simple checks fail to reveal the cause of the problem, the car should be taken to a Toyota dealer or suitably-equipped garage for diagnostic testing. A wiring connector is incorporated in the engine management circuit (under the steering column) into which a special electronic diagnostic tester can be plugged. The tester will locate the fault quickly and simply, alleviating the need to test all the system components individually which is a time-consuming operation that carries a high risk of damaging the ECU. If necessary, the system wiring and wiring connectors can be checked as described in Chapter 12.

3 Ignition coils – removal, testing and refitting

Removal

1 Make sure the ignition is switched off (take out the key).

2 On 1.0 litre and 1.3 litre 2SZ-FE models, remove the air cleaner and inlet duct as described in Chapter 4A.

3 On 1.3 litre models, take off the engine top cover, which is secured by four nuts/bolts.

4 Disconnect the wiring plug from the first coil to be removed **(see illustration)**. Though it seems unlikely that the wiring plugs could be mixed up, it might be safest to disconnect and remove one coil at a time. If all the coils are to be removed, mark them and their respective wiring plugs with labels or tape to indicate their fitted positions (No 1 at the timing chain end).

5 Remove the coil mounting bolt, then pull upwards to remove the coil from its spark plug **(see illustrations)**.

3.4 Disconnect the coil wiring plugs . . .

3.5a . . . then unscrew the coil mounting bolt . . .

3.5b . . . and pull upwards to remove the coil from its spark plug

4.5 Disconnect the knock sensor wiring plug, then unscrew and remove it

Testing

6 Using an ohmmeter, measure the resistances of the ignition coil's primary and secondary windings, and compare with the information given in the Specifications – measure between the two wiring plug terminals, then between each terminal and the connection for the spark plug. Confirm your findings with a Toyota dealer before renewing the coil – a variation in the resistances found is not likely to be significant, but a zero or infinity reading would suggest a problem with the coil.

7 Check for battery voltage at the positive terminal of the coil wiring plug, with the ignition temporarily switched on.

8 Toyota state that a spark test can be carried out, where the spark plug is removed from the engine, refitted to the removed and reconnected coil, and then the engine is cranked to see whether a spark is visible across the plug electrodes. This should only be attempted by the experienced DIYer, as there is a risk the spark could ignite fuel/air mixture rising from the open plug hole, and also a risk of damaging the car's ECU.

Refitting

9 Refitting is a reversal of removal. Repeat for the other coils as necessary.

4 Ignition system sensors – removal and refitting

Note: *Several of the more fuel-related sensors described in Chapter 4A may also have a bearing on the ignition system. Those listed below are simply the most likely to give rise to an ignition system fault.*

Crankshaft position sensor

1 Refer to Chapter 4A, Section 12.

Camshaft position sensor

2 Refer to Chapter 4A, Section 12.

Knock sensor

3 The sensor is used to detect the onset of pinking (pre-ignition or detonation, usually noticed in hot conditions, or when running on sub-standard or low-octane fuel). It is screwed into the engine block, and works by detecting the specific vibrations produced by pinking. When signalled by the knock sensor, the ECU retards the ignition timing until the pinking stops, then advances it slowly until it just recurs, thus maintaining maximum engine efficiency while avoiding the risk of engine damage.

4 To gain access to remove the sensor, first remove the throttle body and inlet manifold as described in Chapter 4A.

5 Disconnect the wiring plug from the sensor, then unscrew and remove it from the engine **(see illustration)**.

6 Refitting is a reversal of removal. It is essential that the sensor is tightened to the specified torque, as failure to do so may prevent it from working properly.

5 Ignition timing – checking and adjustment

Due to the nature of the ignition system, the ignition timing is constantly being monitored and adjusted by the engine management ECU, and nominal values cannot be given. Therefore, it is not possible for the home mechanic to check the ignition timing.

The only way in which the ignition timing can be checked is using special electronic test equipment, connected to the engine management system diagnostic connector (refer to Chapter 4A). No adjustment of the ignition timing is possible. Should the ignition timing be incorrect, then a fault must be present in the engine management system.

Chapter 6
Clutch

Contents

Degrees of difficulty

Easy, suitable for novice with little experience 	**Fairly easy,** suitable for beginner with some experience 	**Fairly difficult,** suitable for competent DIY mechanic 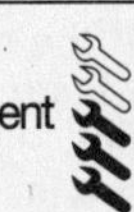	**Difficult,** suitable for experienced DIY mechanic	**Very difficult,** suitable for expert DIY or professional

Specifications

General

Clutch type	Single dry plate, diaphragm spring, hydraulically-operated release mechanism

Clutch disc

Diameter:	
1.0 litre engine models	190.0 mm
1.3 litre engine models	200.0 mm
Friction material thickness (new)	3.5 mm (approximate)
Rivet head depth (minimum)	0.3 mm
Disc run-out (maximum)	0.8 mm

Clutch pedal

Pedal height from floor	144.3 ± 5.0 mm
Pedal free play	5.0 to 15.0 mm
'Bite' point	25.0 mm (minimum) from floor

Torque wrench settings	Nm	lbf ft
Clutch fluid pipe unions	15	11
Master cylinder mounting nuts	12	9
Pressure plate-to-flywheel bolts*	19	14
Release arm support ball-stud	37	27
Slave cylinder mounting bolts	12	9

** Use new bolts.*

1 General information

The clutch consists of a friction disc, a pressure plate assembly, and a release bearing, sandwiched between the engine and the transmission. The clutch is operated hydraulically, with a master cylinder mounted on the bulkhead, attached to the pedal, and a slave cylinder mounted in front of the transmission, operating the clutch release arm. The clutch fluid reservoir is shared with the brake fluid reservoir on the top of the brake master cylinder.

The clutch friction disc is fitted between the engine flywheel and the clutch pressure plate, and is allowed to slide on the transmission input shaft splines.

The pressure plate assembly is bolted to the engine flywheel. When the engine is running, drive is transmitted from the crankshaft, via the flywheel, to the friction disc (these components being clamped securely together by the pressure plate assembly) and from the friction disc to the transmission input shaft.

To interrupt the drive, the spring pressure must be relaxed by the hydraulically-operated release mechanism. Depressing the clutch pedal operates the master cylinder, which in turn operates the slave cylinder and presses the release bearing against the pressure plate spring fingers. This causes the springs to deform and releases the clamping force on the pressure plate.

When the pedal is released, the diaphragm spring forces the pressure plate into contact with the friction linings on the friction disc. The disc is now firmly sandwiched between the pressure plate and the flywheel, thus transmitting engine power to the transmission.

Wear of the friction material on the friction disc is automatically compensated for by the operation of the hydraulic system. As the friction material on the disc wears, the pressure plate moves towards the flywheel, causing the clutch diaphragm spring inner fingers to move outwards. When the clutch pedal is released, excess fluid is expelled through the master cylinder into the fluid reservoir.

Warning: Hydraulic fluid is poisonous. Take care to keep it off bare skin, and in particular not to get splashes in your eyes. The fluid also attacks paintwork and plastics – wash off spillages immediately with cold water. Finally, the fluid is highly inflammable, and should be handled with the same care as petrol. The brake and clutch systems share the same fluid – any work on the clutch system which involves a great loss of fluid may mean that the braking system will have to be checked and bled on completion.

2 Clutch master cylinder – removal and refitting

Note: *Refer to the warning in Section 1 before proceeding.*

Removal

1 At the top of the master cylinder, release the spring clip on the supply hose, and pull off the hose. Either clamp the master cylinder fluid supply hose from the reservoir, or have ready a plug of some kind to fit to the hose end once the hose is disconnected. Plug or tape over the master cylinder pipe stub to prevent fluid loss or dirt entry **(see illustration)**.

2 Unscrew the slave cylinder supply pipe union at the side of the master cylinder. The union may be tight, especially if it has not been disturbed recently – use penetrating fluid (such as WD-40) and, ideally, a proper brake union spanner to loosen it. There will be some loss of fluid as the pipe is removed – wipe up any spillage, and rinse any painted surfaces with water (avoid getting water inside the master cylinder or the disconnected pipe, however).

3 Inside the car, move the driver's seat fully to the rear. To gain the best access to the top of the clutch pedal, consider removing the driver's seat as described in Chapter 11.

4 Using a pair of needle-nosed pliers, unhook and remove the pedal return spring, noting which way round it is fitted **(see illustration 6.2)**.

5 With the same pliers, pull out the spring clip from the clevis pin which secures the master cylinder pushrod. With the clip removed, pull out the clevis pin to detach the clutch pedal **(refer to illustrations 6.3a and 6.3b)**.

6 Remove the two master cylinder mounting nuts inside the car **(see illustration)**. Return to the engine compartment, and withdraw the master cylinder.

7 If the master cylinder is faulty, it must be renewed – at the time of writing, Toyota do not supply a repair kit. Check, however, on parts availability from other sources before purchasing a new unit.

Refitting

8 Refitting is a reversal of removal, noting the following points:

a) *Tighten the mounting nuts and fluid pipe union to the specified torque.*

b) *Ensure that the fluid hose connection is clean, and securely made (if the spring clip is no longer effective, replace it with a Jubilee clip).*

c) *Bleed the clutch on completion, as described in Section 5.*

3 Clutch slave cylinder – removal and refitting

Note: *Refer to the warning in Section 1 before proceeding.*

Removal

1 Anticipating some loss of fluid, unscrew the

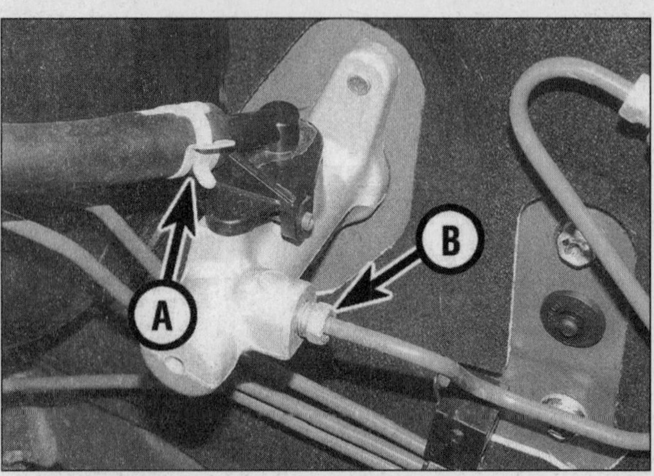

2.1 Clutch master cylinder fluid supply hose (A) and pipe union (B)

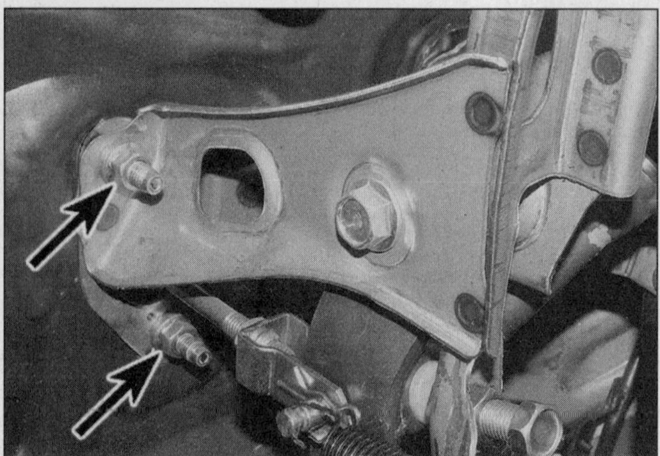

2.6 Clutch master cylinder mounting nuts

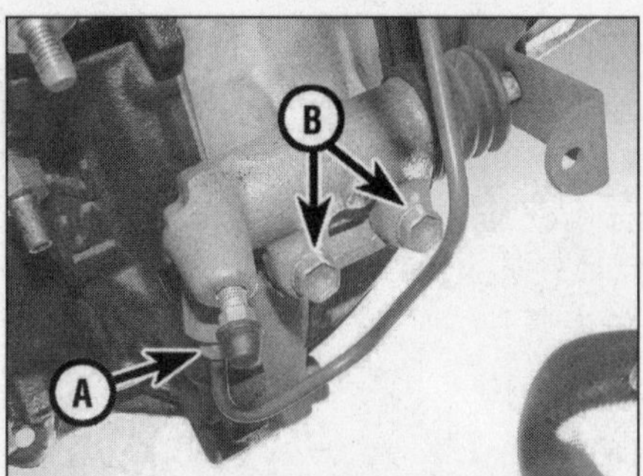

3.2a Slave cylinder union nut (A) and mounting bolts (B)

3.2b Some models have a heat shield fitted over the cylinder

fluid supply pipe union from the slave cylinder. The union may be tight, especially if it has not been disturbed recently – use penetrating fluid (such as WD-40) and, ideally, a proper brake union spanner to loosen it. If possible, cap or tape over the pipe end to reduce fluid loss.

2 Unscrew and remove the two slave cylinder mounting bolts, and withdraw the cylinder from the front of the engine/transmission. On some models, the two slave cylinder bolts are also used to retain a heat shield – note how this is fitted **(see illustrations)**.

3 If the slave cylinder is faulty, it must be renewed – at the time of writing, Toyota do not supply a repair kit. Check, however, on parts availability from other sources before purchasing a new unit.

Refitting

4 Refitting is a reversal of removal, noting the following points:

a) *Tighten the mounting bolts and fluid pipe union to the specified torque.*
b) *Bleed the clutch on completion, as described in Section 5.*

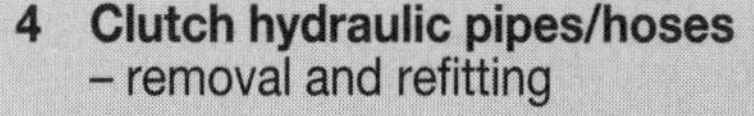

4 Clutch hydraulic pipes/hoses – removal and refitting

Note: *Refer to the warning in Section 1 before proceeding.*

Removal

Low-pressure supply hose

1 Because the clutch supply hose is located low down on the brake fluid reservoir, removing the hose will result in the loss of almost the entire contents. If this were allowed to happen, the amount of air introduced into the braking system would be such that the brakes would have to be completely bled on completion. If possible, therefore, have ready a plug of some kind, to fit to the reservoir once the hose is disconnected.

2 To remove the supply hose, remove the clips then disconnect the hose from the reservoir and master cylinder **(see illustration)**. Plug or tape over the master cylinder pipe stub, to prevent dirt entry into the system.

Pressure pipes

3 To remove the first pressure pipe, first wipe all traces of dirt from the master cylinder and slave cylinder. Unscrew the union connections on the master cylinder and at the bulkhead, then remove the pipe **(see illustration)**. The unions may be tight, especially if they have not been disturbed recently – use penetrating fluid (such as WD-40) and, ideally, a proper brake union spanner to loosen them.

4 The second pressure pipe is fitted between the flexible hose and the slave cylinder. Removal is similar to the other pipe – unscrew the hose-to-pipe union nut is on top of the transmission, and the union at the slave cylinder. The pipe is also clipped to the top of the transmission **(see illustration)**.

High-pressure flexible hose

5 The flexible hose is fitted between the rigid pressure pipes at the bulkhead and the transmission, to allow for engine/transmission movement. To remove the flexible hose, unscrew the union nuts at the hose-to-pipe connections on the bulkhead and transmission.

Refitting

6 Refitting is a reversal of removal, noting the following points:

a) *Tighten the fluid pipe unions to the specified torque.*
b) *Ensure that the fluid hose connections are clean, and securely made (if the spring clips are no longer effective, replace them with Jubilee clips).*
c) *Bleed the clutch on completion, as described in Section 5.*

5 Clutch hydraulic system – bleeding

Note: *Refer to the warning in Section 1 before proceeding.*

1 The correct operation of any hydraulic system is only possible after removing all air from the components and circuit; this is achieved by bleeding the system.

2 During the bleeding procedure, add only clean, unused hydraulic fluid of the recommended type; never re-use fluid that has already been bled from the system. Ensure that sufficient fluid is available before starting work.

3 If there is any possibility of incorrect fluid being already in the system, the hydraulic circuit must be flushed completely with uncontaminated, correct fluid.

4 If hydraulic fluid has been lost from the system, or air has entered because of a leak, ensure that the fault is cured before continuing further.

5 The bleed screw is screwed into the slave

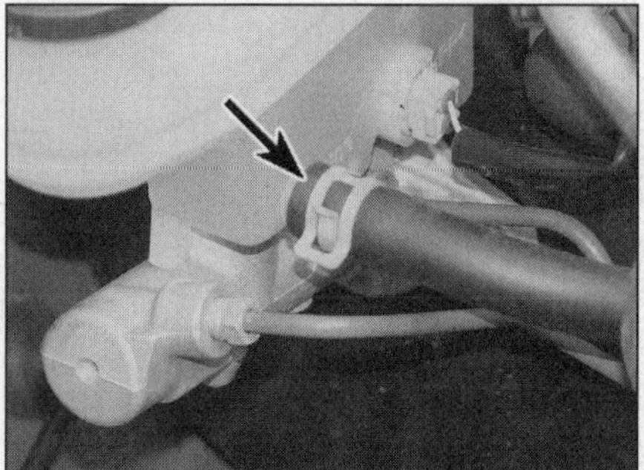

4.2 Clutch supply hose connection at the brake fluid reservoir

4.3 Clutch fluid pipe-to-hose connection at the bulkhead

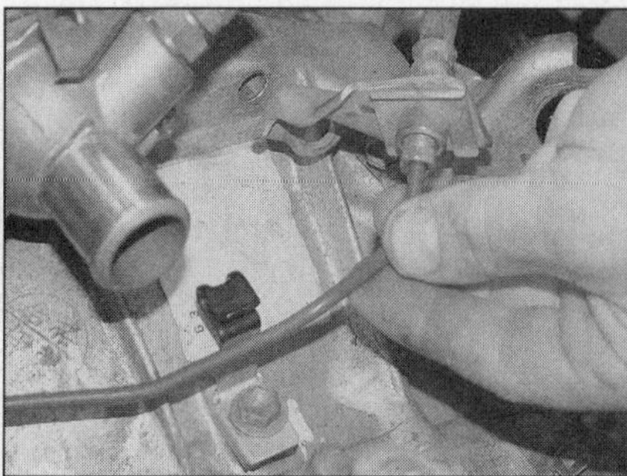

4.4 Unclip the pressure pipe from the top of the transmission

5.5 Clutch hydraulic system bleed screw

6.2 Unhook the pedal return spring using pliers

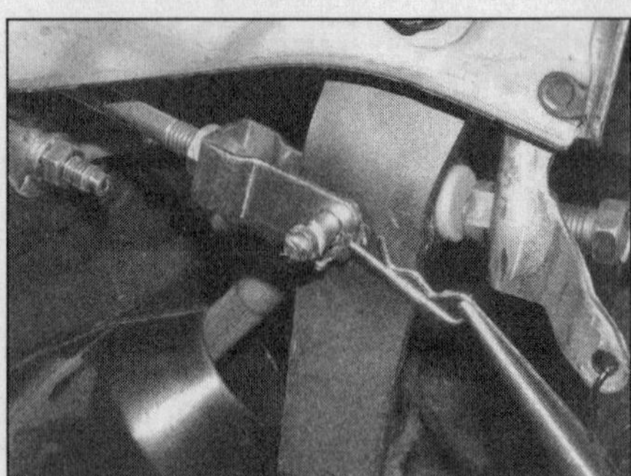

6.3a Pull out the spring clip . . .

cylinder at the front of the transmission **(see illustration)**.

6 First check that all the hydraulic hoses are securely fitted to the master and slave cylinders. Clean any dirt from around the bleed screw.

7 Unscrew the brake master cylinder fluid reservoir cap, and top-up the fluid level to the upper (MAX) level line; refit the cap loosely, and remember to maintain the fluid level at least above the lower (MIN) level line throughout the procedure, or there is a risk of further air entering the system.

8 There is a number of one-man, do-it-yourself bleeding kits currently available from motor accessory shops. It is recommended that one of these kits is used whenever possible, as they greatly simplify the bleeding operation, and reduce the risk of expelled air and fluid being drawn back into the system. If such a kit is not available, the basic (two-man) method must be used.

9 If a kit is to be used, prepare the vehicle as described previously, and follow the kit manufacturer's instructions, as the procedure may vary slightly according to the type being used; generally, they are as outlined below in the relevant sub-section.

Bleeding

10 The procedure for bleeding the clutch is identical to that for bleeding the brakes in Chapter 9, except that (obviously) the clutch pedal should be pumped to expel the fluid, and there is only one bleed screw to worry about. Any of the methods described in Chapter 9 may be used to bleed the clutch.

11 When bleeding is complete, and correct pedal feel is restored, check that the bleed screw is securely tightened and wash off any spilt fluid. Refit the dust cap to the bleed screw.

12 Check the hydraulic fluid level in the reservoir, and top-up if necessary.

13 Discard any hydraulic fluid that has been bled from the system; it will not be fit for re-use.

14 If the clutch is not operating correctly after carrying out the bleeding procedure, the master cylinder or slave cylinder may be faulty.

15 If the clutch system is being bled following a significant loss of fluid, check and if necessary bleed the braking system also, as described in Chapter 9.

6 Clutch pedal – removal, refitting and adjustment

Removal

1 Inside the car, move the driver's seat fully to the rear. To gain the best access to the top of the clutch pedal, consider removing the driver's seat as described in Chapter 11.

2 Using a pair of needle-nosed pliers, unhook and remove the pedal return spring, noting which way round it is fitted **(see illustration)**.

3 With the same pliers, pull out the spring clip from the clevis pin which secures the master cylinder pushrod. With the clip removed, pull out the clevis pin to detach the clutch pedal **(see illustrations)**.

4 Unscrew and remove the pedal pivot bolt/nut, and remove the pedal **(see illustration)**.

Refitting

5 Refitting is a reversal of removal. Tighten the pedal pivot bolt/nut securely, and check the operation of the clutch thoroughly before taking the car out on the road. Adjust the pedal if necessary, as described below.

Adjustment

6 For maximum accuracy, the clutch should be bled as described in Section 5 before carrying out any adjustments.

7 With the pedal released, measure the distance from the floor (directly below the pedal) to the top of the rubber pad (pedal height). Do not lift the pedal when making the measurement.

8 Check the pedal free play by depressing the pedal until resistance is felt, and measure the distance from the fully-released position to this point. It may be easier, therefore, to press the pedal by hand for this check.

9 If the first two measurements are correct, the final check is that the clutch pedal 'bite point' (the point where the clutch begins to engage) should be at least the distance specified from the pedal to the floor.

10 If the pedal height or bite point require adjustment, this is achieved by loosening the locknut and turning the adjuster bolt at the top of the pedal as necessary **(see illustration)**. Some trial-and-error will be required until the height falls into the range specified. Tighten the locknut on completion.

6.3b . . . then slide out the clevis pin to detach the pedal

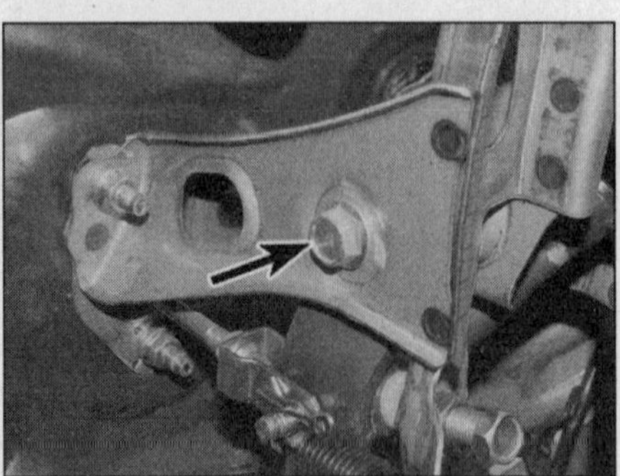

6.4 Clutch pedal pivot bolt

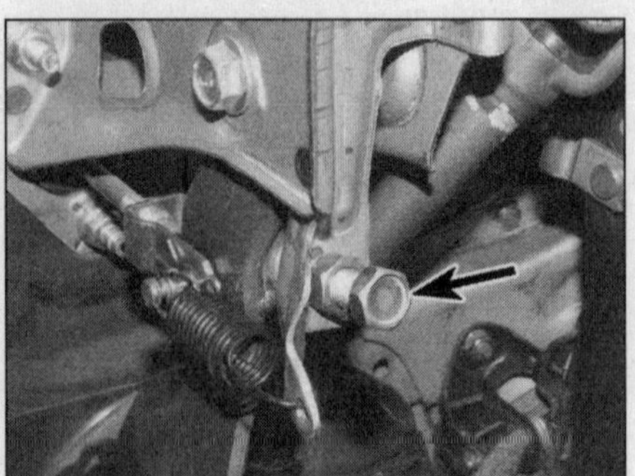

6.10 Pedal stroke adjuster bolt and locknut

11 If the pedal free play is excessive, loosen the locknut on the master cylinder pushrod, and turn the pushrod until the free play dimension is as specified **(see illustration)**. Tighten the locknut on completion.

6.11 Master cylinder pushrod locknut

7 Clutch assembly – removal, inspection and refitting

Warning: Dust created by clutch wear and deposited on the clutch components may contain asbestos, which is a health hazard. DO NOT blow it out with compressed air, or inhale any of it. DO NOT use petrol or petroleum-based solvents to clean off the dust. Brake system cleaner or methylated spirit should be used to flush the dust into a suitable receptacle. After the clutch components are wiped clean with rags, dispose of the contaminated rags and cleaner in a sealed, marked container.

Note: *Although some friction materials may no longer contain asbestos, it is safest to assume that they do, and to take precautions accordingly.*

Removal

1 Unless the complete engine/transmission unit has to be removed from the car (see Chapter 2B), the clutch can be reached by removing the transmission as described in Chapter 7A.

2 Unless a new clutch is being fitted, use chalk or a marker pen to mark the relationship of the pressure plate assembly to the flywheel.

3 Hold the flywheel stationary using a suitable tool engaged with the starter ring gear teeth – a piece of metal can be tightened to one of the bolt holes, or alternatively an assistant can use a wide-bladed screwdriver engaged with the teeth.

4 Working in a diagonal sequence, slacken the pressure plate bolts by half a turn at a time, until spring pressure is released and the bolts can be unscrewed by hand. Discard the bolts – new ones should be used when refitting.

5 Prise the pressure plate assembly off its locating dowels, and collect the friction disc, noting which way round the disc is fitted.

6 Remove the release arm boot from the transmission. Unclip the release arm from the ball-stud, and unclip the release bearing from the arm.

Inspection

Note: *Due to the amount of work necessary to remove and refit clutch components, it is usually considered good practice to renew the clutch friction disc, pressure plate assembly and release bearing as a matched set, even if only one of these is actually worn enough to require renewal. It is also worth considering the renewal of the clutch components on a preventive basis if the engine and/or transmission have been removed for some other reason.*

7 When cleaning clutch components, read first the warning at the beginning of this Section; remove the dust using a clean, dry cloth, and working in a well-ventilated atmosphere.

8 Check the friction disc linings for signs of wear, damage or oil contamination. If the friction material is cracked, burnt, scored or damaged, or if it is contaminated with oil or grease (shown by shiny black patches), the friction disc must be renewed. Check the depth of the rivets below the friction material surface. If any are at or near the surface of the friction material, then the friction disc must be renewed.

9 If the friction material is still serviceable, check that the centre boss splines are unworn, that the torsion springs are in good condition and securely fastened, and that all the rivets are tight. If any wear or damage is found, the friction disc must be renewed.

10 If the friction material is fouled with oil, this must be due to an oil leak from the crankshaft oil seal, or from the transmission input shaft. Renew the seal as described in the appropriate part of Chapter 2A or 7A, before installing the new friction disc.

11 Check the pressure plate assembly for obvious signs of wear or damage; shake it to check for loose rivets or worn or damaged fulcrum rings, and check that the drive straps securing the pressure plate to the cover do not show signs of overheating (such as a deep yellow or blue discoloration). If the diaphragm spring is worn or damaged, or if its pressure is in any way suspect, the pressure plate assembly should be renewed.

12 Examine the machined bearing surfaces of the pressure plate and of the flywheel; they should be clean, completely flat, and free from scratches or scoring. If either is discoloured from excessive heat, or shows signs of cracks, it should be renewed – although minor damage of this nature can sometimes be polished away using emery paper.

13 Check that the release bearing contact surface rotates smoothly and easily, with no sign of noise or roughness. Also check that the surface itself is smooth and unworn, with no signs of cracks, pitting or scoring. If there is any doubt about its condition, the bearing must be renewed.

7.15 Fit the friction disc with the spring hub facing outwards

Refitting

14 On reassembly, ensure that the disc contact surfaces of the flywheel and pressure plate are completely clean, smooth, and free from oil or grease. Use solvent to remove any protective grease from new components.

15 Fit the friction disc so that its spring hub assembly faces away from the flywheel; there may also be a marking showing which way round the plate is to be fitted **(see illustration)**. Depending on the type of centralising tool being used, the friction disc may be held in position at this stage.

16 Refit the pressure plate assembly, aligning the marks made on dismantling (if the original pressure plate is re-used), and locating the pressure plate on its locating dowels. Fit the pressure plate bolts, but tighten them only finger-tight, so that the friction disc can still be moved.

17 The friction disc must now be centralised, so that when the transmission is refitted, its input shaft will pass through the splines at the centre of the friction disc.

18 Centralisation can be achieved by passing a screwdriver or other long bar through the friction disc and into the hole in the crankshaft; the friction disc can then be moved around until it is centred on the crankshaft hole. Alternatively, a clutch-aligning tool can be used to eliminate the guesswork; these can be obtained from most accessory shops. The normal type consists of a spigot bar with several different adapters, but a more recent type consists of a tool which clamps the friction disc to the pressure plate before locating the two items on the flywheel. A home-made aligning tool can be fabricated from a length of metal rod or wooden dowel which fits closely inside the crankshaft hole, and has insulating tape wound around it to match the diameter of the friction disc splined hole.

19 When the friction disc is centralised, tighten the pressure plate bolts evenly and in

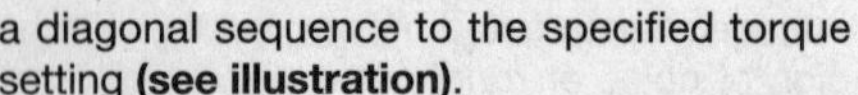

7.19 Tighten the pressure plate bolts to the specified torque

7.20 Apply a little grease to the input shaft splines

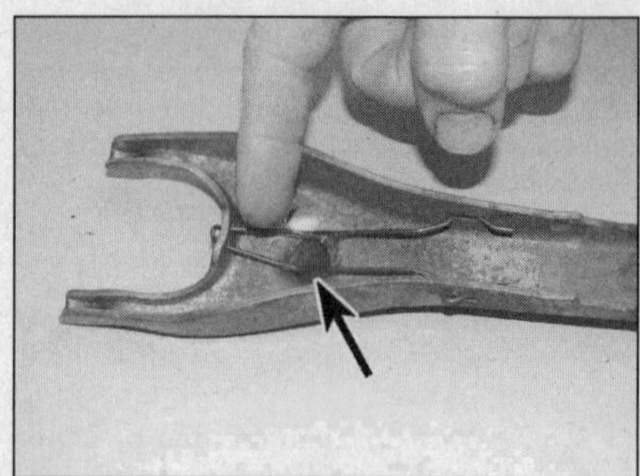

7.21 Apply grease to the clutch release arm pivot

a diagonal sequence to the specified torque setting **(see illustration)**.

20 Apply a thin smear of molybdenum disulphide grease to the splines of the friction disc and the transmission input shaft **(see illustration)**.

Caution: Do not apply too much grease, as there is a risk that it will contaminate the friction disc material.

21 Before refitting the release arm, apply a little grease to the arm pivot, and to the contact surfaces for the slave cylinder pushrod and release bearing **(see illustration)**.

22 Refit the transmission as described in Chapter 7A.

8 Clutch release bearing – removal, inspection and refitting

Removal

1 For access to the clutch release bearing, the transmission must be removed as described in Chapter 7A.

2 Unclip the release bearing from the release arm, and remove it.

Inspection

3 Note that it is often considered worthwhile to renew the release bearing as a matter of course regardless of its condition, considering the amount of work necessary to access it. Check that the contact surface rotates smoothly and easily, with no sign of noise or roughness, and that the surface itself is smooth and unworn, with no signs of cracks, pitting or scoring. If there is any doubt about its condition, the bearing must be renewed.

Refitting

4 Apply a little molybdenum disulphide grease to the release bearing contact points on the release arm.

5 Refit the transmission with reference to Chapter 7A.

Chapter 7 Part A:
Manual transmission

Contents

Degrees of difficulty

Easy, suitable for novice with little experience 	**Fairly easy,** suitable for beginner with some experience 	**Fairly difficult,** suitable for competent DIY mechanic 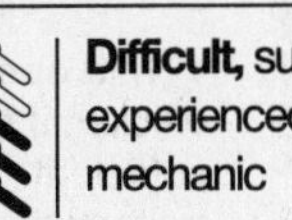	**Difficult,** suitable for experienced DIY mechanic	**Very difficult,** suitable for expert DIY or professional

Specifications

General

Transmission type	Five forward speeds, one reverse. Synchromesh on all forward gears. Gearchange linkage operated by twin cables
Transmission code:	
1.0 litre engine models	C551
1.3 litre engine models	C154
Transmission oil type	See end of *Weekly checks*
Transmission oil capacity	See Chapter 1 Specifications

Gear ratios

1st	3.545:1
2nd	1.913:1
3rd	1.310:1
4th	1.027:1
5th	0.850:1
Reverse	3.214:1
Final drive:	
1.0 litre engine models	4.294:1
1.3 litre engine models	3.250:1

Torque wrench settings

	Nm	lbf ft
Engine/transmission mountings:		
Left-hand mounting bolts	49	36
Rear mounting bracket bolts	49	36
Rear mounting through-bolt	64	47
Gear lever assembly mounting bolts	12	9
Oil filler/level and drain plugs	39	29
Reversing light switch	40	30
Shift/selector cable bracket bolts	11	8
Shift/selector lever assembly bolt	12	9
Starter motor mounting bolts	39	29
Sump-to-transmission stiffener plate bolts	39	29
Transmission-to-engine bolts	64	47
Vehicle speed sensor mounting bolt	11	8

1 General information

This Part of Chapter 7 contains information on the manual transmission. Service procedures for the automatic transmission system are contained in Part B.

The transmission is contained in a cast-aluminium alloy casing bolted to the engine's left-hand end, and consists of the gearbox and final drive differential - often called a transaxle. One of two different units may be fitted, depending on engine size – for the purposes of this manual, the two units differ only in detail.

The new 5-speed transmissions fitted to the Yaris follow a longstanding Toyota tradition of having a cable-actuated gearchange linkage, with gear selection via a floor-mounted lever and two cables.

Drive is transmitted from the crankshaft via the clutch to the input shaft, which has a splined extension to accept the clutch friction disc. From the input shaft, drive is transmitted to the output shaft, from where the drive is transmitted to the differential crownwheel, which rotates with the differential and planetary gears, thus driving the sun gears and driveshafts. The rotation of the planetary gears on their shaft allows the inner roadwheel to rotate at a slower speed than the outer roadwheel when the car is cornering.

The transmission selector mechanism causes the appropriate selector fork to move its respective synchro-sleeve along the output shaft, to lock the gear pinion to the synchro-hub. Since the synchro-hubs are splined to the output shaft, this locks the pinion to the shaft, so that drive can be transmitted. To ensure that gearchanging can be made quickly and quietly, a synchromesh system is fitted to all forward gears, consisting of baulk rings and spring-loaded fingers, as well as the gear pinions and synchro-hubs. The synchromesh cones are formed on the mating faces of the baulk rings and gear pinions.

Transmission overhaul

Because of the complexity of the assembly, possible unavailability of parts and special tools necessary, internal repair procedures for the transmission are not recommended for the home mechanic. The bulk of the information in this Chapter is devoted to removal and refitting procedures.

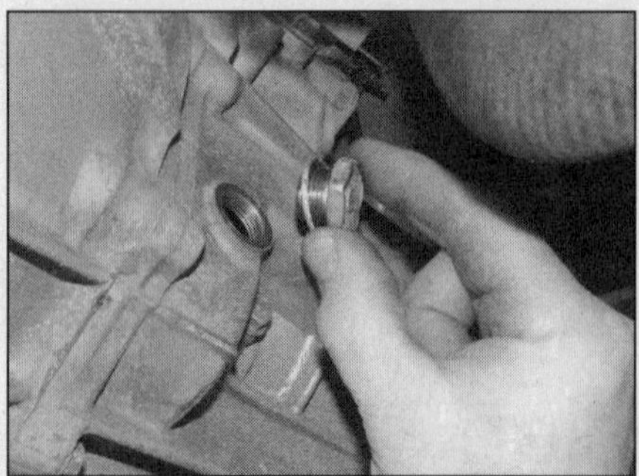
2.4 Transmission oil filler/level plug

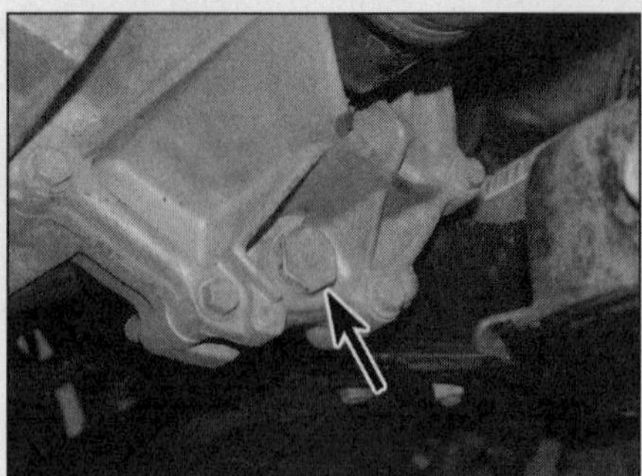
2.5 Transmission oil drain plug

2 Transmission oil renewal

1 This operation is much quicker and more efficient if the car is first taken on a journey of sufficient length to warm the engine/transmission up to normal operating temperature. However, especially on 1.0 litre models, take care to avoid burning yourself on the hot exhaust manifold/downpipe when working underneath the car.

2 Park the car on level ground, switch off the ignition and apply the handbrake firmly. For improved access, jack up the front of the car and support it securely on axle stands (see *Jacking and vehicle support*). Note that the car can be raised at the front only for oil draining, but for level checking, the car must be level (which can be achieved either by lowering the front, or raising the back of the car).

3 Remove the engine lower cover panels from under the car.

4 Remove all traces of dirt, then unscrew the filler/level plug from the front face of the transmission **(see illustration)**. This will probably be very tight – use a good-quality spanner or socket to unscrew it, and take care to avoid personal injury. A new washer should be fitted to the filler/level plug when refitting.

5 Wipe clean the area around the drain plug, which is situated on the base of the transmission, just in front of the left-hand driveshaft inner CV joint **(see illustration)**. Position a suitable container under the drain plug, and unscrew the plug – this will also probably be tight, and will need a new washer when refitting.

6 Allow the oil to drain completely into the container **(see illustration)**. If the oil is hot, take precautions against scalding. Clean the drain plug, being especially careful to wipe any metallic particles off the magnetic insert. Discard the sealing washer; it should be renewed whenever it is disturbed.

7 When the oil has finished draining, clean the drain plug threads and those of the transmission casing, fit a new sealing washer and refit the drain plug, tightening it to the specified torque wrench setting.

8 Refilling the transmission is an awkward operation. Above all, allow plenty of time for the oil level to settle properly before checking it. Note that the car must be parked on flat level ground (or if it is raised, it must be level) when checking the oil level.

9 Fill the transmission with the specified grade of oil (see *Lubricants and fluids*) until the oil just starts to run out **(see illustration)**. Allow any excess oil to flow out until the level stabilises.

10 When the level is correct, clean and refit the filler/level plug (with a new washer), then tighten it to the specified torque.

11 Refit the lower cover panels, and lower the car to the ground.

12 Although not strictly necessary, to ensure maximum accuracy take the car on a short journey so that the new oil is distributed fully around the transmission components, then check the level again on your return.

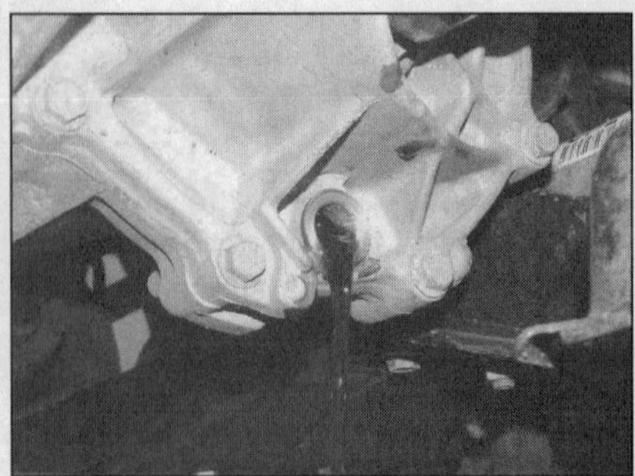
2.6 Remove the drain plug and allow the oil to drain

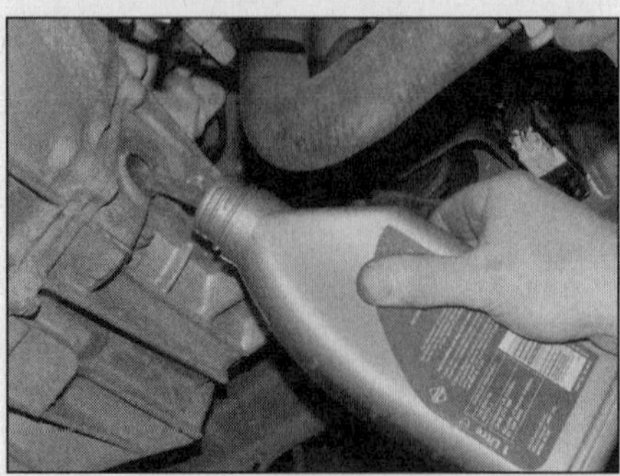
2.9 Fill the transmission until the oil starts to run out

3 Gear lever and gearchange cables – removal and refitting

Removal

Gear lever (gearchange unit)

1 Remove the centre console as described in Chapter 11.

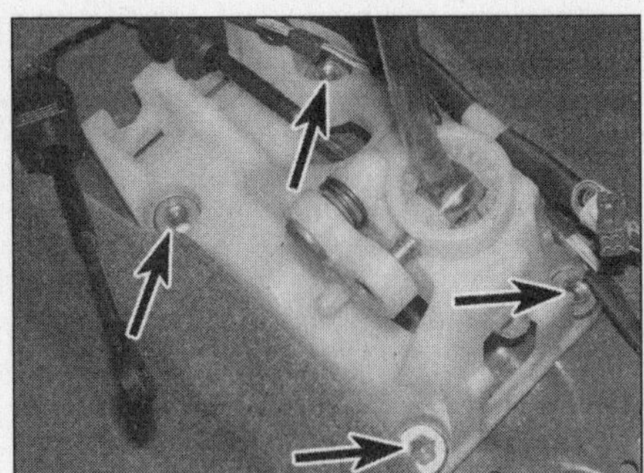
3.4 Gear lever assembly mounting bolts

3.6a On the left-hand cable, pull out the spring clip . . .

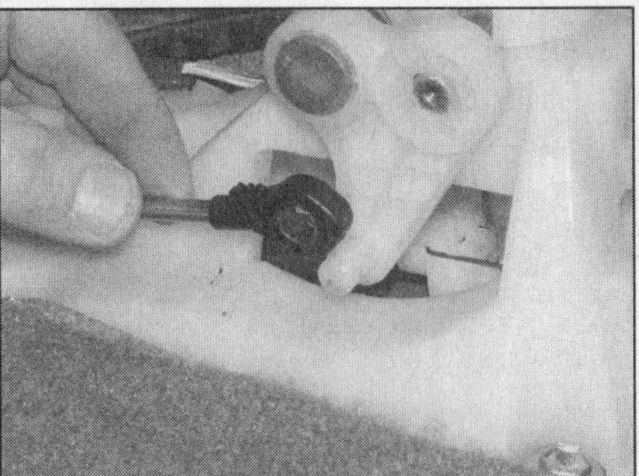
3.6b . . . then unhook the end fitting from the operating lever

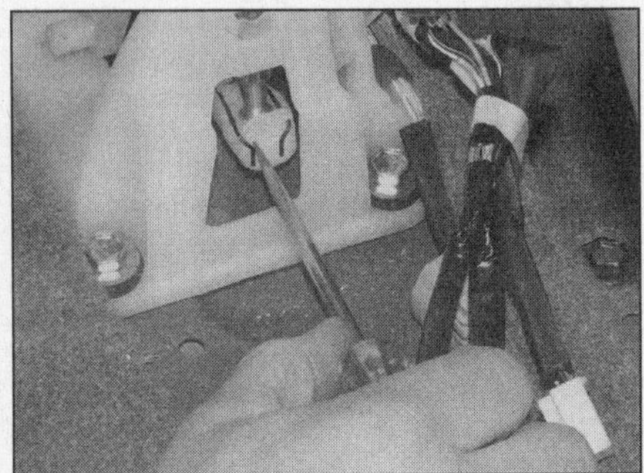
3.6c On the right-hand cable, spread the legs of the spring clip . . .

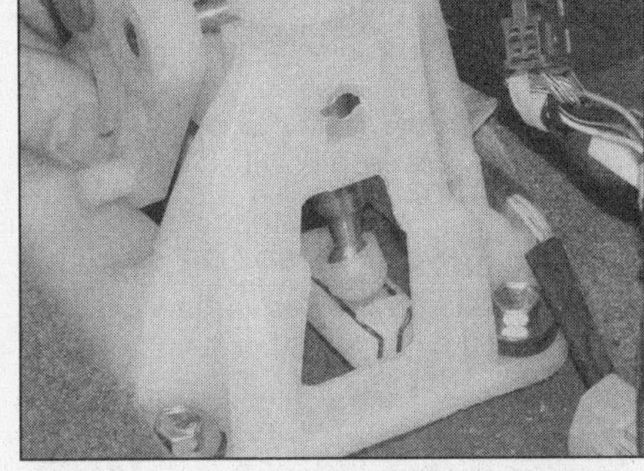
3.6d . . . and pull the end fitting down off the ball fitting

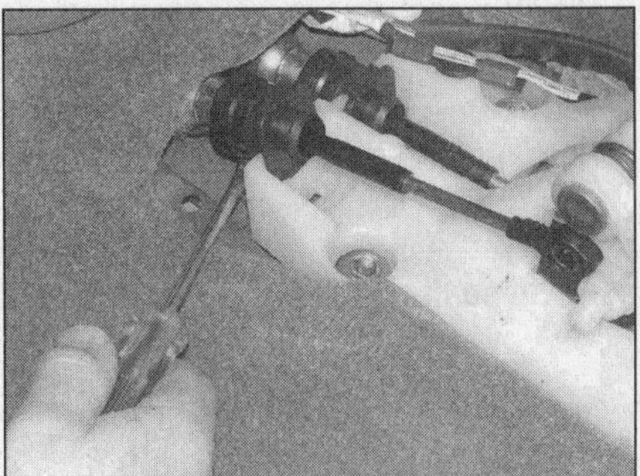
3.7 Both cables are detached at the front by prising upwards

2 Noting their positions for refitting, remove the spring clips and disconnect the two cables from their respective operating levers on the gearchange unit.

3 Lift the cables to detach the retaining plates from the front of the gearchange unit. Move the cables to one side.

4 Remove the four bolts securing the unit to the floor, then lift it out and remove it from the car **(see illustration)**.

Cables

5 Remove the centre console as described in Chapter 11.

6 Noting their positions for refitting, remove the spring clips and disconnect the two cables from their respective operating levers on the gearchange unit **(see illustrations)**.

7 Prise up the cables to detach their collars from the front of the gearchange unit **(see illustration)**.

8 Jack up the front of the car, and support it on axle stands (see *Jacking and vehicle support*).

9 Under the car, remove the two bolts securing the cables' floor plate/grommet, and also the bolt from the cable bracket attached to the underside of the car.

10 With the cables free to move, draw them through from the inside of the car, and let them hang down. Take care not to kink or bend the cables during removal. Check for any further mounting brackets, clips, or ties, and disconnect them as necessary. If preferred, the car can now be lowered to the ground.

11 In the engine compartment, slide out the metal clips used to hold the cables to the support bracket on the transmission, noting their positions. Alternatively (and depending on the nature of the work being carried out), the support bracket itself may be unbolted from the transmission housing, with the cables still attached.

12 Again noting their positions for refitting, pull out the spring clips and recover the washers, then unhook the cable end fittings from the transmission shift/select mechanism. The cables can now be removed completely, taking care not to kink or bend the cables as they are removed.

Refitting

13 Refitting is a reversal of removal. Check that all gears can be selected before taking the car out on the road.

4 Vehicle speed sensor – removal and refitting

Refer to Chapter 4A, Section 12.

5 Reversing light switch – removal and refitting

Removal

1 The switch is located on the top of the transmission, behind the shift/selector lever assembly. With the transmission fitted, the switch is partly obscured by the battery tray **(see illustration)**.

2 Trace the wiring from the switch, and disconnect it at the in-line connector, which is on the front of the unit **(see illustration)**.

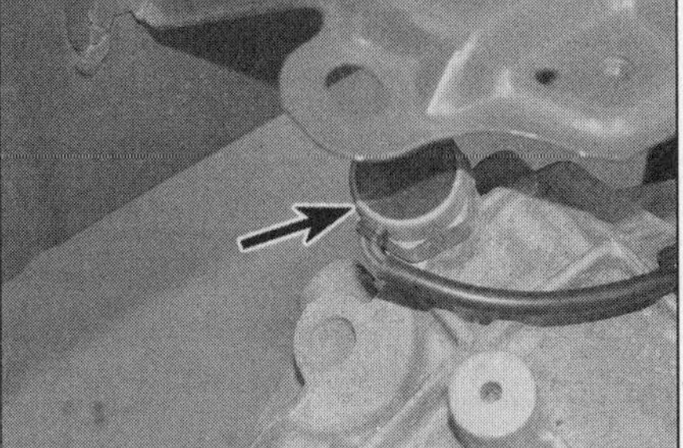
5.1 With the transmission in place, the reversing light switch is below the battery tray

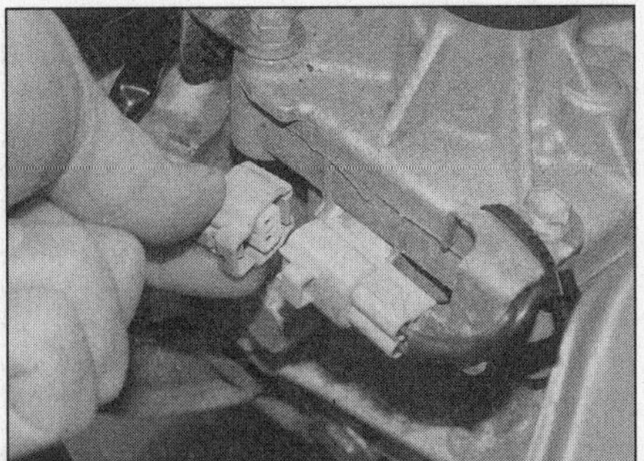
5.2 Disconnect the reversing light switch wiring plug on the front of the transmission

6.4 The driveshaft oil seals can be prised out of the casing

3 Unscrew and remove the switch from the top of the transmission, and remove it.

Refitting

4 Refitting is a reversal of removal. Tighten the switch securely.

6 Oil seals – renewal

1 Oil leaks frequently occur due to wear or deterioration of the driveshaft oil seals, or even the vehicle speed sensor O-ring. Renewal of these seals is relatively easy, since the repairs can be performed without removing the transmission from the car.

Driveshaft oil seals

2 The driveshaft oil seals are located at the sides of the transmission, where the driveshafts enter the transmission. If leakage at the seal is suspected, raise the car and support it securely on axle stands. If the seal is leaking, oil will be found on the side of the transmission below the driveshaft.

3 Refer to Chapter 8 and remove the appropriate driveshaft.

4 Using a large screwdriver or lever, carefully prise the oil seal out of the transmission casing, taking care not to damage the transmission casing **(see illustration)**.

5 Wipe clean the oil seal seating in the transmission casing.

6 Dip the new oil seal in clean oil, then press it a little way into the casing by hand, making sure that it is square to its seating.

7 Using suitable tubing or a large socket, carefully drive the oil seal fully into the casing until it contacts the seating.

8 Refit the driveshaft with reference to Chapter 8.

Vehicle speed sensor oil seal

9 Refer to Chapter 4A, Section 12.

7 Transmission – removal and refitting

Note: *Read through this procedure before starting work to see what is involved, particularly in terms of lifting equipment. Depending on the facilities available, the home mechanic may prefer to remove the engine and transmission together, then separate them on the bench, as described in Chapter 2B. The help of an assistant is highly recommended if the transmission is to be removed (and later refitted) on its own.*

Removal

1 Remove the air cleaner as described in Chapter 4A.

2 Remove the battery as described in Chapter 5A. Also working from the information in Chapter 5A, remove the starter motor.

3 Pull out the spring clips and recover the washers, then unhook the gearchange cable end fittings from the transmission shift/select mechanism, noting their fitted positions **(see illustrations)**. Move the cables clear of the transmission, taking care not to kink or bend them.

4 Again noting their positions for refitting, slide out the metal clips used to hold the gearchange cables to the support bracket on the transmission, noting their positions **(see illustrations)**. Alternatively, the support bracket itself may be unbolted from the transmission housing, with the cables still attached.

5 Unbolt and unclip the rigid pipe from the top of the transmission **(see illustration)**.

6 Unbolt the clutch slave cylinder from the front of the transmission. As the slave cylinder is released, wrap the plunger up with tape **(see illustration)**. If care is taken not to bend the hydraulic pipe, the cylinder need not be

7.3a Pull out the spring clips . . .

7.3b . . . then take off the large washers and lift off the cable end fittings

7.4a Slide out the metal retaining clips . . .

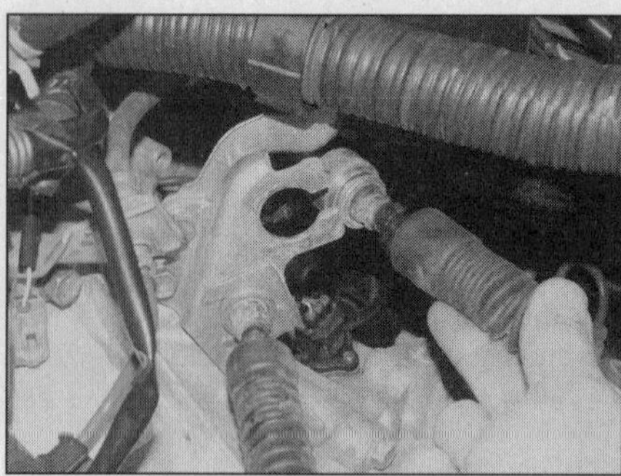

7.4b . . . and unhook the cables from the support bracket

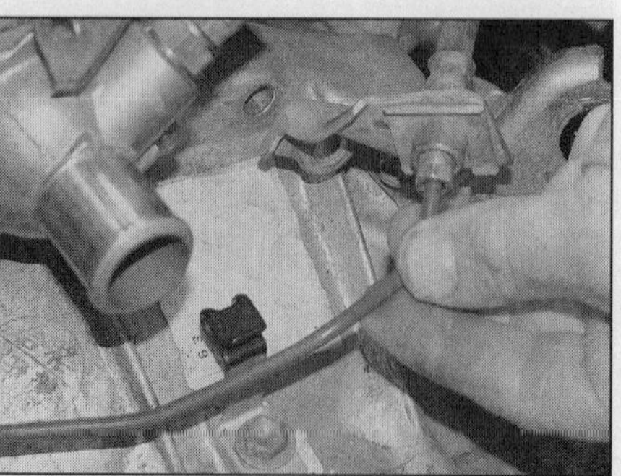

7.5 Unclip and unbolt the clutch fluid hose and pipe from the transmission

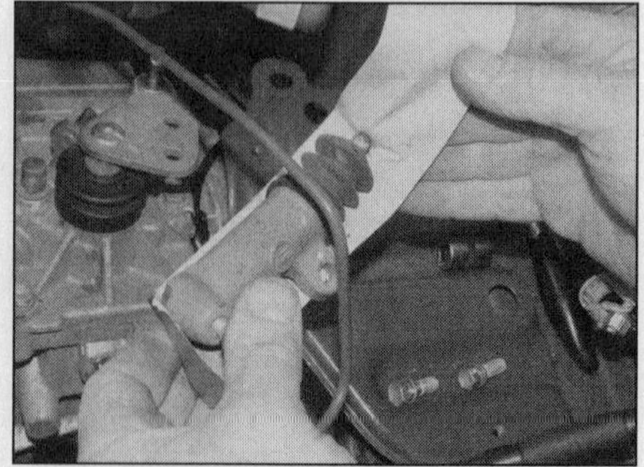

7.6 Unbolt the slave cylinder and wrap the plunger up with tape

7.7 Unbolt the earth strap from the transmission mounting

7.8 Unbolt the engine wiring harness from the gear cable support bracket

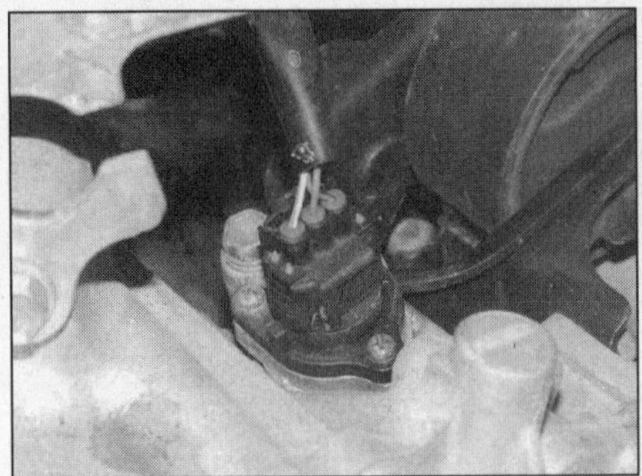
7.9 Unplug the vehicle speed sensor

disconnected, which saves bleeding the clutch later. If possible, tie the cylinder and its pipe up clear of the working area.

7 Unbolt and remove the earth strap from the engine left-hand mounting bracket **(see illustration)**.

8 Unbolt the engine wiring harness from the clip near the gearchange cable support bracket **(see illustration)**.

9 Disconnect the wiring plug from the vehicle speed sensor on top of the transmission **(see illustration)**.

10 Trace the wiring from the reversing light switch and disconnect it at the in-line connector. Unclip the wiring from the transmission **(see illustrations)**.

11 Remove the two uppermost transmission-to-engine bolts – access to these is hampered by the coolant hoses and wiring at the end of the cylinder head, but should still be possible **(see illustration)**.

12 Jack up the front of the car, and support it on axle stands (see *Jacking and vehicle support*). The car must be raised sufficiently that the transmission can be lowered out and removed underneath. Consideration should also be given to the need to support the engine, once the rear and left-hand mountings are disconnected.

13 Unscrew the fasteners and remove the engine left- and right-hand lower covers from under the car.

14 Remove both driveshafts as described in Chapter 8.

15 Just loosen ('crack') the two front transmission-to-engine bolts, but leave them in place for now – this avoids using any substantial force to remove the bolts when the transmission is only supported on a jack **(see illustration)**. Similarly, loosen but do not remove the six bolts securing the sump-to-transmission stiffener plate.

16 Using a substantial hydraulic ('trolley') jack with a block of wood, raise the transmission slightly, to take the weight off its mountings. Supporting the transmission securely in this way can be difficult to achieve – due to its shape, there is a danger the transmission will roll off once disconnected. For this reason, it pays to have an assistant on hand, to steady the unit as it is lowered out.

17 Before the engine rear and left-hand mountings are disconnected, the engine must be supported, preferably from above, using either an engine crane or support bar **(see illustration)**. There must be scope for lowering the transmission end of the engine. If the engine is supported from below, using another jack (and block of wood, to protect the sump), this seriously reduces the working room for removing the transmission. Do not jack under the sump-to-transmission stiffener plate, as this must be removed as part of the procedure.

18 With the engine securely supported, first remove the two lower left-hand mounting-to-

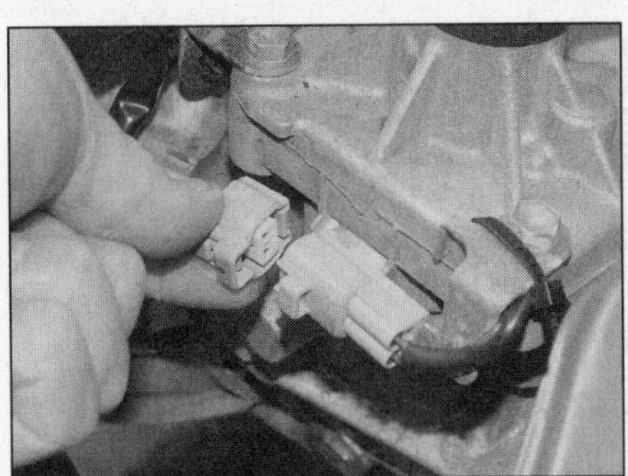
7.10a Disconnect the reversing light switch . . .

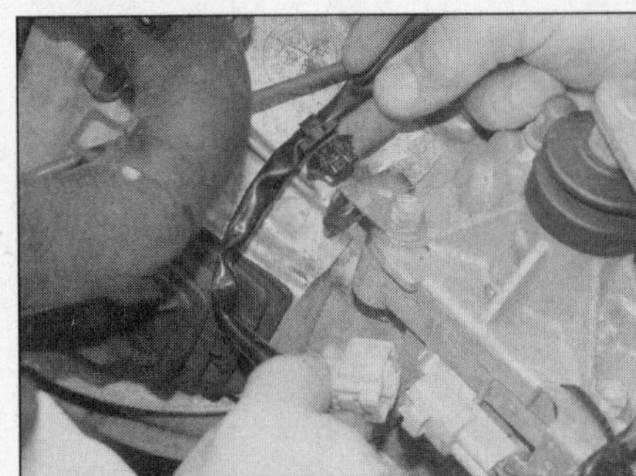
7.10b . . . and unclip the wiring from the transmission

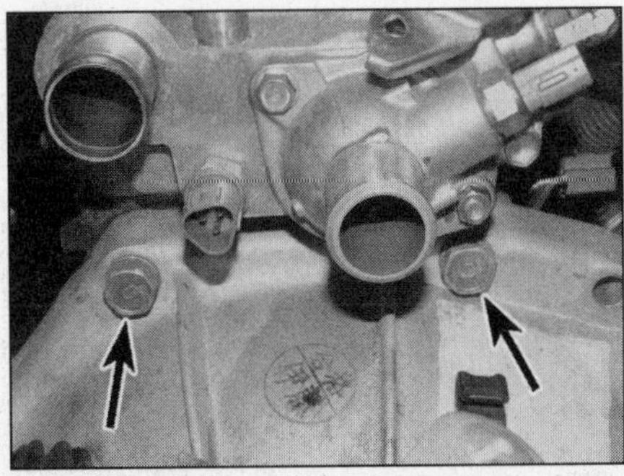
7.11 Two upper transmission bolts – seen without coolant hoses and wiring

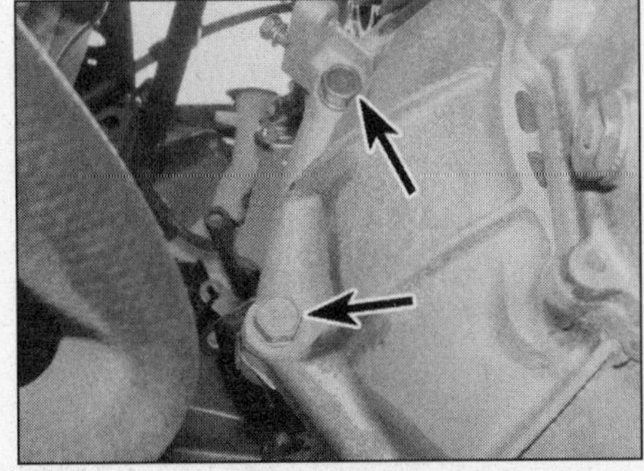
7.15 Loosen the two front transmission-to-engine bolts

7.17 We re-used our DIY support bar from the timing chain cover removal procedure

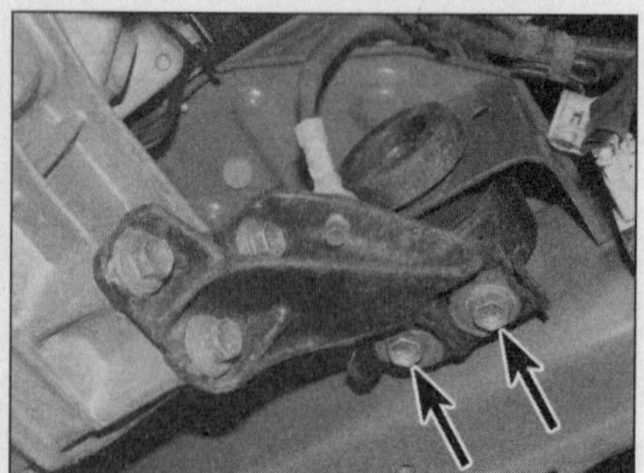

7.18a Either remove the two left-hand mounting-to-body bolts . . .

7.18b . . . or unbolt the mounting completely

7.19a Remove the rear mounting through-bolt and nut . . .

body bolts. Alternatively, unbolt the mounting completely **(see illustrations)**.

19 Remove the through-bolt from the engine rear mounting, then remove three more bolts and take off the mounting bracket **(see illustrations)**.

20 Check that the transmission is securely supported (preferably with the help of an assistant), then remove the five bolts from the sump stiffener plate (where fitted), and take the plate out from under the car **(see illustrations)**. Leave the two front bolts in place for now.

21 Make a final check from below and above that there is nothing left attached to the transmission, nor anything in the way which would prevent the unit from being lowered out.

Before removing the transmission from the engine, it is helpful for refitting to paint or scratch an alignment mark or two across the engine/transmission, so that the transmission can be offered up in approximately the right alignment to engage the dowels.

22 Carefully lower the transmission, checking all the time that nothing is getting caught or stretched. Also take care that the engine right-hand mounting is not being too distorted, or placed under excess strain.

23 Once the transmission is low enough to clear the inner wing, slowly remove the two remaining transmission-to-engine front bolts. As this is done, be prepared for the unit to start separating – have your assistant support it. If the transmission does not separate, prise it gently apart – it is located on dowels, and they may stick **(see illustration)**.

24 As the transmission is withdrawn from the engine, make sure its weight is supported at all times – the transmission input shaft (or the clutch) may otherwise be damaged as it is withdrawn through the clutch assembly bolted to the engine flywheel **(see illustration)**. The adapter plate fitted between the engine and transmission is bolted in place, so should not fall out – unbolt and remove it if required.

25 Once the transmission is clear of the engine, keep the transmission steady on the jack head, and carefully lower it down. With the help of your assistant, remove it from under the car.

26 The clutch components can now be inspected with reference to Chapter 6, and renewed if necessary. Unless they are virtually new, it is worth renewing the clutch components as a matter of course, even if the transmission has been removed for some other reason.

Refitting

27 If removed, refit the clutch components (see Chapter 6). Also ensure that the engine-to-transmission adapter plates are in position on the engine.

28 With the transmission secured to the trolley jack as on removal, raise it into

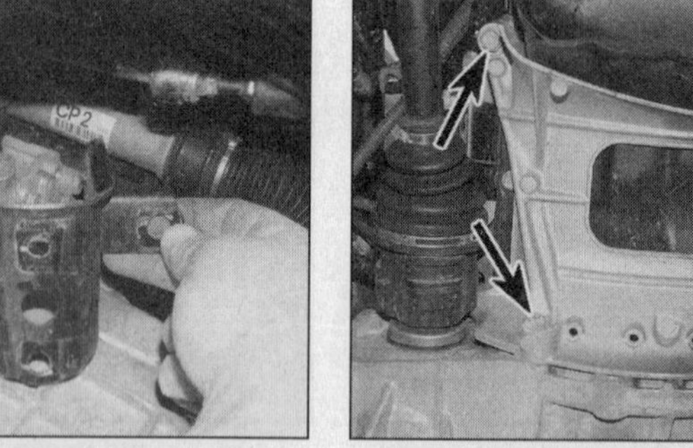

7.19b . . . then unbolt and remove the mounting itself

7.20a Remove the bolts (arrowed) . . .

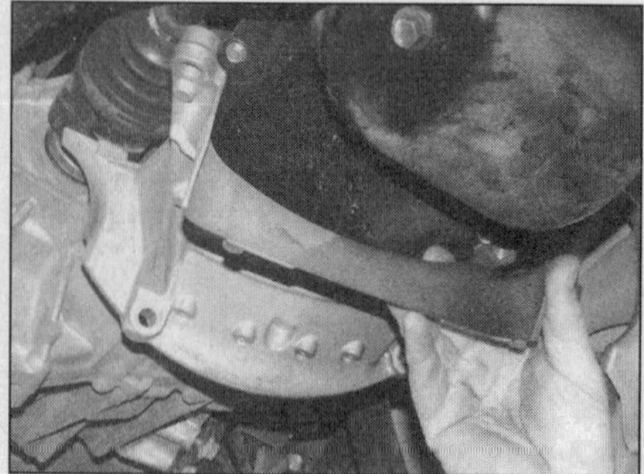

7.20b . . . and take down the stiffener plate

7.23 If necessary, prise the transmission off the engine dowels

7.24 Withdraw the transmission from the engine, keeping it supported

position, and then carefully slide it onto the engine, at the same time engaging the input shaft with the clutch friction disc splines. If marks were made between the transmission and engine on removal, these can be used as a guide to correct alignment.

29 Do not use excessive force to refit the transmission – if the input shaft does not slide into place easily, readjust the angle of the transmission so that it is level, and/or turn the input shaft so that the splines engage properly with the disc. If problems are still experienced, check that the clutch friction disc is correctly centralised (Chapter 6).

30 Once the transmission is successfully mated to the engine, insert as many of the transmission-to-engine bolts as possible, and tighten them progressively, to draw the transmission fully onto the locating dowels.

31 Raise the transmission into position, then refit the engine left-hand and rear mountings. Tighten the bolts hand-tight only at this stage, but sufficiently to support the transmission so that the support bar, engine hoist or supporting jack can be removed.

32 Refit the stiffener plate (where applicable), then tighten its bolts, and the transmission-to-engine bolts, to the specified torque.

33 Tighten the engine mounting bolts to the specified torque.

34 Further refitting is a reversal of removal, noting the following points:

a) Refit the starter motor as described in Chapter 5A.

b) Refit the driveshafts as described in Chapter 8.

c) Refill the transmission with oil as described in Section 2.

8 Transmission overhaul – general information

The overhaul of a manual transmission is a complex (and often expensive) engineering task for the DIY home mechanic to undertake, which requires access to specialist equipment. It involves dismantling and reassembly of many small components, measuring clearances precisely and if necessary, adjusting them by the selection shims and spacers. Internal transmission components are also often difficult to obtain and in many instances, extremely expensive. Because of this, if the transmission develops a fault or becomes noisy, the best course of action is to have the unit overhauled by a specialist repairer or to obtain an exchange reconditioned unit.

Nevertheless, it is not impossible for the more experienced mechanic to overhaul the transmission, if the special tools are available and the job is carried out in a deliberate step-by-step manner, to ensure that nothing is overlooked.

The tools necessary for an overhaul include internal and external circlip pliers, bearing pullers, a slide hammer, a set of pin punches, a dial test indicator, and possibly, a hydraulic press. In addition, a large, sturdy workbench and a vice will be required.

During dismantling of the transmission, make careful notes of how each component is fitted to make reassembly easier and accurate.

Before dismantling the transmission, it will help if you have some idea of where the problem lies. Certain problems can be closely related to specific areas in the transmission which can make component examination and renewal easier. Refer to *Fault diagnosis* at the end of this manual for more information.

Notes

Chapter 7 Part B: Automatic transmission

Contents

Degrees of difficulty

Easy, suitable for novice with little experience

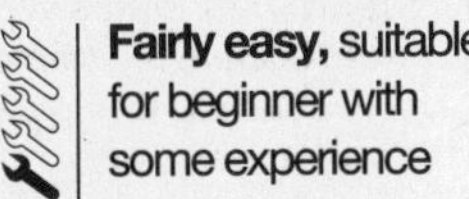

Fairly easy, suitable for beginner with some experience

Fairly difficult, suitable for competent DIY mechanic

Difficult, suitable for experienced DIY mechanic

Very difficult, suitable for expert DIY or professional

Specifications

General

Transmission type number	U440E or U441E
Application	Option on 1.3 litre engine models
Description	Electro-hydraulically controlled planetary gearbox providing four forward speeds and one reverse speed. Drive transmitted through hydrokinetic torque converter. Deselectable overdrive, lock-up clutch on top two speeds, shift lock system
Automatic transmission fluid type	See *Lubricants and fluids*
Automatic transmission fluid capacity	See Chapter 1 Specifications
Torque converter fitted depth (see Section 2)	20.7 mm

Ratios

1st	2.875:1
2nd	1.568:1
3rd	1.000:1
4th (overdrive)	0.697:1
Reverse	2.300:1
Final drive	4.052:1

Torque wrench settings

Torque wrench settings	Nm	lbf ft
Engine/transmission mountings:		
Left-hand mounting bolts	49	36
Rear mounting bracket bolts	49	36
Rear mounting through-bolt	64	47
Rear mounting-to-subframe nuts/bolt	80	59
Fluid drain plug	17	13
Fluid pan bolts	9	7
Neutral start switch mounting nut/bolts	12	9
Selector cable end nut	12	9
Selector lever mounting bolts	12	9
Starter motor mounting bolts	39	29
Sump-to-transmission stiffener plate bolts	39	29
Torque converter-to-driveplate bolts	27	20
Transmission selector lever nut	12	9
Transmission-to-engine bolts	64	47

1 General information

The Toyota U440/U441E automatic transmission has four forward speeds (and one reverse). The automatic gearchanges are electronically-controlled, rather than hydraulically as with previous conventional types, with the transmission control functions incorporated into the engine management ECU. The advantage of electronic management is to provide a faster gearchange response. A kickdown facility is also provided, to enable a faster acceleration response when required.

The transmission consists of three main assemblies, these being the torque converter, which is directly coupled to the engine's driveplate; the final drive unit, which incorporates the differential unit; and the planetary gearbox, with its multi-disc clutches and brake bands. The transmission is lubricated with automatic transmission fluid (ATF).

The torque converter incorporates an automatic lock-up feature, which eliminates any possibility of converter slip in the top two gears; this aids performance and economy. The 'overdrive' 4th gear can be deselected manually, using a button on the selector lever – in this mode, only the first three ratios are used. The control circuit uses input from all the engine management sensors, and can adapt the transmission functions as required – for example, under full-throttle acceleration, upshifts are delayed longer, to make full use of engine power.

Another feature of this transmission is the shift lock system, a safety feature to avoid incorrect operation. Besides the conventional selector lever lock button (to inhibit shifting into R, P, 2 and 1 positions), the shift lock system prevents the lever being moved from P until the ignition is on and the brake pedal is depressed. Correct functioning of the brake stop-light switch is therefore vital for this system to work correctly – see Chapter 9. A further feature of this system is that the ignition key cannot be removed unless the selector lever is in the P position.

A neutral start switch is fitted where the selector cable joins the transmission, to prevent starter motor operation unless the transmission is in P or N. The direct clutch speed sensor determines the roadspeed at which the torque converter 'locks up'.

The transmission kickdown function, which acts to select a lower gear (where possible) on full-throttle acceleration, is incorporated into the throttle position sensor (see Chapter 4A).

Models without ABS are fitted with a vehicle speed sensor, which measures the rotational speed of the transmission final drive, and converts the information into an electronic signal, which is then sent to the speedometer in the instrument panel. The signal is also used as an input by the engine management system ECU. On models with ABS, the car's speed is determined using the information from the ABS wheel sensors, and a speed sensor is not fitted to the transmission.

A fault diagnosis system is integrated into the control unit, but analysis can only be undertaken with specialised equipment. If a malfunction should occur in the transmission electrical system, automatic gear selection will continue, but the changes will be noticeably jerky. It is important that any transmission fault be identified and rectified at the earliest possible opportunity. Delay in doing so will only cause further problems. A Toyota dealer can interrogate the ECU fault memory for stored fault codes, enabling them to pinpoint the fault quickly. Once the fault has been corrected and any fault codes have been cleared, normal transmission operation should be restored.

Because of the need for special test equipment, the complexity of some of the parts, and the need for scrupulous cleanliness when servicing automatic transmissions, the amount which the owner can do is limited. Repairs to the final drive differential are also not recommended. Most major repairs and overhaul operations should be left to a Toyota dealer, who will be equipped with the necessary equipment for fault diagnosis and repair. The information in this Chapter is therefore limited to a description of the removal and refitting of the transmission as a complete unit. The removal, refitting and adjustment of the selector cable is also described.

In the event of a transmission problem occurring, consult a Toyota dealer or transmission specialist before removing the transmission from the car, since the majority of fault diagnosis is carried out with the transmission *in situ*.

2 Automatic transmission – removal and refitting

Note: *Read through this procedure before starting work to see what is involved, particularly in terms of lifting equipment. Depending on the facilities available, the home mechanic may prefer to remove the engine and transmission together, then separate them on the bench, as described in Chapter 2B. The help of an assistant is highly recommended if the transmission is to be removed (and later refitted) on its own.*

Removal

1 Remove the air cleaner as described in Chapter 4A.

2 Remove the battery and battery tray as described in Chapter 5A. Also working from the information in Chapter 5A, remove the starter motor.

3 Remove the nut and washer, and detach the selector cable from the operating lever on the front of the transmission. Slide out the metal clip holding the selector cable to the support bracket, and withdraw the cable **(see illustration)**. Lay it to one side, clear of the transmission, without bending it excessively.

4 Noting their positions for refitting, disconnect the wiring plugs from the following components on and around the transmission **(see illustration)**:

a) Direct clutch speed sensor (on top).
b) Neutral start switch (at the front).
c) Release the clamp and disconnect the solenoid wiring plug.
d) Oxygen sensor.
e) Vehicle speed sensor (on top – only on models without ABS).

5 Unbolt and remove the two earth straps.

6 Unbolt the fluid dipstick/filler tube from the front of the transmission. Pull the tube out of its location, and recover the O-ring at the base – a new one should be used when refitting the tube.

7 Remove the three uppermost transmission-to-engine bolts – access to these is hampered by the coolant hoses and wiring at the end of the cylinder head, but should still be possible.

8 Jack up the front of the car, and support it on axle stands (see *Jacking and vehicle support*). The car must be raised sufficiently that the transmission can be lowered out and removed underneath. Consideration should also be given to the need to support the engine, once the rear and left-hand mountings are disconnected.

9 Unscrew the fasteners and remove the engine left- and right-hand lower covers from under the car.

2.3 The selector cable is clipped to the front of the transmission

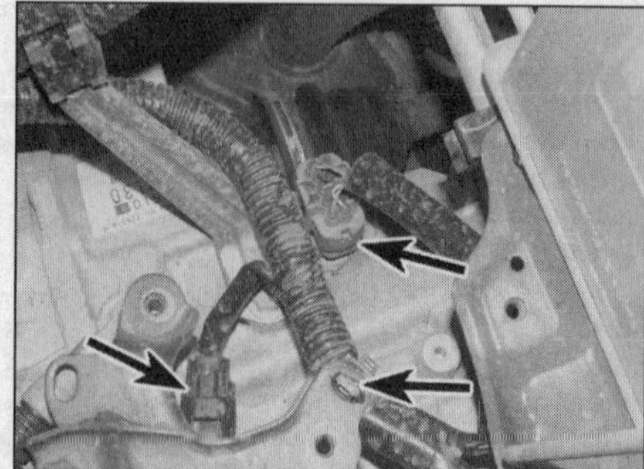

2.4 Disconnect the wiring from the top of the transmission

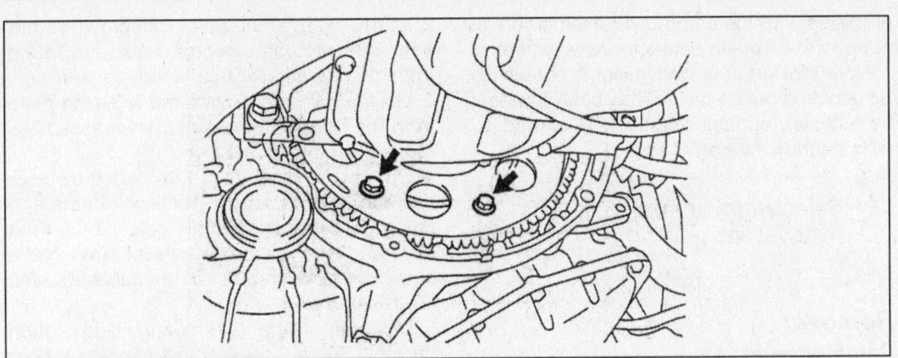

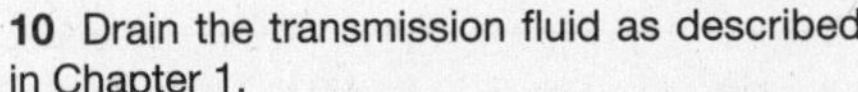

2.15 Turn the crankshaft to access the torque converter mounting bolts

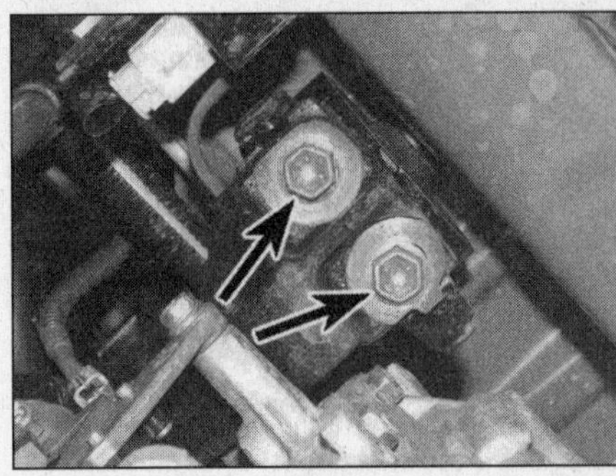

2.19 Left-hand mounting-to-body bolts

10 Drain the transmission fluid as described in Chapter 1.

11 Remove both driveshafts as described in Chapter 8.

12 Refer to Chapter 4B and disconnect the exhaust downpipe from the manifold. Once the wiring for the oxygen sensors has been disconnected, the exhaust can then be lowered onto an axle stand, clear of the transmission, rather than being removed completely.

13 Just loosen ('crack') the two remaining transmission-to-engine bolts (one in front, one at the rear), but leave them in place for now – this avoids using any substantial force to remove the bolts when the transmission is only supported on a jack.

14 Remove the five bolts securing the sump-to-transmission stiffener plate, and lower out the plate for access to the torque converter mounting bolts.

15 Loosen and remove the first of the torque converter mounting bolts, using a suitable tool to jam the driveplate ring gear. Using a spanner or socket on the crankshaft pulley bolt, turn the engine so that the remaining bolts can be removed **(see illustration)**. Note that one of the bolts is marked with grey paint – this bolt must be refitted first, so also note its location.

16 Disconnect the two fluid hoses which run to the radiator – anticipate some fluid spillage as this is done. If possible, clamp the hoses prior to disconnection, and either plug or tape over them to prevent further fluid loss and dirt entry.

17 Using a substantial hydraulic ('trolley') jack with a block of wood, raise the transmission slightly, to take the weight off its mountings. Supporting the transmission securely in this way can be difficult to achieve – due to its shape, there is a danger the transmission will roll off once disconnected. For this reason, it pays to have an assistant on hand, to steady the unit as it is lowered out.

18 Before the engine rear and left-hand mountings are disconnected, the engine must be supported, preferably from above, using either an engine crane or support bar. There must be scope for lowering the transmission end of the engine. If the engine is supported from below, using another jack (and block of wood, to protect the sump), this seriously reduces the working room for removing the transmission.

19 With the engine securely supported, first remove the two lower left-hand mounting-to-body bolts **(see illustration)**.

20 Remove the through-bolt from the engine rear mounting, then remove three more bolts and take off the mounting bracket.

21 Check that the transmission is securely supported (preferably with the help of an assistant), then remove the five bolts from the stiffener plate, and take the plate out from under the car. Leave the two transmission-to-engine bolts in place for now.

22 Make a final check from below and above that there is nothing left attached to the transmission, nor anything in the way which would prevent the unit from being lowered out.

HAYNES HiNT ***Before removing the transmission from the engine, it is helpful for refitting to paint or scratch an alignment mark or two across the engine/transmission, so that the transmission can be offered up in approximately the right alignment to engage the dowels.***

23 Carefully lower the transmission, checking all the time that nothing is getting caught or stretched. Also take care that the engine right-hand mounting is not being too distorted, or placed under excess strain.

24 Once the transmission is low enough to clear the inner wing, slowly remove the two remaining transmission-to-engine bolts. As this is done, be prepared for the unit to start separating – have your assistant support it. If the transmission does not separate, prise it gently apart – it is located on dowels, and they may stick.

25 As the transmission is withdrawn from the engine, make sure its weight is supported at all times – the transmission input shaft (or the torque converter) may otherwise be damaged as it is withdrawn through the converter bolted to the engine driveplate. Recover the adapter plate fitted between the engine and transmission, as it may fall out when the two are separated – note which way round it is fitted.

26 Once the transmission is clear of the engine, keep the transmission steady on the jack head, and carefully lower it down. With the help of your assistant, remove it from under the car. Keep the torque converter pressed into place, otherwise it may fall out. If the unit is to be transported anywhere, bolt a strip of metal across the transmission mating face, and wedge a piece of wood behind to hold the converter.

Refitting

27 Before refitting the transmission, check the fitted depth of the torque converter, as follows. Place a straight-edge horizontally across the mating face of the transmission, and measure directly back from it to one of the converter mounting bolt bosses **(see illustration)**. If the dimension is not as specified, the converter has become dislodged (or incorrectly refitted) and should

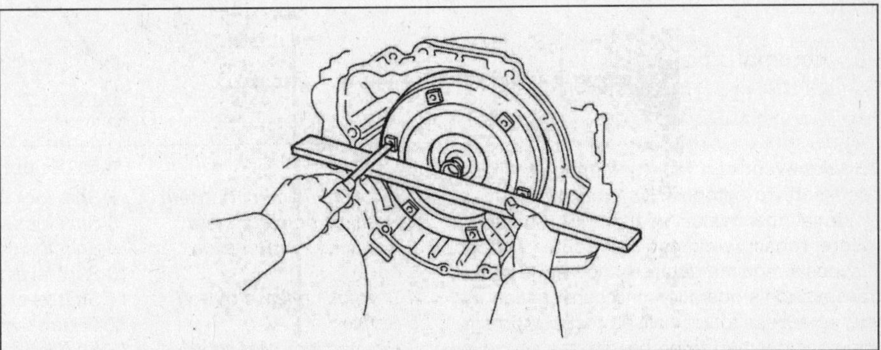

2.27 Measuring the fitted depth of the torque converter

be pressed carefully back into place.

28 With the transmission secured to the trolley jack as on removal, raise it into position, and then carefully slide it onto the engine, at the same time engaging the input shaft with the torque converter. If marks were made between the transmission and engine on removal, these can be used as a guide to correct alignment.

29 Do not use excessive force to refit the transmission – if the input shaft does not slide into place easily, readjust the angle of the transmission so that it is level, and/or turn the input shaft. If problems are still experienced, check that the torque converter is correctly installed (see paragraph 27).

30 Once the transmission is successfully mated to the engine, insert as many of the transmission-to-engine bolts as possible, and tighten them progressively, to draw the transmission fully onto the locating dowels.

31 Raise the transmission into position, then refit the engine left-hand and rear mountings. Tighten the bolts hand-tight only at this stage, but sufficiently to support the transmission so that the support bar, engine hoist or supporting jack can be removed.

32 Refit the stiffener plate, then tighten its bolts, and the transmission-to-engine bolts, to the specified torque.

33 Tighten the engine mounting bolts to the specified torque.

34 Further refitting is a reversal of removal, noting the following points:

a) *When refitting the torque converter bolts, fit the grey-painted one first, to its original location. Tighten all six bolts to the specified torque.*

b) *Refit the starter motor as described in Chapter 5A.*

c) *Refit the driveshafts as described in Chapter 8.*

d) *Refill the transmission with fluid as described in Chapter 1.*

e) *If a new transmission unit has been fitted, it may be necessary to have the ECU reprogrammed, to ensure correct operation – seek the advice of your Toyota dealer. Otherwise, it may take a few miles for the ECU to relearn its values to ensure smooth operation. If the fluid level was checked cold, recheck it after a few miles while it is still hot.*

3 Automatic transmission overhaul – general information

In the event of a fault occurring, it will be necessary to establish whether the fault is electrical, mechanical or hydraulic in nature, before repair work can be contemplated. Diagnosis requires detailed knowledge of the transmission's operation and construction, as well as access to specialised test equipment, and so is deemed to be beyond the scope of this manual. It is therefore essential that problems with the automatic transmission are referred to a Toyota dealer for assessment.

Note that a faulty transmission should not be removed before the car has been assessed by a dealer, as fault diagnosis is carried out with the transmission *in situ*.

4 Selector lever and cable – removal and refitting

Removal

Selector lever

1 Remove the centre console as described in Chapter 11.

2 At the front of the lever, unscrew the nut and withdraw the selector cable end fitting from the operating lever.

3 Lift the cable to detach the retaining plate from the front of the selector lever assembly. Move the cable to one side.

4 On the passenger side of the lever assembly, prise off the shift lock cable end fitting. To release the cable outer at the front of the lever assembly, twist the cable clockwise through 90°. Lift the cable out, and lay it to one side.

5 Disconnect the two wiring plugs, then unscrew the four selector lever assembly floor bolts, and remove the assembly from the car **(see illustrations)**.

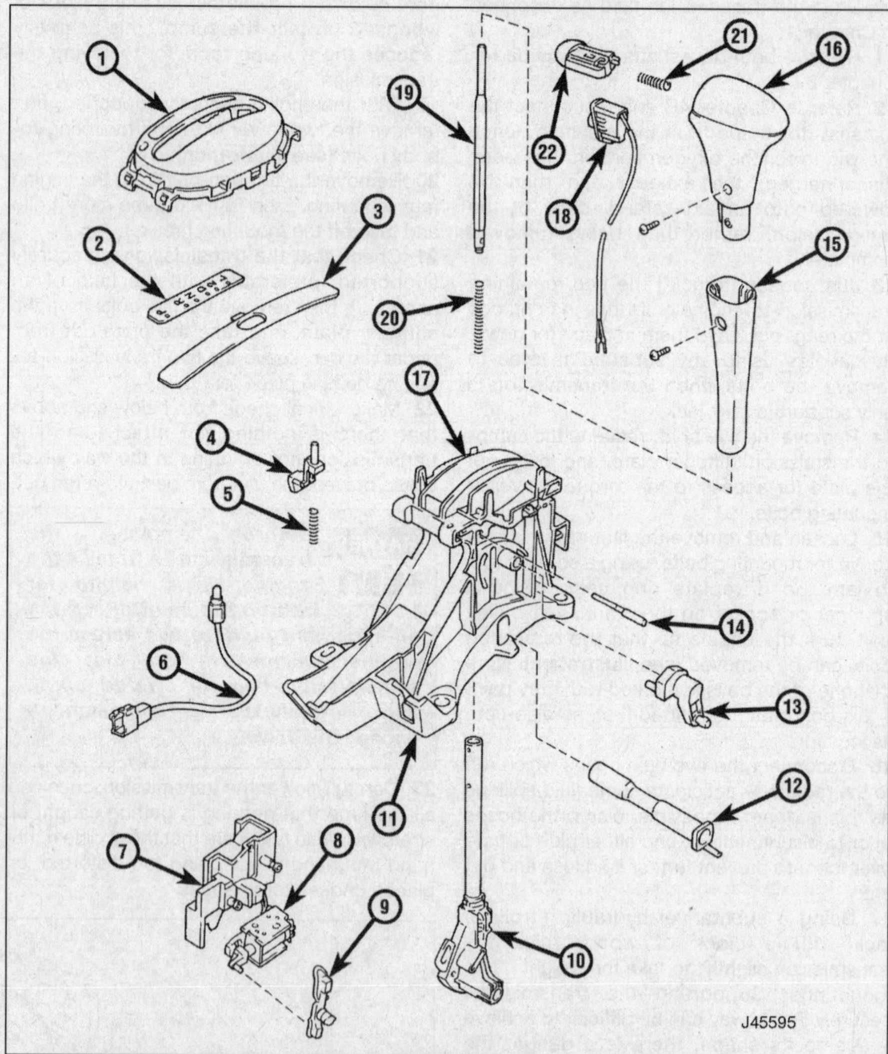

4.5a Selector lever details

1 Position indicator housing
2 Position indicator plate
3 Position indicator slide cover
4 Shift lock release button
5 Spring
6 Position indicator light bulbholder
7 Shift lock unit
8 Shift lock solenoid
9 Shift lock solenoid rod
10 Shift lever sub-assembly
11 Shift lever main assembly
12 Control shaft
13 Shift lock lever
14 Grooved pin
15 Shift lever cover
16 Shift lever knob
17 Shift lever plate
18 Overdrive main switch
19 Detent rod
20 Spring
21 Spring
22 Shift lever button

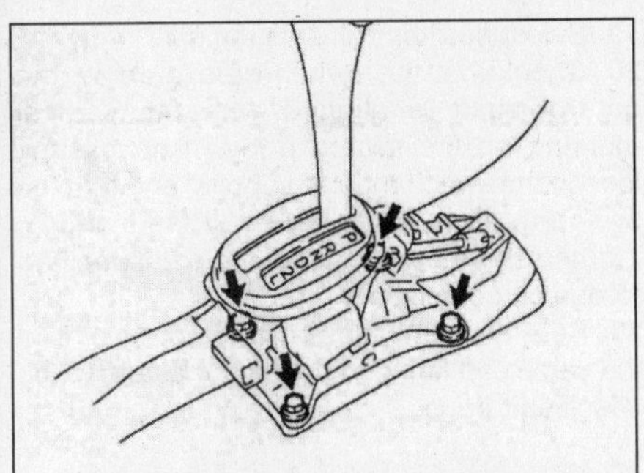

4.5b Selector lever mounting bolts

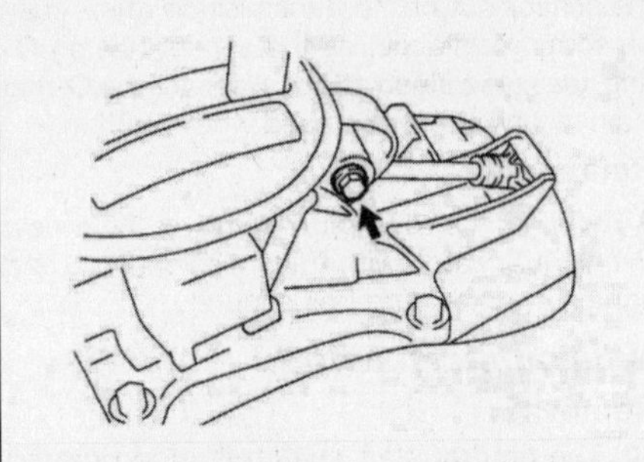

4.13 Remove the nut and washer, and detach the selector cable

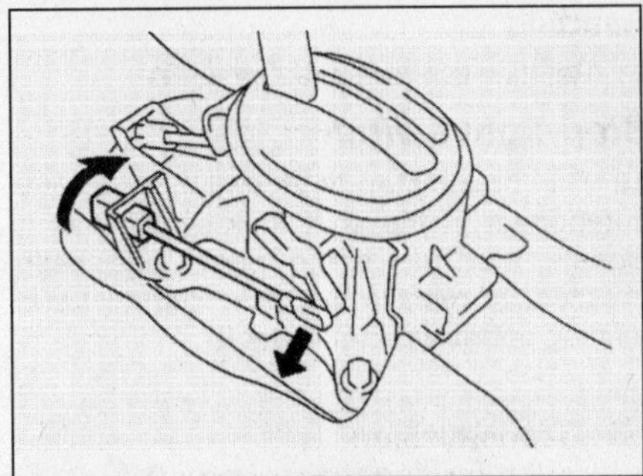

5.5 Release the shift lock cable from the selector lever

Selector cable

6 Remove the centre console as described in Chapter 11.

7 At the front of the selector lever, unscrew the nut and withdraw the selector cable end fitting from the operating lever.

8 Lift the cable to detach the retaining plate from the front of the selector lever assembly.

9 Jack up the front of the car, and support it on axle stands (see *Jacking and vehicle support*).

10 Under the car, remove the two bolts securing the cable's floor plate/grommet, and also the bolt from the cable bracket attached to the underside of the car.

11 With the cable free to move, draw it through from the inside of the car, and let it hang down. Take care not to kink or bend the cable during removal. Check for any further mounting brackets, clips, or ties, and disconnect them as necessary. If preferred, the car can now be lowered to the ground.

12 In the engine compartment, slide out the metal clip used to hold the cable to the support bracket at the front of the transmission.

13 Remove the nut and washer, and detach the selector cable from the operating lever on the front of the transmission **(see illustration)**. The cable can now be removed completely, taking care not to kink or bend the cable as it is removed.

Refitting

14 Refitting is a reversal of removal. Check that all gears can be selected before taking the car out on the road.

5 Shift lock system – component renewal

Description

1 This system is a security/safety device, intended to prevent the car from being left with the transmission in any position other than P. The ignition key cannot be removed from the lock unless P is selected, and once the key has been removed, no other position than P can be selected.

2 This function is provided by means of a cable fitted to the selector linkage at the selector lever, and to the ignition switch assembly. A solenoid unit is fitted to the driver's side of the selector assembly.

Lock cable

Removal

3 Remove the centre console as described in Chapter 11.

4 Remove the steering column lower shroud, which is secured by three screws from underneath, then lift out the upper shroud also.

5 On the passenger side of the lever assembly, prise off the shift lock cable end fitting. To release the cable outer at the front of the lever assembly, twist the cable clockwise through 90° **(see illustration)**. Lift the cable out.

6 Trace the cable forwards, noting how it is routed, and release it from the mounting clip under the centre of the facia. Trace the cable onwards to the back of the ignition switch, releasing it from any further clips or ties.

7 Insert the ignition key, and turn it to the ACC position. At the back of the ignition switch, press the retaining tab on the shift lock cable connector, and pull out the cable **(see illustration)**. Remove the cable from the car.

Refitting

8 Refitting is a reversal of removal, noting the following points:

a) *Ensure the selector lever is in the N position when reconnecting the cable.*

b) *Press and hold the retaining tab on the connector behind the ignition switch, insert the cable end fully, then release the tab and check that the cable is held.*

c) *After hooking on the cable at the selector lever end, operate the spring-loaded adjuster a few times before locking it in position with the cap.*

d) *Check the operation of the system on completion.*

Solenoid unit

Removal

9 Remove the centre console as described in Chapter 11.

10 Disconnect the wiring plug from the solenoid unit, then take out the mounting screw and remove the unit from the selector lever **(see illustration)**.

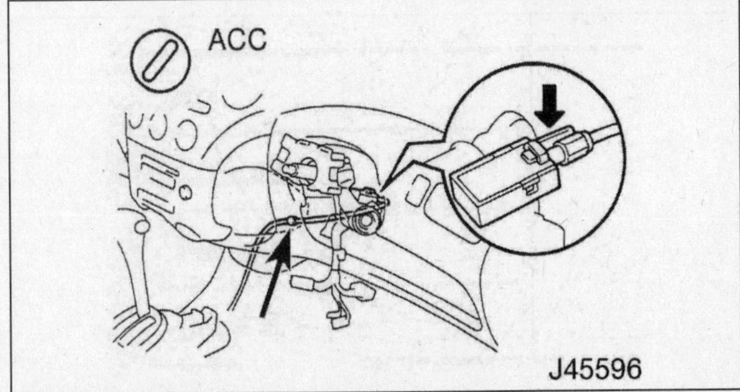

5.7 Disconnect the shift lock cable from the clamp and ignition switch

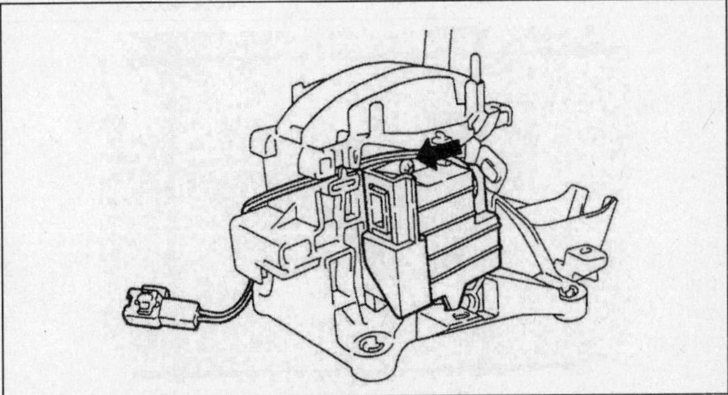

5.10 Remove the solenoid unit mounting screw

Refitting

11 Refitting is a reversal of removal.

Stop-light switch

12 The brake stop-light switch is a vital component in the shift lock system, as it signals that the brake pedal has been pressed, to release the lock. Removal and refitting details are in Chapter 9.

6 Transmission switches/sensors – removal and refitting

Vehicle speed sensor

Note: *The speed sensor is only fitted to models without ABS.*

Removal

1 The sensor is fitted to the top of the transmission, at the rear (just in front of the rear mounting).

2 With the ignition switched off, disconnect the sensor wiring plug.

3 Remove the sensor mounting bolt, and lift the sensor out of the transmission (there may be some resistance, as the sensor has an O-ring seal). Recover the O-ring – a new one should be used when refitting.

4 Using a small screwdriver, prise out the clip fitted below the sensor mounting flange, which secures the sensor to its driven gear.

Refitting

5 Refitting is a reversal of removal. Fit a new O-ring, lubricated with transmission fluid, and tighten the mounting bolt securely.

Direct clutch speed sensor

Removal

6 The sensor is fitted to the top of the transmission, at the rear. To avoid confusion with the vehicle speed sensor, the clutch speed sensor is nearer the battery, and has a wiring plug fitted horizontally rather than vertically.

7 With the ignition switched off, disconnect the sensor wiring plug.

8 Remove the sensor mounting bolt, and lift the sensor out of the transmission (there may be some resistance, as the sensor has an O-ring seal) **(see illustration)**. Recover the O-ring – a new one should be used when refitting.

Refitting

9 Refitting is a reversal of removal. Fit a new O-ring, lubricated with transmission fluid, and tighten the mounting bolt securely.

Neutral start switch

Removal

10 The neutral start switch is incorporated into the selector lever on the front of the transmission.

11 Jack up the front of the car, and support it on axle stands (see *Jacking and vehicle support*). Remove the engine left-hand lower cover panel.

12 Remove the nut and washer, and detach the selector cable from the operating lever on the front of the transmission. Move the cable clear for access to the lever and switch, taking care not to kink or bend the cable.

13 With the ignition switched off, disconnect the switch wiring plug.

14 Unscrew the nut and take off the transmission selector lever, noting how it is fitted.

15 Relieve the staking on the lockwasher behind the operating lever, then take off the washer and unscrew the further nut below it. A new lockwasher should be obtained for refitting.

16 Remove the two mounting bolts, and slide the switch off the transmission control shaft **(see illustration)**.

Refitting

17 Refitting is a reversal of removal, noting the following points:

a) *Tighten all nuts and bolts to the specified torque (where given).*
b) *Use a new lockwasher, staked into position once the nut has been tightened.*
c) *Before tightening the mounting bolts, adjust the switch as described below.*

Adjustment

18 If not already done, disconnect the selector cable and remove the transmission selector lever as described in paragraphs 12 and 14.

19 Select position N inside the car.

20 Check that the switch groove above the control shaft is aligned with the vertical marking on the switch body. If necessary, loosen the switch mounting bolts, and turn the switch to align the groove and the marking. Tighten the mounting bolts to the specified torque on completion.

21 Refit the transmission selector lever and the cable end fitting, tightening the nuts to the specified torque.

7 Oil seals – renewal

1 Oil leaks frequently occur due to wear or deterioration of the driveshaft oil seals, or even the transmission sensor O-ring. Renewal of these seals is relatively easy, since the repairs can be performed without removing the transmission from the car.

Driveshaft oil seals

2 The driveshaft oil seals are located at the sides of the transmission, where the driveshafts enter the transmission. If leakage at the seal is suspected, raise the car and support it securely on axle stands. If the seal is leaking, oil will be found on the side of the transmission below the driveshaft.

3 Refer to Chapter 8 and remove the appropriate driveshaft.

4 Using a large screwdriver or lever, carefully prise the oil seal out of the transmission casing, taking care not to damage the transmission casing.

5 Wipe clean the oil seal seating in the transmission casing.

6 Dip the new oil seal in clean oil, then press it a little way into the casing by hand, making sure that it is square to its seating.

7 Using suitable tubing or a large socket, carefully drive the oil seal fully into the casing until it contacts the seating.

8 Refit the driveshaft with reference to Chapter 8.

Sensor oil seals

9 Refer to Section 6.

6.8 Removing the direct clutch speed sensor

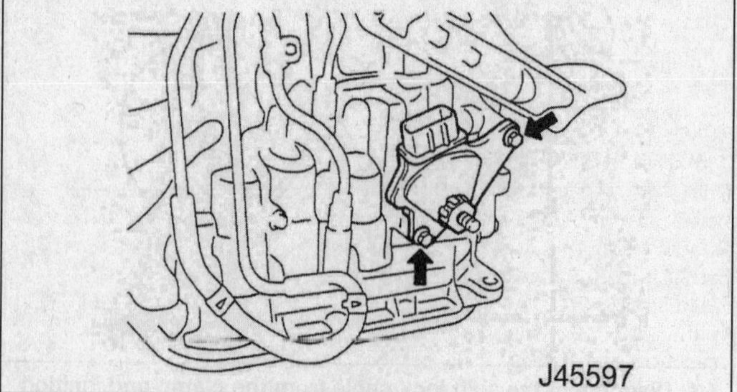

6.16 Remove the neutral start switch mounting bolts

Chapter 8
Driveshafts

Contents

Degrees of difficulty

Easy, suitable for novice with little experience 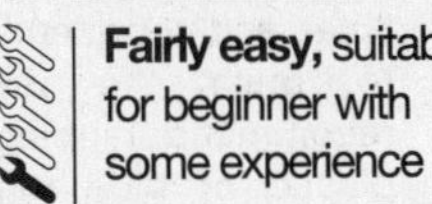	**Fairly easy,** suitable for beginner with some experience 	**Fairly difficult,** suitable for competent DIY mechanic 	**Difficult,** suitable for experienced DIY mechanic 	**Very difficult,** suitable for expert DIY or professional

Specifications

General

Driveshaft type	Solid steel shafts with inner and outer constant velocity (CV) joints. Outer joints of the ball-and-cage (Rzeppa) type, inner joints of the spider-and-yoke (tripod) type. Dynamic damper fitted to right-hand driveshaft
Lubricant:	
Type/specification	Special grease supplied in sachets with gaiter kits – inner and outer joints use different grease types
Quantity (per joint):	
Inner joint	85 to 105 g ('yellow' grease)
Outer joint	80 to 100 g ('grey' grease)

Torque wrench settings	Nm	lbf ft
Driveshaft (hub) nut*	216	159
Lower arm balljoint nut	98	72
Roadwheel nuts	103	76
Swivel hub-to-suspension strut pinch-bolt/nut**:		
Up to May 2002	132	97
May 2002 onwards	142	105
Track rod end nut	49	36

** Use new nut*
** Oiled threads*

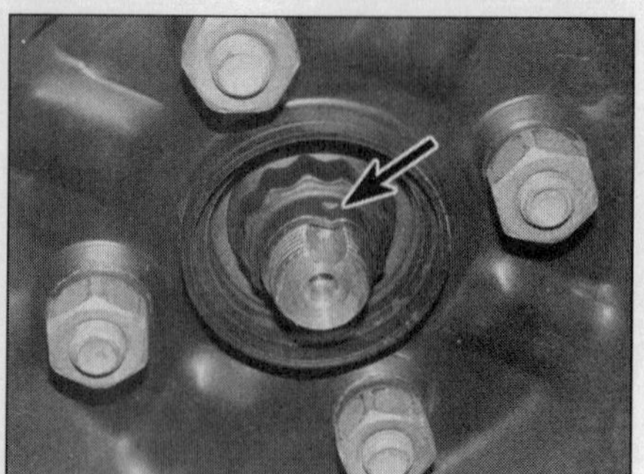
2.2a The driveshaft nut shoulder is staked into the shaft groove

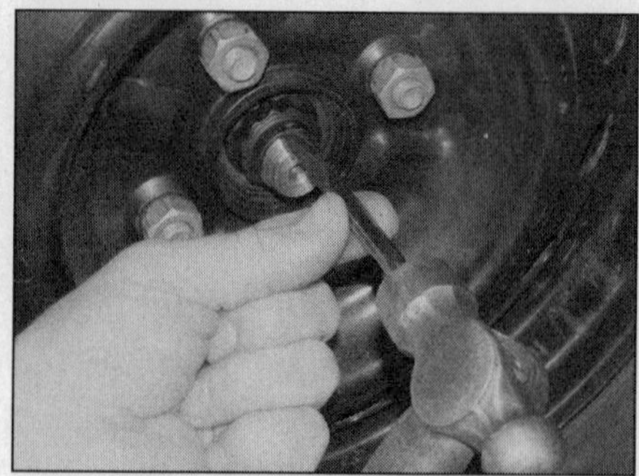
2.2b Tap up the deformed portion of the nut so it can be unscrewed

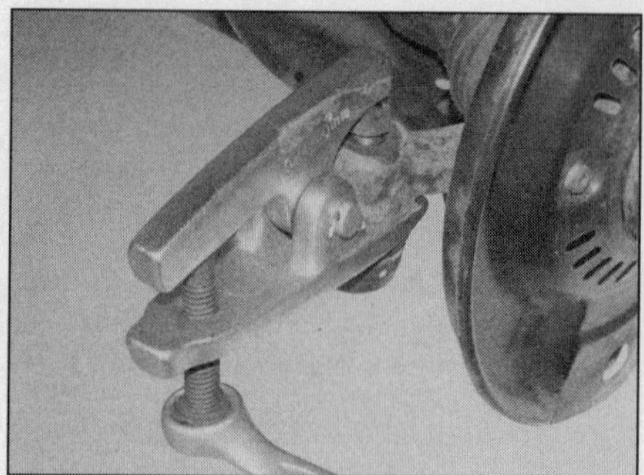
2.6 Separate the track rod end balljoint

1 General information

Drive is transmitted from the differential to the front wheels by means of two, unequal-length driveshafts.

Each driveshaft is fitted with an inner and outer constant velocity (CV) joint. The inner constant velocity joint is of the spider-and-yoke (tripod) type and the outer joint is of the ball-and-cage (Rzeppa) type. Each outer joint is splined to engage with the wheel hub, and is threaded so that it can be fastened to the hub by a large nut. The inner joint is also splined to engage with the differential sunwheel gears.

Approximately halfway along the right-hand driveshaft, a dynamic (vibration) damper weight is attached by two clips.

2 Driveshafts - removal and refitting

Note: *If obtaining a secondhand or reconditioned driveshaft, note that, while all Yaris driveshafts are visually similar, they can vary in length by more than 10 mm, depending on model and where the car was produced. There is no indication in the Toyota material whether the splines are also affected by these detail differences. Quote the VIN when buying new/recon parts, or try always to obtain a shaft from a model the same age and engine size.*

Removal

1 Remove the relevant wheel trim, or the wheel centre cover (alloy wheels) for access to the driveshaft nut.

2 Using a hammer and punch, relieve the staking on the driveshaft nut **(see illustrations)**.

3 Ensure that the handbrake is applied (ideally, have an assistant apply the footbrake), then slacken the driveshaft nut using a suitable socket (30 mm on our car) and extension bar. Loosen the driveshaft nut almost to the end of its threads, but do not remove it at this stage.

Warning: The driveshaft nut is done up extremely tight, and considerable effort will be required to loosen it. Do not use poor-quality, badly-fitting tools for this task, due to the risk of personal injury.

4 Slacken the relevant front wheel nuts, then jack up the front of the car, and support securely on axle stands (see *Jacking and vehicle support*). Remove the roadwheel.

5 Drain the transmission oil or fluid as described in Chapter 1. If this is not done, be prepared for considerable loss of oil or fluid when the driveshafts are removed from the transmission.

6 Extract the split pin from the track rod end balljoint nut, then unscrew the nut and use a balljoint splitter to separate the track rod from the swivel hub **(see illustration)**. Take care not to damage the balljoint rubber during the separation procedure. A new split pin should be used when refitting.

7 Remove the nuts from the two bolts used to secure the swivel hub to the base of the suspension strut. Note which way the bolts are fitted (this should be from the front), then tap the bolts out. Separate the hub from the base of the strut **(see illustrations)**.

8 The splined end of the driveshaft now has to be released from its location in the hub. It's likely that the splines will be very tight (corrosion may even be a factor, if the driveshaft has not been disturbed for some time), and considerable force may be needed to push the driveshaft out. Toyota recommend tapping the shaft out with a plastic or hide mallet **(see illustration)**. If an ordinary hammer is used, place a small piece of wood over the end of the driveshaft - in addition to the loosened driveshaft nut, this will protect the threads from damage.

9 Once the splines have been released, remove the driveshaft nut and discard it - the nut is only intended to be used once.

10 Pull the hub outwards, and pull the

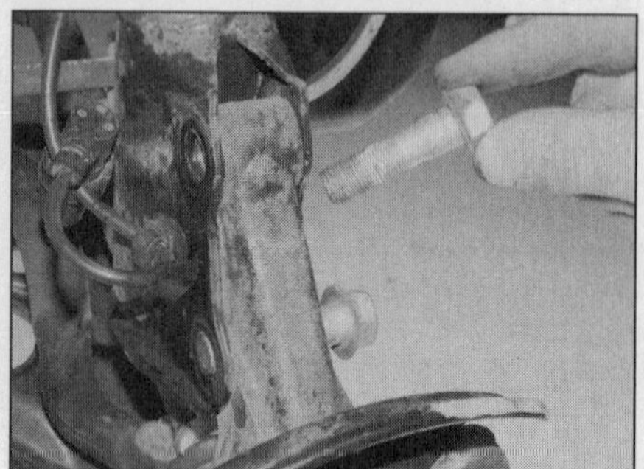
2.7a Remove the strut-to-hub bolts . . .

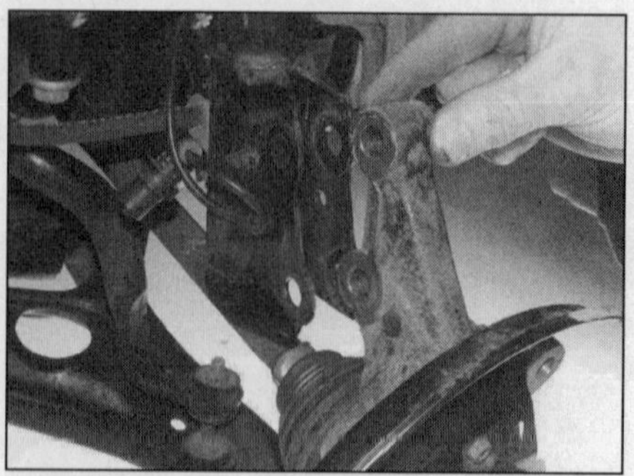
2.7b . . . and separate the hub from the base of the strut

2.8 Tap out the driveshaft splined end

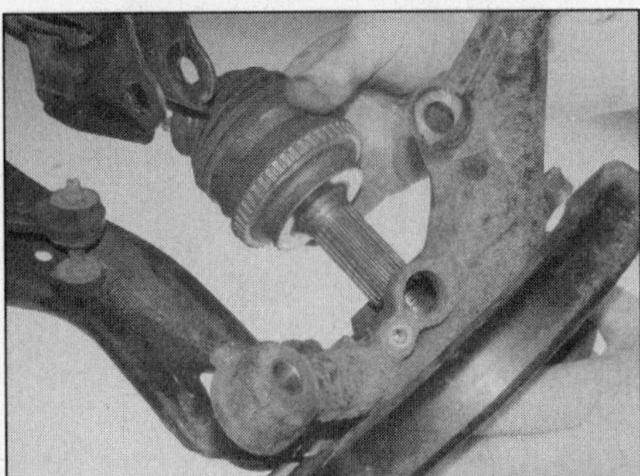

2.10 Separate the driveshaft from the inside of the hub

2.11 Prising out the inner joint, using a wood block, pry bar and exhaust clamp (arrowed)

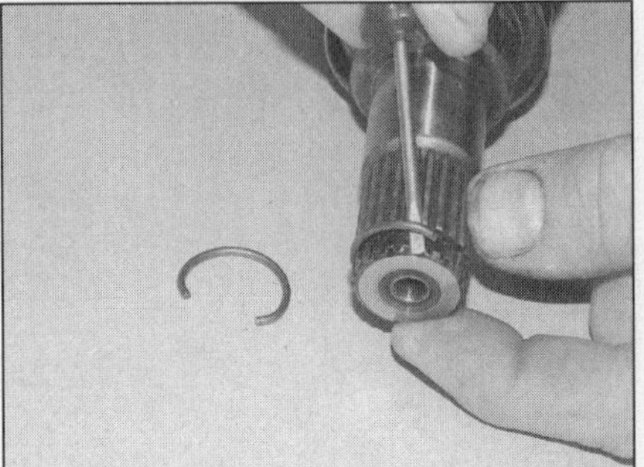

2.14 Prise out the old driveshaft circlip, and have a new one ready for refitting

driveshaft inwards, to separate the splined end from the hub **(see illustration)**. It is helpful to have an assistant on hand, to pull either the hub or the shaft. Do not bend the driveshaft excessively at any stage, or the joints may be damaged – the inner and outer joints should not be bent through more than 18° and 45° respectively. Do not let the driveshaft hang down under its own weight – tie it up level if necessary.

11 The driveshafts are held into the transmission by a spring circlip, which can take some effort to release. Using a suitable drift on the shoulder of the driveshaft inner joint, tap the joint out of the transmission. Alternatively, use a pry bar with a block of wood behind to prise the inner joint out – we also fitted an exhaust clamp at the inner end of the joint to provide a better leverage point **(see illustration)**. Take care not to damage the driveshaft boot or the securing clips. Be prepared for a small amount of oil/fluid loss when the driveshaft releases (or a large amount, if the transmission was not drained).

12 Manoeuvre the driveshaft out of position, ensuring that the constant velocity joints are not placed under excessive strain, and remove the driveshaft from underneath the car.

13 Whilst the driveshaft is removed, plug the differential aperture with a clean, lint-free cloth to prevent dirt getting in.

14 Extract the circlip from the groove on the inner end of the driveshaft, and obtain a new one **(see illustration)**.

15 Check the condition of the differential oil seals, and if necessary renew them as described in Chapter 7.

Caution: If the car is lowered back onto its wheels while the driveshafts are removed, this could cause damage to the wheel bearings, especially if the car is moved. The Toyota special tool for this eventuality is a very large bolt (identical in diameter to the driveshaft) which fits through the hub and supports the bearing – if a large enough bolt could be obtained, a home-made substitute could be made.

Refitting

16 Locate the new circlip in the groove on the inner end of the driveshaft, and turn the clip so its open side is facing downwards.

17 Lubricate the driveshaft inner splines with transmission oil/fluid. Carefully refit the driveshaft into the transmission, taking care not to damage the oil seal. Turn the driveshaft until it engages the splines on the differential gears.

18 Push the driveshaft fully home, so that the circlip engages. Try pulling the shaft out, to make sure the circlip is fully engaged.

19 Apply a little molybdenum disulphide grease to the driveshaft outer splines. Pull the hub outwards, and insert the outer end of the driveshaft. Turn the driveshaft to engage the splines in the hub, and fully push on the hub.

20 Screw on the new driveshaft nut, and use it to draw the driveshaft fully through the hub. Delay fully tightening the nut until the wheel is back on, and the car has been lowered to the ground.

21 Locate the hub onto the base of the suspension strut, and secure with the two bolts, inserted from the front. Tap the bolts through if necessary. Tighten the nuts to the specified torque.

22 Locate the track rod end balljoint into the swivel hub. Tighten the nut to the specified torque, then secure with a new split pin. If the split pin hole is not lined up, the nut may be tightened up to a further 60°.

23 Fill the transmission, and check the level as described in Chapter 1.

24 Refit the wheel, and lower the car to the ground. Tighten the wheel nuts to the specified torque.

25 Fully tighten the driveshaft nut to the specified torque, then stake the nut into the driveshaft groove. Finally, refit the wheel trim (or centre cover).

3 Driveshaft inner joint gaiter – renewal

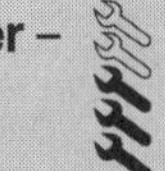

1 The inner joint gaiter is best renewed with the driveshaft removed from the car, as described in Section 2. Note that if both the inner and outer gaiters are being renewed at the same time, the outer gaiter can only be removed from the inner end of the driveshaft, once the inner joint and gaiter have been removed.

2 If required, mount the driveshaft in a vice.

3 Note the fitted location of both of the inner joint gaiter retaining clips, then release the clips from the gaiter, and slide the gaiter back along the driveshaft a little way **(see illustrations)**.

4 Mark the driveshaft in relation to the joint housing, to ensure correct refitting.

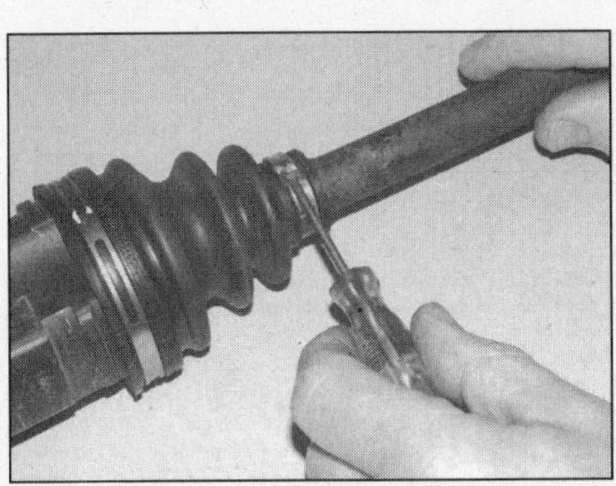

3.3a Using a screwdriver, release the inner joint gaiter's smaller . . .

3.3b . . . and larger-diameter clips

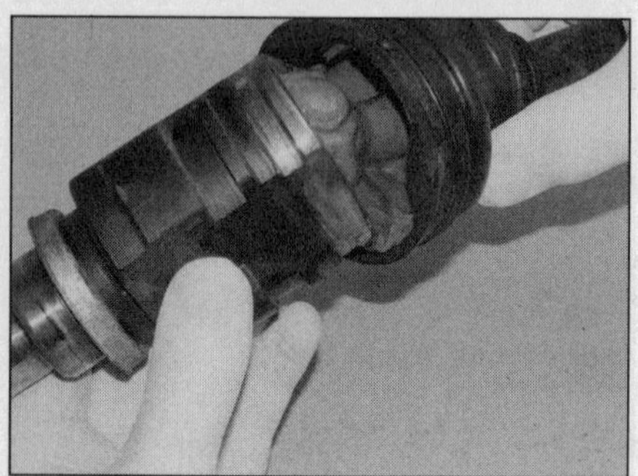

3.5 Separate the inner joint from the tripod

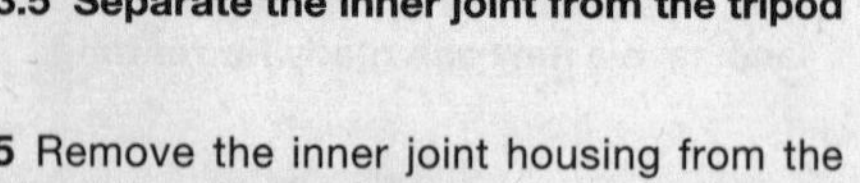

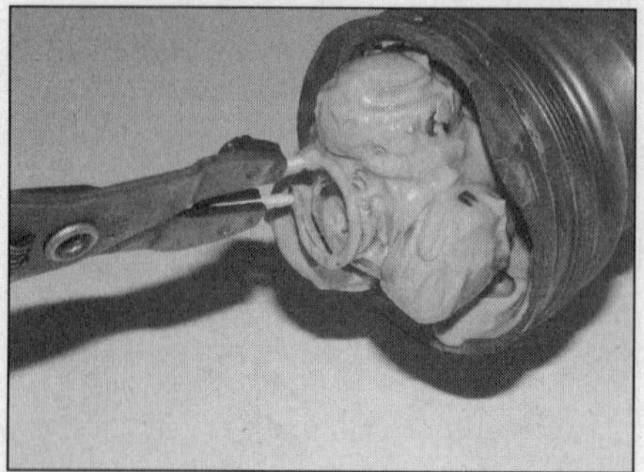

3.6 Extract the circlip from the end of the driveshaft

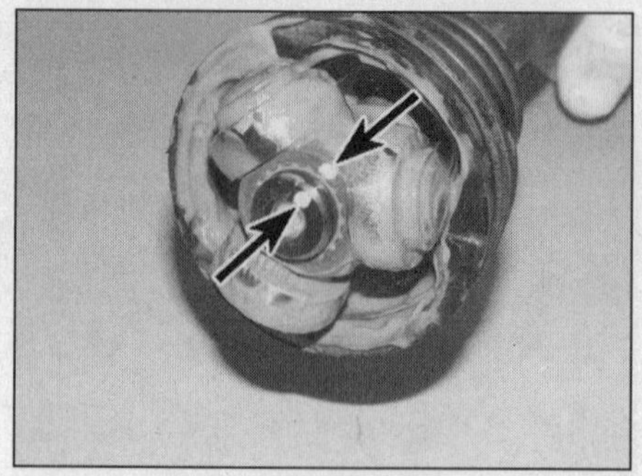

3.7 Mark the tripod in relation to the shaft

5 Remove the inner joint housing from the tripod **(see illustration)**.

6 Extract the circlip retaining the tripod on the driveshaft **(see illustration)**.

7 Check that the inner end of the driveshaft is marked in relation to the splined tripod hub. If not, use dabs of paint on the driveshaft and one end of the tripod **(see illustration)**.

8 Using a soft-metal or wooden drift on the tripod centre hub (not on the outer rollers), tap off the tripod from the end of the driveshaft **(see illustration)**.

9 Finally, slide off the inner gaiter **(see illustration)**.

10 If the outer gaiter is also to be renewed, remove it with reference to Section 4. If working on the right-hand driveshaft, first mark the fitted position of the dynamic damper. Use a screwdriver to prise open the damper securing clips either side, and slide the damper off the shaft.

11 Clean the driveshaft, and obtain a new joint retaining circlip. The gaiter retaining clips must also be renewed.

12 Slide the new gaiter on the driveshaft, together with new clips.

13 On the right-hand driveshaft, refit the dynamic damper to its previously-marked position, and secure by closing the clips.

14 Refit the tripod on the driveshaft splines, if necessary using a soft-faced mallet and a suitable socket to drive it fully onto the splines. It must be fitted with the previously-made marks aligned **(see illustration)**. Secure it in position using a new circlip. Ensure that the circlip is fully engaged in its groove.

15 Scoop out all of the old grease from the joint housing, then pack the joint and gaiter with new grease (see Specifications at the beginning of this Chapter). Guide the joint housing onto the tripod joint, making sure that the previously-made marks are aligned.

16 Slide the gaiter along the driveshaft, and locate it on the tripod joint housing. The small-diameter end of the gaiter must be located in the groove on the driveshaft, while the larger end of the gaiter should also locate in a groove on the housing.

17 Ensure that the gaiter is not twisted or distorted, then insert a small screwdriver under the lip of the gaiter at the housing end. This will allow trapped air to escape.

18 Remove the screwdriver, then fit the retaining clips and tighten them **(see illustrations)**.

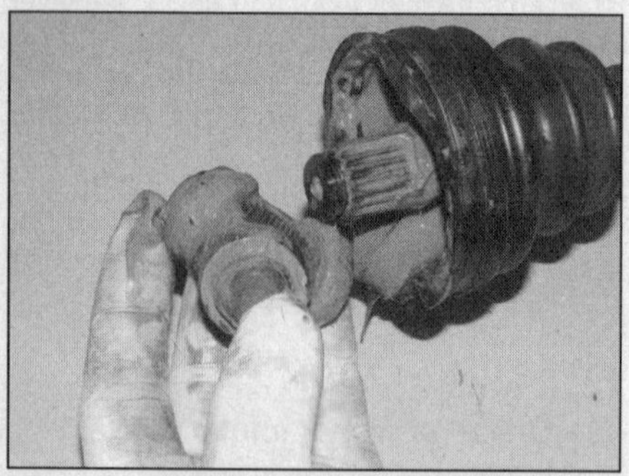

3.8 Tap the tripod off the shaft

3.9 Slide off the inner joint gaiter

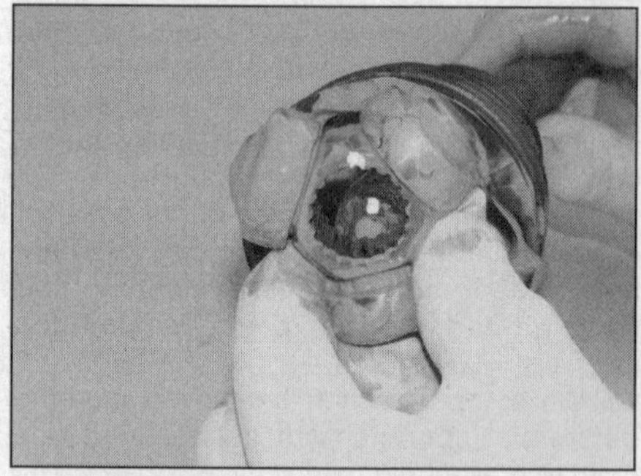

3.14 Line up the paint marks when refitting the tripod

3.18a Fit new gaiter retaining clips . . .

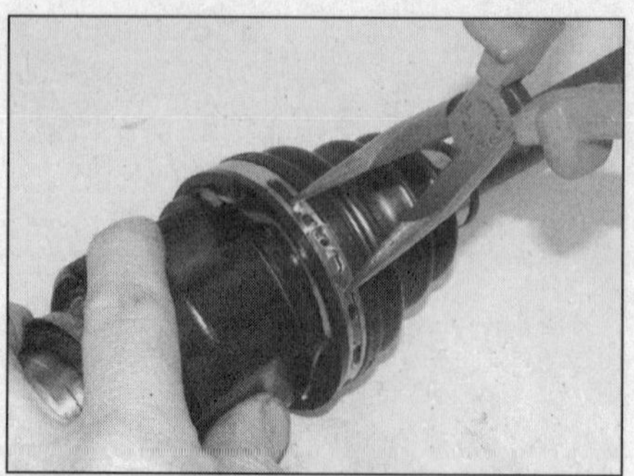

3.18b . . . and secure them using pliers

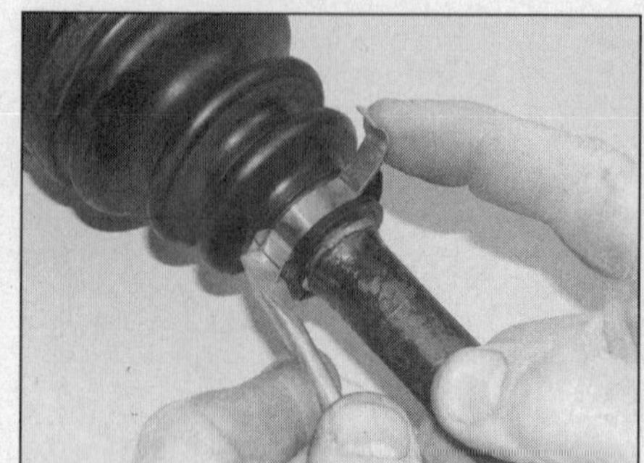

3.18c The smaller clip has an over-centre catch

4.3a Using a screwdriver, release the outer joint gaiter's smaller . . .

4.3b . . . and larger-diameter clips . . .

4.3c . . . then slide the gaiter off the CV joint, and off the inner end of the shaft

4 Driveshaft outer joint gaiter – renewal

1 The outer CV joint gaiter can only be renewed by removing the inner gaiter first as described in Section 3.

2 If required, mount the driveshaft in a vice.

3 Note the fitted location of both of the outer joint gaiter retaining clips, then release the clips from the gaiter, and slide the gaiter back along the driveshaft, and off the inner end **(see illustrations)**.

4 Slide the new gaiter (together with new clips) onto the driveshaft.

5 Scoop out all of the old grease, then pack the joint and gaiter with new grease (see Specifications at the beginning of this Chapter). Take care that the fresh grease does not become contaminated with dirt or grit as it is being applied.

6 Move the gaiter along the driveshaft, and locate it over the joint and onto the outer CV joint housing **(see illustration)**. The small-diameter end of the gaiter must be located in the groove on the driveshaft.

7 Ensure that the gaiter is not twisted or distorted, then insert a small screwdriver under the lip of the gaiter at the housing end, to allow any trapped air to escape.

8 Remove the screwdriver, fit the retaining clips in their previously-noted positions, and tighten them **(see illustration)**.

4.6 Locate the gaiter onto the CV joint

4.8 The outer joint gaiter clips are secured using special pliers, but side-cutters may be used

5 Driveshafts – inspection and joint renewal

1 If any of the checks described in the relevant part of Chapter 1 reveal apparent excessive wear or play in any driveshaft joint, first remove the wheel trim (or centre cover), and check the condition of the driveshaft nut. As it should have been staked in place when it was fitted, it is unlikely to be loose. If this is a concern, however, relieve the staking with a hammer and punch, and check that it is tightened to the specified torque. Repeat this check on the other side of the car.

2 Road test the car, and listen for a metallic clicking from the front as the car is driven slowly in a circle on full-lock. If a clicking noise is heard, this indicates wear in the outer constant velocity joint, which means that the joint must be renewed; reconditioning is not possible.

3 The outer CV joint is part of the driveshaft, and is not available separately.

4 If vibration, consistent with roadspeed, is felt through the car when accelerating, there is a possibility of wear in the inner tripod joints.

5 To renew an inner tripod joint, remove the driveshaft as described in Section 2, then separate the joint from the driveshaft with reference to Section 3.

Notes

Chapter 9
Braking system

Contents

Degrees of difficulty

Easy, suitable for novice with little experience 

Fairly easy, suitable for beginner with some experience 

Fairly difficult, suitable for competent DIY mechanic 

Difficult, suitable for experienced DIY mechanic

Very difficult, suitable for expert DIY or professional

Specifications

Brake pedal

Pedal height	129.0 to 139.0 mm
Pedal free play	1 to 3 mm
Stop-light switch clearance	0.5 to 2.4 mm

Front brakes

Type	Ventilated disc, with single sliding-piston caliper
Disc diameter	235.0 mm
Disc thickness:	
New	18.0 mm
Minimum	16.0 mm
Maximum disc thickness variation	0.025 mm
Maximum disc/hub run-out (installed)	0.050 mm
Caliper piston diameter	51.0 mm
Brake pad thickness (minimum)	1.0 mm

Rear drum brakes

Type	Leading and trailing shoes, with automatic adjusters
Drum internal diameter:	
New	200.0 mm
Maximum	201.0 mm
Brake shoe thickness (minimum)	1.0 mm

Torque wrench settings	Nm	lbf ft
ABS hydraulic unit to body	19	14
ABS wheel sensor securing bolts	8	6
ABS wiring bracket bolt	29	21
Brake disc splash shield bolts	8	6
Brake pedal mounting bracket nuts	13	10
Brake pedal pivot shaft nut	37	27
Brake pipe unions	15	11
Caliper guide pin bolts:		
Models made in Japan*	25	18
Models made in France*	32	24
Caliper hose union	30	22
Caliper mounting bracket (carrier) bolts	88	65
LSPV mounting bolts	19	14
LSPV link rod nut	13	10
Master cylinder-to-servo mounting nuts:		
Models made in Japan*	13	10
Models made in France*	20	15
Rear hub bolt	52	38
Rear wheel cylinder mounting bolt	10	7
Roadwheel nuts	103	76
Servo pushrod locknut:		
Models made in Japan*	26	19
Models made in France*	22	16

** Refer to 'Vehicle identification' for more information.*

1 General information

The braking system is of diagonally-split, dual-circuit design, with ventilated discs at the front, and drum brakes at the rear. Yaris models from May 2003 have an anti-lock braking system (ABS) as standard, and it was available as an option on earlier models. The front calipers are of single sliding-piston design, using asbestos-free pads. The rear drum brakes are of the leading and trailing shoe type, and are self-adjusting.

The vacuum servo unit uses inlet manifold depression (generated only when the engine is running) to boost the effort applied by the driver at the brake pedal and transmits this increased effort to the master cylinder pistons.

A load-sensitive proportioning valve (LSPV) is fitted to the rear brake circuit on models without ABS, to prevent rear wheel lock-up under hard braking by limiting the flow of fluid to the rear wheel cylinders. The valve is attached to the rear axle, and regulates the flow of fluid according to the weight being carried over the rear wheels.

Models with ABS are also equipped with Electronic Brake force Distribution (EBD). Simply, this is an electronically-managed version of the rear brake regulator valves fitted to non-ABS models – to prevent rear wheel lock-up, the ABS unit software limits the brake fluid pressure supplied to the rear wheels.

The handbrake is cable-operated, and acts on the rear brakes. The cables operate on the rear trailing brake shoe operating levers.

Models with ABS have a conventional brake system, together with an ABS hydraulic unit fitted between the master cylinder and the four brake units at each wheel. For more information on the system, refer to Section 15.

Precautions

The car's braking system is one of its most important safety features. When working on the brakes, there are a number of points to be aware of, to ensure that your health (or even your life) is not being put at risk.

- ***When servicing any part of the system, work carefully and methodically – do not take short-cuts; also observe scrupulous cleanliness when overhauling any part of the hydraulic system.***
- ***Always renew components in axle sets, where applicable – this means renewing brake pads, shoes, etc, on BOTH sides, even if only one set of pads is worn, or one wheel cylinder is leaking (for example). In the instance of uneven brake wear, the cause should be investigated and fixed (on front brakes, sticking caliper pistons is a likely problem).***
- ***Use only genuine Toyota parts, or at least those of known good quality.***
- ***Although genuine Toyota brake pads and shoes are asbestos-free, the dust created by wear of non-genuine parts may contain asbestos, which is a health hazard. Never blow it out with compressed air, and don't inhale any of it.***
- ***DO NOT use petroleum-based solvents to clean brake parts; use brake cleaner or methylated spirit only.***
- ***DO NOT allow any brake fluid, oil or grease to contact the brake pads or disc.***

Warning: Brake fluid is poisonous. Take care to keep it off bare skin, and in particular not to get splashes in your eyes. The fluid also attacks paintwork and plastics – wash off spillages immediately with cold water. Finally, brake fluid is highly inflammable, and should be handled with the same care as petrol.

2 Front brake pads – renewal

Note: *Refer to the precautions in Section 1 before proceeding. The pads fitted to Yaris models made in Japan differ significantly from those made in France – check where your car was made before ordering, referring to 'Vehicle identification' if necessary.*

1 Apply the handbrake. Loosen the front wheel nuts, then jack up the front of the car and support it on axle stands (see *Jacking and vehicle support*). Remove the front wheels. Work on one brake assembly at a time, using the assembled brake for reference if necessary.

2 Slacken and remove the lower caliper guide

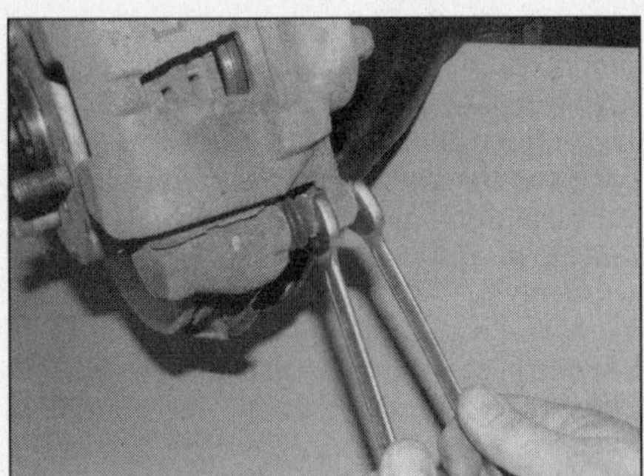
2.2a Using one spanner to hold the guide pin, unscrew . . .

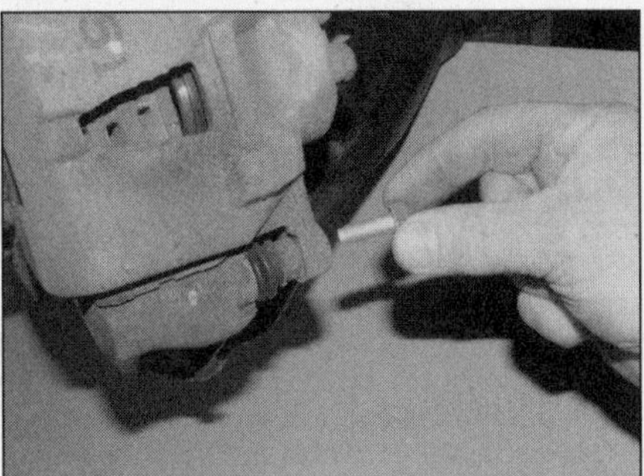
2.2b . . . and remove the guide pin bolt

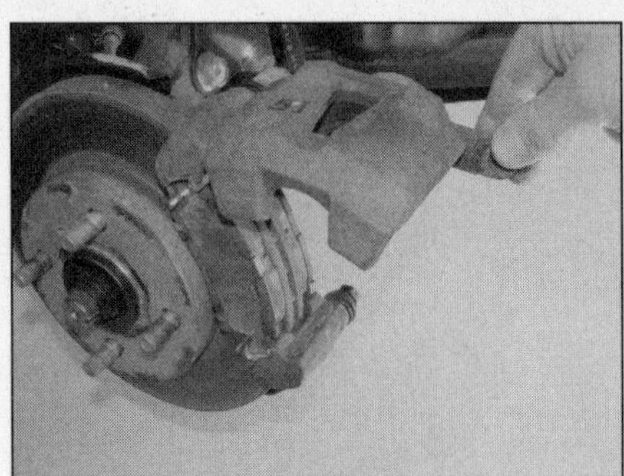
2.3 Swing the caliper upwards to access the pads

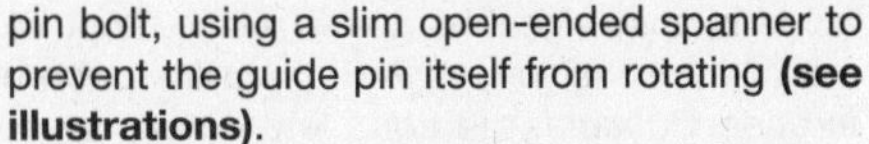

pin bolt, using a slim open-ended spanner to prevent the guide pin itself from rotating **(see illustrations)**.

3 With the lower guide pin bolt removed, pivot the caliper upwards **(see illustration)**.

Models made in Japan

4 Make a note of how the pad upper and lower support plates are fitted, as they are liable to fall out when the pads are removed.

5 Withdraw the two brake pads, which each have an anti-squeal shim, from the caliper mounting bracket **(see illustration)**.

Models made in France

6 Unclip the brake pads (which have integral anti-squeal shims) and remove them.

All models

7 First measure the thickness of each brake pad's friction material (not including the backing plate). If either pad is worn at any point to the specified minimum thickness or less, all four pads must be renewed. Also, the pads should be renewed if any are fouled with oil or grease; there is no satisfactory way of degreasing friction material, once contaminated. If any of the brake pads are worn unevenly, or are fouled with oil or grease, trace and rectify the cause before reassembly.

8 If the brake pads are still serviceable, carefully clean them using a clean, fine wire brush or similar, paying particular attention to the sides and back of the metal backing. If the pads are 'glazed' (have a shiny appearance) it may be helpful to roughen the surface of the friction material in order to restore the pads' braking effectiveness. Clean out the grooves in the friction material (where applicable), and pick out any large embedded particles of dirt or debris. Carefully clean the pad locations in the caliper body/mounting bracket.

9 Prior to fitting the pads, check that the spacers are free to slide easily in the caliper body bushes, and are a reasonably tight fit. Brush the dust and dirt from the caliper and piston, but *do not* inhale it, as it may contain asbestos, which is a health hazard. Inspect the dust seal around the piston for damage, and the piston for evidence of fluid leaks, corrosion or damage. If attention to any of these components is necessary, refer to Section 3.

10 The caliper piston must be pushed back into the caliper to make room for the new pads – this may require considerable effort. Either use a G-clamp, sliding-jaw (water pump) pliers, or suitable pieces of wood as levers **(see illustration)**.

Caution: Pushing back the piston causes a reverse-flow of brake fluid, which has been known to 'flip' the master cylinder rubber seals, resulting in a total loss of braking. To avoid this, clamp the caliper flexible hose and open the bleed screw – as the piston is pushed back, the fluid can be directed into a suitable container using a hose attached to the bleed screw. Close the screw just before the piston is pushed fully back, to ensure no air enters the system.

11 If the recommended method of opening a bleed screw before pushing back the piston is not used, the fluid level in the reservoir will rise, and possibly overflow. Make sure that there is sufficient space in the brake fluid reservoir to accept the displaced fluid and, if necessary, syphon some off first. Any brake fluid spilt on paintwork should be washed off with clean water, without delay – brake fluid is also a highly-effective paint-stripper.

12 Where applicable, refit the pad upper and lower support plates to the mounting bracket **(see illustration)**.

13 Although not essential, it is useful to apply a little copper brake grease to the edges of the pads in the areas which will slide in the mounting bracket (such as the end lugs, or

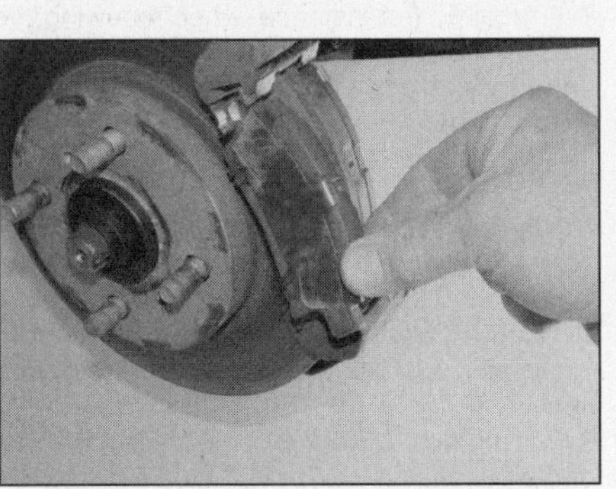
2.5 Withdraw the pads and anti-squeal shims from the mounting bracket

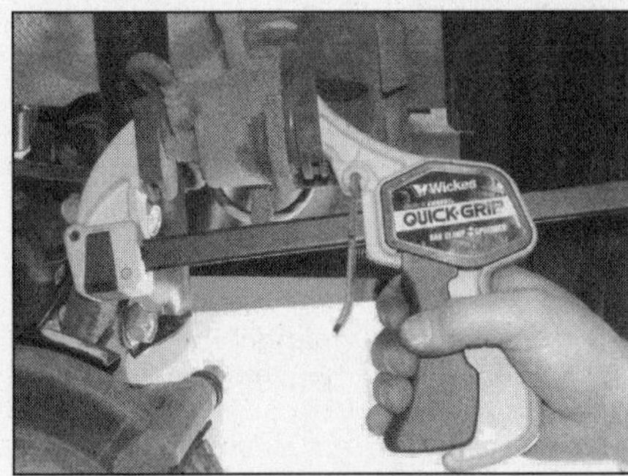

2.10 Using a DIY clamping tool to squeeze back the caliper pistons

2.12 If removed, refit the pad support plates to the mounting bracket

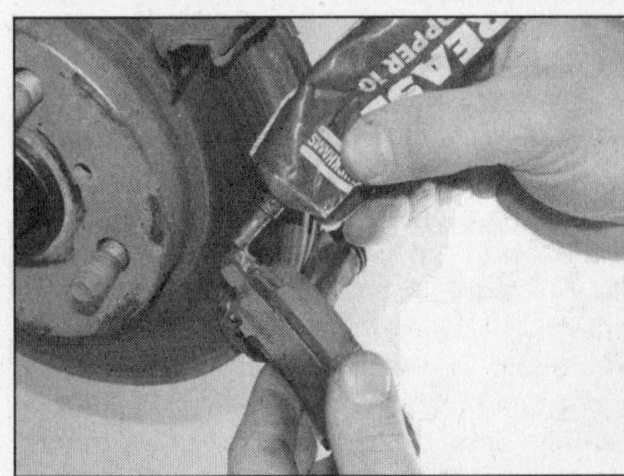
2.13 Apply a little copper grease to the pad-to-bracket surfaces

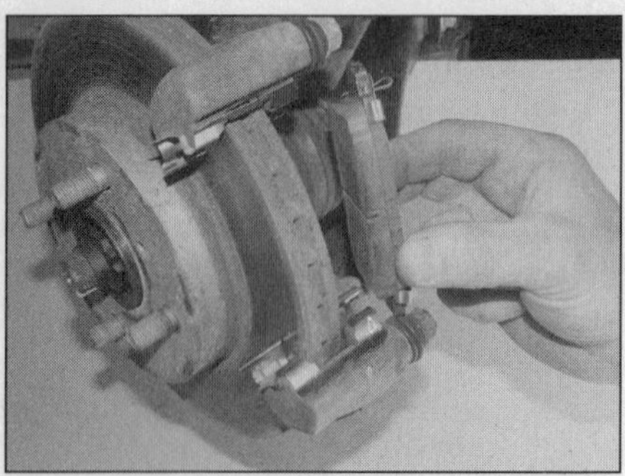

2.14 Fit the new pads into the mounting bracket

'ears') **(see illustration)**. Though anti-squeal shims are fitted, there is no harm in applying a little brake grease to the backs of the pads, where they will contact the caliper pistons. Ensure that no grease ends up on the pad friction material, or on the disc.

14 Install the pads and anti-squeal shims, ensuring that the friction material of each pad is against the brake disc **(see illustration)**. On genuine Toyota pads, the inner pad may have a wear indicator plate – if so, this should be facing upwards.

15 Pivot the caliper down into position. Install the guide pin bolt, tightening it to the specified torque setting while retaining the guide pin with an open-ended spanner.

16 On completion, firmly depress the brake pedal a few times, to bring the pads to their normal working position. Check the level of the brake fluid in the reservoir, and top-up if necessary.

17 Give the car a short road test, to make sure that the brakes are functioning correctly, and to bed-in the new linings to the contours of the disc. New linings will not provide maximum braking efficiency until they have bedded-in; avoid heavy braking as far as possible for the first hundred miles or so.

3 Front brake caliper – removal, overhaul and refitting

Note: *Refer to the precautions in Section 1 before proceeding.*

Removal

1 Apply the handbrake. Loosen the front wheel nuts, then jack up the front of the car and support it on axle stands (see *Jacking and vehicle support*). Remove the appropriate front wheel.

2 If the caliper is to be completely removed (as opposed to simply being unbolted and moved aside for other servicing work to be carried out) fit a brake hose clamp to the flexible hose leading to the caliper. This will minimise brake fluid loss during subsequent operations. Loosen the union on the caliper end of the flexible brake hose. Once loosened, do not try to unscrew the hose at this stage.

3 Remove the brake pads as described in Section 2.

4 Holding the upper guide pin using one spanner, unscrew and remove the upper guide pin bolt **(see illustration)**.

5 The caliper can now be removed from the mounting bracket. If it is simply to be unbolted and moved aside, support it from a convenient point under the wheel arch, using a piece of wire, string, or a cable-tie **(see illustration)**. Do not allow the caliper to hang unsupported on its flexible hose.

6 To remove the caliper completely, support it in one hand, and prevent the hydraulic hose from turning with the other hand. Unscrew the caliper from the hose, making sure that the hose is not twisted unduly or strained. Once the caliper is detached, plug the open hydraulic unions in the caliper and hose, to keep out dust and dirt.

7 If required (for instance, when renewing the discs), the caliper carrier bracket can be unbolted from the hub carrier **(see illustration)**.

Overhaul

Note: *Before starting work, check on the availability of parts (caliper overhaul kit/seals).*

8 With the caliper on the bench, brush away all traces of dust and dirt, but take care not to inhale any dust, as it may be harmful to your health.

9 Pull the dust cover rubber seal from the end of the piston.

10 Apply low air pressure to the fluid inlet union, to eject the piston. Only low air pressure is required for this, such as is produced by a foot-operated tyre pump.

Caution: The piston may be ejected with some force. Position a thin piece of wood between the piston and the caliper body to prevent damage to the end face of the piston in the event of it being ejected suddenly.

11 Using a suitable blunt instrument, prise the piston seal from the groove in the cylinder bore. Take care not to scratch the surface of the bore.

12 Clean the piston and caliper body with methylated spirit, and allow to dry. Examine the surfaces of the piston and cylinder bore for wear, damage and corrosion. If the piston alone is unserviceable, a new piston must be obtained, along with seals. If the cylinder bore is unserviceable, the complete caliper must be renewed. The seals must be renewed, regardless of the condition of the other components.

13 Coat the piston and seals with clean brake fluid, then manipulate the piston seal into the groove in the cylinder bore.

14 Push the piston squarely into its bore, taking care not to damage the seal.

15 Fit the dust cover rubber seal onto the piston and caliper, then depress the piston fully.

Refitting

16 Refit the caliper by reversing the removal operations. Make sure that the flexible brake hose is not twisted. Tighten the mounting bolts and wheel nuts to the specified torque.

17 Bleed the brake circuit according to the procedure given in Section 11, remembering to remove the brake hose clamp from the flexible hose. Make sure there are no leaks from the hose connections. Test the brakes carefully before returning the car to normal service.

4 Front brake disc – inspection, removal and refitting

Note: *Refer to the precautions in Section 1 before proceeding.*

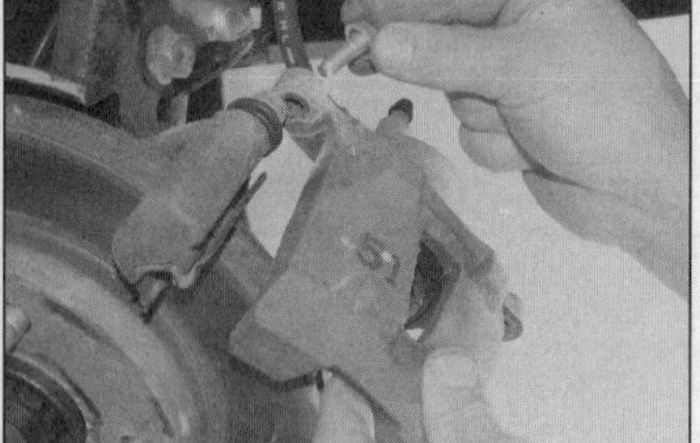

3.4 Unscrew the upper guide pin bolt, and the caliper can be removed

3.5 If the caliper is not being removed completely, hang it up inside the wheel arch

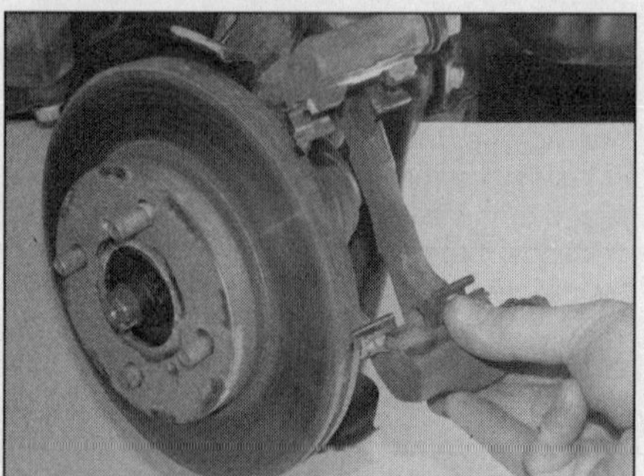

3.7 Unbolt and remove the caliper mounting bracket if necessary

Inspection

1 Apply the handbrake. Loosen the relevant wheel nuts, jack up the front of the car and support it on axle stands. Remove the appropriate front wheel.

2 Remove the front brake caliper from the disc with reference to Section 3, and undo the two caliper bracket securing bolts **(see illustration)**. Do not disconnect the flexible hose. Support the caliper on an axle stand, or suspend it out of the way with a piece of wire, taking care to avoid straining the flexible hose.

3 Temporarily refit two of the wheel nuts to diagonally-opposite studs, with the flat sides of the nuts against the disc. Tighten the nuts progressively, to hold the disc firmly.

4 Scrape any corrosion from the disc. Rotate the disc, and examine it for deep scoring, grooving or cracks. Using a micrometer, measure the thickness of the disc in several places. The minimum thickness is stamped on the disc hub. Light wear and scoring is normal, but if excessive, the disc should be removed, and either reground by a specialist, or renewed. If regrinding is undertaken, the minimum thickness must be maintained. Obviously, if the disc is cracked, it must be renewed.

5 Using a dial gauge or a flat metal block and feeler gauges, check that the disc run-out 10 mm from the outer edge does not exceed the limit given in the Specifications. To do this, fix the measuring equipment, and rotate the disc, noting the variation in measurement as the disc is rotated. The difference between the minimum and maximum measurements recorded is the disc run-out.

6 If the run-out is greater than the specified amount, check for variations of the disc thickness as follows. Mark the disc at eight positions 45° apart then, using a micrometer, measure the disc thickness at the eight positions, 15 mm in from the outer edge. If the variation between the minimum and maximum readings is greater than the specified amount, the disc should be renewed.

7 The hub face run-out can also be checked in a similar way. First remove the disc as described later in this Section, fix the measuring equipment, then slowly rotate the hub, and check that the run-out does not exceed the amount given in the Specifications. If the hub face run-out is excessive, this should be corrected (by renewing the hub bearings – see Chapter 10) before rechecking the disc run-out.

Removal

8 With the wheel and caliper removed, remove the wheel nuts which were temporarily refitted in paragraph 3.

9 Mark the disc in relation to the hub, if it is to be refitted.

10 Remove the washer/retaining clip(s) (where fitted), and withdraw the disc over the wheel studs **(see illustration)**.

4.2 Caliper mounting bracket bolts (arrowed)

Refitting

11 Make sure that the disc and hub mating surfaces are clean, then locate the disc on the wheel studs. Align the previously-made marks if the original disc is being refitted.

12 Refit the washer/retaining clip(s), where applicable.

13 Refit the brake caliper and carrier bracket.

14 Refit the wheel, and lower the car to the ground. Tighten wheel nuts to their specified torque.

15 Test the brakes carefully before returning the car to normal service.

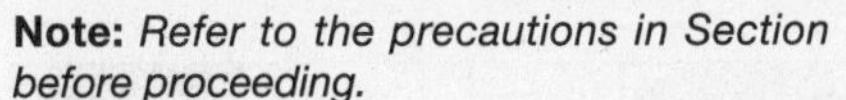

5 Rear brake drum – removal, inspection and refitting

Note: *Refer to the precautions in Section 1 before proceeding.*

Removal

1 Chock the front wheels, release the handbrake and engage 1st gear. Loosen the relevant wheel nuts, jack up the rear of the car and support it on axle stands (see *Jacking and vehicle support*). Remove the appropriate rear wheel.

2 It should be possible to pull the drum off by hand – if not, first check that the handbrake is fully released. Removal often means turning the drum, and trying to pull a little at either side. Another option is to try loosening the handbrake adjuster nut inside the car (refer to Section 19). Do not use too much force in removing the drum, or the shoe components could be damaged.

5.3a Fit two suitable bolts into the holes provided, and tighten them evenly . . .

4.10 Removing the brake disc

3 Toyota have provided two small bolt holes in the drum, which can be used to draw the drum off. Screw two suitable bolts into these holes, and tighten them evenly to pull the drum off **(see illustrations)**.

4 The last option is to prise out the rubber inspection plug in the brake backplate. Insert a slim, flat-bladed screwdriver through the hole, and try to turn the toothed wheel which operates the shoe adjuster – flick the blade end of the screwdriver upwards to turn the adjuster the right way.

5 With the brake drum removed, clean the dust from the drum, brake shoes, wheel cylinder and backplate, using brake cleaner or methylated spirit. Take care not to inhale the dust, as it may contain asbestos.

Inspection

6 Clean the inside surfaces of the brake drum, then examine the internal friction surface for signs of scoring or cracks. If the drum was difficult to remove, this may have been due to a wear lip on the outer edge. If it is cracked, deeply scored, or has worn to a diameter greater than the maximum given in the Specifications, then it should be renewed, together with the drum on the other side.

7 Regrinding of the brake drum is not recommended.

8 Check the wheel cylinder for signs of fluid leakage. A clue to a cylinder which may have just started leaking is a build-up of black brake dust around the cylinder rubber boots. Carefully lift their rubber boots with a small

5.3b . . . to draw the drum off without damaging the shoes

6.2 Note how the components are fitted before dismantling

6.3 Clean up the brake assembly and backplate as far as possible

6.4a Use pliers to depress and twist the cups . . .

screwdriver, and look for dampness. Renew if necessary, as described in Section 7.

If one wheel cylinder is found to be leaking, the one on the opposite side should also be at least checked. With safety in mind, it may be advisable to renew the other one as a matter of course – the likelihood is, it too will fail soon.

Refitting

9 Refitting is a reversal of removal, noting the following points:

a) Secure the drum using a new clip or star washer (where applicable).

b) With the wheel refitted and the car lowered to the ground, apply the footbrake and handbrake fully several times, to centre up the shoes and to set the automatic adjuster.

c) Test the brakes carefully before returning the car to normal service.

6 Rear brake shoes – renewal

Note: *Refer to the precautions in Section 1 before proceeding.*

1 Chock the front wheels, release the handbrake and engage 1st gear. Loosen the relevant wheel nuts, jack up the rear of the car and support it on axle stands (see *Jacking and vehicle support*). Remove the rear wheels.

Work on one brake assembly at a time, using the assembled brake for reference if necessary.

2 Before going any further, note the fitted position of the springs and the brake shoes (if possible, take a digital picture) **(see illustration)**.

3 Clean the components with brake cleaner, and allow to dry **(see illustration)**. Position a tray beneath the backplate, to catch the fluid and residue.

4 Remove the two shoe hold-down springs, use a pair of pliers to depress and twist the cups so that they can be withdrawn off the pins. Remove the hold-down pins from the backplate **(see illustrations)**.

5 Noting how it is fitted, unhook and remove the shoe lower spring, using a pair of thin-nosed pliers if necessary **(see illustration)**.

6 Pull out the rear shoe, and use the thin-nosed pliers to unhook the handbrake cable end fitting from the operating lever **(see illustrations)**.

7 Disconnect the top ends of the shoes from the wheel cylinder, taking care not to damage the rubber boots, and remove the shoe

6.4b . . . which releases the cups and hold-down springs . . .

6.4c . . . and allows the pins to be withdrawn from the rear

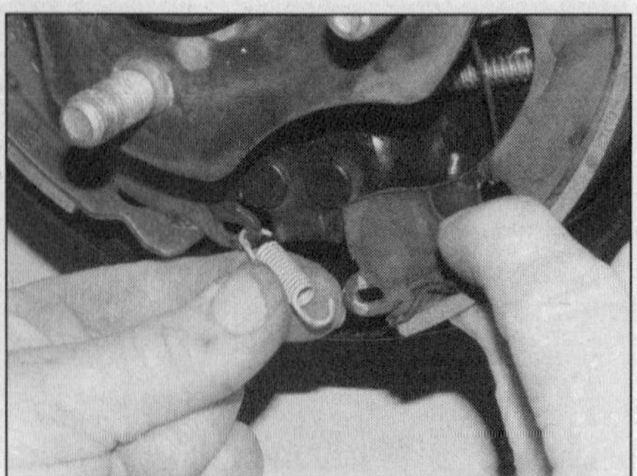

6.5 Unhook and remove the shoe lower spring

6.6a Pull the handbrake cable end fitting rearwards . . .

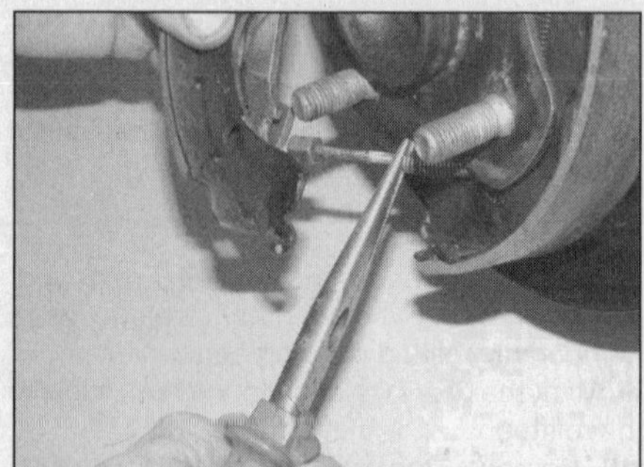

6.6b . . . then lift it to unhook it from the rear shoe

6.7 Carefully detach the tops of the shoes from the wheel cylinder, and remove the assembly

assembly from the backplate **(see illustration)**.

8 To prevent the wheel cylinder pistons from being accidentally ejected, fit a suitable elastic band or wire lengthways over the cylinder/pistons **(see illustration)**. DO NOT press the brake pedal while the shoes are removed.

9 Working on a clean bench, pull the leading shoe from the strut and brake shoe adjuster, noting how it is attached, then unhook the upper return spring from the shoes. Pull the adjustment strut to release it from the trailing brake shoe, and remove the strut rear return spring **(see illustrations)**.

10 If the wheel cylinder shows signs of fluid leakage, or if there is any reason to suspect it of being defective, inspect it now, as described in the next Section.

11 Clean the backplate, and apply small amounts of high-melting-point brake grease to the brake shoe contact points. Be careful not to get grease on any friction surfaces.

12 Lubricate the sliding components of the brake shoe adjuster with a little high-melting-point brake grease, but leave the serrations on the eccentric cam clean.

13 Fit the new brake shoes using a reversal of the removal procedure, but set the adjuster to its minimum length before assembling it to the trailing shoe.

14 Carry out the renewal procedures on the remaining rear brake.

15 Before refitting the drum, check its condition as described in Section 5.

16 With the drum in position, refit the wheel.

6.8 Wrap an elastic band around the wheel cylinder while the shoes are removed

17 Lower the car to the ground, and tighten the wheel nuts to the specified torque.

18 Depress the brake pedal several times, in order to operate the self-adjusting mechanism and set the shoes at their normal operating position.

19 Make several forward and reverse stops, and operate the handbrake fully two or three times (adjust the handbrake as required – see Section 19). Give the car a road test, to make sure that the brakes are functioning correctly, and to bed-in the new shoes to the contours of the drum. Remember that the new shoes will not give full braking efficiency until they have bedded-in.

7 Rear wheel cylinder – removal, overhaul and refitting

Note: *Refer to the precautions in Section 1 before proceeding. Also bear in mind that if the brake shoes have been contaminated by fluid leaking from the wheel cylinder, they must be renewed. The shoes on BOTH sides of the car must be renewed, even if they are only contaminated on one side.*

Removal

1 Remove the brake drum as described in Section 6. If the wheel cylinders have been leaking, there will probably be a significant build-up of brake dust on the failed seals (the dust sticks to the leaking fluid). A leak can be confirmed by carefully prising up the outer lip of the seal – any wetness means a new cylinder will be needed.

2 In recent years, the availability of wheel cylinder repair kits has greatly decreased, but it may still be worth asking. Wheel cylinders do not have to be fitted in pairs (providing they are the same size), but if one is leaking, it's reasonable to assume the other one soon will be too. If the leak has been going on for some time, it may be serious enough to have contaminated the brake shoes, in which case new shoes should be fitted on BOTH sides.

3 Minimise fluid loss either by removing the master cylinder reservoir cap, and then tightening it down onto a piece of polythene to obtain an airtight seal, or by using a brake hose clamp, a G-clamp, or similar tool, to clamp the flexible hose at the nearest convenient point to the wheel cylinder.

4 Pull the brake shoes apart at their top ends, so that they are just clear of the wheel cylinder. The automatic adjuster will hold the shoes in this position, so that the cylinder can be withdrawn.

5 Wipe away all traces of dirt around the hydraulic union at the rear of the wheel cylinder, then undo the union nut **(see illustration)**. This nut may well be very tight – it pays to apply penetrating oil (or WD-40) in advance, and to use a proper brake spanner when loosening it.

6 Unscrew the bolt securing the wheel cylinder to the backplate.

7 Withdraw the wheel cylinder from the backplate so that it is clear of the brake shoes. Plug the open hydraulic unions, to prevent the entry of dirt, and to minimise further fluid loss whilst the cylinder is detached.

Overhaul

8 No overhaul procedures or parts were available at the time of writing – check availability of spares before dismantling. Renewing a wheel cylinder as a unit is recommended.

Refitting

9 Wipe clean the backplate and remove the plug from the end of the hydraulic pipe. Fit the cylinder onto the backplate and screw in the hydraulic union nut by hand, being careful not to cross-thread it.

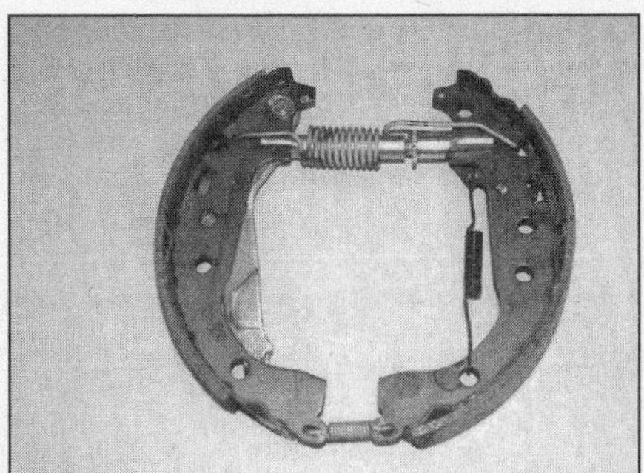
6.9a Driver's-side shoe assembly – front view

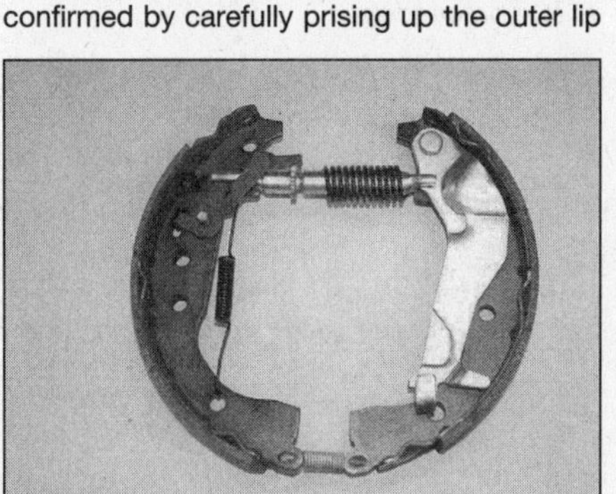
6.9b Driver's-side shoe assembly – rear view

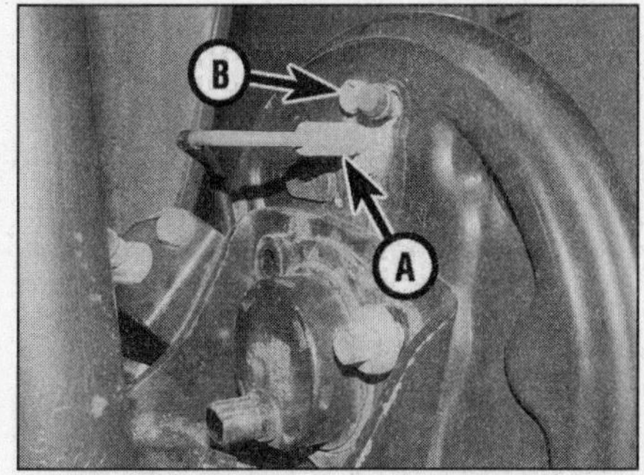

7.5 Wheel cylinder union nut (A) and mounting bolt (B)

10 Tighten the mounting bolt, then fully tighten the hydraulic union nut.

11 Retract the automatic brake adjuster mechanism, so that the brake shoes engage with the pistons of the wheel cylinder. To do this, prise the shoes apart slightly, turn the automatic adjuster to its minimum position, and release the shoes.

12 Remove the clamp from the flexible brake hose, or the polythene from the master cylinder (as applicable).

13 Refit the brake drum with reference to Section 6.

14 Bleed the hydraulic system as described in Section 11. Providing suitable precautions were taken to minimise loss of fluid, it should only be necessary to bleed the relevant rear brake.

15 Test the brakes carefully before returning the car to normal service.

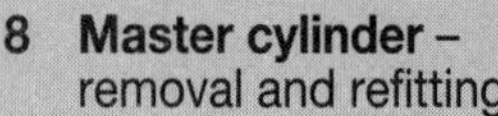

8 Master cylinder – removal and refitting

Note: *Refer to the precautions in Section 1 before proceeding.*

Removal

1 Disconnect the wiring plug for the fluid level warning sensor from the side of the reservoir.

2 Draw off the hydraulic fluid from the reservoir, using an old battery hydrometer or similar. Alternatively, raise the car, remove the wheels, then slacken the front bleed nipples and drain the fluid from the reservoir.

3 Disconnect the clutch master cylinder supply hose from the reservoir. Plug or cap the hose, to prevent fluid loss or dirt entry.

4 Identify the locations of the brake pipes on the master cylinder, then unscrew the union nuts and disconnect the pipes **(see illustration)**. These nuts may well be very tight – it pays to apply penetrating oil (or WD-40) in advance, and to use a proper brake spanner when loosening them.

5 Undo the master cylinder securing nuts, then withdraw the master cylinder from the studs on the servo unit **(see illustration)**. Recover the O-ring – a new one will be needed when refitting.

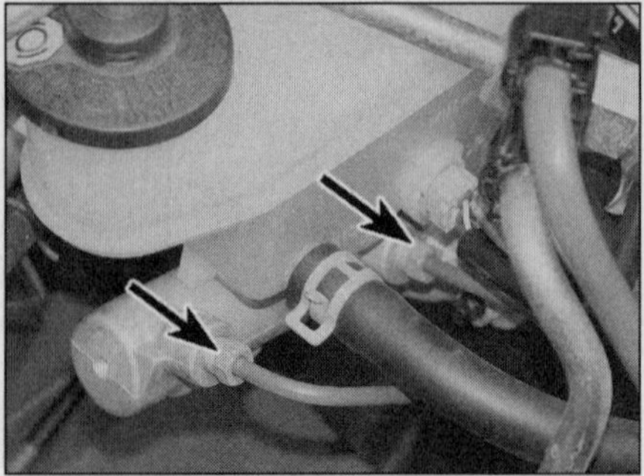

8.4 Unscrew the fluid unions on the side of the master cylinder

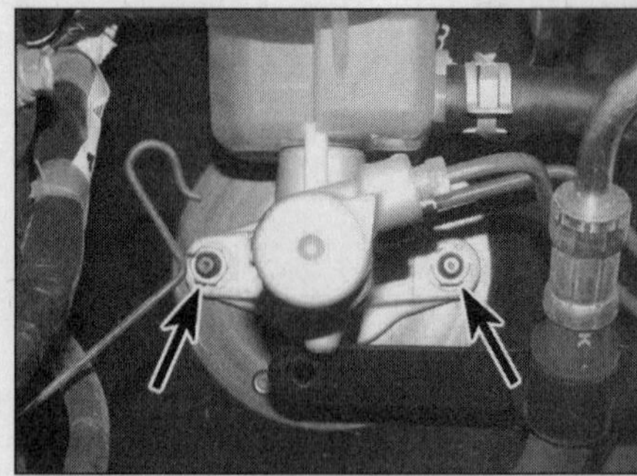

8.5 Unscrew the master cylinder mounting nuts

6 If required, the reservoir can be removed from the cylinder, by extracting the mounting pin and lifting the reservoir off. Recover the two reservoir seals, and fit new ones when reassembling.

7 If the master cylinder is faulty, it must be renewed. At the time of writing, no overhaul kits were available.

Refitting

8 Refitting is a reversal of the removal procedure, noting the following points:

a) Clean the contact surfaces of the master cylinder and servo, and locate a new O-ring on the back of the master cylinder.

b) Refit and tighten the nuts to the specified torque.

c) Carefully insert the brake pipes in the apertures in the master cylinder, then tighten the union nuts. Make sure that the nuts enter their threads correctly.

d) Fill the reservoir with fresh brake fluid.

e) Bleed the brake hydraulic system as described in Section 11. Depending on the amount of fluid lost, it may also be necessary to bleed the clutch as described in Chapter 6.

f) Test the brakes carefully before returning the car to normal service.

9 Brake pedal – removal, refitting and adjustment

Note: *Refer to the precautions in Section 1 before proceeding.*

Removal

1 Working inside the car, move the driver's seat fully to the rear (or remove it completely as described in Chapter 11) to allow maximum working area.

2 Raise the pedal by hand, and use a pair of pliers to unhook and remove the pedal return spring **(see illustration)**.

3 Use the same pliers to pull out the spring clip used to secure the servo pushrod clevis pin **(see illustration)**. Pull out the clevis pin and detach the pushrod from the pedal.

4 Unscrew the pedal pivot bolt nut, then slide out the bolt and remove the pedal from the car **(see illustration)**. Recover the pedal pivot bushes – if they appear worn, obtain new ones for reassembly.

5 If required, the pedal mounting bracket can also be removed – it is secured to the bulkhead by the four servo unit mounting nuts, and by a further bolt to the facia crossmember.

Refitting

6 Prior to refitting the pedal, apply a little grease to the pivot shaft, pedal bushes and actuator rods.

7 Refitting is a reversal of the removal procedure, but make sure that the pedal bushes and servo operating rod are correctly located.

8 Check and adjust the pedal height if necessary as described below.

Adjustment

Note: *For maximum accuracy, the brakes should be bled as described in Section 11 before carrying out any adjustments.*

9.2 Brake pedal return spring

9.3 Spring clip used to secure servo pushrod clevis pin

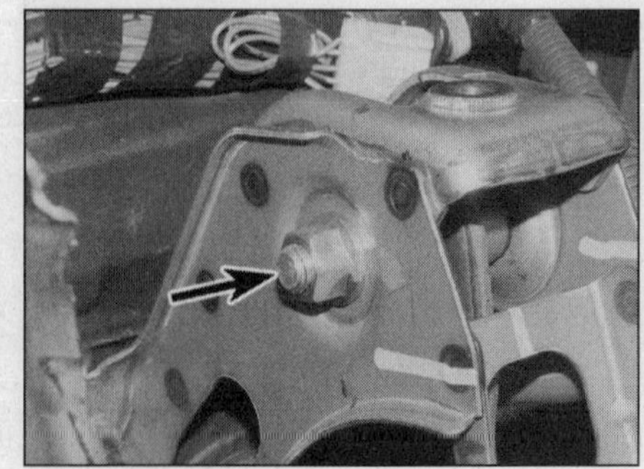

9.4 Brake pedal pivot bolt nut

9 With the pedal released, measure the distance from the floor (directly below the pedal), and compare with the specified dimension.

10 If adjustment is necessary, first disconnect the wiring plug from the stop-light switch. Loosen the switch locknut and remove the switch from the pedal bracket.

11 Loosen the locknut on the brake servo pushrod, and turn the adjuster as required until the pedal height falls within the specified range. Tighten the locknut to the specified torque on completion.

12 Refit the stop-light switch and reconnect its wiring plug.

13 Have an assistant on hand, to check the operation of the brake lights. Push the brake pedal in by hand, approximately 5 to 10 mm. With the pedal in this position, adjust the stop-light switch so that the brake lights are just going out.

14 Release the pedal, then slowly press it by hand, and check that the brake lights are on before the pedal has travelled 15 mm. The stop-light can also be adjusted by measuring the clearance between the switch plunger and the top of the pedal, and comparing with that specified.

15 Now press the pedal repeatedly using your foot, until the vacuum in the servo is dissipated and the pedal has a firm feel.

16 Check the pedal free play by depressing the pedal with your hand until resistance is felt – this should be no more than a very few millimetres. If the free play is incorrect, recheck the servo pushrod adjustment. Incorrect free play suggests a problem elsewhere in the braking system.

17 On completion, test the brakes carefully before returning the car to normal service.

10 Hydraulic pipes and hoses – inspection, removal and refitting

Note: *Refer to the precautions in Section 1 before proceeding.*

Inspection

1 Jack up the front and rear of the car, and support on axle stands. Make sure the car is safely supported on a level surface.

2 Check for signs of leakage at the pipe unions, then examine the flexible hoses for signs of cracking, chafing and fraying **(see illustration)**.

3 The brake pipes should be examined carefully for signs of dents, corrosion or other damage. Corrosion should be scraped off, and if the depth of pitting is significant, the pipes renewed. This is particularly likely in those areas underneath the car body where the pipes are exposed and unprotected.

4 Renew any defective brake pipes and/or hoses.

Removal

5 If a section of pipe or hose is to be removed, loss of brake fluid can be reduced by unscrewing the filler cap, and completely sealing the top of the reservoir with cling film or adhesive tape. Alternatively, the reservoir can be emptied (see Section 11).

6 To remove a section of pipe, hold the adjoining hose union nut with a spanner to prevent it from turning, then unscrew the union nut at the end of the pipe, and release it. Repeat the procedure at the other end of the pipe, then release the pipe by pulling out the clips attaching it to the body.

7 Where the union nuts are exposed to the full force of the weather, they can sometimes be quite tight. If an open-ended spanner is used, burring of the flats on the nuts is not uncommon, and for this reason it is preferable to use a split ring (brake) spanner, which will engage all the flats. If such a spanner is not available, self-locking grips may be used as a last resort; these may well damage the nuts, but if the pipe is to be renewed, this does not matter.

8 To further minimise the loss of fluid when disconnecting a flexible brake line from a rigid pipe, clamp the hose as near as possible to the pipe to be detached, using a brake hose clamp or a pair of self-locking grips with protected jaws.

9 To remove a flexible hose, first clean the ends of the hose and the surrounding area, then unscrew the union nuts from the hose ends. Remove the spring clip, and withdraw the hose from the support bracket **(see illustrations)**. Where applicable, unscrew the hose from the caliper.

10 Brake pipes supplied with flared ends and union nuts can be obtained individually or in sets from Toyota dealers or accessory shops. The pipe is then bent to shape, using the old pipe as a guide, and is ready for fitting. Be careful not to kink or crimp the pipe when bending it; ideally, a proper pipe-bending tool should be used.

Refitting

11 Refitting of the pipes and hoses is a reversal of removal. Make sure that all brake pipes are securely supported in their clips, and ensure that the hoses are not kinked. Check also that the hoses are clear of all suspension components and underbody fittings, and will remain clear during movement of the suspension and steering.

12 On completion, bleed the hydraulic system as described in Section 11.

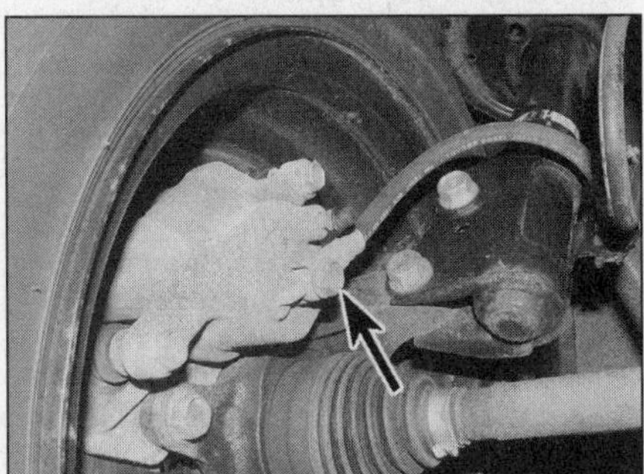
10.2 Front caliper flexible hose and union bolt (arrowed)

10.9a Front brake flexible hose union inside wheel arch

10.9b Front hose mounting bracket bolt (arrowed) inside suspension strut

10.9c Rear brake flexible hose union and body mounting bracket

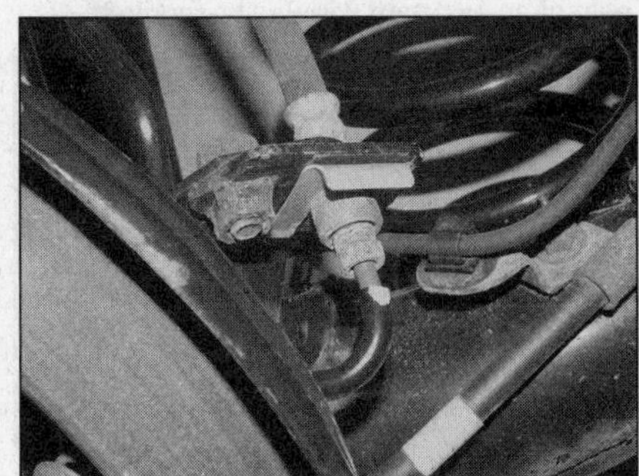
10.9d Rear brake flexible hose union inboard of backplate

11 Hydraulic system – bleeding

Note: *Refer to the precautions in Section 1 before proceeding.*

1 If the master cylinder has been disconnected and reconnected, then the complete system (all circuits) must be bled of air. If a component of one circuit has been disturbed, then only that particular circuit need be bled.

2 Bleeding should start with the furthest bleed nipple from the master cylinder, followed by the next one until the bleed nipple nearest the master cylinder is bled last.

3 There are many do-it-yourself 'one-man' brake bleeding kits available from motor accessory shops, and it is recommended that one of these kits be used wherever possible, as they greatly simplify the brake bleeding operation. Follow the kit manufacturer's instructions in conjunction with the following procedure. If a pressure-bleeding kit is obtained, then it will not be necessary to depress the brake pedal in the following procedure.

4 During the bleeding operation, do not allow the brake fluid level in the reservoir to drop below the minimum mark. If the level is allowed to fall so far that air is drawn in, the whole procedure will have to be started again from scratch. **Note:** *On models fitted with ABS, the ignition must be switched off (take out the key).* Only use new fluid for topping-up, preferably from a freshly-opened container. Never re-use fluid bled from the system.

5 Before starting, check that all rigid pipes and flexible hoses are in good condition, and that all hydraulic unions are tight. Take great care not to allow hydraulic fluid to come into contact with the car paintwork, otherwise the finish will be seriously damaged. Wash off any spilt fluid immediately with cold water.

Bleeding

Basic (two-man) method

6 Collect together a clean glass jar of reasonable size, a suitable length of plastic or rubber tubing which is a tight fit over the bleed screw, and a ring spanner to fit the screw. The help of an assistant will also be required.

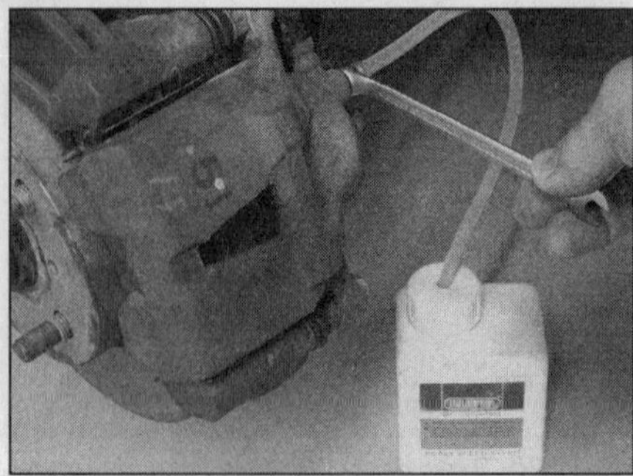

11.15 Using a one-man brake bleeding kit

7 Remove the dust cap from the first screw in the sequence. Fit the spanner and tube to the screw, place the other end of the tube in the jar, and pour in sufficient fluid to cover the end of the tube.

8 Ensure that the master cylinder reservoir fluid level is maintained at least above the MIN level line throughout the procedure.

9 Have the assistant fully depress the brake pedal several times to build-up pressure, then maintain it on the final downstroke.

10 While pedal pressure is maintained, unscrew the bleed screw (approximately one turn) and allow the compressed fluid and air to flow into the jar. The assistant should maintain pedal pressure, following it down to the floor if necessary, and should not release it until instructed to do so. When the flow stops, tighten the bleed screw again, have the assistant release the pedal slowly, and recheck the reservoir fluid level.

11 Repeat the steps given in paragraphs 9 and 10 until the fluid emerging from the bleed screw is free from air bubbles. If the master cylinder has been drained and refilled, and air is being bled from the first screw in the sequence, allow approximately five seconds between cycles for the master cylinder passages to refill.

12 When no more air bubbles appear, tighten the bleed screw securely, remove the tube and spanner, and refit the dust cap. Do not overtighten the bleed screw.

13 Repeat the procedure on the remaining screws in the sequence, until all air is removed from the system and the brake pedal feels firm again.

Using a one-way valve kit

14 As their name implies, these kits consist of a length of tubing with a one-way valve fitted, to prevent expelled air and fluid being drawn back into the system; some kits include a translucent container, which can be positioned so that the air bubbles can be more easily seen flowing from the end of the tube.

15 The kit is connected to the bleed screw, which is then opened **(see illustration)**. The user returns to the driver's seat, depresses the brake pedal with a smooth, steady stroke, and slowly releases it; this is repeated until the expelled fluid is clear of air bubbles.

16 Note that these kits simplify work so much that it is easy to forget the master cylinder reservoir fluid level; ensure that this is maintained at least above the MIN level line at all times.

Using a pressure-bleeding kit

17 These kits are usually operated by the reservoir of pressurised air contained in the spare tyre. However, note that it will probably be necessary to reduce the pressure to a lower level than normal; refer to the instructions supplied with the kit.

18 By connecting a pressurised, fluid-filled container to the master cylinder reservoir, bleeding can be carried out simply by opening each screw in turn (in the specified sequence), and allowing the fluid to flow out until no more air bubbles can be seen in the expelled fluid.

19 This method has the advantage that the large reservoir of fluid provides an additional safeguard against air being drawn into the system during bleeding.

20 Pressure-bleeding is particularly effective when bleeding 'difficult' systems, or when bleeding the complete system at the time of routine fluid renewal.

All methods

21 When bleeding is complete, and firm pedal feel is restored, wash off any spilt fluid, tighten the bleed screws securely, and refit their dust caps.

22 Check the hydraulic fluid level in the master cylinder reservoir, and top-up if necessary (see *Weekly checks*).

23 Discard any hydraulic fluid that has been bled from the system; it will not be fit for re-use.

24 Check the feel of the brake pedal. If it feels at all spongy, air must still be present in the system, and further bleeding is required. Failure to bleed satisfactorily after a reasonable repetition of the bleeding procedure may be due to worn master cylinder seals.

25 Check the clutch operation on completion; it may be necessary to bleed the clutch hydraulic system with reference to Chapter 6.

12 Vacuum servo unit – testing, removal and refitting

Note: *Refer to the precautions in Section 1 before proceeding.*

Testing

1 To test the operation of the servo unit, depress the footbrake four or five times to dissipate the vacuum, then start the engine while keeping the footbrake depressed. As the engine starts, there should be a noticeable give in the brake pedal as vacuum builds-up. Allow the engine to run for at least two minutes, and then switch it off. If the brake pedal is now depressed again, it should be possible to hear a hiss from the servo when the pedal is depressed. After four or five applications, no further hissing should be heard, and the pedal should feel harder.

2 Before assuming that a problem exists in the servo unit itself, inspect the non-return valve as described in the next Section.

Removal

3 Refer to Section 8 and remove the master cylinder.

4 Release the spring clip, then pull off the vacuum hose from the connection on the front of the servo unit.

5 Remove the wiper motor and linkage as described in Chapter 12.

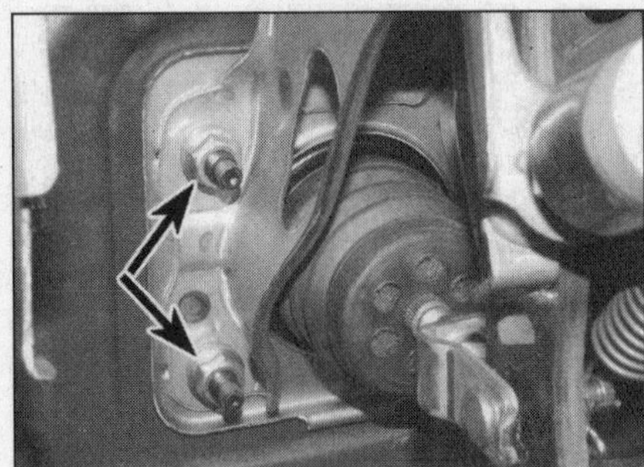

12.11 Two of the four brake servo mounting nuts

13.2 Disconnect the vacuum hose from the servo

13.4 Disconnect the servo vacuum hose from the inlet manifold – 1.0 litre shown

6 On left-hand-drive models, remove the ABS hydraulic unit as described in Section 16.
7 On right-hand-drive models with hydraulic power steering, using the information in Chapter 10, loosen the power steering pump mountings, and move it aside as necessary.
8 Working inside the car, move the driver's seat fully to the rear, to allow maximum working room.
9 Raise the brake pedal by hand, and use a pair of pliers to unhook and remove the pedal return spring **(refer to illustration 9.2)**.
10 Use the same pliers to pull out the spring clip used to secure the servo pushrod clevis pin. Pull out the clevis pin and detach the pushrod from the brake pedal **(refer to illustration 9.3)**.
11 Have an assistant support the servo unit under the bonnet, then unscrew and remove the four nuts from the brake pedal mounting bracket **(see illustration)**.
12 Have your assistant carefully withdraw the servo unit into the engine compartment – this will also loosen the pedal mounting bracket inside the car, but it will remain in place thanks to the upper bolt to the facia crossmember.
13 Recover the servo mounting gasket – a new one should be used when refitting.

Refitting

14 Refitting is a reversal of the removal procedure, noting the following points:

a) *Make sure the new gasket is correctly positioned on the servo.*
b) *Refit the master cylinder as described in Section 8.*
c) *Test the brakes carefully before returning the car to normal service.*

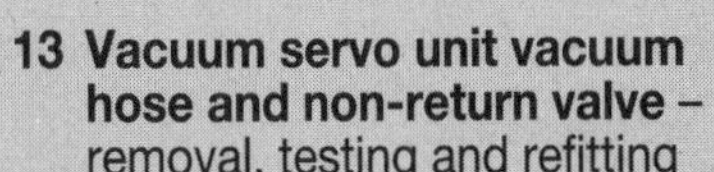

13 Vacuum servo unit vacuum hose and non-return valve – removal, testing and refitting

Note: *Refer to the precautions in Section 1 before proceeding.*

Removal

1 With the engine switched off, depress the brake pedal four or five times, to dissipate any remaining vacuum from the servo unit.
2 Release the spring clip and disconnect the vacuum hose at the servo unit **(see illustration)**.
3 Remove the non-return valve by pulling it free from the rubber grommet. If it is reluctant to move, prise it free, using a screwdriver with its blade inserted under the flange.
4 Detach the vacuum hose from the inlet manifold connection **(see illustration)**.
5 If the hose or the fixings are damaged or in poor condition, they must be renewed.

Testing

6 Examine the non-return valve for damage and signs of deterioration, and renew it if necessary. The valve may be tested by blowing through its connecting hoses in both directions. It should only be possible to blow from the servo end towards the inlet manifold.

Refitting

7 Refitting is a reversal of the removal procedure. If fitting a new non-return valve, ensure that it is fitted the correct way round.

14 Load-sensitive proportioning valve (LSPV) – removal and refitting

Note: *Refer to the precautions in Section 1 before proceeding. On models with ABS, the LSPV function is superseded by a system known as EBD (Electronic Brake force Distribution) – see Section 15.*

Removal

1 Loss of brake fluid can be reduced during this procedure by unscrewing the filler cap, and completely sealing the top of the reservoir with cling film or adhesive tape. Alternatively, the reservoir can be emptied (see Section 11).
2 Jack up the rear of the car, and support it on axle stands (see *Jacking and vehicle support*). Release the handbrake.
3 The valve assembly is located just in front of the rear axle, on the passenger side. To remove the valve, first unbolt and remove the handbrake cable mounting bracket on that side, and move the cable clear as far as possible.
4 Preferably using a proper brake spanner, loosen and remove the four brake pipe unions from the valve body. Anticipate some spillage of fluid as this is done.
5 Unscrew the nut and disconnect the valve link rod from the bracket on the rear axle. Particularly if the same valve is to be refitted, do not loosen the adjuster lock bolt fitted below the spring on the link rod.
6 Remove the three mounting bolts, and withdraw the valve and its mounting bracket from under the car. If required, the valve can be separated from the bracket by removing the two through-bolts.

Refitting

7 Refitting is a reversal of removal, noting the following points:

a) *If a new valve is being fitted, it should be set up by a Toyota dealer, using a special setting jig. However, set the new valve's link rod dimension to the same length as the old one, using the adjuster lockbolt, as an initial setting. Drive the car with care until the valve has been properly set up.*
b) *Tighten the mounting bolts, link rod nut and brake pipe union nuts to the specified torque.*
c) *Bleed the braking system as described in Section 11.*

15 Anti-lock braking system (ABS) – general information

ABS is fitted to many Yaris models as standard. The system comprises a hydraulic regulator unit and the four roadwheel sensors. The regulator unit contains the electronic control unit (ECU), the hydraulic solenoid valves and the electrically-driven return pump. The purpose of the system is to prevent the wheel(s) locking during heavy braking. This is achieved by automatic release of the brake on the relevant wheel, followed by re-application of the brake.

The solenoid valves are controlled by the ECU, which itself receives signals from the four wheel sensors fitted to the wheel hubs which monitor the speed of rotation of each wheel. By comparing these signals, the ECU can determine the speed at which the vehicle

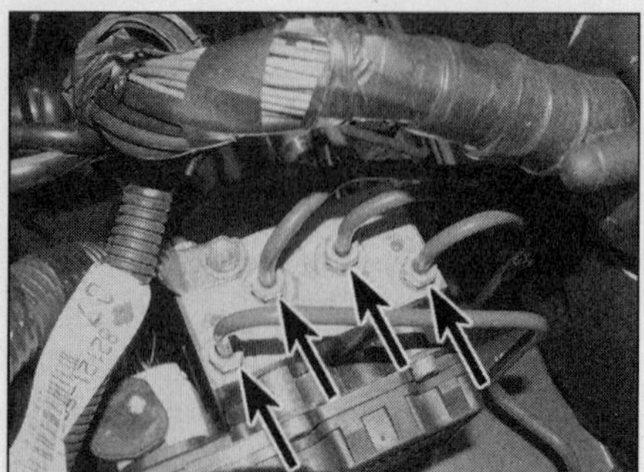

16.3 Disconnect the four brake pipes from the top of the unit

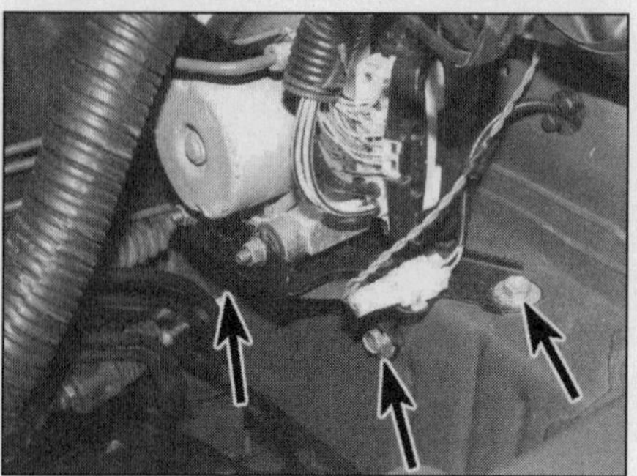

16.4 Unbolt the ABS unit mounting bracket from the inner wing

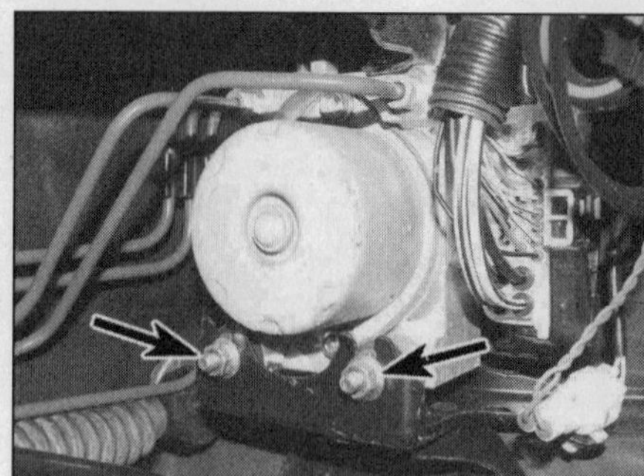

16.5 ABS unit-to-mounting bracket nuts

is travelling – this information is used instead of a vehicle speed sensor signal on some models. It can use this speed to determine when a wheel is decelerating at an abnormal rate, compared to the speed of the car, and therefore predicts when a wheel is about to lock. During normal operation, the system functions in the same way as a non-ABS braking system.

If the ECU senses that a wheel is about to lock, it closes the relevant outlet solenoid valves in the hydraulic unit, which then isolates the relevant brake(s) on the wheel(s) which is/are about to lock from the master cylinder, effectively sealing-in the hydraulic pressure.

If the speed of rotation of the wheel continues to decrease at an abnormal rate, the ECU opens the inlet solenoid valves on the relevant brake(s), and operates the electrically-driven return pump which pumps the hydraulic fluid back into the master cylinder, releasing the brake. Once the speed of rotation of the wheel returns to an acceptable rate, the pump stops; the solenoid valves switch again, allowing the hydraulic master cylinder pressure to return to the caliper, which then re-applies the brake. This cycle can be carried out many times a second.

The action of the solenoid valves and return pump creates pulses in the hydraulic circuit. When the ABS system is functioning, these pulses can be felt through the brake pedal.

The operation of the ABS system is entirely dependent on electrical signals. To prevent the system responding to any inaccurate signals, a built-in safety circuit monitors all signals received by the ECU. If an inaccurate signal or low battery voltage is detected, the ABS system is automatically shut-down, and the warning light on the instrument panel is illuminated, to inform the driver that the ABS system is not operational. Normal braking should still be available, however.

The Yaris is also equipped with an additional safety feature called EBD (Electronic Brake force Distribution), which automatically apportions braking effort between the front and rear wheels. The EBD function is built into the system's software, and the intention is to limit braking effort (fluid pressure) to the rear wheels, to further prevent them locking up under heavy braking.

If a fault does develop in the any of these systems, the vehicle must be taken to a Toyota dealer or suitably-equipped specialist for fault diagnosis and repair.

16 ABS hydraulic unit – removal and refitting

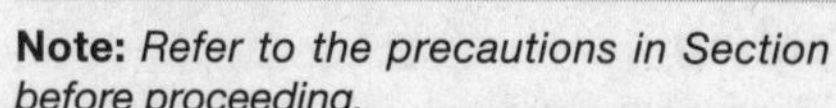

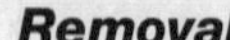

Note: *Refer to the precautions in Section 1 before proceeding.*

Removal

1 The ABS unit is somewhat inaccessible, at the rear of the engine compartment on the passenger's side. Access may be improved by unbolting the windscreen scuttle panel, as described in the windscreen wiper motor removal procedure in Chapter 12.

2 Disconnect the wiring multi-plug from the ABS unit.

3 Taking precautions against the spillage of brake fluid, and noting their positions for refitting, unscrew the six brake pipe unions on the top and side of the unit, and disconnect the pipes **(see illustration)**. Use a proper brake spanner on the unions, to avoid rounding them off if they are tight.

4 Unbolt the mounting bracket from the inner wing, and remove the hydraulic unit from the engine compartment, together with its mounting bracket **(see illustration)**.

5 If required, the hydraulic unit can be separated from its mounting bracket, after removing the two nuts **(see illustration)**.

17.7 Unscrew the mounting bolt and remove the sensor from the hub

Refitting

6 Refitting is a reversal of removal. Ensure that the multi-plug is securely connected, and that the brake pipe unions are tightened to the specified torque. On completion, bleed the hydraulic system as described in Section 11.

17 ABS wheel sensors – testing, removal and refitting

Note: *Refer to the precautions in Section 1 before proceeding.*

Testing

1 Checking of the sensors is done before removal, connecting a voltmeter to the disconnected sensor multi-plug. Using an analogue (moving coil) meter is not practical, since the meter does not respond quickly enough. A digital meter having an ac facility may be used to check that the sensor is operating correctly.

2 To do this, raise the relevant wheel then disconnect the wiring to the ABS sensor and connect the meter to it.

3 Spin the wheel and check that the output voltage is between 1.5 and 2.0 volts, depending on how fast the wheel is spun.

4 Alternatively, an oscilloscope may be used to check the output of the sensor – an alternating current will be traced on the screen, of magnitude depending on the speed of the rotating wheel.

5 If the sensor output is low or zero, renew the sensor.

Removal

Front wheel sensor

6 Apply the handbrake and loosen the relevant front wheel nuts. Jack up the front of the car and support it on axle stands. Remove the wheel.

7 Unscrew the sensor mounting bolt from the hub and withdraw the sensor **(see illustration)**. The sensors can prove difficult to remove, due to corrosion – try soaking the sensor in penetrating oil (or WD-40). Do not use any great force to remove a sensor, or it may be damaged. If the sensor does not have to be removed, unclip and disconnect its wiring instead.

8 Unbolt the sensor wiring support bracket inside the wheel arch **(see illustration)**.

9 Carefully detach the sensor wiring grommet from the wheel arch **(see illustration)**, then trace the wiring inside the engine compartment and disconnect the multi-plug. Withdraw the sensor and wiring.

Rear wheel sensor

10 The rear wheel sensor is pressed into the rear hub, which can be removed as described in Chapter 10 for rear wheel bearing renewal. A puller will then be needed to extract the sensor, and a press is required to fit the new one. Due to the likely cost of a new sensor (and the risk of damaging it), and the tools required, this is a job best left to a Toyota dealer.

Refitting

11 Refitting is a reversal of the removal procedure.

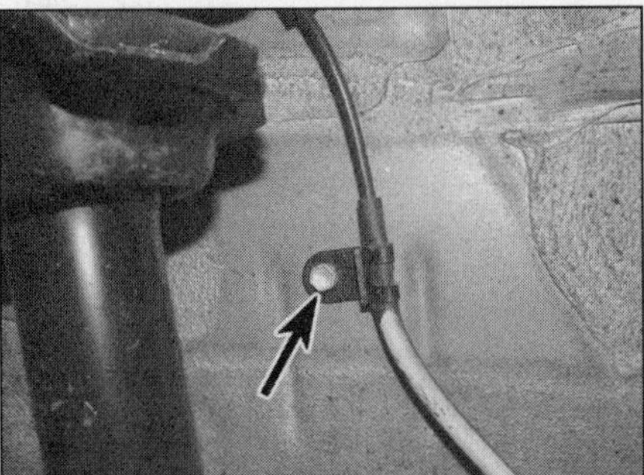

17.8 Unbolt the sensor wiring inside the wheel arch

17.9 Prise out the sensor wiring grommet

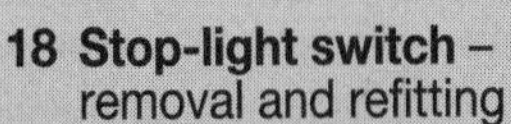

18 Stop-light switch – removal and refitting

Note: *Refer to the precautions in Section 1 before proceeding.*

Removal

1 Working inside the car, move the driver's seat fully to the rear, to allow maximum working space.

2 Disconnect the wiring plug from the stop-light switch at the top of the brake pedal bracket **(see illustration)**.

3 Loosen the switch locknut and withdraw the switch from the bracket **(see illustration)**.

Refitting

4 Refitting is a reversal of removal. Once the switch has been fitted and reconnected, check the operation of the switch as follows.

5 Have an assistant on hand, to check the operation of the brake lights. Push the brake pedal in by hand, approximately 5 to 10 mm. With the pedal in this position, adjust the stop-light switch so that the brake lights are just going out.

6 Release the pedal, then slowly press it by hand, and check that the brake lights are on before the pedal has travelled 15 mm. The stop-light can also be adjusted by measuring the clearance between the switch plunger and the top of the pedal, and comparing with that specified.

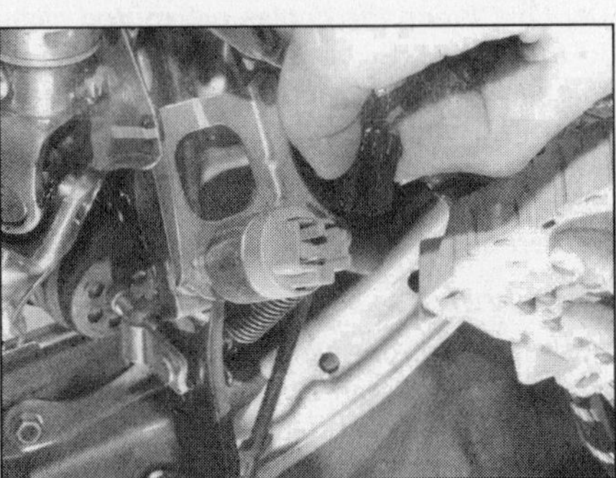

18.2 Disconnect the stop-light switch wiring plug

18.3 Stop-light switch locknut

19 Handbrake lever – removal, refitting and adjustment

Note: *Refer to the precautions in Section 1 before proceeding.*

Removal

1 Chock the front wheels, and engage 1st gear or P on automatics.

2 Though not essential, access to the handbrake lever is greatly improved by removing one of the front seats, as described in Chapter 11.

3 Remove the centre console as described in Chapter 11.

4 Loosen the handbrake locknut, then unscrew it and the adjuster nut completely, and disconnect the link rod from the lever. Alternatively, unhook the equaliser bar from the cable end fittings at the rear **(see illustrations)**.

5 Disconnect the electrical connector from the handbrake warning light switch **(see illustration)**.

6 Remove the two bolts securing the lever

19.4a Loosen the locknut and adjuster nut . . .

19.4b . . . and unhook the equaliser bar from the cables

19.5 Unplug the handbrake warning light switch

19.6 Remove the two mounting bolts and remove the lever assembly

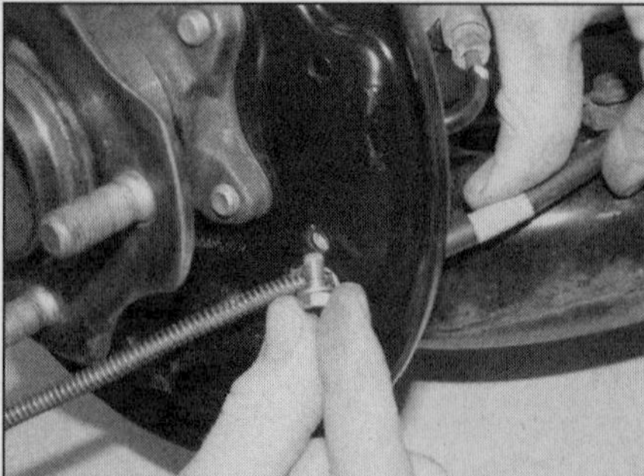

20.3 Remove the cable support bracket bolt inside the backplate

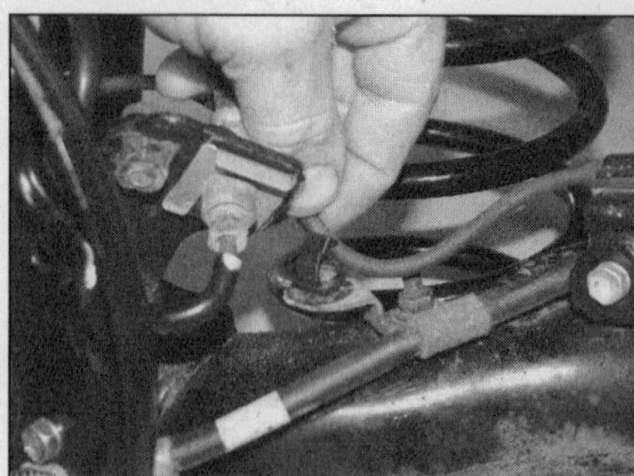

20.4a Where necessary, unclip the ABS wiring from its bracket . . .

assembly to the floor, and remove it from the car **(see illustration)**.

Refitting

7 Refitting is a reversal of removal.

8 When refitting the lever, it will be necessary to reset and adjust the mechanism, as described below.

Adjustment

9 Refer to the adjustment procedure in Chapter 1. If new cables have been fitted, recheck the adjustment after (say) one month or 1000 miles.

20 Handbrake cables – removal and refitting

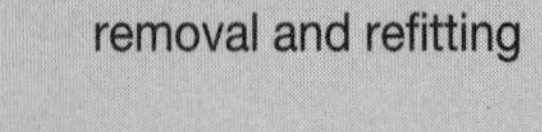

Note: *Refer to the precautions in Section 1 before proceeding.*

Caution: Since the cables are routed close to the exhaust system in several places, this procedure should only be attempted when the engine and exhaust system are completely cool. The engine should have been switched off for at least a few hours (preferably, after it has been left overnight).

Removal

1 Chock the front wheels, and engage 1st gear or P on automatics. Loosen the wheel nuts on the relevant rear wheel, then jack up the rear of the car and support it on axle stands (see *Jacking and vehicle support*). Fully release the handbrake lever.

2 Remove the brake shoes as described in Section 6.

3 Unscrew the cable support bracket bolt to free the cable from the brake backplate **(see illustration)**.

4 Where applicable, unclip the ABS sensor wiring from the support clip, then unscrew the first cable support bracket nut, on the rear suspension arm **(see illustrations)**.

5 With the support bracket free, the cable end can be withdrawn from the brake backplate **(see illustration)**.

6 Trace the cable forwards, unbolting the support brackets to free it from the underside of the car **(see illustrations)**. Note how it is routed for refitting.

7 At the front, unscrew the bolt which secures the cable to the floor where it enters the car **(see illustration)**.

8 Remove the centre console as described in Chapter 11.

9 Unhook the cable from the equaliser bar behind the handbrake lever **(see illustration)**, then feed it downwards and out from under the car.

20.4b . . . then unscrew the handbrake cable support bracket nut (arrowed)

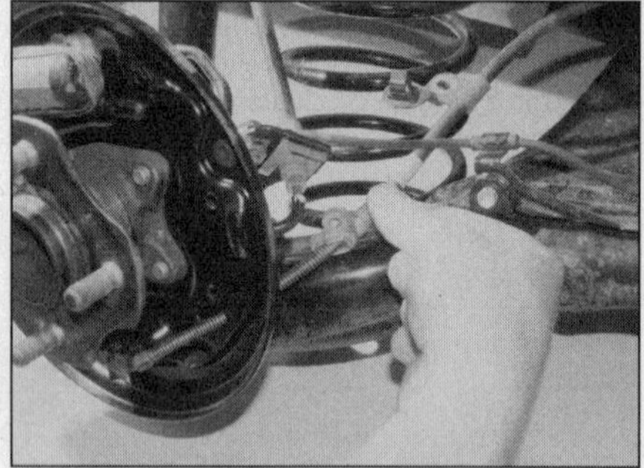

20.5 Withdraw the cable from the backplate

20.6a Handbrake cable support bracket in front of rear axle pivot . . .

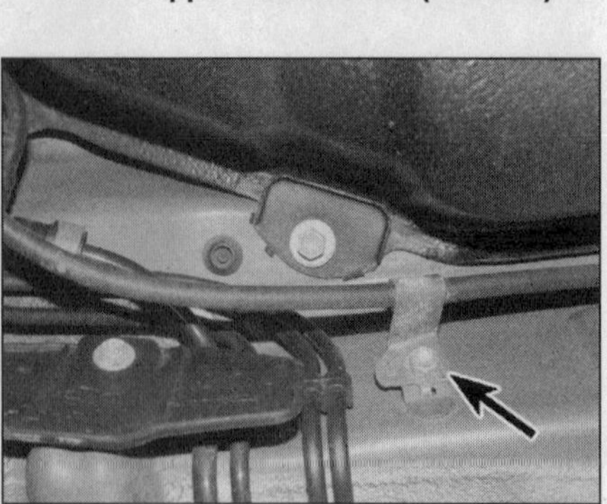

20.6b . . . and across the back of the car (arrowed)

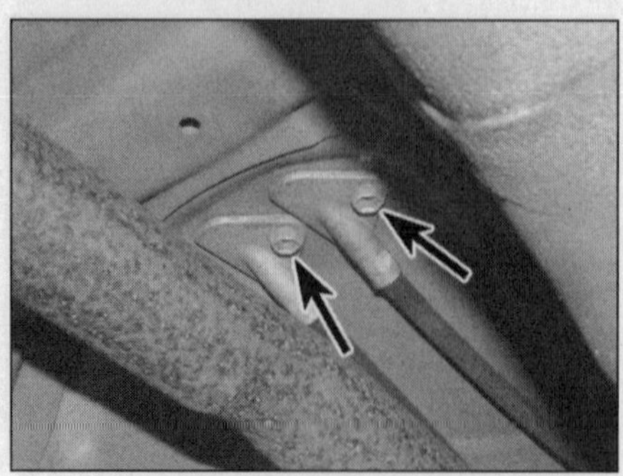

20.7 Handbrake cable front mounting bolts to floor

20.9 Unhook the cable end fitting from the equaliser bar

10 If one cable is being renewed due to wear or other problems, consider renewing them both as a pair, to ensure even operation.

Refitting

11 Refitting is a reversal of the removal procedure, noting the following points:

a) Make sure that the cable end fittings are correctly located, and that the cables are routed as before, without any kinks or sharp bends.

b) Adjust the handbrake as described in Section 19.

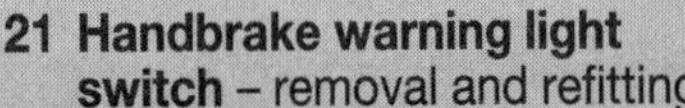

21 Handbrake warning light switch - removal and refitting

Note: *Although not absolutely necessary, access to the handbrake switch is greatly improved if the driver's seat is removed as described in Chapter 11.*

Removal

1 Remove the centre console as described in Chapter 11.

21.2 The switch mounting screw is masked by the lever link rod

21.3 Note the fitted position of the locknut and adjuster nut

2 The mounting screw for the switch appears at first to be accessible from the driver's side, but the handbrake lever link rod prevents putting a screwdriver onto the screw head **(see illustration)**.

3 Note the position of the handbrake adjuster and locknuts (if the threaded section beyond the locknut is measured, the nuts can be reset to this position, avoiding re-adjusting the handbrake on completion) **(see illustration)**.

4 Loosen the locknut and adjuster nut, to create enough slack at the equaliser bar to unhook the cables **(refer to illustration 20.9)**.

5 Lift the equaliser bar and link rod upwards, and the warning light switch can be unscrewed **(see illustration)**.

6 Disconnect the switch wiring plug, and remove it from the lever bracket **(see illustrations)**.

Refitting

7 Refitting is a reversal of removal. If necessary, check the handbrake adjustment as described in Chapter 1.

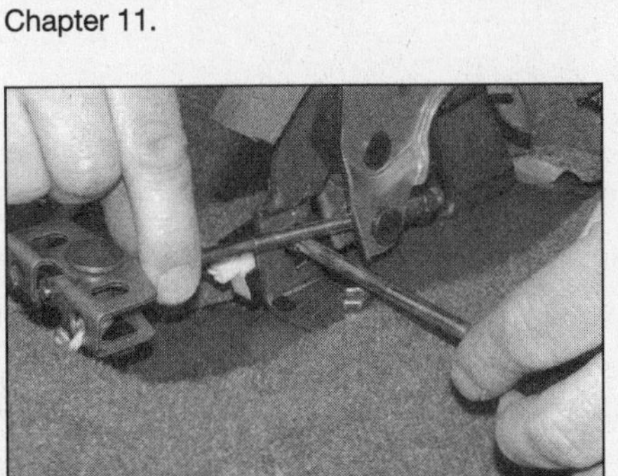

21.5 Lift the link rod upwards, and remove the mounting screw

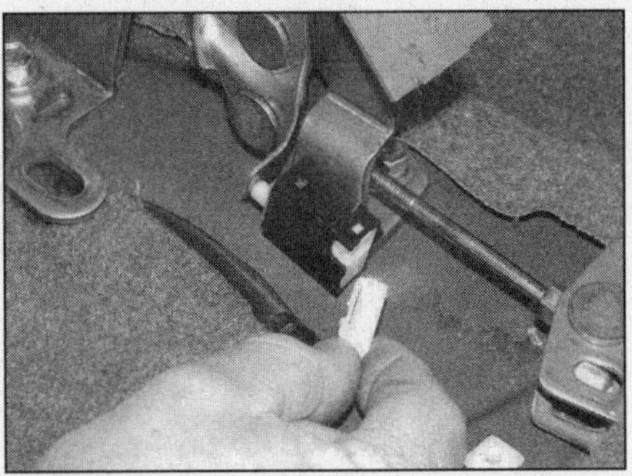

21.6a Disconnect the switch wiring plug . . .

21.6b . . . and remove the switch from the bracket

Notes

Chapter 10
Suspension and steering

Contents

Degrees of difficulty

Easy, suitable for novice with little experience 	**Fairly easy,** suitable for beginner with some experience 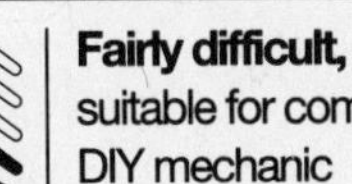	**Fairly difficult,** suitable for competent DIY mechanic	**Difficult,** suitable for experienced DIY mechanic	**Very difficult,** suitable for expert DIY or professional

Specifications

Wheel alignment and steering angles

Front wheel toe-setting	0 ± 2 mm
Front wheel camber:	
All models	-0° 35' ± 45'
Maximum side-to-side variation	30'
Front wheel castor:	
Manual steering	0° 35' ± 45'
Power steering	1° 33' ± 45'
Maximum side-to-side variation	30'
Steering axis inclination:	
All models	10° 05' ± 45'
Maximum side-to-side variation	30'
Rear wheel camber:	
Up to May 2002	-1° 00' ± 45'
May 2002 onwards	-0° 56' ± 25'
Maximum side-to-side variation	30'
Rear wheel toe-setting	2.8 mm (toe-in) ± 3.0 mm

Torque wrench settings

	Nm	lbf ft
Front suspension		
Anti-roll bar bracket bolts	19	14
Anti-roll bar drop link nuts	18	13
Brake caliper mounting bracket (carrier) bolts	88	65
Brake disc splash shield bolts	8	6
Brake hose/wiring support bracket-to-strut	29	21
Driveshaft (hub) nut*	216	159
Lower arm balljoint nut	98	72
Lower arm front pivot bolt	88	65
Lower arm rear mounting bolt	132	97
Subframe mounting bolts:		
Front bolts	70	52
Rear bolts	116	86
Subframe reinforcement bracket bolts	47	35
Suspension strut piston rod nut*	33	24
Suspension strut top mounting nuts	39	29
Swivel hub-to-suspension strut pinch-bolt/nut**:		
Up to May 2002	132	97
May 2002 onwards	142	105
Rear suspension		
Rear hub mounting bolts	52	38
Shock absorber lower mounting nut	49	36
Shock absorber upper mounting top nut	25	18
Steering		
Power steering pump:		
Front mounting bolt	21	15
Pressure pipe union bolt	54	40
Side mounting bolts	44	32
Steering column intermediate shaft pinch-bolts	28	21
Steering column mounting bolts	21	15
Steering rack fluid unions	49	36
Steering rack securing bolts	74	55
Steering wheel securing nut:		
Japan-made models without electric power steering***	34	25
All other models	50	37
Track rod end balljoint nut:		
Up to May 2002	49	36
May 2002 onwards	33	24
Track rod end locknuts	47	35
Roadwheels		
Roadwheel nuts	103	76

** Use new nut/bolt.*
** Oiled threads.*
**** Refer to 'Vehicle identification'.*

1 General information

The front suspension is of independent type, with a subframe, MacPherson struts, lower arms, and an anti-roll bar. The struts, which incorporate coil springs and integral shock absorbers, are attached at their upper ends to the reinforced strut mountings on the body shell. The lower end of each strut is bolted to the top of a cast swivel hub, which carries the hub, and the brake disc and caliper. The hubs run within non-adjustable bearings in the swivel hubs. The lower end of each swivel hub is attached, via a balljoint, to a pressed-steel lower arm assembly. The balljoints are integral with the lower arms. Each lower arm is attached at its inboard end to the subframe, via flexible rubber bushes, and controls both lateral and fore-and-aft movement of the front wheels. An anti-roll bar is fitted to all models. The anti-roll bar is mounted on the subframe, and is connected to the suspension struts via vertical drop links.

The rear suspension is semi-independent, with a U-section beam welded between pressed-steel trailing arms. This U-section beam allows a limited torsional flexibility, giving each rear wheel a certain degree of independent movement, whilst maintaining optimum track and wheel camber control. This type of arrangement is called a 'twist beam' rear axle. The axle is attached to the body via rubber bushes which are designed to allow a certain amount of 'rear steering' (toe correction) during fast cornering. The rear suspension commonly used on small cars is separate springs and shock absorbers. The compact springs are mounted under the car, so only the shock absorber housings encroach on the boot area, resulting in more boot space. The shock absorbers are bolted to the trailing arm section of the rear axle at the base, and to the body housings at the top. The rear hubs are integral with the stub axles which are bolted to the rear of the trailing arms, and the brake drums are separate.

The steering is of conventional rack-and-pinion type, incorporating a collapsible safety column. The column is joined to the steering rack via a flexible coupling. The steering rack is mounted on the front suspension subframe. The steering rack track rods are attached via the track rod ends to the steering arms on the swivel hubs.

All but a few base Yaris models (and virtually all those sold in the UK) are equipped with power steering. Most models have a conventional 'hydraulic' system, with a pump which is belt-driven from the crankshaft pulley, a fluid reservoir, and interconnecting hoses. Some later models may be equipped with an 'electric' system, with a motor incorporated into the steering column to provide the turning assistance; on these models, any references to power steering pipes, hoses and fluid can be disregarded. The two systems can be distinguished by the presence (or otherwise) of a power steering fluid reservoir in the engine compartment (refer to *Weekly checks*). It appears most likely that models built in France will have the electric system – refer to *Vehicle identification* for details on establishing the country of origin.

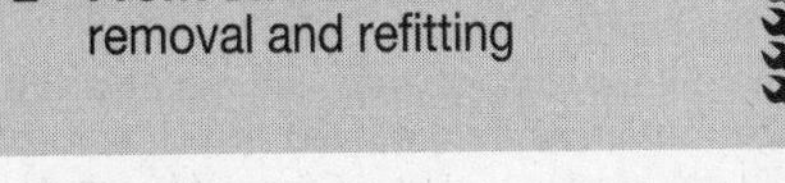

2 Front swivel hub – removal and refitting

Removal

1 Remove the relevant wheel trim, or the wheel centre cover (alloy wheels) for access to the driveshaft nut.

2 Using a hammer and punch, relieve the staking on the driveshaft nut.

3 Ensure that the handbrake is applied (ideally, have an assistant apply the footbrake), then slacken the driveshaft nut using a suitable socket (30 mm on our car) and extension bar. Loosen the driveshaft nut almost to the end of its threads, but do not remove it at this stage.

Warning: The driveshaft nut is done up extremely tight, and considerable effort will be required to loosen it. Do not use poor-quality, badly-fitting tools for this task, due to the risk of personal injury.

4 Apply the handbrake, slacken the relevant front wheel nuts, then jack up the front of the car and support securely on axle stands (see *Jacking and vehicle support*). Remove the roadwheel and the engine lower cover.

5 Unscrew the bolts securing the brake caliper mounting bracket to the swivel hub, then slide the caliper/bracket assembly from the swivel hub and brake disc (there is no need to remove the brake pads). Suspend the caliper/bracket assembly from the strut coil spring using wire or string – do not allow the caliper to hang on the brake hose.

6 Mark the brake disc in relation to the hub (assuming it is to be refitted), then remove any retaining clips or washers holding it in place, and withdraw it from the hub.

7 On models with ABS, unscrew the wheel sensor retaining bolt, then withdraw the wheel sensor from the top of the hub. Provided the sensor is placed out of the way, there is no need to disconnect its wiring. **Note:** *The sensors can prove difficult to remove, due to corrosion – try soaking the sensor in penetrating oil (or WD-40). Do not use any great force to remove a sensor, or it may be damaged.*

8 Remove the split pin, then slacken the track rod end balljoint nut, and unscrew it as far as the ends of the threads.

9 Disconnect the track rod end balljoint from the swivel hub using a balljoint separator tool (leave the nut fitted to protect the threads), taking care not to damage the balljoint rubber seal **(see illustration)**. Once the balljoint has been released, remove the balljoint nut.

10 Remove the spring clip, then slacken the lower arm balljoint nut, and unscrew it as far as the ends of the threads. Push the end of the lower arm down to free the balljoint from the swivel hub. If the balljoint is very tight, it may be necessary to lever down using a large screwdriver, or similar tool, but take care not to damage the balljoint rubber seal **(see illustrations)**.

11 Remove the nuts from the two bolts used to secure the swivel hub to the base of the suspension strut. Note which way the bolts are fitted (this should be from the front), then support the hub and tap the bolts out **(see illustrations)**.

12 The splined end of the driveshaft now has to be released from its location in the hub. It's likely that the splines will be very tight (corrosion may even be a factor, if the driveshaft has not been disturbed for some time), and considerable force may be needed to push the driveshaft out. Toyota recommend tapping the shaft out with a plastic or hide mallet. If an ordinary hammer is used, place a small piece of wood over the end of the driveshaft – in addition to the loosened driveshaft nut, this will protect the threads from damage **(see illustration)**.

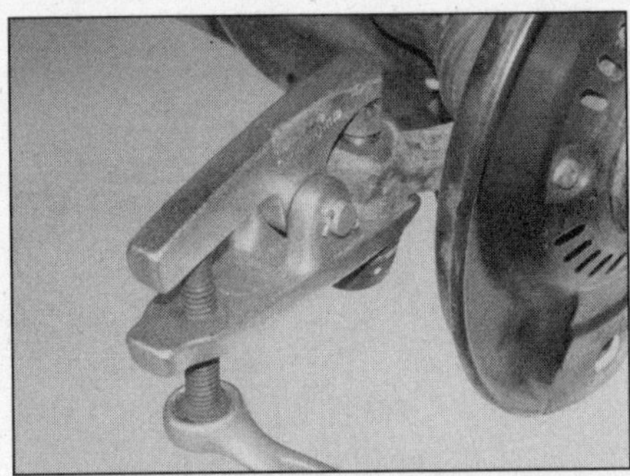

2.9 Separate the track rod end balljoint

2.10a Remove the lower balljoint nut spring clip . . .

2.10b . . . then use a balljoint separator tool to release the balljoint

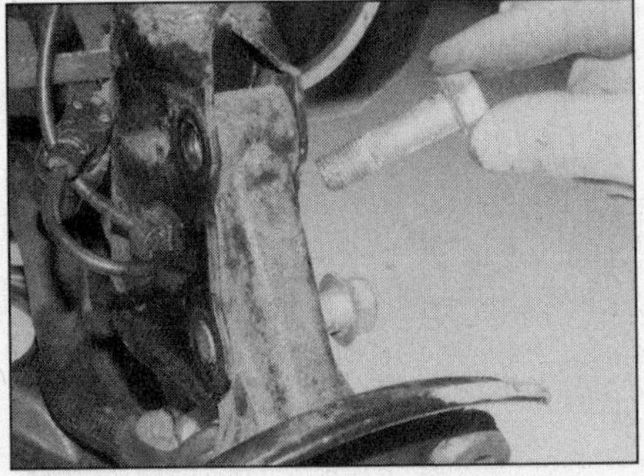

2.11a Remove the strut-to-hub bolts . . .

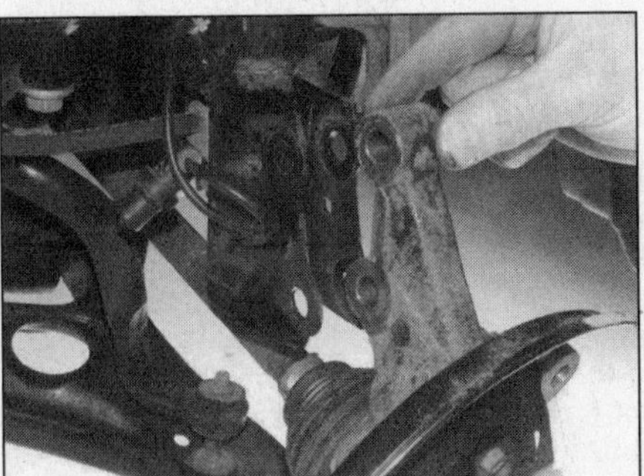

2.11b . . . and separate the hub from the base of the strut

2.12 Tap the splined end of the driveshaft to release it from the hub

2.14a Pull the driveshaft out from the inside of the hub . . .

2.14b . . . then remove it completely

13 Once the splines have been released, remove the driveshaft nut and discard it – the nut is only intended to be used once.

14 Pull the hub outwards, and pull the driveshaft inwards, to separate the splined end from the hub. It is helpful to have an assistant on hand, to pull either the hub or the shaft. Do not bend the driveshaft excessively at any stage, or the joints may be damaged – the inner and outer joints should not be bent through more than 18° and 45° respectively. Do not let the driveshaft hang down under its own weight – tie it up level if necessary. Pull off the hub, and remove it **(see illustrations)**.

Refitting

15 Refitting is a reversal of removal, bearing in mind the following points:

a) *Fit the swivel hub-to-strut bolts in from the front, and oil the nut threads before fitting.*

b) *Use a new split pin and spring clip on the track rod end and lower arm balljoint nuts respectively, and a new driveshaft nut.*

c) *The track rod end and lower arm balljoint nuts can both be tightened up to 60° past their torque value, if necessary, to fit the split pin/spring clip.*

d) *Do not fully tighten the driveshaft nut until the car is resting on its wheels.*

e) *Tighten all fixings to the specified torque.*

f) *Have the front wheel alignment checked on completion.*

3 Front hub bearings – renewal

Note: *A press, a suitable puller, or similar improvised tools will be required for this operation. Obtain a bearing overhaul kit before proceeding.*

1 With the swivel hub removed as described in Section 2, proceed as follows.

2 The bearing removal process involves three stages – removing the hub flange (where the wheel mounts), tapping off the inner race from the hub flange, then driving out the bearing itself from the hub.

3 The hub flange must first be removed from the bearing/swivel hub assembly. It is preferable to use a press to do this, but it is possible to drive out the hub using a metal tube of suitable diameter. Alternatively, a suitable puller can be used.

4 Have an assistant hold the hub assembly over a work surface then, using a metal bar, tube, or socket of suitable diameter, drive the hub flange through the bearing and remove it **(see illustrations)**. This process will destroy the bearing, as the inner race will separate with the flange.

5 The bearing inner race left on the hub flange must now be removed, which is most easily done using a puller. Otherwise, grip the edge of the flange in a vice, and tap the race off with a chisel, taking care not to damage the flange's bearing surface **(see illustrations)**. Tap the race at the top and both sides (even turn the flange over in the vice) to stop it jamming as it comes off.

6 Now the bearing itself must be removed. First, remove the large bearing retaining circlip, using a pair of circlip pliers **(see illustration)**.

7 After applying a generous amount of spray

3.4a Using a metal tube and socket . . .

3.4b . . . to drive through the hub flange

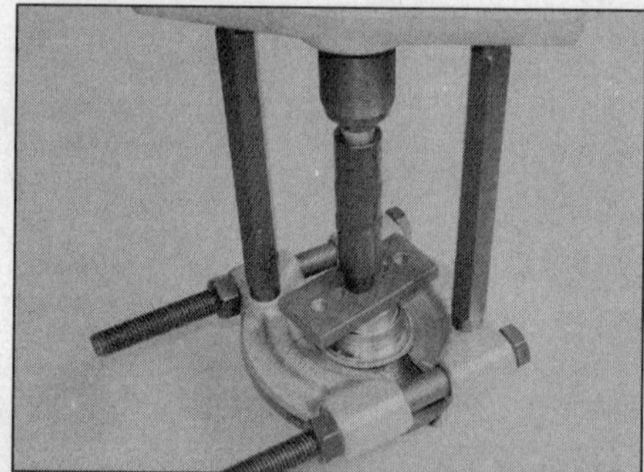

3.5a Removing the bearing inner race is most easily done using a puller

3.5b Use a chisel between the hub flange and the inner race . . .

3.5c . . . then remove the inner race

3.6 Extract the bearing circlip

3.7 Drive out the old bearing using a large tube or socket

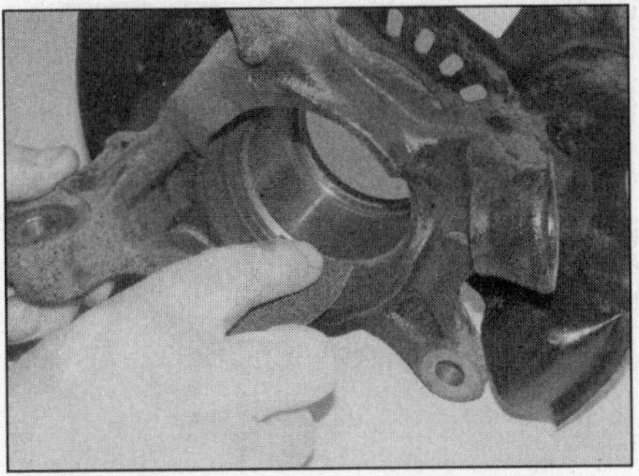
3.8a Remove any burrs from the hub carrier using emery paper . . .

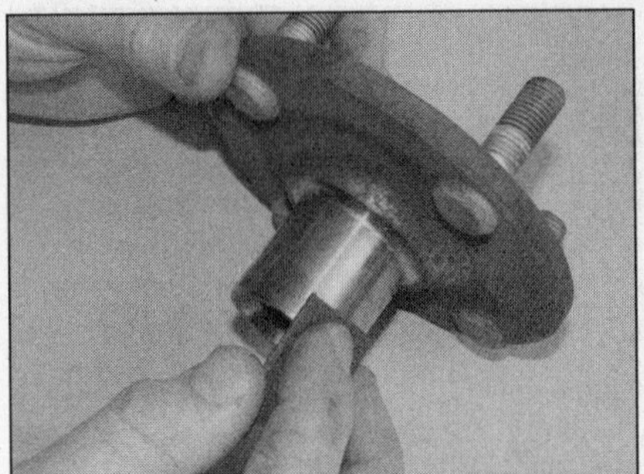
3.8b . . . if necessary, the hub flange should also be cleaned

3.9a Offer the new bearing into position . . .

3.9b . . . and gently tap it in squarely to initially locate it

3.10 Using a threaded rod and spacers to press in the new bearing

lubricant, we were able to drive the bearing out, using a large socket **(see illustration)**. Mount the swivel hub across two large blocks of wood (or even bricks) – putting it across the open jaws of a vice might result in damage to the vice, owing to the amount of force which will be necessary.

8 Using emery paper, clean off any burrs or raised edges from the hub flange and hub carrier, which might stop the components going back together **(see illustrations)**.

9 Apply a light coat of lubricant to the inside of the hub carrier, and to the outside of the new bearing. Start fitting the bearing by offering it squarely into the carrier, then give it a few light taps with the hammer all round to locate it – keep the bearing square as this is done, or it will jam **(see illustrations)**.

10 Fitting the bearing by tapping it in all the way with a hammer will likely damage it. We used a length of threaded bar (available from motor factors, DIY stores, etc), with a nut, some large washers and a drilled plate on the outside of the hub carrier. With the old bearing, a large socket, another washer, and a nut on the inside, the whole assembly was mounted in a vice, and the nuts tightened to press the new bearing in place **(see illustration)**.

11 The hub carrier bearing housing has a flange, so the bearing can be pressed in until fully home. When the bearing is in place, refit the bearing retaining circlip.

12 The hub flange can be pressed into the new bearing using a very similar method to the one just used **(see illustrations)**.

13 On completion, refit the swivel hub as described in Section 2.

4 Front suspension strut – removal, overhaul and refitting

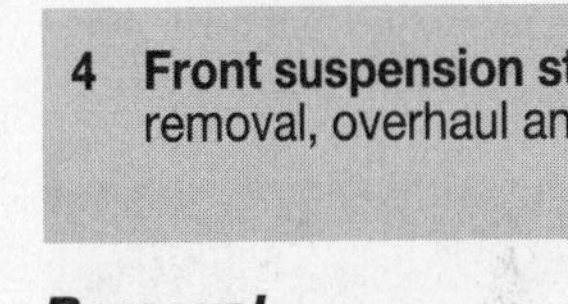

Removal

1 Apply the handbrake, slacken the relevant front wheel nuts, then jack up the front of the car and support securely on axle stands (see *Jacking and vehicle support*). Remove the roadwheel and the engine lower cover.

2 Where applicable, use a small screwdriver to release the clip securing the ABS wiring to the hub **(see illustration)**.

3 Remove the retaining bolt securing the brake flexible hose (and ABS wiring, where applicable) support bracket to the suspension

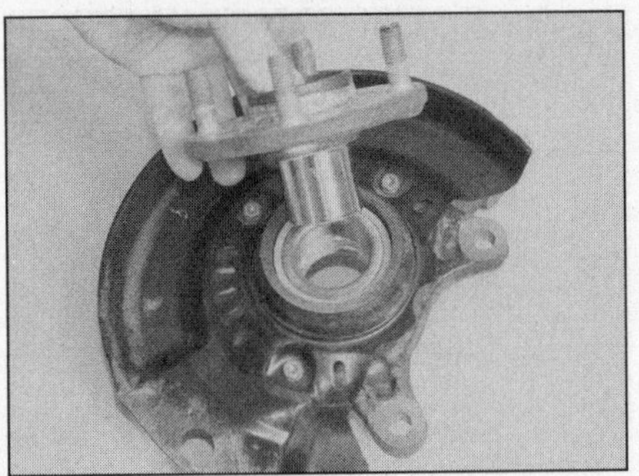
3.12a Offer the hub flange into the new bearing . . .

3.12b . . . and press it into the new bearing using a threaded rod and spacers

4.2 Use a small screwdriver to release the ABS wiring clip

4.3a Remove the bolt on the inside of the strut . . .

4.3b . . . which secures the brake hose and ABS wiring

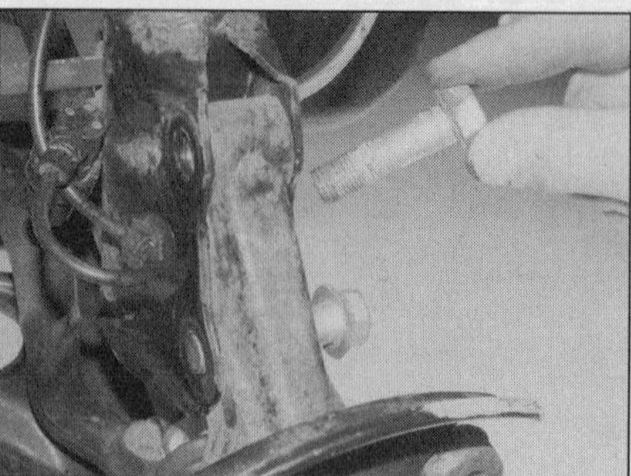
4.4a Remove the strut-to-hub bolts . . .

strut. Release the hose and wiring from the strut **(see illustrations)**.

4 Remove the nuts from the two bolts used to secure the swivel hub to the base of the suspension strut. Note which way the bolts are fitted (this should be from the front). Tap the bolts out, then separate the strut base from the hub **(see illustrations)**.

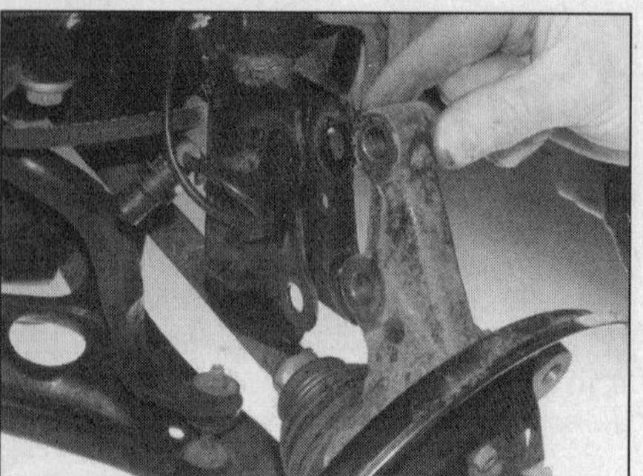
4.4b . . . and separate the hub from the base of the strut

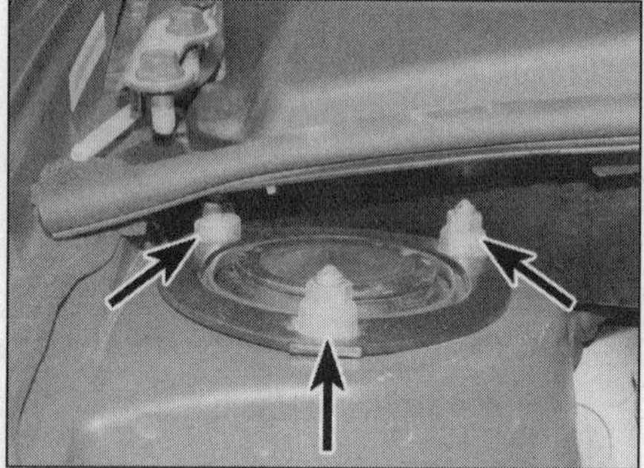
4.5 The rearmost strut mounting nuts are hidden under the scuttle panel

5 All that's holding the strut in place now are the three top mounting nuts on top of the inner wing. Access to these nuts is hampered by the scuttle panel below the windscreen, but it is possible to unscrew and remove them using a spanner **(see illustration)**. However, tightening them on completion to the specified torque will be impossible, so it is recommended that the scuttle panel is removed as follows.

6 Remove the windscreen wiper motor as described in Chapter 12.

7 Remove the bolts securing the metal scuttle panel below the wiper motor, and withdraw it. Access to the strut top mounting nuts is now greatly improved **(see illustrations)**.

8 Support the strut from under the wheel arch then, working in the engine compartment, unscrew the three suspension strut top mounting nuts. Lower the strut out, and remove it under the wheel arch. Recover the strut top mounting plate **(see illustrations)**.

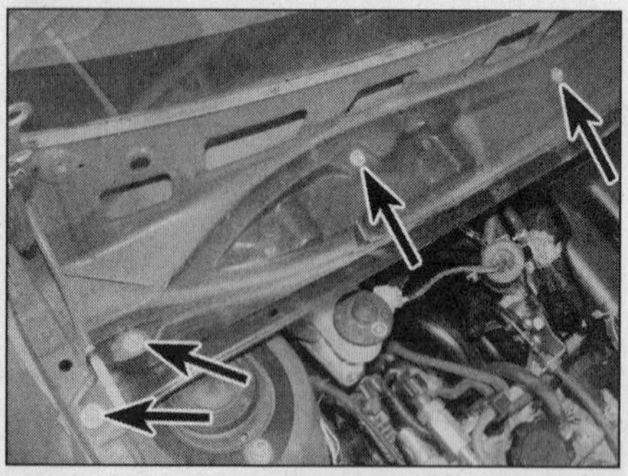

Overhaul

Note: *A spring compressor tool will be required for this operation.*

9 With the suspension strut resting on a bench, or clamped in a vice, fit a spring compressor tool, and compress the coil spring to relieve the pressure on the spring seats. Ensure that the compressor tool is securely located on the spring, in accordance with the tool manufacturer's instructions.

4.7a Remove the bolts . . .

4.7b . . . and lift out the scuttle panel

4.7c With the scuttle panel removed, the strut mounting nuts are accessible

4.8a Lower the strut from under the wheel arch . . .

4.8b . . . and recover the strut top mounting plate

4.10 Remove the strut centre cap (seen in-car)

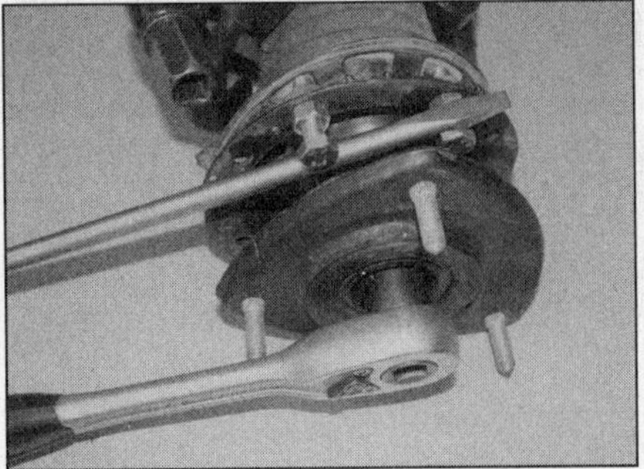

4.11a Counterhold the lower mounting using two bolts and a screwdriver . . .

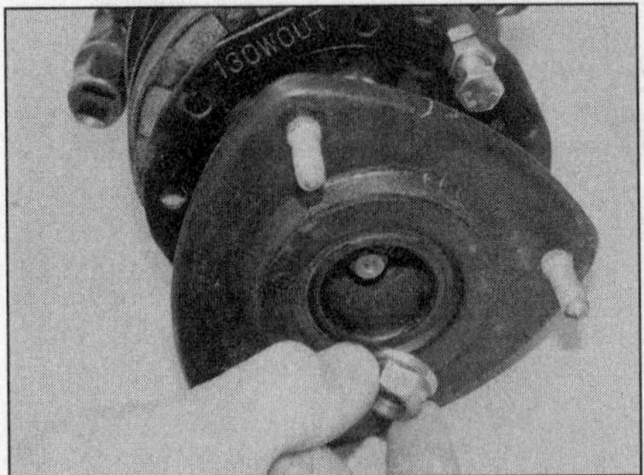

4.11b . . . then remove and discard the piston rod centre nut

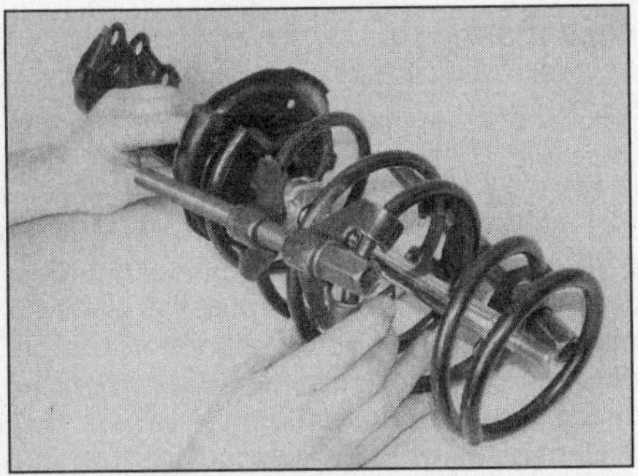

4.18a Slide the compressed spring over the strut . . .

4.18b . . . and locate the spring end in the lower seat

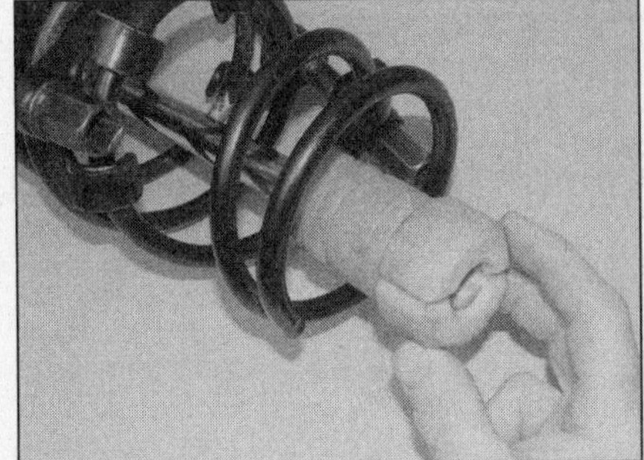

4.19 Fit the rubber bump stop over the strut piston

10 Remove the centre cap from the top of the strut **(see illustration)**.

11 The strut upper spring seat must now be prevented from turning while the piston rod centre nut is loosened. Holes are provided in the spring seat flange, into which two short bolts can be tightened. With two such bolts fitted in the flange, pass a sturdy screwdriver between them, then loosen and remove the centre nut **(see illustrations)**. Discard the nut, and obtain a new one for refitting.

12 Remove the top mounting plate, dust seal, spacer (where fitted), upper spring seat/bearing, the dust boot, the spring (with compressor tool still fitted), and the rubber bump stop.

13 With the strut assembly now completely dismantled, examine all the components for wear, damage or deformation, and check the thrust bearing for smoothness of operation. Renew any of the components as necessary.

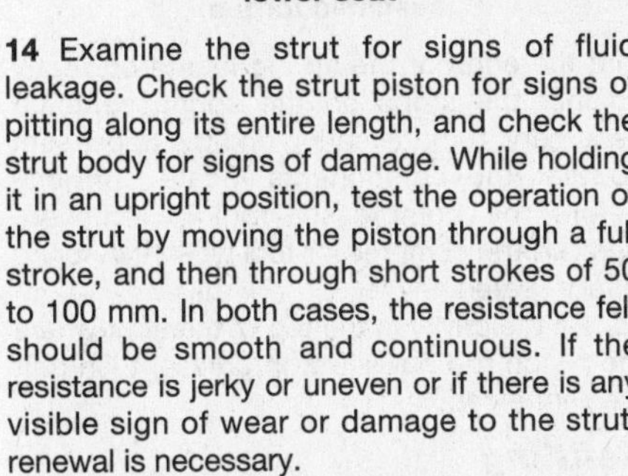

14 Examine the strut for signs of fluid leakage. Check the strut piston for signs of pitting along its entire length, and check the strut body for signs of damage. While holding it in an upright position, test the operation of the strut by moving the piston through a full stroke, and then through short strokes of 50 to 100 mm. In both cases, the resistance felt should be smooth and continuous. If the resistance is jerky or uneven or if there is any visible sign of wear or damage to the strut, renewal is necessary.

15 If any doubt exists as to the condition of the coil spring, carefully remove the spring compressors and check the spring for distortion and signs of cracking. Renew the spring if it is damaged or distorted, or if there is any doubt as to its condition.

16 Inspect all other components for damage or deterioration, and renew any that are suspect.

17 If the spring compressor tool has been removed from the spring, refit it and compress the spring sufficiently to enable it to be refitted to the strut.

18 Slide the spring over the strut, and position it so that the lower end of the spring is resting against the stop on the lower seat **(see illustrations)**.

19 Fit the rubber bump stop onto the strut piston **(see illustration)**.

20 Slide the dust boot into position, and turn it so that the triangular mark on its top surface faces the outside of the car (ie, towards the strut's roadwheel) **(see illustrations)**.

21 Refit the upper spring seat, and rotate it as necessary to position the stop against the upper end of the spring – in this position, the OUT marking on top should align with the triangular mark on the dust boot (facing outwards) **(see illustrations)**.

4.20a Slide the dust boot over the bump stop . . .

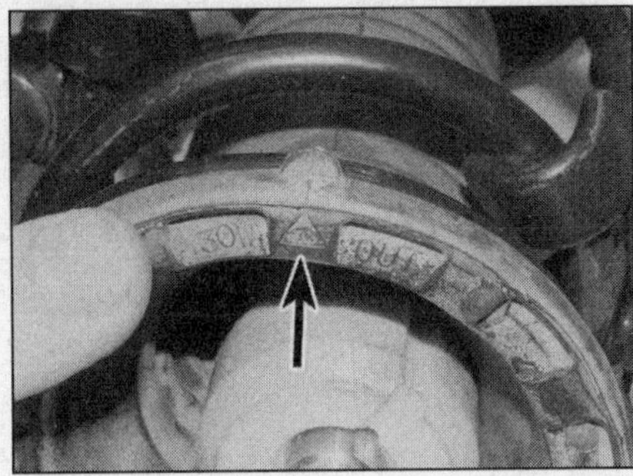

4.20b . . . and align the top over the spring so that the triangle mark faces outwards

4.21a Refit the upper spring seat . . .

4.21b . . . and turn it to align with the triangle mark on the dust boot

4.22a Refit the dust seal . . .

4.22b . . . followed by the upper mounting plate

4.23 Fit a new nut, and tighten it to the specified torque

22 Fit the spacer (where applicable), dust seal, and the top mounting plate **(see illustrations)**.

23 Fit a new piston rod nut, and tighten to the specified torque. Prevent the upper spring seat from turning using a screwdriver between the bolts as for loosening **(see illustration)**. This job must be done before the spring compressor is released, otherwise there will be insufficient room for the bolts or the screwdriver – for the same reason, the bolts used must be removed before releasing the spring.

24 Slowly slacken the spring compressor tool to relieve the tension in the spring. Check that the ends of the spring locate correctly against the stops on the spring seats. If necessary, turn the spring and the upper seat so that the components locate correctly before the compressor tool is removed. Remove the compressor tool when the spring is fully seated.

25 Fill the cavity in the top of the strut where the piston rod nut sits with grease, then refit the centre cap.

Refitting

26 Refitting is a reversal of removal, bearing in mind the following points:

a) Fit the swivel hub-to-strut bolts in from the front, and oil the nut threads before fitting.

b) Tighten all fixings to the specified torque.

c) Have the front wheel alignment checked on completion.

5 Front suspension anti-roll bar – removal and refitting

Note: *If it is wished to renew just the anti-roll bar drop links and/or bushes, this can be accomplished with much less additional dismantling than described below for removing the bar itself.*

Removal

1 Apply the handbrake, loosen the front wheel nuts, then jack up the front of the car and support it on axle stands (see *Jacking and vehicle support*). Remove both front wheels and the engine lower covers.

2 Remove the split pin either side, then unscrew and remove the track rod balljoint nuts. Using a balljoint separator tool if necessary, detach the track rods from the swivel hubs **(see illustration)**.

3 On models with hydraulic power steering, anticipating some fluid spillage, unscrew the feed and return pipe unions, and disconnect the pipes from the steering rack. Plug or tape over the open unions, to prevent further fluid loss or dirt entry.

4 Unbolt the steering pipe support bracket from the subframe. The steering pipes can now be moved aside as necessary, to access and remove the anti-roll bar.

5 Referring to Chapter 4B if necessary, unbolt the exhaust system for access to the anti-roll bar. It may be found that the exhaust need only be unbolted at the front, and lowered, rather than practically removed completely, for sufficient access to be gained.

6 Holding the drop link against rotation using a spanner on the flats, remove the upper and lower nuts, and disconnect both links from the

5.2 Separate the track rod end balljoint

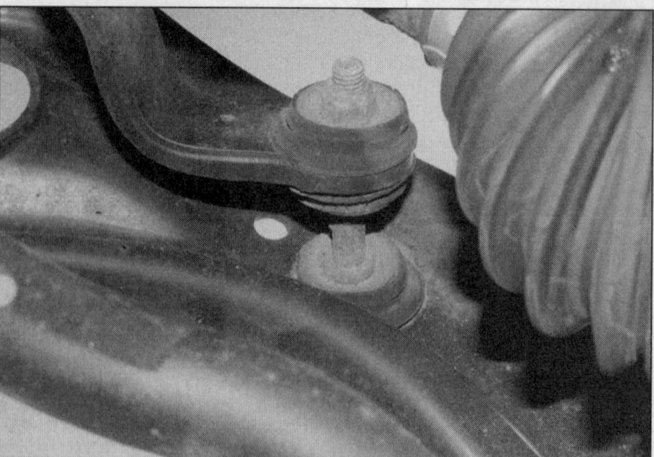
5.6 Anti-roll bar-to-lower arm drop link

lower arms **(see illustration)**. Recover the washers and rubbers, noting the fitted order and orientation of all components as they are removed.

7 Remove the two bolts securing each clamp to the subframe, then lift the clamp from the anti-roll bar. The rubber bushes are split, and can be removed once the clamps are taken off **(see illustration)**.

8 Manoeuvre the anti-roll bar out between the subframe, suspension arms, exhaust system, and the underside of the car. Take great care not to damage the disconnected power steering pipes as the roll bar is withdrawn.

Refitting

9 Refitting is a reversal of removal, bearing in mind the following points:

a) Tighten all fixings to the specified torque.
b) Use a new split pin on the track rod end balljoint nuts.
c) The track rod end balljoint nuts can be tightened up to 60° past their torque value, if necessary, to fit the split pin.
d) On models with hydraulic power steering, top-up and bleed the power steering system as described in Section 19.
e) Refit the exhaust system with reference to Chapter 4B.
f) Have the front wheel alignment checked on completion.

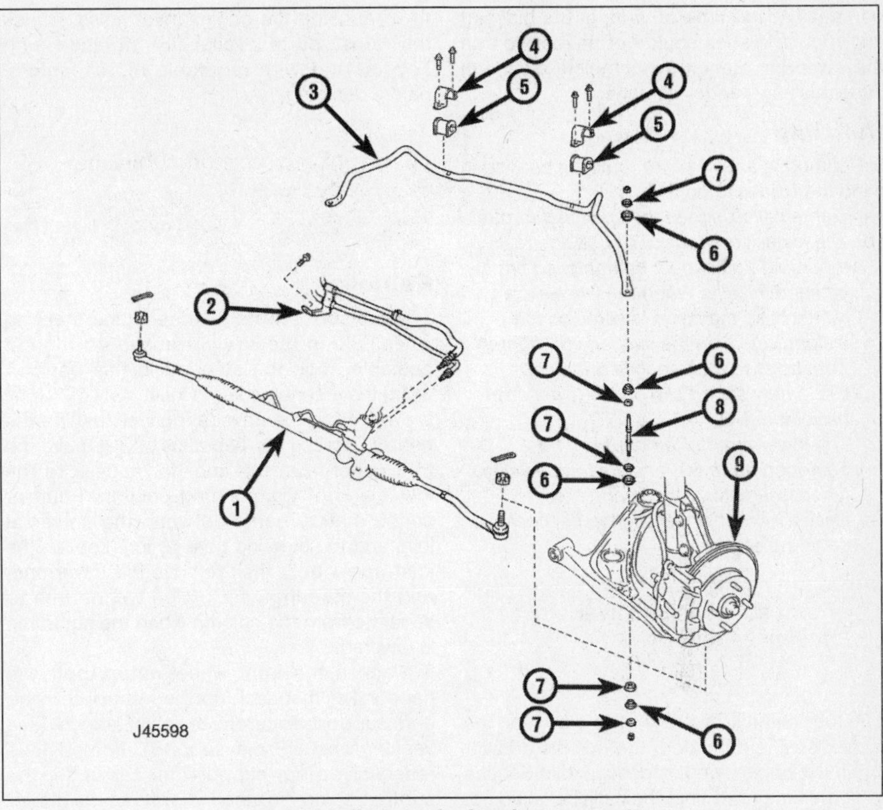

5.7 Anti-roll bar and related components

1 *Steering rack*
2 *Steering fluid pipe support bracket*
3 *Anti-roll bar*
4 *Anti-roll bar clamp*
5 *Anti-roll bar bush*
6 *Drop link rubber*
7 *Drop link washer*
8 *Drop link*
9 *Lower arm*

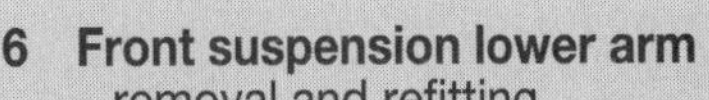

6 Front suspension lower arm – removal and refitting

Removal

1 Slacken the front wheel nuts on the side concerned, then apply the handbrake, jack up the front of the car, and support securely on axle stands (see *Jacking and vehicle support*). Remove the roadwheel and the engine lower cover.

2 Remove the spring clip, then unscrew the lower arm balljoint nut. Push the end of the lower arm down to free the balljoint from the swivel hub. If the balljoint is very tight, it may be necessary to lever down using a large screwdriver, or similar tool, but take care not to damage the balljoint rubber seal **(see illustrations)**.

3 Holding the drop link against rotation using a spanner on the flats, remove the lower nut, and disconnect the link from the lower arm **(see illustration)**. Recover the washers and bushes, noting the fitted order and orientation of all components as they are removed (temporarily refit them to the base of the link, if wished).

4 Remove the lower arm front pivot bolt, then unscrew the rear mounting bolt and remove the lower arm from under the car **(see illustration)**.

Overhaul

5 Examine the rubber bushes and the suspension lower balljoint for wear and

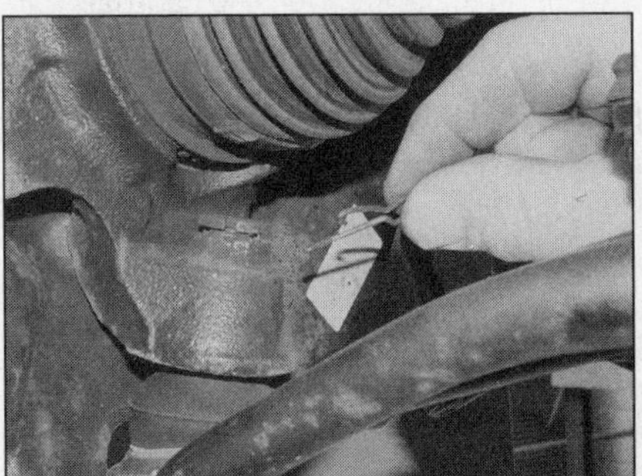

6.2a Remove the spring clip . . .

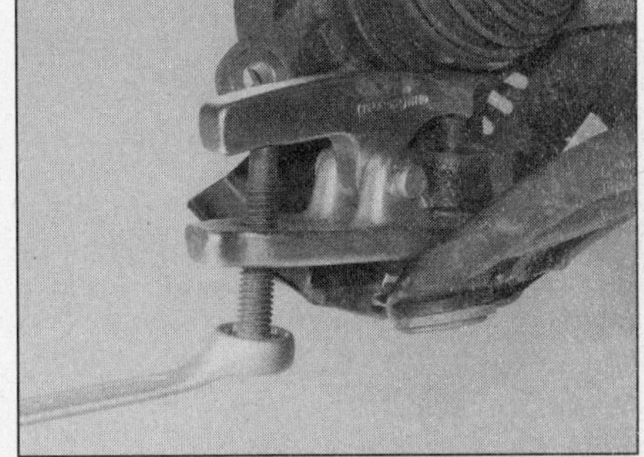

6.2b . . . and separate the lower arm balljoint

6.3 Anti-roll bar drop link lower nut

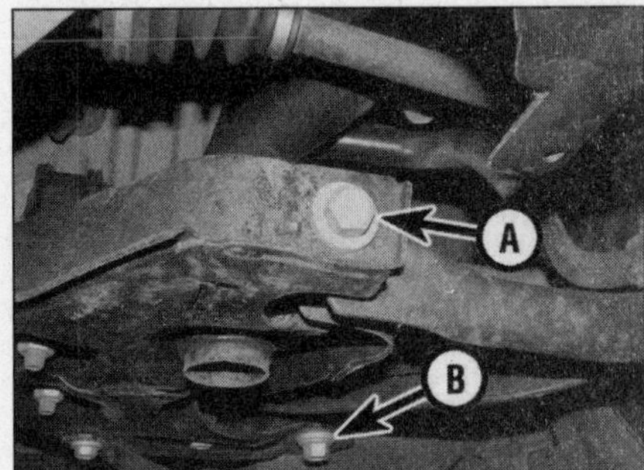

6.4 Lower arm pivot bolt (A) and rear mounting bolt (B)

damage. At the time of writing, the balljoint and rubber bushes could not be renewed on the lower arm. Renew the complete lower arm if there is any wear or damage.

Refitting

6 Refitting is a reversal of removal, bearing in mind the following points:

a) *Tighten all fixings to the specified torque.*
b) *The lower arm front pivot bolt and rear mounting bolt should be tightened firmly by hand initially. When the wheels are refitted and the car is lowered so the weight is fully on the suspension, tighten both bolts to their specified torques.*
c) *Use a new spring clip on the lower arm balljoint nut.*
d) *The lower arm balljoint nut can be tightened up to 60° past its torque value, if necessary, to fit the spring clip.*
e) *Have the front wheel alignment checked on completion.*

7 Front suspension lower arm balljoint – renewal

If the lower arm balljoint is worn, or the rubber seal is damaged, the complete lower arm must be renewed as described in Section 6. At the time of writing, the balljoint could not be renewed separately from the lower arm, as it is riveted in place during manufacture. However, balljoint repair kits have become available over time for other similarly-affected models – with these, the original rivets are drilled out, and the new balljoint is bolted onto the arm using the original rivet holes. Check the latest parts availability situation with Toyota, and with reputable motor factors, before deciding.

8 Front suspension subframe – removal and refitting

Removal

1 Make sure the front wheels (and steering wheel) are in the straight-ahead position. If possible, lock the steering in this position using the steering column lock.

2 Working in the driver's footwell, behind the pedals, release the two clips and remove the trim panel from the floor for access to the lower end of the steering column. Paint or scribe match-marks between the universal joint and the steering gear pinion. Loosen the joint upper bolt, then remove the lower one, and the steering gear pinion will be free to separate from the column when the subframe is lowered.

3 Slacken the front wheel nuts. Apply the handbrake, then jack up the front of the car, and support securely on axle stands (see *Jacking and vehicle support*). For obvious reasons, do not support the car under the subframe, nor in such a way as to hinder lowering the subframe out. Remove the roadwheels and the engine lower covers.

4 Remove the split pin each side, then slacken the track rod end balljoint nut, and unscrew it as far as the ends of the threads.

5 Disconnect the track rod end balljoints from the swivel hubs using a balljoint separator tool (leave the nuts fitted to protect the threads), taking care not to damage the balljoint rubber seals. Once the balljoints have been released, remove the balljoint nuts.

6 Remove the spring clip each side, then slacken the lower arm balljoint nut, and unscrew it as far as the ends of the threads. Push the ends of the lower arms down to free the balljoints from the swivel hubs. If a balljoint is very tight, it may be necessary to lever down using a large screwdriver, or similar tool, but take care not to damage the balljoint rubber seal.

7 Referring to Chapter 4B if necessary, unbolt and remove the exhaust system. If the exhaust is only unbolted at the front, remember that the subframe (a heavy assembly) will have to be lowered to disengage the steering column, then moved forwards to clear the exhaust.

8 On models with hydraulic power steering, anticipating some fluid spillage, unscrew the feed and return pipe unions, and disconnect the pipes from the steering rack. Plug or tape over the open unions, to prevent further fluid loss or dirt entry.

9 Unbolt the steering pipe support bracket from the subframe **(see illustration)**.

10 Unbolt and remove the subframe reinforcement bars fitted to the rear either side **(see illustration)**.

11 Remove the two nuts and single bolt used to secure the engine rear mounting to the subframe. When the subframe is lowered, the mounting's studs may need to be tapped upwards. The engine/transmission will be less stable once the mounting has been undone, but will still be safely supported on the left- and right-hand mountings.

12 Support the subframe from below, using at least two substantial jacks (one either side).

13 With the subframe securely supported, progressively loosen the four mounting bolts. There are two at the rear, into the car floor, and one more each side at the front, on a curved spur up to the base of the chassis leg **(see illustrations)**.

14 When all the bolts have been removed, check once more that nothing is still attached to the subframe, and that nothing is still fitted which would hinder it from being lowered. With the help of an assistant, lower the subframe and remove it from under the car. In doing so, the steering gear pinion will be being disengaged from the column splines, and the engine rear mounting studs will also be coming through their subframe holes.

Refitting

15 With the help of an assistant, position the subframe on the jacks, then raise the jack to lift the subframe into position under the car. Line up the mounting holes and fit the rear mounting studs through as the subframe is raised into position. Also engage the steering gear pinion splines with those of the column inside the car.

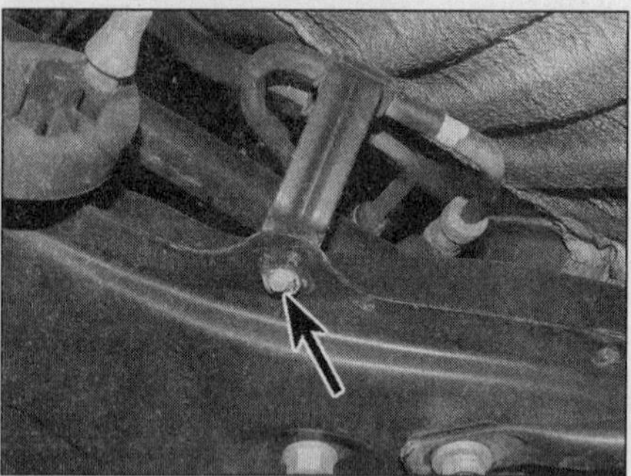

8.9 Steering fluid pipe bracket bolt

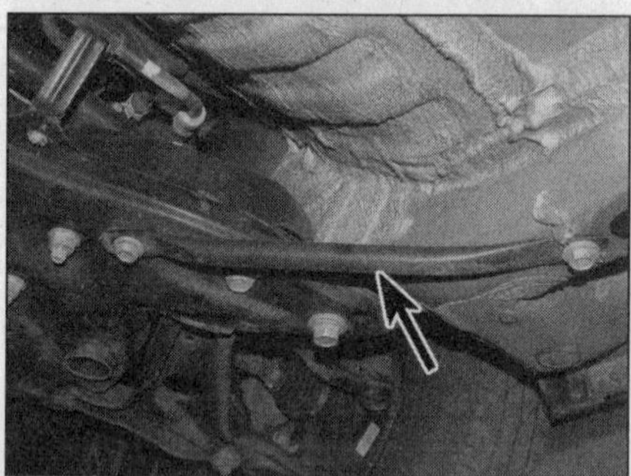

8.10 Subframe reinforcement bar

8.13a Subframe rear mounting bolt

8.13b Subframe front mounting bolt

9.6 Disconnect the ABS sensor wiring plug using a screwdriver

9.7a Remove the four hub mounting bolts . . .

9.7b . . . and withdraw the hub through the brake shoes

16 The remainder of refitting is a reversal of removal, noting the following points:

a) Tighten all fixings to the specified torque.
b) On models with hydraulic power steering, top-up and bleed the power steering system as described in Section 19.
c) Have the front wheel alignment checked on completion.

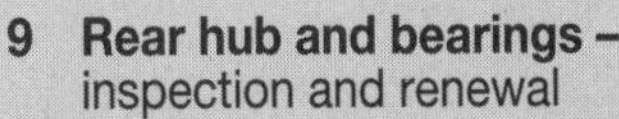

9 Rear hub and bearings - inspection and renewal

Note: *The rear hub and bearing are a sealed unit. If the rear bearings are worn, a new hub must be fitted. On models with ABS, the rear wheel sensor is fitted to the hub, and while it can be removed and fitted to the new unit, this is a job for a Toyota dealer (refer to Chapter 9, Section 17).*

Inspection

1 The rear hub bearings are non-adjustable.

2 To check the bearings for excessive wear, chock the front wheels, then jack up the rear of the vehicle and support it on axle stands. Fully release the handbrake.

3 Grip the rear wheel at the top and bottom, and attempt to rock it. If excessive movement is noted, or if there is any roughness or vibration felt when the wheel is spun, it is indicative that the hub bearings are worn.

Removal

4 Loosen the rear wheel nuts, then chock the front wheels (or engage a gear). Jack up the rear of the car, and support it on axle stands (see *Jacking and vehicle support*). Remove the rear wheel.

5 Remove the brake drum as described in Chapter 9. While the drum is removed, it would make sense to inspect the rear brake components for wear, and the wheel cylinder for signs of fluid leakage.

6 On models with ABS, disconnect the wiring plug for the rear wheel sensor from the back of the hub. A small screwdriver is useful to release the wiring plug catch **(see illustration)**.

7 Loosen the four bolts securing the hub (and brake backplate) to the trailing arm. Support the hub and backplate, and remove the four bolts. Withdraw the hub through the rear shoe assembly **(see illustrations)**.

If the hub is reluctant to move, this is probably due to corrosion between the hub and backplate. To remove the hub, loosely refit the four bolts, and use a punch on each of the bolt heads in turn to release the hub. Take care to avoid damaging the ABS sensor, where applicable.

8 Temporarily refit the four bolts to hang the backplate onto, and cable-tie the backplate to the trailing arm, to prevent straining the brake pipe and handbrake cable.

Refitting

9 Refitting is a reversal of removal, noting the following points:

a) On models with ABS, if a new hub is being fitted, the rear wheel sensor should be transferred to the new hub by a Toyota dealer.
b) When refitting the hub, clean away any corrosion on its mating surfaces with the backplate, and apply a little copper grease to make future removal easier.
c) Tighten all fixings to the specified torque.
d) Refit the brake drum as described in Chapter 9.

10 Rear shock absorber - removal and refitting

Removal

1 Working in the boot, prise off the upper trim cover from the top of the shock absorber, then pull off the rubber cover underneath for access to the two top nuts **(see illustrations)**.

2 Using a spanner to hold the lower nut, loosen the top nut and remove it. Now using a

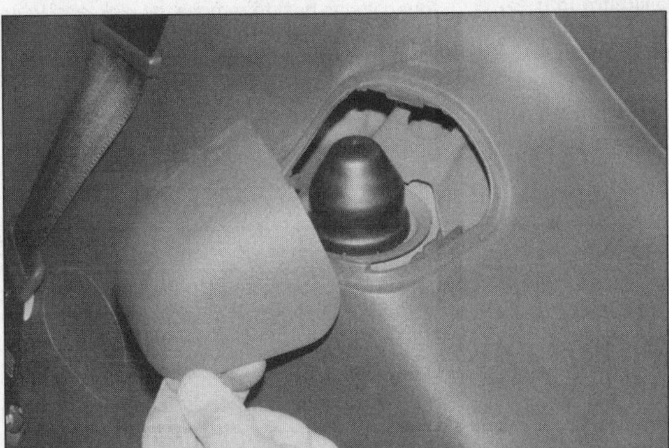

10.1a Prise off the plastic trim panel inside the boot . . .

10.1b . . . then pull off the shock absorber rubber cover

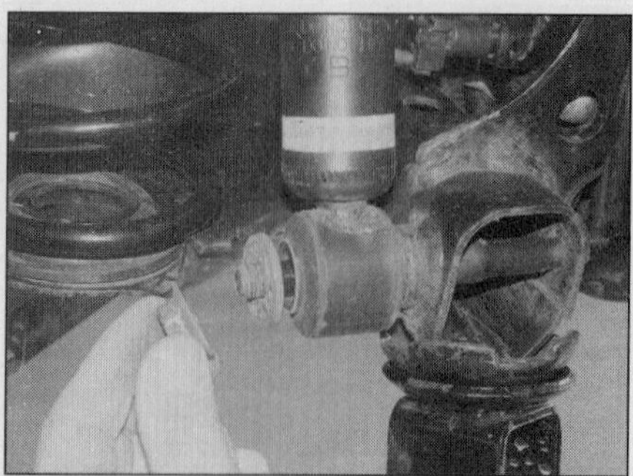
10.4a Remove the lower mounting nut and washer . . .

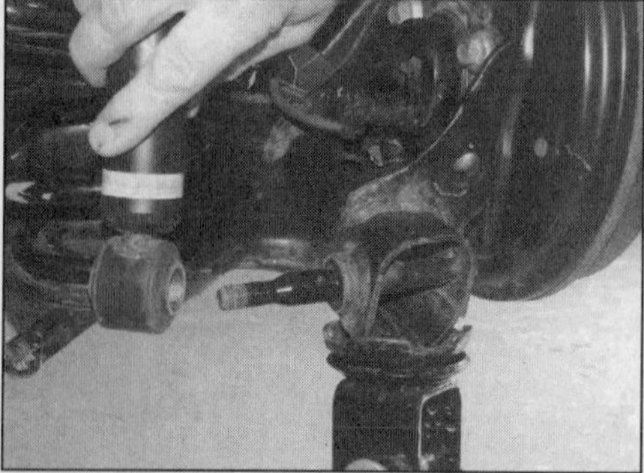
10.4b . . . then slide the shock absorber off its mounting

10.5a Remove the shock absorber from under the wheel arch . . .

10.5b . . . then recover the upper mounting washer . . .

10.5c . . . and rubber bush from inside the boot

small spanner to hold the piston rod flats at the top (if necessary), loosen the shock absorber lower nut. Leave the lower nut fitted just by a few threads, until the lower mounting has been removed and the shock absorber is ready to be lowered out.

3 Slacken the relevant rear wheel nuts. Chock the front wheels, select 1st gear, then jack up the rear of the car, and support securely on axle stands (see *Jacking and vehicle support*). Remove the rear roadwheel.

4 Support the 'trailing arm' section of the beam axle using a trolley jack, then unscrew the shock absorber lower mounting nut. Take off the nut, recover the washer, then slide the bottom end of the shock absorber off its mounting **(see illustrations)**.

5 Lower the trailing arm on the jack. Support the shock absorber, then remove the upper mounting nut, and remove the unit from under the wheel arch. Recover the shock absorber top washer and rubber bush from the mounting inside the boot **(see illustrations)**.

Refitting

6 Ensure that the shock absorber is fully reassembled before offering it into position – check that the upper mounting(s) have been refitted (or transferred to the new unit, where applicable) **(see illustration)**.

7 Fit the lower mounting nut first, and tighten it by hand only at this stage.

8 Raise the trailing arm using the jack, and fit the top mounting through the hole under the wheel arch. Fit the upper mounting and washer, then fit and tighten the first nut so that 15 to 18 mm of the piston rod is showing above its top surface **(see illustration)**.

9 Fit the second nut to the first, then hold the first nut in position, and tighten the second to the specified torque **(see illustration)**. Refit the rubber cover and plastic trim.

10 Refit the wheel, then lower the car to the ground, and tighten the wheel nuts to the specified torque.

11 Bounce the rear of the car a couple of times to settle the rear suspension, then tighten the shock absorber lower mounting nut to the specified torque.

11 Rear spring – removal and refitting

Removal

1 Slacken the rear wheel nuts. Chock the front wheels, select 1st gear, then jack up the rear of the car, and support securely on axle stands (see *Jacking and vehicle support*). Remove both rear roadwheels.

2 Support the 'trailing arm' section of the beam axle using a trolley jack, then unscrew the shock absorber lower mounting nut. Take off the nut, recover the washer, then slide the bottom end of the shock absorber off its mounting.

3 Slowly lower the trailing arms on the jack, until the spring tension is released, and the springs can be pulled out of their location. We found it was best to remove the jack, and then press down the trailing arm to remove the spring – make sure, however, that no excess

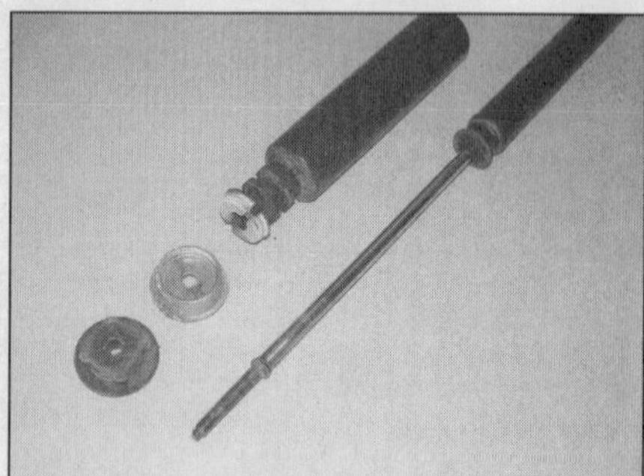
10.6 Shock absorber and upper mounting components

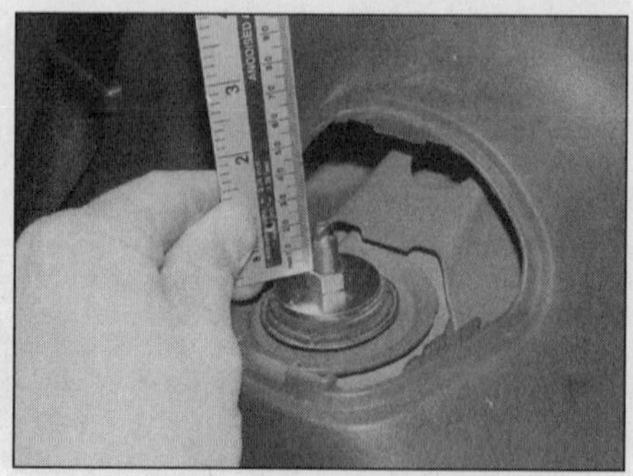
10.8 Checking the thread protrusion after tightening the lower nut

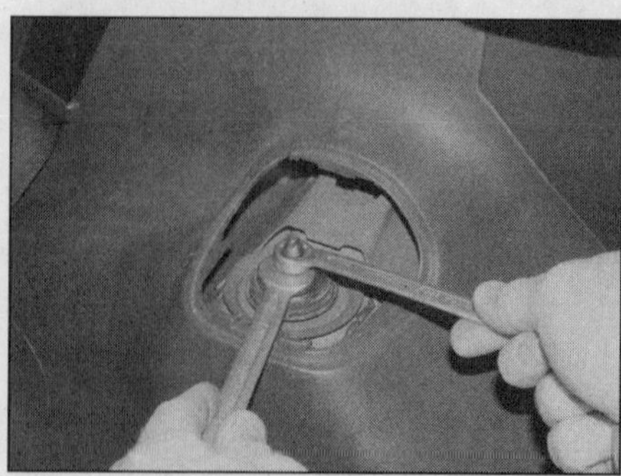
10.9 Tighten the upper nut onto the lower one

strain is placed on the brake hose **(see illustrations)**.

4 Recover the spring upper and lower mounting rubbers, noting how they are fitted **(see illustrations)**. If they are in poor condition, fit new ones.

Refitting

5 Refitting is a reversal of removal, noting the following points:

a) *Make sure the spring is properly engaged in the upper and lower mounts.*
b) *Delay fully tightening the shock absorber lower mounting nut to its specified torque until the car is resting on its wheels.*

11.3a Lower the trailing arm on the jack until the spring tension is released

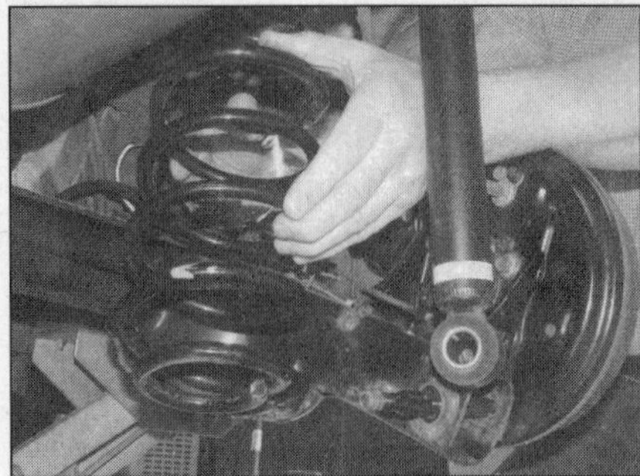

11.3b Press down on the trailing arm, and remove the spring

11.4a Recover the spring upper . . .

11.4b . . . and lower mounting rubbers

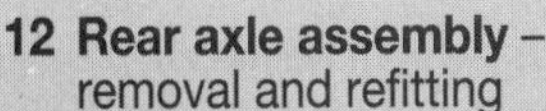

12 Rear axle assembly – removal and refitting

Removal

1 Slacken the rear wheel nuts. Chock the front wheels, select 1st gear or P on automatics, then jack up the rear of the car, and support securely on axle stands (see *Jacking and vehicle support*). Remove the rear roadwheels.

2 Disconnect the rear brake flexible hoses from the rigid pipes leading to the backplates. Anticipate some fluid spillage – if possible, clamp the hoses before disconnecting them. Slide out the metal clip used to secure the hose each side, and move the hoses clear of the axle **(see illustration)**.

3 Unbolt the brackets for the handbrake cable, and (where applicable) the ABS sensor wiring, from the rear axle **(see illustration)**. Move the cables and wiring clear as far as possible, so that it does not get caught up when the axle is lowered.

4 Remove the rear hubs as described in Section 9. Instead, however, of securing the brake backplates roughly back into their fitted positions, tie them up clear of the axle once the hubs have been removed.

5 Remove the rear springs as described in Section 11.

6 Support the rear axle using two substantial jacks, one at each end. Having an assistant will also be useful – the axle is a heavy and awkward assembly to remove without help.

7 Make a final check that nothing is still attached to the axle which would hamper its removal.

8 With the axle securely supported, unscrew and remove the pivot bolt each side **(see illustration)**. Lower the axle on the jacks, making sure that nothing gets caught, until it can be withdrawn from under the car.

Refitting

9 Refitting of the axle assembly is a reversal of removal, bearing in mind the following points:

a) *Do not fully tighten the axle mounting bolts, or the shock absorber lower mounting nuts, until the weight of the car is resting on its wheels.*
b) *Tighten all fixings to the specified torque.*
c) *Refit the springs and rear hubs as described in Sections 11 and 9 respectively.*
d) *Bleed the brakes as described in Chapter 9.*

13 Rear axle pivot bushes – renewal

1 Remove the rear axle as described in Section 12.

2 Make alignment marks between the bush housing and the end of the bush.

3 Using a hammer and chisel, straighten the bent-over sections of the metal internal collar.

4 Using a metal tube of suitable diameter, flat washers and a long bolt and nut, draw the bush out of its location.

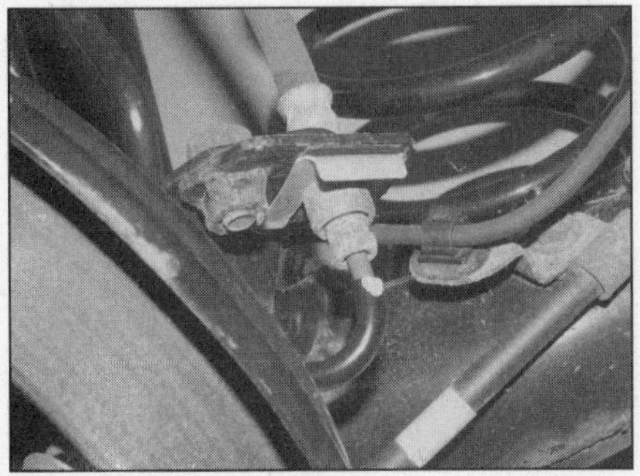

12.2 Brake hose-to-pipe union on the rear axle

12.3 Unbolt the cable brackets and unclip the ABS wiring

12.8 Rear axle pivot bolt

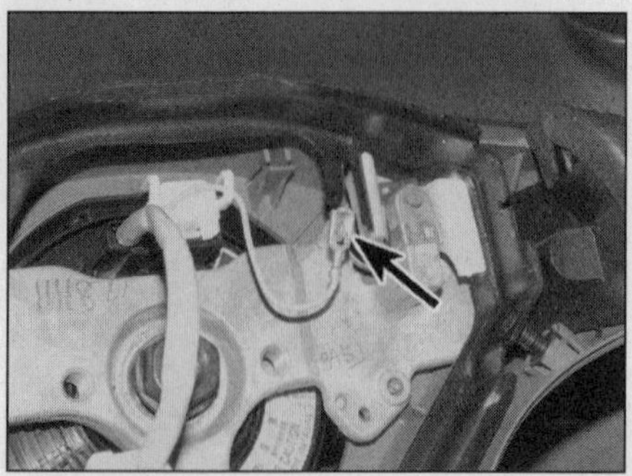
14.3 Disconnect the earth wire at the top of the wheel

14.6 Grip the wheel either side, and pull it off the splines

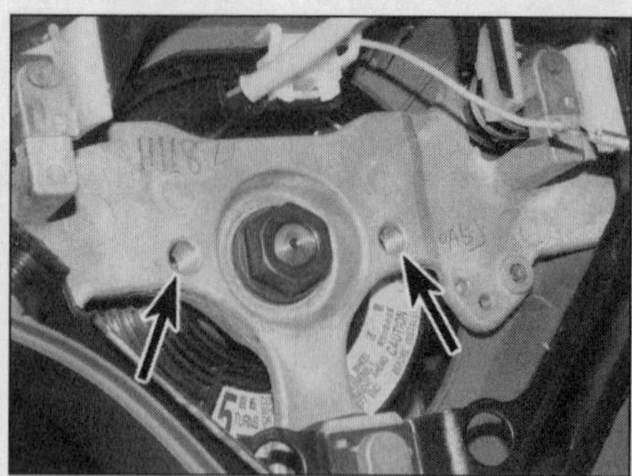
14.7a Two threaded holes are provided, either side of the nut . . .

5 Thoroughly clean the bush housing in the trailing arm.
6 Lubricate the bush housing, and the new bush, with a soapy solution (eg, washing-up liquid) to aid fitting.
7 Locate the new bush in position against the housing, together with the metal tube, washers, bolt and nut used for removal. Align the line made on the side of the bush with the alignment mark made before removal on the trailing arm, then draw the bush into the housing until it is fully engaged.
8 Repeat the procedure for the remaining bush.
9 On completion, refit the rear axle as described in Section 12.

14 Steering wheel – removal and refitting

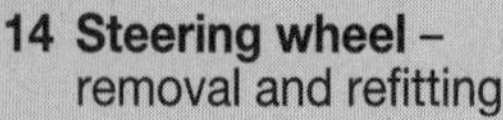

Removal

1 Disconnect the battery negative lead, and position the lead away from the battery (also see *Disconnecting the battery*). Wait at least one minute before proceeding. If this waiting period is not observed, there is a danger of accidentally activating the airbag(s).
2 Remove the airbag unit from the steering wheel as described in Chapter 12.
3 Disconnect the small earth wire at the top of the wheel **(see illustration)**.
4 Ensure that the front wheels are pointing in the straight-ahead position, and if possible, engage the steering lock in this position.
5 Prevent the steering wheel turning by grasping the rim firmly, then unscrew and remove the steering wheel securing nut. Do not rely on the steering column lock to prevent the wheel turning, as this may damage the lock.

Don't unscrew the nut all the way – leave it in by a thread or two. This way, if excess effort is needed to pull the wheel off its splines, the wheel won't suddenly fly off and cause injury.

6 Grip the steering wheel on each side (or top and bottom), then pull and withdraw it from the splines on the end of the column. Once the wheel has released, remove the securing nut completely, and withdraw the wheel **(see illustration)**.
7 The wheel may prove difficult to remove from its splines. Toyota have provided two M8 threaded holes in the wheel hub, for use with a puller **(see illustrations)**. If a puller is not available, a home-made alternative can be made as follows.
8 Use a thick metal strip, approx 85 mm long. Drill two holes in the strip, centres 55 mm apart. Use two M8 bolts (which must be no more than 20 mm long, otherwise they will screw into the airbag clockspring behind) tightened evenly to pull the wheel off. To protect the end of the column, refit the steering wheel nut before the puller, leaving the nut just proud of the column **(see illustration)**.

Refitting

9 Make sure that the front wheels are pointing in the straight-ahead position, then fit the steering wheel to the column.
10 Refit the steering wheel securing nut, and tighten to the specified torque – again, do not rely on the steering column lock to hold the wheel as the nut is tightened.
11 The remainder of the refitting procedure is a reversal of removal. Refit the airbag unit as described in Chapter 12.

15 Steering column – removal and refitting

Removal

1 Disconnect the battery negative lead, and position the lead away from the battery (also see *Disconnecting the battery*). Wait at least one minute before proceeding. If this waiting period is not observed, there is a danger of accidentally activating the airbag(s).
2 Remove the airbag unit from the steering wheel as described in Chapter 12.
3 Move the driver's seat fully to the rear, to allow maximum working area.
4 Remove the three screws securing the steering column lower shroud, and lower it out. Two of the three screws are at the front edge of the shroud (turn the wheel for access), with the third underneath **(see illustrations)**.
5 Remove the two front screws from the lower shroud, turning the steering wheel as

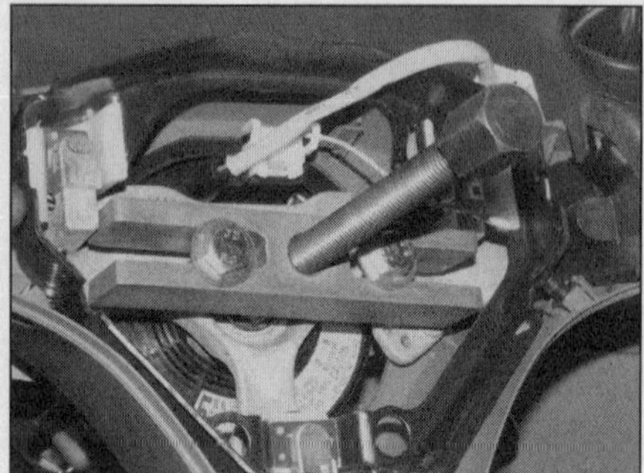
14.7b . . . for use with a puller

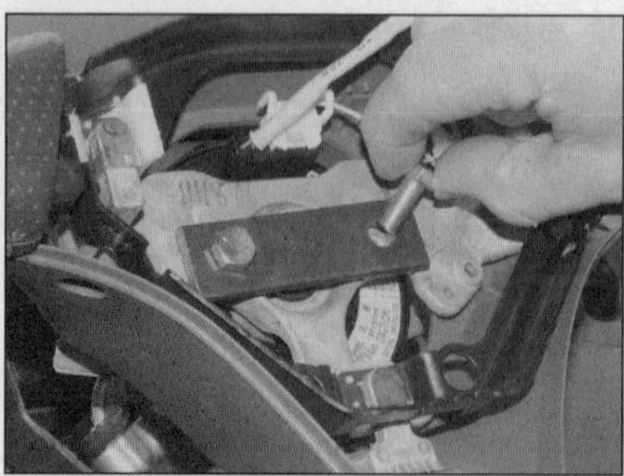
14.8 Fitting a home-made puller to remove the wheel

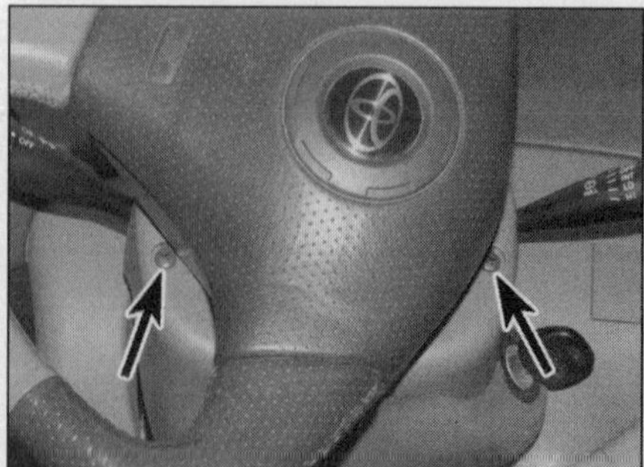
15.4a Turn the steering wheel so both front screws can be seen

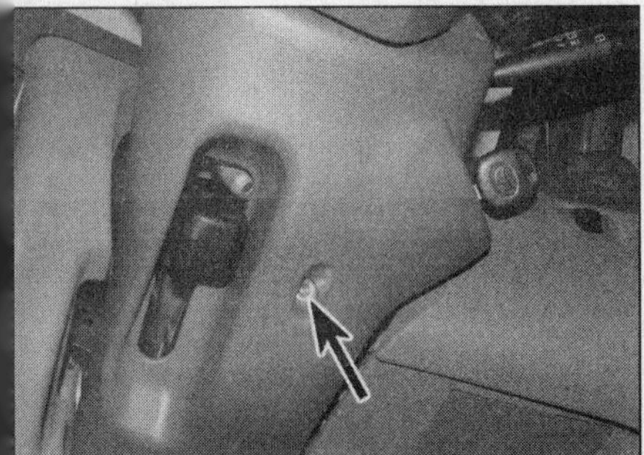
15.4b The lower shroud also has a screw underneath

15.5 Removing the upper shroud – note central clip

15.8 Unclip and remove the column lower trim panel

15.9 Loosen the universal joint upper bolt, and remove the lower one

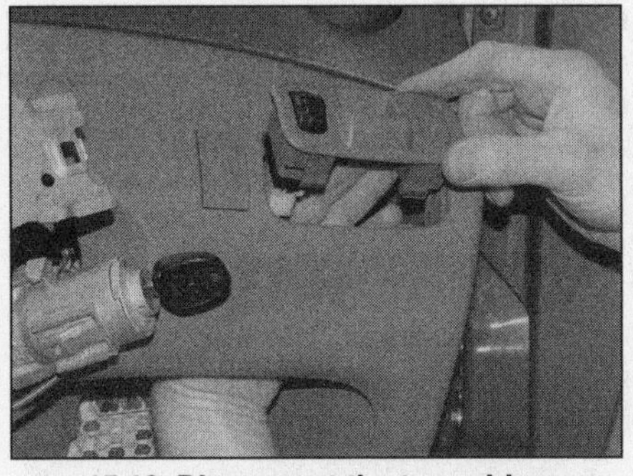
15.10 Disconnect the two wiring connectors behind the ignition switch

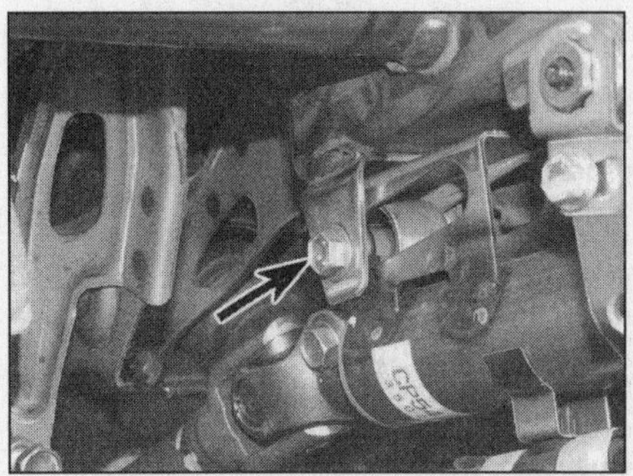
15.11a Steering column lower mounting bolt

necessary for access. Once the two screws have been removed, the upper shroud can be manoeuvred out. The upper shroud has a clip in the centre, which must be accurately located when refitting **(see illustration)**.

6 Remove the airbag clockspring and steering column switches as described in Chapter 12.

7 On models with automatic transmission, disconnect the shift lock cable from the ignition switch as described in Chapter 7B, and unclip the cable from the steering column as necessary.

8 Working in the driver's footwell, behind the pedals, release the two clips and remove the trim panel from the floor for access to the lower end of the steering column **(see illustration)**.

9 Paint or scribe match-marks between the universal joint and the steering gear pinion. Loosen the joint upper bolt, then remove the lower one, and the steering column can be separated from the steering gear pinion **(see illustration)**.

10 Disconnect the two wiring connectors from the ignition switch, noting their fitted positions **(see illustration)**.

11 Remove the column lower mounting bolt (about halfway down, inserted from the side) and the two upper bolts (fitted into captive nuts, from underneath) **(see illustrations)**. Access to the column mountings is certainly easier with the facia lower section removed as described in Chapter 11, but should still be possible.

12 Unclip the column from its upper mounting, and carefully withdraw the column from the car **(see illustration)**.

Refitting

13 Refitting is a reversal of removal, bearing in mind the following points:

a) Tighten all fixings to the specified torque.

b) Refit the driver's airbag and the clockspring unit as described in Chapter 12.

16 Steering rack rubber gaiters – renewal

1 Remove the relevant track rod end as described in Section 20.

2 Remove the inboard and outboard securing clips, then slide the gaiter off the end of the track rod.

3 Thoroughly clean the track rod, then slide the new gaiter into position.

4 Fit the gaiter securing clips, using new clips if necessary, making sure that the gaiter is not twisted.

5 Refit the track rod end as described in Section 20.

17 Steering rack – removal and refitting

Removal

1 Access to the steering rack is best achieved by removing the subframe as described in Section 8. However, since the

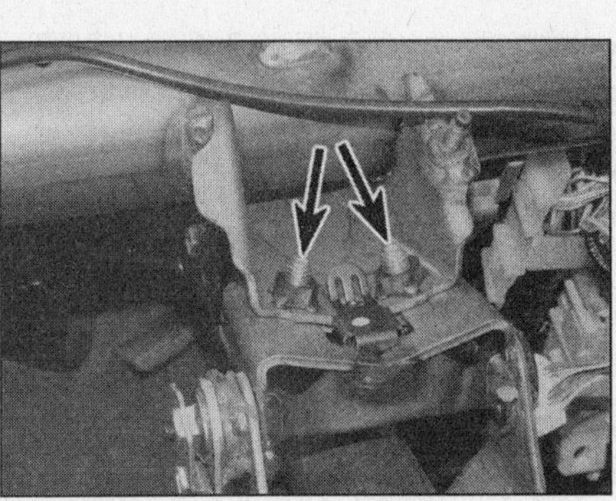
15.11b Column upper bolts fit from below into captive nuts

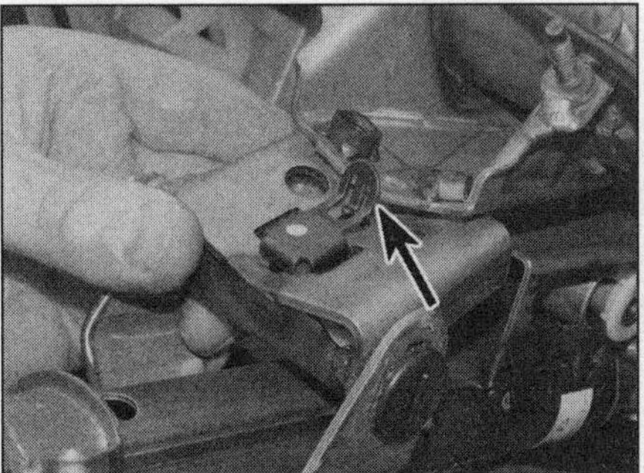
15.12 Unclip the column from its top mounting, and remove it

17.2a Two of the four steering rack mounting nuts under the subframe

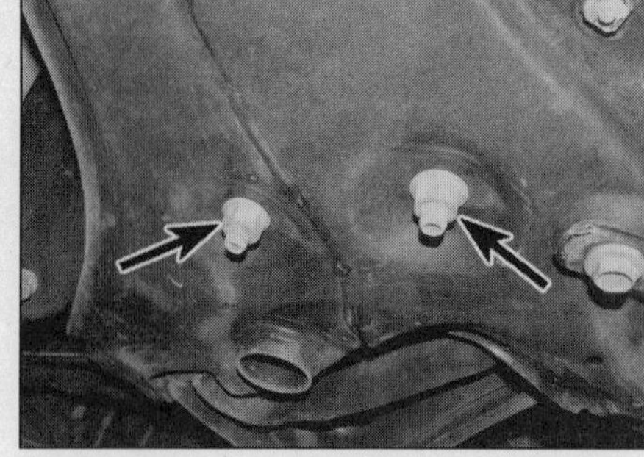
17.2b Steering rack mounting bolts and fluid pipes

17.3 One end of the rack has a clamp attaching it to the subframe

steering rack nuts can be accessed from under the car with the subframe in place, it may be possible to slide the steering rack out to the side. If this approach is chosen, proceed as described in Section 8 to disconnect the steering column, track rod ends, fluid pipes, etc.

2 Remove the four steering rack mounting bolts, and recover the nuts **(see illustrations)**.

3 Lift off the steering rack mounting clamp, and remove the rubber bush fitted below **(see illustration)**.

4 If a new steering rack is being fitted, the lower intermediate shaft will probably have to be removed, and transferred to the new unit. Mark the shaft in relation to the rack body (in a location which can easily be duplicated on the new unit), then remove the pinch-bolt and lift out the shaft.

Refitting

5 Refitting is a reversal of removal, noting the following points:

a) Tighten all fixings to the specified torque.
b) Refit the subframe as described in Section 8.
c) On models with hydraulic power steering, fill and bleed the power steering system as described in Section 19.

18 Power steering pump – removal and refitting

Note: *Only models with the hydraulic power steering system have a pump (see Section 1).*

Removal

1 Remove the auxiliary drivebelt as described in Chapter 1.

2 If the pump is being removed because a new one is being fitted, the fluid pipes are best disconnected first (as described in paragraphs 3 and 4). If not, the pump can be unbolted and moved aside.

3 Release the clips and disconnect the low-pressure fluid hose from the rear of the power steering pump – anticipate some loss of fluid as this is done. Plug or cover the pipe ends.

4 Unscrew the high-pressure union bolt and disconnect the fluid supply pipe from the front of the pump. Recover the gasket from the joint, noting how it is arranged – a new one should be fitted on reassembly.

1.0 litre and 1.3 litre 2SZ-FE engines

5 The pump is secured by three mounting bolts – one on a bracket to the front of the engine, and two more which are accessed through the pump pulley spokes (turn the pulley as necessary) **(see illustrations)**. Remove the bolts, supporting the pump as the last one is loosened, and lift off the pump. Try and keep the pump level, to reduce further fluid spillage as it is removed.

6 If the fluid pipes have not been detached, the pump assembly will not clear the engine front panel, and so cannot be moved aside. First, unbolt the fluid pipe support bracket at the rear of the engine. Remove the two bolts at the pump end of the engine front panel, then pull the panel back to allow the pump assembly to pull round the front of the engine and out of the way **(see illustrations)**.

18.5a Power steering pump-to-head bracket

18.5b Turn the pump pulley to access two of the power steering pump bolts . . .

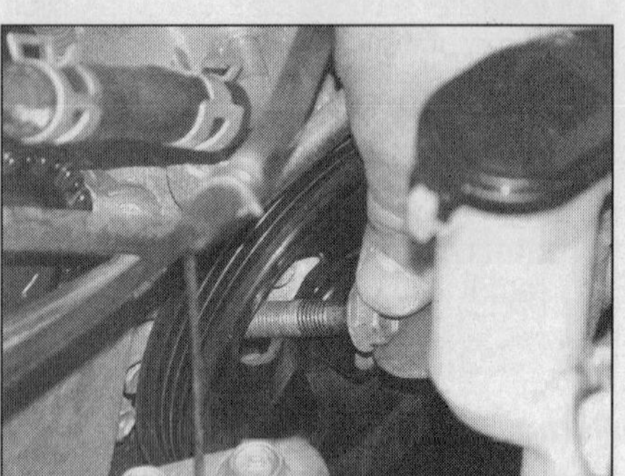
18.5c . . . then unscrew and remove them through the pulley

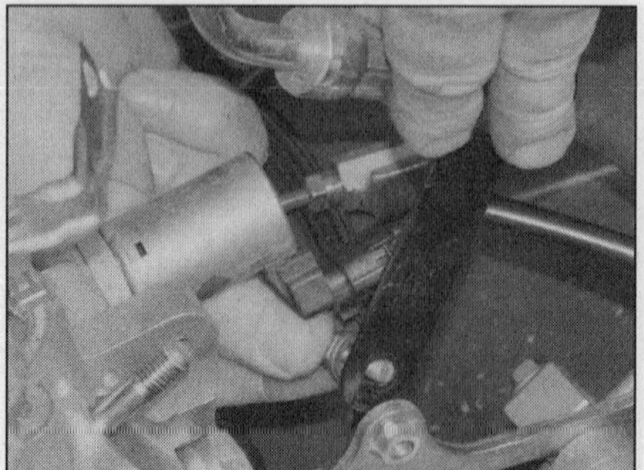
18.6a Unbolt the fluid pipe support bracket behind the engine . . .

18.6b . . . then unbolt the front panel end nearest the pump . . .

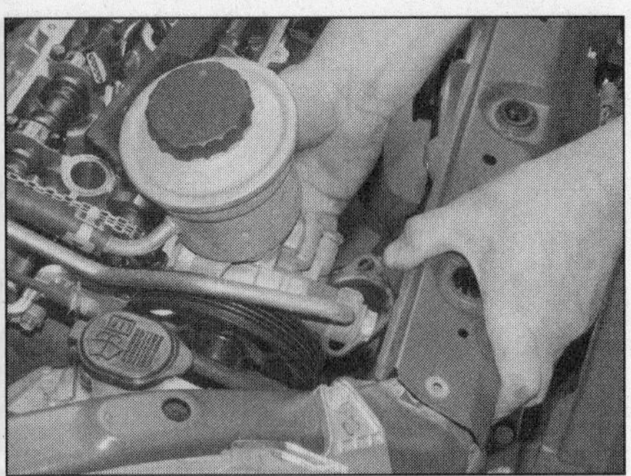

18.6c . . . and pull the panel back to swing the pump round

1.3 litre 2NZ-FE engine

7 Access to the power steering pump is not particularly good, and may in fact be easier from below. Remove the three bolts securing the fluid reservoir to the top of the pump, and lift it clear. Remove the two nuts and through-bolts which secure the pump to the back of the engine, and withdraw the pump.

Refitting

8 Refitting is a reversal of removal, noting the following points:

a) *Use a new gasket when refitting the high-pressure pipe, and tighten the union nut to the specified torque.*
b) *Tighten all fixings to the specified torque.*
c) *Refit the auxiliary drivebelt as described in Chapter 1.*
d) *On completion, fill and bleed the power steering system as described in Section 19.*

19 Power steering hydraulic system – bleeding

Note: *This Section only applies to models with the hydraulic power steering system (see Section 1).*

1 Check the power steering fluid level as described in *Weekly checks*. If the system has been drained, fill the reservoir very slowly with clean fluid, until the level reaches the MAX line. Make sure the fluid is agitated as little as possible, to reduce aeration.

2 Jack up the front of the car, and support it on axle stands (see *Jacking and vehicle support*).

3 With the engine switched off, turn the steering wheel slowly from lock to lock several times.

4 Lower the car to the ground.

5 Ensure that the fluid level does not drop below the MIN line during the following procedure. If the system is completely empty, the fluid in the reservoir will disappear very quickly when the engine is started.

6 Start the engine, and allow it to idle for a few minutes.

7 Turn the steering wheel slowly until it reaches full lock. Hold the steering wheel on full lock for two or three seconds (no longer), then turn the wheel slowly to the opposite lock, and repeat.

8 Repeat the process of turning the wheel from lock to lock several times, then centre the steering and switch off the engine.

9 Check for air bubbles in the fluid reservoir – if air bubbles are visible, the system requires further bleeding.

10 On completion, check and if necessary top-up the fluid level once more.

11 If problems with air in the system persist, leave the car overnight, then repeat the bleeding procedure.

20 Track rod end – removal and refitting

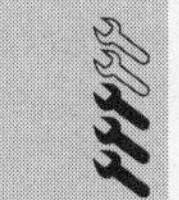

Note: *A balljoint separator tool will be required for this operation. Where applicable, Nyloc-type self-locking nuts must be renewed on refitting.*

Removal

1 Slacken the relevant front wheel nuts. Apply the handbrake, then jack up the front of the car, and support securely on axle stands (see *Jacking and vehicle support*). Remove the roadwheel.

2 Pull out the split pin, then slacken the track rod end balljoint nut, and unscrew it as far as the ends of the threads **(see illustration)**.

3 Disconnect the track rod end balljoint from the swivel hub using a balljoint separator tool (leave the nut fitted to protect the threads), taking care not to damage the balljoint rubber seal **(see illustration)**. Once the balljoint has been released, remove the balljoint nut.

4 If the same track rod is to be refitted, mark its position relative to the steering rack. Slacken the track rod end locknut, then unscrew the track rod end from the track rod, counting the number of turns necessary to remove it.

Refitting

5 Screw the track rod end onto the track rod the number of turns noted during removal (or until the marks line up, where applicable), then tighten the locknut while holding the balljoint in position.

6 Engage the track rod end balljoint pin with the swivel hub, then the nut. Tighten the nut to the specified torque, then fit a new split pin. The nut may be tightened by up to an extra 60° if necessary until the split pin fits.

7 Refit the roadwheel, then lower the car to the ground, and tighten the wheel nuts.

8 Check the front wheel alignment at the earliest opportunity.

21 Wheel alignment and steering angles – general information

Front wheel alignment

1 Accurate front wheel alignment is essential to precise steering and for even tyre wear. Before considering the steering angles, check that the tyres are correctly inflated, that the front wheels are not buckled, the hub bearings are not worn, and that the steering linkage and front suspension are in good order, without slackness or wear at the joints.

2 Wheel alignment consists of four factors:

Camber, is the angle at which the roadwheels are set from the vertical when viewed from the front or rear of the car. Positive camber is the angle (in degrees) that the wheels are tilted outwards at the top from the vertical. The camber angle is given for reference only, and cannot be adjusted.

Castor, is the angle between the steering axis and a vertical line when viewed from each side of the car. Positive castor is indicated

20.2a The track rod end nut and split pin may be corroded . . .

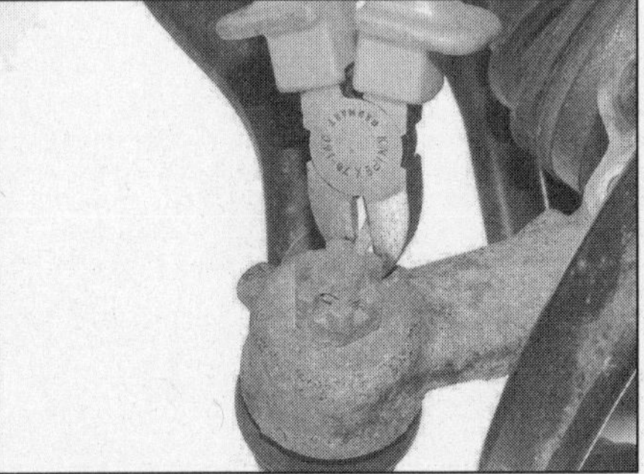

20.2b . . . so the split pin might need persuading to remove

20.3 Use a balljoint splitter to separate the track rod end

when the steering axis is inclined towards the rear of the car at its upper end. This angle is not adjustable.

Steering axis inclination (kingpin inclination), is the angle, when viewed from the front or rear of the car, between the vertical and an imaginary line drawn between the upper and lower front suspension strut mountings. This angle is not adjustable.

Toe, is the amount by which the distance between the front inside edges of the roadwheel rim differs from that between the rear inside edges. If the distance between the front edges is less than that at the rear, the wheels are said to toe-in. If the distance between the front inside edges is greater than that at the rear, the wheels toe-out.

3 Owing to the need for precision gauges to measure the small angles of the steering and suspension settings, it is preferable that checking of camber and castor is left to a service station having the necessary equipment. Camber and castor is set during production of the car, and any deviation from the specified angle will be due to accident damage or gross wear in the suspension mountings.

4 To check the front wheel alignment, first make sure that the lengths of both track rods are equal when the steering is in the straight-ahead position. The track rod lengths can be adjusted if necessary by releasing the locknuts from the track rod ends and rotating the track rods. If necessary, self-locking grips can be used to rotate the track rods.

5 Obtain a tracking gauge. These are available in various forms from accessory stores, or one can be fabricated from a length of steel tubing suitably cranked to clear the sump and transmission, and having a setscrew and locknut at one end.

6 With the gauge, measure the distances between the two wheel inner rims (at hub height) at the rear of the wheel. Push the car forward to rotate the wheel through 180° (half a turn) and measure the distance between the wheel inner rims, again at hub height, at the front of the wheel. This last measurement should differ from the first by the appropriate toe-in which is given in the Specifications. The car must be on level ground.

7 If the toe-in is found to be incorrect, release the track rod end locknuts and turn both track rods equally **(see illustration)**. Only turn them a quarter-of-a-turn at a time before rechecking the alignment. If necessary use self-locking grips to turn the track rods – **do not** grip the threaded part of the track rod during adjustment. It is important not to allow the track rods to become unequal in length during adjustment, otherwise the alignment of the steering wheel will become incorrect and tyre scrubbing will occur on turns.

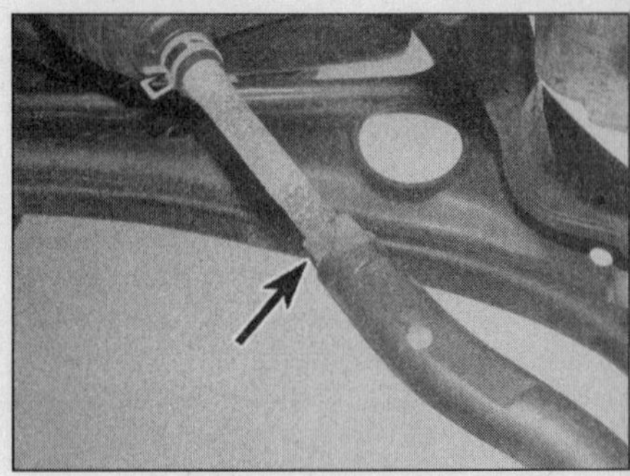

21.7 Track rod end locknut

8 On completion tighten the locknuts without disturbing the setting. Check that the track rod end balljoint is at the centre of its arc of travel (ie, not twisted to the front or rear).

Rear wheel alignment

9 Figures are provided in the Specifications for rear wheel camber and toe-setting, for reference only. No adjustment is possible, so any significant deviation from the quoted figures is likely to be due to accident damage, or possibly to poor reassembly. Refer to paragraph 2 for a description of the settings.

Chapter 11
Bodywork and fittings

Contents

Degrees of difficulty

Easy, suitable for novice with little experience 

Fairly easy, suitable for beginner with some experience 

Fairly difficult, suitable for competent DIY mechanic 

Difficult, suitable for experienced DIY mechanic 

Very difficult, suitable for expert DIY or professional

Specifications

Torque wrench settings	Nm	lbf ft
Bumper mountings	13	10
Bonnet hinge bolts	11	8
Door check strap bolts	30	22
Door hinge bolts:		
Front	43	32
Rear	25	18
Tailgate	11	8
Door lock striker:		
Doors	23	17
Tailgate	11	8
Front seat mounting bolts	37	27
Rear seat hinge bolts	37	27
Seat belt mounting bolts	41	30

1 General information

The bodyshell is of three- and five-door Hatchback configurations, and is made of pressed-steel sections. Most components are welded together, but some use is made of structural adhesives. The front wings are bolted on.

The bonnet, doors and some other vulnerable panels are made of zinc-coated metal, and are further protected by being coated with an anti-chip primer prior to being sprayed.

Extensive use is made of plastic materials, mainly in the interior, but also in exterior components. The front and rear bumpers are injection-moulded from a synthetic material which is very strong, and yet light (the Yaris' lower rear bumper is metal, however). Plastic components such as wheel arch liners are fitted to the underside of the car, to improve the body's resistance to corrosion.

2 Maintenance – bodywork and underframe

The general condition of a car's bodywork is the one thing that significantly affects its value. Maintenance is easy, but needs to be regular. Neglect, particularly after minor damage, can lead quickly to further deterioration and costly repair bills. It is important also to keep watch on those parts of the car not immediately visible, for instance the underside, inside all the wheel arches, and the lower part of the engine compartment.

The basic maintenance routine for the bodywork is washing – preferably with a lot of water, from a hose. This will remove all the loose solids which may have stuck to the car. It is important to flush these off in such a way as to prevent grit from scratching the finish. The wheel arches and underframe need washing in the same way, to remove any accumulated mud which will retain moisture and tend to encourage rust. Paradoxically enough, the best time to clean the underframe and wheel arches is in wet weather, when the mud is thoroughly wet and soft. In very wet weather, the underframe is usually cleaned of large accumulations automatically, and this is a good time for inspection.

Periodically, except on models with a wax-based underbody protective coating, it is a good idea to have the whole of the underframe of the car steam-cleaned, engine compartment included, so that a thorough inspection can be carried out to see what minor repairs and renovations are necessary. Steam-cleaning is available at many garages, and is necessary for the removal of the accumulation of oily grime, which sometimes is allowed to become thick in certain areas. If steam-cleaning facilities are not available, there are one or two excellent grease solvents available, which can be brush-applied; the dirt can then be simply hosed off. Note that these methods should not be used on cars with wax-based underbody protective coating, or the coating will be removed. Such cars should be inspected annually, preferably just prior to Winter, when the underbody should be washed down, and any damage to the wax coating repaired. Ideally, a completely fresh coat should be applied. It would also be worth considering the use of such wax-based protection for injection into door panels, sills, box sections, etc, as an additional safeguard against rust damage, where such protection is not provided by the manufacturer.

After washing paintwork, wipe off with a chamois leather to give an unspotted clear finish. A coat of clear protective wax polish will give added protection against chemical pollutants in the air. If the paintwork sheen has dulled or oxidised, use a cleaner/polisher combination to restore the brilliance of the shine. This requires a little effort, but such dulling is usually caused because regular washing has been neglected. Care needs to be taken with metallic paintwork, as special non-abrasive cleaner/polisher is required to avoid damage to the finish. Always check that the door and ventilator opening drain holes and pipes are completely clear, so that water can be drained out. Brightwork should be treated in the same way as paintwork. Windscreens and windows can be kept clear of the smeary film which often appears, by the use of proprietary glass cleaner. Never use any form of wax, or other body or chromium polish, on glass.

3 Maintenance – upholstery and carpets

Mats and carpets should be brushed or vacuum-cleaned regularly, to keep them free of grit. If they are badly stained, remove them from the car for scrubbing or sponging, and make quite sure they are dry before refitting. Seats and interior trim panels can be kept clean by wiping with a damp cloth. If they do become stained (which can be more apparent on light-coloured upholstery), use a little liquid detergent and a soft nail brush to scour the grime out of the grain of the material. Do not forget to keep the headlining clean in the same way as the upholstery. When using liquid cleaners inside the car, do not over-wet the surfaces being cleaned. Excessive damp could get into the seams and padded interior, causing stains, offensive odours or even rot. If the inside of the car gets wet accidentally, it is worthwhile taking some trouble to dry it out properly, particularly where carpets are involved. *Do not leave oil or electric heaters inside the car for this purpose.*

4 Minor body damage – repair

Repairs of minor scratches

If the scratch is very superficial, and does not penetrate to the metal of the bodywork, repair is very simple. Lightly rub the area of the scratch with a paintwork renovator, or a very fine cutting paste, to remove loose paint from the scratch, and to clear the surrounding bodywork of wax polish. Rinse the area with clean water.

In the case of metallic paint (and some solid colours), the most commonly-found scratches are not in the basecoat paint, but in the lacquer top coat, and appear white. If care is taken, these can sometimes be rendered less obvious by very careful use of paintwork renovator (which would otherwise not be used on metallic paintwork); otherwise, repair of these scratches can be achieved by applying lacquer with a fine brush.

Apply touch-up paint to the scratch using a fine paint brush; continue to apply fine layers of paint until the surface of the paint in the scratch is level with the surrounding paintwork. Allow the new paint at least two weeks to harden, then blend it into the surrounding paintwork by rubbing the scratch area with a paintwork renovator or a very fine cutting paste. Finally, apply wax polish.

Where the scratch has penetrated right through to the metal of the bodywork, causing the metal to rust, a different repair technique is required. Remove any loose rust from the bottom of the scratch with a penknife, then apply rust-inhibiting paint, to prevent the formation of rust in the future. Using a rubber or nylon applicator, fill the scratch with bodystopper paste. If required, this paste can be mixed with cellulose thinners, to provide a very thin paste which is ideal for filling narrow scratches. Before the stopper-paste in the scratch hardens, wrap a piece of smooth cotton rag around the top of a finger. Dip the finger in cellulose thinners, and quickly sweep it across the surface of the stopper-paste in the scratch; this will ensure that the surface of the stopper-paste is slightly hollowed. The scratch can now be painted over as described earlier in this Section.

Repairs of dents

When deep denting of the bodywork has taken place, the first task is to pull the dent out, until the affected bodywork almost attains its original shape. There is little point in trying to restore the original shape completely, as the metal in the damaged area will have stretched on impact, and cannot be reshaped fully to its original contour. It is better to bring the level of the dent up to a point which is about 3 mm below the level of the surrounding bodywork. In cases where the dent is very shallow anyway, it is not worth trying to pull it out at all. If the underside of the dent is accessible, it can be hammered out gently from behind, using a mallet with a wooden or plastic head. Whilst doing this, hold a suitable block of wood firmly against the outside of the panel, to absorb the impact from the hammer blows and thus prevent a large area of the bodywork from being 'belled-out'.

Should the dent be in a section of the bodywork which has a double skin, or some other factor making it inaccessible from behind, a different technique is called for. Drill several small holes through the metal inside the area – particularly in the deeper section. Then screw long self-tapping screws into the holes, just sufficiently for them to gain a good purchase in the metal. Now the dent can be pulled out by pulling on the protruding heads of the screws with a pair of pliers.

The next stage of the repair is the removal of the paint from the damaged area, and from an inch or so of the surrounding 'sound' bodywork. This is accomplished most easily by using a wire brush or abrasive pad on a power drill, although it can be done just as effectively by hand, using sheets of abrasive paper. To complete the preparation for filling, score the surface of the bare metal with a screwdriver or the tang of a file, or alternatively, drill small holes in the affected area. This will provide a really good 'key' for the filler paste.

To complete the repair, see the Section on filling and respraying.

Repairs of rust holes or gashes

Remove all paint from the affected area, and from an inch or so of the surrounding 'sound' bodywork, using an abrasive pad or a wire brush on a power drill. If these are not available, a few sheets of abrasive paper will do the job most effectively. With the paint removed, you will be able to judge the severity of the corrosion, and therefore decide whether to renew the whole panel (if this is possible) or to repair the affected area. New body panels are not as expensive as most people think, and it is often quicker and more satisfactory to fit a new panel than to attempt to repair large areas of corrosion.

Remove all fittings from the affected area, except those which will act as a guide to the original shape of the damaged bodywork (eg body side mouldings etc). Then, using tin snips or a hacksaw blade, remove all loose metal and any other metal badly affected by corrosion. Hammer the edges of the hole inwards, in order to create a slight depression for the filler paste.

Wire-brush the affected area to remove the powdery rust from the surface of the remaining metal. Paint the affected area with rust-inhibiting paint; if the back of the rusted area is accessible, treat this also.

Before filling can take place, it will be necessary to block the hole in some way. This can be achieved by the use of aluminium or plastic mesh, or aluminium tape.

Aluminium or plastic mesh, or glass-fibre matting, is probably the best material to use for a large hole. Cut a piece to the approximate size and shape of the hole to be filled, then position it in the hole so that its edges are below the level of the surrounding bodywork. It can be retained in position by several blobs of filler paste around its periphery.

Aluminium tape should be used for small or very narrow holes. Pull a piece off the roll, trim it to the approximate size and shape required, then pull off the backing paper (if used) and stick the tape over the hole; it can be overlapped if the thickness of one piece is insufficient. Burnish down the edges of the tape with the handle of a screwdriver or similar, to ensure that the tape is securely attached to the metal underneath.

Filling and respraying

Before using this Section, see the Sections on dent, deep scratch, rust holes and gash repairs.

Many types of bodyfiller are available, but generally speaking, those proprietary kits which contain a tin of filler paste and a tube of resin hardener are best for this type of repair. A wide, flexible plastic or nylon applicator will be found invaluable for imparting a smooth and well-contoured finish to the surface of the filler.

Mix up a little filler on a clean piece of card or board – measure the hardener carefully (follow the maker's instructions on the pack), otherwise the filler will set too rapidly or too slowly. Using the applicator, apply the filler paste to the prepared area; draw the applicator across the surface of the filler to achieve the correct contour and to level the surface. As soon as a contour that approximates to the correct one is achieved, stop working the paste – if you carry on too long, the paste will become sticky and begin to 'pick-up' on the applicator. Continue to add thin layers of filler paste at 20-minute intervals, until the level of the filler is just proud of the surrounding bodywork.

Once the filler has hardened, the excess can be removed using a metal plane or file. From then on, progressively-finer grades of abrasive paper should be used, starting with a 40-grade production paper, and finishing with a 400-grade wet-and-dry paper. Always wrap the abrasive paper around a flat rubber, cork, or wooden block – otherwise the surface of the filler will not be completely flat. During the smoothing of the filler surface, the wet-and-dry paper should be periodically rinsed in water. This will ensure that a very smooth finish is imparted to the filler at the final stage.

At this stage, the 'dent' should be surrounded by a ring of bare metal, which in turn should be encircled by the finely 'feathered' edge of the good paintwork. Rinse the repair area with clean water, until all of the dust produced by the rubbing-down operation has gone.

Spray the whole area with a light coat of – this will show up any imperfections in the surface of the filler. Repair these imperfections with fresh filler paste or bodystopper, and once more smooth the surface with abrasive paper. If bodystopper is used, it can be mixed with cellulose thinners, to form a really thin paste which is ideal for filling small holes. Repeat this spray-and-repair procedure until you are satisfied that the surface of the filler, and the feathered edge of the paintwork, are perfect. Clean the repair area with clean water, and allow to dry fully.

The repair area is now ready for final spraying. Paint spraying must be carried out in a warm, dry, windless and dust-free atmosphere. This condition can be created artificially if you have access to a large indoor working area, but if you are forced to work in the open, you will have to pick your day very carefully. If you are working indoors, dousing the floor in the work area with water will help to settle the dust which would otherwise be in the atmosphere. If the repair area is confined to one body panel, mask off the surrounding panels; this will help to minimise the effects of a slight mis-match in paint colours. Bodywork fittings (eg chrome strips, door handles etc) will also need to be masked off. Use genuine masking tape, and several thicknesses of newspaper, for the masking operations.

Before commencing to spray, agitate the aerosol can thoroughly, then spray a test area (an old tin, or similar) until the technique is mastered. Cover the repair area with a thick coat of primer; the thickness should be built up using several thin layers of paint, rather than one thick one. Using 400 grade wet-and-dry paper, rub down the surface of the primer until it is really smooth. While doing this, the work area should be thoroughly doused with water, and the wet-and-dry paper periodically rinsed in water. Allow to dry before spraying on more paint.

Spray on the top coat, again building up the thickness by using several thin layers of paint. Start spraying at the top of the repair area, and then, using a side-to-side motion, work downwards until the whole repair area and about two inches of the surrounding original paintwork is covered. Remove all masking material 10 to 15 minutes after spraying on the final coat of paint.

Allow the new paint at least two weeks to harden, then, using a paintwork renovator or a very fine cutting paste, blend the edges of the paint into the existing paintwork. Finally, apply wax polish.

Plastic components

With the use of more and more plastic body components by the car manufacturers (eg bumpers. spoilers, and in some cases, major body panels), rectification of more serious damage to such items has become a matter of either entrusting repair work to a specialist in this field, or renewing complete components. Repair of such damage by the DIY owner is not really feasible, owing to the cost of the equipment and materials required for effecting such repairs. The basic technique involves making a groove along the line of the crack in the plastic, using a rotary burr in a power drill. The damaged part is then welded back together, using a hot air gun to heat up and fuse a plastic filler rod into the groove. Any excess plastic is then removed, and the area rubbed down to a smooth finish. It is important that a filler rod of the correct plastic is used, as body components can be made of a variety of different types (eg polycarbonate, ABS, polypropylene).

Damage of a less serious nature (abrasions, minor cracks etc) can be repaired by the DIY owner using a two-part epoxy filler repair. Once mixed in equal, this is used in similar fashion to the bodywork filler used on metal panels. The filler is usually cured in twenty to thirty minutes, ready for sanding and painting.

If the owner is renewing a complete component himself, or if he has repaired it with epoxy filler, he will be left with the problem of finding a suitable paint for finishing which is compatible with the type of plastic used. At one time, the use of a universal paint was not possible, owing to the complex range of plastics encountered in body component applications. Standard paints, generally speaking, will not bond to plastic or rubber satisfactorily, but suitable paints to match any plastic or rubber finish, can be obtained from dealers. However, it is now possible to obtain a plastic body parts finishing kit which consists of a pre-primer treatment, a primer and coloured top coat. Full instructions are normally supplied with a kit, but basically, the method of use is to first apply the pre-primer to the component concerned, and allow it to dry for up to 30 minutes. Then the primer is applied, and left to dry for about an hour before finally applying the special-coloured top coat. The result is a correctly-coloured component, where the paint will flex with the plastic or rubber, a property that standard paint does not normally posses.

5 Major body damage – repair

Where serious damage has occurred, or large areas need renewal due to neglect, it means that complete new panels will need welding-in, and this is best left to professionals. If the damage is due to impact, it will also be necessary to check completely the alignment of the bodyshell, and this can only be carried out accurately by a Toyota dealer using special jigs. If the body is left misaligned, it is primarily dangerous, as the car will not handle properly, and secondly, uneven stresses will be imposed on the steering, suspension and possibly transmission, causing abnormal wear, or complete failure, particularly to such items as the tyres.

6 Bumpers – removal and refitting

Front bumper

Removal

1 Open the bonnet, and prise out the single clip from the top edge of the bumper, in the centre **(see illustration)**.

2 Working in the wheel arch, remove the single screw/fastener used to secure the top rear corner of the bumper on each side **(see illustration)**.

3 Jack up the front of the car, and support it on axle stands (see *Jacking and vehicle support*).

4 Remove the engine undercover panels (see Chapter 1, Section 3).

5 Remove the two remaining bolts which secure the bumper lower trim piece at either end, and remove the trim **(see illustrations)**.

6 Prise out and remove the plastic trim clips used to secure the front part of the wheel arch liner, and pull it away from the bumper **(see illustrations)**.

7 On models with front foglights, reach up behind the light unit and disconnect the wiring plug each side.

8 The bumper is now secured by a total of four clips – one at each end, and one just inside the lower corner of each headlight.

6.1 Prise up and remove the central clip

6.2 Remove the bumper end screw inside the wheel arch

6.5a Remove the two bolts . . .

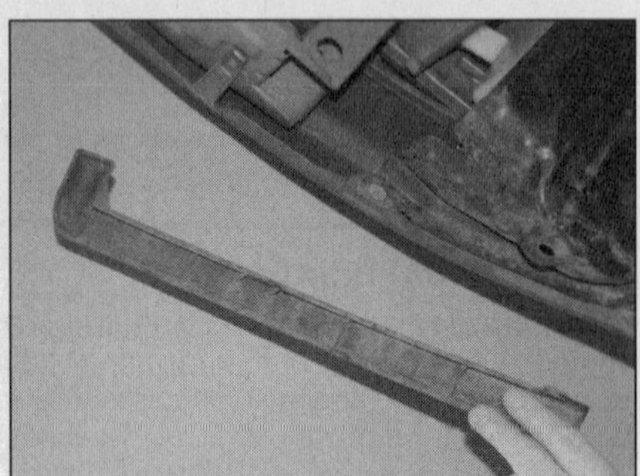

6.5b . . . and take off the trim piece

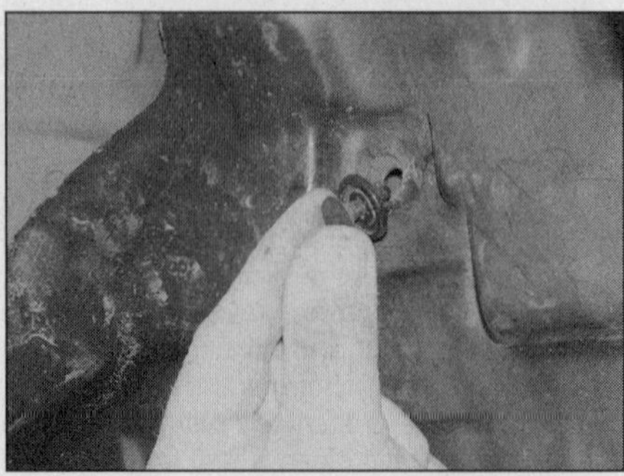

6.6a Prise out the clips securing the front section of the wheel arch liner . . .

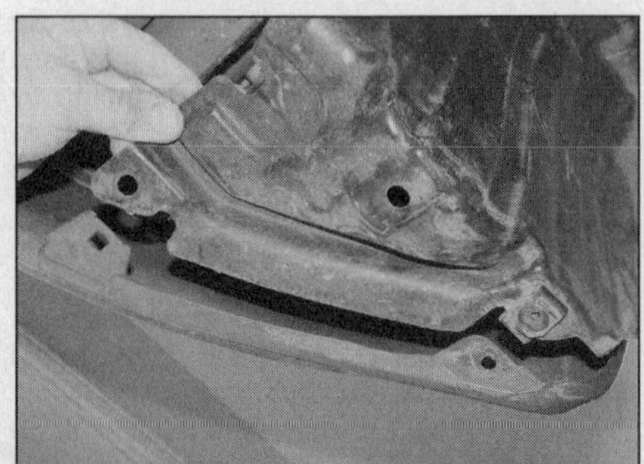

6.6b . . . and release it from the bumper

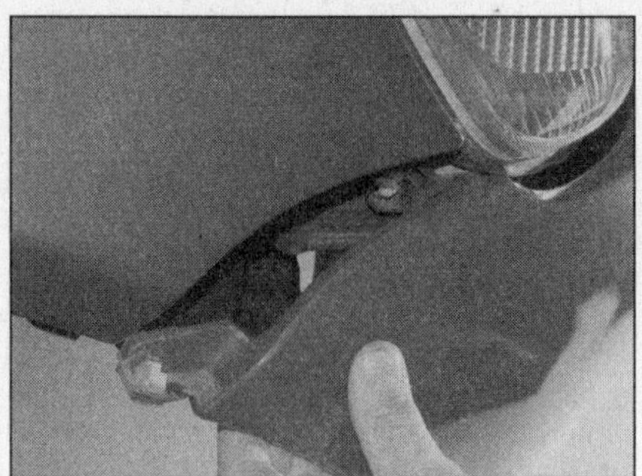

6.9 Pull the bumper end outwards to release the end clips

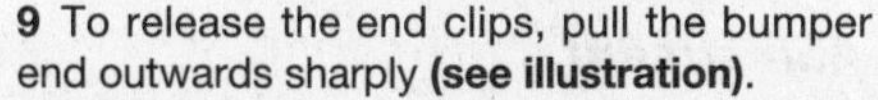

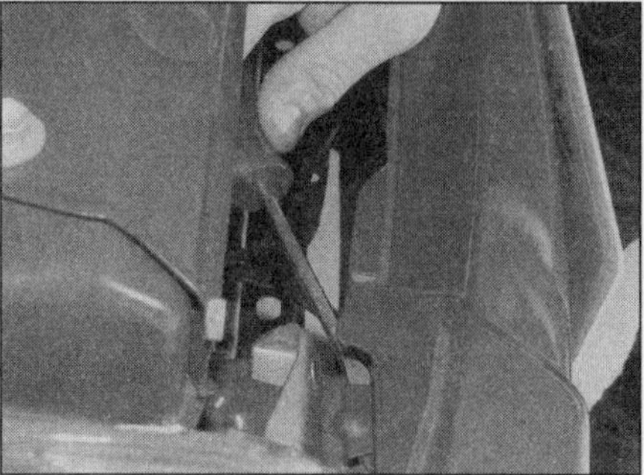

6.10a Prise up the metal centre clips using a screwdriver . . .

6.10b . . . then pull the bumper forwards . . .

9 To release the end clips, pull the bumper end outwards sharply **(see illustration)**.

10 The two centre clips are made of metal, and can be prised upwards using a screwdriver - once this has been done, the bumper can be pulled forwards and removed from the car **(see illustrations)**.

Refitting

11 Refitting is a reversal of removal. Have an assistant available to help align the bumper, and tighten the mountings securely.

Rear bumper

Note: *The rear bumper is in two sections. The main (upper) section is made of plastic, and is removed first. If required, the metal lower section can then be unbolted and removed.*

Removal

12 Jack up the rear of the car, and support it on axle stands (see *Jacking and vehicle support*).

13 In the rear wheel arch each side, unclip and unbolt the rear mudflap from the bumper. Unscrew and remove the retaining bolt inside the wheel arch each side **(see illustrations)**.

14 Open the tailgate, and remove the two bolts from the corners of the tailgate aperture **(see illustration)**.

15 The bumper plastic (upper) section is now held in place by two different types of clip. Approximately 10 cm in from each end, a very stiff plastic plug-and-socket clip secures the end of the bumper to the car - pull sharply outwards on the bumper end to detach it **(see illustration)**.

6.10c . . . and remove it from the car

6.13a Remove the bolt securing the mudflap . . .

6.13b . . . then unclip and remove it from the edge of the rear bumper

6.13c Unscrew the upper-to-lower bumper section bolt inside the wheel arch

16 Pull the plastic section of the bumper rearwards to detach the four folded-over edge clips used to secure it to the metal lower section **(see illustration)**. If any of the clips come off with the plastic bumper, refit them to the lower section.

17 Reach inside the bumper, and twist off the bulbholders from the number plate lights (on

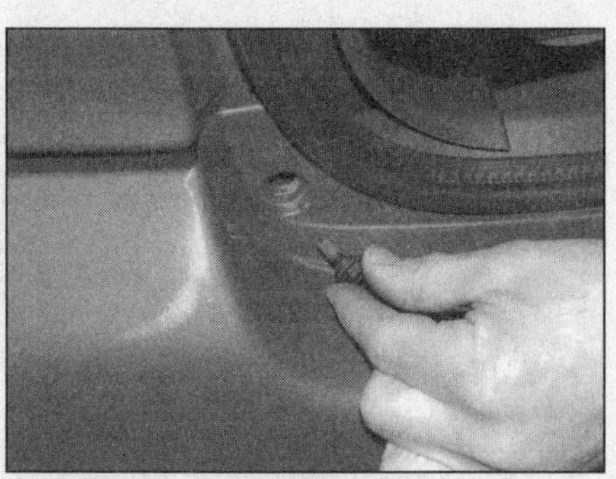

6.14 Remove the upper bolt either side of the tailgate

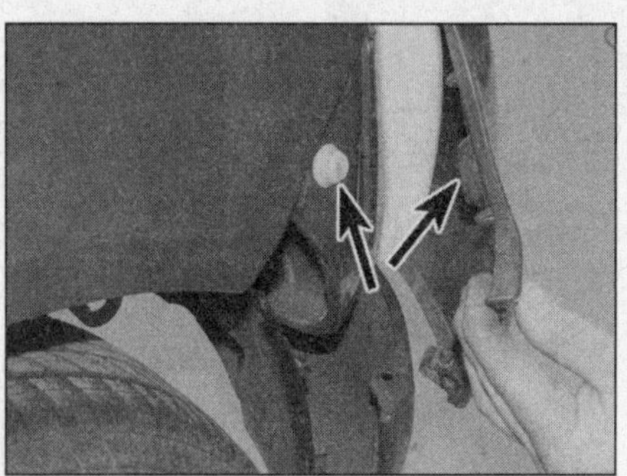

6.15 Pull the bumper end outwards to detach the plug-and-socket clip

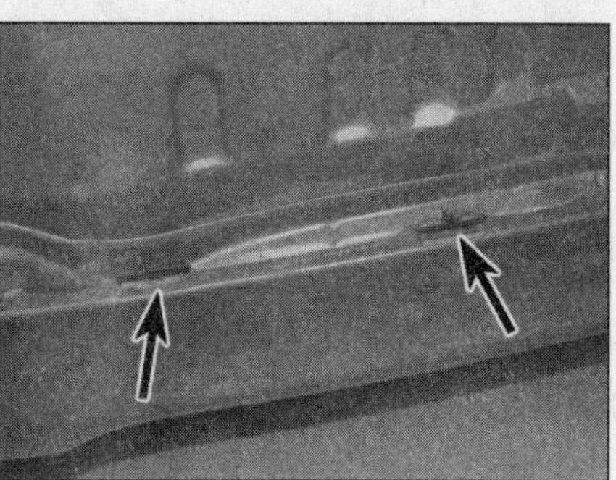

6.16 Two of the plastic edge clips used to hold the bumper sections together

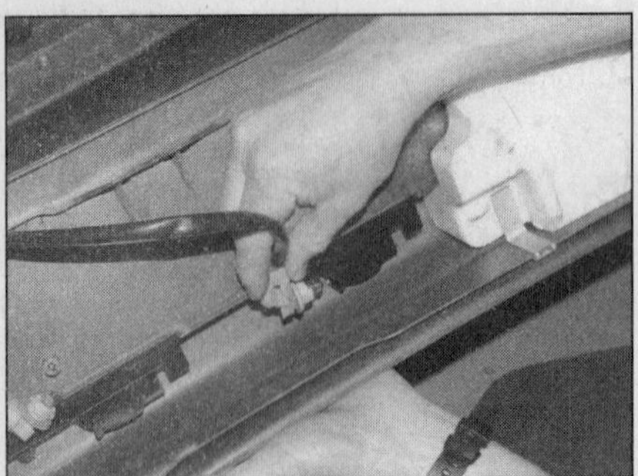

6.17a Twist off the number plate light bulbholders . . .

6.18a One of the bumper lower section retaining nuts on top . . .

models with rear parking sensors, also disconnect the wiring plug from each sensor). Remove the bumper from the car **(see illustrations)**.

18 If required, the bumper lower section can also be removed. The metal lower section is secured by two nuts and two bolts along the top edge, and a further two bolts (one each side) underneath **(see illustrations)**.

Refitting

19 Refitting is a reversal of removal, noting the following points:

a) On models with rear parking sensors, if a new bumper is being fitted, these may be supplied without the holes for the sensors. If so, the old bumper will have to be used as a template, and suitable holes cut.

b) Have an assistant available to help align the bumper, and tighten the mountings securely.

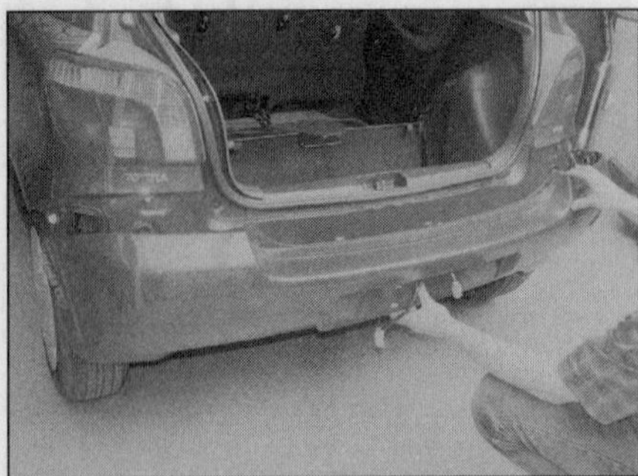

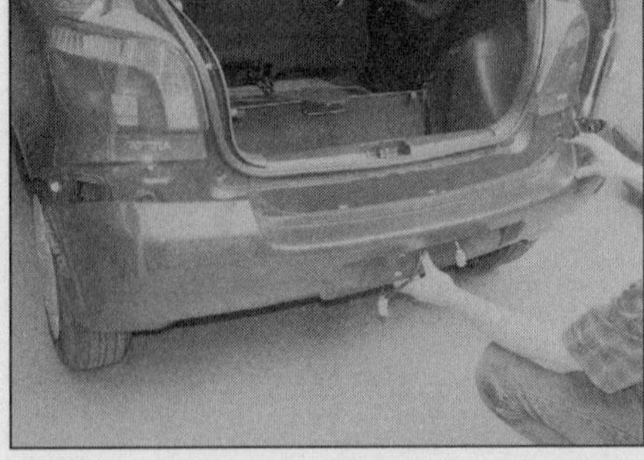

6.17b . . . and remove the bumper from the car

6.18b . . . and one of the lower bolts

7 Bonnet – removal, refitting and adjustment

Removal

1 Open the bonnet, and support it on its stay.

2 Using a marker pen or paint, mark around the hinge positions on the bonnet.

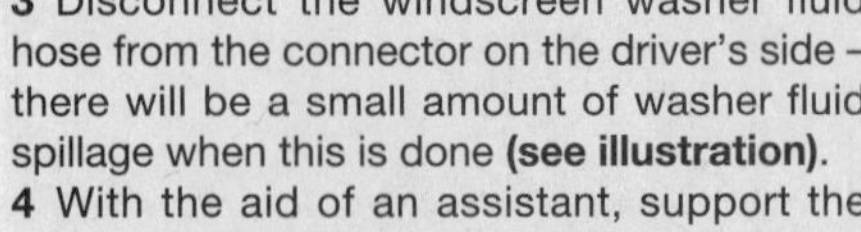

3 Disconnect the windscreen washer fluid hose from the connector on the driver's side – there will be a small amount of washer fluid spillage when this is done **(see illustration)**.

4 With the aid of an assistant, support the bonnet, and unscrew the four bolts securing the bonnet to the hinges **(see illustration)**.

5 Lift off the bonnet.

Refitting

6 Align the marks made on the bonnet before removal with the hinges, then refit and tighten the bonnet securing bolts.

7 Reconnect the washer hose, ensuring that it is pushed firmly onto the connector.

8 Check the bonnet adjustment as follows.

Adjustment

9 Close the bonnet, and check that there is an equal gap at each side, between the bonnet and the wing panels. Check also that the bonnet sits flush in relation to the surrounding body panels.

10 The bonnet should close smoothly and positively without excessive pressure. If this is not the case, adjustment will be required.

11 To adjust the bonnet alignment, slacken the bonnet securing bolts, and move the bonnet on the bolts as required (the bolt holes in the hinges are elongated). To adjust the bonnet closure, adjustable bump stops are fitted to the body front panel. These may be raised or lowered by screwing in or out as necessary. If desired, the bonnet lock can be adjusted as described in Section 9.

8 Bonnet release cable – removal and refitting

Note: *If the cable has broken, use the information in this Section to establish which end of the cable has failed – if the break is inside the car, it may be possible to remove the release lever as described below, and operate the remains of the cable to get the bonnet open. If the break is under the bonnet,*

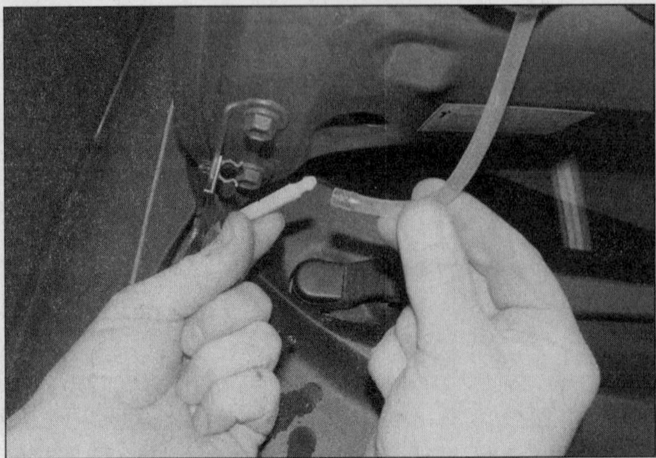

7.3 Disconnect the windscreen washer supply hose

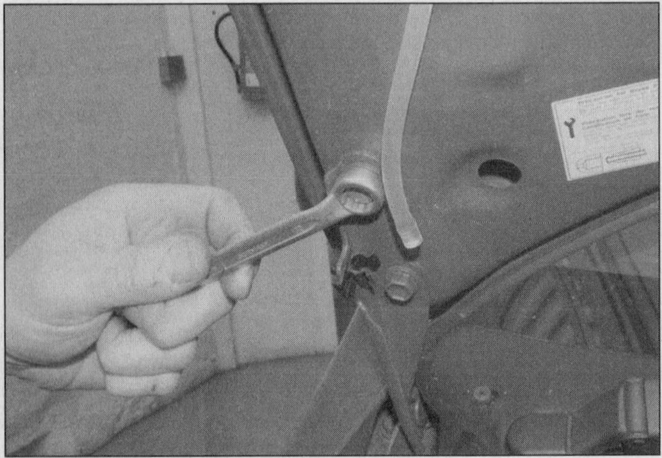

7.4 With the bonnet supported, unscrew the four hinge bolts

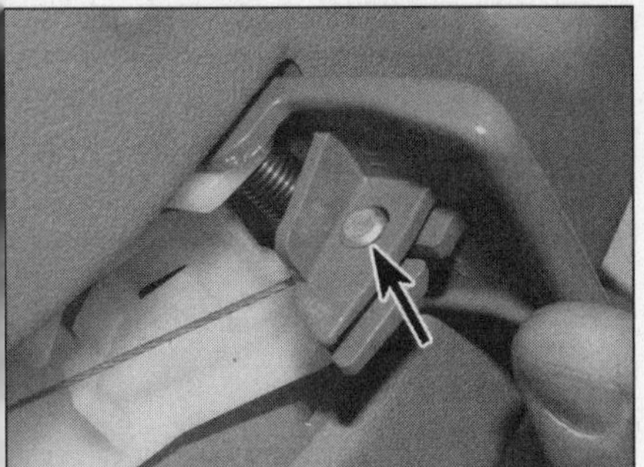

8.2a Pull out the release lever and unhook the cable end fitting . . .

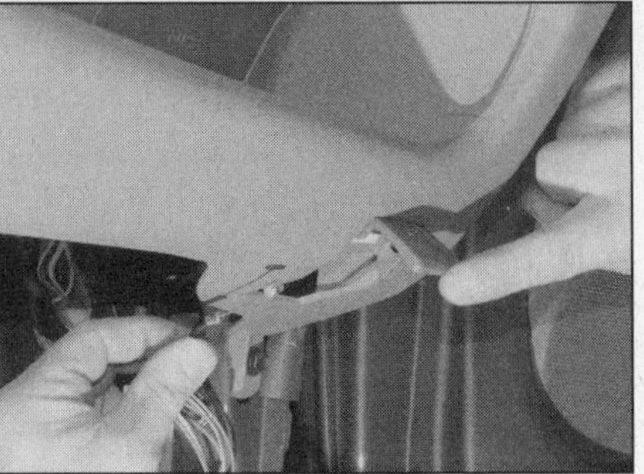

8.2b . . . then release the outer cable and withdraw it under the facia

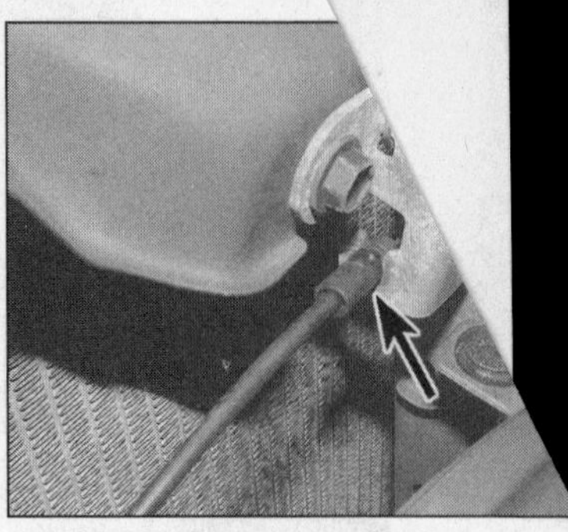

8.3 Unclip the outer cable from the sl the bonnet lock

there are two ways the bonnet may be opened – through the radiator grille aperture, or from underneath. Even with the bonnet shut, it may still be possible to operate the lock through the grille with minimal damage, though access to the cable will be poor. From underneath, with the car jacked up and supported on axle stands, access to the bonnet lock operating lever may be a little better.

Removal

1 The bonnet release lever is located on the lower facia panel, to the right of the steering wheel.

2 Pull out the release lever, and unclip the cable end fitting from underneath it. Release the outer cable from the mounting bracket, and withdraw it under the facia **(see illustrations)**.

3 Under the bonnet, prise out the outer cable end fitting from its slot in the bonnet lock **(see illustration)**, then unhook the inner cable from the lock operating lever.

4 Release the cable from the clips and brackets in the engine compartment, noting its routing.

5 Tie a length of string to the end of the cable at the release lever inside the car, then carefully pull the cable through the bulkhead grommet into the engine compartment.

6 Untie the string from the end of the cable, and leave it in position to aid refitting.

Refitting

7 Refitting is a reversal of removal, but tie the string to the release lever end of the cable, and use the string to pull the cable into position. Ensure that the cable is routed as noted before removal, and make sure that the bulkhead grommet is correctly seated.

9 Bonnet lock – removal and refitting

Removal

1 Open the bonnet, then unscrew the three securing bolts, and remove the lock assembly **(see illustrations)**.

2 Prise out the outer cable end fitting from its slot in the bonnet lock, then unhook the inner cable from the lock operating lever **(see illustration)**.

Refitting

3 Refitting is a reversal of removal. If necessary, the position of the lock can be altered to adjust the lock operation, by moving the lock within the elongated holes.

10 Door – removal and refitting

Removal

1 Open the door, and disconnect the wiring plug at the front edge.

2 Unbolt the door check strap from the door, or from the door pillar **(see illustration)**.

3 Ensure that the door is adequately supported, with the aid of an assistant, or using wooden blocks or similar under th bottom edge of the door (take care not to damage the paintwork).

4 Mark the position of the hinges on the body or on the door, then unscrew the bolts and remove the door from the car.

Refitting

5 Refitting is a reversal of removal.

11 Door inner trim panel – removal and refitting

Front door

Removal

1 On models with manual front windows, remove the winder handle as described in paragraph 9.

9.1a Unscrew the bonnet lock mounting bolts . . .

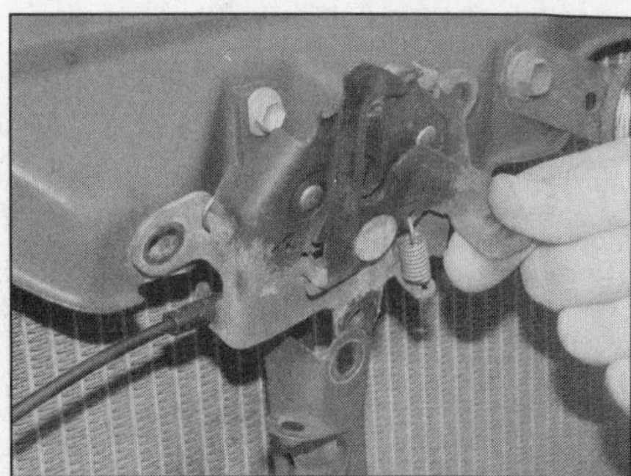

9.1b . . . and remove it from the front panel

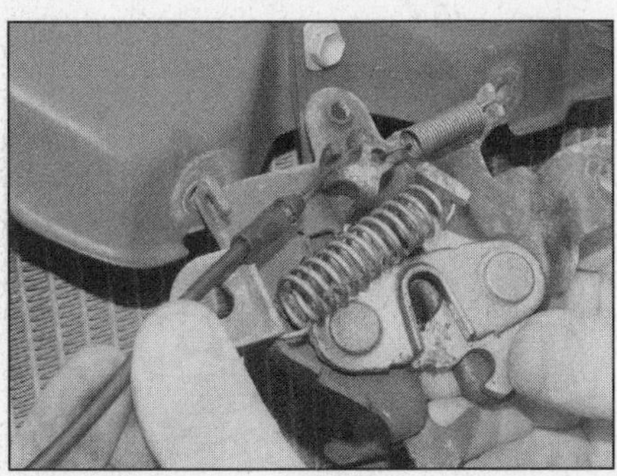

9.2 Unhook the cable from the bonnet lock

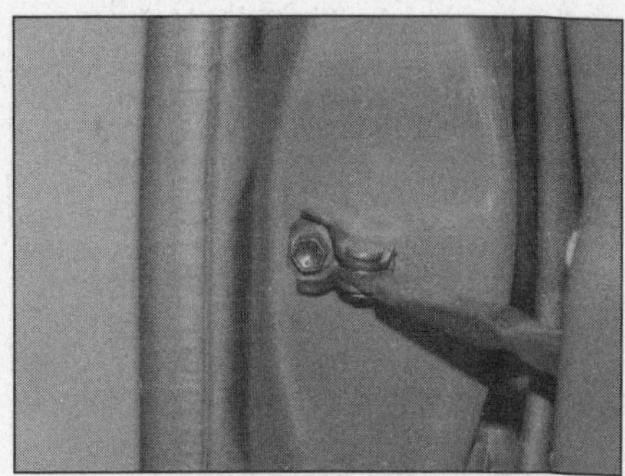

10.2 Door check strap bolt on the door pillar

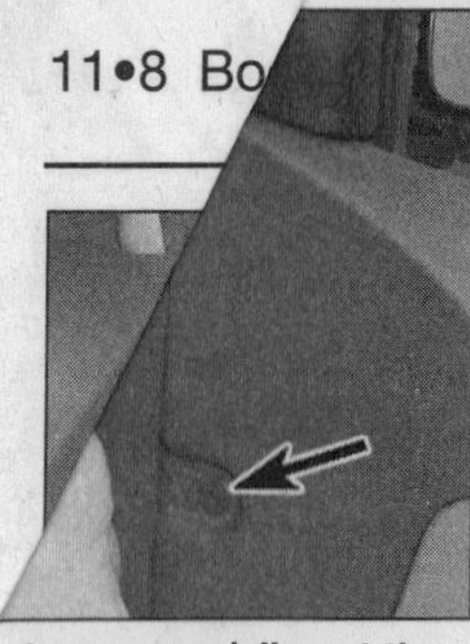

…e two screw/clips at the … the door trim panel

…oor fully open, remove the two … from the front edge of the panel …ation). Take care not to mark or … e trim panel.

…ove the screw above the door lock …dle, and the one inside the door pull handle **(see illustrations)**.

4 On five-door models, remove the screw/clip at the rear of the trim panel **(see illustration)**. Again, take care not to mark or damage the trim panel.

5 On models with electric windows, carefully prise up the window switch panel (this can be done without tools), then disconnect the wiring plug underneath **(see illustrations)**.

6 The door trim panel is now secured by a number of plastic clips, all round the sides and base. Start at one of the bottom corners, and prise the panel with a wide-bladed tool to release the first few clips. Work along the base of the panel, then up the sides, releasing the clips as you go. Finally, the panel should be lifted to unhook the top edge from the door glass channel, and over the door lock button **(see illustrations)**.

7 To access the door inner components, it will usually be necessary to remove the plastic membrane from the door. Unbolt the door pull handle bracket, and remove it. Use a sharp knife to slice along the bead of mastic, and carefully peel back the plastic without tearing it **(see illustrations)**.

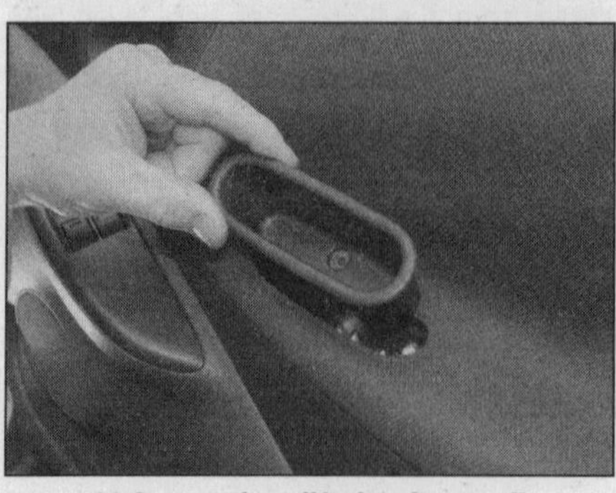

11.3a Remove the screw above the door lock handle . . .

11.3b . . . and the one inside the door pull . . .

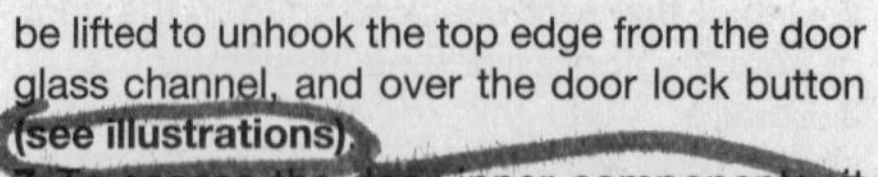

11.3c . . . then lift the door pull out

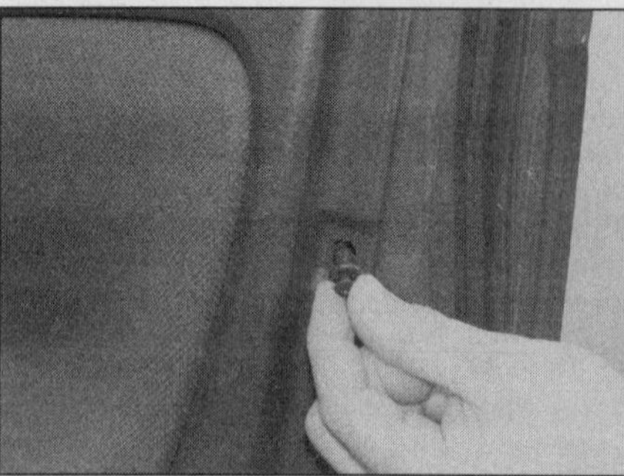

11.4 On five-door models, remove the screw/clip at the back

11.5a Prise up the window switch panel . . .

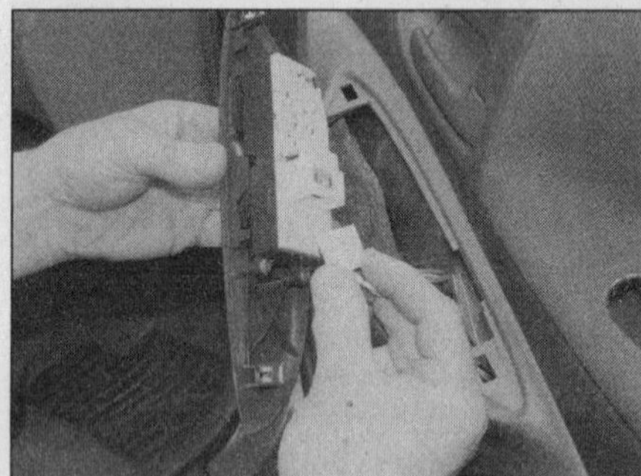

11.5b . . . and disconnect the wiring plug

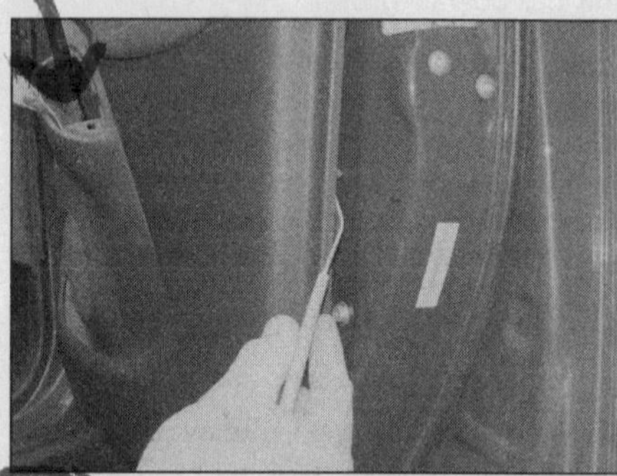

11.6a Prise the panel to release the clips . . .

11.6b . . . then lift it over the door lock button

11.7a Unbolt and remove the door pull handle bracket . . .

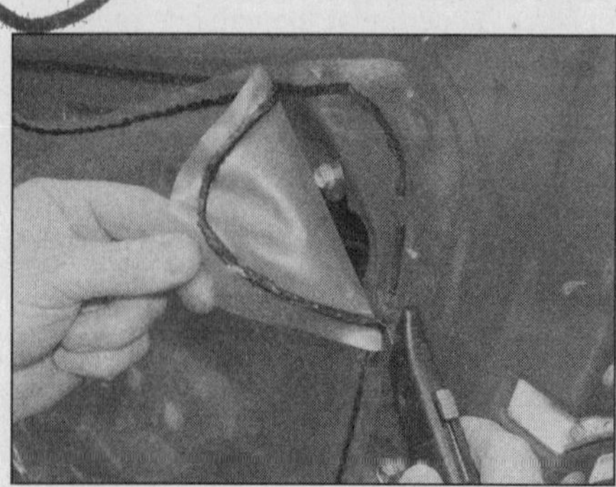

11.7b . . . then slice along the bead of mastic securing the plastic membrane

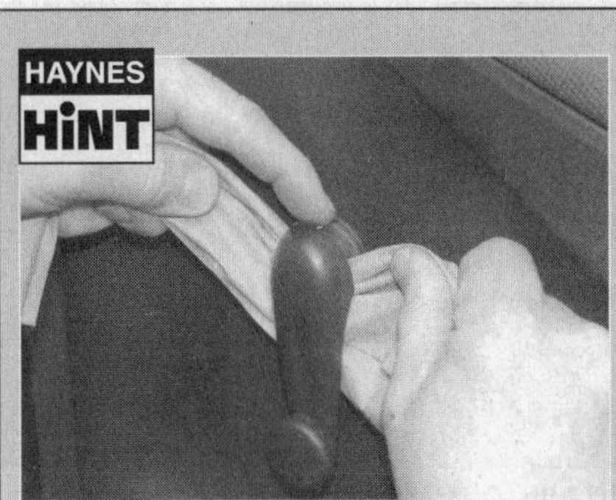

Prise the winder handle to open a gap between it and the circular disc behind. Work the edge of a piece of (clean) cloth/rag into the gap behind the handle, either from the top or underneath. Using a 'sawing' action, work the cloth side to side, and also pull the ends of the cloth up (or down). It may take some time, but what you're trying to do is snag the ends of the spring clip holding the handle in place – when you do, the sawing action should work the clip off, allowing the handle to be pulled from the splines. A little patience is required, but it will work. Keep an eye on where the spring clip goes, though.

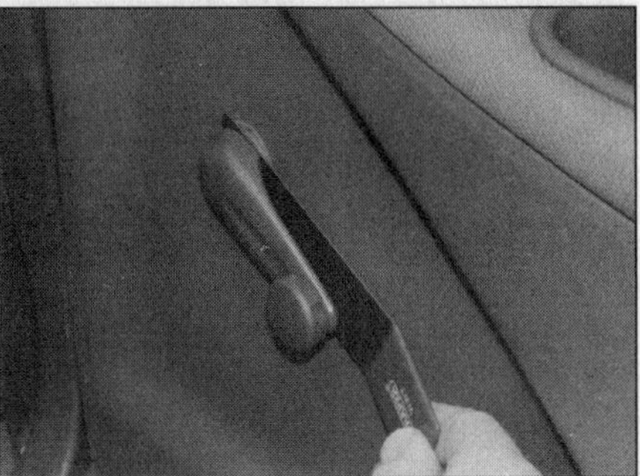

11.9a Release the window winder spring clip with a special tool (if available) . . .

11.9b . . . then recover and refit the spring clip to the handle, and take off the trim disc

11.10a Remove the screw above the door lock handle . . .

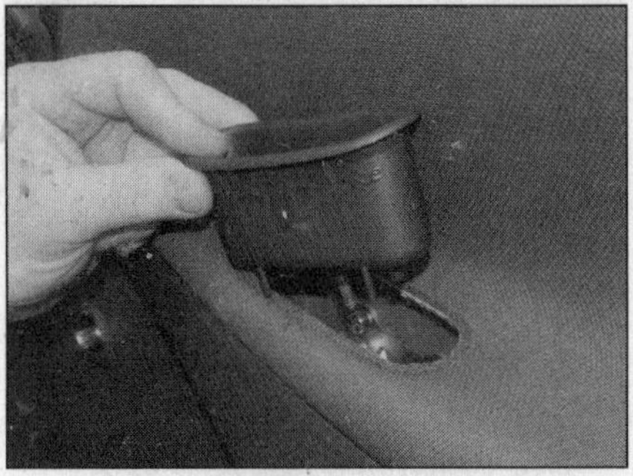

11.10b . . . and the one inside the door pull, then lift the door pull out

Refitting

8 Refitting is a reversal of removal. Before starting, check to see whether any trim clips have been left on the door, and transfer them to the trim panel.

Rear door

Removal

9 On models with manual rear windows, use a hooked piece of wire or a similar tool to release the window regulator handle securing clip from the shaft – if neither of these is available, see the **Haynes Hint**. Pull off the regulator handle, and recover the spring clip and the trim disc **(see illustrations)**.

10 Remove the screw above the door lock handle, and the one inside the door pull handle **(see illustrations)**.

11 The door trim panel is now secured by a number of plastic clips, all round the sides and base. Start at one of the bottom corners, and prise the panel with a wide-bladed tool to release the first few clips. Work along the base of the panel, then up the sides, releasing the clips as you go. Finally, the panel should be lifted to unhook the top edge from the door glass channel, and over the door lock button **(see illustration)**.

12 On models with electric rear windows, disconnect the window switch wiring plug from the back, and the panel can be removed completely.

13 If required, remove the door membrane using a similar method to that described in paragraph 7.

Refitting

14 Refitting is a reversal of removal. Before starting, check to see whether any trim clips have been left on the door, and transfer them to the trim panel.

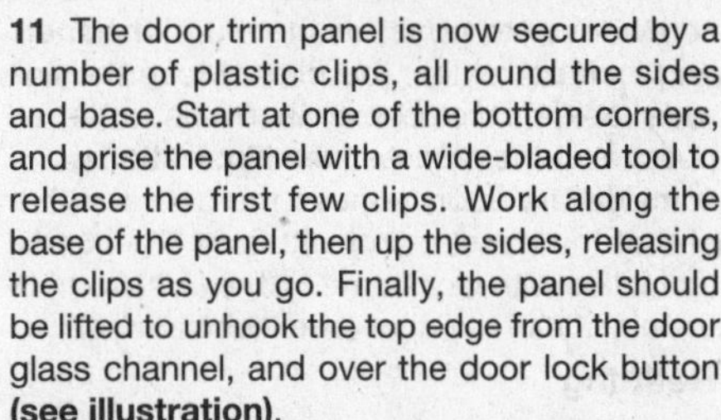

12 Door handles and lock components – removal and refitting

Interior handle

Removal

1 Remove the door inner trim panel as described in Section 11.

2 Unclip the door lock handle from the door, first releasing its locating peg at the rear edge **(see illustration)**.

3 Unhook the cable end from the handle, and the handle can be removed **(see illustration)**.

11.11 Prise off the door trim panel, and lift it away

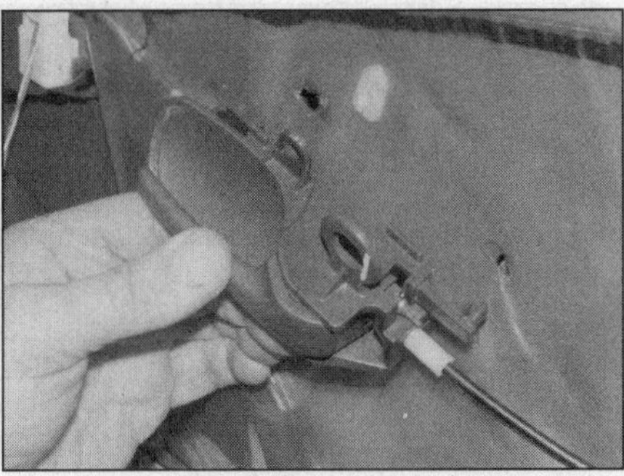

12.2 Unclip the interior handle – note the locating peg at the rear

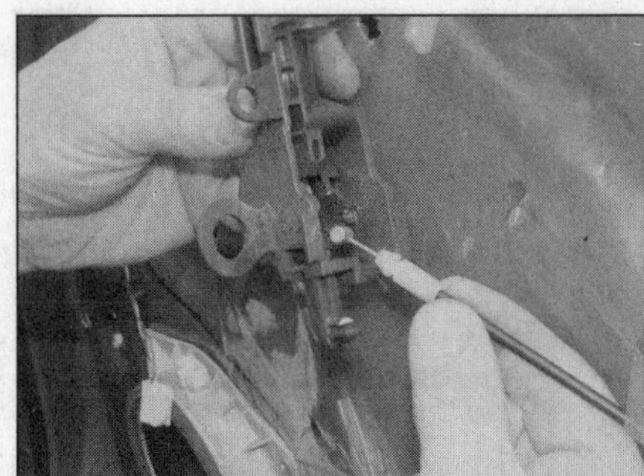

12.3 Unhook the cable end fitting and remove the handle

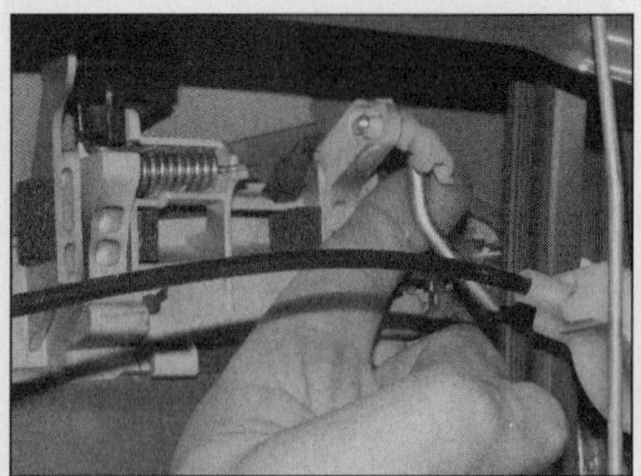
12.8a Lift up the handle link rod clip to release it . . .

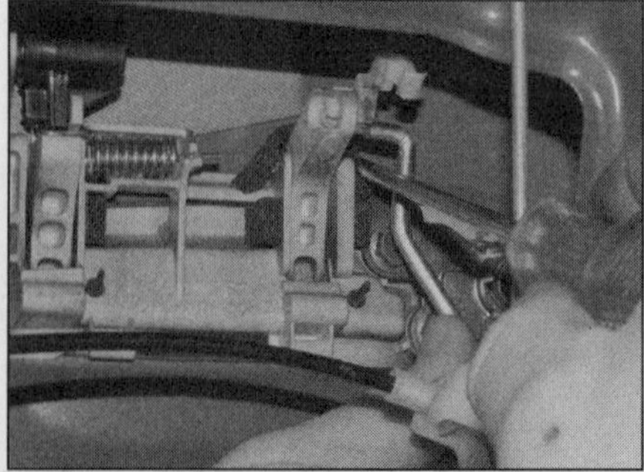
12.8b . . . then use a screwdriver to slide the link rod off sideways

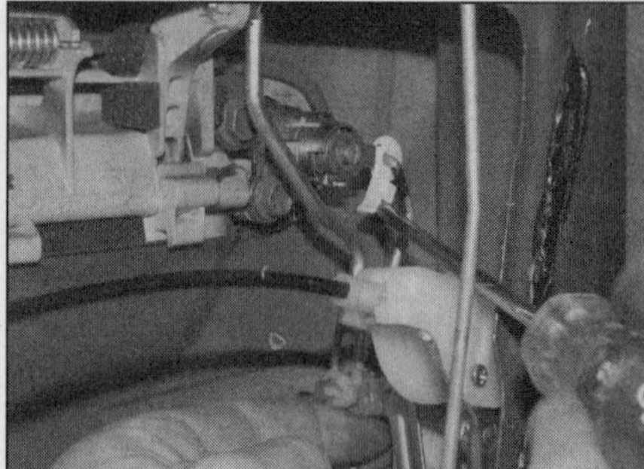
12.8c On the front door, the lock barrel link rod is similarly removed

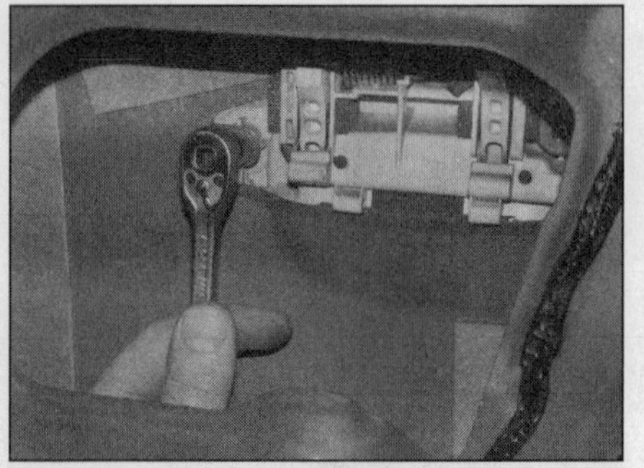
12.9a Remove the bolt at the front . . .

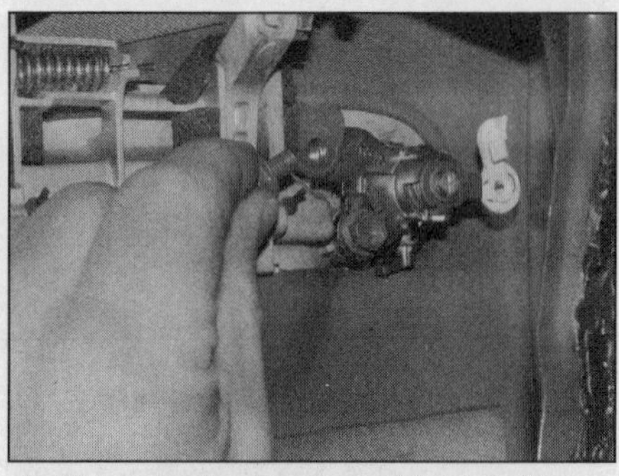
12.9b . . . and at the rear of the handle . . .

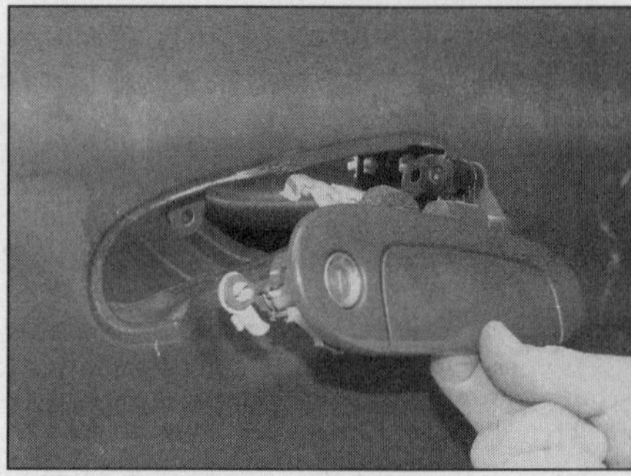
12.9c . . . and remove the handle from the door

4 To remove the cable, the plastic membrane will also have to be peeled off, as described in Section 11. Unclip the cable from the door clip, then unhook the end fitting from the lock assembly.

Refitting

5 Refitting is a reversal of removal. Refit the door trim panel with reference to Section 11.

Exterior handle

Removal

6 Remove the door inner trim panel as described in Section 11, and peel back the plastic membrane.

7 On the rear door handle (5-door models), the door glass rear guide channel will have to be removed for access, and possibly the rear lock assembly also (see Section 13 and later in this Section respectively).

8 Noting how they are fitted, use a screwdriver to prise off the exterior handle and lock barrel link rod clips. Move the link rods aside, disturbing them as little as possible in the process **(see illustrations)**.

9 Inside the door, remove the bolt at either end of the handle, and withdraw the handle (complete with lock barrel on the front door) to the outside of the door **(see illustrations)**.

Refitting

10 Refitting is a reversal of removal. Check the operation of the handle (and lock barrel, where applicable) before refitting the trim panel as described in Section 11.

Front lock barrel

Removal

11 Remove the exterior handle as described previously in this Section.

12 Remove the single mounting bolt, and withdraw the lock barrel from the handle **(see illustration)**.

Refitting

13 Refitting is a reversal of removal.

Front lock

Removal

14 Remove the door trim panel as described in Section 11, and peel back the plastic membrane.

15 Unscrew the knob from the top of the door lock pop-up button **(see illustration)**.

16 Unclip the door lock interior handle from the door, first releasing its locating peg at the rear edge.

17 Unhook the cable end from the handle, and release the door lock operating cable from its clip on the door **(see illustration)**.

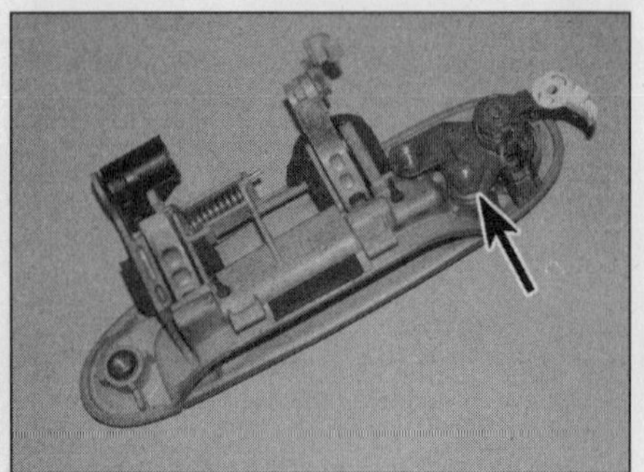
12.12 Lock barrel mounting bolt (arrowed)

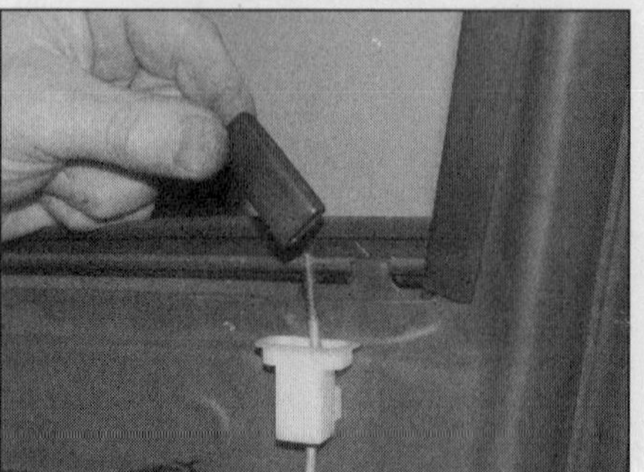
12.15 Unscrew and remove the door lock button

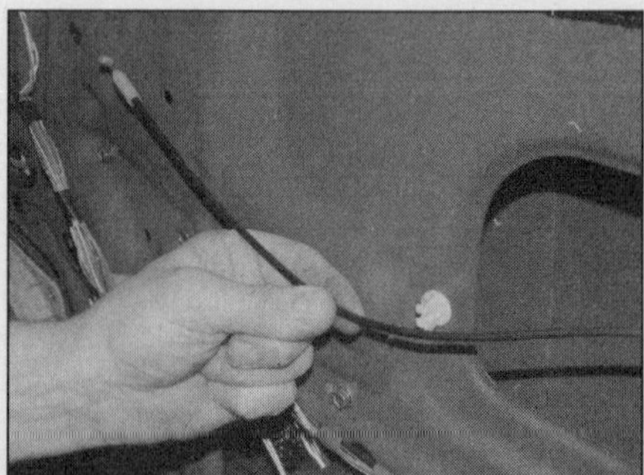
12.17 Unclip the lock operating cable from the door

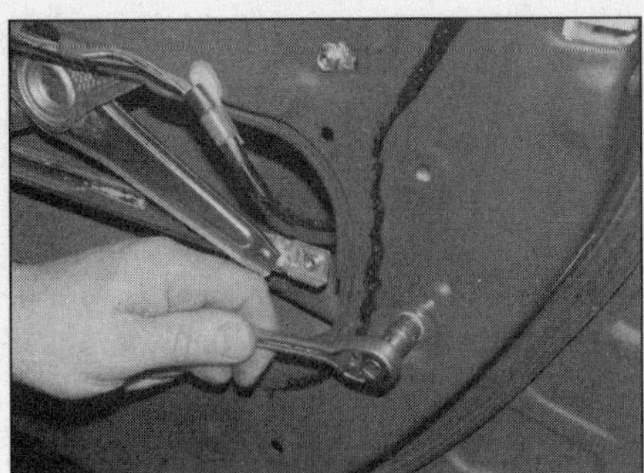
12.19a Remove the door window guide channel bolt . . .

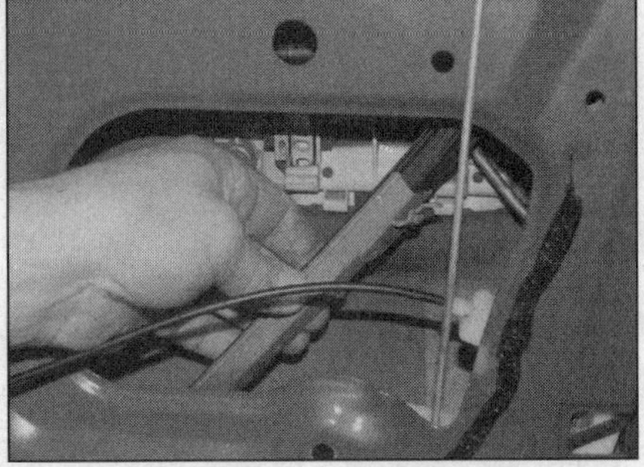
12.19b . . . then unclip it at the top, and move it clear of the lock assembly

12.20a Remove the three Torx screws at the rear . . .

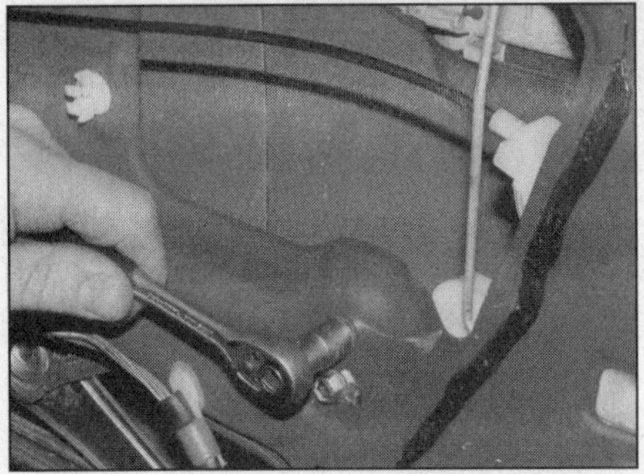
12.20b . . . and, where applicable, the bolt inside

12.21a Slide the lock downwards, and disconnect the central locking wiring plug

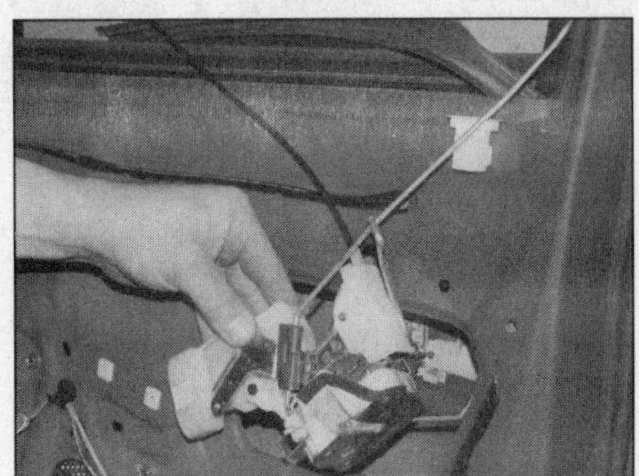
12.21b Remove the lock and link rods from the door

18 Noting how they are fitted, use a screwdriver to prise off the exterior handle and lock barrel link rod clips (see paragraph 8). Move the link rods aside, disturbing them as little as possible in the process.

19 To improve access to the lock, remove the door window rear guide channel, which is clipped in at the top, and secured by a single bolt at the base. Move the channel down and forwards – it can be laid in the bottom of the door, but don't forget to refit it **(see illustrations)**.

20 The lock itself is secured by three screws on the back edge of the door (models with central locking have a further lock securing bolt on the inside of the door). Remove the fasteners, and withdraw the lock downwards **(see illustrations)**.

21 On models with central locking, disconnect the wiring plug from the lock, and remove it from the door **(see illustrations)**.

Refitting

22 Refitting is a reversal of removal, bearing in mind the following points:

a) *Lubricate the moving parts of the lock assembly with multi-purpose grease before refitting.*
b) *The three lock securing screws on the back edge of the door should have their threads cleaned and coated with thread-locking fluid before refitting them.*
c) *Check the operation of the lock mechanism before refitting the door inner trim panel.*
d) *Refit the door trim panel with reference to Section 11.*

Rear lock

Removal

23 Remove the door trim panel as described in Section 11, and peel back the plastic membrane.

24 Unscrew the knob from the top of the door lock pop-up button.

25 Unclip the door lock interior handle from the door, first releasing its locating peg at the rear edge **(see illustration)**.

26 Unhook the cable end from the interior handle **(see illustration)**. With the membrane peeled back, release the door lock operating cable and the door lock button link rod from the clip on the door.

27 To improve access to the lock, the door glass rear guide channel will have to be removed as described in Section 13.

28 Noting how they are fitted, use a screwdriver to separate the exterior handle and lock button link rods from the plastic link piece. There is an access hole in the door, through which a screwdriver can be used **(see illustration)**. Move the link rods aside,

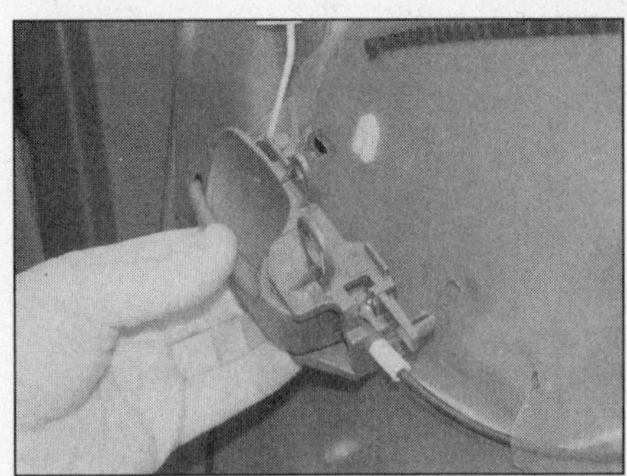
12.25 Unclip the interior handle from the door

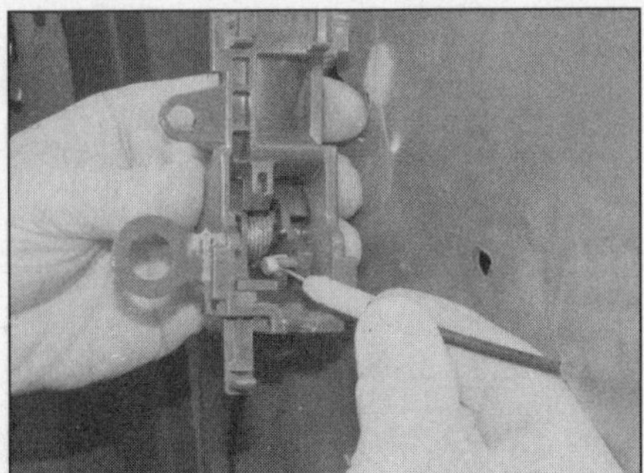
12.26 Release the door lock cable end fitting from the interior handle

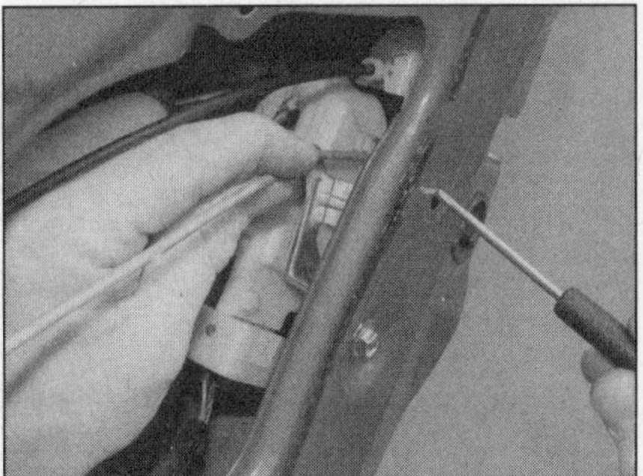
12.28 Use a screwdriver through the access hole to help unclip the link rods

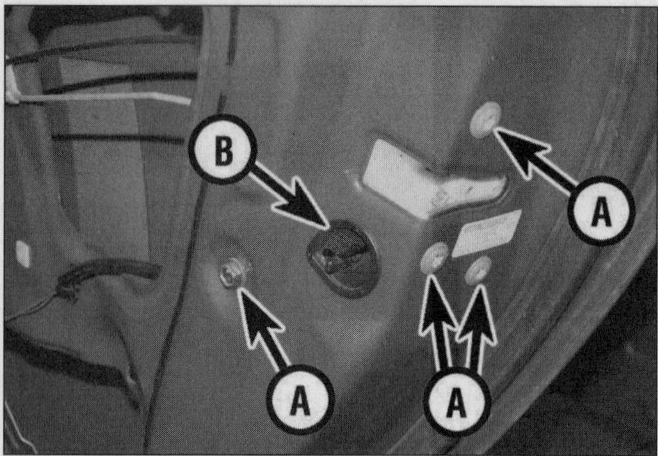

12.29 Rear door lock fasteners (A) and childproof lock (B)

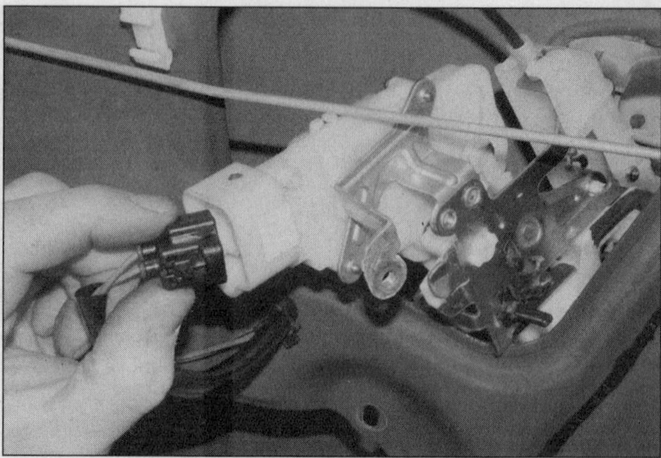
12.30a Disconnect the central locking wiring plug . . .

12.30b . . . and remove the lock from the door

disturbing them as little as possible in the process.

29 The lock itself is secured by three screws on the back edge of the door (models with central locking have a further lock securing bolt on the inside of the door). Remove the fasteners, and withdraw the lock downwards, unhooking the childproof lock operating knob in the process (if preferred, the rubber grommet around the knob can be prised out) **(see illustration)**.

30 On models with central locking, disconnect the wiring plug from the lock, and remove it from the door **(see illustrations)**.

Refitting

31 Refitting is a reversal of removal, bearing in mind the following points:

a) Lubricate the moving parts of the lock assembly with multi-purpose grease before refitting.

b) The three lock securing screws on the back edge of the door should have their threads cleaned and coated with thread-locking fluid before refitting them.

c) Check the operation of the lock mechanism before refitting the door inner trim panel.

d) Refit the door trim panel with reference to Section 11.

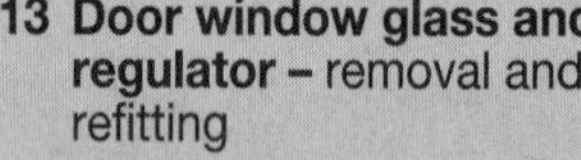

13 Door window glass and regulator – removal and refitting

Front door window

Removal

1 Remove the door trim panel as described in Section 11.

2 Reconnect the electric window switch (or window winder handle), and lower the glass until the door glass retaining bolts are visible in the access holes in the inner panel **(see illustrations)**.

3 Unscrew the glass retaining bolts, then lift the glass and remove it from the door **(see illustrations)**.

Refitting

4 Refitting is a reversal of removal, noting the following points:

a) Tighten the glass retaining bolts securely.

b) Refit the door trim panel as described in Section 11.

Front regulator

Removal

5 Remove the door window glass as described previously in this Section.

13.2a Door glass front retaining bolt has its own access hole

13.2b Door glass rear retaining bolt is more accessible

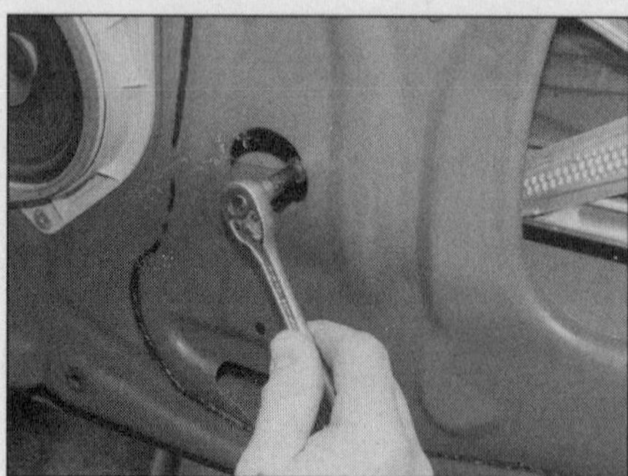
13.3a Unscrew the retaining bolts . . .

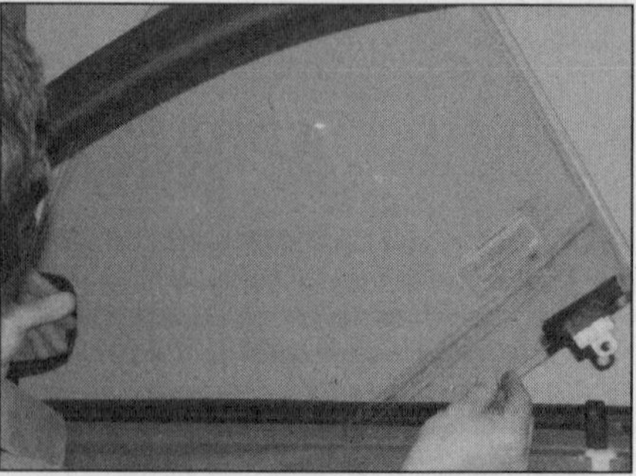
13.3b . . . then lift the glass out of the door

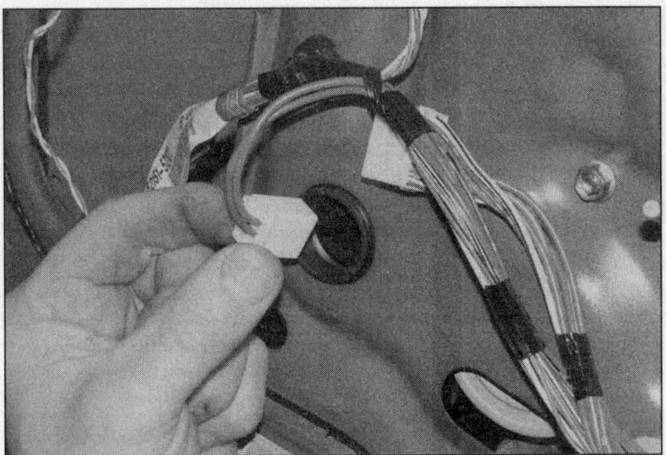

13.6 Disconnect the electric window wiring plug

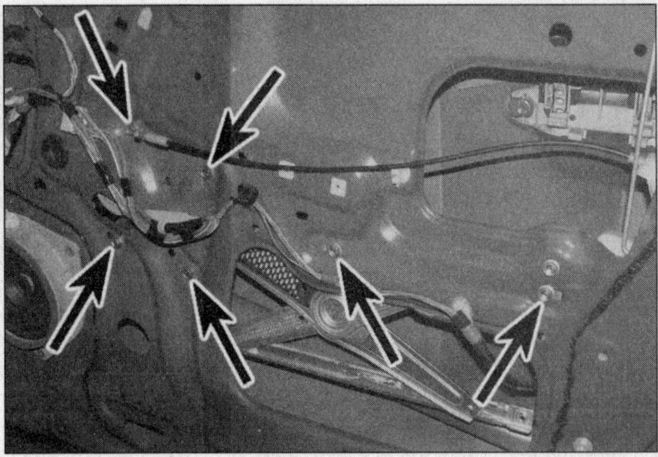

13.7a Electric window regulator securing bolts (arrowed)

6 On models with electric windows, disconnect the wiring plug from the motor **(see illustration)**.

7 The window regulator is secured by five bolts on models with manual windows, or six bolts on electric windows. Remove the bolts and withdraw the regulator from the door **(see illustrations)**.

Refitting

8 Refitting is a reversal of removal, noting the following points:

a) Lubricate the moving parts of the regulator with multi-purpose grease before refitting.

b) Check the operation of the window regulator mechanism before refitting the door trim panel.

Rear window

Removal

9 Remove the door trim panel as described in Section 11, then open the window as far as possible.

10 Unclip the door sliding glass runner from the top and two sides of the window frame, and pull upwards to remove it **(see illustration)**.

11 Pull off the door seal at the upper rear corner, and remove the window rear guide channel top screw **(see illustration)**.

12 Remove the two bolts securing the base of the rear guide channel, then remove the guide channel from the door **(see illustrations)**.

13 Slide the rear fixed glass and its rubber seal forwards, and remove it from the door **(see illustration)**. If required, the rubber seal can then be removed from the glass.

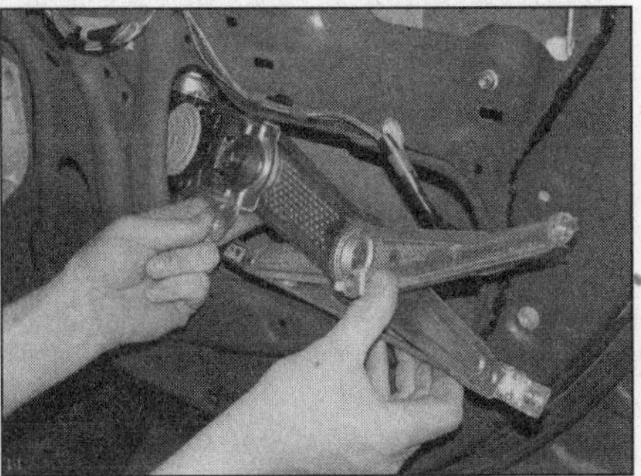

13.7b Removing the regulator assembly

13.10 Unclip and remove the glass runner from the window frame

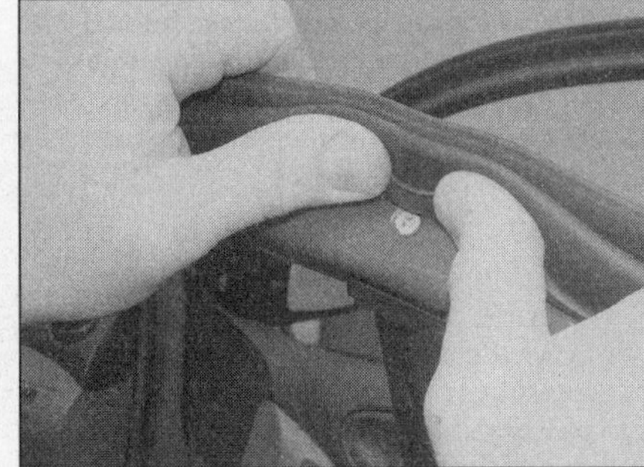

13.11 Pull back the door seal for access to the guide channel screw

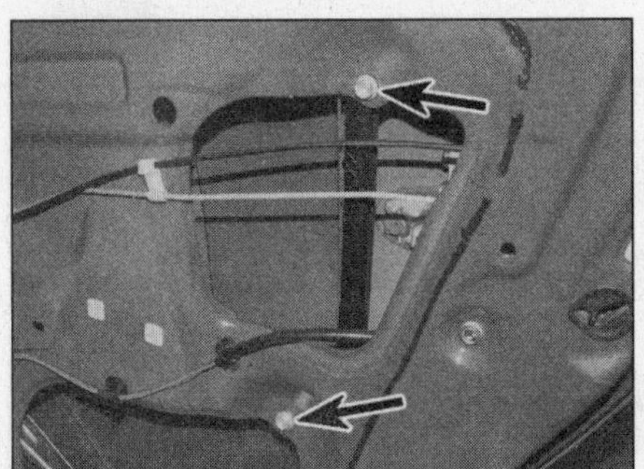

13.12a Remove the two rear guide channel bolts . . .

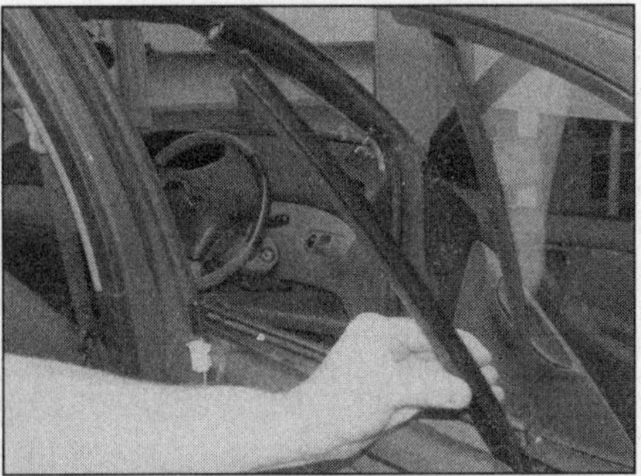

13.12b . . . then slide the channel up and out of the door

13.13 Slide the rear glass forwards and remove it from the door frame

13.14a Slide the door glass rearwards off the regulator . . .

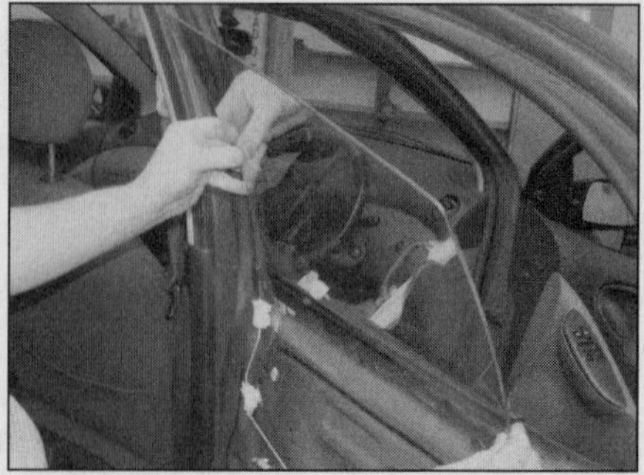

13.14b . . . and remove the glass from the door

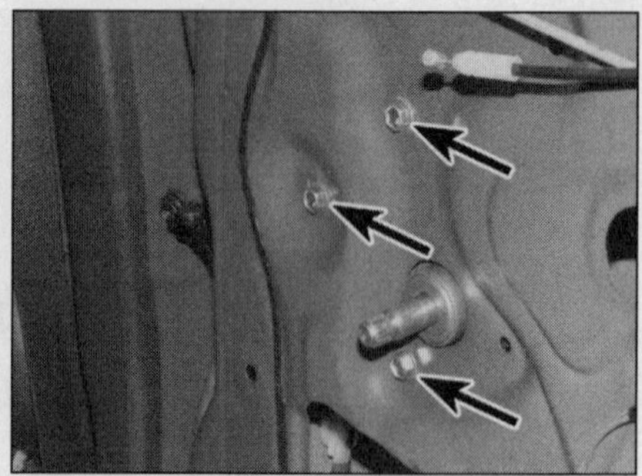

13.18 Rear window regulator securing bolts (arrowed)

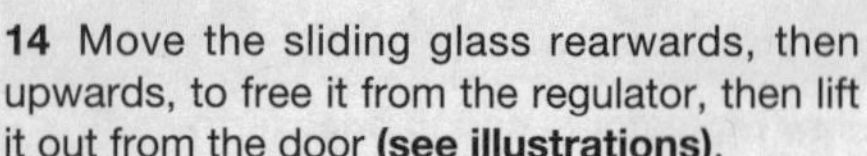

14 Move the sliding glass rearwards, then upwards, to free it from the regulator, then lift it out from the door **(see illustrations)**.

Refitting

15 Refitting is a reversal of removal, noting the following points:

a) Check the operation of the window regulator mechanism before refitting the door trim panel.

b) Refit the door trim panel as described in Section 11.

Rear regulator

Removal

16 Remove the door window glass as described previously in this Section.

17 On models with electric windows, disconnect the wiring plug from the motor.

18 The window regulator is secured by two bolts on models with manual windows, or three bolts on electric windows **(see illustration)**. Remove the bolts and withdraw the regulator from the door.

Refitting

19 Refitting is a reversal of removal, noting the following points:

a) Lubricate the moving parts of the regulator with multi-purpose grease before refitting.

b) Check the operation of the window regulator mechanism before refitting the door trim panel.

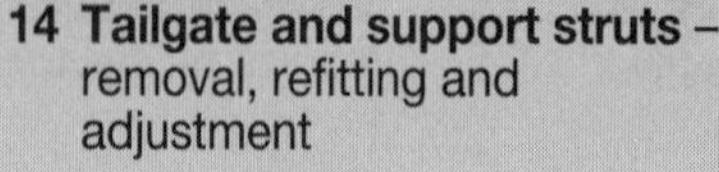

14 Tailgate and support struts – removal, refitting and adjustment

Tailgate

Removal

1 Remove the high-level brake light as described in Chapter 12.

2 Also with reference to Chapter 12, disconnect the wiring from the rear wiper motor.

3 On models with central locking, refer to Section 15 and disconnect the wiring from the tailgate lock.

4 As far as possible, release all the tailgate wiring from any clips or ties, as it must all be fed back through the top of the tailgate and removed **(see illustration)**.

5 Disconnect the washer tube from the jet, and feed it back into the tailgate. Taking care not to damage the paintwork, prise out the tailgate washer jet **(see illustrations)**.

6 Using a pencil or marker pen, mark the position of the hinges on the tailgate to aid refitting.

7 Support the tailgate, and disconnect the support struts as described later in this Section.

8 Prise out the rubber gaiters at the top of the tailgate, and carefully start to pull through the wiring and washer tube **(see illustrations)**. If the same tailgate is being refitted, tie on some lengths of string to the various wiring plugs beforehand – the string can then be untied when it emerges from the top of the tailgate,

14.4 Disconnect the heated rear window wiring plugs either side, and feed them and the grommets back inside the tailgate

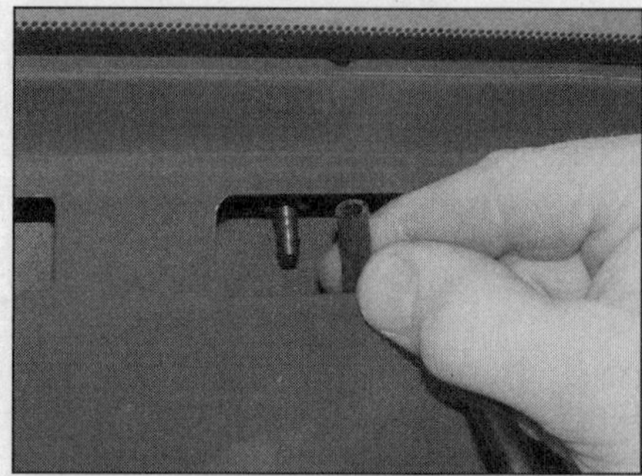

14.5a Pull off the tailgate washer jet supply tube . . .

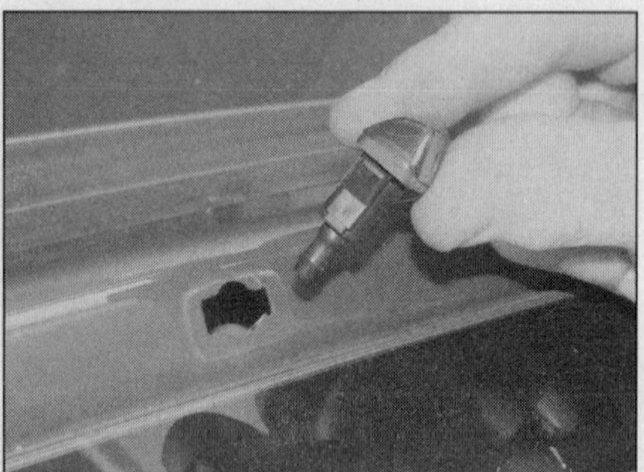

14.5b . . . then carefully prise out the washer jet and remove it

14.8a Prise out the rubber gaiter for the wiring (right-hand side) . . .

14.8b . . . and the one for the washer tube (centre)

14.9 Tailgate hinge bolts

14.12 Remove the two bolts and take off the tailgate strut mounting plate

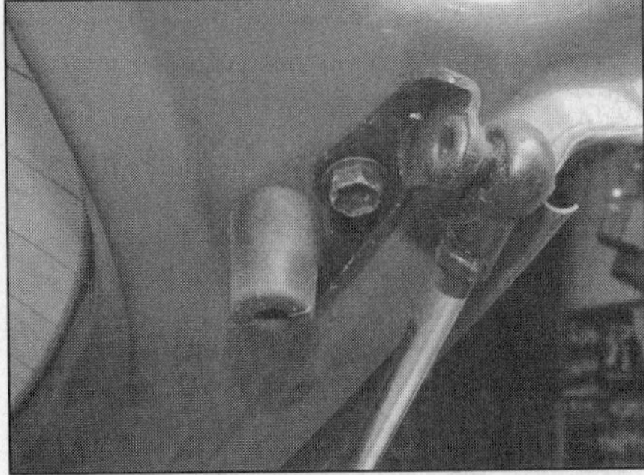
14.13 Prise off the tailgate strut ball-stud

and left in place to pull the wires back through.

9 Ensure that the tailgate is adequately supported, ideally with the aid of an assistant, then unscrew the bolts securing the hinges to the tailgate **(see illustration)**, and lift the tailgate from the car.

Refitting

10 Refitting is a reversal of removal, bearing in mind the following points:

a) Make sure that the hinges are aligned with the marks made before removal.

b) Where applicable, use the string to pull the wiring harness and the washer fluid hose into position in the tailgate.

c) On completion, check the alignment of the tailgate with the surrounding body panels and, if necessary, adjust the position of the tailgate hinges within the elongated holes until satisfactory alignment is achieved.

Support struts

Removal

11 Open the tailgate, and support it in the open position, using a wooden prop or similar tool. Note that the tailgate is heavy, and will fall closed if either of the support struts are disconnected.

12 Working at the car body end of the strut, remove the two bolts and detach the strut mounting plate **(see illustration)**.

13 At the tailgate end, either prise off the ball-stud fitting to remove the strut, or remove two further bolts and take off the mounting bracket **(see illustration)**.

Refitting

14 Refitting is a reversal of removal.

15 Tailgate lock components – removal and refitting

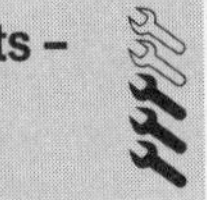

Lock

Removal

1 Open the tailgate, and remove the inner trim panel, which is secured by a total of eight push-in clips **(see illustrations)**.

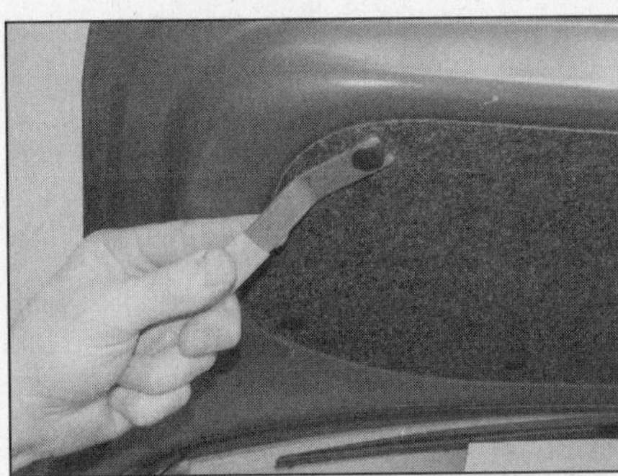
15.1a Prise out the plastic clips . . .

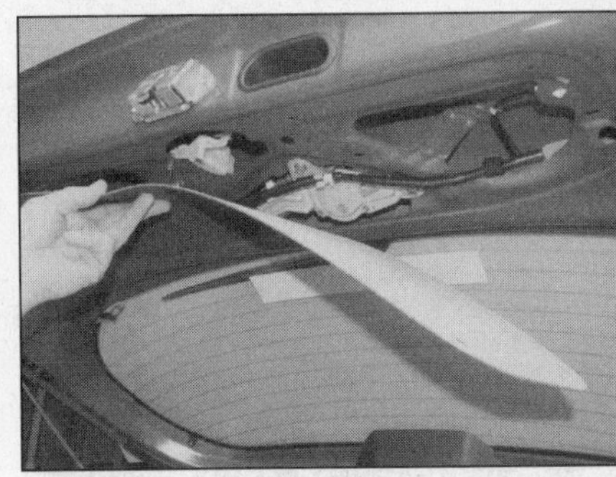
15.1b . . . and take off the tailgate trim panel

2 Unscrew the three lock securing screws, and manipulate the lock out from the tailgate **(see illustrations)**.

Refitting

3 Refitting is a reversal of removal, but check the operation of the lock mechanism before refitting the tailgate trim panel.

Lock barrel

Removal

4 Remove the lock as described previously in this Section.

5 Remove the single bolt securing the lock barrel assembly to the tailgate **(see illustration)**.

6 Twist the lock barrel assembly to release it

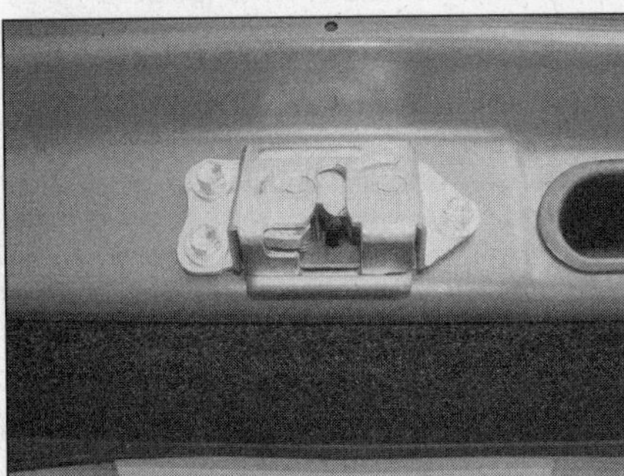
15.2a Remove the three lock mounting bolts . . .

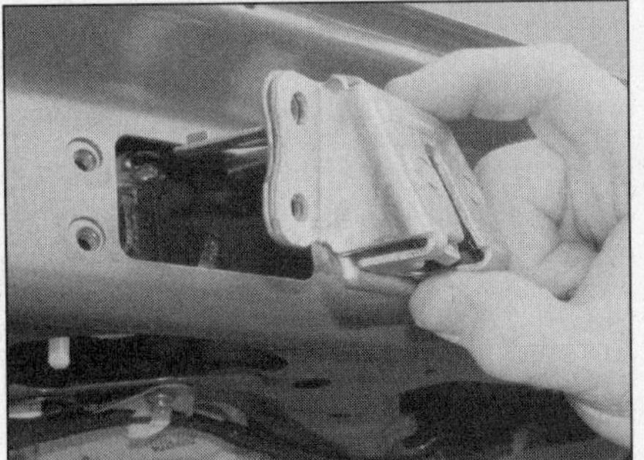
15.2b . . . and withdraw the lock from the tailgate

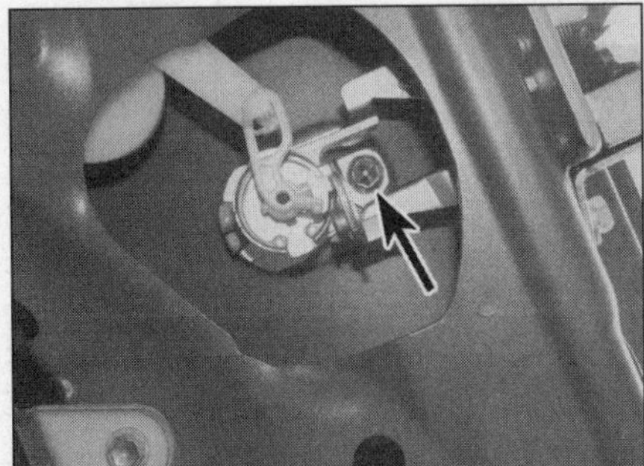
15.5 Remove the lock barrel mounting bolt (arrowed)

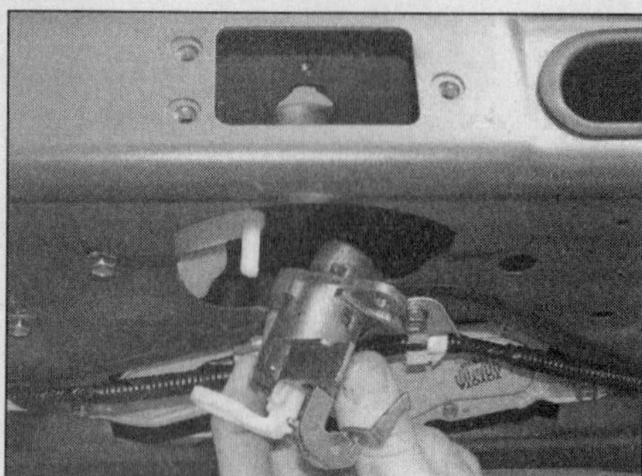

15.6 Twist and release the lock barrel, and unhook it from the actuator

15.7c . . . and pull out the lock barrel

from the tailgate, then unhook it from the actuator lever (central locking models only) and remove it **(see illustration)**.

7 If required, the lock barrel can be removed from its mounting sleeve by releasing the

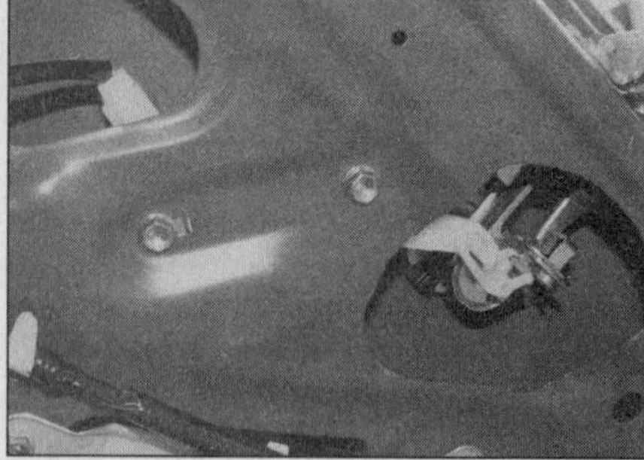

15.11 Remove the two actuator bolts . . .

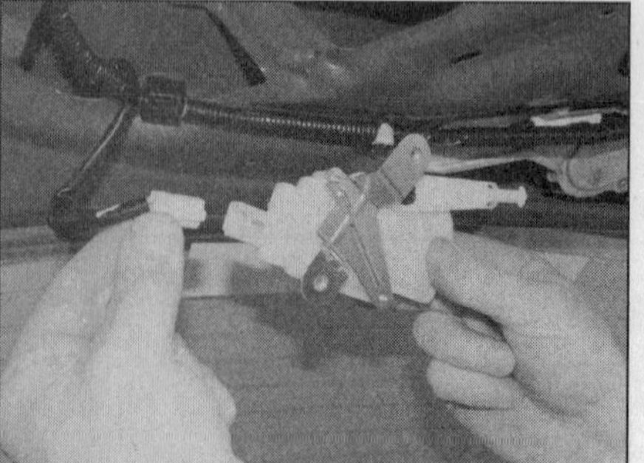

15.12 . . . then unhook the lever and disconnect the wiring plug

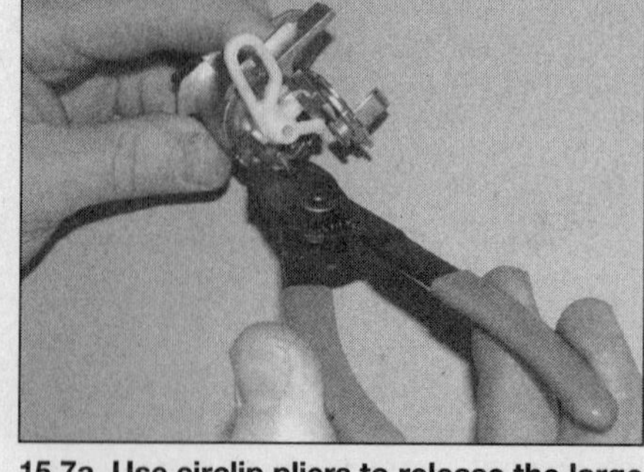

15.7a Use circlip pliers to release the large circlip . . .

15.8 If required, the lock barrel trim can be unclipped from the tailgate

large circlip and taking out the pushbutton spring **(see illustrations)**.

8 The lock barrel trim can now be unclipped from the outside of the tailgate, and removed **(see illustration)**.

Refitting

9 Refitting is a reversal of removal, bearing in mind the following points:

a) Make sure the lock barrel is twisted firmly into place, and that the actuator lever (where applicable) is fully located by pressing it firmly into position.

b) Check the operation of the lock mechanism before refitting the tailgate trim panel.

Lock actuator

Removal

10 Open the tailgate, and remove the inner trim panel, which is secured by a total of eight push-in clips.

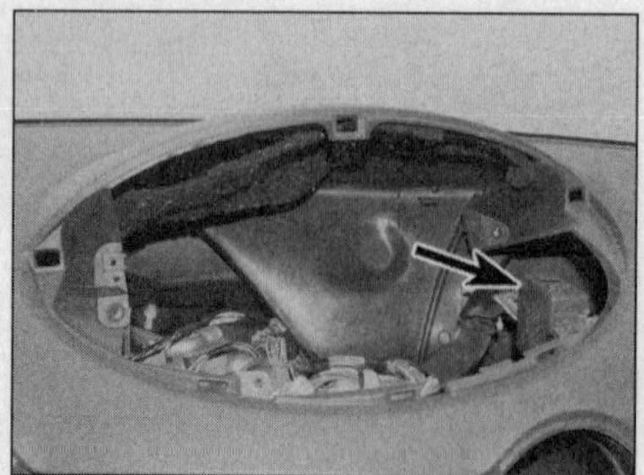

16.8 The door lock control unit is next to the instrument panel

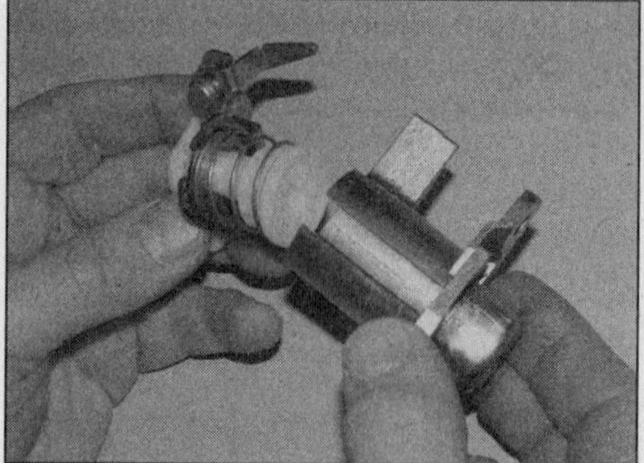

15.7b . . . then extract the pushbutton spring . . .

11 Remove the two bolts securing the actuator to the tailgate **(see illustration)**.

12 Unhook the actuator lever from the lock barrel, then disconnect the wiring plug and remove it **(see illustration)**.

Refitting

13 Refitting is a reversal of removal, but check the operation of the mechanism before refitting the tailgate trim panel.

16 Central locking system components – removal and refitting

Door lock motor

1 The door lock motors are an integral part of the lock assemblies. Removal and refitting is part of the door lock removal and refitting procedure in Section 12.

Door lock microswitch

2 The door lock microswitches (fitted to the front doors) are an integral part of the lock assemblies. Removal and refitting is part of the door lock removal and refitting procedure in Section 12.

Remote control

Battery renewal

3 Remove the small screw from the key fob, and take off the key cover.

4 Lift out the battery case from the key, and prise off the case cover.

5 The battery is held in place (positive + side up) by four separate retaining clips. Carefully prise the smaller two clips aside to release the battery, and slide it out of its holder.

6 Fit the new battery the same way up as the old one, and ensure it is held securely by the clips.

7 Reassemble the key fob, and test the operation (the key indicator light should come on when the key is pressed).

Door lock control unit

8 The door lock control unit is fitted to the crossmember below the upper facia panel, near the instrument cluster **(see illustration)**. Either remove the cluster as described in

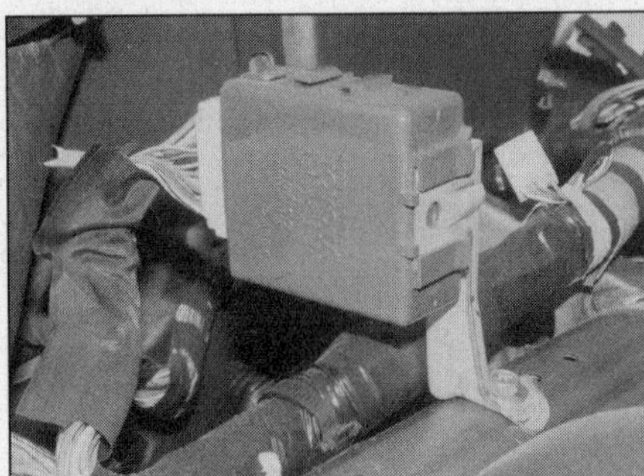
16.9 Disconnect the wiring plug and unbolt the unit from the crossmember

17.2 Electric window motor securing screws

18.2 Unclip and remove the mirror trim panel

Chapter 12, or the upper section of the facia panel as described in Section 26, for access.

9 Disconnect the wiring plug, then unbolt and remove the unit from the crossmember **(see illustration)**.

10 Refitting is a reversal of removal.

Remote locking receiver unit

11 The remote locking receiver unit is fitted to the crossmember below the upper facia panel, above the steering column. Remove the upper section of the facia panel as described in Section 26 for access.

12 Disconnect the wiring plug, then unbolt and remove it from the crossmember.

13 Refitting is a reversal of removal.

17 Electric window components – removal and refitting

Window switches

1 Refer to Chapter 12, Section 4.

Window motors

2 Remove the regulator as described in Section 13. Unscrew the three motor securing screws, and withdraw the motor from the regulator **(see illustration)**.

3 Refitting is a reversal of removal.

18 Exterior mirrors and associated components – removal and refitting

Mirror

Removal

1 Remove the door trim panel as described in Section 11.

2 Carefully unclip the triangular trim panel from inside the mirror base **(see illustration)**.

3 On electric mirrors, disconnect the mirror wiring plug.

4 Remove the three mirror mounting nuts, supporting the mirror from outside as the last is removed, and withdraw the mirror (and wiring, where applicable) from the door **(see illustrations)**.

Refitting

5 Refitting is a reversal of removal, noting the following points:

a) Check the condition of the mirror-to-body seal – any damage here could result in water entering the car.

b) Tighten the mirror mounting nuts securely.

c) Refit the door trim panel as described in Section 11.

Mirror motor

6 The motor is integral with the mirror, and cannot be renewed separately. If faulty, the complete mirror assembly must be renewed.

Mirror switch

Removal

7 Carefully prise the door mirror switch panel from the facia – use a piece of card, or wrap the tool blade in tape, to prevent damage to the facia.

8 Disconnect the switch wiring plug, and remove the switch.

Refitting

9 Refitting is a reversal of removal. Check the operation of the switch before clipping the panel back into place.

Mirror glass

Warning: If the mirror glass is broken, wear gloves to protect your hands.

Removal

10 The mirror glass can be removed with the mirror in place if preferred (this avoids removing the door trim panel as described in Section 11).

11 Using a screwdriver to prise in the two cut-out locations at the bottom, prise off the lower edge of the glass, which is secured by two clips to its mounting plate **(see illustration)**.

12 Unhook the glass from the two upper mountings, and remove it downwards **(see**

18.4a Unscrew the three mirror mounting nuts . . .

18.4b . . . then withdraw the mirror from the door

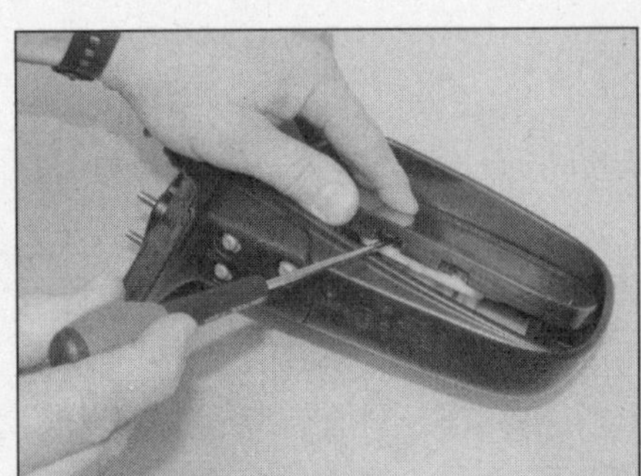
18.11 Prise the mirror glass off its mounting plate from below

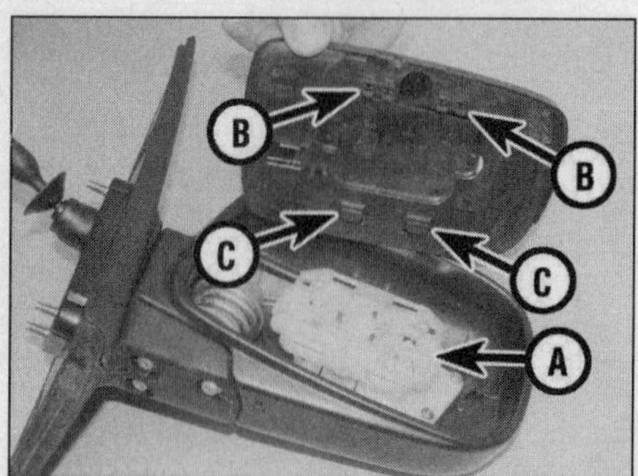

18.12 Mirror glass removed, showing mounting plate (A), lower clips (B) and upper hooks (C)

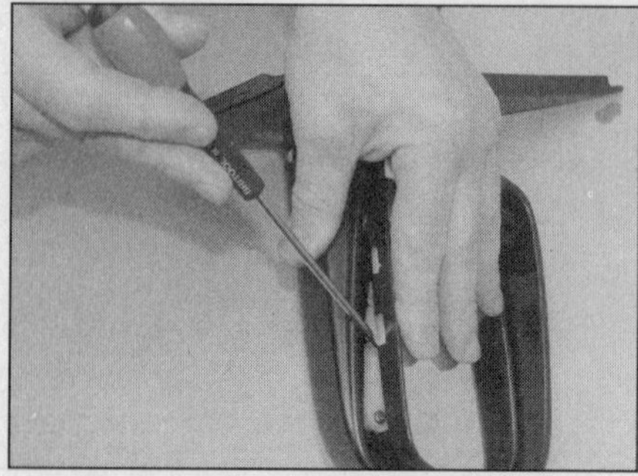
18.13 Use a screwdriver under the mounting plate, and press the glass to engage the clips

21.7a The fuel filler flap is operated via a plunger at the rear

illustration). On models with electric mirrors, disconnect the wiring plug as necessary.

Refitting

13 Refitting is a reversal of removal. Hook the glass in at the top, then press it firmly on the bottom edge to engage the two clips. Use a flat-bladed screwdriver under the glass mounting plate to provide a surface to bear against when engaging the clips **(see illustration)**.

19 Windscreen, side and tailgate glass – general information

These areas of glass are secured by the tight fit of the weatherseal in the body aperture, and are bonded in position with a special adhesive. Renewal of such fixed glass is a difficult, messy and time-consuming task, which is considered beyond the scope of the home mechanic. It is difficult, unless one has plenty of practice, to obtain a secure, waterproof fit. Furthermore, the task carries a high risk of breakage; this applies especially to the laminated glass windscreen. In view of this, owners are strongly advised to have this sort of work carried out by one of the many specialist windscreen fitters.

Removal of the fixed rear door window glass on 5-door models is covered in Section 13.

20 Sunroof – general information

Due to the complexity of the sunroof mechanism, considerable expertise is required to repair, renew or adjust the sunroof components successfully. Removal of the roof first requires the headlining to be removed, which is a tedious operation, and not a task to be undertaken lightly. Therefore, any problems with the sunroof should be referred to a Toyota dealer.

21 Body exterior fittings – removal and refitting

Bumpers

1 Refer to Section 6.

Scuttle cover panel

2 Refer to the windscreen wiper motor removal procedure in Chapter 12.

Wheel arch liners

3 The wheel arch liners are secured by a combination of self-tapping screws and push-fit clips.

4 With all the fasteners removed, pull the liner down from the arch and remove it.

Body trim strips and badges

5 The various body trim strips and badges are held in position with a special adhesive. Removal requires the trim/badge to be heated, to soften the adhesive, and then cut away from the surface. Due to the high risk of damage to the paintwork during this operation, it is recommended that this task should be entrusted to a Toyota dealer or bodyshop.

Fuel filler flap and operating cable

Note: *This procedure assumes the flap can still be opened. The cable operates a spring-loaded plunger inside the flap, at the rear – provided the cable hasn't broken right at the flap end, the plunger can be operated by pulling on the inner cable, at any point along its length. On UK-market cars, the cable runs down the passenger side, across the front of the rear seat, then down to the lever by the driver's seat.*

Removal

6 The filler flap itself is riveted in place, so the only way to remove it would be to drill out the rivets.

7 The operating cable can be removed as follows. Inside the filler flap, twist the locking collar on the cable end/plunger, and pull out the cable from the bodywork **(see illustrations)**.

8 Remove the left-hand parcel shelf support panel as described in Section 24. It's also helpful to remove the rear seat, and the driver's seat, as described in Section 22.

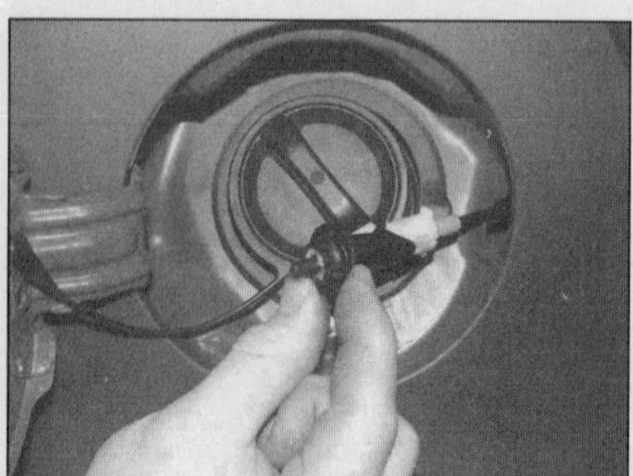
21.7b Twist the locking collar and pull out the cable end

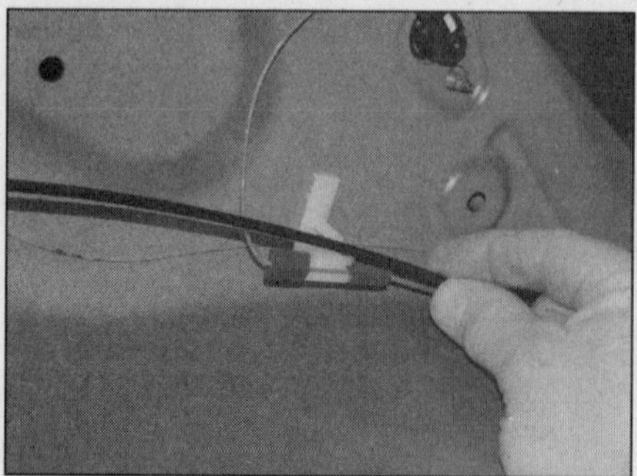
21.9a Unclip the operating cable behind the rear side trim panel . . .

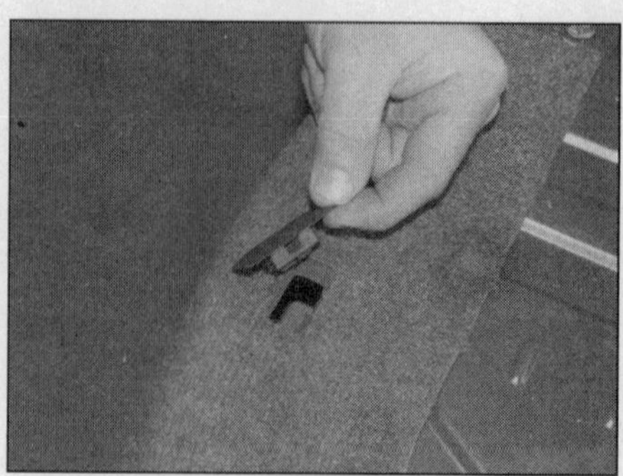
21.9b . . . then prise up the carpet retaining clips . . .

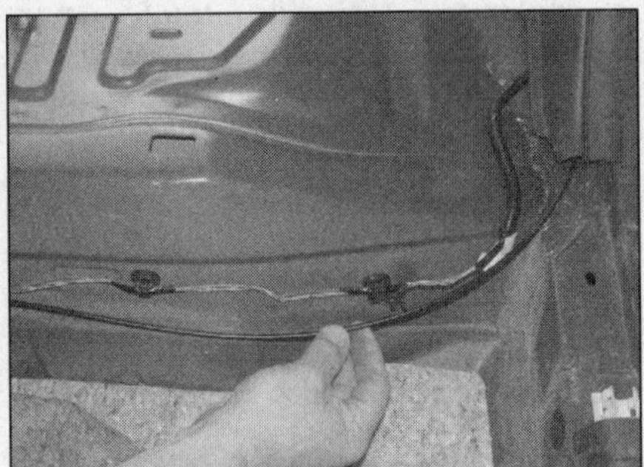

21.9c . . . and unclip the cable along the front of the back seat

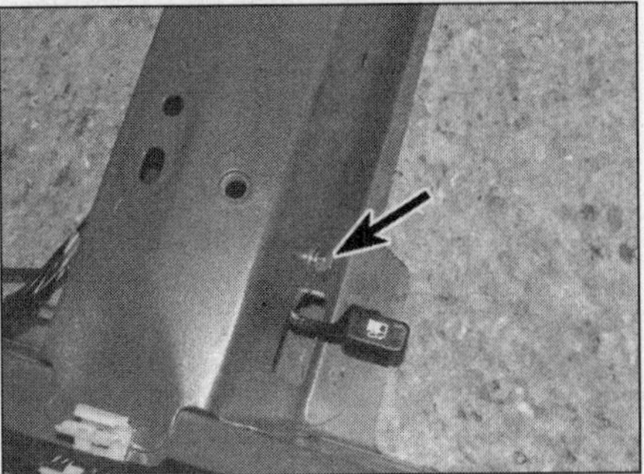

21.11a Unscrew the operating lever mounting bolt . . .

21.11b . . . then withdraw the lever and unhook the cable

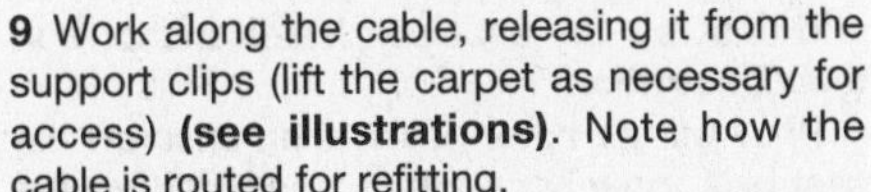

9 Work along the cable, releasing it from the support clips (lift the carpet as necessary for access) **(see illustrations)**. Note how the cable is routed for refitting.

10 Release the carpet in the area next to the driver's seat by removing the B-pillar and door sill trim panels, as described in Section 24.

11 Unscrew the operating lever mounting bolt, and pull the operating lever forwards from the seat mounting crossmember. Unhook the cable end fitting from the lever, and remove the cable through the hole at the fuel filler flap **(see illustrations)**.

Refitting

12 Refitting is a reversal of removal. Make sure the cable is not kinked or twisted, and check its operation before refitting the parts removed for access.

22 Seats – removal and refitting

Front seat

Warning: On later models with side airbags (denoted by SRS AIRBAG tags on the outside of the seat back), disconnect the battery negative lead (see 'Disconnecting the battery'), then wait for two minutes before proceeding. If this waiting period is not observed, there is danger of activating the airbag system.

1 Slide the seat fully rearwards, then unscrew the two front bolts securing the seat rails to the floor **(see illustration)**.

2 Slide the seat fully forwards, use a screwdriver to prise off the seat sliding rail rear covers (note which fits where, as they are not interchangeable), then unscrew the two rear bolts **(see illustrations)**.

3 Check under and around the seat for any wiring (typically, this will only be on models fitted with side airbags or a seat belt warning light), and disconnect it as necessary.

4 Lift the seat, complete with mounting rails, and remove it from the car **(see illustration)**.

5 Refitting is a reversal of removal, but tighten the seat mounting bolts to the specified torque.

Rear seat

Split folding type

6 Prise off the seat hinge covers at the front edge of the rear seat, and unscrew the bolts underneath **(see illustrations)**.

7 Slide the rear seat forwards as far as possible, and fold the backrest forwards.

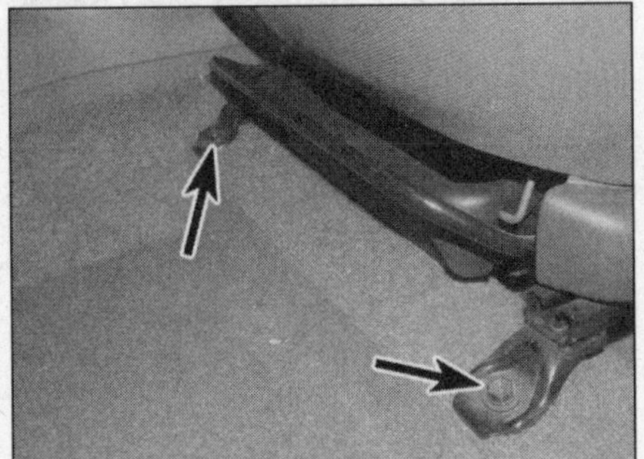

22.1 With the front seat fully back, the seat rail mounting bolts can be seen

22.2a Unclip the cover from the seat inner rail . . .

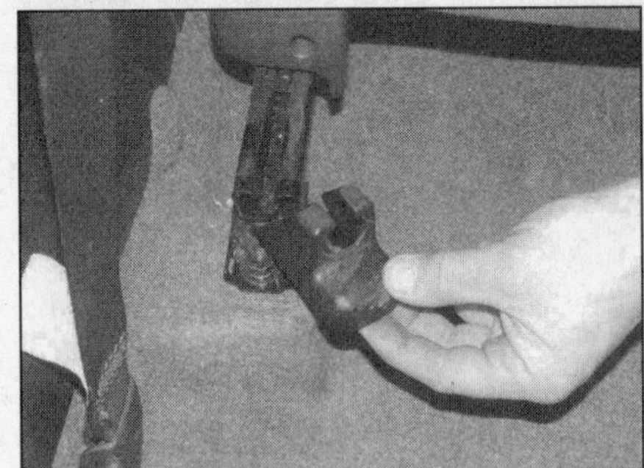

22.2b . . . and from the outer rail, for access to the bolts

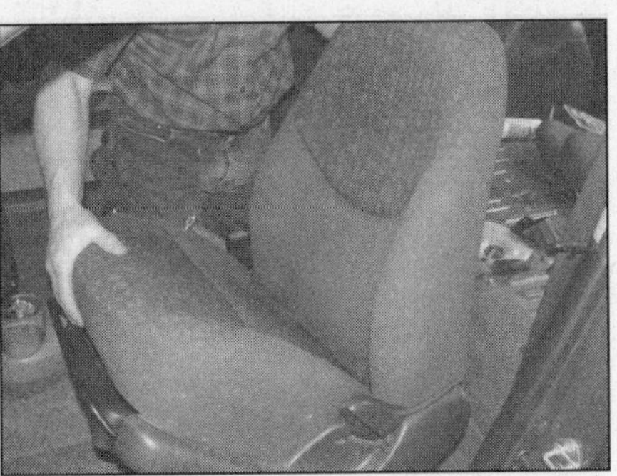

22.4 Remove the front seat from the car

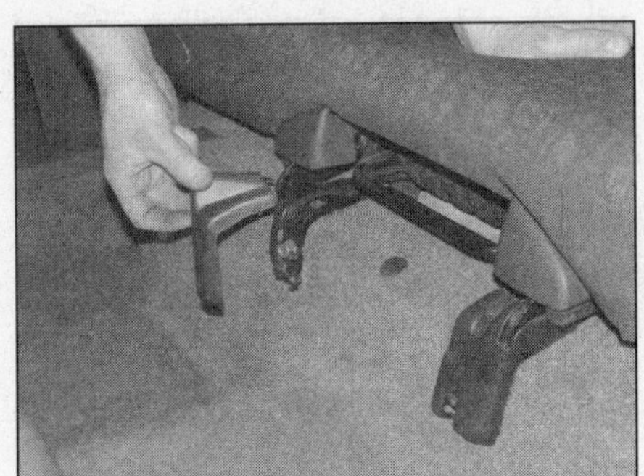

22.6a Working in the rear seat footwell, prise off the hinge covers . . .

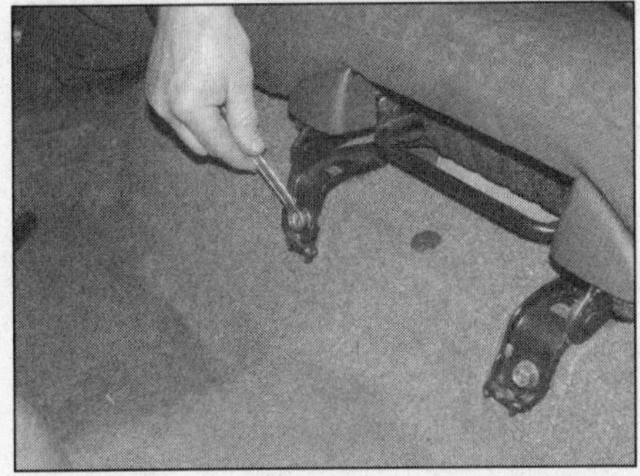

22.6b . . . then unscrew the bolts underneath

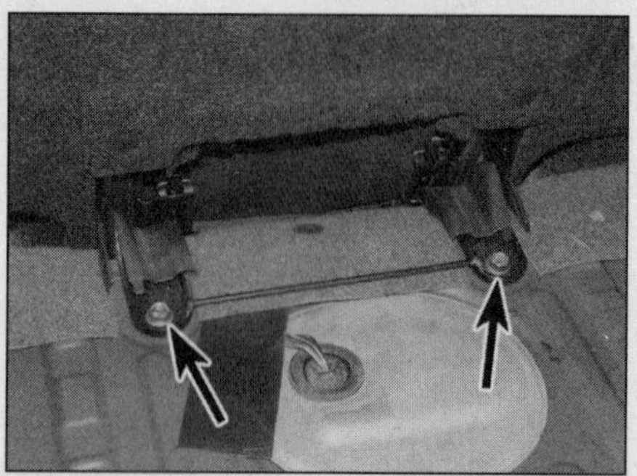

22.8a Unscrew the hinge bolts behind the seat . . .

22.8b . . . then unlock it from the floor using the lever, and remove

8 Remove the two bolts from the rear of the seat hinges, then unlock the seat and remove it **(see illustrations)**. The rear seat is a heavy assembly – have an assistant on hand to help.

9 Refitting is a reversal of removal, but tighten the seat hinge bolts to the specified torque.

Bench type

10 Release the backrest catches, and fold the backrest forwards.

11 Unclip the carpet from the base of the seat, which is secured by five clips, then fold the carpet up either side for access to the hinge bolts.

12 Remove the bolt each side securing the backrest to the hinge, and remove the backrest from the car.

13 If required, the hinge each side can be removed by unbolting it from the car.

14 The seat cushion is held in place by a single bolt at the rear, and by two clips at the front. Unscrew the rear bolt, then lift the cushion out of the front clips, and remove it.

15 Refitting is a reversal of removal, but tighten the seat hinge bolts to the specified torque.

23 Seat belt components – removal and refitting

Front belt

Removal

Warning: Disconnect the battery negative lead (see 'Disconnecting the battery'), then wait for two minutes before proceeding. If this waiting period is not observed, there is danger of activating the seat belt tensioner.

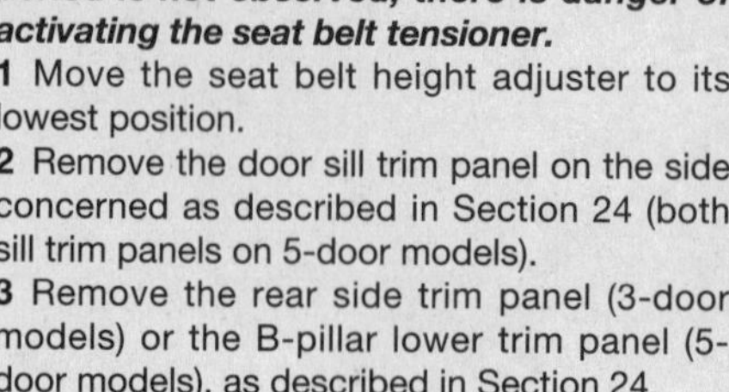

1 Move the seat belt height adjuster to its lowest position.

2 Remove the door sill trim panel on the side concerned as described in Section 24 (both sill trim panels on 5-door models).

3 Remove the rear side trim panel (3-door models) or the B-pillar lower trim panel (5-door models), as described in Section 24.

4 On 3-door models, unscrew the bolt at each end of the seat belt lower anchor rail (attached to the outside of the seat), then slide the end of the belt off the rail.

5 On 5-door models, prise off the outer cover, and unscrew the seat belt lower anchor bolt **(see illustration)**.

6 Prise off the outer cover, then unscrew the seat belt upper anchor bolt, and withdraw the upper anchor from the car **(see illustrations)**.

7 Disconnect the wiring plug for the seat belt pretensioner from the inertia reel, by first lifting the (white) locking clip, then pulling off the yellow plug **(see illustrations)**.

8 Remove the two bolts securing the inertia reel **(see illustration)**, and lift it and the seat belt out of the car.

Refitting

9 Refitting is a reversal of removal, but tighten the seat belt bolts to the specified torque.

Front belt stalk

Removal

Note: *On models from May 2003 onwards,*

23.5 Prise off the cover to access the lower anchor bolt

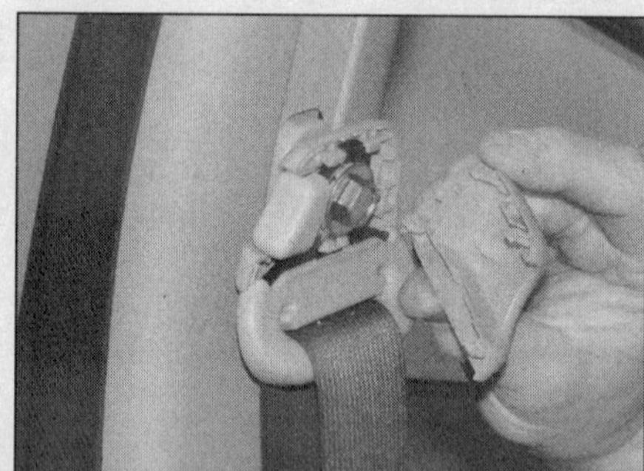

23.6a Unclip the trim cover . . .

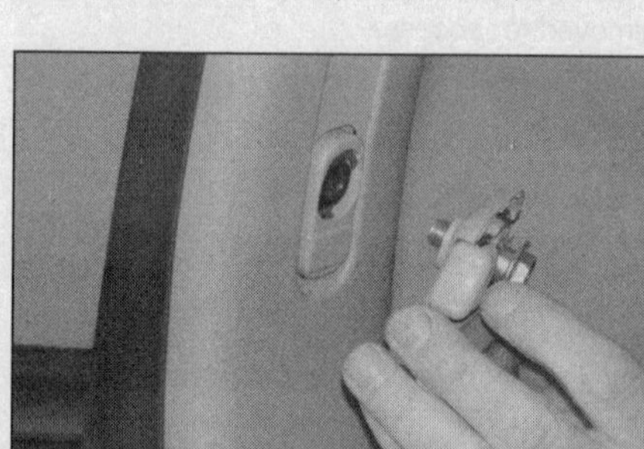

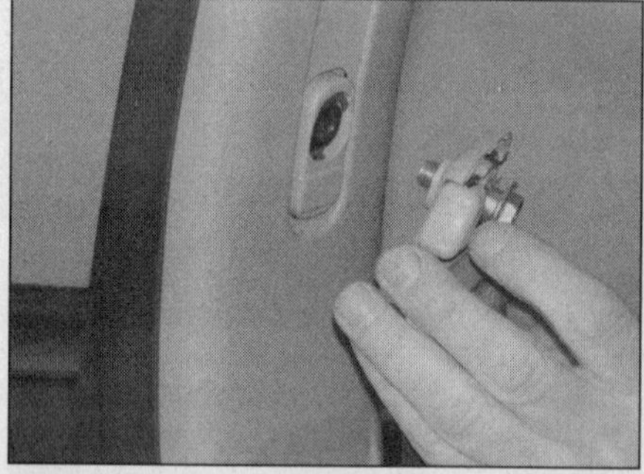

23.6b . . . then unscrew the seat belt upper bolt

23.7a Lift the locking clip . . .

23.7b . . . then pull off the pretensioner wiring plug

23.8 Front seat belt inertia reel mounting bolts

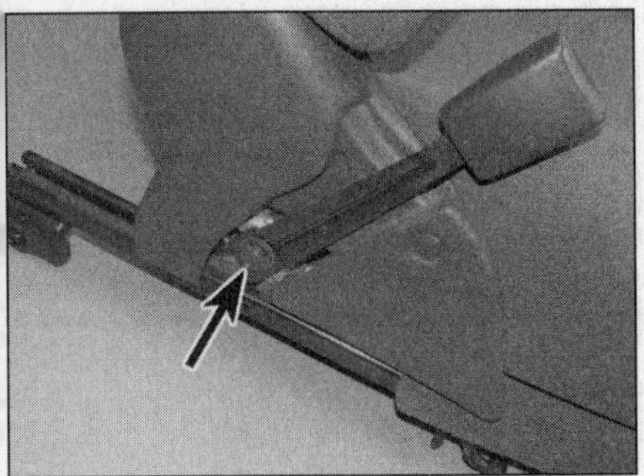
23.10 Front seat belt stalk mounting bolt (seen with seat removed)

23.13 Front seat belt height adjuster bolts

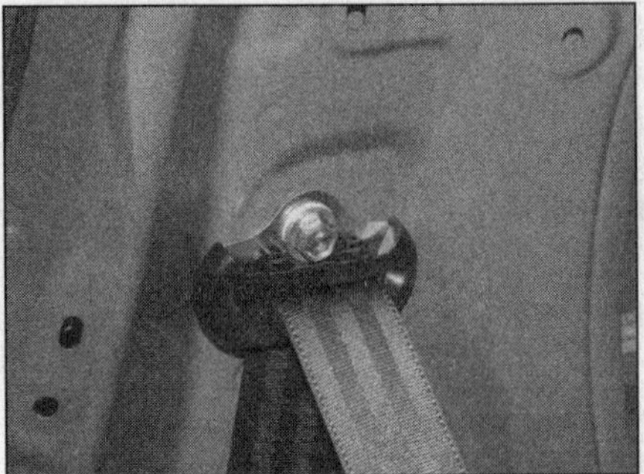
23.18 Rear seat side belt upper anchor bolt

front seat belt stalks with pretensioner assemblies were fitted across the range. It is not recommended that one of these assemblies be tampered with, as there is a risk of setting it off. Consult a Toyota dealer for more information.

10 Slide the front seat fully rearwards to gain access to the stalk mounting bolt **(see illustration)**. Unscrew the bolt, and remove the stalk from the seat frame.

Refitting

11 Refitting is a reversal of removal, bearing in mind the following points:

a) *Make sure that the stalk is angled towards the seat.*

b) *Tighten the securing bolt to the specified torque.*

Front belt height adjuster

Removal

12 Remove the B-pillar trim panels as described in Section 24.

13 The height adjuster is secured by two bolts, one top and one bottom **(see illustration)**. Remove the bolts and withdraw the adjuster from the car.

Refitting

14 Refitting is a reversal of removal. Tighten the bolts to the specified torque.

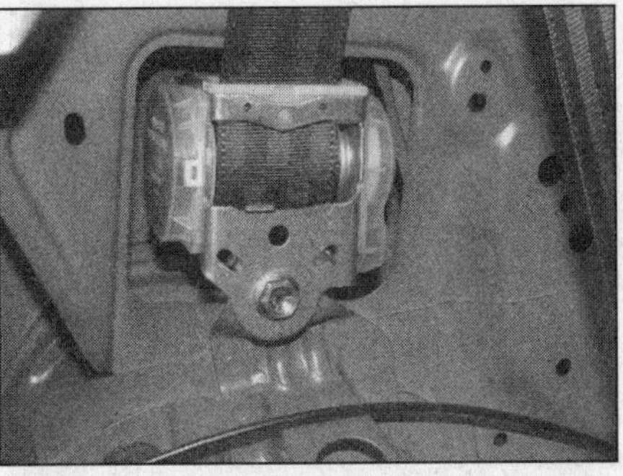
23.19 Rear seat side belt inertia reel and mounting bolt

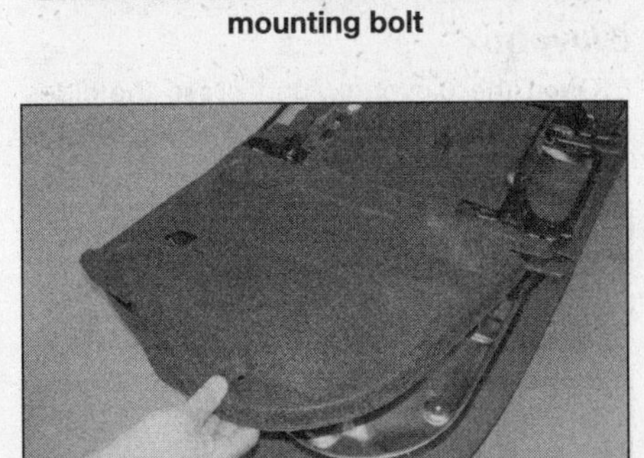
23.23a Unclip and remove the carpet trim panel from the base of the rear seat

Rear inertia reel belt

Removal

15 Fold the rear seat (backrest and cushion) fully forwards.

16 Alternatively, remove the rear seat completely, as described in Section 22 (this is essential on models without the split folding rear seat).

17 Remove the rear side window trim panel (3-door models) or the C-pillar trim panel (5-door models) as described in Section 24. Also remove the parcel shelf support panel on the side concerned.

18 Unscrew the seat belt upper anchor bolt, and withdraw the upper anchor from the car **(see illustration)**.

19 Remove the inertia reel mounting bolt, then lift out the inertia reel **(see illustration)**.

Refitting

20 Refitting is a reversal of removal. Tighten the bolts to the specified torque.

Rear buckles and lap belt

Removal

21 Remove the rear seat as described in Section 22.

22 The buckles and lap belt are bolted to the seat cushion frame, inside the seat. The first option for removal is to prise back the seat material, and gain access to the mounting bolt from the top **(see illustration)**.

23 If this does not work, turn the rear seat assembly over, and using a screwdriver or similar tool remove the clips securing the carpet panels to the base of the seat either side. Limited access to the bolt can now be gained, but take care – the seat support panel has sharp edges **(see illustrations)**.

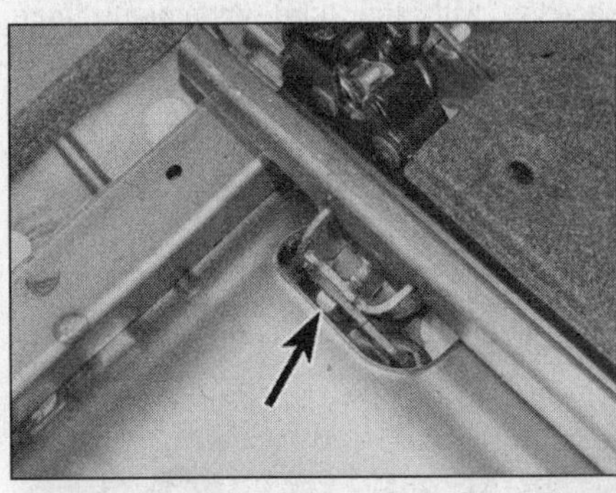
23.22 Pull back the seat material for access to the seat belt buckle bolt

23.23b The seat belt buckle bolt can now be seen, but the metal edges are sharp

Refitting

24 Refitting is a reversal of removal. Tighten the bolts to the specified torque.

24 Interior trim and fittings – removal and refitting

General

1 The interior trim panels are secured by a combination of clips and screws, with easily-broken plastic clips featuring heavily. Removal and refitting is generally self-explanatory, noting that it may be necessary to remove or

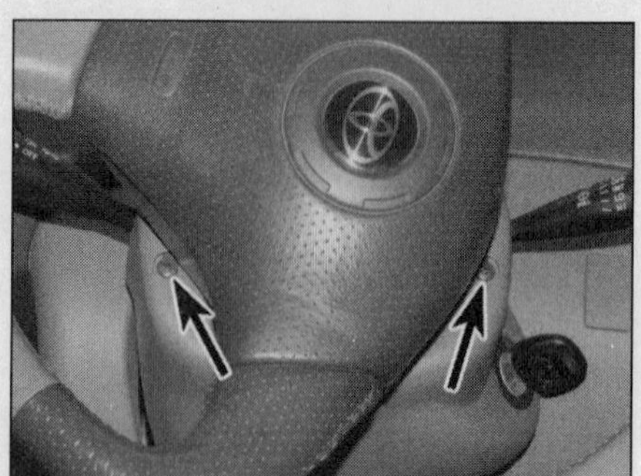
24.3a Turn the steering wheel so both front screws can be seen

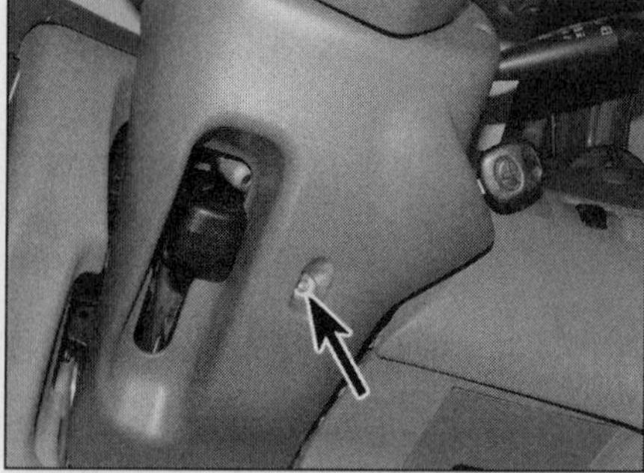
24.3b The lower shroud also has a screw underneath

24.4 Removing the upper shroud – note central clip

loosen surrounding panels to allow a particular panel to be removed. The following paragraphs describe the removal and refitting of the major panels in more detail.

Door inner trim panels

2 Refer to Section 11.

Steering column shrouds

Lower shroud

3 Remove the three screws securing the steering column lower shroud, and lower it out. Two of the three screws are at the front edge of the shroud (turn the wheel for access), with the third underneath **(see illustrations)**.

Upper shroud

4 Remove the two front screws from the lower shroud, turning the steering wheel as necessary for access. Once the two screws have been removed, the upper shroud can be manoeuvred out. The upper shroud has a clip in the centre, which must be accurately located when refitting **(see illustration)**.

Both shrouds

5 Refitting is a reversal of removal. If both shrouds have been removed, refit the upper one first.

Glovebox

6 Open the glovebox, and press the sides inwards to release the lid stops. Withdraw the lid from the facia, and remove it **(see illustrations)**.

24.6a Open the glovebox, and press the sides inwards . . .

24.6b . . . then remove the glovebox from the facia

7 Refitting is a reversal of removal.

Footwell trim panels

8 Prise up the front edge of the sill trim panel, to free the footwell trim panel. Work round the edges of the panel, freeing the remaining clips, until the panel can be lifted out **(see illustration)**. The footwell trim panel locates over a stud in the bulkhead at the front edge.

9 Refitting is a reversal of removal. Align the panel on the bulkhead stud at the front, then clip into place.

Sill trim panels

10 Pull away the rubber door seals as necessary in the area of the sill trim panels.

11 The sill trim panels are clipped in place – use a wide-bladed tool to release them, starting at one end of the panel, and pulling the panel back as it is released **(see illustrations)**. Check whether any of the clips pull out of the panel to be left on the car – transfer them back to the panel before refitting.

12 Refitting is a reversal of removal.

A-pillar trim panel

13 Open the door, and carefully prise the rubber door seal from the edge of the door aperture.

14 The A-pillar trim panels are clipped in place. Several clips are used, and some are

24.8 Removing a footwell trim panel

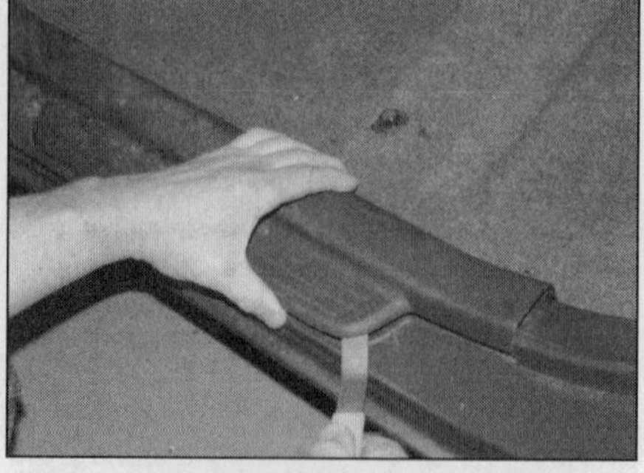
24.11a Use a wide-bladed tool to prise up the panel . . .

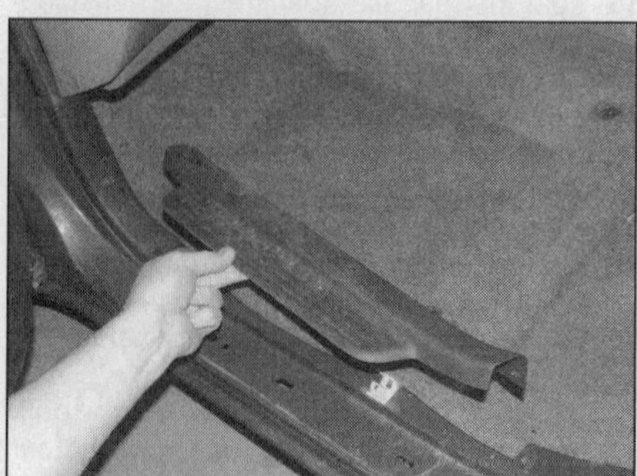
24.11b . . . then release the clips and remove it

24.14 Removing an A-pillar trim panel

quite stiff to release – start at the top of the panel, and pull the panel back as it is released **(see illustration)**. Check whether any of the clips pull out of the panel to be left on the car – transfer them back to the panel before refitting.

15 Refitting is a reversal of removal.

B-pillar trim panels (5-door)

Note: *The B-pillar trim is in two sections – the larger lower section must be removed first if the upper section is to be removed.*

16 Remove both sill trim panels as described previously in this Section. Detach the rubber weatherstrip from the B-pillar as necessary to free the edges of the trim panel.

17 The B-pillar lower trim panel is clipped in place. Several clips are used, and some are quite stiff to release – start at the top of the panel, and pull the panel back as it is released **(see illustration)**.

18 To remove the upper trim panel, unclip the trim cover, and unscrew the seat belt upper anchor bolt **(see illustrations)**.

19 Unclip the upper trim panel, and remove it **(see illustration)**.

20 Refitting is a reversal of removal.

Rear trim panels

Rear side trim panel (3-door)

21 Fold the rear seat (backrest and cushion) fully forwards. Alternatively, remove the rear seat completely, as described in Section 22 (this is essential, on models without the split folding rear seat).

22 Remove the sill trim panel as described earlier in this Section. If preferred, it may be possible to free the rear side trim panel by just prising up the sill panel at the rear, rather than removing it completely.

23 Detach the rubber weatherstrip from the B-pillar as necessary to free the edges of the trim panel.

24 Unclip the side trim panel at the base, then work round the edges of the panel, freeing the remaining clips, until the panel can be lifted out.

25 Refitting is a reversal of removal.

Rear window trim panel (3-door)

26 Detach the rubber weatherstrip from the B-pillar as necessary to free the edges of the trim panel.

24.17 Unclip and remove the B-pillar lower trim panel

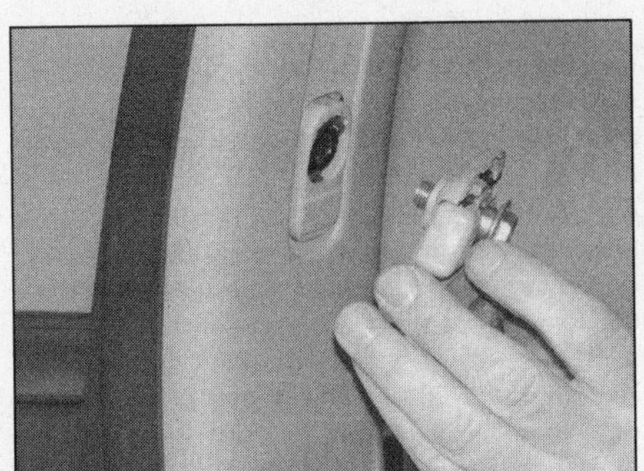

24.18b . . . then unscrew the seat belt upper bolt

27 The window trim panel is overlapped by the rear side trim panel below it, so either remove the panel as described earlier in this Section, or just prise it away at the top.

28 Similarly, the window trim panel is overlapped by the parcel shelf support panel – either remove the panel as described in later in this Section, or just free the top edge.

29 Fold the rear seat (backrest and cushion) fully forwards. Alternatively, remove the rear seat completely, as described in Section 22 (this is essential on models without the split folding rear seat).

30 Unscrew the rear seat belt lower mounting bolt. When the trim panel is ready to come out, the belt buckle and lower anchor will have to be passed through it.

31 Remove the trim panel mounting bolt from in front of the rear window.

24.36 Remove the C-pillar trim panel front screw/clip

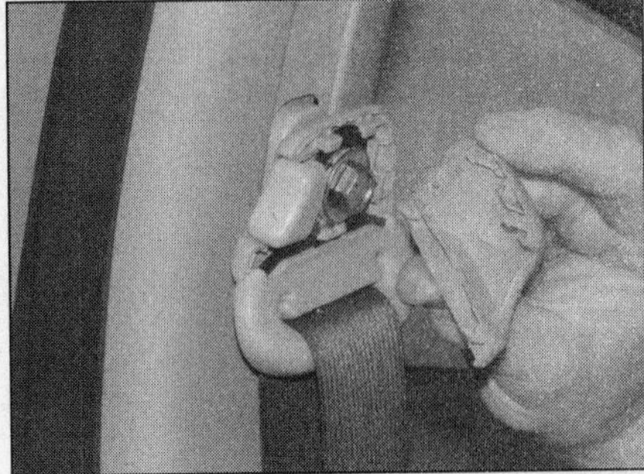

24.18a Unclip the trim cover . . .

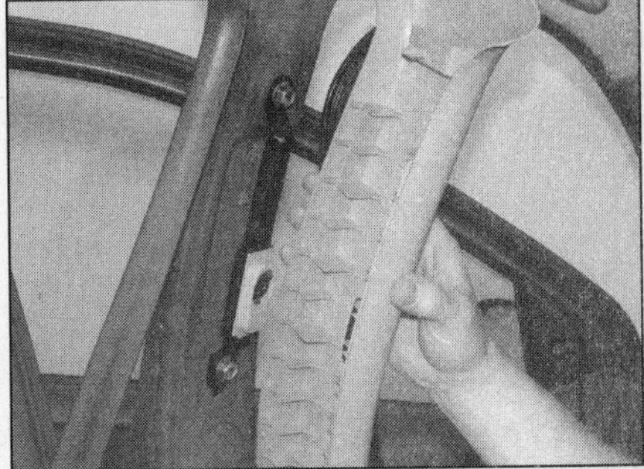

24.19 Unclip and remove the B-pillar upper trim panel

32 Prise out the two trim panel clips fitted below the rear window.

33 Work round the edges of the panel, freeing the remaining clips, until the panel can be lifted out. Pass the rear belt buckle and anchor through as the panel is removed.

34 Refitting is a reversal of removal. Tighten the rear seat belt lower anchor bolt to the specified torque.

C-pillar trim panel (5-door)

35 Remove the parcel shelf support panel as described later in this Section.

36 Remove the screw/clip at the lower front corner of the panel **(see illustration)**.

37 Work round the edges of the panel, freeing the remaining clips, until the panel can be lifted out. Pass the rear belt buckle and anchor through as the panel is removed **(see illustration)**.

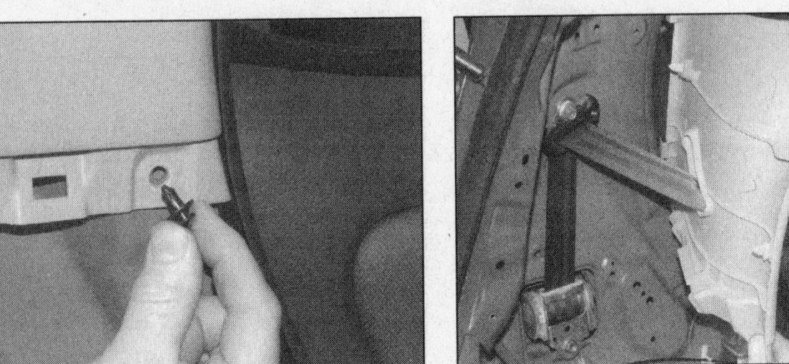

24.37 Release the trim panel clips, and pass the seat belt through

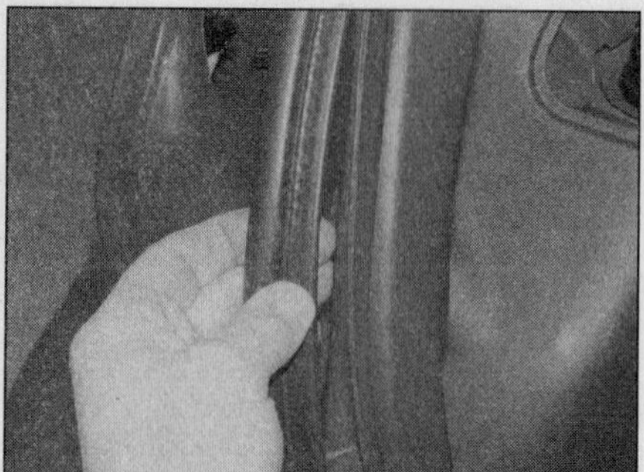

24.38 Pull off the tailgate weatherstrip around the panel edges

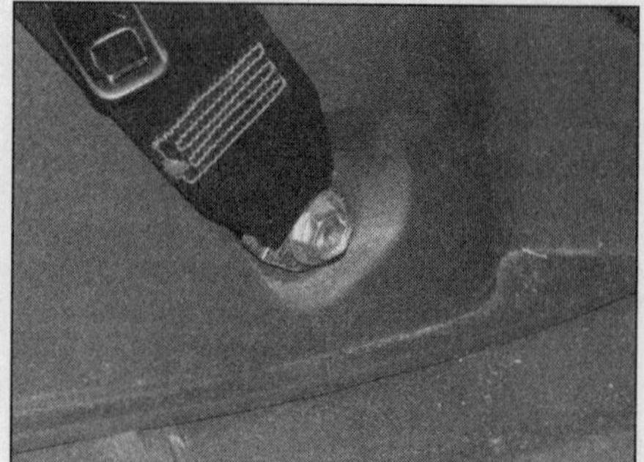

24.43a Unscrew the seat belt lower mounting bolt . . .

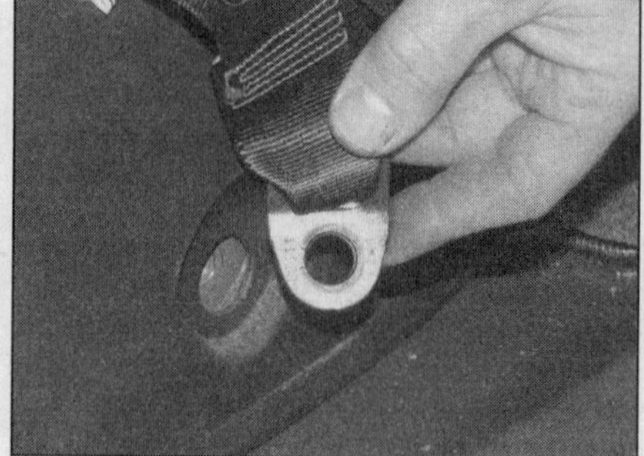

24.43b . . . and free the seat belt anchor plate

Parcel shelf support panel

38 Detach the rubber weatherstrip from the tailgate aperture as necessary to free the edges of the trim panel **(see illustration)**.

39 Remove the parcel shelf.

40 Fold the rear seat (backrest and cushion) fully forwards. Alternatively, remove the rear seat completely, as described in Section 22 (this is essential on models without the split folding rear seat).

41 On 3-door models, remove the rear side trim panel as described previously in this Section. If preferred, it may be possible to free the parcel shelf support panel by releasing the rear side trim panel at the rear edge.

42 On 5-door models, remove the rear door sill trim panel as described previously in this Section. If preferred, it may be possible to free the parcel shelf support panel by releasing the sill trim panel at the rear edge.

43 Unscrew the rear seat belt lower mounting bolt **(see illustrations)**.

44 The panel is secured by one screw at its upper rear corner, and by a screw/clip lower down, just inside the boot **(see illustrations)**.

45 Once these have been removed, work round the edges of the panel, freeing the remaining clips, until the panel can be lifted out **(see illustration)**. Where applicable, disconnect the boot light wiring plug as the panel is removed.

Carpets

46 The passenger compartment floor carpet is in several pieces, and is secured along the edges by various types of clips.

47 Carpet removal and refitting is reasonably straightforward, but time-consuming, due to the fact that all adjoining trim panels must be released, and the seats and centre console must be removed.

Headlining

48 The headlining is clipped to the roof, and can be withdrawn only once all fittings such as the grab handles, sun visors, sunroof, front, centre and rear pillar trim panels, and associated components have been removed. The door, tailgate and sunroof aperture weatherseals will also have to be prised clear.

49 Note that headlining removal requires considerable skill and experience if it is to be carried out without damage, and is therefore best entrusted to an expert.

Sun visors

50 Remove the two sun visor hinge screws, and remove the sun visor from the roof **(see illustration)**. The holding clips are secured by just one screw.

51 Refitting is a reversal of removal.

Grab handles

52 Carefully prise sideways the grab handle end covers. Remove the two mounting screws (one at each end) and remove the grab handle from the roof **(see illustration)**.

53 Refitting is a reversal of removal.

24.44a Remove the screw at the upper rear corner . . .

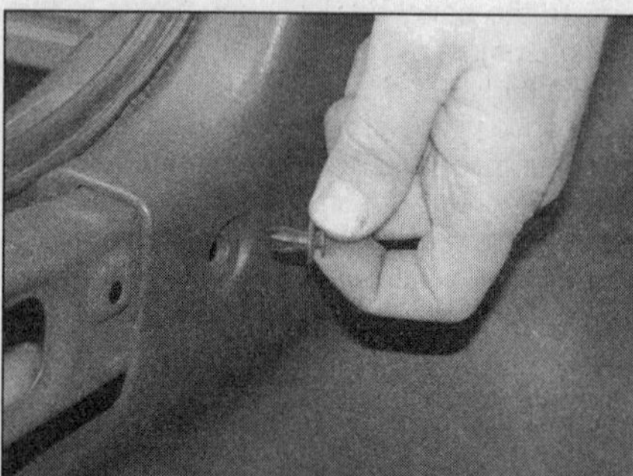

24.44b . . . and the screw/clip just inside the tailgate aperture

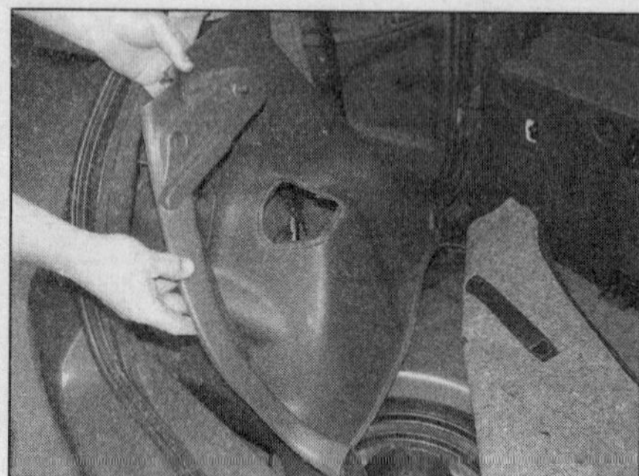

24.45 Release the remaining clips and remove the trim panel

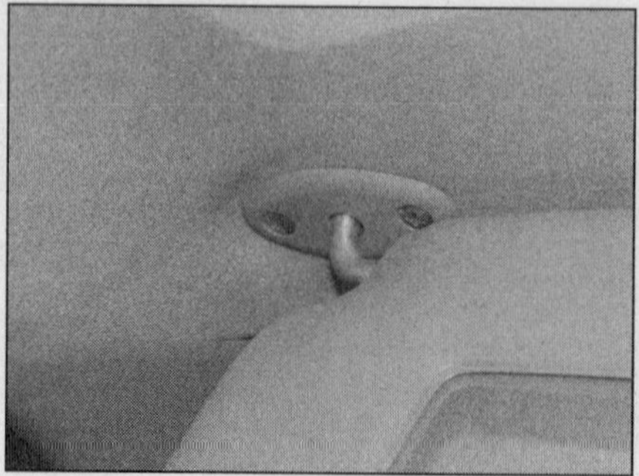

24.50 Sun visor hinge screws

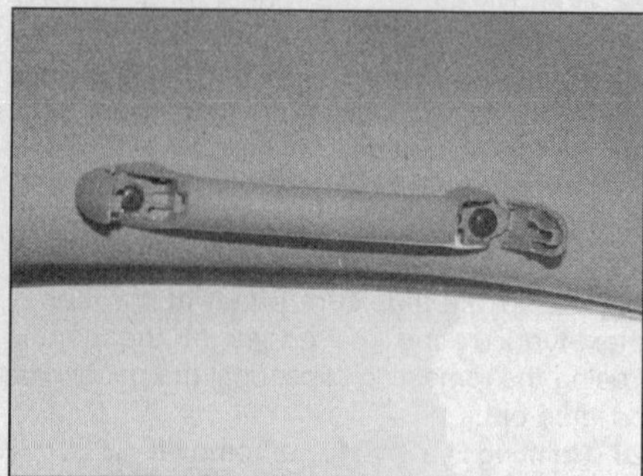

24.52 Prise out the grab handle end covers and remove the mounting screws

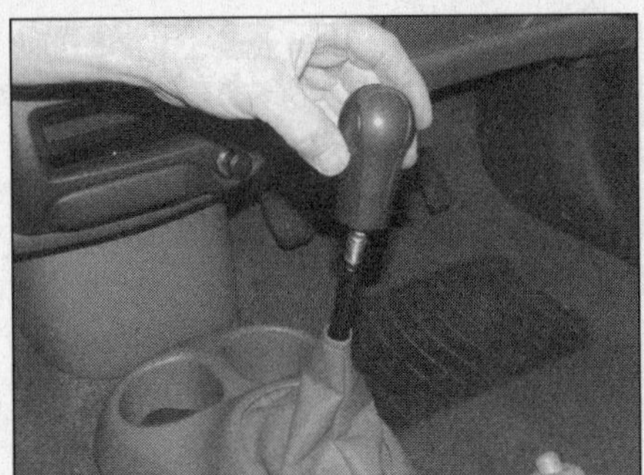

25.1 Unscrew the gear knob

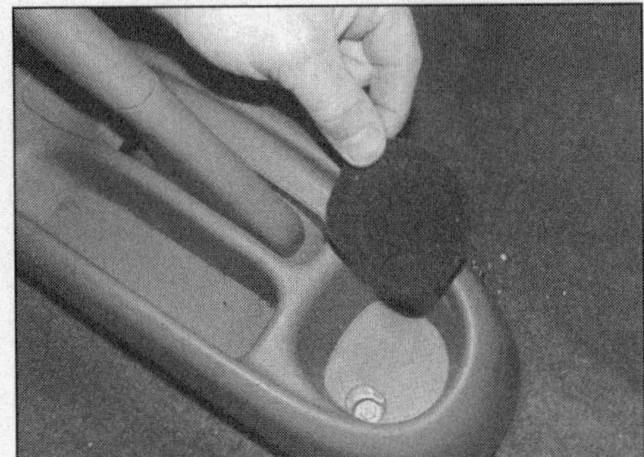

25.2a Lift out the mat from the storage compartment . . .

25.2b . . . then unscrew the bolt underneath

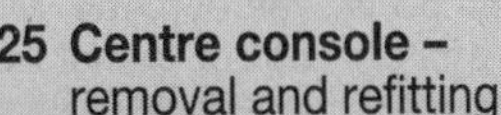

25 Centre console – removal and refitting

Removal

1 On manual transmission models, unscrew the gear knob **(see illustration)**.

2 Lift out the mat from the rearmost storage compartment in the console, and remove the bolt underneath **(see illustrations)**.

3 Unclip the trim panel in front of the handbrake lever **(see illustration)**.

4 Lift the console off its mounting clips, and lift it over the handbrake lever **(see illustration)**. On manual transmission models, feed the gaiter up over the gear lever. Disconnect the wiring plugs from the console switches as necessary, and remove the console from the car.

Refitting

5 Refitting is a reversal of removal.

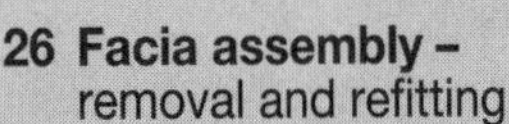

26 Facia assembly – removal and refitting

Removal

Note: *The facia panel is in two sections (upper and lower), with a large metal crossmember underneath it. Depending on the other work being carried out, not all of the facia sections may need to be removed. It is strongly recommended that this Section is read through thoroughly before starting the procedure.*

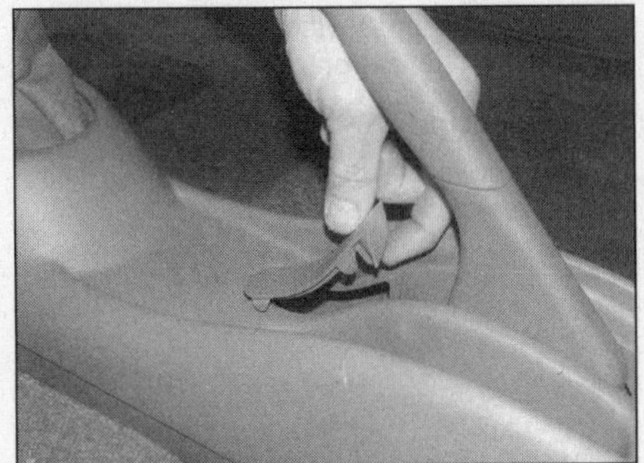

25.3 Unclip the trim in front of the handbrake lever

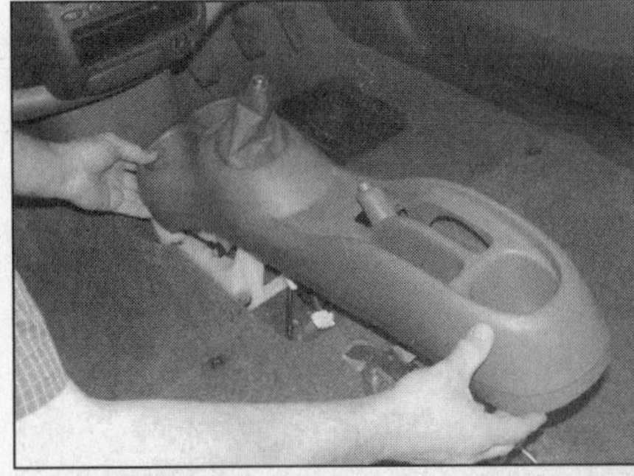

25.4 Lift the console over the handbrake and gear levers, and remove

Upper section

1 Disconnect the battery negative lead, with reference to *Disconnecting the battery*, then wait for two minutes before proceeding. If this waiting period is not observed, there is danger of activating the airbags.

2 Remove the footwell trim panels, A-pillar trim panels and the glovebox as described in Section 24.

3 Remove the steering wheel as described in Chapter 10.

4 Remove the airbag rotary connector ('clockspring') as described in Chapter 12.

5 Also referring to Chapter 12, remove the steering column switches, and the headlight beam adjuster switch panel to the right of the steering column.

6 Remove the facia speakers and the instrument panel as described in Chapter 12.

7 Remove the heater control panel as described in Chapter 3. If just the upper section of the facia is being removed, only the front section of the heater control panel need be removed.

8 Working through the glovebox aperture, unscrew and remove the single central bolt from the facia crossmember. On models with a passenger airbag, this bolt secures the airbag unit; disconnect the airbag wiring connector (by pressing and sliding back the locking catch) also visible inside the glovebox aperture **(see illustrations)**.

9 The facia upper section is secured by four small screws – one at each end in the speaker

26.8a Remove the crossmember bolt visible above the glovebox aperture

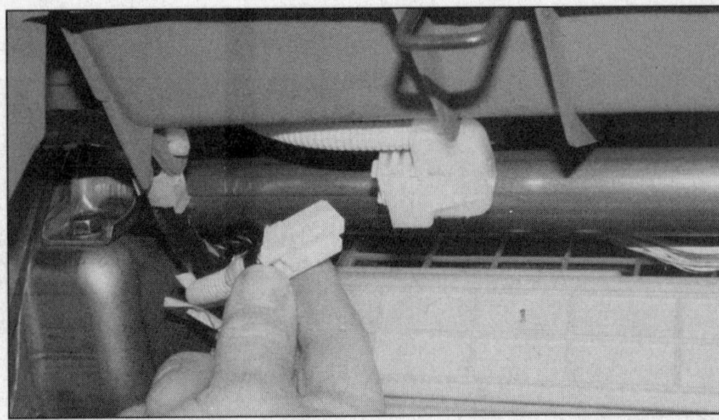

26.8b Where applicable, disconnect the passenger airbag wiring plug

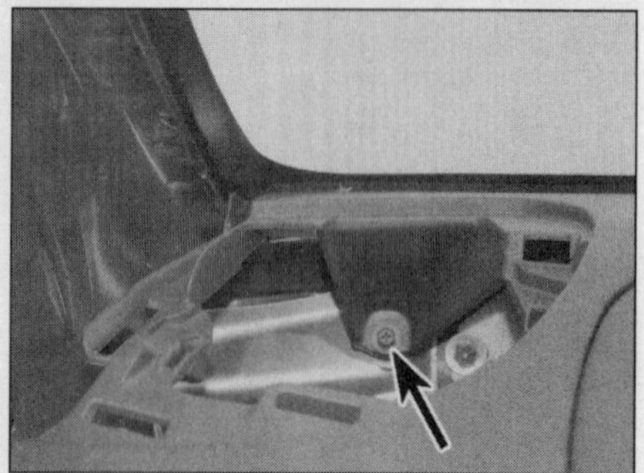
26.9a The facia upper section has a screw at each end . . .

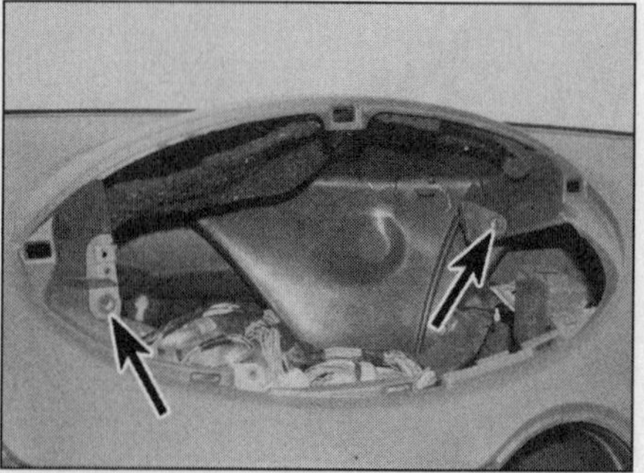
26.9b . . . and two in the instrument panel aperture

26.10 Push the facia upper section upwards to release the clips

holes, and two in the instrument panel aperture **(see illustrations)**. Remove the screws, noting their locations.

10 The upper section of the facia panel may now be removed, by pushing it upwards from below to release the clips fitted all along its front and rear edges. Remove the panel from the car **(see illustration)**.

Lower section

11 To remove the lower section of the facia, start by removing the ashtray.

12 If not already done, remove the rear section of the heater control panel, as described in Chapter 3.

13 Remove the radio main unit as described in Chapter 12.

14 Pull the bonnet release lever, and unhook the cable end fitting from it as described in Section 8.

15 The lower section of the facia panel is secured by two nuts and a central bolt on top, a bolt either end on the bottom, and a central screw below the radio aperture. A plastic push-in fastener either end secures the facia to the crossmember, with a further clip at the base in the passenger footwell. Remove the various fasteners, noting their locations, then lift the panel off the crossmember **(see illustrations)**.

16 Disconnect the wiring plugs and release the harness behind the panel as it is removed **(see illustrations)**. Two small screws are used to secure the fusebox to the lower facia,

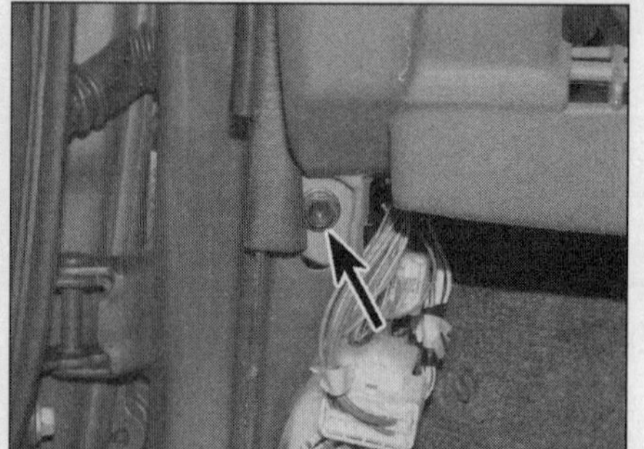
26.15a One of the lower section bottom mounting bolts

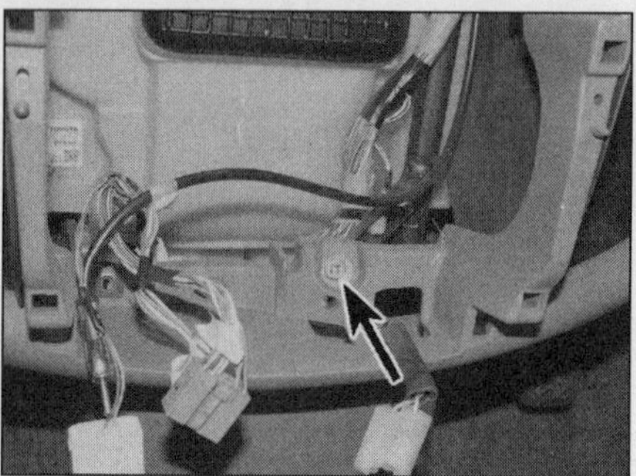
26.15b Remove the central screw (arrowed)

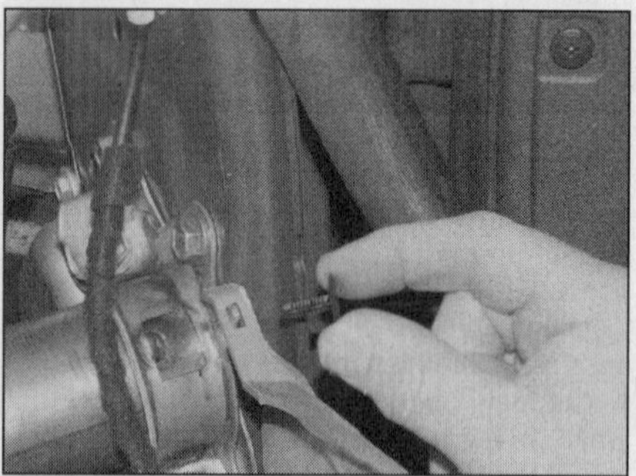
26.15c Prise out the plastic clip at each end . . .

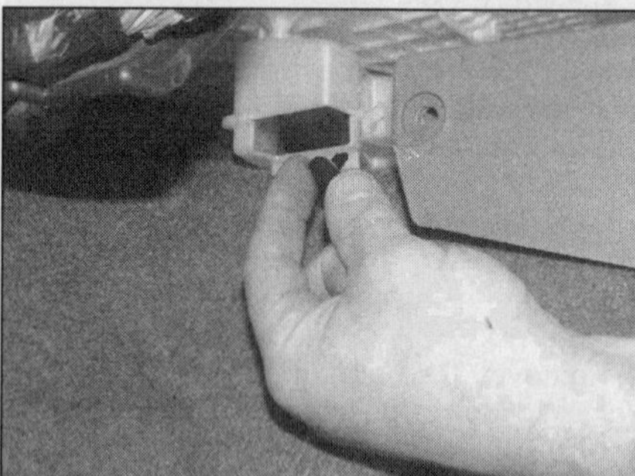
26.15d . . . and the one in the passenger footwell

26.16a Disconnect the wiring plugs inside the glovebox aperture . . .

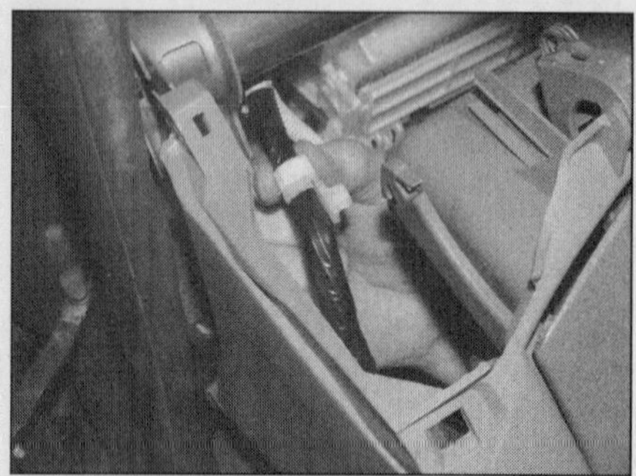
26.16b . . . then unclip the harness from the back of the facia . . .

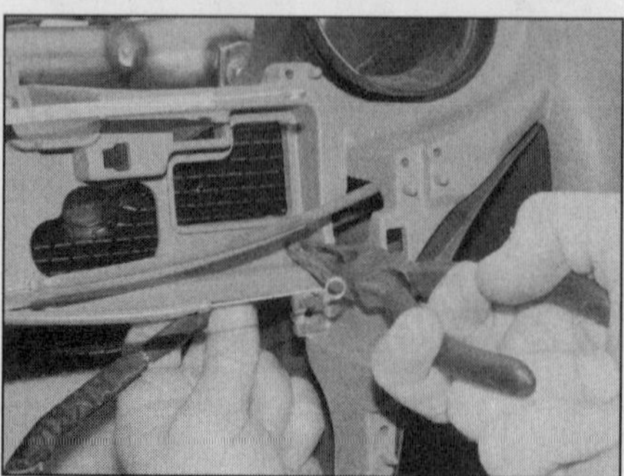
26.16c . . . and from various other points

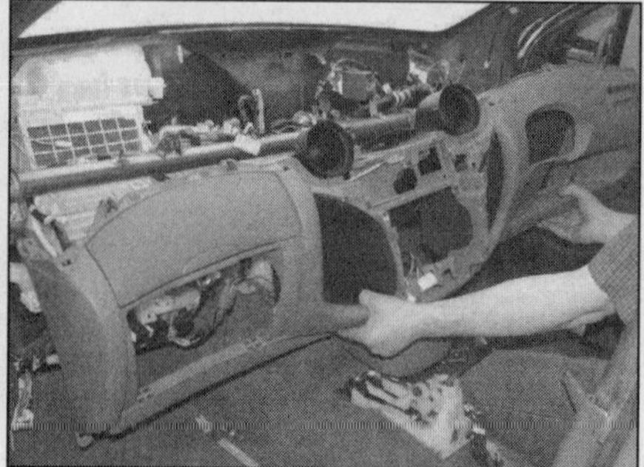
26.16d With everything detached from it, lift out the facia lower section

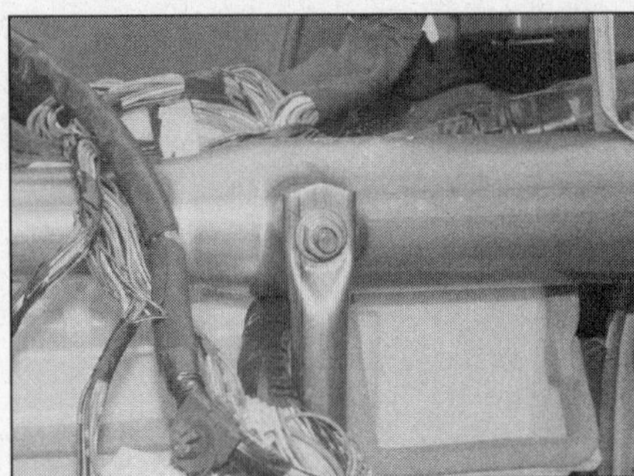

26.19a Remove the centre brace upper mounting nut . . .

26.19b . . . pull back the carpet to access the lower mounting

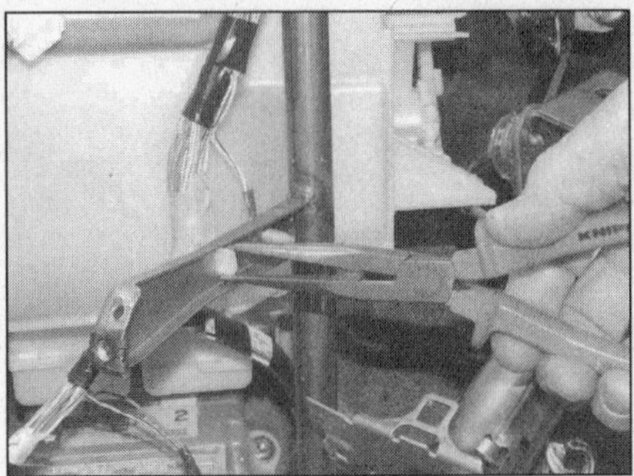

26.19c Unclip the wiring harness, and unbolt the earth strap behind . . .

on the driver's side. Once all the wiring has been disconnected, lift the panel off the steering column and out of the car.

Crossmember

17 To remove the facia crossmember, first unbolt the steering column from it, release the upper clip, and lower it clear of the crossmember (refer to Chapter 10 if necessary). Tie the column up to the brake pedal bracket, or lower it to the floor.

18 Remove the centre console as described in Section 25.

19 Unbolt the central brace fitted between the crossmember and the floor. Release the wiring harness from it, then unscrew the earth strap bolt and remove the brace **(see illustrations)**.

20 Disconnect the wiring plugs from the central locking relay and control unit, or unbolt them from the crossmember, and move them clear **(see illustration)**.

21 Release the wiring harness from the crossmember, and move it clear, noting how it is routed and attached.

22 Disconnect the top row of plugs from the fusebox, then remove the two nuts securing it to the crossmember, together with a further nut used to secure the wiring plug bracket, and move the fusebox rearwards off its studs **(see illustrations)**.

23 Remove the eight bolts securing the crossmember in position, and remove it from the car **(see illustrations)**.

26.19d . . . then remove the brace from the car

26.20 Unbolt the central locking control unit from the crossmember

26.22a Disconnect the upper plugs from the fusebox . . .

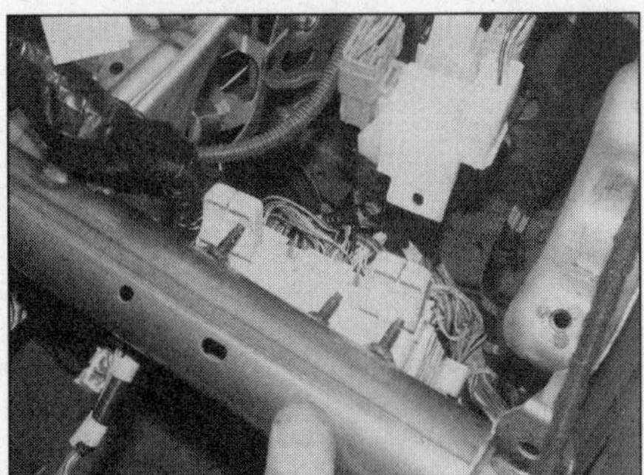

26.22b . . . then remove the nuts at the back, and slide it off

Refitting

24 Refitting is a reversal of removal, bearing in mind the following points:

a) If the facia is being refitted at a later date, ensure that the battery is disconnected before starting. It is dangerous, for example, to reconnect the airbag wiring with the battery connected.

b) Ensure that the wiring harness is securely reconnected to the facia crossmember, and is routed as before.

c) Tighten all bolts securely.

26.23a Unbolt the crossmember clamps at each end . . .

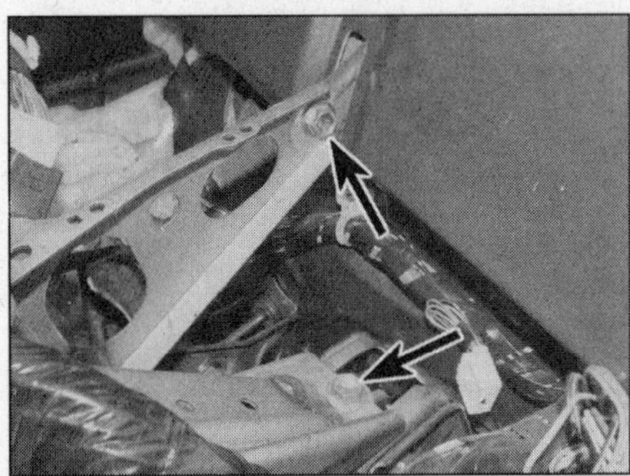

26.23b . . . and remove the bolts from the braces behind the steering column . . .

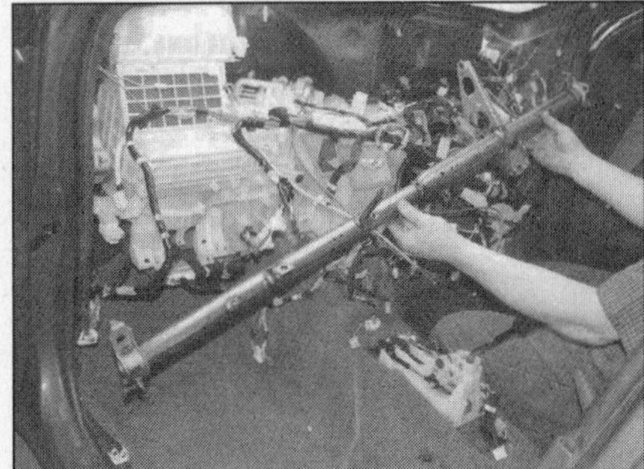

26.23c . . . then remove the crossmember from the car

Notes

Chapter 12
Body electrical system

Contents

Degrees of difficulty

Easy, suitable for novice with little experience 	**Fairly easy,** suitable for beginner with some experience 	**Fairly difficult,** suitable for competent DIY mechanic 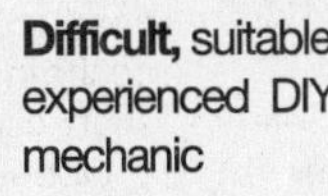	**Difficult,** suitable for experienced DIY mechanic	**Very difficult,** suitable for expert DIY or professional

Specifications

General

System type	12 volt, negative-earth

Fuses

Refer to label inside fusebox lid

Bulbs

	Type	Wattage
Front direction indicator light	Bayonet-fit	21 (amber)
Front direction indicator side repeater light	–*	5
Front foglight	HB4	51
Front sidelight	Push-fit	5
Headlight	H4	55/60
High-level stop-light	Push-fit	16
Interior light	Festoon	10
Luggage compartment light	Festoon	5
Map reading lights	Push-fit	6
Number plate light	Push-fit	5
Rear direction indicator light	Bayonet-fit	21**
Rear foglight	Bayonet-fit	21
Reversing light	Bayonet-fit	21
Stop/tail light	Bayonet-fit	21/5

** Bulbs not available separately – renew light unit.*
*** May be an amber bulb on some models.*

Torque wrench settings

	Nm	lbf ft
Airbag control unit mounting bolts	20	15
Airbag sensor mounting bolts	20	15

1 General information and precautions

Warning: Before carrying out any work on the electrical system, read through the precautions given in 'Safety first!' at the beginning of this manual, and in Chapter 5A.

The electrical system is of 12 volt negative-earth type. Power for the lights and all electrical accessories is supplied by a lead-acid type battery, which is charged by the alternator.

This Chapter covers repair and service procedures for the various electrical components not associated with engine. Information on the battery, alternator and starter motor can be found in Chapter 5A.

It should be noted that, prior to working on any component in the electrical system, the battery negative terminal should first be disconnected, to prevent the possibility of electrical short-circuits and/or fires.

Caution: Before disconnecting the battery, refer to 'Disconnecting the battery' in the Reference Section.

2 Electrical fault finding – general information

Note: *Refer to the precautions given in 'Safety first!' and at the beginning of Chapter 5A before starting work. The following tests relate to testing of the main electrical circuits, and should not be used to test delicate electronic circuits (such as anti-lock braking systems), particularly where an electronic control module is used.*

General

1 A typical electrical circuit consists of an electrical component, any switches, relays, motors, fuses, fusible links or circuit breakers related to that component, and the wiring and connectors which link the component to both the battery and the chassis. To help to pinpoint a problem in an electrical circuit, wiring diagrams are included at the end of this Chapter.

2 Before attempting to diagnose an electrical fault, first study the appropriate wiring diagram, to obtain a more complete understanding of the components included in the particular circuit concerned. The possible sources of a fault can be narrowed down by noting whether other components related to the circuit are operating properly. If several components or circuits fail at one time, the problem is likely to be related to a shared fuse or earth connection.

3 Electrical problems usually stem from simple causes, such as loose or corroded connections, a faulty earth connection, a blown fuse, a melted fusible link, or a faulty relay (refer to Section 3 for details of testing relays). Visually inspect the condition of all fuses, wires and connections in a problem circuit before testing the components. Use the wiring diagrams to determine which terminal connections will need to be checked, in order to pinpoint the trouble-spot.

4 The basic tools required for electrical fault-finding include a circuit tester or voltmeter (a 12 volt bulb with a set of test leads can also be used for certain tests); a self-powered test light (sometimes known as a continuity tester); an ohmmeter (to measure resistance); a battery and set of test leads; and a jumper wire, preferably with a circuit breaker or fuse incorporated, which can be used to bypass suspect wires or electrical components. Before attempting to locate a problem with test instruments, use the wiring diagram to determine where to make the connections.

5 To find the source of an intermittent wiring fault (usually due to a poor or dirty connection, or damaged wiring insulation), a 'wiggle' test can be performed on the wiring. This involves wiggling the wiring by hand, to see if the fault occurs as the wiring is moved. It should be possible to narrow down the source of the fault to a particular section of wiring. This method of testing can be used in conjunction with any of the tests described in the following sub-Sections.

6 Apart from problems due to poor connections, two basic types of fault can occur in an electrical circuit – open-circuit, or short-circuit.

7 Open-circuit faults are caused by a break somewhere in the circuit, which prevents current from flowing. An open-circuit fault will prevent a component from working, but will not cause the relevant circuit fuse to blow.

8 Short-circuit faults are caused by a 'short' somewhere in the circuit, which allows the current flowing in the circuit to 'escape' along an alternative route, usually to earth. Short-circuit faults are normally caused by a breakdown in wiring insulation, which allows a feed wire to touch either another wire, or an earthed component such as the bodyshell. A short-circuit fault will normally cause the relevant circuit fuse to blow.

Finding an open-circuit

9 To check for an open-circuit, connect one lead of a circuit tester or voltmeter to either the negative battery terminal or a known good earth.

10 Connect the other lead to a connector in the circuit being tested, preferably nearest to the battery or fuse.

11 Switch on the circuit, bearing in mind that some circuits are live only when the ignition switch is moved to a particular position.

12 If voltage is present (indicated either by the tester bulb lighting or a voltmeter reading, as applicable), this means that the section of the circuit between the relevant connector and the battery is problem-free.

13 Continue to check the remainder of the circuit in the same fashion.

14 When a point is reached at which no voltage is present, the problem must lie between that point and the previous test point with voltage. Most problems can be traced to a broken, corroded or loose connection.

Finding a short-circuit

15 To check for a short-circuit, first disconnect the load(s) from the circuit (loads are the components which draw current from a circuit, such as bulbs, motors, heating elements, etc).

16 Remove the relevant fuse from the circuit and connect a circuit tester or voltmeter to the fuse connections.

17 Switch on the circuit, bearing in mind that some circuits are live only when the ignition switch is moved to a particular position.

18 If voltage is present (indicated either by the tester bulb lighting or a voltmeter reading as applicable), this means that there is a short-circuit.

19 If no voltage is present, but the fuse still blows with the load(s) connected, this indicates an internal fault in the load(s).

Finding an earth fault

20 The battery negative terminal is connected to 'earth' – the metal of the engine/transmission unit and the car body – and most systems are wired so that they only receive a positive feed, the current returning via the metal of the car body. This means that the component mounting and the body form part of that circuit. Loose or corroded mountings can therefore cause a range of electrical faults, ranging from total failure of a circuit, to a puzzling partial fault.

21 In particular, lights may shine dimly (especially when another circuit sharing the same earth point is in operation), motors (eg, wiper motors or the radiator cooling fan motor) may run slowly, and the operation of one circuit may have an apparently-unrelated effect on another.

22 Note that on many vehicles, earth straps are used between certain components, such as the engine/transmission and the body, usually where there is no metal-to-metal contact between components, due to flexible rubber mountings, etc.

23 To check whether a component is properly earthed, disconnect the battery, and connect one lead of an ohmmeter to a known good earth point. Connect the other lead to the wire or earth connection being tested. The resistance reading should be zero; if not, check the connection as follows.

24 If an earth connection is thought to be faulty, dismantle the connection, and clean back to bare metal both the bodyshell and the wire terminal or the component earth connection mating surface. Be careful to remove all traces of dirt and corrosion, then use a knife to trim away any paint, so that a clean metal-to-metal joint is made.

25 On reassembly, tighten the joint fasteners

3.2 Additional fuses are located in the engine compartment fusebox

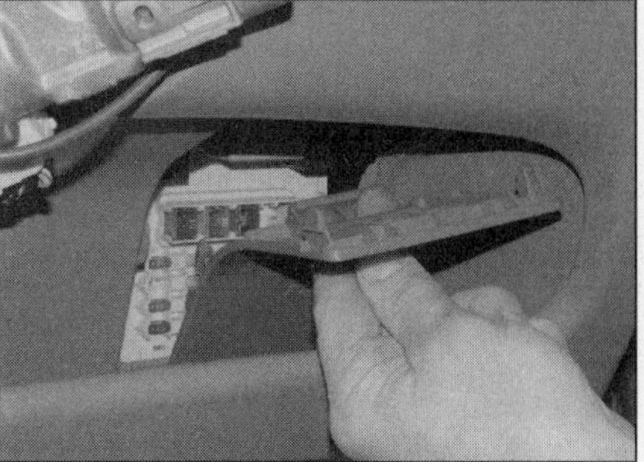

3.3 Unclip the fusebox lid inside the car

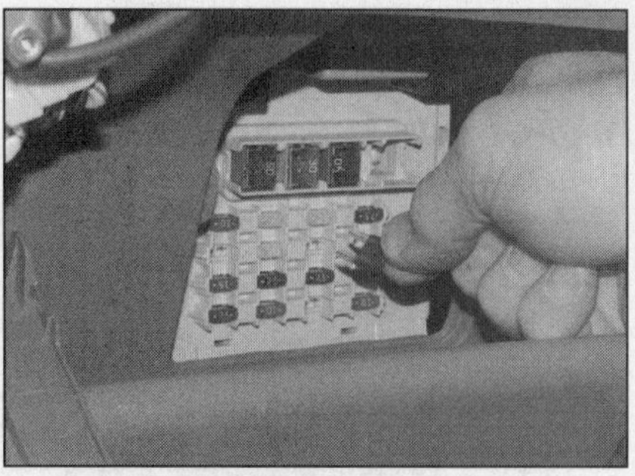

3.6 Pull the fuse out, using pliers if necessary

securely; if a wire terminal is being refitted, use serrated washers between the terminal and the bodyshell, to ensure a clean and secure connection.

26 When the connection is remade, prevent the onset of corrosion in the future by applying a coat of petroleum jelly or silicone-based grease, or by spraying on (at regular intervals) a proprietary ignition sealer.

3 Fuses and relays – general information

Fuses

1 Fuses are designed to break a circuit when a predetermined current is reached, in order to protect the components and wiring which could be damaged by excessive current flow. Any excessive current flow will be due to a fault in the circuit, usually a short-circuit (see Section 2).

2 The main fuses are located in the fusebox, behind a panel in the driver's storage tray. Additional fuses are located in a second fusebox in the engine compartment, next to the battery **(see illustration)**.

3 Unclip the fusebox lid from the back of the driver's storage tray, and remove it for access to the fuses **(see illustration)**. In the case of the engine compartment fusebox, the lid unclips and can be lifted off.

4 A blown fuse can be recognised from its melted or broken wire.

5 To remove a fuse, first ensure that the relevant circuit is switched off. Taking out the ignition key is a start, but several circuits are live even with the ignition off – for maximum safety, disconnect the battery (see *Disconnecting the battery*).

6 Pull the fuse from its location, using thin-nosed pliers if necessary **(see illustration)**.

7 Before renewing a blown fuse, trace and rectify the cause, and always use a fuse of the correct rating. Never substitute a fuse of a higher rating, or make temporary repairs using wire or metal foil; more serious damage, or even fire, could result.

8 Note that the fuses are colour-coded as follows. Refer to the markings on the back of the fusebox lids for details of the circuits protected. Also note that the Yaris uses the later-type 'mini' fuses.

Colour	Rating
Orange	*5A*
Red	*10A*
Blue	*15A*
Yellow	*20A*
Clear or white	*25A*
Green	*30A*

9 Larger 'midi' fuses will also be found in the engine compartment fusebox. Since many of these are rated in excess of 30 amps, if any of these is found to have blown, it indicates a serious wiring fault, which should be investigated – just fitting a new fuse may cause further problems.

Relays

10 A relay is an electrically-operated switch, which is used for the following reasons:

a) *A relay can switch a heavy current remotely from the circuit in which the current is flowing, allowing the use of lighter-gauge wiring and switch contacts.*

b) *A relay can receive more than one control input, unlike a mechanical switch.*

c) *A relay can have a timer function – for example, the intermittent wiper relay.*

11 The relays are divided between the under-facia fusebox and the engine compartment fusebox. Some models may feature a separate relay box on the bulkhead, behind the engine compartment fusebox. Typically, the flasher relay and main power relay will be inside the car, with the rest under the bonnet. The central locking relay is located (with the central locking control unit) under the upper section of the facia, mounted on the crossmember – see Chapter 11.

12 If a circuit or system controlled by a relay develops a fault, and the relay is suspect, operate the system. If the relay is functioning, it should be possible to hear it 'click' as it is energised. If this is the case, the fault lies with the components or wiring of the system.

13 If the relay is not being energised, then either the relay is not receiving a main supply or a switching voltage, or the relay itself is faulty. Testing is by the substitution of a known good unit, but be careful – while some relays are identical in appearance and in operation, others look similar but perform different functions.

14 To remove a relay, first ensure that the relevant circuit is switched off. The relay can then simply be pulled out from the socket, and pushed back into position.

4 Switches – removal and refitting

Note: *Before removing any switch, disconnect the battery negative lead, and position the lead away from the battery (also see 'Disconnecting the battery').*

Ignition switch/steering lock

Steering column lock cylinder

1 Remove the steering column shrouds as described in Chapter 11, Section 24.

2 Disconnect the wiring plug, then unclip and slide off the anti-theft immobiliser transceiver unit from the ignition switch/steering lock assembly **(see illustrations)**.

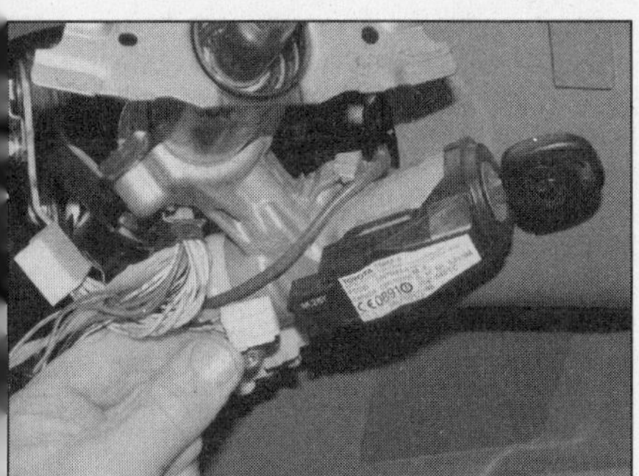

4.2a Disconnect the wiring plug from the immobiliser unit . . .

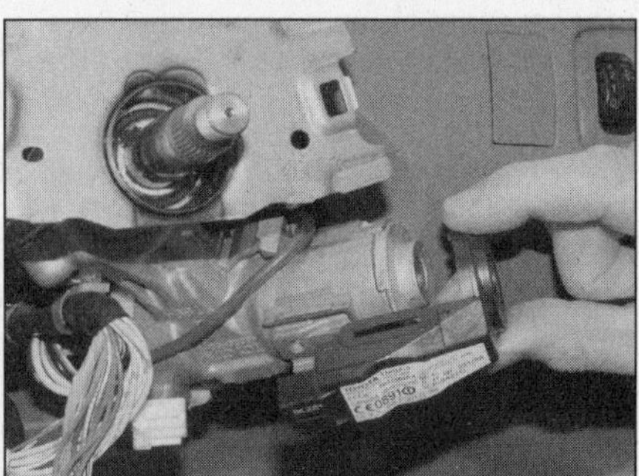

4.2b . . . then unclip it and slide it off

4.4 Depress the locking pin and slide out the lock barrel

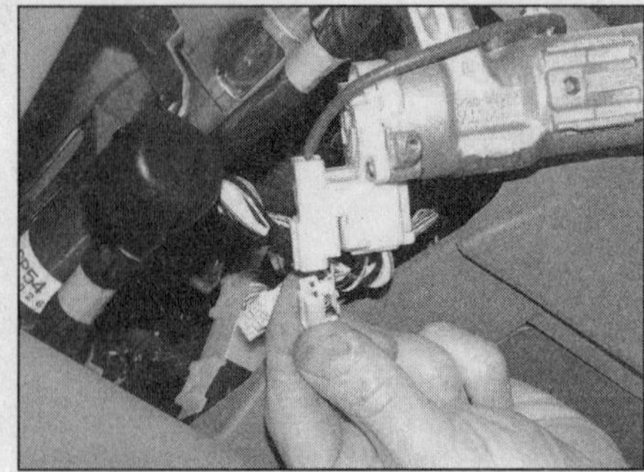

4.7a Disconnect the wiring plug from the thick blue wire . . .

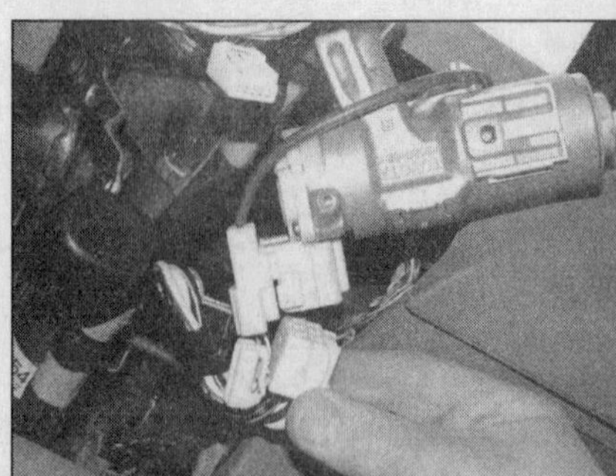

4.7b . . . then disconnect the main ignitior switch wiring plug

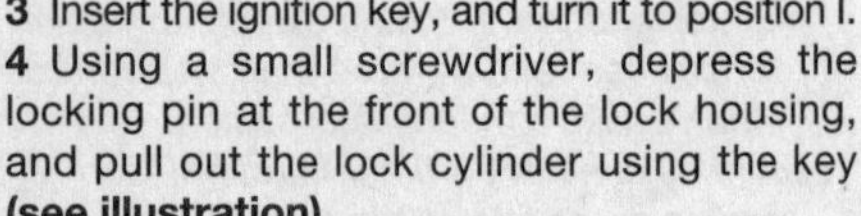

3 Insert the ignition key, and turn it to position I.
4 Using a small screwdriver, depress the locking pin at the front of the lock housing, and pull out the lock cylinder using the key **(see illustration)**.
5 To refit the lock cylinder, push the assembly into the lock housing, until the locking pin engages, then turn the ignition key to position 0 and withdraw the key.

Ignition switch

Caution: Do not remove the ignition switch whilst the steering column lock cylinder is removed.

6 Remove the steering column shrouds as described in Chapter 11, Section 24.
7 Where applicable, disconnect the wiring plug from the thick blue wire behind the switch itself, then disconnect the main ignition switch wiring plug **(see illustrations)**.
8 Remove the two switch retaining screws at the rear, then the switch is withdrawn from the steering column mounting bracket **(see illustrations)**.
9 Refitting is a reversal of removal, but make sure that switch engages correctly.

Steering column switches

10 Remove the steering column shrouds as described in Chapter 11, Section 24.
11 Disconnect the wiring plug from the base of the switch **(see illustration)**.
12 Use a small screwdriver to depress the release tab on the front of the switch, then withdraw the switch sideways and remove it **(see illustrations)**.
13 Refitting is a reversal of removal.

Heated rear window switch

14 Remove the heater blower motor switc as described in Chapter 3.
15 The heated rear window switch is integra with the blower switch, and cannot b renewed separately.
16 Refitting is a reversal of removal.

Hazard warning light switch

17 Remove the heater blower motor switcl as described in Chapter 3.
18 The hazard warning light switch is integra with the blower switch, and cannot b renewed separately.
19 Refitting is a reversal of removal.

Air conditioning switch

20 Remove the heater blower motor switcl as described in Chapter 3.
21 The air conditioning switch is integral witl the blower switch, and cannot be renewec separately.
22 Refitting is a reversal of removal.

Electric mirror switch

23 Taking care not to mark the facia, prise out the switch panel until it is free.
24 Disconnect the wiring plug(s) from the back of the switch panel, and withdraw the assembly from the facia.
25 The mirror switch is integral with the othe switches on the panel, and is not available separately.
26 Refitting is a reversal of removal.

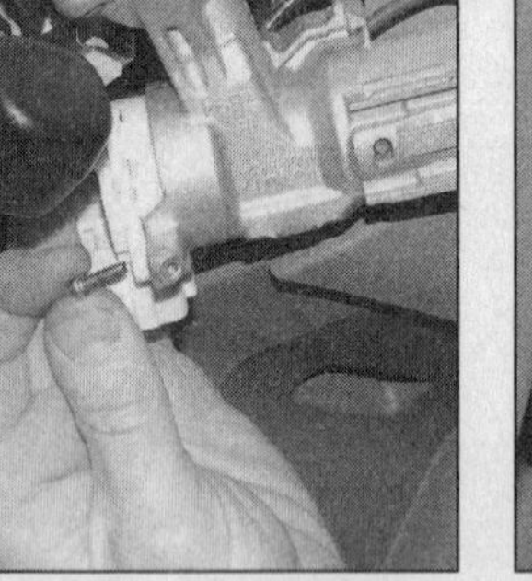

4.8a Remove the two switch securing screws . . .

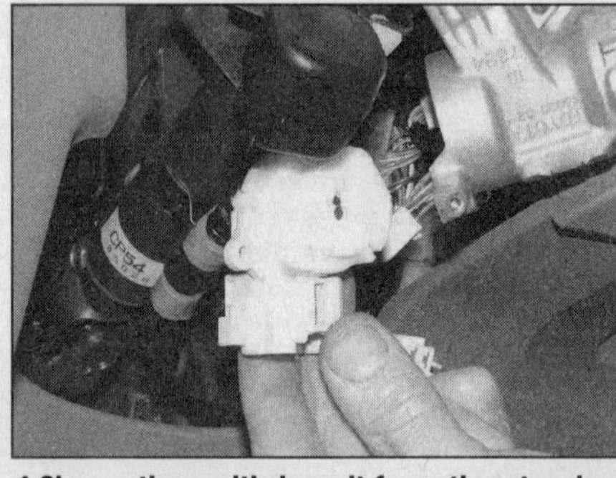

4.8b . . . then withdraw it from the steering column

4.11 Disconnect the column switch wiring plug

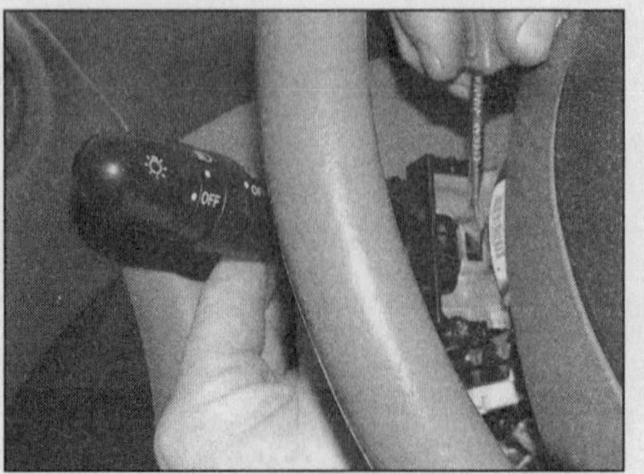

4.12a Depress the tab on the front of the switch . . .

4.12b . . . and slide it out sideways

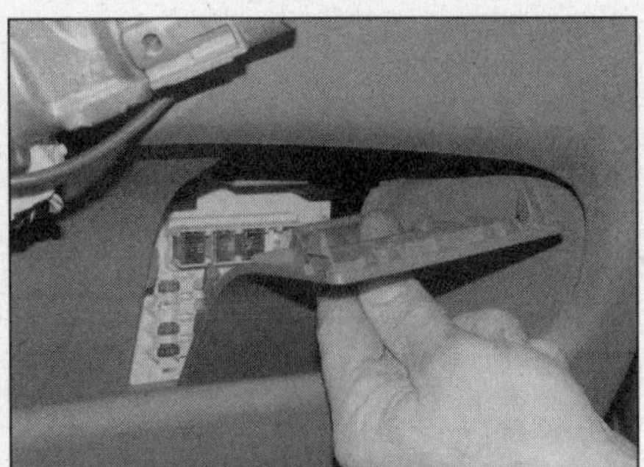
4.27a Remove the fusebox lid . . .

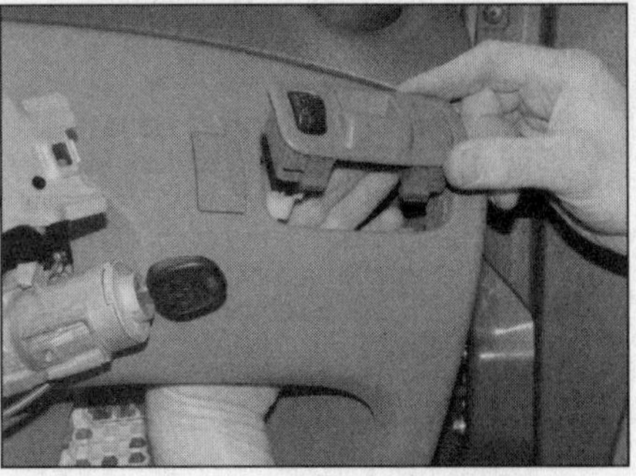
4.27b . . . then reach in behind the facia and push out the switch panel

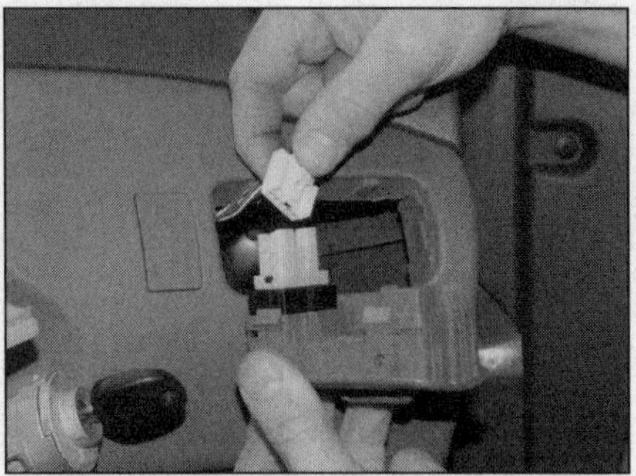
4.28 Disconnect the wiring plug from the switch . . .

Headlight beam adjuster

27 Remove the fusebox lid, and push out the switch panel from behind **(see illustrations)**.

28 Disconnect the wiring plug(s) from the back of the switch panel, and withdraw the assembly from the facia **(see illustration)**.

29 Push the beam adjuster switch backwards out of the panel, and remove it **(see illustration)**.

30 Refitting is a reversal of removal.

Rear foglight switch

Note: *Depending on model, the foglight switch is located either on the facia panel (as described below), or is incorporated in the steering column switch for the lights.*

31 Taking care not to mark the facia, prise out the switch panel until it is free.

32 Disconnect the wiring plug(s) from the back of the switch panel, and withdraw the assembly from the facia.

33 The rear foglight switch is integral with the other switches on the panel, and is not available separately.

34 Refitting is a reversal of removal.

Blower motor switch

35 The switch can only be removed from the back of the heater control panel, which is removed as described in Chapter 3.

Audio remote control switch

36 Remove the steering column shrouds as described in Chapter 11, Section 24.

37 Disconnect the wiring plug from the switch assembly.

38 Remove the securing screws, and take out the switch.

39 Refitting is a reversal of removal.

Electric window switches

40 Taking care not to mark the trim, prise out the switch panel from the door (this can be done without using tools). Work round the panel until it is free **(see illustration)**.

41 Disconnect the wiring plug(s) from the window switch assembly, and withdraw the assembly from the door trim panel. Unscrew the switch panel mounting screws on the underside, and separate the switch proper from its trim piece **(see illustrations)**.

42 Refitting is a reversal of removal.

Centre console switches

43 Taking care not to mark the trim, prise out the switch panel from the console. Work round the panel until it is free.

44 Disconnect the wiring plug(s) from the switch assembly, and withdraw the assembly from the console.

45 Refitting is a reversal of removal.

Door courtesy light switches

46 Open the relevant door. Remove the screw securing the switch to the door frame, and prise the switch out of its location **(see illustration)**.

47 Disconnect the wiring plug and remove

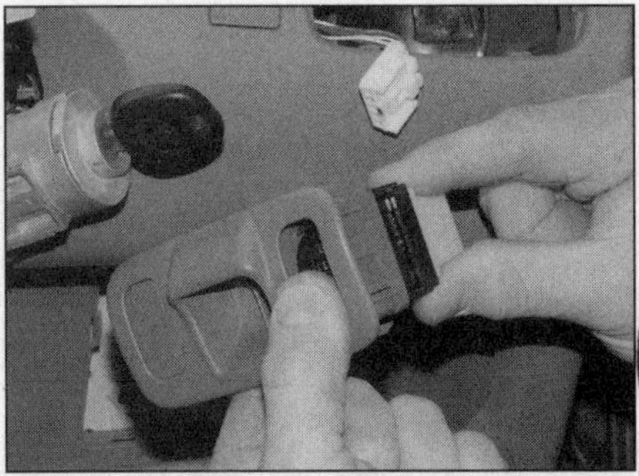
4.29 . . . then push the switch backwards out of the panel

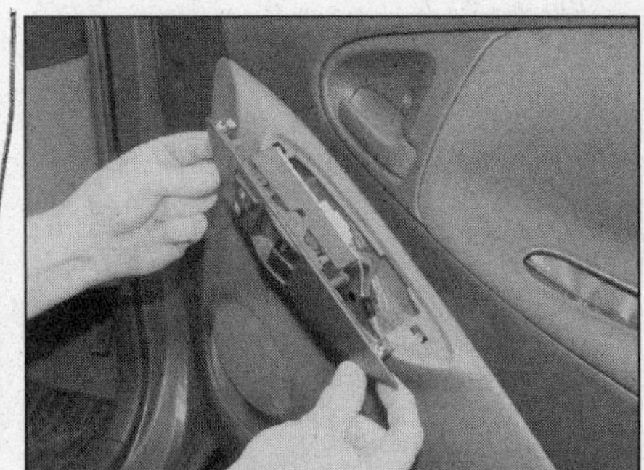
4.40 The window switch panel can be unclipped from the door without using tools

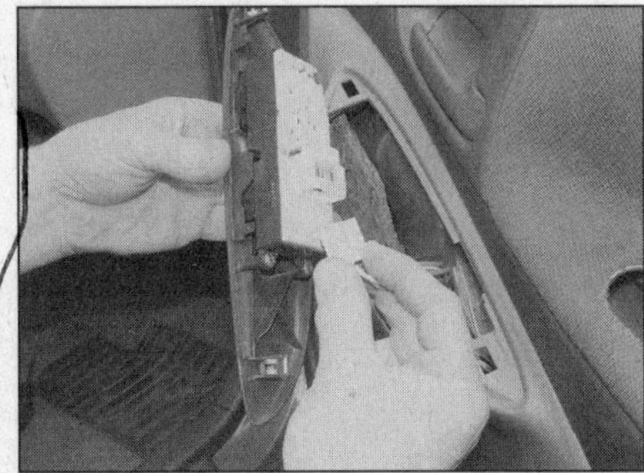
4.41a Disconnect the switch wiring plug, and remove it

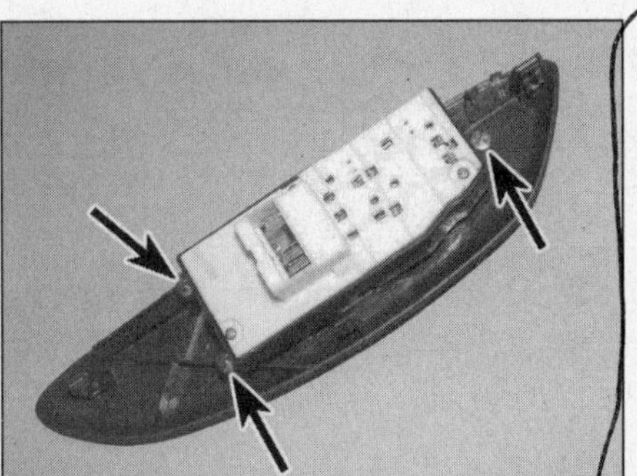
4.41b The switch panel is secured to the trim piece by three screws (arrowed)

4.46 Remove the mounting screw and withdraw the switch

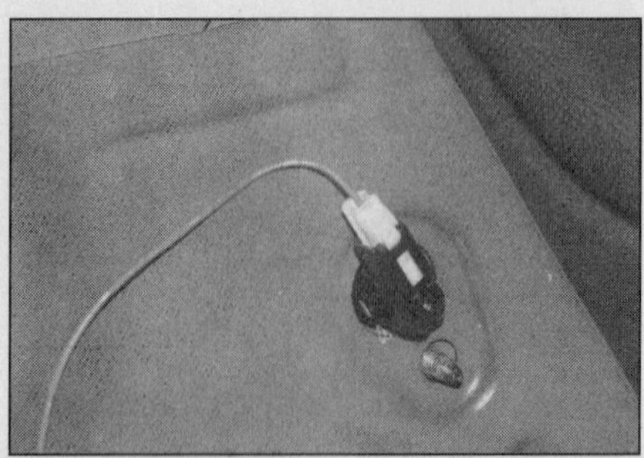

4.47 Rear door switch seen from inside, with parcel shelf support panel removed

the switch. Make sure that the wiring does not drop back into the aperture by using tape or string to secure it **(see illustration)**.

48 Refitting is a reversal of removal.

Handbrake-on warning switch

49 Refer to Chapter 9.

Stop-light switch

50 Refer to Chapter 9.

5 Bulbs (exterior lights) – renewal

1 Whenever a bulb is renewed, note the following points:

a) Disconnect the battery negative lead before starting work (see 'Disconnecting the battery').

b) Remember that, if the light has just been in use, the bulb may be extremely hot.

c) Always check the bulb contacts and holder, ensuring that there is clean metal-to metal contact between the bulb and its live(s) and earth. Clean off any corrosion or dirt before fitting a new bulb.

d) Wherever bayonet-type bulbs are fitted (see Specifications), ensure that the live contact(s) bear firmly against the bulb contact.

e) Always ensure that the new bulb is of the correct rating, and that it is completely clean before fitting it; this applies particularly to headlight/foglight bulbs (see below).

Headlight

Note: *Access to the headlight bulbholders is not great. On the passenger side, it may be helpful to remove the battery (Chapter 5A), or at least to remove the top clamp and move it a little, to improve things. Removing the headlight is quite involved (see Section 7) but may be the only option otherwise.*

2 Pull the wiring plug from the rear of the bulb, then pull off the rubber cover **(see illustration)**.

3 Release the bulb's wire retaining clip by unhooking it sideways at the top, then pivot the clip down. Withdraw the bulb **(see illustrations)**.

4 When handling the new bulb, use a tissue or clean cloth, to avoid touching the glass with the fingers; moisture and grease from the skin can cause blackening and rapid failure of this type of bulb. If the glass is accidentally touched, wipe it clean using methylated spirit.

5 Install the new bulb, ensuring that its locating tabs are correctly seated in the light cut-outs. Secure the bulb in position with the spring clip.

6 Refit the rubber cover, ensuring that a good seal is made to the back of the headlight. Reconnect the wiring plug.

Front sidelight

7 Refer to the note before paragraph 2 before starting. Disconnect the wiring plug from the bulbholder. Twist the bulbholder anti-clockwise, and pull it from the rear of the headlight **(see illustration)**.

8 Pull out the wedge-base bulb from the holder, and fit a new one firmly into place **(see illustration)**.

9 Refit the bulbholder, twisting it firmly into place to secure it.

Front direction indicator light

10 Turn the steering wheel to give the best access to the front of the wheel arch.

11 Remove the three cross-head screws at the front edge (and at least two more push-in clips) securing the front half of the wheel arch liner, and pull the liner back for access to the bulbholder.

12 Disconnect the wiring plug from the bulbholder. Twist the bulbholder anti-clockwise, and withdraw it from the light unit.

13 Depress and twist the bulb anti-clockwise to remove it **(see illustration)**.

14 Fit the new bulb, then twist the bulbholder clockwise into the back of the light.

15 Refit the wheel arch liner screws to complete.

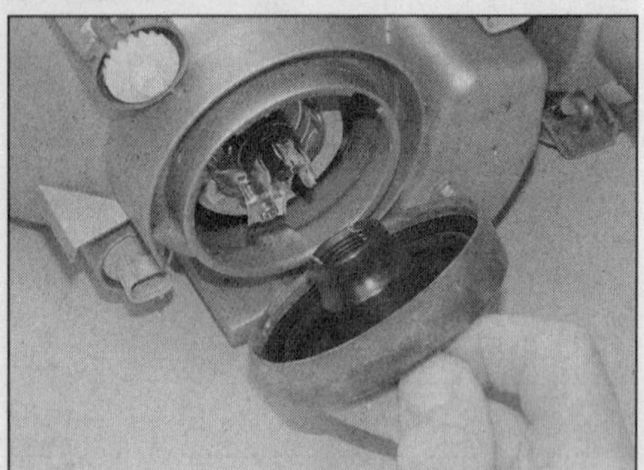

5.2 Pull off the rubber cover for access to the headlight bulb

5.3a Unhook the wire clip at the top . . .

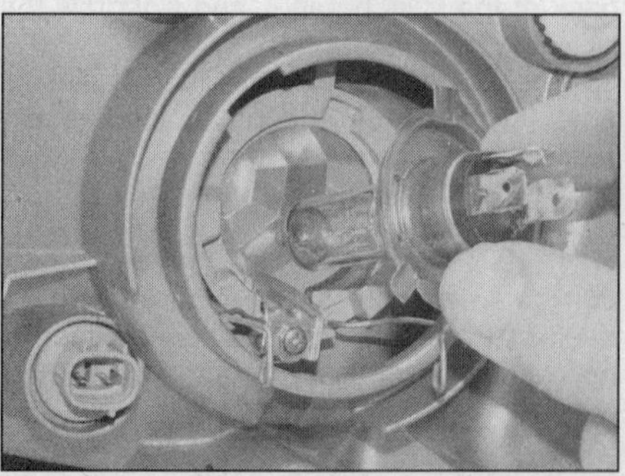

5.3b . . . then hinge it down and remove the bulb

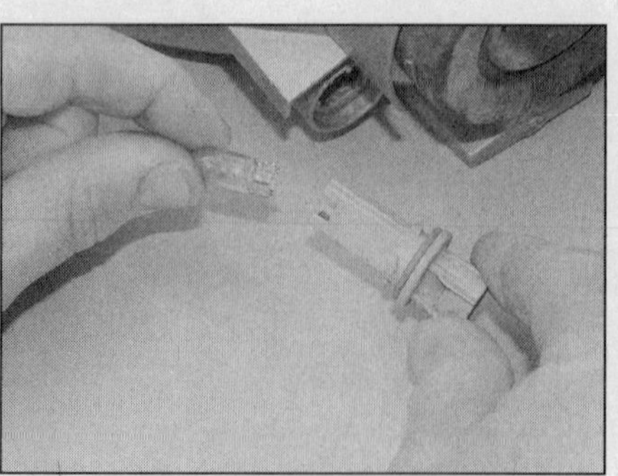

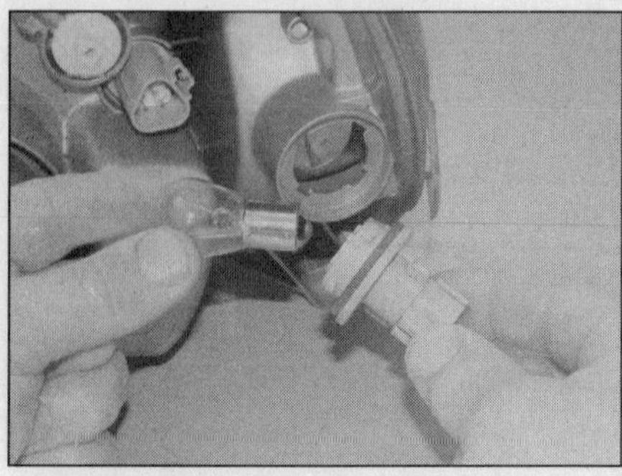

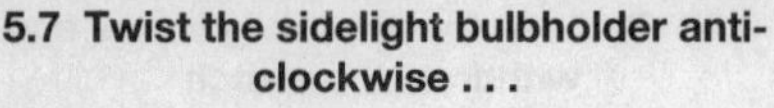

5.7 Twist the sidelight bulbholder anti-clockwise . . .

5.8 . . . and pull out the wedge-base bulb

5.13 Removing the bayonet-fit indicator bulb (headlight removed)

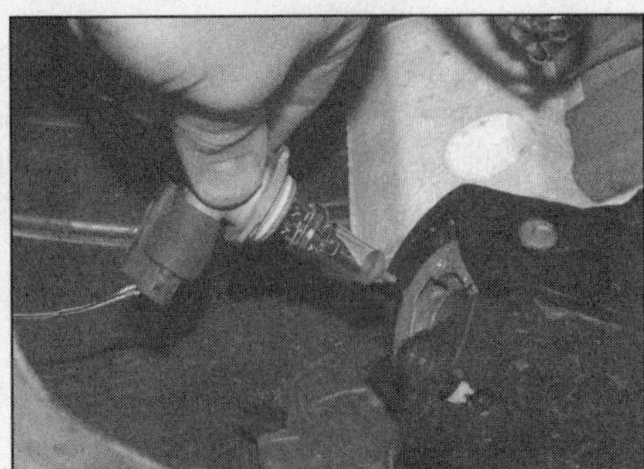
5.19 Twist the foglight bulb anti-clockwise and withdraw it

5.23 Slide the light unit forwards against the spring, and unhook it at the back

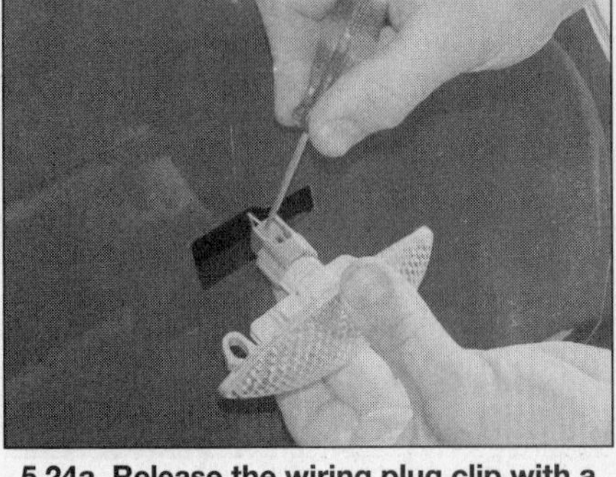
5.24a Release the wiring plug clip with a screwdriver . . .

Front foglight

16 Turn the steering wheel to give the best access to the front of the wheel arch.

17 Remove the three cross-head screws securing the front half of the wheel arch liner, and pull the liner back for access to the bulbholder.

18 Press the back of the wiring plug, and pull it down to disconnect it.

19 Twist the bulb anti-clockwise to remove it from the back of the light unit **(see illustration)**.

20 The bulb is unusual in having its wiring socket integrated with it – for this reason, this type of bulb may only be readily obtainable from Toyota dealers.

21 When handling the new bulb, use a tissue or clean cloth, to avoid touching the glass with the fingers; moisture and grease from the skin can cause blackening and rapid failure of this type of bulb. If the glass is accidentally touched, wipe it clean using methylated spirit.

22 Fit the new bulb, twisting it clockwise into the back of the light unit to secure. Reconnect the wiring plug, then refit the wheel arch liner screws.

Indicator side repeater light

23 Slide the light unit to the front, against its internal spring clip. Hold the light against the spring tension, and unhook its rear edge **(see illustration)**.

24 Withdraw the light unit, and disconnect the wiring plug, using a small screwdriver if necessary **(see illustrations)**. To avoid the possibility of the wiring and plug disappearing back inside the hole in the wing, tape it temporarily in place.

25 The bulb is not available separately, and in the event of failure, a new light unit must be obtained.

26 Refitting is a reversal of removal.

Rear lights

27 Open the tailgate, and unclip the trim panel from the back of the light unit, for access to the bulbholders **(see illustration)**.

28 Twist the required bulbholder anti-clockwise and remove it from the light **(see illustration)**. One of the bulbholders has the rear light unit wiring plug attached, but this does not have to be disconnected for bulb renewal.

29 Any of the bayonet-fitting bulbs can now be removed by pressing and turning them anti-clockwise **(see illustration)**.

30 Fit the new bulb(s), then clip the bulbholder back onto the light unit. Clip the trim panel back into place.

Number plate light

31 Taking care not to damage the paintwork, prise the number plate light from the bumper using a small screwdriver **(see illustrations)**.

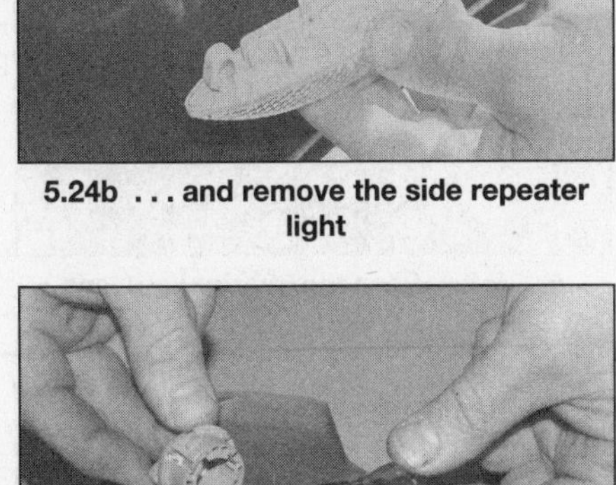
5.24b . . . and remove the side repeater light

5.27 Unclip the trim panel from the back of the light unit

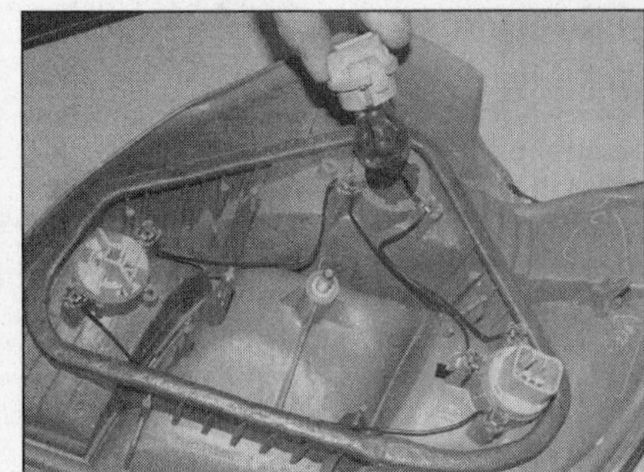
5.28 Twist and remove the bulbholder . . .

5.29 . . . then push and twist out the bayonet bulb

5.31a Using a small screwdriver . . .

5.31b . . . prise out the number plate light

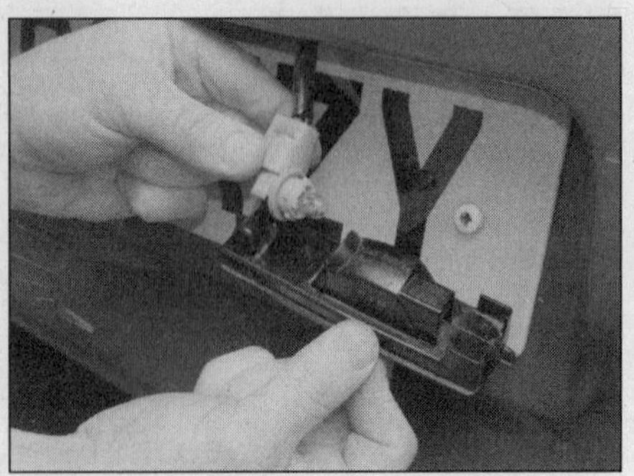
5.32 Twist off the bulbholder . . .

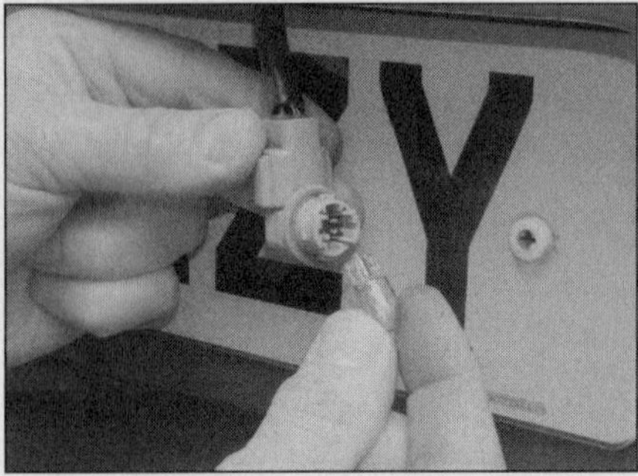
5.33 . . . and pull out the wedge-base bulb

5.35 Unclip the cover from the high-level stop-light

5.36a Remove the mounting bolt . . .

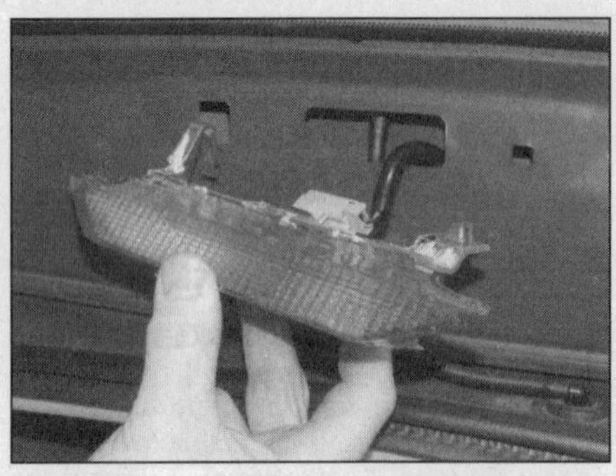
5.36b . . . then unclip the light from the tailgate

5.37 Twist the bulbholder out of the light . . .

32 Twist the bulbholder anti-clockwise from the light **(see illustration)**.
33 Pull out the wedge-base bulb, and press a new one into place **(see illustration)**.
34 Refitting is a reversal of removal.

High-level stop-light

35 Open the tailgate, and unclip the cover downwards from the back of the light **(see illustration)**.
36 Remove the single mounting bolt, then unclip and withdraw the light from the tailgate **(see illustrations)**.
37 Twist the bulbholder anti-clockwise from the light, and remove it **(see illustration)**.
38 The bulb is a push-fit in its holder – pull the old one out, and press in a new one **(see illustration)**.
39 Refitting is a reversal of removal.

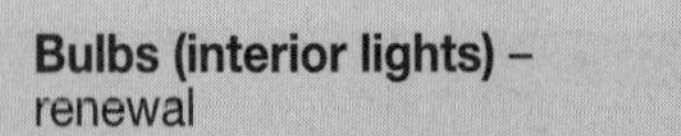

6 Bulbs (interior lights) – renewal

General

1 Refer to Section 5, paragraph 1.

Interior and map reading lights

2 Carefully prise the light unit lens down at the side, using a small screwdriver **(see illustration)**.
3 Pull the festoon-type interior light bulb from the sprung contacts **(see illustration)**.
4 On models with map reading lights, hinge back the contact plate and remove the push-fit bulb.
5 Fit the new bulb using a reversal of the removal procedure.
6 If required, the light unit can be removed completely by removing the two mounting screws and disconnecting the wiring plug **(see illustration)**.

Luggage compartment light

7 Carefully prise the light unit out from the trim panel.
8 Pull the festoon-type interior light bulb from the sprung contacts.
9 Fit the new bulb using a reversal of the removal procedure.

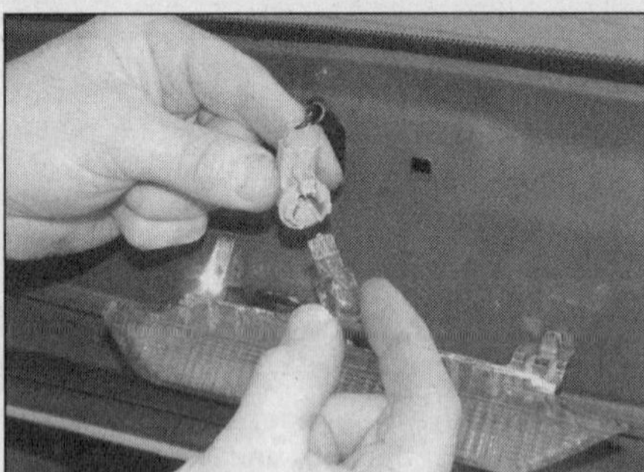
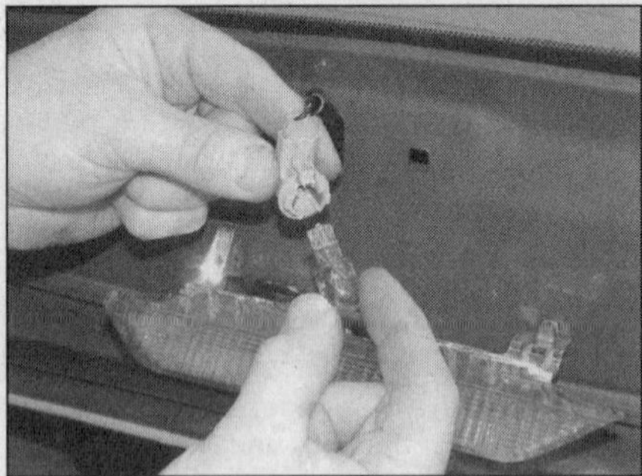
5.38 . . . and pull out the wedge-base bulb

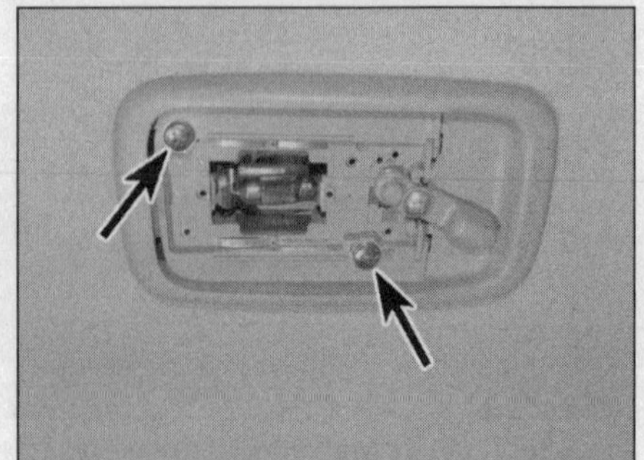
6.2 Prise down the interior light lens

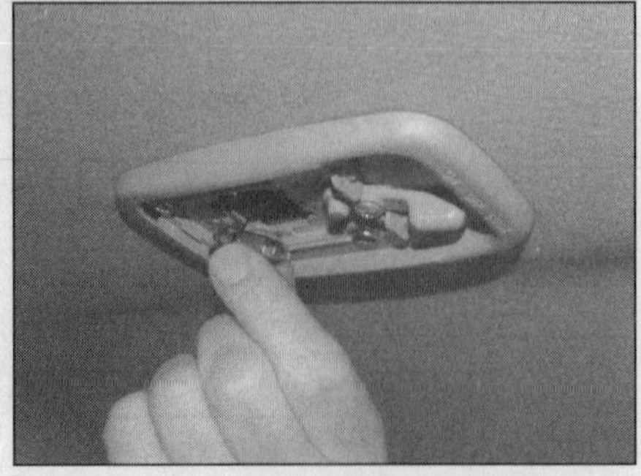
6.3 Pull the bulb from the spring contacts

6.6 Interior light mounting screws

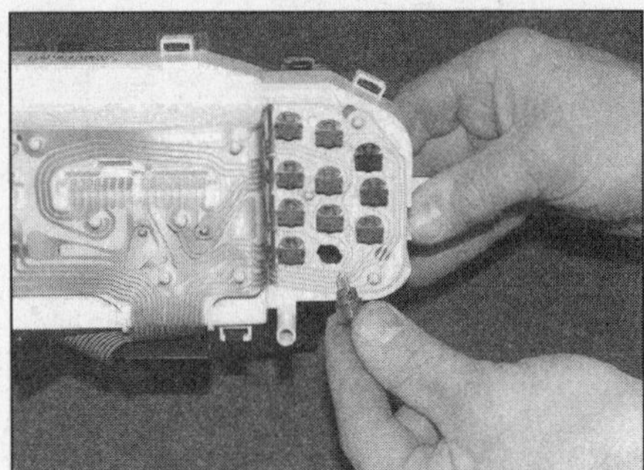

6.11 Twist the bulbholders from the back of the instrument panel

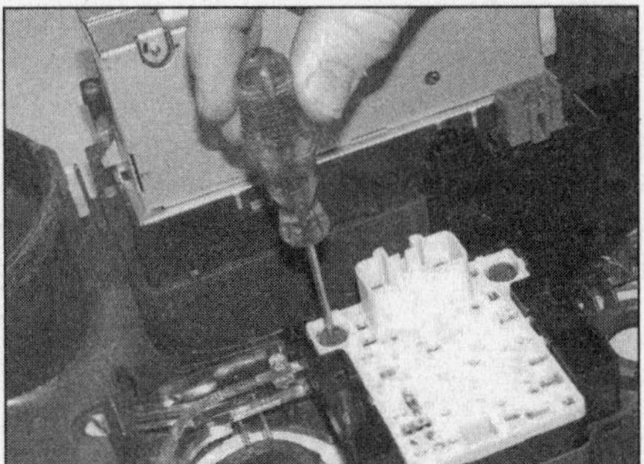

6.15a Unscrew the bulbholder using a screwdriver . . .

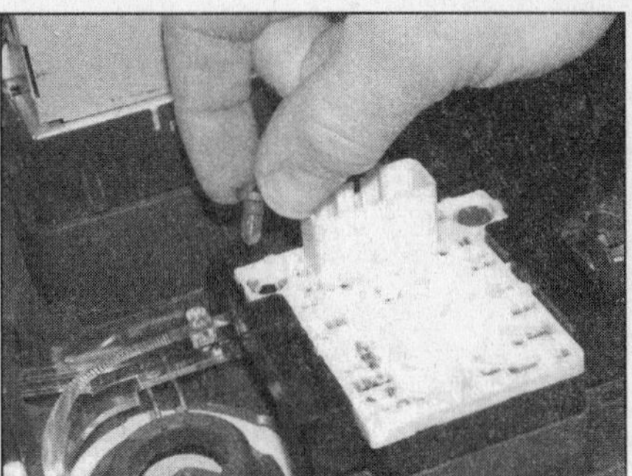

6.15b . . . and withdraw it from the heater control panel

Instrument panel illumination

10 Remove the instrument panel as described in Section 10.

11 Twist the relevant bulbholder anti-clockwise and remove it from the rear of the panel **(see illustration)**. Depending on type, the instrument panel bulbs will either be one-piece items (with integral bulbs), or will have a wedge-base bulb, which can be pulled out.

12 Refit the instrument panel as described in Section 10.

Switch illumination

13 The bulbs are integral with the switches, and cannot be renewed separately.

Heater control illumination

14 Remove the heater control panel as described in Chapter 3.

15 Twist the relevant bulbholder anti-clockwise using a screwdriver in the slot provided, and remove it from the rear of the panel. The bulb appears to be integral with the holder **(see illustrations)**.

16 Refit the heater control panel as described in Chapter 3.

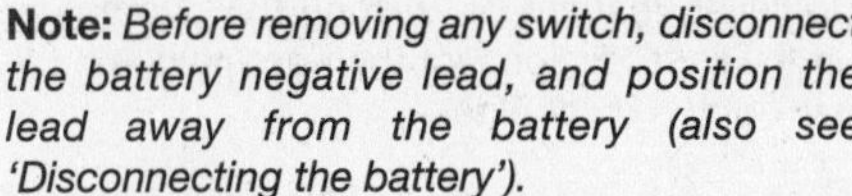

7 Exterior light units – removal and refitting

Note: *Before removing any switch, disconnect the battery negative lead, and position the lead away from the battery (also see 'Disconnecting the battery').*

Headlight

1 Remove the front bumper as described in Chapter 11.

2 Remove the two headlight securing screws on the top of the unit, and lift the mountings to release them from the front panel **(see illustrations)**.

3 Using a screwdriver, prise up the retaining tab at the front lower corner of the light unit to release it **(see illustration)**.

4 Pull the unit forwards slightly, to disconnect the outer rear securing clip **(see illustration)**.

5 Slide the unit forwards, then disconnect the four wiring connectors from the back of the headlight – three bulbholders, one adjustment motor – and remove it **(see illustrations)**.

6 Note that, in the event of damage to the headlight, the lens can be unclipped (six clips in total) and a new one fitted. In this case, check the condition of the seal fitted between the lens and the light unit.

7 Refitting is a reversal of removal.

Front direction indicator light

8 The front indicator is integral with the headlight.

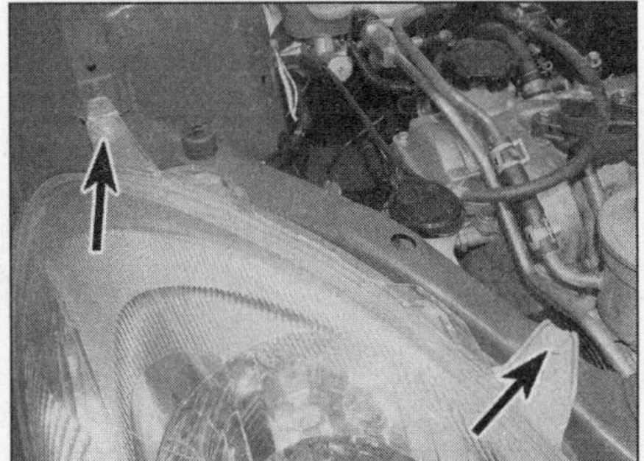

7.2a Remove the two upper mounting screws . . .

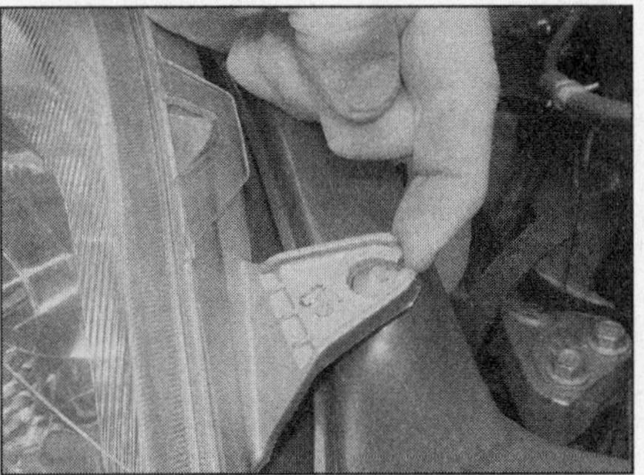

7.2b . . . and lift the mounting tabs to release them

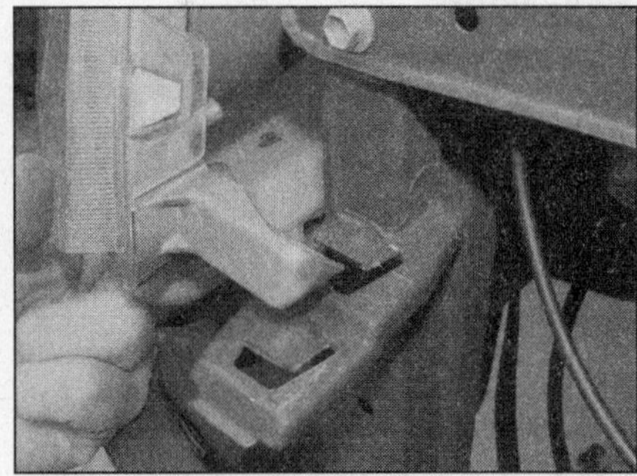

7.3 Prise up the metal clip to release the headlight

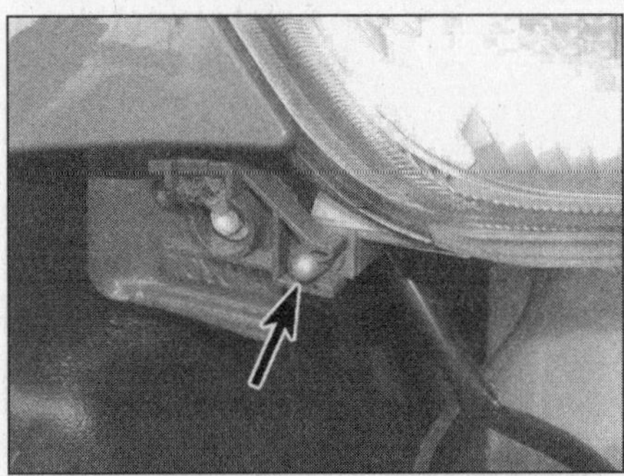

7.4 Pull the headlight forwards to detach the outer clip

7.5a Pull the headlight forwards . . .

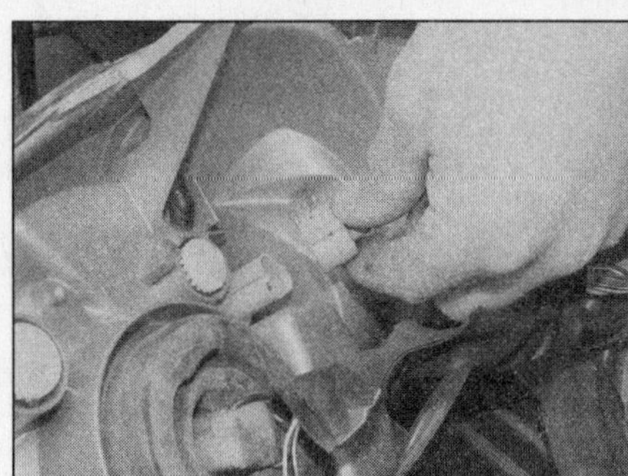

7.5b . . . then disconnect the four wiring plugs on the back, and remove it

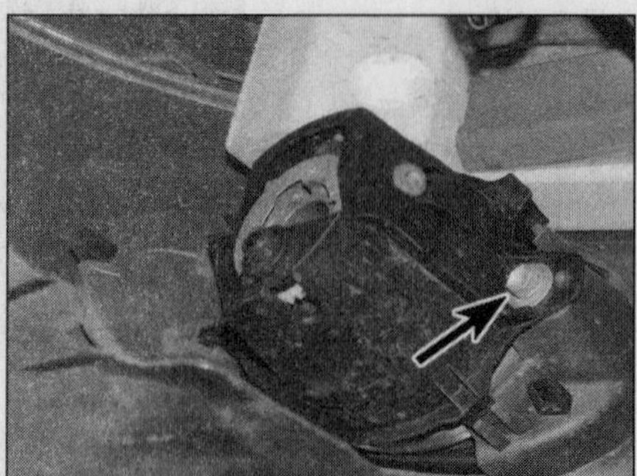
7.13 Undo the mounting bolt (arrowed) then unclip and remove the foglight

7.16 Unclip the trim panel from the back of the light unit

7.17 Disconnect the single wiring plug from the bulbholder

Front foglight

9 Turn the steering wheel to give the best access to the front of the wheel arch.

10 Remove the three cross-head screws securing the front half of the wheel arch liner, and pull the liner back for access to the bulbholder.

11 Press the back of the wiring plug, and pull it down to disconnect it.

12 Taking care not to damage the paintwork, prise the foglight front trim panel from the bumper using a small screwdriver.

13 Remove the mounting bolt at the back, then unclip and remove the light from the bumper **(see illustration)**.

14 Refitting is a reversal of removal.

Indicator side repeater light

15 The procedure is described as part of the bulb renewal procedure in Section 5.

Rear lights

16 Open the tailgate, and unclip the trim panel from the back of the light unit, for access to the bulbholders **(see illustration)**.

17 Disconnect the wiring plug from the bulbholder **(see illustration)**.

18 Support the light from outside, then unscrew and remove the central nut from the back of the light **(see illustration)**.

19 Remove the light from the car – it may be stuck on the body seal **(see illustration)**.

20 Refitting is a reversal of removal. Check the condition of the body seal before fitting the light – if necessary, fit a new one to prevent water leaks.

Rear number plate light

21 The procedure is described as part of the bulb renewal procedure in Section 5. However, instead of twisting the bulbholder off the light, disconnect the wiring plug on the back of the bulbholder.

High-level stop-light

22 The procedure is described as part of the bulb renewal procedure in Section 5. However, instead of twisting the bulbholder off the light, disconnect the wiring plug on the back of the bulbholder.

8 Headlight adjuster components – removal and refitting

Adjuster switch

1 Refer to Section 4.

Adjuster motor

2 The motor is integral with the headlight, and is not available separately. The headlight is removed as described in Section 7.

9 Headlight beam alignment – general information

1 All models are equipped with an electrical vertical beam adjuster unit – this can be used to adjust the headlight beam to compensate for the relevant load which the car is carrying. An adjuster switch is provided on the facia. Refer to the car's handbook for further information.

2 Accurate adjustment of the headlight beam is only possible using optical beam-setting equipment, and this work should therefore be carried out by a Toyota dealer or suitably-equipped workshop.

3 For reference, the headlights can be finely adjusted by rotating the adjuster screws fitted to the rear of each light unit **(see illustration)**. The vertical adjustment screw is mounted at the outer end of the headlight. The horizontal adjustment screw is mounted at the inner end of the headlight.

10 Instrument panel – removal and refitting

1 The digital instrument display fitted to most Yaris models is so unusual it deserves special mention. The display seen is in fact an enlarged virtual image – the system features a vacuum fluorescent display tube, which projects the image of the digits onto a magnifying mirror. Besides creating a display which is easily read from many angles, this type of digital dash is less susceptible to reflections and direct sunlight.

Removal

2 Disconnect the battery negative lead, and position the lead away from the battery (also see *Disconnecting the battery*).

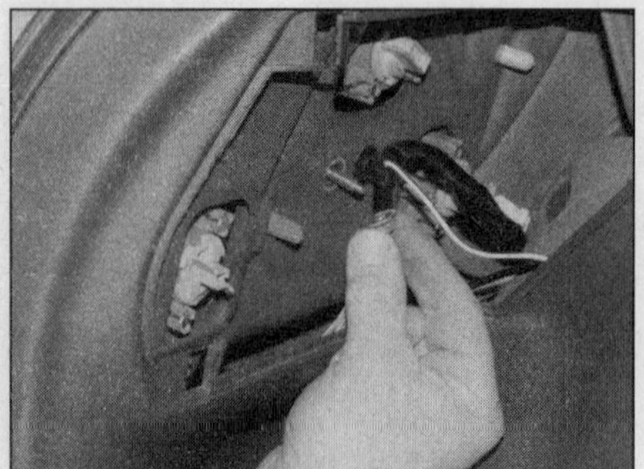
7.18 Unscrew the central nut . . .

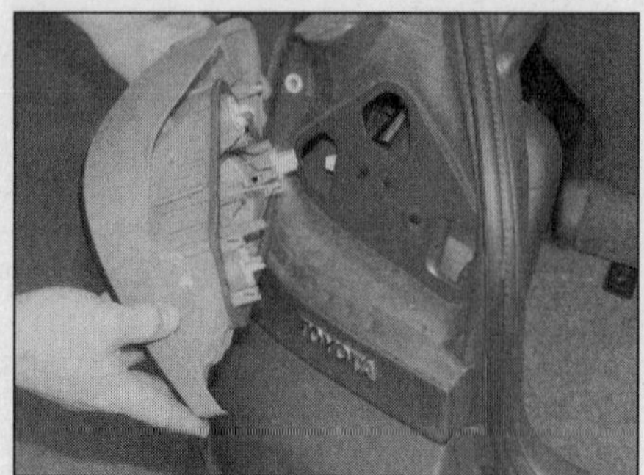
7.19 . . . and withdraw the light unit from the car

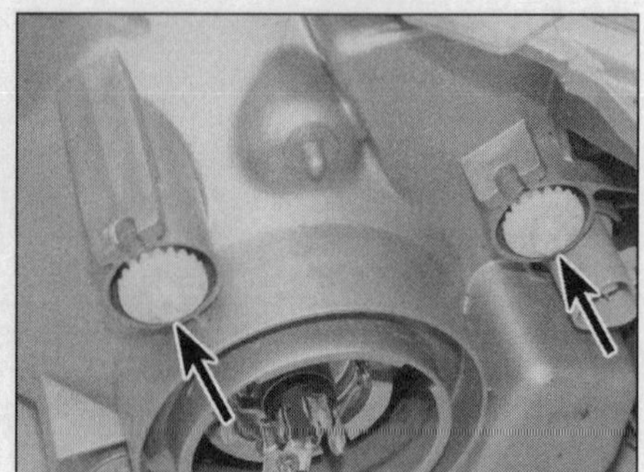
9.3 Headlight beam adjusters

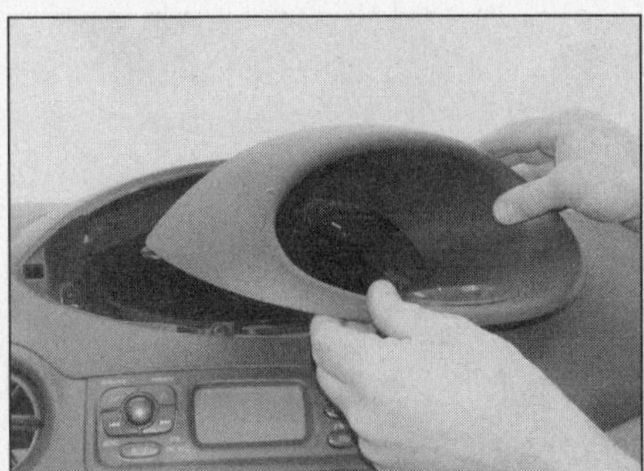
10.3 Release the instrument panel surround . . .

10.4 . . . and disconnect the wiring plug

10.5 Remove the four instrument panel mounting screws

10.6a Disconnect the wiring plug at the side . . .

10.6b . . . and the two from the back of the instrument panel

3 Taking care not to mark the trim, prise out the instrument panel surround from the facia (we found it was possible to remove this just by pulling). Work round the surround until it is free, and lift it out **(see illustration)**.

4 Disconnect the surround wiring plug, and remove it **(see illustration)**.

5 Remove the mounting screw either side of the instrument panel, and two more at the front, and withdraw it **(see illustration)**.

6 Disconnect the wiring plugs from the side and back of the panel, and remove it from the facia **(see illustrations)**.

Refitting

7 Refitting is a reversal of removal.

11 Clock/multi-function display panel – removal and refitting

Removal

1 Remove the heater control panel as described in Chapter 3.

2 Turn the panel over, and remove the two screws securing the display panel.

3 Withdraw the display panel from the heater panel.

Refitting

4 Refitting is a reversal of removal. Refit the heater control panel as described in Chapter 3.

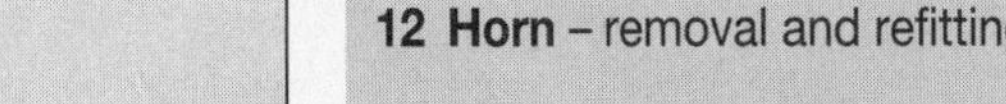

12 Horn – removal and refitting

Removal

1 Open the bonnet, and disconnect the wiring plug **(see illustration)**.

2 Unscrew the single horn mounting bolt, and withdraw the horn from its mounting **(see illustration)**.

Refitting

3 Refitting is a reversal of removal.

13 Wiper arms – removal and refitting

Removal

1 Operate the wiper motor, then switch it off so that the wiper arm returns to the 'park' position.

Stick a piece of masking tape along the edge of the wiper blade, to use as an alignment aid on refitting.

12.1 Disconnect the horn wiring plug

12.2 Unscrew the horn mounting bolt, and remove the unit

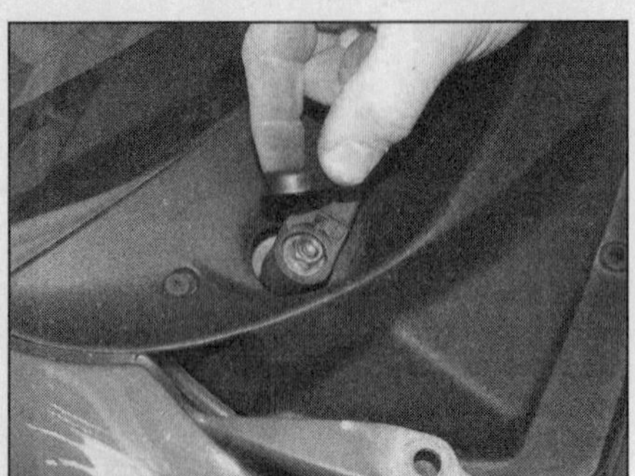

13.2a Prise off the windscreen wiper arm nut cover . . .

13.2b . . . then unscrew and remove the nut

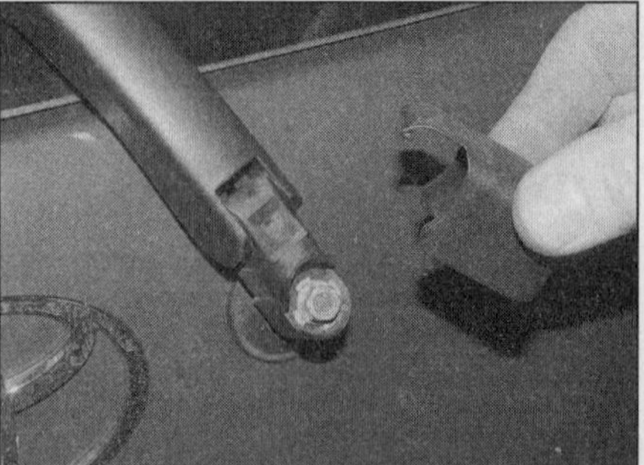

13.2c Prise the tailgate wiper arm cover up, or off completely, to access the nut beneath

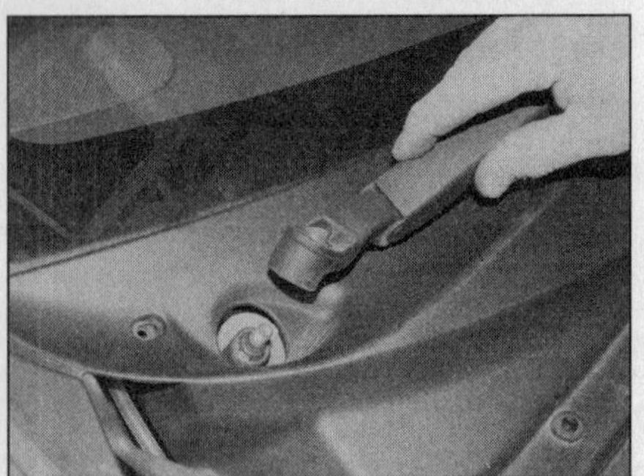

13.3a Remove the windscreen wiper arm off the splines

13.3b Unscrew the nut, then work the tailgate wiper arm off the splined spindle

2 Prise off the wiper arm spindle nut cover, then slacken and remove the spindle nut **(see illustrations)**.

3 Lift the blade off the glass, and pull the wiper arm off its spindle **(see illustrations)**. Note that on some models, the wiper arms may be very tight on the spindle splines – it should be possible to lever the arm off the spindle, using a flat-bladed screwdriver (take care not to damage the scuttle cover panel). In extreme cases, it may even be necessary to use a small puller to free the arm.

Refitting

4 Ensure that the wiper arm and spindle splines are clean and dry, then refit the arm to the spindle. Where applicable, align the wiper blade with the tape fitted on removal.

5 Refit the spindle nut, tightening it securely, and clip the nut cover back into position.

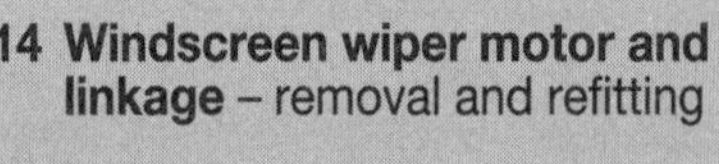

14 Windscreen wiper motor and linkage – removal and refitting

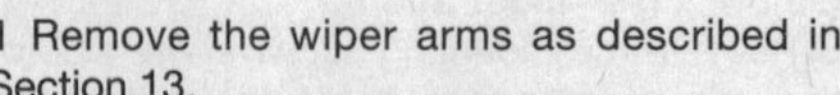

Removal

1 Remove the wiper arms as described in Section 13.

2 Peel off the rubber weatherstrip along the edge of the windscreen lower cover panel.

3 Unclip the central section of the cover panel, and remove it **(see illustration)**.

4 Unscrew and prise out the various screw/clip fasteners from the two remaining cover panels, then unclip and remove them **(see illustrations)**.

5 Disconnect the wiper motor wiring plug **(see illustration)**.

6 Remove the three bolts, and lift out the wiper motor and linkage from below the

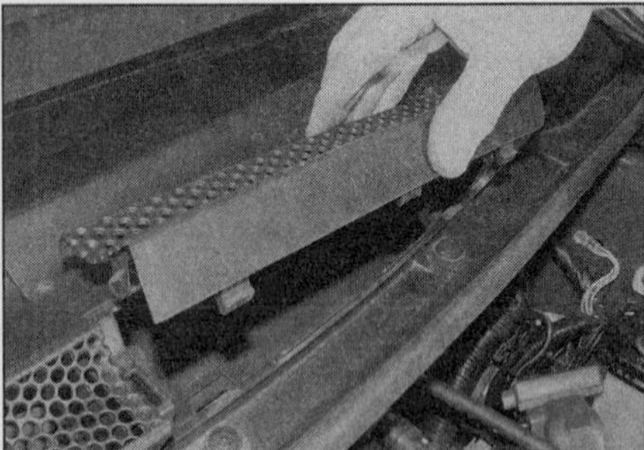

14.3 Unclip the central section of the cover panel

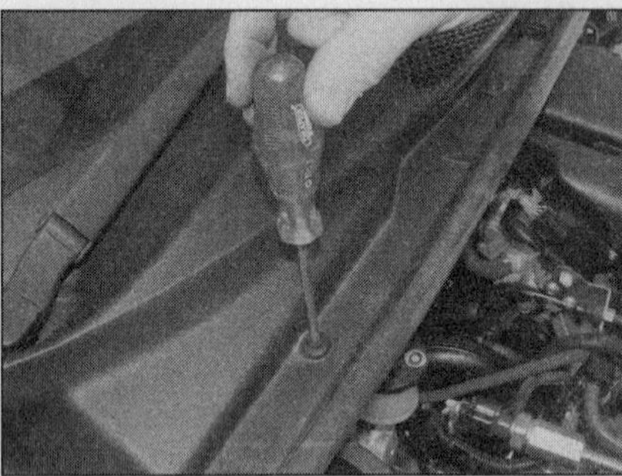

14.4a Unscrew the cover panel screw/clip fasteners . . .

14.4b . . . then prise them out

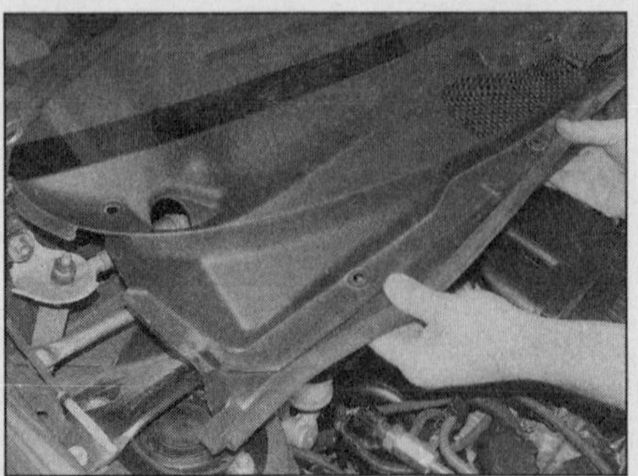

14.4c Unclip and remove the two panel halves

14.5 Disconnect the wiring plug from the wiper motor

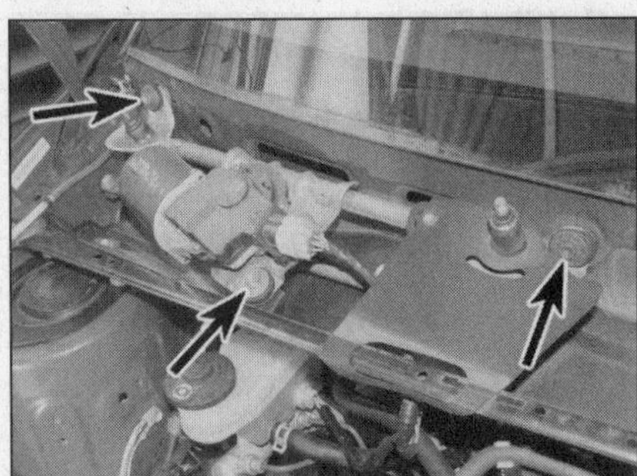

14.6a Remove the wiper motor assembly mounting bolts . . .

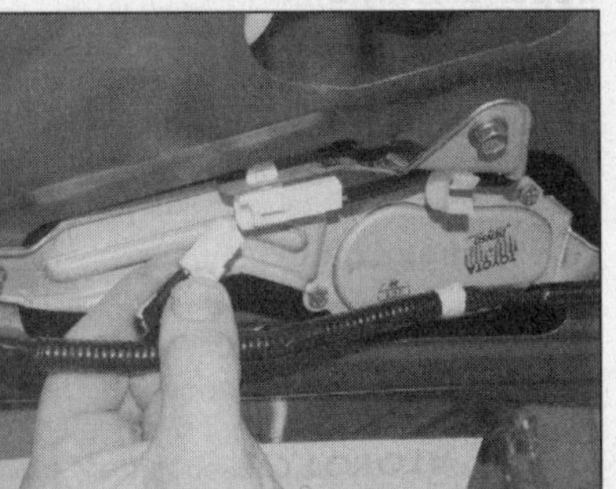

15.3 Disconnect the wiper motor wiring plug

windscreen **(see illustrations)**. If the wiper motor and linkage is being removed for access to another component, this is all the dismantling which is required. To separate the motor and linkage, proceed as follows.

7 Remove the nut (and recover the washer) from the motor spindle.

8 Before removing the wiper motor itself, paint or scribe a mark across the motor spindle and the mounting frame.

9 Remove the three screws, and separate the wiper motor from the frame.

Refitting

10 Refitting is a reversal of removal, bearing in mind the following points:

a) Ensure that the motor spindle is in the 'parked' position (align the marks made before removal), then refit the washer and tighten the nut.

14.6b . . . and lift out the wiper motor and linkage

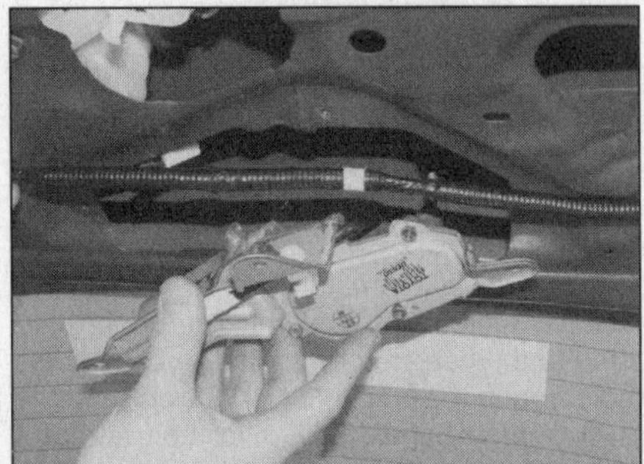

15.4 Remove the three mounting bolts, and withdraw the wiper motor

b) Tighten all fasteners securely.

c) Refit the wiper arms with reference to Section 13.

15 Tailgate wiper motor – removal and refitting

Removal

1 Remove the wiper arm as described in Section 13.

2 Open the tailgate, and remove the inner trim panel, which is secured by eight push-in clips.

3 Disconnect the wiper motor wiring plug **(see illustration)**.

4 Remove the three motor mounting bolts, and remove the motor from the tailgate **(see illustration)**. If the grommet/spacer on the outside of the tailgate is loose, remove it for safekeeping until the wiper motor is refitted.

Refitting

5 Refitting is a reversal of removal. Tighten the mounting bolts securely.

16 Windscreen/tailgate washer system components – removal and refitting

Washer fluid reservoir

Removal

1 Remove the front bumper as described in Chapter 11.

2 Remove the driver's-side headlight as described in Section 7.

3 Disconnect the wiring plug from the washer pump **(see illustration)**.

4 Anticipate some spillage of washer fluid (have a suitable container ready), then disconnect the washer hoses, noting their fitted locations.

5 Remove the reservoir mounting bolts, then lift the reservoir to disengage the mounting pegs on the inner wing **(see illustrations)**. Manoeuvre it out from its location, taking care not to damage the filler neck.

Refitting

6 Refitting is a reversal of removal. Make sure the washer hoses are securely reconnected to their original positions.

Washer fluid pump

Removal

7 Proceed as described in paragraphs 1 to 4.

8 Prise the pump from the reservoir, and recover the rubber sealing grommet.

Refitting

9 Examine the rubber sealing grommet, and renew if necessary.

10 Refitting is a reversal of removal, but take care not to push the grommet into the reservoir when refitting the pump. Make sure that the pump is securely fitted in its sealing grommet, and make sure that the fluid hose(s) are securely reconnected.

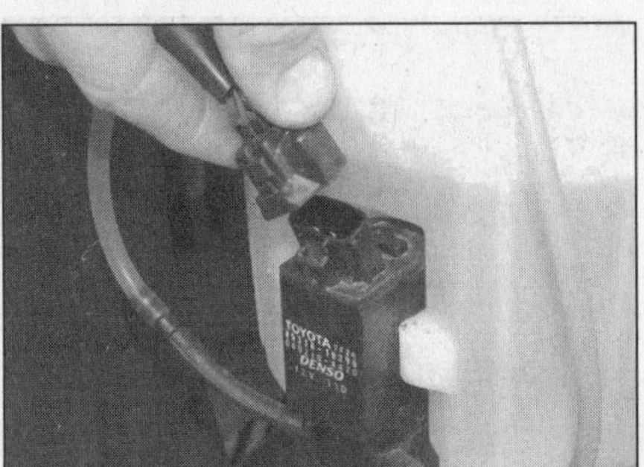

16.3 Disconnect the wiring plug from the washer pump

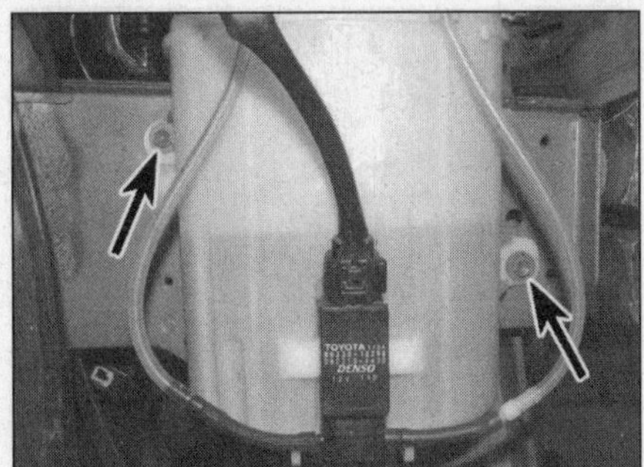

16.5a Washer reservoir mounting bolts

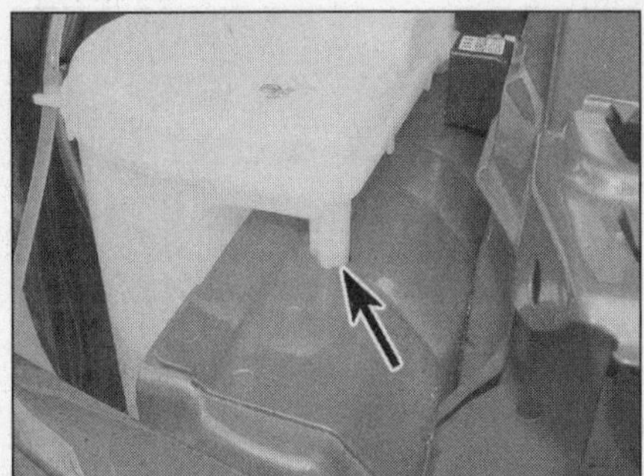

16.5b Reservoir is also mounted on pegs to the inner wing

Windscreen washer jet

Removal

11 Taking care not to damage the paintwork, carefully prise the washer jet from the outside of the bonnet.

12 Disconnect the washer hose from the jet, and remove it completely. Tape the hose to the bonnet if possible, to stop it dropping down inside.

Refitting

13 Refitting is a reversal of removal, but make sure that the fluid hose connections are securely remade.

Tailgate washer jet

Removal

14 Remove the high-level stop-light as described in Section 7.

15 Anticipating some fluid spillage, disconnect the fluid hose from the base of the jet **(see illustration)**. Tape the hose to the tailgate if possible, to stop it dropping down inside.

16 Taking care not to damage the paintwork, carefully prise the washer jet from the top of the tailgate **(see illustration)**.

Refitting

17 Refitting is a reversal of removal, but make sure that the fluid hose connection is securely remade.

16.15 Disconnect the fluid hose from the jet

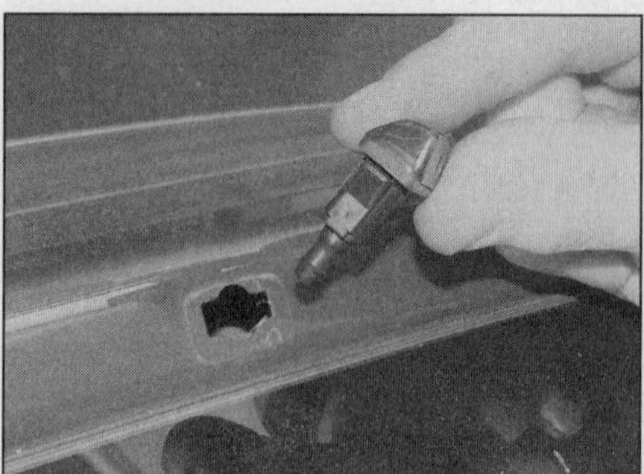

16.16 Prise out and remove the jet from the tailgate

17 Radio unit – removal and refitting

Removal

1 The audio equipment fitted to the Yaris is typically split into two units. The upper unit, fitted to the heater control panel, contains the radio frequency and volume controls, and the LCD display panel. The lower unit (either a cassette or CD player), is fitted to the lower section of the facia, and is the 'main' unit, with all the speaker and aerial connections. Also note that the Yaris audio equipment does not have a security code – all that will be lost when disconnecting it are any preset radio stations.

Upper display unit

2 Remove the heater control (front) panel as described in Chapter 3.

3 Remove the two screws at the rear on the top, then release the clips below, and withdraw the unit from the panel **(see illustrations)**.

Lower 'main' unit

4 Remove the heater control (front) panel as described in Chapter 3. To gain the best access to the unit's two upper mounting screws, the rear section of the heater control panel should also be unclipped from the facia, but it is not necessary to disconnect the heater control cables.

5 Pull out the ashtray, and remove it.

6 Remove the four screws (two above, two below inside the ashtray aperture) securing the unit to the facia **(see illustrations)**.

7 Pull the unit forwards to release the

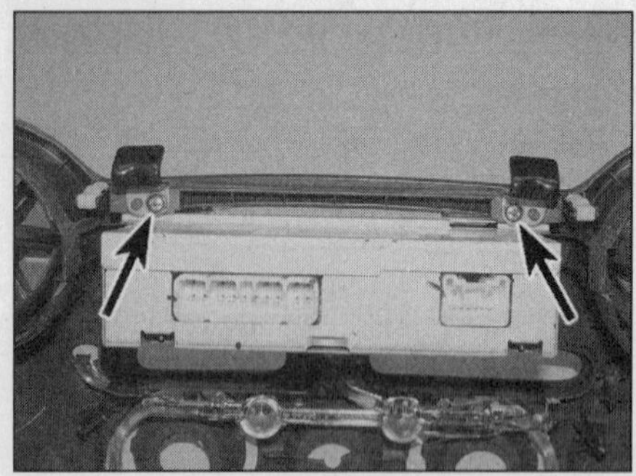

17.3a Remove the two screws on the top . . .

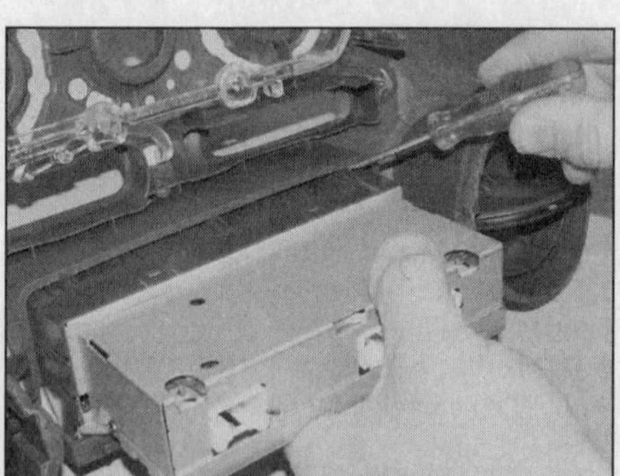

17.3b . . . then release the tabs on the lower edge using a screwdriver . . .

17.3c . . . and remove the display unit from the heater control panel

17.6a Remove the two upper screws . . .

17.6b . . . and the two screws in the ashtray aperture, on the left . . .

17.6c . . . and on the right-hand side

17.7 Pull the unit forwards to release the four mounting clips

mounting clips (one at each corner), and withdraw it **(see illustration)**.

8 Disconnect the power and speaker wiring plugs, the aerial lead, and the cigar lighter wiring plug, and remove the unit **(see illustrations)**.

Refitting

9 Refitting is a reversal of removal. Refit the heater control panel as described in Chapter 3.

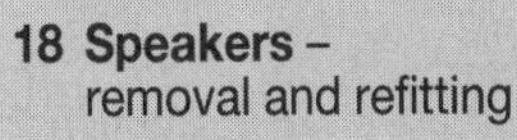

18 Speakers – removal and refitting

Door speaker

1 Remove the front door trim panel as described in Chapter 11.

2 Disconnect the speaker wiring plug **(see illustration)**.

3 The door speakers are secured to the inner door panel by three rivets **(see illustration)**. Using a 4 mm drill bit, drill out the rivets and remove the speaker from the door.

4 It is advisable to vacuum up the drilling debris from the inside of the door before refitting.

5 Refitting is a reversal of removal. The speaker is best riveted back into place; if a rivet gun is not available, consider carefully before using other methods to secure it. Bolts or self-tapping screws which are too long may catch on the window or its regulator.

Facia speaker

6 Taking care not to damage the facia, first prise up the speaker cover at the rear, then pull it rearwards to release the mounting lugs from under the windscreen **(see illustration)**.

7 Using a short screwdriver, remove the two speaker mounting screws.

8 Lift the speaker out of its location, disconnect its wiring plug, and remove it from the facia **(see illustration)**.

9 Refitting is a reversal of removal.

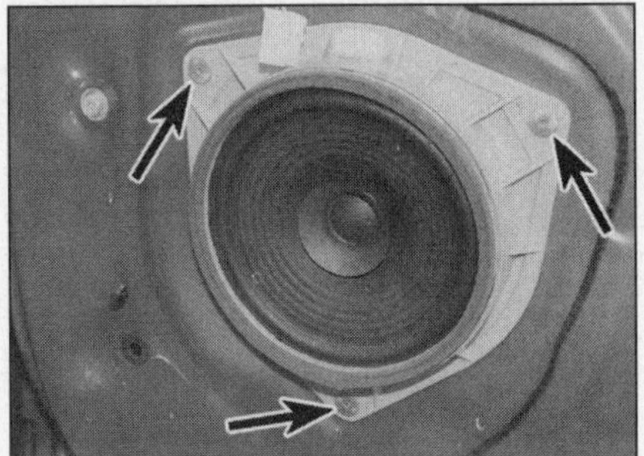
18.3 The speaker is secured by three rivets, which must be drilled out

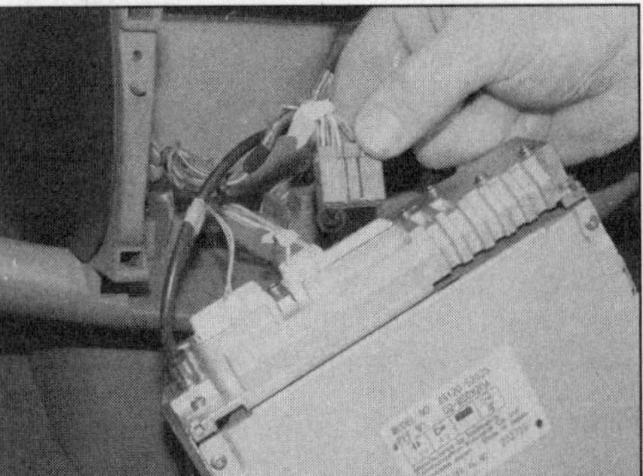
17.8a Disconnect the power and speaker plugs . . .

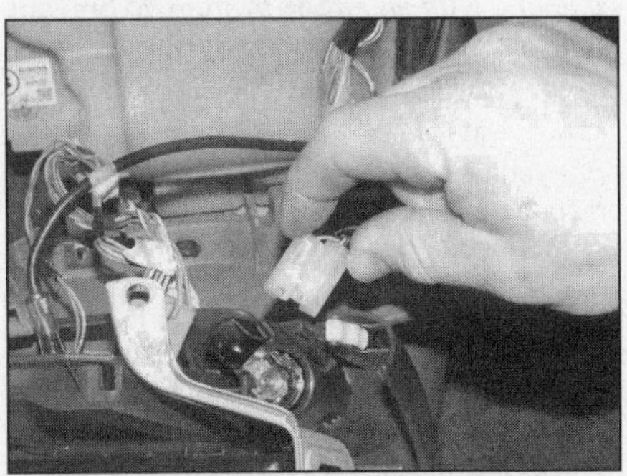
17.8c . . . as well as the cigar lighter wiring plug

17.8b . . . and the aerial lead from the main unit . . .

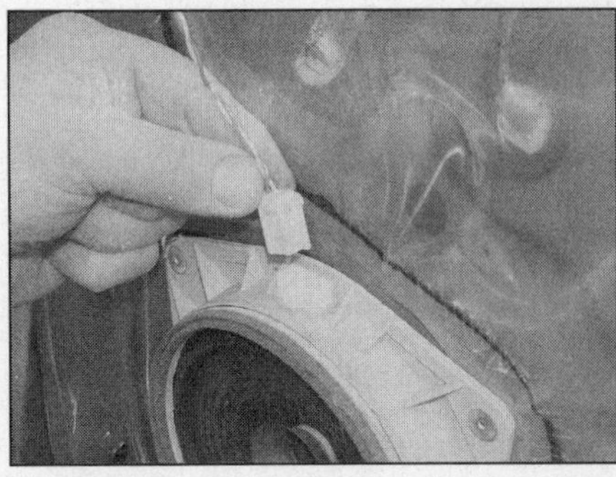
18.2 Disconnect the wiring plug from the door speaker

19 Radio aerial – removal and refitting

Removal

1 If only the aerial mast is to be removed, this can be unscrewed from the aerial base.

2 Removing the aerial base requires that the headlining must be unclipped and lowered at the front, which is not a job to be undertaken lightly. It is advisable to remove the grab handles and sun visors (as described in Chapter 11, Section 24), and even the interior light (Section 6). The front door rubber seals will also need to be pulled away from the door frames.

3 Remove the radio unit as described in Section 17.

4 The aerial lead runs across the top of the lower section of the facia (remove the upper section for access, as described in Chapter 11). From there, it runs up the driver's A-pillar, and across to the base of the aerial, where it is secured by a nut.

5 Once the aerial lead has been disconnected, remove the aerial base fasteners, and remove the base from the roof. Recover the sealing grommet.

Refitting

6 Refitting is a reversal of removal.

18.6 Lift up the speaker cover at the rear, and remove it

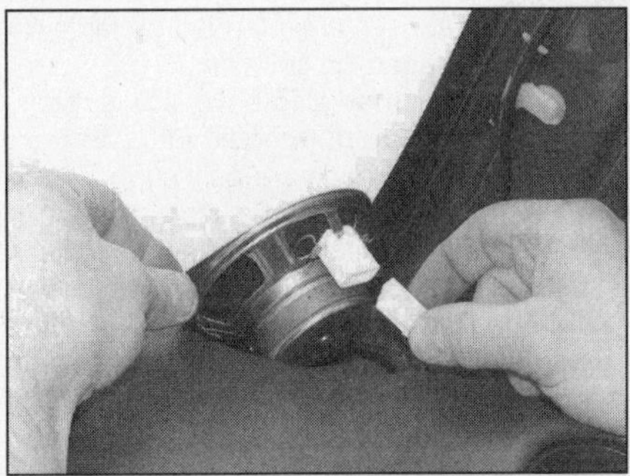
18.8 Remove the two screws, disconnect the wiring plug, and remove the speaker

20 Anti-theft immobiliser – general information

An engine immobiliser system is fitted as standard to all models, and the system is operated automatically every time the ignition key is inserted/removed.

The immobiliser system ensures that the car can only be started using the original Toyota keys supplied with the car when new. Each key contains an electronic chip (transponder) which is programmed with a code. When the key is inserted into the ignition switch, it uses the current present in the sensor coil (which is fitted to the switch housing) to send a signal to the immobiliser electronic control unit (ECU). The ECU checks this code every time the ignition is switched on. If the key code does not match the ECU code, the ECU will disable the fuel pump and ignition circuits to prevent the engine being started.

The security indicator light on the facia panel indicates when the system is active. Should the light continue to flash once the ignition key has been inserted, the engine will not start – the most likely reason for this being the use of an uncoded key.

If the ignition key is lost, a new one can be obtained from a Toyota dealer. They have access to the correct key code for the immobiliser system of your car, and will be able to supply a new coded key.

If you have any spare keys cut, if they are not coded correctly, they will only open the doors, etc, and will not be capable of starting the engine. For this reason, it may be best to have any spare keys supplied by your Toyota dealer.

21 Airbag system – general information, precautions and system de-activation

General information

Driver's and front seat passenger's airbags are fitted as standard equipment on most models. The driver's airbag is fitted to the steering wheel centre pad, while the passenger's unit is fitted to the top of the facia. These airbags are intended to deploy in the event of a head-on collision.

Later models may also have side airbags, which fire from modules built into the front seats. The side airbags are only supposed to be triggered in the event of a lateral impact.

The system is armed only when the ignition is switched on. However, a reserve power source maintains a power supply to the system in the event of a break in the main electrical supply. The system is activated by 'g' sensors (deceleration sensors), incorporated in the electronic control unit. All models have separate sensors, bolted to each of the front chassis legs, while models with side airbags have further sensors in the B-pillars (and in the front doors on 3-door models). Note that the electronic control unit also controls the front seat belt tensioners, fitted to all models.

The airbags are inflated by gas generators, which force the bags out from their locations. Although these are safety items, their deployment is violently rapid, and this may cause injury if they are triggered unintentionally.

Precautions

Warning: The following precautions must be observed when working on vehicles equipped with an airbag system, to prevent the possibility of personal injury.

General precautions

The following precautions **must** be observed when carrying out work on a vehicle equipped with an airbag:

a) Do not disconnect the battery with the engine running.
b) Before carrying out any work in the vicinity of the airbag, removal of any of the airbag components, or any welding work on the car, de-activate the system as described in the following sub-Section.
c) Do not attempt to test any of the airbag system circuits using test meters or any other test equipment.
d) If the airbag warning light comes on, or any fault in the system is suspected, consult a Toyota dealer without delay. Do not attempt to carry out fault diagnosis, or any dismantling of the components.

When handling an airbag

a) Transport the airbag by itself, bag upwards.
b) Do not put your arms around the airbag.
c) Carry the airbag close to the body, bag outwards.
d) Do not drop the airbag or expose it to impacts.
e) Do not attempt to dismantle the airbag unit.
f) Do not connect any form of electrical equipment to any part of the airbag circuit.

When storing an airbag unit

a) Store the unit in a cupboard with the airbag upwards.
b) Do not expose the airbag to temperatures above 80°C.
c) Do not expose the airbag to flames.
d) Do not attempt to dispose of the airbag – consult a Toyota dealer.
e) Never refit an airbag which is known to be faulty or damaged.

De-activation of airbag system

The system must be de-activated as follows, before carrying out any work on the airbag components or surrounding area.

a) Switch off the ignition.
b) Remove the ignition key.
c) Switch off all electrical equipment.
d) Disconnect the battery negative lead (see 'Disconnecting the battery').
e) Insulate the battery negative terminal and the end of the battery negative lead to prevent any possibility of contact.
*f) **Wait for at least two minutes** before carrying out any further work.*

22 Airbag system components – removal and refitting

Warning: Refer to the precautions given in Section 21 before attempting to carry out work on the airbag components.

Driver's airbag

Removal

1 De-activate the airbag system as described in Section 21. The airbag unit is an integral part of the steering wheel centre pad.

2 The airbag's two Torx screws are fitted to the back of the steering wheel centre pad, and are recessed **(see illustration)**. It is likely the screws will be quite tight, especially if they have not been disturbed recently – use only the proper tools to remove them. The screws cannot be removed completely – when the screw head is flush with the back of the wheel pad, it has been released.

3 To free the airbag unit completely, carefully pull away the back section of the wheel boss each side – this will pull the airbag screws out a fraction, and allow the airbag to be released **(see illustration)**.

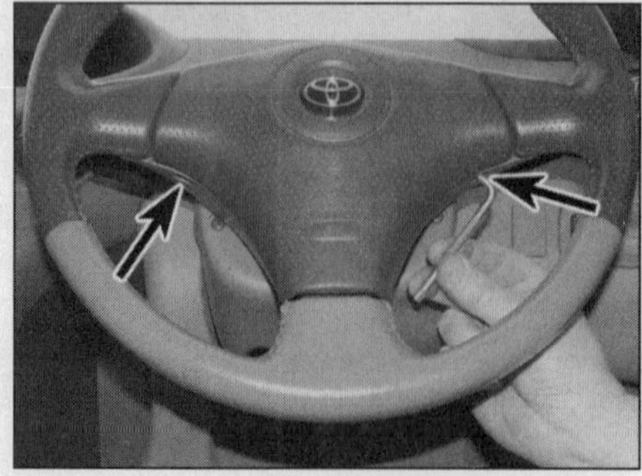

22.2 Driver's airbag Torx screw locations

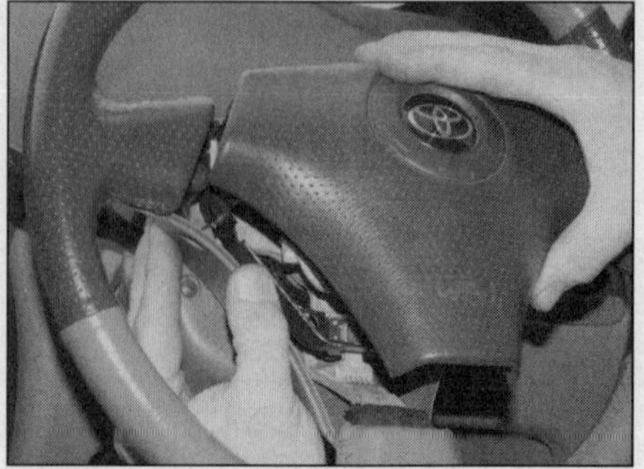

22.3 Pull back the edges of the wheel boss to free the airbag

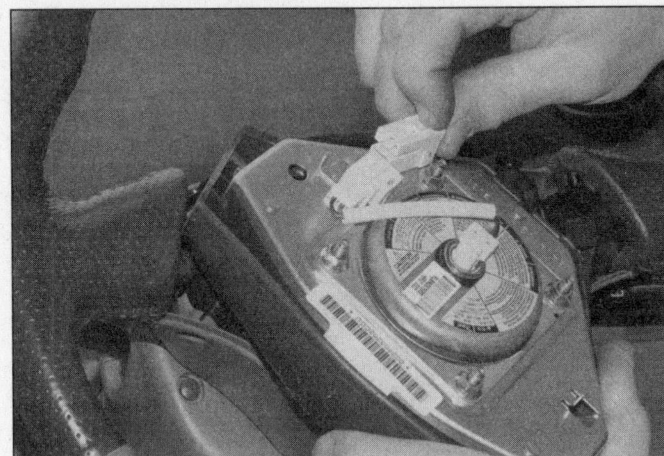
22.4 Press and slide back the locking catch on the airbag wiring plug

22.9 Passenger airbag retaining nuts

22.15a Slide back the catch and disconnect the airbag wiring plug . . .

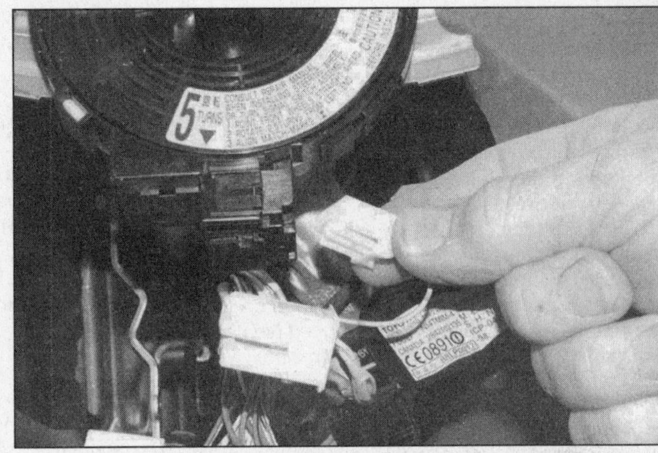
22.15b . . . and the horn connector from the clockspring

4 Lift the unit from the wheel, and disconnect the wiring plug as follows, according to type:

a) *Press and slide back the locking catch **(see illustration)**.*

b) *Prise up the small yellow section on the back of the plug, then prise the main body of the plug up to disconnect it.*

5 Remove the airbag and store it in a safe place, with reference to the precautions in Section 21.

Refitting

6 Refitting is a reversal of removal, noting the following points:

a) *The battery must still be disconnected when reconnecting the airbag wiring.*

b) *Ensure that the airbag wiring plug is securely reconnected.*

c) *Tighten the airbag Torx screws securely.*

Passenger's airbag

Removal

7 De-activate the airbag system as described in Section 21.

8 Remove the upper section of the facia panel as described in Chapter 11.

9 Turn the facia panel over, and remove the two airbag retaining nuts **(see illustration)**.

10 Carefully prise up the six clips round the edge of the airbag, and release the unit from the facia.

Refitting

11 Refitting is a reversal of removal, bearing in mind the following points:

a) *The battery must still be disconnected when reconnecting the airbag wiring.*

b) *Make sure that the wiring harness is routed as noted before removal, and that the connectors are reconnected to their original positions.*

c) *Make sure that the wiring connectors are securely reconnected.*

d) *Tighten the airbag mounting nuts securely.*

Airbag clockspring (rotary connector)

Removal

12 Remove the driver's airbag unit as described previously in this Section.

13 Remove the steering wheel as described in Chapter 10.

14 Remove the steering column shrouds as described in Chapter 11, Section 24.

15 Noting their positions for refitting, disconnect the (yellow) airbag wiring plug and the (white) horn connector from the clockspring **(see illustrations)**.

16 If the clockspring will be off the car for any length of time, secure it using tape so that it is not turned **(see illustration)**.

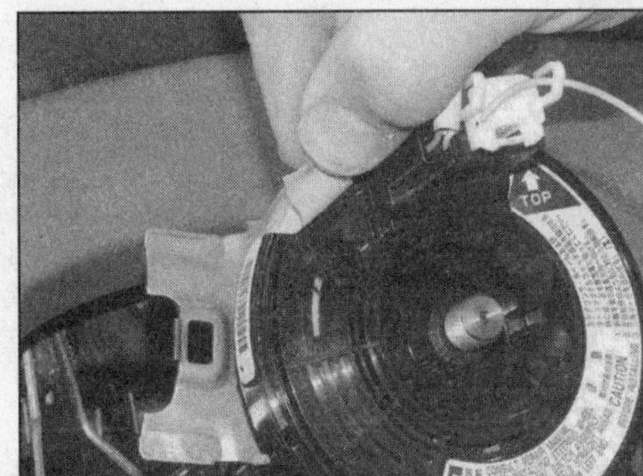
22.16 Secure the clockspring in its centred position using a piece of tape

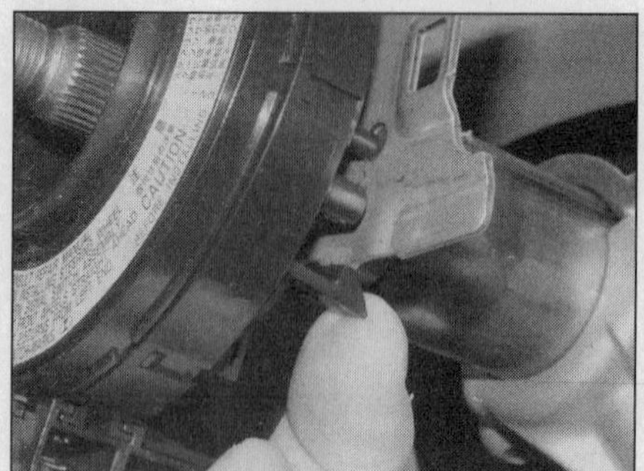

22.17a Release the plastic clip either side . . .

22.17b . . . and the metal one, at the top . . .

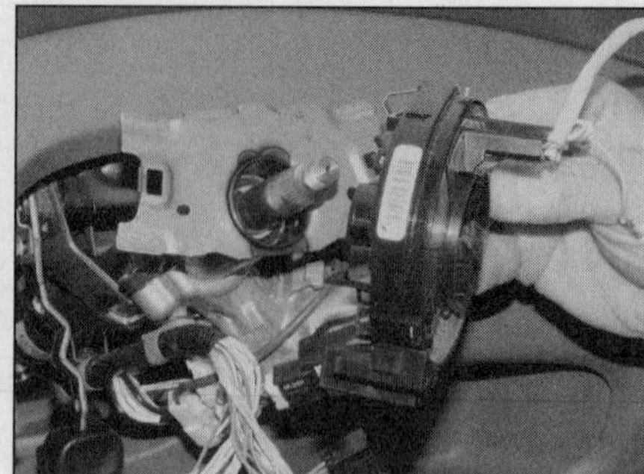

22.17c . . . then withdraw the clockspring without turning it

17 Release the clips at the back of the unit (one each side, one at the top), then withdraw the clockspring unit from the column – take care not to turn it as it is removed **(see illustrations)**.

Refitting

18 Refitting is a reversal of removal.

19 Before refitting the steering wheel, the clockspring unit should be centralised (unless it is known absolutely that the steering wheel was centralised before removal, and that the clockspring has not been turned during or since its removal).

20 First, turn the clockspring anti-clockwise gently, until resistance is felt. Now turn the clockspring about two and a half turns clockwise, until the arrowhead markings on the front face and outer cover are aligned **(see illustration)**. **Note:** *It is not enough to simply align the marks – the unit must be centralised first, with the marks as confirmation.*

21 Refit the steering wheel as described in Chapter 10.

Side airbags

22 The side airbags are located internally within the front seat backrest, and no attempt should be made to remove them. Any suspected problems with the side airbag system should be referred to a Toyota dealer.

Airbag control unit

Removal

23 The airbag control unit is located behind the curved trim panel in front of the centre console. Before removing the control unit, de-activate the airbag system as described in Section 21.

24 Prise out the trim clip from the side of the trim panel, then unclip and remove the panel from under the facia.

25 Disconnect the wiring plugs from the front of the sensor. If there is any chance of incorrectly refitting them, mark them for position first.

26 Remove the four T40 Torx bolts used to secure the sensor, and remove it from the floor.

Refitting

27 Refitting is a reversal of removal, bearing in mind the following points:

a) *The battery must still be disconnected when reconnecting the airbag wiring.*
b) *Make sure that the wiring connectors are securely reconnected.*
c) *Tighten the mounting bolts to the specified torque – this is essential if the sensors inside the unit are to operate correctly.*

Airbag sensors

Front impact sensors

28 The sensors are located under the bonnet, on the front chassis legs **(see illustration)**. Before removing the sensors, de-activate the airbag system as described in Section 21.

29 To remove the passenger-side sensor, on 1.0 litre models, remove the bolt securing the air cleaner duct to the inner wing, and move the duct to one side; on 1.3 litre models, remove the air cleaner as described in Chapter 4A.

30 Disconnect the sensor wiring plug by squeezing the sides of the outer sleeve and separating the connector halves.

31 Unscrew the two sensor mounting bolts, and withdraw the sensor.

32 Refitting is a reversal of removal, bearing in mind the following points:

a) *The battery must still be disconnected when reconnecting the wiring.*
b) *Make sure that the wiring connectors are securely reconnected.*
c) *Tighten the mounting bolts to the specified torque – this is essential if the sensors are to operate correctly.*

Side impact sensors

33 The sensors are located in the B-pillars,

22.20 Centre the clockspring as described, then align the arrowhead marks

22.28 Airbag front impact sensor

23.1 Air temperature sensor is located on the brace below the bonnet lock

23.2 Prise out the sensor to release the clip from the brace

above the seat belt inertia reel. On 3-door models, an additional side impact sensor is located inside the door, towards the rear. Before removing the sensors, de-activate the airbag system as described in Section 21.

34 On 3-door models, remove either the door trim panel or the rear side trim panel (depending on which side impact sensor is being worked on), as described in Chapter 11.

35 On 5-door models, remove the B-pillar trim panel as described in Chapter 11, Section 24.

36 Disconnect the sensor wiring plug by squeezing the sides of the outer sleeve and separating the connector halves.

37 Unscrew the two sensor mounting bolts, and withdraw the sensor.

38 Refitting is a reversal of removal, bearing in mind the following points:

a) The battery must still be disconnected when reconnecting the wiring.

b) Make sure that the wiring connectors are securely reconnected.

c) Tighten the mounting bolts to the specified torque – this is essential if the sensors are to operate correctly.

23 Ambient air temperature sensor – removal and refitting

Removal

1 The air temperature sensor, used to provide the information for the display panel on the facia, is located on the central brace below the bonnet lock at the front of the car **(see illustration)**.

2 Prise out the sensor mounting clip, and remove the sensor from the brace **(see illustration)**.

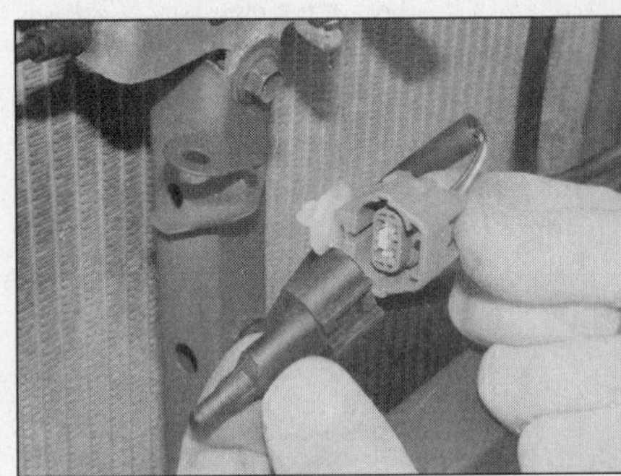

23.3 Disconnect the wiring plug and remove the sensor

3 Disconnect the wiring plug, and remove the sensor from the car **(see illustration)**.

Refitting

4 Refitting is a reversal of removal.

YOYOTA YARIS wiring diagrams

Diagram 1

Key to symbols

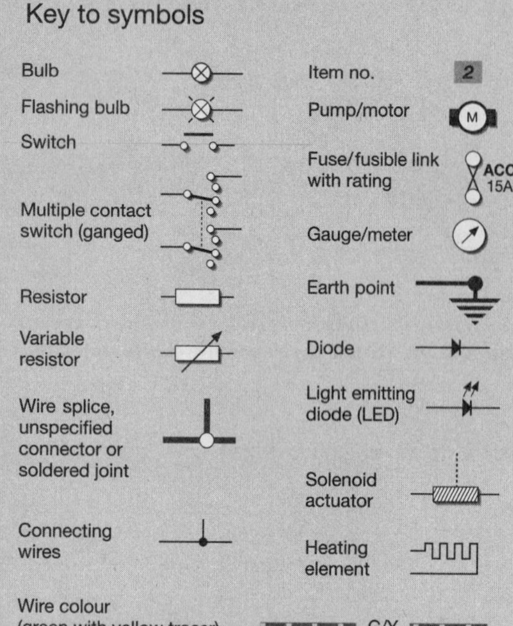

Dashed outline denotes part of a larger item, containing in this case an electronic or solid state device.

3 Unspecified connector, pin 3
E/2 Connector E, pin 2

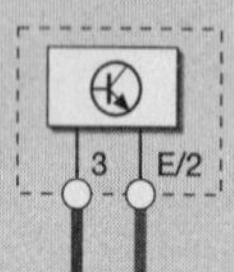

Engine fuse/relay box 7

Fuse	Rating	Circuit protected
DOME	15A	Instrument cluster, interior light, multi-display, audio system, central locking
EFI	15A	Engine control
HORN	15A	Horn
AM2	15A	Charging system, instrument cluster, electronic transmission indicator, engine control, multi-display, safety restraint system
ST	30A	Starting & charging
H-LP LH	10A	Headlight
H-LP RH	10A	Headlight
CL-ACT2	30A	Toyota Freetronic transmission
RDI	30A	Radiator & condenser fan
HTR SUB1	50A	Cabin heater
HTR SUB2	50A	Cabin heater

Earth locations

E1 RH inner wing
E2 On block
E3 Near battery
E4 LH kick panel
E5 Behind centre console
E6 RH kick panel
E7 Behind LH tail light
E8 Behind RH tail light

Passenger compartment fusebox 5

Fuse	Rating	Circuit protected
AM1	50A	ACC, GAUGE, WIPER, ECU-IG, S-HTR & DEF fuses
POWER	30A	Electric windows
HTR	40A	Air conditioning & heater blower
GAUGE	10A	ABS, air conditioning, reversing light, charging, instrument cluster, central locking, automatic transmission indicator, engine control, lights on buzzer, electric windows, Toyota Freetronic transmission, direction indicator & hazard warning lights, heater blower
DEF	25A	Heated rear window & mirrors
D/L	25A	Central locking
TAIL	7.5A	Side, tail & number plate light, rear foglight & switch illumination
WIPER	20A	Front & rear wash/wipe
ECU-B	7.5A	Rear foglight, Toyota Freetronic transmission
ACC	15A	Electric mirrors, cigar lighter & audio system
ECU-IG	7.5A	Heater blower, safety restraint system
OBD	7.5A	Automatic transmission indicator & engine control
HAZ	10A	Direction indicators & hazard warning lights
A/C	7.5A	Air conditioning & heater blower
STOP	10A	Antilock brakes, automatic transmission indicator, engine control, stop light & Toyota Freetronic transmission

Front view of passenger compartment fusebox (fuse layout)

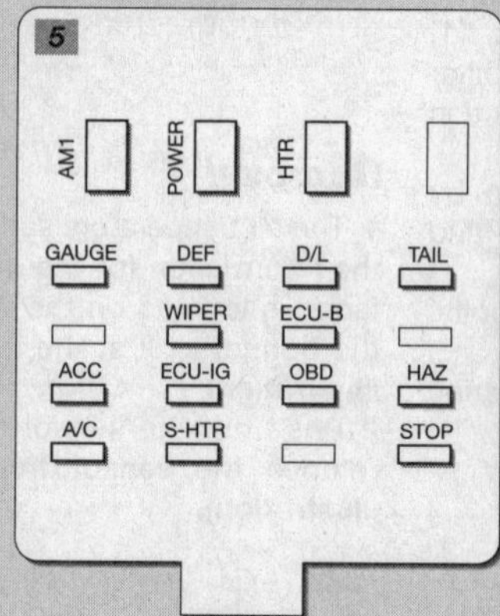

Rear view of passenger compartment fusebox (connector layout)

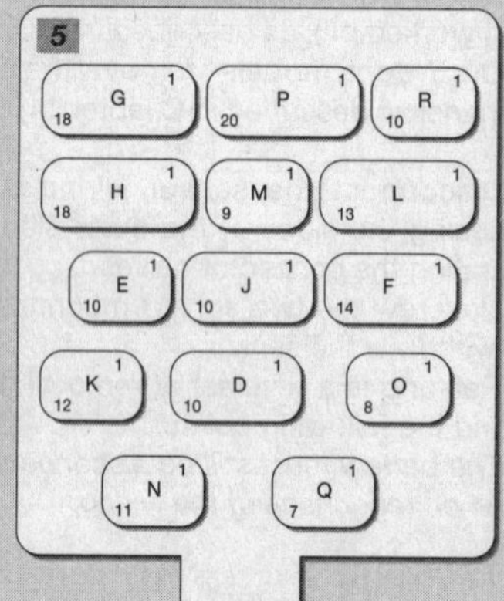

Front view of engine fuse/relay box (fuse layout)

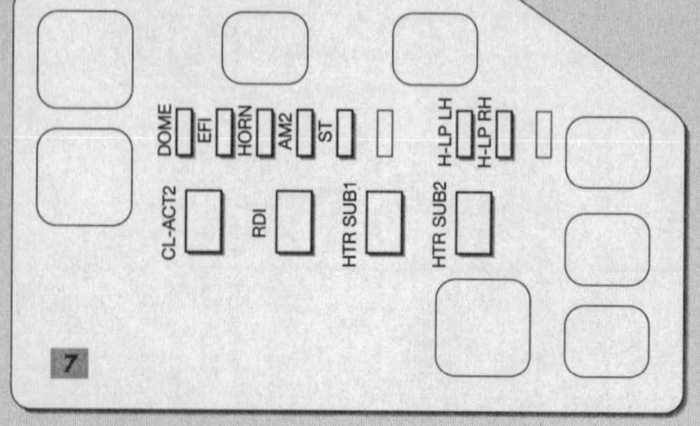

H33156

Diagram 2

Wire colours

L	Blue	**V**	Violet
Br	Brown	**W**	White
Y	Yellow	**O**	Orange
Gr	Grey	**R**	Red
G	Green	**B**	Black
Sb	Sky blue	**Lg**	Light green
P	Pink		

Key to items

1 Battery
2 Ignition switch
3 Starter motor
4 Alternator
5 Passenger compartment fusebox
6 Engine fusible link box
7 Engine fuse/relay box
   a = starter relay
8 Transmission switch
9 High level stop light
10 LH rear light unit
   a = stop light
   b = reversing light
   c = tail light
11 RH rear light unit
   a = stop light
   c = tail light
12 Reversing light switch
13 Stop light switch
14 Combination switch
   a = light switch
   b = dip switch
15 LH headlight
16 RH headlight
17 LH front sidelight
18 RH front sidelight
21 LH number plate light
22 RH number plate light

H33157

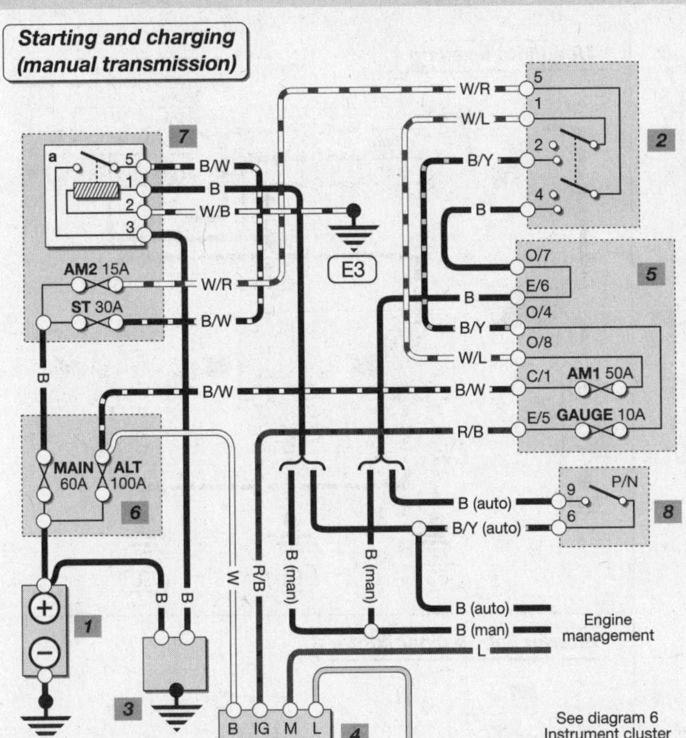

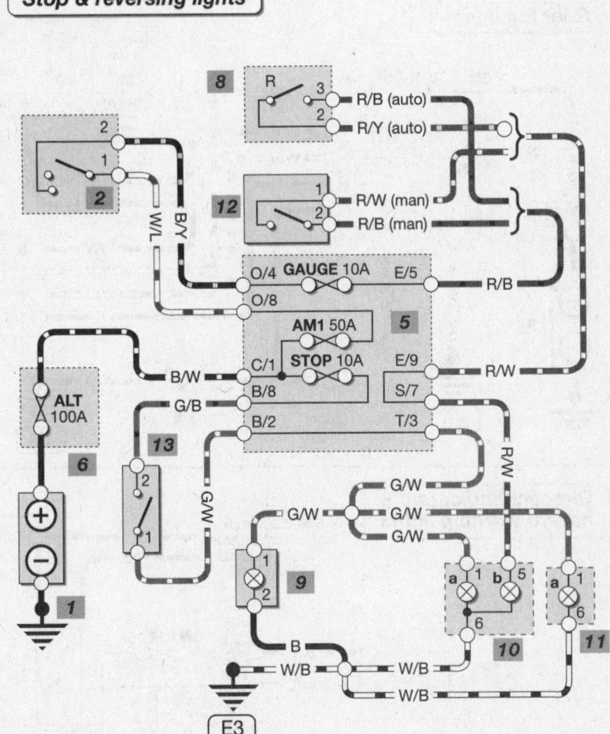

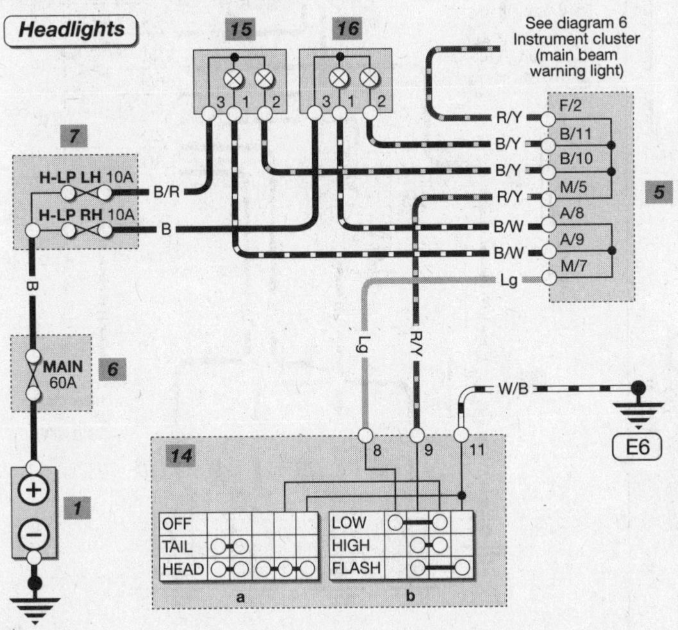

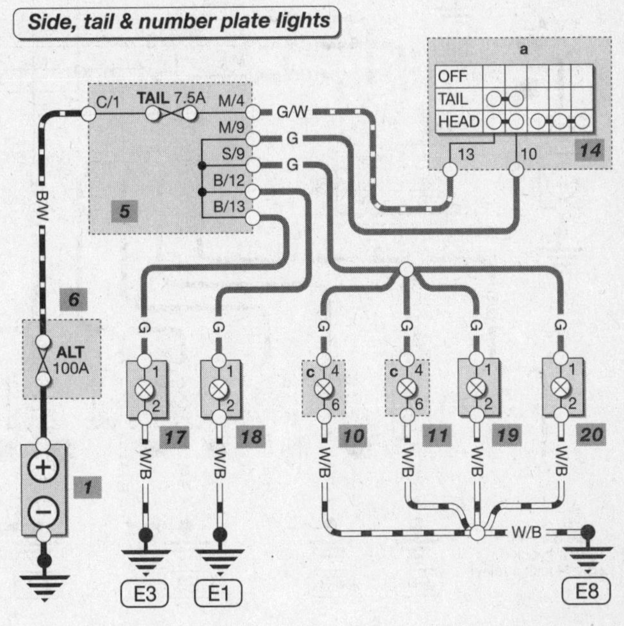

Diagram 3

Wire colours

L	Blue	**V**	Violet
Br	Brown	**W**	White
Y	Yellow	**O**	Orange
Gr	Grey	**R**	Red
G	Green	**B**	Black
Sb	Sky blue	**Lg**	Light green
P	Pink		

Key to items

1 Battery
2 Ignition switch
5 Passenger compartment fusebox
  a = direction indicator flasher relay
6 Engine fusible link box
7 Engine fuse/relay box
10 LH rear light unit
  d = direction indicator
11 RH rear light unit
  b = foglight
  d = direction indicator
14 Combination switch
  a = light switch
  c = direction indicator switch
24 Rear foglight switch
25 Hazard warning light switch
26 LH front direction indicator
27 LH front indicator side repeater
28 RH front direction indicator
29 RH front indicator side repeater
30 Headlight levelling switch
31 LH headlight levelling actuator
32 RH headlight levelling actuator
33 Interior light
34 Cigar lighter
35 Driver's door switch
36 Passenger's door switch
37 LH rear door switch
38 RH rear door switch

H33158

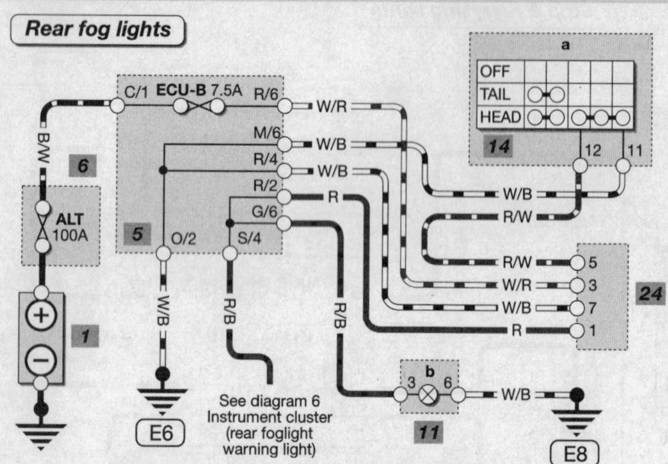

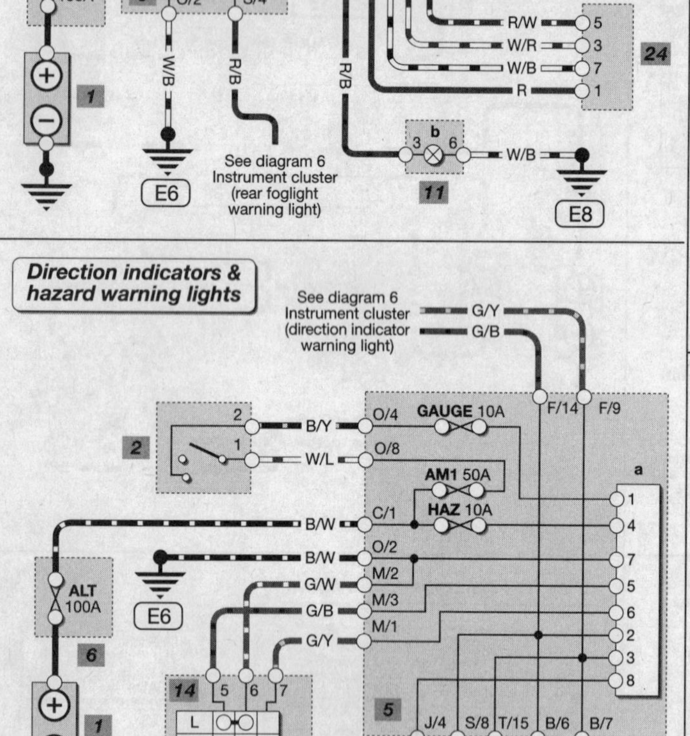

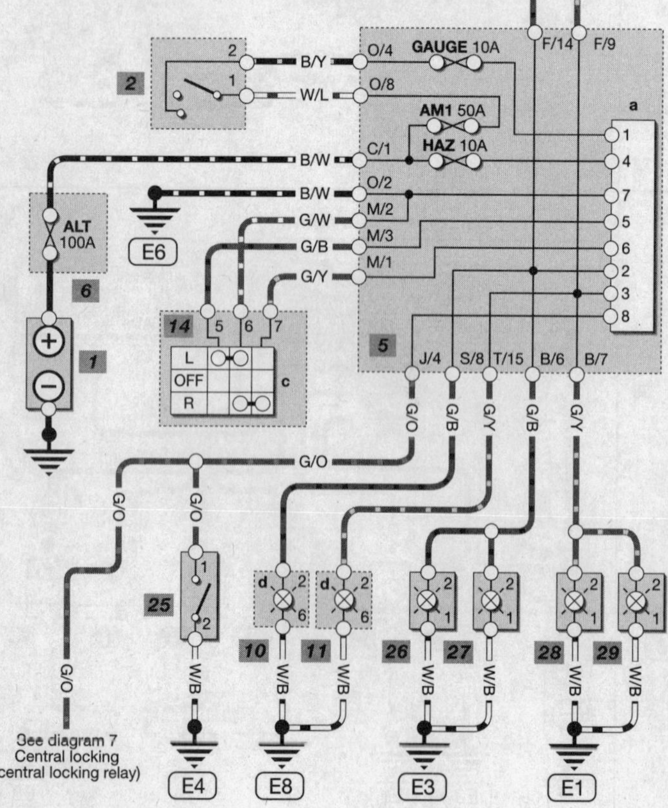

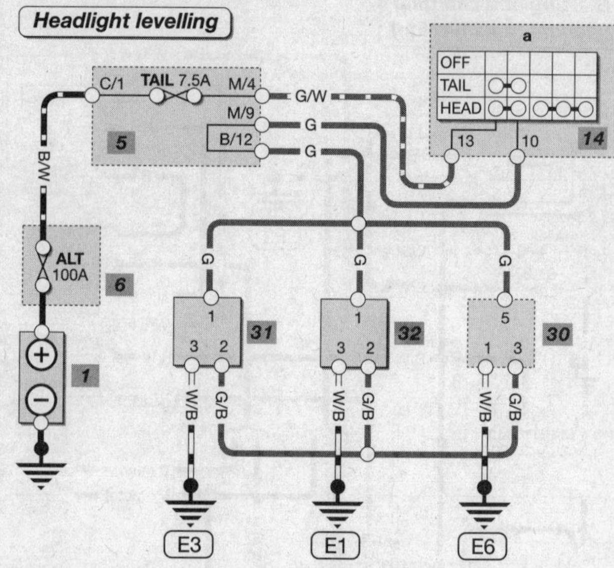

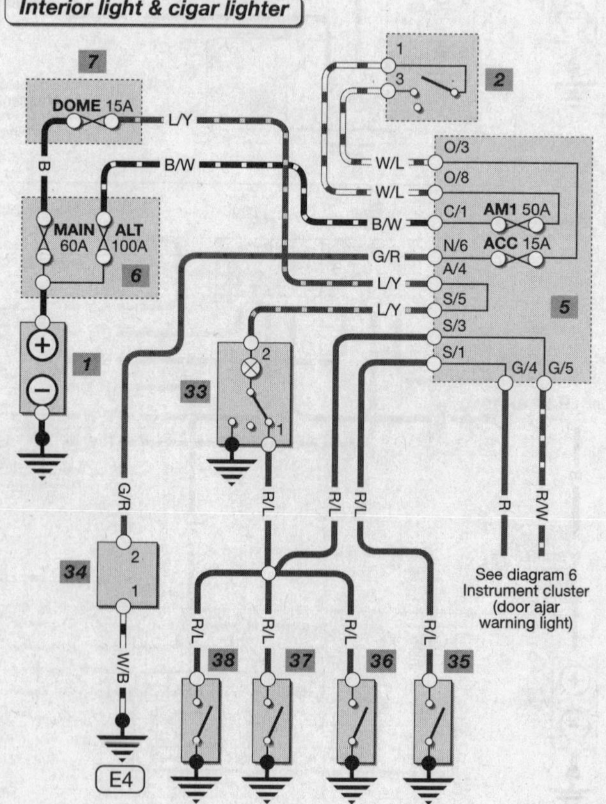

Diagram 4

Wire colours

L	Blue	V	Violet
Br	Brown	W	White
Y	Yellow	O	Orange
Gr	Grey	R	Red
G	Green	B	Black
Sb	Sky blue	Lg	Light green
P	Pink		

Key to items

1 Battery
2 Ignition switch
5 Passenger compartment fusebox
b = heater relay
6 Engine fusible link box
7 Engine fuse/relay box
b = horn relay
14 Combination switch
a = light switch
24 Rear foglight switch
30 Headlight levelling switch
40 Overdrive main switch
41 Multiple display
42 Rear door lock control switch
43 Heater blower switch
44 Radio unit
45 Heater blower motor and resistors
46 Horn
47 Horn switch
48 LH mirror assembly
49 RH mirror assembly
50 Mirror control switch

H33159

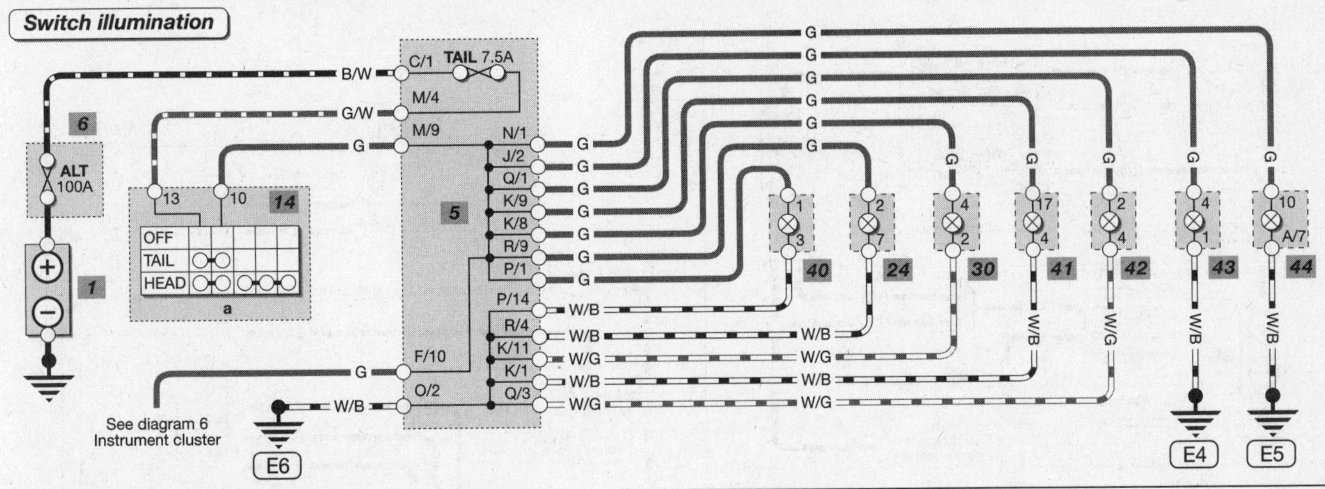

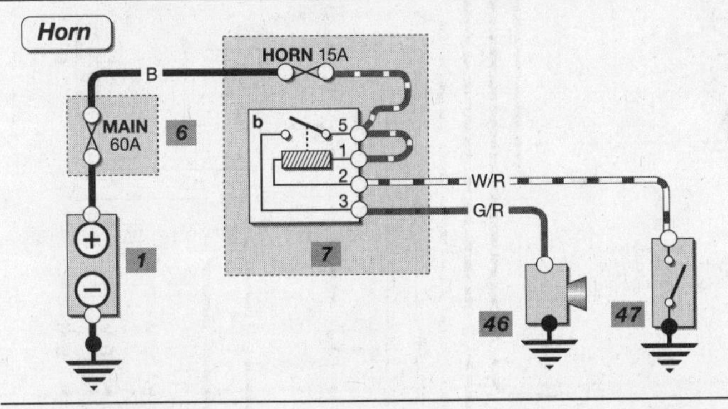

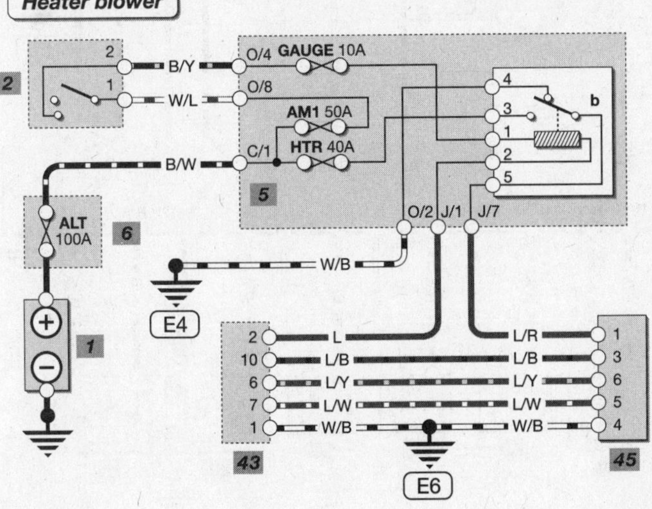

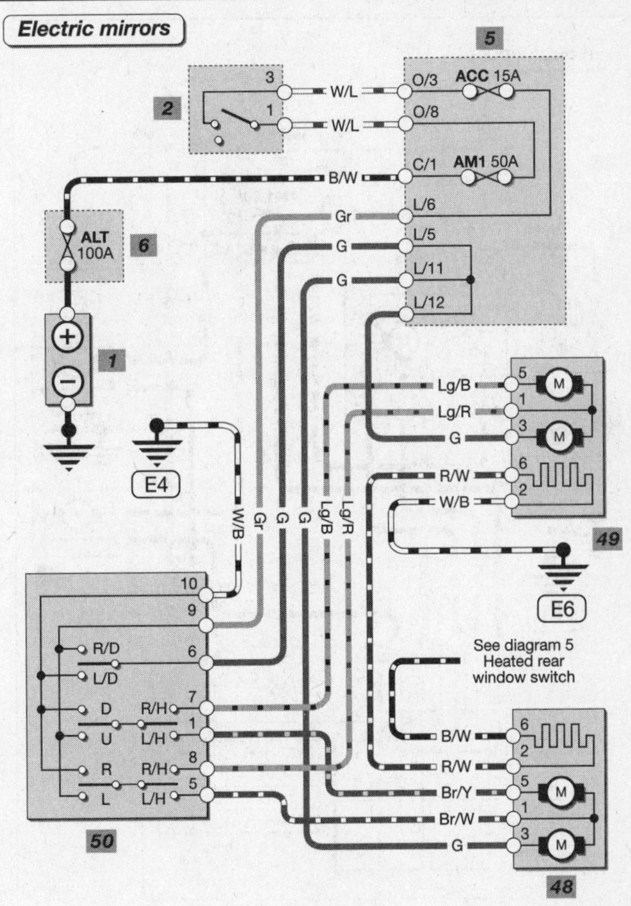

Diagram 5

Wire colours

L	Blue	**V**	Violet
Br	Brown	**W**	White
Y	Yellow	**O**	Orange
Gr	Grey	**R**	Red
G	Green	**B**	Black
Sb	Sky blue	**Lg**	Light green
P	Pink		

Key to items

1 Battery
2 Ignition switch
5 Passenger compartment fusebox
6 Engine fusible link box
7 Engine fuse/relay box
53 Heated rear window switch
54 Heated rear window
55 Wash/wipe switch
a = front
b = rear
56 Front wiper motor
57 Rear wiper motor
58 Washer pump
59 SRS control unit
60 Diagnostic socket
61 Driver's airbag
62 Passenger's airbag
63 LH seatbelt pretensioner
64 RH seatbelt pretensioner
65 LH front airbag sensor
66 RH front airbag sensor

H33160

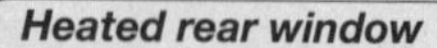

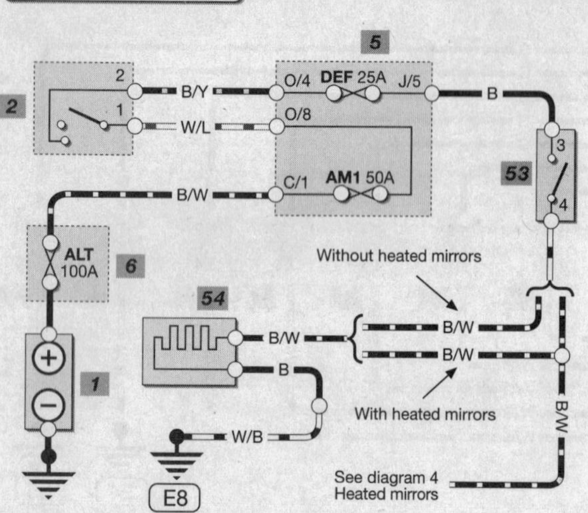

Wash/wipe

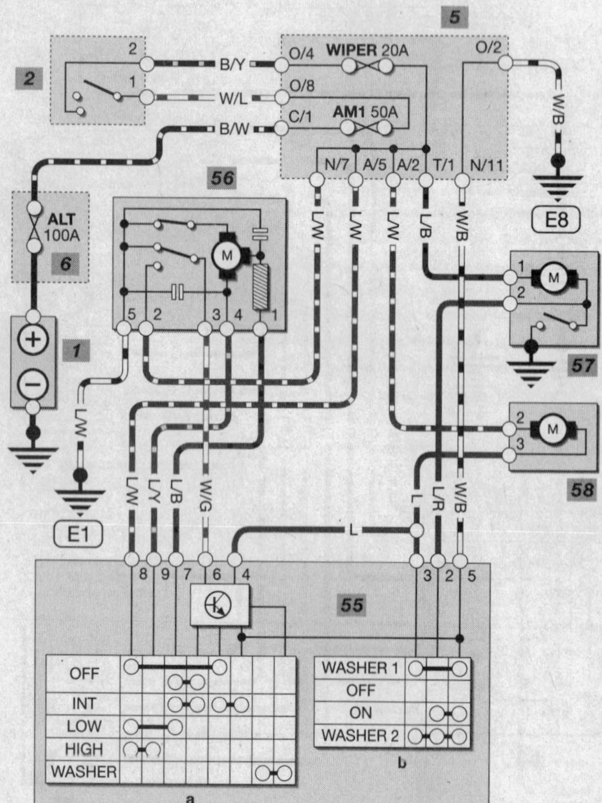

Safety restraint system

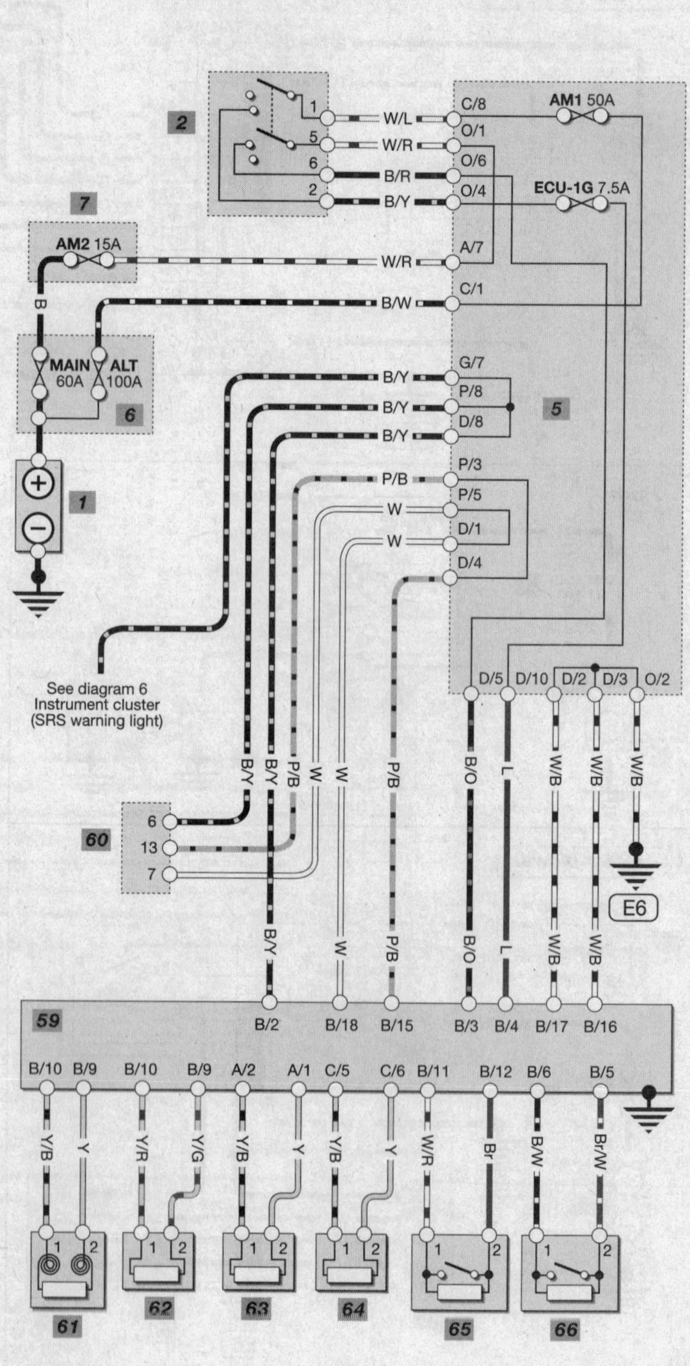

Wire colours

L	Blue	**V**	Violet
Br	Brown	**W**	White
Y	Yellow	**O**	Orange
Gr	Grey	**R**	Red
G	Green	**B**	Black
Sb	Sky blue	**Lg**	Light green
P	Pink		

Key to items

1 Battery
2 Ignition switch
5 Passenger compartment fusebox
6 Engine fusible link box
7 Engine fuse/relay box
69 Low brake fluid warning switch
70 Handbrake switch
71 Vehicle speed sensor
72 Fuel gauge sender unit
73 Coolant temperature sensor
74 Odometer/trip meter switch
75 Front passenger seatbelt warning light
76 Oil pressure switch

77 Instrument cluster
a = digital sisplay unit
b = buzzer
c = control unit
d = seatbelt warning light
e = 'Freetronic' warning light
f = door ajar warning light
g = alternator warning light
h = SRS warning light
i = ABS warning light
j = brake system warning light
k = 'O/D off' warning light
l = low oil pressure warning light

77 Instrument cluster continued
m = low coolant temp. warning light
n = high coolant temp. warning light
o = engine man. warning light
p = main beam warning light
q = LH indicator warning light
r = RH indicator warning light
s = rear foglight warning light

Diagram 6

H33161

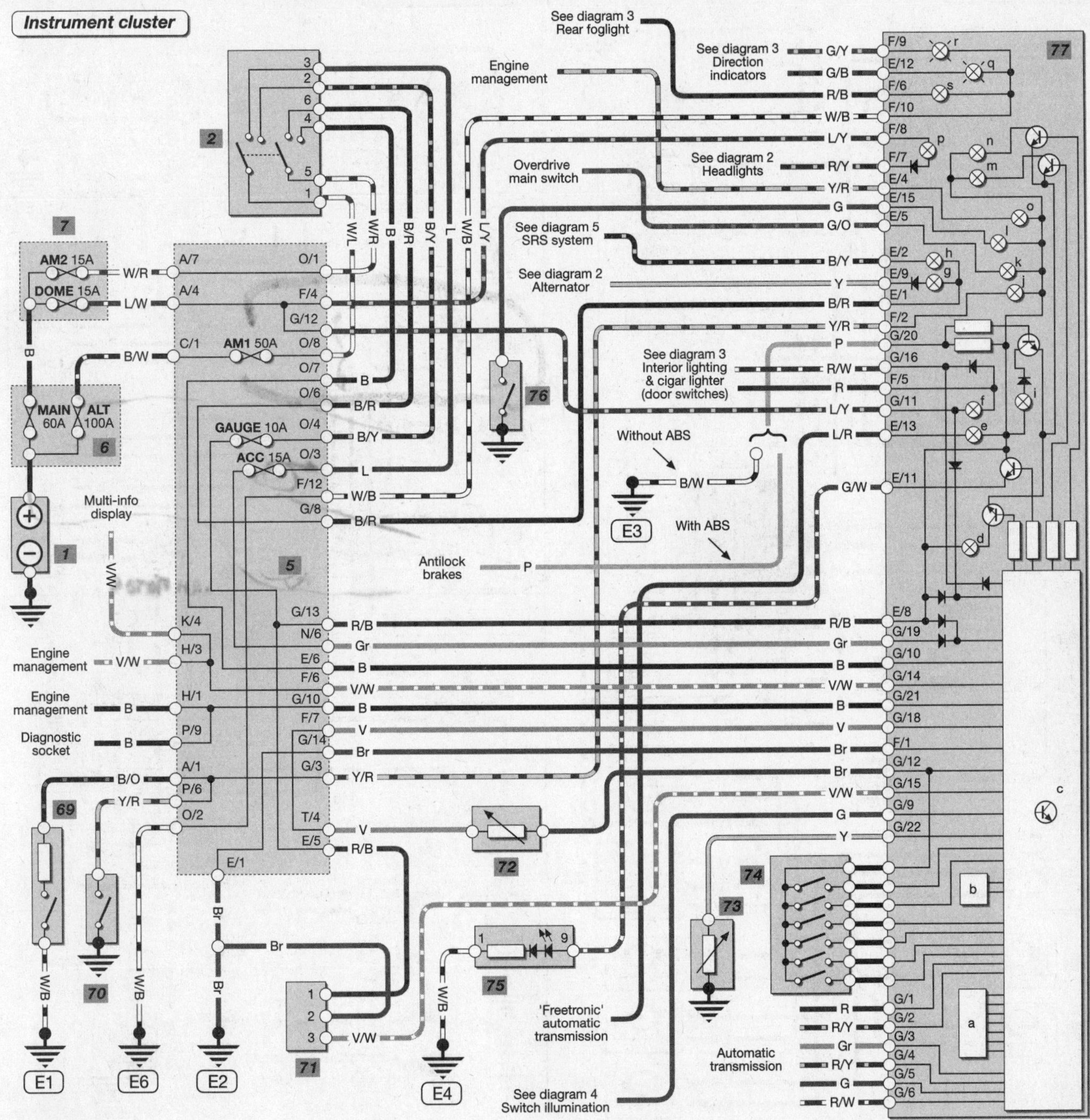

Diagram 7

Wire colours

L	Blue	V	Violet
Br	Brown	W	White
Y	Yellow	O	Orange
Gr	Grey	R	Red
G	Green	B	Black
Sb	Sky blue	Lg	Light green
P	Pink		

* Models with rear electric windows

Key to items

1 Battery
2 Ignition switch
5 Passenger compartment fusebox
c = electric window relay
6 Engine fusible link box
7 Engine fuse/relay box
42 Rear door lock control switch
44 Radio unit
80 Central locking control unit
81 Central locking remote receiver
82 Door lock control switch
83 Driver's door lock switch
84 Passenger's door lock switch
85 Driver's door lock motor
86 Passenger's door lock motor
87 LH rear door lock motor
88 RH rear door lock motor
89 Tailgate lock motor
90 Unlock warning switch
91 Electric window master switch
92 LH front window control switch
93 LH rear window control switch
94 RH rear window control switch
95 LH front window motor
96 RH front window motor
97 LH rear window motor (if fitted)
98 RH rear window motor (if fitted)
99 LH front dashboard speaker
100 RH front dashboard speaker
101 LH front door speaker
102 RH front door speaker

H33162

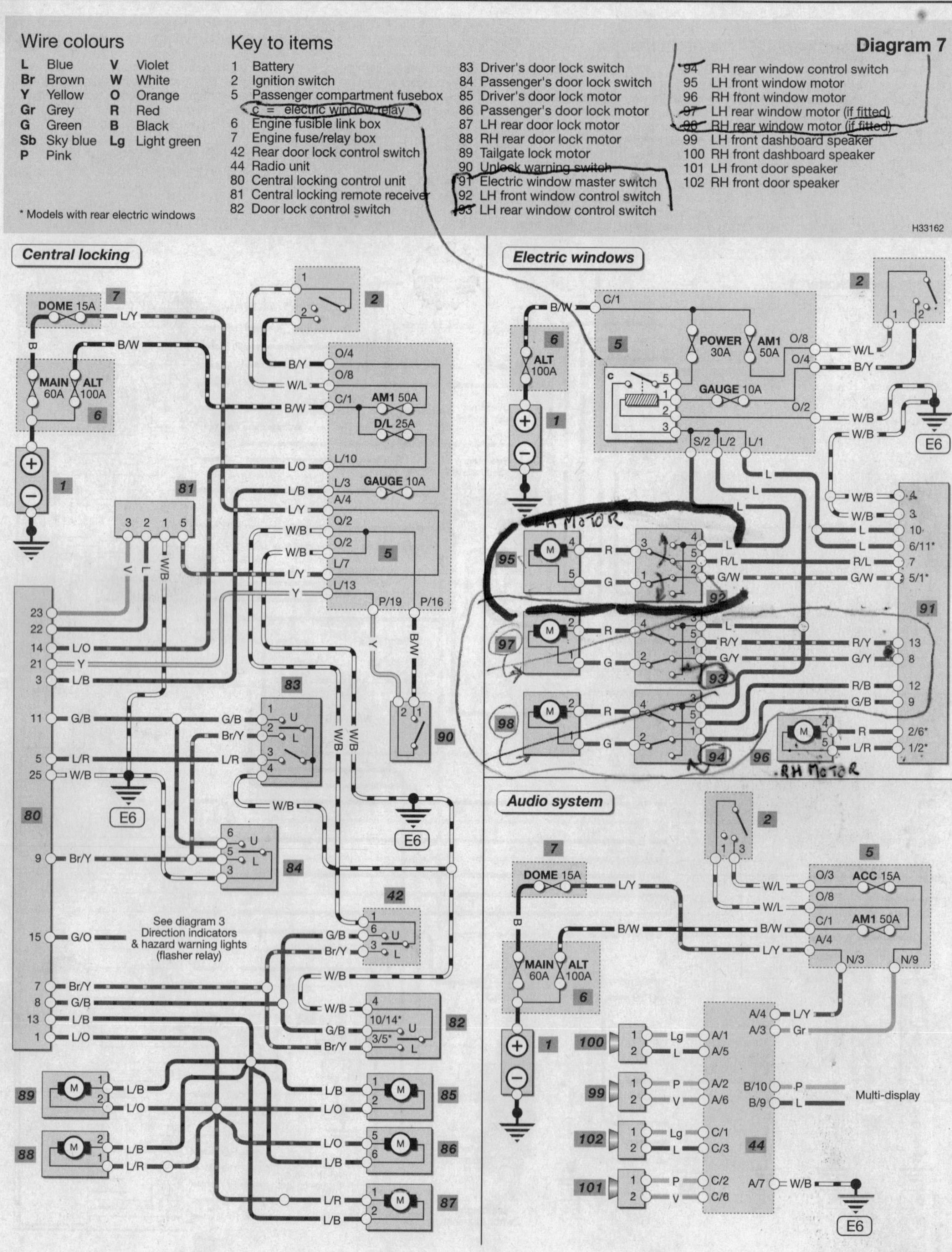

Dimensions and Weights

Note: *All figures are approximate, and may vary according to model. Refer to manufacturer's data for exact figures.*

Dimensions

Overall length	3615 to 3640 mm
Overall width	1660 mm
Overall height (unladen)	1500 mm
Wheelbase	2370 mm

Weights

Kerb weight	805 to 825 kg
Maximum gross vehicle weight	1335 to 1395 kg
Maximum towing weight	400 kg

Conversion factors

Length (distance)

Inches (in)	x 25.4	= Millimetres (mm)	x 0.0394	= Inches (in)
Feet (ft)	x 0.305	= Metres (m)	x 3.281	= Feet (ft)
Miles	x 1.609	= Kilometres (km)	x 0.621	= Miles

Volume (capacity)

Cubic inches (cu in; in^3)	x 16.387	= Cubic centimetres (cc; cm^3)	x 0.061	= Cubic inches (cu in; in^3)
Imperial pints (Imp pt)	x 0.568	= Litres (l)	x 1.76	= Imperial pints (Imp pt)
Imperial quarts (Imp qt)	x 1.137	= Litres (l)	x 0.88	= Imperial quarts (Imp qt)
Imperial quarts (Imp qt)	x 1.201	= US quarts (US qt)	x 0.833	= Imperial quarts (Imp qt)
US quarts (US qt)	x 0.946	= Litres (l)	x 1.057	= US quarts (US qt)
Imperial gallons (Imp gal)	x 4.546	= Litres (l)	x 0.22	= Imperial gallons (Imp gal)
Imperial gallons (Imp gal)	x 1.201	= US gallons (US gal)	x 0.833	= Imperial gallons (Imp gal)
US gallons (US gal)	x 3.785	= Litres (l)	x 0.264	= US gallons (US gal)

Mass (weight)

Ounces (oz)	x 28.35	= Grams (g)	x 0.035	= Ounces (oz)
Pounds (lb)	x 0.454	= Kilograms (kg)	x 2.205	= Pounds (lb)

Force

Ounces-force (ozf; oz)	x 0.278	= Newtons (N)	x 3.6	= Ounces-force (ozf; oz)
Pounds-force (lbf; lb)	x 4.448	= Newtons (N)	x 0.225	= Pounds-force (lbf; lb)
Newtons (N)	x 0.1	= Kilograms-force (kgf; kg)	x 9.81	= Newtons (N)

Pressure

Pounds-force per square inch (psi; lbf/in^2; lb/in^2)	x 0.070	= Kilograms-force per square centimetre (kgf/cm^2; kg/cm^2)	x 14.223	= Pounds-force per square inch (psi; lbf/in^2; lb/in^2)
Pounds-force per square inch (psi; lbf/in^2; lb/in^2)	x 0.068	= Atmospheres (atm)	x 14.696	= Pounds-force per square inch (psi; lbf/in^2; lb/in^2)
Pounds-force per square inch (psi; lbf/in^2; lb/in^2)	x 0.069	= Bars	x 14.5	= Pounds-force per square inch (psi; lbf/in^2; lb/in^2)
Pounds-force per square inch (psi; lbf/in^2; lb/in^2)	x 6.895	= Kilopascals (kPa)	x 0.145	= Pounds-force per square inch (psi; lbf/in^2; lb/in^2)
Kilopascals (kPa)	x 0.01	= Kilograms-force per square centimetre (kgf/cm^2; kg/cm^2)	x 98.1	= Kilopascals (kPa)
Millibar (mbar)	x 100	= Pascals (Pa)	x 0.01	= Millibar (mbar)
Millibar (mbar)	x 0.0145	= Pounds-force per square inch (psi; lbf/in^2; lb/in^2)	x 68.947	= Millibar (mbar)
Millibar (mbar)	x 0.75	= Millimetres of mercury (mmHg)	x 1.333	= Millibar (mbar)
Millibar (mbar)	x 0.401	= Inches of water (inH_2O)	x 2.491	= Millibar (mbar)
Millimetres of mercury (mmHg)	x 0.535	= Inches of water (inH_2O)	x 1.868	= Millimetres of mercury (mmHg)
Inches of water (inH_2O)	x 0.036	= Pounds-force per square inch (psi; lbf/in^2; lb/in^2)	x 27.68	= Inches of water (inH_2O)

Torque (moment of force)

Pounds-force inches (lbf in; lb in)	x 1.152	= Kilograms-force centimetre (kgf cm; kg cm)	x 0.868	= Pounds-force inches (lbf in; lb in)
Pounds-force inches (lbf in; lb in)	x 0.113	= Newton metres (Nm)	x 8.85	= Pounds-force inches (lbf in; lb in)
Pounds-force inches (lbf in; lb in)	x 0.083	= Pounds-force feet (lbf ft; lb ft)	x 12	= Pounds-force inches (lbf in; lb in)
Pounds-force feet (lbf ft; lb ft)	x 0.138	= Kilograms-force metres (kgf m; kg m)	x 7.233	= Pounds-force feet (lbf ft; lb ft)
Pounds-force feet (lbf ft; lb ft)	x 1.356	= Newton metres (Nm)	x 0.738	= Pounds-force feet (lbf ft; lb ft)
Newton metres (Nm)	x 0.102	= Kilograms-force metres (kgf m; kg m)	x 9.804	= Newton metres (Nm)

Power

Horsepower (hp)	x 745.7	= Watts (W)	x 0.0013	= Horsepower (hp)

Velocity (speed)

Miles per hour (miles/hr; mph)	x 1.609	= Kilometres per hour (km/hr; kph)	x 0.621	= Miles per hour (miles/hr; mph)

Fuel consumption*

Miles per gallon, Imperial (mpg)	x 0.354	= Kilometres per litre (km/l)	x 2.825	= Miles per gallon, Imperial (mpg)
Miles per gallon, US (mpg)	x 0.425	= Kilometres per litre (km/l)	x 2.352	= Miles per gallon, US (mpg)

Temperature

Degrees Fahrenheit = (°C x 1.8) + 32

Degrees Celsius (Degrees Centigrade; °C) = (°F - 32) x 0.56

** It is common practice to convert from miles per gallon (mpg) to litres/100 kilometres (l/100km), where mpg x l/100 km = 282*

Spare parts are available from many sources, including maker's appointed garages, accessory shops, and motor factors. To be sure of obtaining the correct parts, it will sometimes be necessary to quote the vehicle identification number (see *Vehicle identification*). If possible, it can also be useful to take the old parts along for positive identification. Items such as starter motors and alternators may be available under a service exchange scheme – any parts returned should always be clean.

Our advice regarding spare part sources is as follows.

Officially-appointed garages

This is the best source of parts which are peculiar to your car, and which are not otherwise generally available (eg badges, interior trim, certain body panels, etc). It is also the only place at which you should buy parts if the car is still under warranty.

Accessory shops

These are very good places to buy materials and components needed for the maintenance of your car (oil, air and fuel filters, spark plugs, light bulbs, drivebelts, oils and greases, brake pads, touch-up paint, etc). Components of this nature sold by a reputable shop are of the same standard as those used by the car manufacturer.

Besides components, these shops also sell tools and general accessories, usually have convenient opening hours, charge lower prices, and can often be found not far from home. Some accessory shops have parts counters where the components needed for almost any repair job can be purchased or ordered.

Motor factors

Good factors will stock all the more important components which wear out comparatively quickly, and can sometimes supply individual components needed for the overhaul of a larger assembly (eg brake seals and hydraulic parts, bearing shells, pistons, valves, alternator brushes). They may also handle work such as cylinder block reboring, crankshaft regrinding and balancing, etc.

Tyre and exhaust specialists

These outlets may be independent, or members of a local or national chain. They frequently offer competitive prices when compared with a main dealer or local garage, but it will pay to obtain several quotes before making a decision. When researching prices, also ask what 'extras' may be added – for instance, fitting a new valve and balancing the wheel are both commonly charged on top of the price of a new tyre.

Other sources

Beware of parts or materials obtained from market stalls, car boot sales or similar outlets. Such items are not invariably sub-standard, but there is little chance of compensation if they do prove unsatisfactory. In the case of safety-critical components such as brake pads, there is the risk not only of financial loss but also of an accident causing injury or death.

Second-hand components or assemblies obtained from a car breaker can be a good buy in some circumstances, but this sort of purchase is best made by the experienced DIY mechanic.

Vehicle identification

Modifications are a continuing and unpublicised process in car manufacture, quite apart from major model changes. Spare parts manuals and lists are compiled upon a numerical basis, the individual vehicle identification numbers being essential to correct identification of the component concerned.

When ordering spare parts, always give as much information as possible. Quote the car model, year of manufacture, body and engine numbers as appropriate.

The *vehicle identification plate* is located on the driver's inner wing **(see illustration)**. In addition to many other details, it carries the Vehicle Identification Number (VIN), maximum vehicle weight information, and codes for interior trim and body colours.

The *Vehicle Identification Number (VIN)* is given on the vehicle identification plate. On models manufactured in Japan (TMC), it is also stamped on the engine compartment bulkhead, below the windscreen **(see illustration)**. On later models assembled at the Toyota plant in France (TMMF), the VIN is stamped into the floor, below one of the front seats – an access flap is provided.

The *body number and paint code numbers* are located on the vehicle identification plate.

The *engine number* is stamped in the following locations, according to engine type:

a) *On the 1.0 litre and 1.3 litre 2SZ-FE engines, it is stamped on the transmission end of the block, at the front **(see illustration)**.*

b) *On the 1.3 litre 2NZ-FE engine, it is stamped on the front of the block, behind the inlet manifold **(see illustration)**.*

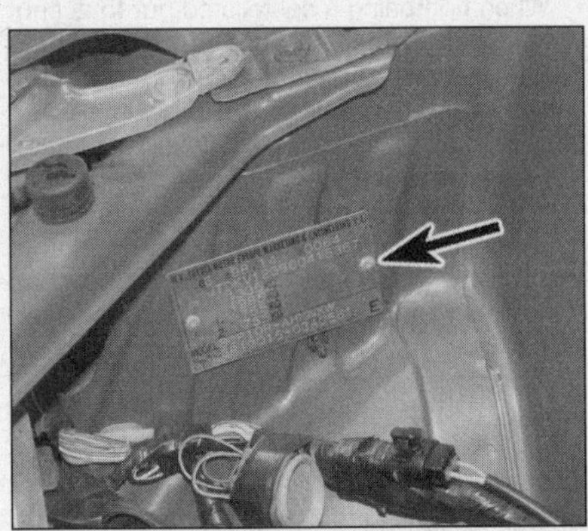

The vehicle identification plate is located on the driver's inner wing

The VIN also appears at the top of the bulkhead, behind the windscreen scuttle panel

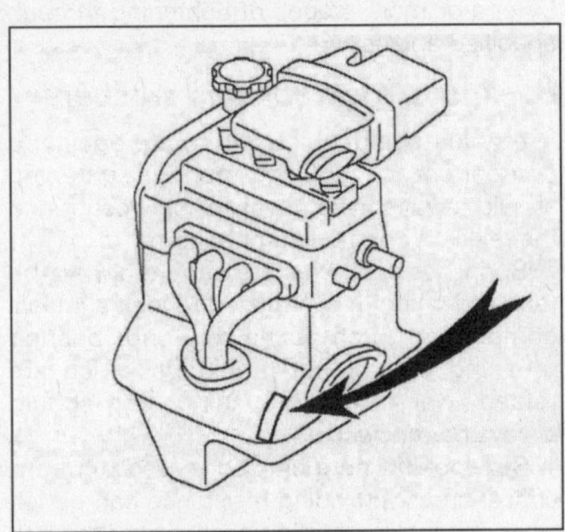

Engine number location – 1.0 litre and 1.3 litre 2SZ-FE engines

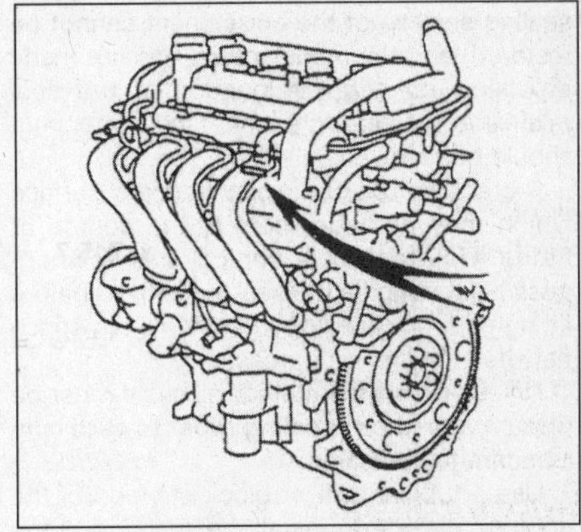

Engine number location – 1.3 litre 2NZ-FE engine

Whenever servicing, repair or overhaul work is carried out on the car or its components, observe the following procedures and instructions. This will assist in carrying out the operation efficiently and to a professional standard of workmanship.

Joint mating faces and gaskets

When separating components at their mating faces, never insert screwdrivers or similar implements into the joint between the faces in order to prise them apart. This can cause severe damage which results in oil leaks, coolant leaks, etc upon reassembly. Separation is usually achieved by tapping along the joint with a soft-faced hammer in order to break the seal. However, note that this method may not be suitable where dowels are used for component location.

Where a gasket is used between the mating faces of two components, a new one must be fitted on reassembly; fit it dry unless otherwise stated in the repair procedure. Make sure that the mating faces are clean and dry, with all traces of old gasket removed. When cleaning a joint face, use a tool which is unlikely to score or damage the face, and remove any burrs or nicks with an oilstone or fine file.

Make sure that tapped holes are cleaned with a pipe cleaner, and keep them free of jointing compound, if this is being used, unless specifically instructed otherwise.

Ensure that all orifices, channels or pipes are clear, and blow through them, preferably using compressed air.

Oil seals

Oil seals can be removed by levering them out with a wide flat-bladed screwdriver or similar implement. Alternatively, a number of self-tapping screws may be screwed into the seal, and these used as a purchase for pliers or some similar device in order to pull the seal free.

Whenever an oil seal is removed from its working location, either individually or as part of an assembly, it should be renewed.

The very fine sealing lip of the seal is easily damaged, and will not seal if the surface it contacts is not completely clean and free from scratches, nicks or grooves. If the original sealing surface of the component cannot be restored, and the manufacturer has not made provision for slight relocation of the seal relative to the sealing surface, the component should be renewed.

Protect the lips of the seal from any surface which may damage them in the course of fitting. Use tape or a conical sleeve where possible. Lubricate the seal lips with oil before fitting and, on dual-lipped seals, fill the space between the lips with grease.

Unless otherwise stated, oil seals must be fitted with their sealing lips toward the lubricant to be sealed.

Use a tubular drift or block of wood of the appropriate size to install the seal and, if the seal housing is shouldered, drive the seal down to the shoulder. If the seal housing is unshouldered, the seal should be fitted with its face flush with the housing top face (unless otherwise instructed).

Screw threads and fastenings

Seized nuts, bolts and screws are quite a common occurrence where corrosion has set in, and the use of penetrating oil or releasing fluid will often overcome this problem if the offending item is soaked for a while before attempting to release it. The use of an impact driver may also provide a means of releasing such stubborn fastening devices, when used in conjunction with the appropriate screwdriver bit or socket. If none of these methods works, it may be necessary to resort to the careful application of heat, or the use of a hacksaw or nut splitter device.

Studs are usually removed by locking two nuts together on the threaded part, and then using a spanner on the lower nut to unscrew the stud. Studs or bolts which have broken off below the surface of the component in which they are mounted can sometimes be removed using a stud extractor. Always ensure that a blind tapped hole is completely free from oil, grease, water or other fluid before installing the bolt or stud. Failure to do this could cause the housing to crack due to the hydraulic action of the bolt or stud as it is screwed in.

When tightening a castellated nut to accept a split pin, tighten the nut to the specified torque, where applicable, and then tighten further to the next split pin hole. Never slacken the nut to align the split pin hole, unless stated in the repair procedure.

When checking or retightening a nut or bolt to a specified torque setting, slacken the nut or bolt by a quarter of a turn, and then retighten to the specified setting. However, this should not be attempted where angular tightening has been used.

For some screw fastenings, notably cylinder head bolts or nuts, torque wrench settings are no longer specified for the latter stages of tightening, "angle-tightening" being called up instead. Typically, a fairly low torque wrench setting will be applied to the bolts/nuts in the correct sequence, followed by one or more stages of tightening through specified angles.

Locknuts, locktabs and washers

Any fastening which will rotate against a component or housing during tightening should always have a washer between it and the relevant component or housing.

Spring or split washers should always be renewed when they are used to lock a critical component such as a big-end bearing retaining bolt or nut. Locktabs which are folded over to retain a nut or bolt should always be renewed.

Self-locking nuts can be re-used in non-critical areas, providing resistance can be felt when the locking portion passes over the bolt or stud thread. However, it should be noted that self-locking stiffnuts tend to lose their effectiveness after long periods of use, and should then be renewed as a matter of course.

Split pins must always be replaced with new ones of the correct size for the hole.

When thread-locking compound is found on the threads of a fastener which is to be re-used, it should be cleaned off with a wire brush and solvent, and fresh compound applied on reassembly.

Special tools

Some repair procedures in this manual entail the use of special tools such as a press, two or three-legged pullers, spring compressors, etc. Wherever possible, suitable readily-available alternatives to the manufacturer's special tools are described, and are shown in use. In some instances, where no alternative is possible, it has been necessary to resort to the use of a manufacturer's tool, and this has been done for reasons of safety as well as the efficient completion of the repair operation. Unless you are highly-skilled and have a thorough understanding of the procedures described, never attempt to bypass the use of any special tool when the procedure described specifies its use. Not only is there a very great risk of personal injury, but expensive damage could be caused to the components involved.

Environmental considerations

When disposing of used engine oil, brake fluid, antifreeze, etc, give due consideration to any detrimental environmental effects. Do not, for instance, pour any of the above liquids down drains into the general sewage system, or onto the ground to soak away. Many local council refuse tips provide a facility for waste oil disposal, as do some garages. If none of these facilities are available, consult your local Environmental Health Department, or the National Rivers Authority, for further advice.

With the universal tightening-up of legislation regarding the emission of environmentally-harmful substances from motor vehicles, most vehicles have tamperproof devices fitted to the main adjustment points of the fuel system. These devices are primarily designed to prevent unqualified persons from adjusting the fuel/air mixture, with the chance of a consequent increase in toxic emissions. If such devices are found during servicing or overhaul, they should, wherever possible, be renewed or refitted in accordance with the manufacturer's requirements or current legislation.

OIL BANK LINE
0800 66 33 66
www.oilbankline.org.uk

Note: It is antisocial and illegal to dump oil down the drain. To find the location of your local oil recycling bank, call this number free.

The jack supplied with the car's tool kit should only be used for changing the roadwheels – see *Wheel changing* at the front of this book. When carrying out any other kind of work, raise the car using a hydraulic (or 'trolley') jack, and always supplement the jack with axle stands positioned under the jacking/support points. If the roadwheels do not have to be removed, consider using wheel ramps – if wished, these can be placed under the wheels once the car has been raised using a hydraulic jack, and then lowered onto the ramps so that it is resting on its wheels.

Only ever jack the car up on a solid, level surface. If there is even a slight slope, take great care that the car cannot move as the wheels are lifted off the ground. Jacking up on an uneven or gravelled surface is not recommended, as the weight of the car will not be evenly distributed, and the jack may slip as the car is raised.

As far as possible, do not leave the car unattended once it has been raised, particularly if children are playing nearby.

Before jacking up the front of the car, ensure that the handbrake is firmly applied. When jacking up the rear of the car, place wooden chocks in front of the front wheels, and engage first gear **(see illustration)**.

To raise the front and/or rear of the car, use the jacking/support points at the front and rear ends of the door sills, which are located between two notches in the sill's lower flange **(see illustration)**. Position a block of wood with a groove cut in it on the jack head to prevent the car's weight resting on the sill edge; align the sill edge with the groove in the wood so that the car's weight is spread evenly over the surface of the block. Supplement the jack with axle stands (also with slotted blocks of wood) positioned as close as possible to the jacking points.

When using a hydraulic jack or axle stands, always try to position the jack head or axle stand head under one of the relevant jacking points.

Providing care is taken (and a block of wood is used to spread the load), the centre of the front subframe, and the protrusion just inside the rear bumper lower edge, may be used as support points **(see illustration)**. It may be safe also to use reinforced areas of the floor pan ('chassis legs'), particularly those in the region of suspension mountings, as support points – consult a Toyota dealer for advice before using anything other than the approved jacking points, however.

Do not jack the car under any other part of the sill, sump, floorpan, or directly under any of the steering or suspension components, including the rear axle. Avoid trapping cables, fuel pipes and brake pipes, and do not compress the suspension.

Never work under, around, or near a raised vehicle, unless it is adequately supported on stands. Do not rely on a jack alone, as even a hydraulic jack could fail under load.

Wheel chocks should be used when jacking the rear of the car

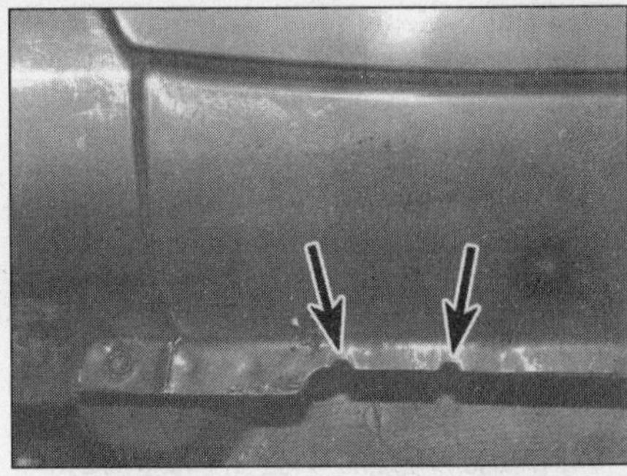

Door sill jacking points are located between the two notches on the sill flange

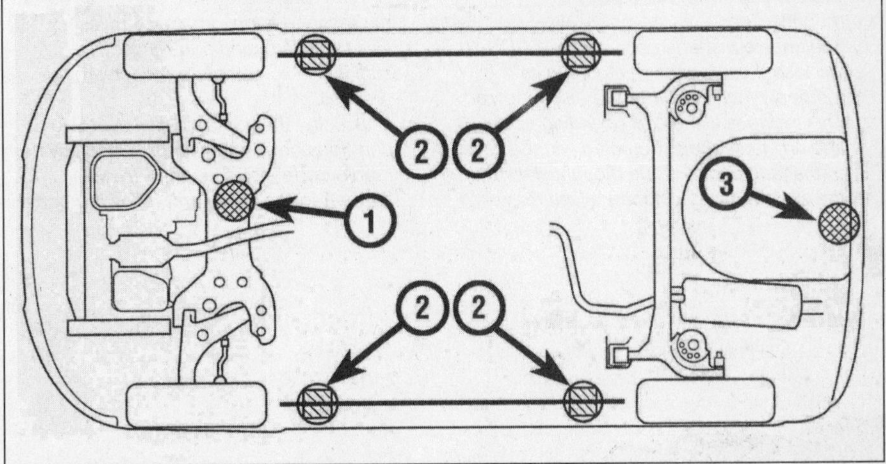

Vehicle jacking and support points

1 Centre of front subframe
2 Door sill front and rear jacking points
3 Reinforced pad inside centre of rear bumper

Disconnecting the battery

Several systems fitted to the car require battery power to be available at all times, either to ensure that their continued operation (such as the clock) or to maintain control unit memories (such as that in the engine management system's ECU) which would be wiped if the battery were to be disconnected. Whenever the battery is to be disconnected therefore, first note the following, to ensure that there are no unforeseen consequences of this action:

a) *First, on any vehicle with central locking, it is a wise precaution to remove the key from the ignition, and to keep it with you, so that it does not get locked in, if the central locking should engage accidentally when the battery is reconnected.*

b) *The engine management system's ECU will lose the information stored in its memory when the battery is disconnected. This includes idling and operating values, and any fault codes detected – in the case of the fault codes, if it is thought likely that the system has developed a fault for which the corresponding code has been logged, the car must be taken to a Toyota dealer for the codes to be read, using the special diagnostic equipment necessary for this. Whenever the battery is disconnected, the information relating to idle speed control and other operating values will have to be re-programmed into the unit's memory. The ECU does this automatically, but until then, there may be surging, hesitation, erratic idle and a generally inferior level of performance. To allow the ECU to relearn these values, start the engine and run it as close to idle speed as possible until it reaches its normal operating temperature, then run it for approximately two minutes at 1200 rpm. Next, drive the car as far as necessary – approximately 5 miles of varied driving conditions is usually sufficient – to complete the relearning process.*

c) *Unusually, the standard-fit Toyota audio unit does not have a security code system ('radio code'), so the worst that will happen to the audio unit following battery disconnection is the loss of any radio presets.*

Devices known as 'memory-savers' (or 'code-savers') can be used to avoid some of the above problems. Precise details vary according to the device used. Typically, it is plugged into the cigarette lighter, and is connected by its own wires to a spare battery; the car's own battery is then disconnected from the electrical system, leaving the 'memory-saver' to pass sufficient current to maintain audio unit security codes and ECU memory values, and also to run permanently-live circuits such as the clock, all the while isolating the battery in the event of a short-circuit occurring while work is carried out.

Warning: Some of these devices allow a considerable amount of current to pass, which can mean that many of the car's systems are still operational when the main battery is disconnected. If a 'memory-saver' is used, ensure that the circuit concerned is actually 'dead' before carrying out any work on it!

Introduction

A selection of good tools is a fundamental requirement for anyone contemplating the maintenance and repair of a motor vehicle. For the owner who does not possess any, their purchase will prove a considerable expense, offsetting some of the savings made by doing-it-yourself. However, provided that the tools purchased meet the relevant national safety standards and are of good quality, they will last for many years and prove an extremely worthwhile investment.

To help the average owner to decide which tools are needed to carry out the various tasks detailed in this manual, we have compiled three lists of tools under the following headings: *Maintenance and minor repair, Repair and overhaul*, and *Special*. Newcomers to practical mechanics should start off with the *Maintenance and minor repair* tool kit, and confine themselves to the simpler jobs around the vehicle. Then, as confidence and experience grow, more difficult tasks can be undertaken, with extra tools being purchased as, and when, they are needed. In this way, a *Maintenance and minor repair* tool kit can be built up into a *Repair and overhaul* tool kit over a considerable period of time, without any major cash outlays. The experienced do-it-yourselfer will have a tool kit good enough for most repair and overhaul procedures, and will add tools from the *Special* category when it is felt that the expense is justified by the amount of use to which these tools will be put.

Maintenance and minor repair tool kit

The tools given in this list should be considered as a minimum requirement if routine maintenance, servicing and minor repair operations are to be undertaken. We recommend the purchase of combination spanners (ring one end, open-ended the other); although more expensive than open-ended ones, they do give the advantages of both types of spanner.

☐ *Combination spanners:*
Metric - 8 to 19 mm inclusive
☐ *Adjustable spanner - 35 mm jaw (approx.)*
☐ *Spark plug spanner (with rubber insert) - petrol models*
☐ *Spark plug gap adjustment tool - petrol models*
☐ *Set of feeler gauges*
☐ *Brake bleed nipple spanner*
☐ *Screwdrivers:*
Flat blade - 100 mm long x 6 mm dia
Cross blade - 100 mm long x 6 mm dia
Torx - various sizes (not all vehicles)
☐ *Combination pliers*
☐ *Hacksaw (junior)*
☐ *Tyre pump*
☐ *Tyre pressure gauge*
☐ *Oil can*
☐ *Oil filter removal tool*
☐ *Fine emery cloth*
☐ *Wire brush (small)*
☐ *Funnel (medium size)*
☐ *Sump drain plug key (not all vehicles)*

Repair and overhaul tool kit

These tools are virtually essential for anyone undertaking any major repairs to a motor vehicle, and are additional to those given in the *Maintenance and minor repair* list. Included in this list is a comprehensive set of sockets. Although these are expensive, they will be found invaluable as they are so versatile - particularly if various drives are included in the set. We recommend the half-inch square-drive type, as this can be used with most proprietary torque wrenches.

The tools in this list will sometimes need to be supplemented by tools from the *Special* list:

☐ *Sockets (or box spanners) to cover range in previous list (including Torx sockets)*
☐ *Reversible ratchet drive (for use with sockets)*
☐ *Extension piece, 250 mm (for use with sockets)*
☐ *Universal joint (for use with sockets)*
☐ *Flexible handle or sliding T "breaker bar" (for use with sockets)*
☐ *Torque wrench (for use with sockets)*
☐ *Self-locking grips*
☐ *Ball pein hammer*
☐ *Soft-faced mallet (plastic or rubber)*
☐ *Screwdrivers:*
Flat blade - long & sturdy, short (chubby), and narrow (electrician's) types
Cross blade – long & sturdy, and short (chubby) types
☐ *Pliers:*
Long-nosed
Side cutters (electrician's)
Circlip (internal and external)
☐ *Cold chisel - 25 mm*
☐ *Scriber*
☐ *Scraper*
☐ *Centre-punch*
☐ *Pin punch*
☐ *Hacksaw*
☐ *Brake hose clamp*
☐ *Brake/clutch bleeding kit*
☐ *Selection of twist drills*
☐ *Steel rule/straight-edge*
☐ *Allen keys (inc. splined/Torx type)*
☐ *Selection of files*
☐ *Wire brush*
☐ *Axle stands*
☐ *Jack (strong trolley or hydraulic type)*
☐ *Light with extension lead*
☐ *Universal electrical multi-meter*

Sockets and reversible ratchet drive

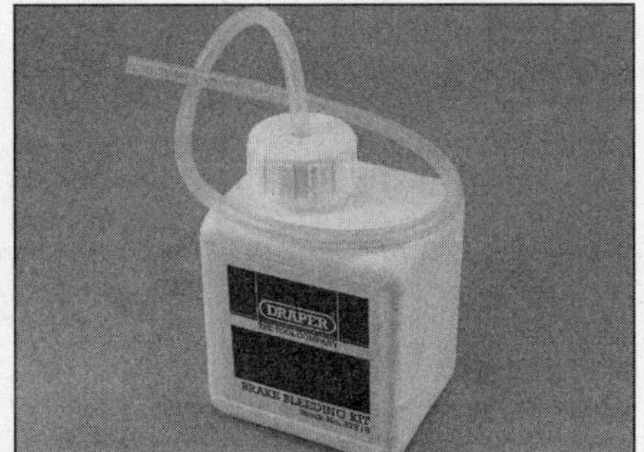

Brake bleeding kit

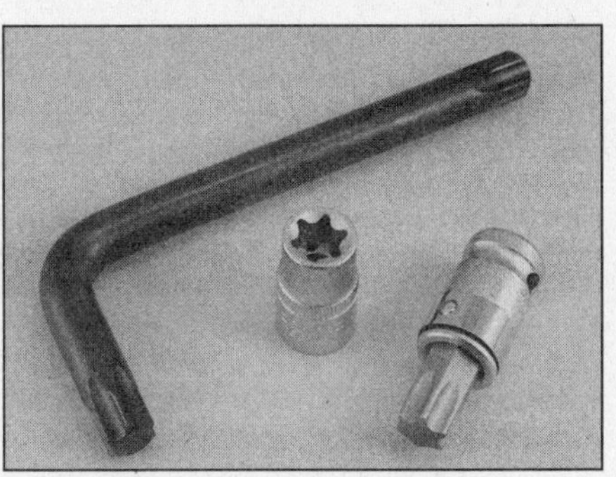

Torx key, socket and bit

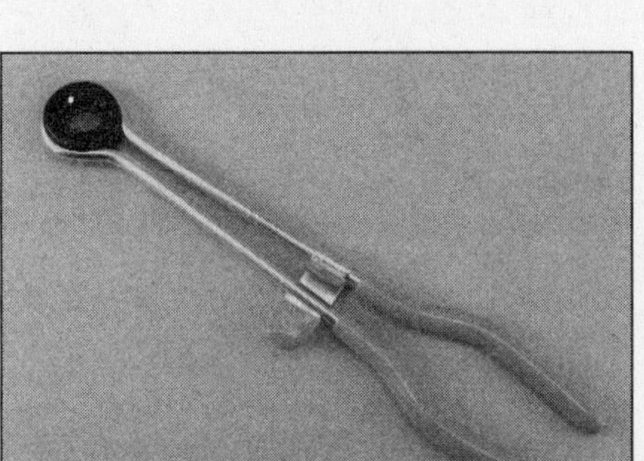

Hose clamp

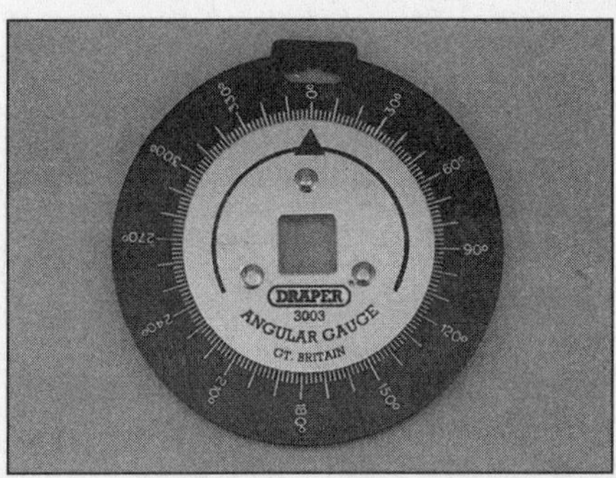

Angular-tightening gauge

Special tools

The tools in this list are those which are not used regularly, are expensive to buy, or which need to be used in accordance with their manufacturers' instructions. Unless relatively difficult mechanical jobs are undertaken frequently, it will not be economic to buy many of these tools. Where this is the case, you could consider clubbing together with friends (or joining a motorists' club) to make a joint purchase, or borrowing the tools against a deposit from a local garage or tool hire specialist. It is worth noting that many of the larger DIY superstores now carry a large range of special tools for hire at modest rates.

The following list contains only those tools and instruments freely available to the public, and not those special tools produced by the vehicle manufacturer specifically for its dealer network. You will find occasional references to these manufacturers' special tools in the text of this manual. Generally, an alternative method of doing the job without the vehicle manufacturers' special tool is given. However, sometimes there is no alternative to using them. Where this is the case and the relevant tool cannot be bought or borrowed, you will have to entrust the work to a dealer.

- ☐ *Angular-tightening gauge*
- ☐ *Valve spring compressor*
- ☐ *Valve grinding tool*
- ☐ *Piston ring compressor*
- ☐ *Piston ring removal/installation tool*
- ☐ *Cylinder bore hone*
- ☐ *Balljoint separator*
- ☐ *Coil spring compressors (where applicable)*
- ☐ *Two/three-legged hub and bearing puller*
- ☐ *Impact screwdriver*
- ☐ *Micrometer and/or vernier calipers*
- ☐ *Dial gauge*
- ☐ *Stroboscopic timing light*
- ☐ *Dwell angle meter/tachometer*
- ☐ *Fault code reader*
- ☐ *Cylinder compression gauge*
- ☐ *Hand-operated vacuum pump and gauge*
- ☐ *Clutch plate alignment set*
- ☐ *Brake shoe steady spring cup removal tool*
- ☐ *Bush and bearing removal/installation set*
- ☐ *Stud extractors*
- ☐ *Tap and die set*
- ☐ *Lifting tackle*
- ☐ *Trolley jack*

Buying tools

Reputable motor accessory shops and superstores often offer excellent quality tools at discount prices, so it pays to shop around.

Remember, you don't have to buy the most expensive items on the shelf, but it is always advisable to steer clear of the very cheap tools. Beware of 'bargains' offered on market stalls or at car boot sales. There are plenty of good tools around at reasonable prices, but always aim to purchase items which meet the relevant national safety standards. If in doubt, ask the proprietor or manager of the shop for advice before making a purchase.

Care and maintenance of tools

Having purchased a reasonable tool kit, it is necessary to keep the tools in a clean and serviceable condition. After use, always wipe off any dirt, grease and metal particles using a clean, dry cloth, before putting the tools away. Never leave them lying around after they have been used. A simple tool rack on the garage or workshop wall for items such as screwdrivers and pliers is a good idea. Store all normal spanners and sockets in a metal box. Any measuring instruments, gauges, meters, etc, must be carefully stored where they cannot be damaged or become rusty.

Take a little care when tools are used. Hammer heads inevitably become marked, and screwdrivers lose the keen edge on their blades from time to time. A little timely attention with emery cloth or a file will soon restore items like this to a good finish.

Working facilities

Not to be forgotten when discussing tools is the workshop itself. If anything more than routine maintenance is to be carried out, a suitable working area becomes essential.

It is appreciated that many an owner-mechanic is forced by circumstances to remove an engine or similar item without the benefit of a garage or workshop. Having done this, any repairs should always be done under the cover of a roof.

Wherever possible, any dismantling should be done on a clean, flat workbench or table at a suitable working height.

Any workbench needs a vice; one with a jaw opening of 100 mm is suitable for most jobs. As mentioned previously, some clean dry storage space is also required for tools, as well as for any lubricants, cleaning fluids, touch-up paints etc, which become necessary.

Another item which may be required, and which has a much more general usage, is an electric drill with a chuck capacity of at least 8 mm. This, together with a good range of twist drills, is virtually essential for fitting accessories.

Last, but not least, always keep a supply of old newspapers and clean, lint-free rags available, and try to keep any working area as clean as possible.

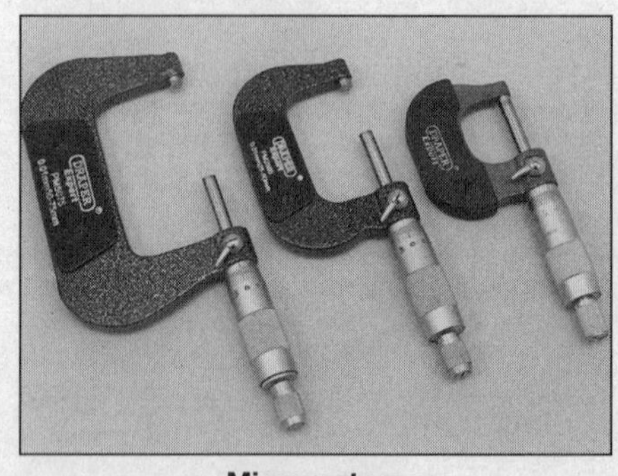
Micrometers

Dial test indicator ("dial gauge")

Strap wrench

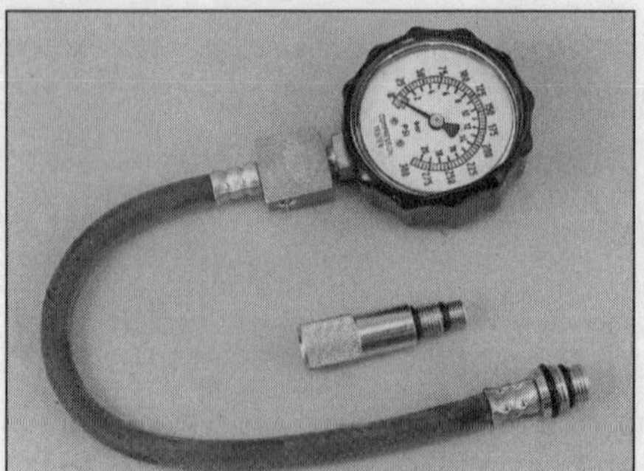
Compression tester

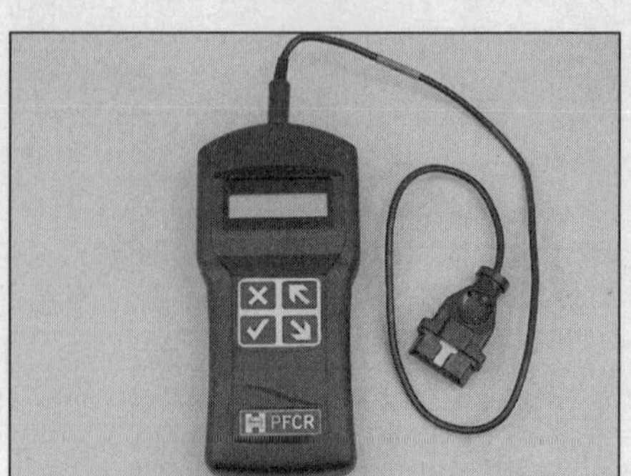

Fault code reader

This is a guide to getting your vehicle through the MOT test. Obviously it will not be possible to examine the vehicle to the same standard as the professional MOT tester. However, working through the following checks will enable you to identify any problem areas before submitting the vehicle for the test.

Where a testable component is in borderline condition, the tester has discretion in deciding whether to pass or fail it. The basis of such discretion is whether the tester would be happy for a close relative or friend to use the vehicle with the component in that condition. If the vehicle presented is clean and evidently well cared for, the tester may be more inclined to pass a borderline component than if the vehicle is scruffy and apparently neglected.

It has only been possible to summarise the test requirements here, based on the regulations in force at the time of printing. Test standards are becoming increasingly stringent, although there are some exemptions for older vehicles.

An assistant will be needed to help carry out some of these checks.

The checks have been sub-divided into four categories, as follows:

1 Checks carried out **FROM THE DRIVER'S SEAT**

2 Checks carried out **WITH THE VEHICLE ON THE GROUND**

3 Checks carried out **WITH THE VEHICLE RAISED AND THE WHEELS FREE TO TURN**

4 Checks carried out on **YOUR VEHICLE'S EXHAUST EMISSION SYSTEM**

1 Checks carried out FROM THE DRIVER'S SEAT

Handbrake

☐ Test the operation of the handbrake. Excessive travel (too many clicks) indicates incorrect brake or cable adjustment.

☐ Check that the handbrake cannot be released by tapping the lever sideways. Check the security of the lever mountings.

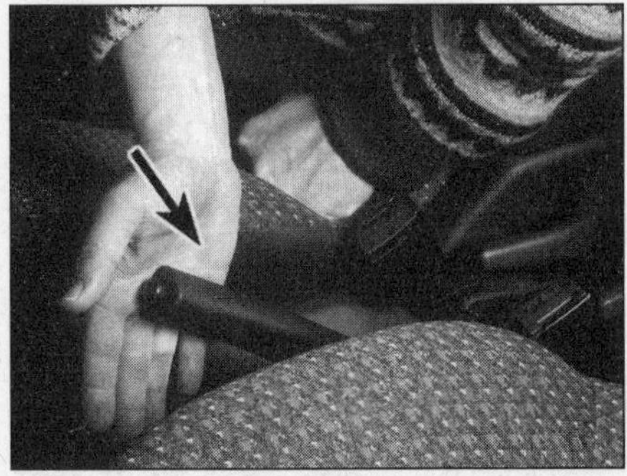

Footbrake

☐ Depress the brake pedal and check that it does not creep down to the floor, indicating a master cylinder fault. Release the pedal, wait a few seconds, then depress it again. If the pedal travels nearly to the floor before firm resistance is felt, brake adjustment or repair is necessary. If the pedal feels spongy, there is air in the hydraulic system which must be removed by bleeding.

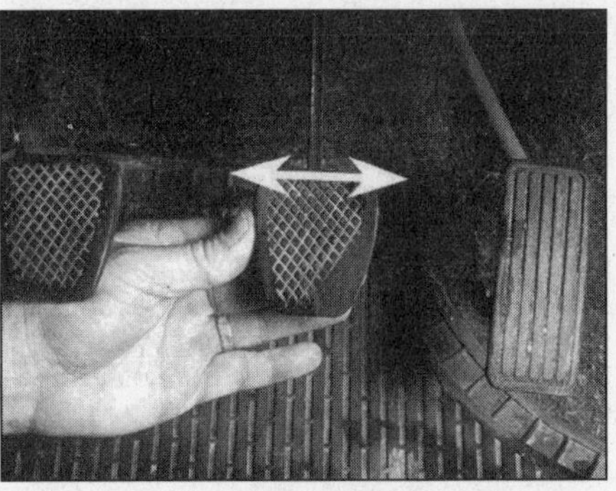

☐ Check that the brake pedal is secure and in good condition. Check also for signs of fluid leaks on the pedal, floor or carpets, which would indicate failed seals in the brake master cylinder.

☐ Check the servo unit (when applicable) by operating the brake pedal several times, then keeping the pedal depressed and starting the engine. As the engine starts, the pedal will move down slightly. If not, the vacuum hose or the servo itself may be faulty.

Steering wheel and column

☐ Examine the steering wheel for fractures or looseness of the hub, spokes or rim.

☐ Move the steering wheel from side to side and then up and down. Check that the steering wheel is not loose on the column, indicating wear or a loose retaining nut. Continue moving the steering wheel as before, but also turn it slightly from left to right.

☐ Check that the steering wheel is not loose on the column, and that there is no abnormal

movement of the steering wheel, indicating wear in the column support bearings or couplings.

Windscreen, mirrors and sunvisor

☐ The windscreen must be free of cracks or other significant damage within the driver's field of view. (Small stone chips are acceptable.) Rear view mirrors must be secure, intact, and capable of being adjusted.

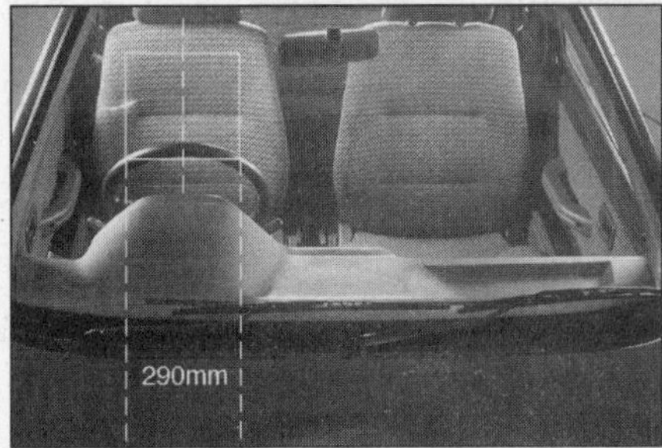

☐ The driver's sunvisor must be capable of being stored in the "up" position.

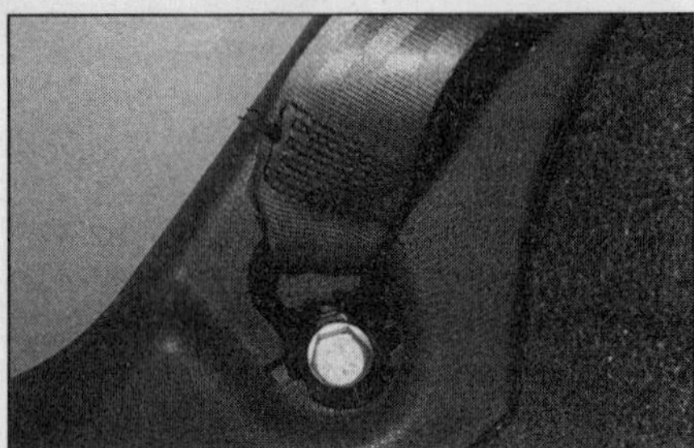

Seat belts and seats

Note: *The following checks are applicable to all seat belts, front and rear.*

☐ Examine the webbing of all the belts (including rear belts if fitted) for cuts, serious fraying or deterioration. Fasten and unfasten each belt to check the buckles. If applicable, check the retracting mechanism. Check the security of all seat belt mountings accessible from inside the vehicle.

☐ Seat belts with pre-tensioners, once activated, have a "flag" or similar showing on the seat belt stalk. This, in itself, is not a reason for test failure.

☐ The front seats themselves must be securely attached and the backrests must lock in the upright position.

Doors

☐ Both front doors must be able to be opened and closed from outside and inside, and must latch securely when closed.

2 Checks carried out WITH THE VEHICLE ON THE GROUND

Vehicle identification

☐ Number plates must be in good condition, secure and legible, with letters and numbers correctly spaced – spacing at (A) should be at least twice that at (B).

☐ The VIN plate and/or homologation plate must be legible.

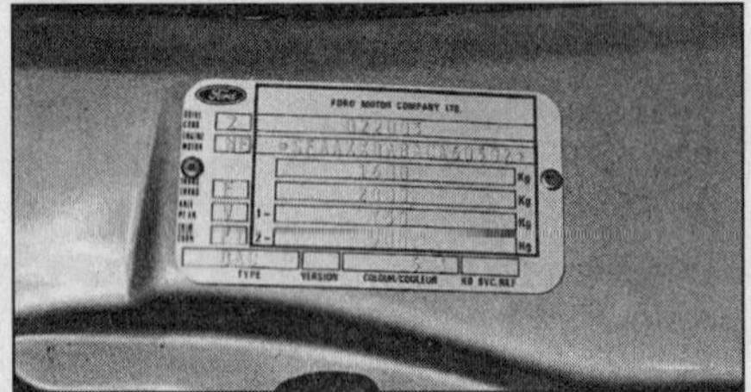

Electrical equipment

☐ Switch on the ignition and check the operation of the horn.

☐ Check the windscreen washers and wipers, examining the wiper blades; renew damaged or perished blades. Also check the operation of the stop-lights.

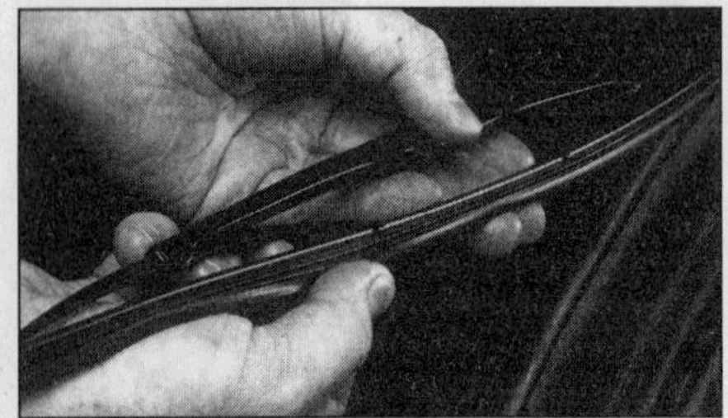

☐ Check the operation of the sidelights and number plate lights. The lenses and reflectors must be secure, clean and undamaged.

☐ Check the operation and alignment of the headlights. The headlight reflectors must not be tarnished and the lenses must be undamaged.

☐ Switch on the ignition and check the operation of the direction indicators (including the instrument panel tell-tale) and the hazard warning lights. Operation of the sidelights and stop-lights must not affect the indicators - if it does, the cause is usually a bad earth at the rear light cluster.

☐ Check the operation of the rear foglight(s), including the warning light on the instrument panel or in the switch.

☐ The ABS warning light must illuminate in accordance with the manufacturers' design. For most vehicles, the ABS warning light should illuminate when the ignition is switched on, and (if the system is operating properly) extinguish after a few seconds. Refer to the owner's handbook.

Footbrake

☐ Examine the master cylinder, brake pipes and servo unit for leaks, loose mountings, corrosion or other damage.

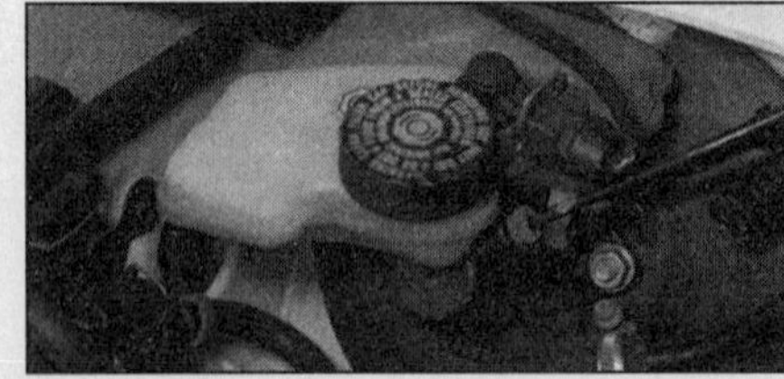

☐ The fluid reservoir must be secure and the fluid level must be between the upper (**A**) and lower (**B**) markings.

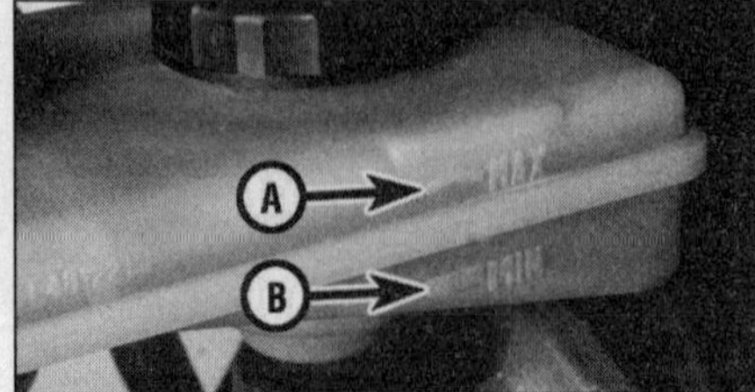

☐ Inspect both front brake flexible hoses for cracks or deterioration of the rubber. Turn the steering from lock to lock, and ensure that the hoses do not contact the wheel, tyre, or any part of the steering or suspension mechanism. With the brake pedal firmly depressed, check the hoses for bulges or leaks under pressure.

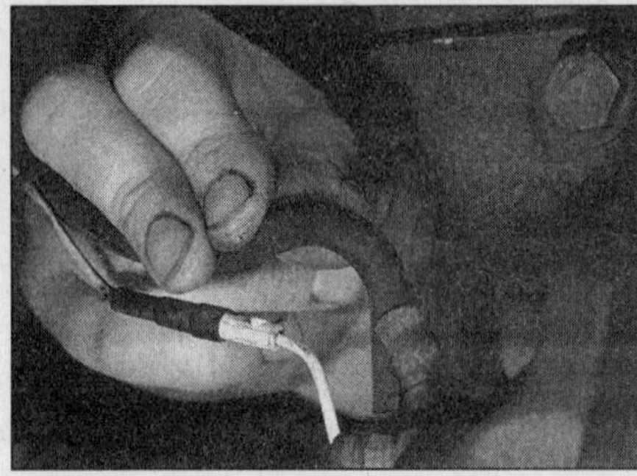

Steering and suspension

☐ Have your assistant turn the steering wheel from side to side slightly, up to the point where the steering gear just begins to transmit this movement to the roadwheels. Check for excessive free play between the steering wheel and the steering gear, indicating wear or insecurity of the steering column joints, the column-to-steering gear coupling, or the steering gear itself.

☐ Have your assistant turn the steering wheel more vigorously in each direction, so that the roadwheels just begin to turn. As this is done, examine all the steering joints, linkages, fittings and attachments. Renew any component that shows signs of wear or damage. On vehicles with power steering, check the security and condition of the steering pump, drivebelt and hoses.

☐ Check that the vehicle is standing level, and at approximately the correct ride height.

Shock absorbers

☐ Depress each corner of the vehicle in turn, then release it. The vehicle should rise and then settle in its normal position. If the vehicle continues to rise and fall, the shock absorber is defective. A shock absorber which has seized will also cause the vehicle to fail.

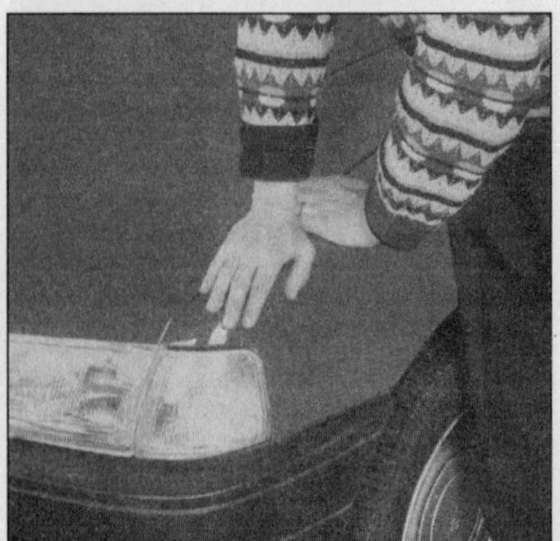

Exhaust system

□ Start the engine. With your assistant holding a rag over the tailpipe, check the entire system for leaks. Repair or renew leaking sections.

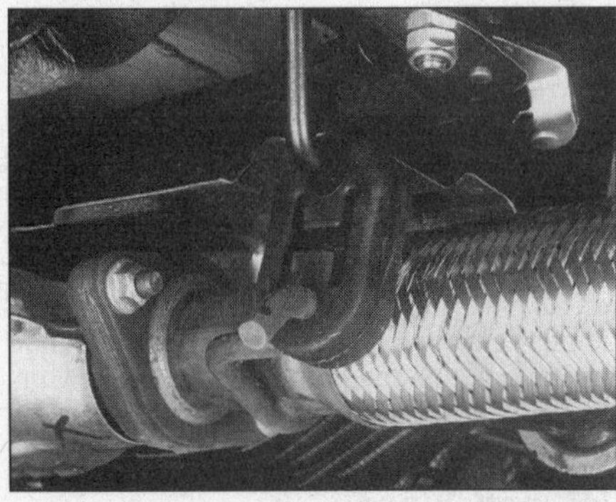

3 Checks carried out WITH THE VEHICLE RAISED AND THE WHEELS FREE TO TURN

Jack up the front and rear of the vehicle, and securely support it on axle stands. Position the stands clear of the suspension assemblies. Ensure that the wheels are clear of the ground and that the steering can be turned from lock to lock.

Steering mechanism

□ Have your assistant turn the steering from lock to lock. Check that the steering turns smoothly, and that no part of the steering mechanism, including a wheel or tyre, fouls any brake hose or pipe or any part of the body structure.

□ Examine the steering rack rubber gaiters for damage or insecurity of the retaining clips. If power steering is fitted, check for signs of damage or leakage of the fluid hoses, pipes or connections. Also check for excessive stiffness or binding of the steering, a missing split pin or locking device, or severe corrosion of the body structure within 30 cm of any steering component attachment point.

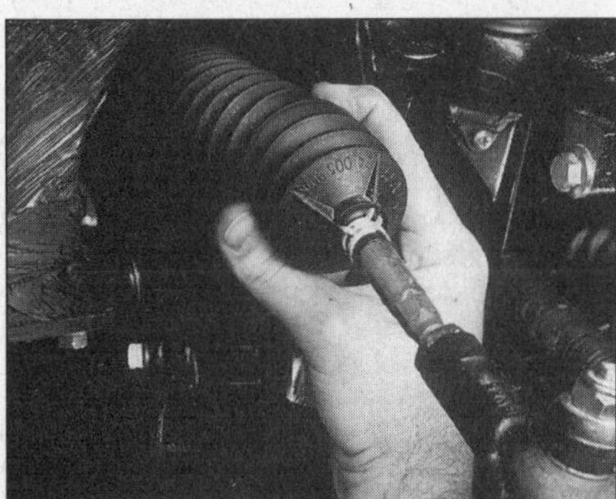

Front and rear suspension and wheel bearings

□ Starting at the front right-hand side, grasp the roadwheel at the 3 o'clock and 9 o'clock positions and rock gently but firmly. Check for free play or insecurity at the wheel bearings, suspension balljoints, or suspension mountings, pivots and attachments.

□ Now grasp the wheel at the 12 o'clock and 6 o'clock positions and repeat the previous inspection. Spin the wheel, and check for roughness or tightness of the front wheel bearing.

□ If excess free play is suspected at a component pivot point, this can be confirmed by using a large screwdriver or similar tool and levering between the mounting and the component attachment. This will confirm whether the wear is in the pivot bush, its retaining bolt, or in the mounting itself (the bolt holes can often become elongated).

□ Carry out all the above checks at the other front wheel, and then at both rear wheels.

Springs and shock absorbers

□ Examine the suspension struts (when applicable) for serious fluid leakage, corrosion, or damage to the casing. Also check the security of the mounting points.

□ If coil springs are fitted, check that the spring ends locate in their seats, and that the spring is not corroded, cracked or broken.

□ If leaf springs are fitted, check that all leaves are intact, that the axle is securely attached to each spring, and that there is no deterioration of the spring eye mountings, bushes, and shackles.

□ The same general checks apply to vehicles fitted with other suspension types, such as torsion bars, hydraulic displacer units, etc. Ensure that all mountings and attachments are secure, that there are no signs of excessive wear, corrosion or damage, and (on hydraulic types) that there are no fluid leaks or damaged pipes.

□ Inspect the shock absorbers for signs of serious fluid leakage. Check for wear of the mounting bushes or attachments, or damage to the body of the unit.

Driveshafts (fwd vehicles only)

□ Rotate each front wheel in turn and inspect the constant velocity joint gaiters for splits or damage. Also check that each driveshaft is straight and undamaged.

Braking system

□ If possible without dismantling, check brake pad wear and disc condition. Ensure that the friction lining material has not worn excessively, (A) and that the discs are not fractured, pitted, scored or badly worn (B).

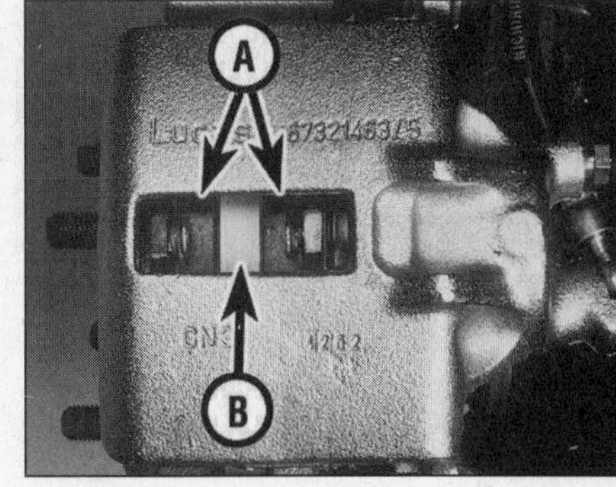

□ Examine all the rigid brake pipes underneath the vehicle, and the flexible hose(s) at the rear. Look for corrosion, chafing or insecurity of the pipes, and for signs of bulging under pressure, chafing, splits or deterioration of the flexible hoses.

□ Look for signs of fluid leaks at the brake calipers or on the brake backplates. Repair or renew leaking components.

□ Slowly spin each wheel, while your assistant depresses and releases the footbrake. Ensure that each brake is operating and does not bind when the pedal is released.

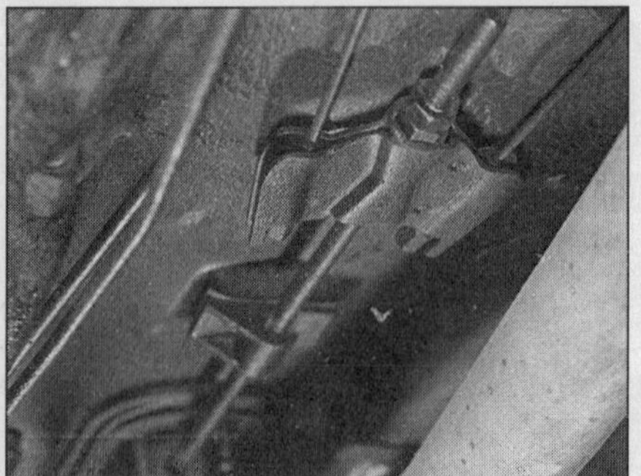

☐ Examine the handbrake mechanism, checking for frayed or broken cables, excessive corrosion, or wear or insecurity of the linkage. Check that the mechanism works on each relevant wheel, and releases fully, without binding.

☐ It is not possible to test brake efficiency without special equipment, but a road test can be carried out later to check that the vehicle pulls up in a straight line.

Fuel and exhaust systems

☐ Inspect the fuel tank (including the filler cap), fuel pipes, hoses and unions. All components must be secure and free from leaks.

☐ Examine the exhaust system over its entire length, checking for any damaged, broken or missing mountings, security of the retaining clamps and rust or corrosion.

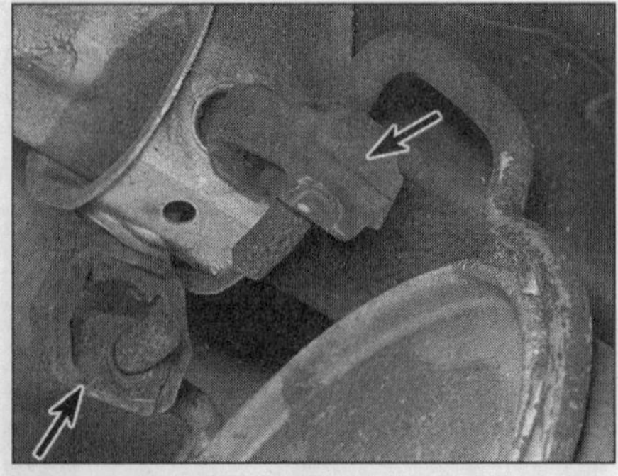

Wheels and tyres

☐ Examine the sidewalls and tread area of each tyre in turn. Check for cuts, tears, lumps, bulges, separation of the tread, and exposure of the ply or cord due to wear or damage. Check that the tyre bead is correctly seated on the wheel rim, that the valve is sound and properly seated, and that the wheel is not distorted or damaged.

☐ Check that the tyres are of the correct size for the vehicle, that they are of the same size and type on each axle, and that the pressures are correct.

☐ Check the tyre tread depth. The legal minimum at the time of writing is 1.6 mm over at least three-quarters of the tread width. Abnormal tread wear may indicate incorrect front wheel alignment.

Body corrosion

☐ Check the condition of the entire vehicle structure for signs of corrosion in load-bearing areas. (These include chassis box sections, side sills, cross-members, pillars, and all suspension, steering, braking system and seat belt mountings and anchorages.) Any corrosion which has seriously reduced the thickness of a load-bearing area is likely to cause the vehicle to fail. In this case professional repairs are likely to be needed.

☐ Damage or corrosion which causes sharp or otherwise dangerous edges to be exposed will also cause the vehicle to fail.

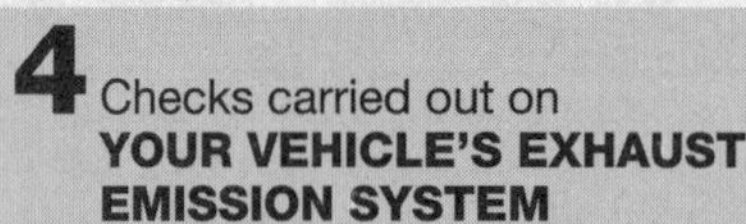

4 Checks carried out on **YOUR VEHICLE'S EXHAUST EMISSION SYSTEM**

Petrol models

☐ Have the engine at normal operating temperature, and make sure that it is in good tune (ignition system in good order, air filter element clean, etc).

☐ Before any measurements are carried out, raise the engine speed to around 2500 rpm, and hold it at this speed for 20 seconds. Allow the engine speed to return to idle, and watch for smoke emissions from the exhaust tailpipe. If the idle speed is obviously much too high, or if dense blue or clearly-visible black smoke comes from the tailpipe for more than 5 seconds, the vehicle will fail. As a rule of thumb, blue smoke signifies oil being burnt (engine wear) while black smoke signifies unburnt fuel (dirty air cleaner element, or other carburettor or fuel system fault).

☐ An exhaust gas analyser capable of measuring carbon monoxide (CO) and hydrocarbons (HC) is now needed. If such an instrument cannot be hired or borrowed, a local garage may agree to perform the check for a small fee.

CO emissions (mixture)

☐ At the time of writing, for vehicles first used between 1st August 1975 and 31st July 1986 (P to C registration), the CO level must not exceed 4.5% by volume. For vehicles first used between 1st August 1986 and 31st July 1992 (D to J registration), the CO level must not exceed 3.5% by volume. Vehicles first used after 1st August 1992 (K registration) must conform to the manufacturer's specification. The MOT tester has access to a DOT database or emissions handbook, which lists the CO and HC limits for each make and model of vehicle. The CO level is measured with the engine at idle speed, and at "fast idle". The following limits are given as a general guide:

At idle speed -
CO level no more than 0.5%
At "fast idle" (2500 to 3000 rpm) -
CO level no more than 0.3%
(Minimum oil temperature 60°C)

☐ If the CO level cannot be reduced far enough to pass the test (and the fuel and ignition systems are otherwise in good condition) then the carburettor is badly worn, or there is some problem in the fuel injection system or catalytic converter (as applicable).

HC emissions

☐ With the CO within limits, HC emissions for vehicles first used between 1st August 1975 and 31st July 1992 (P to J registration) must not exceed 1200 ppm. Vehicles first used after 1st August 1992 (K registration) must conform to the manufacturer's specification. The MOT tester has access to a DOT database or emissions handbook, which lists the CO and HC limits for each make and model of vehicle. The HC level is measured with the engine at "fast idle". The following is given as a general guide:

At "fast idle" (2500 to 3000 rpm) -
HC level no more than 200 ppm
(Minimum oil temperature 60°C)

☐ Excessive HC emissions are caused by incomplete combustion, the causes of which can include oil being burnt, mechanical wear and ignition/fuel system malfunction.

Diesel models

☐ The only emission test applicable to Diesel engines is the measuring of exhaust smoke density. The test involves accelerating the engine several times to its maximum unloaded speed.

Note: *It is of the utmost importance that the engine timing belt is in good condition before the test is carried out.*

☐ The limits for Diesel engine exhaust smoke, introduced in September 1995 are:

Vehicles first used before 1st August 1979:
Exempt from metered smoke testing, but must not emit "dense blue or clearly visible black smoke for a period of more than 5 seconds at idle" or "dense blue or clearly visible black smoke during acceleration which would obscure the view of other road users".

Non-turbocharged vehicles first used after 1st August 1979: 2.5m^{-1}

Turbocharged vehicles first used after 1st August 1979: 3.0m^{-1}

☐ Excessive smoke can be caused by a dirty air cleaner element. Otherwise, professional advice may be needed to find the cause.

Engine

- ☐ Engine fails to rotate when attempting to start
- ☐ Engine rotates, but will not start
- ☐ Engine difficult to start when cold
- ☐ Engine difficult to start when hot
- ☐ Starter motor noisy or excessively-rough in engagement
- ☐ Engine starts, but stops immediately
- ☐ Engine misfires, or idles unevenly
- ☐ Engine stalls, or lacks power
- ☐ Engine backfires
- ☐ Engine noises
- ☐ Oil consumption excessive
- ☐ Oil pressure warning light illuminated with engine running

Cooling system

- ☐ Overheating
- ☐ Overcooling
- ☐ External coolant leakage
- ☐ Internal coolant leakage
- ☐ Corrosion

Fuel and exhaust systems

- ☐ Fuel consumption excessive
- ☐ Fuel leakage and/or fuel odour
- ☐ Black smoke in exhaust
- ☐ Blue or white smoke in exhaust
- ☐ Excessive noise or fumes from exhaust system

Clutch

- ☐ Pedal travels to floor – no pressure or very little resistance
- ☐ Clutch fails to disengage (unable to select gears)
- ☐ Clutch slips (engine speed increases, with no increase in vehicle speed)
- ☐ Judder as clutch is engaged
- ☐ Noise when depressing or releasing clutch pedal

Manual transmission

- ☐ Noisy in neutral with engine running
- ☐ Noisy in one particular gear
- ☐ Difficulty engaging gears
- ☐ Jumps out of gear
- ☐ Vibration
- ☐ Lubricant leaks

Driveshafts

- ☐ Vibration when accelerating or decelerating
- ☐ Clicking or knocking noise on turns (at slow speed on full-lock)

Automatic transmission

- ☐ Fluid leakage
- ☐ Transmission fluid brown, or has burned smell
- ☐ General gear selection problems
- ☐ Transmission will not downshift (kickdown) with accelerator fully depressed
- ☐ Engine will not start in any gear, or starts in gears other than Park or Neutral
- ☐ Transmission slips, shifts roughly, is noisy, or has no drive in forward or reverse gears

Braking system

- ☐ Car pulls to one side under braking
- ☐ Noise (grinding or high-pitched squeal) when brakes applied
- ☐ Excessive brake pedal travel
- ☐ Brake pedal feels spongy when depressed
- ☐ Excessive brake pedal effort required to stop vehicle
- ☐ Judder felt through brake pedal or steering wheel when braking
- ☐ Brakes binding
- ☐ Rear wheels locking under normal braking

Suspension and steering

- ☐ Car pulls to one side
- ☐ Wheel wobble and vibration
- ☐ Excessive pitching and/or rolling around corners, or during braking
- ☐ Wandering or general instability
- ☐ Excessively-stiff steering
- ☐ Excessive play in steering
- ☐ Lack of power assistance
- ☐ Tyre wear excessive

Electrical system

- ☐ Battery will only hold a charge for a few days
- ☐ Ignition (no-charge) warning light remains illuminated with engine running
- ☐ Ignition (no-charge) warning light fails to come on
- ☐ Lights inoperative
- ☐ Instrument readings inaccurate or erratic
- ☐ Horn faults
- ☐ Windscreen/tailgate wiper faults
- ☐ Windscreen/tailgate washer faults
- ☐ Electric window faults
- ☐ Central locking system faults

Introduction

The car owner who does his or her own maintenance according to the recommended service schedules should not have to use this section of the manual very often. Modern component reliability is such that, provided those items subject to wear or deterioration are inspected or renewed at the specified intervals, sudden failure is comparatively rare. Faults do not usually just happen as a result of sudden failure, but develop over a period of time. Major mechanical failures in particular are usually preceded by characteristic symptoms over hundreds or even thousands of miles. Those components which do occasionally fail without warning are often small and easily carried in the car.

With any fault-finding, the first step is to decide where to begin investigations. Sometimes this is obvious, but on other occasions, a little detective work will be necessary. The owner who makes half a dozen haphazard adjustments or replacements may be successful in curing a fault (or its symptoms), but will be none the wiser if the fault recurs, and ultimately may have spent more time and money than was necessary. A calm and logical approach will be found to be more satisfactory in the long run. Always take into account any warning signs or abnormalities that may have been noticed in the period preceding the fault – power loss, high or low gauge readings, unusual smells, etc – and remember that failure of components such as fuses may only be pointers to some underlying fault.

The pages which follow provide an easy reference guide to the more common problems which may occur during the operation of the car. These problems and their possible causes are grouped under headings denoting various components or systems, such as Engine, Cooling system, etc. The Chapter and/or Section which deals with the problem is also shown in brackets. Whatever the fault, certain basic principles apply. These are as follows:

Verify the fault. This is simply a matter of being sure that you know what the symptoms are before starting work. This is particularly important if you are investigating a fault for someone else, who may not have described it very accurately.

Don't overlook the obvious. For example, if the car won't start, is there fuel in the tank? (Don't take anyone else's word on this particular point, and don't trust the fuel gauge either!) If an electrical fault is indicated, look for loose or broken wires before using the test gear.

Cure the disease, not the symptom. Substituting a flat battery with a fully-charged one will get you off the hard shoulder, but if the underlying cause is not attended to, the new battery will go the same way.

Don't take anything for granted. Particularly, don't forget that a 'new' component may itself be defective (especially if it's been rattling around in the boot for months), and don't leave components out of a fault diagnosis sequence just because they are new or recently fitted. When you do finally diagnose a difficult fault, you'll probably realise that all the evidence was there from the start.

Consider what work, if any, has recently been carried out. Many faults arise through careless or hurried work. For instance, if any work has been performed under the bonnet, could some of the wiring have been dislodged or incorrectly routed, or a hose trapped? Have all the fasteners been properly tightened? Were new, genuine parts and new gaskets used? There is often a certain amount of detective work to be done in this case, as an apparently-unrelated task can have far-reaching consequences.

Engine

Engine fails to rotate when attempting to start

- ☐ Battery terminal connections loose or corroded (*Weekly checks*).
- ☐ Battery discharged or faulty (Chapter 5A).
- ☐ Broken, loose or disconnected wiring in the starting circuit (Chapter 5A).
- ☐ Defective starter solenoid or ignition switch (Chapter 5A or 12).
- ☐ Defective starter motor (Chapter 5A).
- ☐ Flywheel ring gear or starter pinion teeth loose or broken (Chapter 2A or 5A).
- ☐ Engine earth strap broken or disconnected.
- ☐ Engine suffering 'hydraulic lock' (eg from water ingested after traversing flooded roads, or from a serious internal coolant leak) – consult a Toyota dealer for advice.
- ☐ Automatic transmission shift lock fault, footbrake not depressed, or faulty stop-light switch (Chapter 7B or 9).

Engine rotates, but will not start

- ☐ Fuel tank empty.
- ☐ Battery discharged or inadequate capacity (engine rotates slowly) (Chapter 5A).
- ☐ Battery terminal connections loose or corroded (*Weekly checks*).
- ☐ Ignition components damp or damaged (Chapter 1 or 5B)
- ☐ Worn, faulty or incorrectly-gapped spark plugs (Chapter 1)
- ☐ Immobiliser faulty or incorrectly used, or 'uncoded' ignition key being used (Chapter 12).
- ☐ Crankshaft sensor, or other engine management system sensor, fault (Chapter 4A)
- ☐ Air filter element dirty or clogged (Chapter 1).
- ☐ Blockage in exhaust system (Chapter 4B).
- ☐ Low cylinder compressions (Chapter 2A)
- ☐ Valve timing incorrect, possibly through a poorly-fitted timing chain (Chapter 2A).
- ☐ Major mechanical failure (eg camshaft drive) (Chapter 2A).

Engine difficult to start when cold

- ☐ Battery discharged (Chapter 5A).
- ☐ Battery terminal connections loose or corroded (see *Weekly checks*).
- ☐ Worn, faulty or incorrectly-gapped spark plugs (Chapter 1).
- ☐ Other ignition system fault (Chapter 5B).
- ☐ Fuel system fault (Chapter 4A).
- ☐ Wrong grade of engine oil used (*Weekly checks* or Chapter 1).
- ☐ Low cylinder compressions (Chapter 2A)

Engine difficult to start when hot

- ☐ Air filter element dirty or clogged (Chapter 1).
- ☐ Fuel system fault (Chapter 4A).
- ☐ Low cylinder compressions (Chapter 2A).

Starter motor noisy or excessively-rough

- ☐ Starter pinion or flywheel ring gear teeth loose or broken (Chapter 2A or 5A).
- ☐ Starter motor mounting bolts loose or missing (Chapter 5A).
- ☐ Starter motor internal components worn or damaged (Chapter 5A).

Engine starts, but stops immediately

- ☐ Loose or faulty electrical connections in the ignition circuit (Chapter 1 or 5B).
- ☐ Vacuum leak at the throttle body, inlet manifold or associated hoses (Chapter 4A).
- ☐ Blocked injectors/fuel system fault (Chapter 4A).
- ☐ Fuel very low in tank.
- ☐ Restriction in fuel feed.
- ☐ Air cleaner dirty, or blockage in air intake system (Chapter 1 or 4A).
- ☐ Blockage in exhaust system (Chapter 4B).

Engine misfires, or idles unevenly

- ☐ Air cleaner dirty or blockage in air intake system (Chapter 1 or 4A).
- ☐ Vacuum leak at the throttle body, inlet manifold or associated hoses (Chapter 4A).
- ☐ Worn, faulty or incorrectly-gapped spark plugs (Chapter 1).
- ☐ Valve clearances incorrect (Chapter 2A).
- ☐ Uneven or low cylinder compressions (Chapter 2A)
- ☐ Camshaft lobes worn (Chapter 2A).
- ☐ Timing chain incorrectly fitted (Chapter 2A).
- ☐ Blocked injectors/fuel injection system fault (Chapter 4A).
- ☐ Valve(s) sticking, valve spring(s) weak or broken, or poor compressions (Chapter 2A).
- ☐ Overheating (Chapter 3).
- ☐ Cylinder head gasket blown (Chapter 2A).

Engine stalls, or lacks power

- ☐ Fuel filter choked (Chapter 4A).
- ☐ Fuel pump faulty, or delivery pressure low (Chapter 4A).
- ☐ Valve clearances incorrect (Chapter 2A).
- ☐ Vacuum leak at the throttle body, inlet manifold or associated hoses (Chapter 4A).
- ☐ Worn, faulty or incorrectly-gapped spark plugs (Chapter 1).
- ☐ Faulty ignition coils (Chapter 5B).
- ☐ Uneven or low cylinder compressions (Chapter 2A).
- ☐ Blocked injector/fuel system fault (Chapter 4A).
- ☐ Blocked catalytic converter (Chapter 4B).
- ☐ Engine overheating (Chapter 3).
- ☐ Air filter element blocked (Chapter 1).
- ☐ Accelerator cable problem (Chapter 4A).
- ☐ Throttle position sensor fault (Chapter 4A).
- ☐ Engine management warning light on (fault code in system) (Chapter 4A).
- ☐ Timing chain worn, or incorrectly fitted (Chapter 2A).
- ☐ Brakes binding (Chapter 1 or 9).
- ☐ Clutch slipping (Chapter 6).

Engine backfires

- ☐ Timing chain incorrectly fitted (Chapter 2A).
- ☐ Vacuum leak at the throttle body, inlet manifold or associated hoses (Chapter 4A).
- ☐ Blocked catalytic converter (Chapter 4B).
- ☐ Ignition coil(s) faulty (Chapter 5B).

Engine (continued)

Engine noises

Pre-ignition (pinking) or knocking during acceleration or under load

- ☐ Ignition system fault (Chapter 1 or 5B).
- ☐ Incorrect grade of spark plug (Chapter 1).
- ☐ Incorrect grade (or type) of fuel used (Chapter 4A).
- ☐ Vacuum leak at the throttle body, inlet manifold or associated hoses (Chapter 4A).
- ☐ Excessive carbon build-up in cylinder head/pistons (Chapter 2A or 2B).
- ☐ Blocked injector/fuel injection system fault (Chapter 4A).

Whistling or wheezing noises

- ☐ Leaking inlet manifold or throttle body gasket (Chapter 4A).
- ☐ Leaking exhaust manifold gasket, or pipe-to-manifold joint (Chapter 4B).
- ☐ Leaking vacuum hose (Chapter 4 or 9).
- ☐ Blowing cylinder head gasket (Chapter 2A).
- ☐ Partially blocked or leaking crankcase ventilation system (Chapter 4B).

Tapping or rattling noises

- ☐ Worn camshaft(s) (Chapter 2A)
- ☐ Ancillary component fault (coolant pump, alternator, etc) (Chapter 3, 5A, etc).
- ☐ Valve clearances incorrect (Chapter 2A).

Knocking or thumping noises

- ☐ Worn big-end bearings (regular heavy knocking, perhaps less under load) (Chapter 2B).
- ☐ Worn main bearings (rumbling and knocking, perhaps worsening under load) (Chapter 2B).
- ☐ Piston slap – most noticeable when cold, caused by piston/bore wear (Chapter 2B).
- ☐ Ancillary component fault (coolant pump, alternator, etc) (Chapter 3, 5A, etc).
- ☐ Engine mountings worn or defective (Chapter 2A).
- ☐ Front suspension or steering components worn (Chapter 10).

Oil consumption excessive

- ☐ External leakage (standing or running) – eg timing chain cover, crankshaft oil seals (Chapter 2A).
- ☐ New engine not yet run-in.
- ☐ Engine oil incorrect grade/poor quality, or oil level too high (*Weekly checks*).
- ☐ Crankcase ventilation system obstructed (Chapter 1 or 4B).
- ☐ Burning oil due to general engine wear – pistons and/or bores, valve stem oil seals, etc (Chapter 2B).

Oil pressure warning light illuminated with engine running

- ☐ Low oil level or incorrect oil grade (*Weekly checks*).
- ☐ Engine oil and filter change overdue (Chapter 1).
- ☐ Faulty oil pressure warning light switch (Chapter 2A).
- ☐ Worn engine bearings and/or oil pump (Chapter 2A or 2B).
- ☐ High engine operating temperature (Chapter 3).
- ☐ Oil pick-up strainer clogged – remove sump to check (Chapter 2A).

Cooling system

Overheating

- ☐ Insufficient coolant in system (*Weekly checks*).
- ☐ Thermostat faulty (Chapter 3).
- ☐ Radiator core blocked or grille restricted (Chapter 3).
- ☐ Radiator electric cooling fan or coolant temperature sensor faulty (Chapter 3).
- ☐ Pressure cap faulty (Chapter 3).
- ☐ Inaccurate coolant temperature gauge sender (Chapter 3).
- ☐ Airlock in cooling system (Chapter 1).
- ☐ Engine management system fault (Chapter 4A).
- ☐ Blockage in exhaust system (Chapter 4B).
- ☐ Cylinder head gasket blown (Chapter 2A).

Overcooling

- ☐ Thermostat faulty (Chapter 3).
- ☐ Inaccurate coolant temperature gauge sender (Chapter 3).

External coolant leakage

- ☐ Deteriorated or damaged hoses or hose clips (Chapter 1).
- ☐ Radiator core or heater matrix leaking (Chapter 3).
- ☐ Pressure cap faulty (Chapter 1).
- ☐ Water pump or thermostat housing leaking (Chapter 3).
- ☐ Boiling due to overheating (Chapter 3).
- ☐ Core plug leaking (Chapter 2B).

Internal coolant leakage

- ☐ Leaking cylinder head gasket (Chapter 2A).
- ☐ Cracked cylinder head or cylinder bore (Chapter 2A or 2B).

Corrosion

- ☐ Infrequent draining and flushing (Chapter 1).
- ☐ Incorrect antifreeze mixture, or inappropriate antifreeze type (*Weekly checks* and Chapter 1).

Fuel and exhaust systems

Fuel consumption excessive

- ☐ New engine not yet run-in.
- ☐ Air cleaner element dirty, or blockage in air intake system (Chapter 1 or 4A).
- ☐ Fuel system fault (Chapter 4A).
- ☐ Crankcase ventilation system blocked (Chapter 4B).
- ☐ Unsympathetic driving style, or adverse conditions.
- ☐ Tyres under-inflated (see *Weekly checks*).
- ☐ Brakes binding (Chapter 1 or 9).
- ☐ Fuel leak, causing apparent high consumption (Chapter 1 or 4A).
- ☐ Valve timing incorrect, possibly through a poorly-fitted timing chain (Chapter 2A).

Fuel leakage and/or fuel odour

- ☐ Damaged or corroded fuel tank, pipes or connections (Chapter 1).
- ☐ Evaporative emissions system fault (Chapter 4B).

Black smoke in exhaust

- ☐ Air cleaner element dirty, or blockage in air intake system (Chapter 1 or 4A).
- ☐ Fuel system fault (Chapter 4A).

Fuel and exhaust systems (continued)

Blue or white smoke in exhaust

- ☐ Engine oil incorrect grade or poor quality, or fuel passing into sump (worn piston rings/bores).
- ☐ Air cleaner element dirty, or blockage in air intake system (Chapter 1 or 4A).
- ☐ Injector(s) faulty (Chapter 4A).
- ☐ Blocked or damaged emissions system hoses or components (Chapter 4B).
- ☐ General engine wear – pistons and/or bores, valve stem oil seals, etc (Chapter 2B).
- ☐ Cylinder head gasket blown – white smoke (Chapter 2A).

Excessive noise or fumes from exhaust system

- ☐ Leaking exhaust system or manifold joints (Chapter 1 or 4B).
- ☐ Leaking, corroded or damaged silencers or pipe (Chapter 1 or 4B).
- ☐ Oxygen sensors loose or damaged (Chapter 4B).
- ☐ Broken mountings, causing body or suspension contact (Chapter 1 or 4B).

Clutch

Pedal travels to floor – no pressure or very little resistance

- ☐ Air in hydraulic system/faulty master or slave cylinder (Chapter 6).
- ☐ Faulty hydraulic release system (Chapter 6).
- ☐ Clutch pedal return spring detached or broken (Chapter 6).
- ☐ Broken clutch release bearing or fork (Chapter 6).
- ☐ Broken diaphragm spring in clutch pressure plate (Chapter 6).

Clutch fails to disengage (unable to select gears)

- ☐ Air in hydraulic system/faulty master or slave cylinder (Chapter 6).
- ☐ Faulty hydraulic release system (Chapter 6).
- ☐ Clutch disc sticking on transmission input shaft splines (Chapter 6).
- ☐ Clutch disc sticking to flywheel or pressure plate (Chapter 6).
- ☐ Faulty pressure plate assembly (Chapter 6).
- ☐ Clutch release mechanism worn or incorrectly assembled (Chapter 6).

Clutch slips (engine speed increases, with no increase in vehicle speed)

- ☐ Faulty hydraulic release system (Chapter 6).
- ☐ Clutch disc linings excessively worn (Chapter 6).
- ☐ Clutch disc linings contaminated with oil or grease (Chapter 6).
- ☐ Faulty pressure plate or weak diaphragm spring (Chapter 6).

Judder as clutch is engaged

- ☐ Clutch disc linings contaminated with oil or grease (Chapter 6).
- ☐ Clutch disc linings excessively worn (Chapter 6).
- ☐ Faulty or distorted pressure plate or diaphragm spring (Chapter 6).
- ☐ Worn or loose engine/transmission mountings (Chapter 2A).
- ☐ Clutch disc hub or transmission input shaft splines worn (Chapter 6 or 7A).

Noise when depressing or releasing clutch pedal

- ☐ Worn clutch release bearing (Chapter 6).
- ☐ Worn or dry clutch pedal bushes (Chapter 6).
- ☐ Worn or dry clutch master cylinder piston (Chapter 6).
- ☐ Faulty pressure plate assembly (Chapter 6).
- ☐ Pressure plate diaphragm spring broken (Chapter 6).
- ☐ Broken clutch disc cushioning springs (Chapter 6).

Manual transmission

Noisy in neutral with engine running

- ☐ Lack of oil (Chapter 1).
- ☐ Input shaft bearings worn (noise apparent with clutch pedal released, but not when depressed) (Chapter 7A).*
- ☐ Clutch release bearing worn (noise apparent with clutch pedal depressed, possibly less when released) (Chapter 6).

Noisy in one particular gear

- ☐ Worn, damaged or chipped gear teeth (Chapter 7A).*

Difficulty engaging gears

- ☐ Clutch fault (Chapter 6).
- ☐ Worn or damaged gear cables (Chapter 7A).
- ☐ Worn synchroniser assemblies (Chapter 7A).*

Jumps out of gear

- ☐ Worn or damaged gear cables (Chapter 7A).
- ☐ Worn synchroniser assemblies (Chapter 7A).*
- ☐ Worn selector forks (Chapter 7A).*

Vibration

- ☐ Lack of oil (Chapter 1).
- ☐ Worn bearings (Chapter 7A).*

Lubricant leaks

- ☐ Leaking differential side gear oil seal (Chapter 7A).
- ☐ Leaking housing joint (Chapter 7A).*
- ☐ Leaking input shaft oil seal (Chapter 7A).*
- ☐ Leaking selector shaft oil seal (Chapter 7A).

** Although the corrective action necessary to remedy the symptoms described is beyond the scope of the home mechanic, the above information should be helpful in isolating the cause of the condition, so that the owner can communicate clearly with a professional mechanic.*

Driveshafts

Vibration when accelerating or decelerating

- ☐ Worn inner constant velocity joint (Chapter 1 or 8).
- ☐ Bent or distorted driveshaft (Chapter 8).
- ☐ Right-hand driveshaft vibration damper loose or missing (Chapter 8).
- ☐ Loose or damaged driveshaft nut (Chapter 1 or 8).

Clicking or knocking noise on turns (at slow speed on full-lock)

- ☐ Lack of constant velocity joint lubricant (Chapter 8).
- ☐ Worn outer constant velocity joint (Chapter 1 or 8).
- ☐ Loose or damaged driveshaft nut (Chapter 1 or 8).

Automatic transmission

Note: *Due to the complexity of the automatic transmission, it is difficult for the home mechanic to properly diagnose and service this unit. For problems other than the following, the car should be taken to a dealer service department or automatic transmission specialist. Do not be too hasty in removing the transmission if a fault is suspected, as most of the testing is carried out with the unit still fitted.*

Fluid leakage

☐ Automatic transmission fluid is usually dark (and often red) in colour. Fluid leaks should not be confused with engine oil, which can easily be blown onto the transmission by airflow.

☐ To determine the source of a leak, first remove all built-up dirt and grime from the transmission housing and surrounding areas using a degreasing agent, or by steam-cleaning. Drive the car at low speed, so airflow will not blow the leak far from its source. Raise and support the car, and determine where the leak is coming from.

General gear selection problems

☐ Chapter 7B deals with the shift lock and selector cable on the automatic transmission. The following are common problems which may be cable-related:

a) *Engine starting in gears other than Park or Neutral.*
b) *Indicator panel indicating a gear other than the one actually being used.*
c) *Car moves when in Park or Neutral.*
d) *Poor gear shift quality or erratic gear changes.*

☐ Refer to Chapter 7B to check, and possibly renew, the cables.

Transmission will not downshift (kickdown) with accelerator pedal fully depressed

☐ Low transmission fluid level (Chapter 1).
☐ Throttle position sensor faulty (Chapter 4A).
☐ Engine management system problem (Chapter 4A).
☐ Selector cable stretched (Chapter 7B).

Engine will not start in any gear, or starts in gears other than Park or Neutral

☐ Shift lock system faulty (Chapter 7B).
☐ Selector cable stretched (Chapter 7B).

Transmission slips, shifts roughly, is noisy, or has no drive in forward or reverse gears

☐ There are many probable causes for the above problems, but unless there is a very obvious reason (such as a loose or corroded wiring plug connection on or near the transmission), the car should be taken to a Toyota dealer for the fault to be diagnosed. The transmission control unit incorporates a self-diagnosis facility, and any fault codes can quickly be read and interpreted by a Toyota dealer with the proper diagnostic equipment.

Braking system

Note: *Before assuming that a brake problem exists, make sure that the tyres are in good condition and correctly inflated, that the front wheel alignment is correct, and that the car is not loaded with weight in an unequal manner. Apart from checking the condition of all pipe and hose connections, any faults occurring on the Anti-lock Braking System (ABS) should be referred to a Toyota dealer for diagnosis.*

Car pulls to one side under braking

☐ Worn, defective, damaged or contaminated front or rear brake pads/shoes on one side (Chapter 1).
☐ Seized or partially-seized front caliper, or leaking rear wheel cylinder (Chapter 9).
☐ A mixture of brake pad/shoe lining materials fitted between sides (Chapter 1).
☐ Brake caliper mounting bolts loose (Chapter 9).
☐ Rear hub/brake backplate mounting bolts loose (Chapter 9).
☐ Worn or damaged steering or suspension components (Chapter 10).

Noise (grinding or high-pitched squeal) when brakes applied

☐ Brake pad or shoe friction lining material worn down to metal backing Chapter 1).
☐ Excessive corrosion of brake disc or drum (may be apparent after the car has been standing for some time) (Chapter 1).

Excessive brake pedal travel

☐ Inoperative rear brake self-adjust mechanism (Chapter 9).
☐ Rear wheel cylinders leaking (Chapter 9).
☐ Faulty master cylinder (Chapter 9).
☐ Air in hydraulic system (Chapter 9).

Brake pedal feels spongy when depressed

☐ Air in hydraulic system (Chapter 9).
☐ Rear wheel cylinders leaking (Chapter 9).
☐ Deteriorated flexible rubber brake hoses (Chapter 9).
☐ Master cylinder mounting nuts loose (Chapter 9).
☐ Faulty master cylinder (Chapter 9).

Excessive brake pedal effort required to stop car

☐ Faulty vacuum servo unit (Chapter 9).
☐ Disconnected, damaged or insecure brake servo vacuum hoses (Chapter 9).
☐ Primary or secondary hydraulic circuit failure (Chapter 9).
☐ Seized brake caliper or wheel cylinder piston(s) (Chapter 9).
☐ Brake pads or brake shoes incorrectly fitted (Chapter 9).
☐ Incorrect grade of brake pads or brake shoes fitted (Chapter 1).
☐ Brake pads or brake shoe linings contaminated (Chapter 1).

Judder felt through brake pedal or steering wheel when braking

☐ Excessive run-out or distortion of front discs or rear discs/drums (Chapter 9).
☐ Brake pad or brake shoe linings worn (Chapter 1).
☐ Brake caliper or rear brake backplate mounting bolts loose (Chapter 9).
☐ Wear in suspension or steering components or mountings (Chapter 10).

Brakes binding

☐ Seized brake caliper or wheel cylinder piston(s) (Chapter 9).
☐ Faulty handbrake mechanism (Chapter 9).
☐ Faulty master cylinder (Chapter 9).

Rear wheels locking under normal braking

☐ Rear brake pad/shoe linings contaminated (Chapter 1).
☐ Faulty brake pressure regulator valves, or ABS unit (Chapter 9).

Suspension and steering

Note: *Before diagnosing suspension or steering faults, be sure that the trouble is not due to incorrect tyre pressures, mixtures of tyre types, or binding brakes.*

Car pulls to one side

- ☐ Defective tyre (Chapter 1).
- ☐ Excessive wear in suspension or steering components (Chapter 10).
- ☐ Incorrect front wheel alignment (Chapter 10).
- ☐ Accident damage to steering or suspension components (Chapter 10).

Wheel wobble and vibration

- ☐ Front roadwheels out of balance (vibration felt mainly through the steering wheel) (Chapter 1).
- ☐ Rear roadwheels out of balance (vibration felt throughout the car) (Chapter 1).
- ☐ Roadwheels damaged or distorted (Chapter 1).
- ☐ Faulty or damaged tyre (*Weekly checks*).
- ☐ Worn steering or suspension joints, bushes or components (Chapter 10).
- ☐ Roadwheel nuts loose (Chapter 1).
- ☐ Wear in driveshaft joint, or loose driveshaft nut (vibration worst when under load) (Chapter 1 or 8).

Excessive pitching and/or rolling around corners, or during braking

- ☐ Defective shock absorbers (Chapter 10).
- ☐ Broken or weak coil spring and/or suspension components (Chapter 10).
- ☐ Worn or damaged anti-roll bar or mountings (Chapter 10).

Wandering or general instability

- ☐ Incorrect front wheel alignment (Chapter 10).
- ☐ Worn steering or suspension joints, bushes or components (Chapter 10).
- ☐ Tyres out of balance (*Weekly checks*).
- ☐ Faulty or damaged tyre (*Weekly checks*).
- ☐ Roadwheel nuts loose (Chapter 1).
- ☐ Defective shock absorbers (Chapter 10).

Excessively-stiff steering

- ☐ Lack of steering gear lubricant (Chapter 10).
- ☐ Seized track-rod end balljoint or suspension balljoint (Chapter 10).
- ☐ Broken or slipping auxiliary drivebelt (hydraulic power steering) (Chapter 1).
- ☐ Faulty power steering motor, blown fuse, or damaged wiring (electric power steering) (Chapter 10).
- ☐ Incorrect front wheel alignment (Chapter 10).
- ☐ Steering rack or column bent or damaged (Chapter 10).

Excessive play in steering

- ☐ Worn steering column universal joint (Chapter 10).
- ☐ Worn steering track-rod end balljoints (Chapter 10).
- ☐ Worn rack-and-pinion steering gear (Chapter 10).
- ☐ Worn steering or suspension joints, bushes or components (Chapter 10).

Lack of power assistance

- ☐ Broken or slipping auxiliary drivebelt (hydraulic power steering) (Chapter 1).
- ☐ Faulty power steering motor, blown fuse, or damaged wiring (electric power steering) (Chapter 10).
- ☐ Incorrect power steering hydraulic fluid level (*Weekly checks*).
- ☐ Restriction in power steering hydraulic fluid hoses (Chapter 10).
- ☐ Faulty power steering pump (hydraulic power steering) (Chapter 10).
- ☐ Faulty rack-and-pinion steering gear (Chapter 10).

Tyre wear excessive

Tyres worn on inside or outside edges

- ☐ Tyres under-inflated (wear on both edges) (*Weekly checks*).
- ☐ Incorrect camber or castor angles (wear on one edge only) (Chapter 10).
- ☐ Worn steering or suspension joints, bushes or components (Chapter 10).
- ☐ Excessively-hard cornering.
- ☐ Accident damage.

Tyre treads exhibit feathered edges

- ☐ Incorrect toe setting (Chapter 10).

Tyres worn in centre of tread

- ☐ Tyres over-inflated (*Weekly checks*).

Tyres worn on inside and outside edges

- ☐ Tyres under-inflated (*Weekly checks*).

Tyres worn unevenly

- ☐ Tyres out of balance (*Weekly checks*).
- ☐ Excessive wheel or tyre run-out (Chapter 1).
- ☐ Worn shock absorbers (Chapter 10).
- ☐ Faulty tyre (*Weekly checks*).

Electrical system

Note: *For problems associated with the starting system, refer to the faults listed under Engine earlier in this Section.*

Battery will only hold a charge for a few days

- ☐ Battery defective internally (Chapter 5A).
- ☐ Battery electrolyte level low (Chapter 5A).
- ☐ Battery terminal connections loose or corroded (*Weekly checks*).
- ☐ Auxiliary drivebelt worn or slipping (Chapter 1).
- ☐ Alternator not charging at correct output (Chapter 5A).
- ☐ Alternator or voltage regulator faulty (Chapter 5A).
- ☐ Short-circuit causing continual battery drain (Chapters 5A and 12).

Ignition (no-charge) warning light remains illuminated with engine running

- ☐ Auxiliary drivebelt broken, worn, or slipping (Chapter 1).
- ☐ Alternator brushes worn, sticking, or dirty (Chapter 5A).
- ☐ Alternator brush springs weak or broken (Chapter 5A).
- ☐ Internal fault in alternator or voltage regulator (Chapter 5A).
- ☐ Disconnected or loose wiring in charging circuit (Chapter 5A).

Ignition (no-charge) warning light fails to come on

- ☐ Warning light bulb blown (Chapter 12).
- ☐ Broken, disconnected, or loose wiring in warning light circuit (Chapters 5A and 12).
- ☐ Alternator faulty (Chapter 5A).

Lights inoperative

- ☐ Bulb blown (Chapter 12).
- ☐ Corrosion of bulb or bulbholder contacts (Chapter 12).
- ☐ Blown fuse (Chapter 12).
- ☐ Faulty relay (Chapter 12).
- ☐ Broken, loose, or disconnected wiring (Chapter 12).
- ☐ Faulty switch (Chapter 12).

Electrical system (continued)

Instrument readings inaccurate or erratic

Gauges give no reading

- ☐ Faulty gauge sender unit (Chapter 3 or 4A).
- ☐ Wiring open-circuit (Chapter 12).
- ☐ Faulty gauge (Chapter 12).

Gauges give continuous maximum reading

- ☐ Faulty gauge sender unit (Chapter 3 or 4A).
- ☐ Wiring short-circuit (Chapter 12).
- ☐ Faulty gauge (Chapter 12).

Horn faults

Horn fails to operate

- ☐ Blown fuse (Chapter 12).
- ☐ Cable or cable connections loose or disconnected (Chapter 12).
- ☐ Faulty switch (Chapter 12).
- ☐ Faulty horn (Chapter 12).

Horn emits intermittent or unsatisfactory sound

- ☐ Cable connections loose (Chapter 12).
- ☐ Horn mountings loose (Chapter 12).
- ☐ Faulty horn (Chapter 12).

Horn operates all the time

- ☐ Horn push either earthed or stuck down (Chapter 12).
- ☐ Horn cable to horn push earthed (Chapter 12).

Windscreen/tailgate wiper faults

Wipers fail to operate, or operate very slowly

- ☐ Wiper blades stuck to screen, or linkage seized (Chapter 12).
- ☐ Blown fuse (Chapter 12).
- ☐ Cable or cable connections loose or disconnected (Chapter 12).
- ☐ Faulty switch (Chapter 12).
- ☐ Faulty relay (Chapter 12).
- ☐ Faulty wiper motor (Chapter 12).

Wiper blades sweep over the wrong area of glass

- ☐ Wiper arms incorrectly-positioned on spindles (Chapter 12).
- ☐ Excessive wear of wiper linkage (Chapter 12).
- ☐ Wiper motor or linkage mountings loose or insecure (Chapter 12).

Wiper blades fail to clean the glass effectively

- ☐ Wiper blade rubbers worn or perished (*Weekly checks*).
- ☐ Wiper arm tension springs broken, or arm pivots seized (Chapter 12).
- ☐ Insufficient windscreen washer additive to adequately remove road film (*Weekly checks*).

Windscreen/tailgate washer faults

One or more washer jets inoperative

- ☐ Blocked washer jet (*Weekly checks* or Chapter 12).
- ☐ Disconnected, kinked or restricted fluid hose (Chapter 12).
- ☐ Insufficient fluid in washer reservoir (*Weekly checks*).

Washer pump fails to operate

- ☐ Broken or disconnected wiring or connections (Chapter 12).
- ☐ Blown fuse (Chapter 12).
- ☐ Faulty washer switch (Chapter 12).
- ☐ Faulty washer pump (Chapter 12).

Washer pump runs for some time before fluid is emitted from jets

- ☐ Faulty one-way valve in fluid supply hose (Chapter 12).

Electric window faults

Window glass will only move in one direction

- ☐ Faulty switch (Chapter 12).

Window glass slow to move

- ☐ Regulator seized or damaged, or lack of lubrication (Chapter 11).
- ☐ Door internal components or trim fouling regulator (Chapter 11).
- ☐ Faulty motor (Chapter 12).

Window glass fails to move

- ☐ Blown fuse (Chapter 12).
- ☐ Faulty relay (Chapter 12).
- ☐ Broken or disconnected wiring or connections (Chapter 12).
- ☐ Faulty motor (Chapter 12).

Central locking system faults

Complete system failure

- ☐ Blown fuse (Chapter 12).
- ☐ Faulty control unit or relay (Chapter 11).
- ☐ Broken or disconnected wiring or connections (Chapter 12).

Latch locks but will not unlock, or unlocks but will not lock

- ☐ Faulty master switch (Chapter 12).
- ☐ Faulty lock (Chapter 11).
- ☐ Faulty relay (Chapter 12).

One lock motor fails to operate

- ☐ Broken or disconnected wiring or connections (Chapter 12).
- ☐ Faulty lock motor (Chapter 11).
- ☐ Fault in door latch (Chapter 11).

A

ABS (Anti-lock brake system) A system, usually electronically controlled, that senses incipient wheel lockup during braking and relieves hydraulic pressure at wheels that are about to skid.
Air bag An inflatable bag hidden in the steering wheel (driver's side) or the dash or glovebox (passenger side). In a head-on collision, the bags inflate, preventing the driver and front passenger from being thrown forward into the steering wheel or windscreen.
Air cleaner A metal or plastic housing, containing a filter element, which removes dust and dirt from the air being drawn into the engine.
Air filter element The actual filter in an air cleaner system, usually manufactured from pleated paper and requiring renewal at regular intervals.

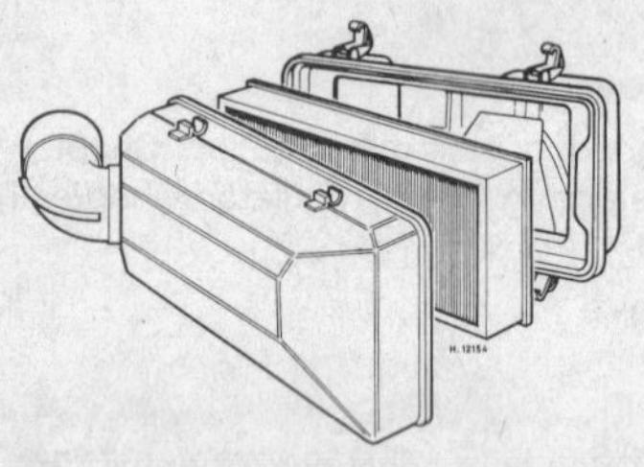

Air filter

Allen key A hexagonal wrench which fits into a recessed hexagonal hole.
Alligator clip A long-nosed spring-loaded metal clip with meshing teeth. Used to make temporary electrical connections.
Alternator A component in the electrical system which converts mechanical energy from a drivebelt into electrical energy to charge the battery and to operate the starting system, ignition system and electrical accessories.
Ampere (amp) A unit of measurement for the flow of electric current. One amp is the amount of current produced by one volt acting through a resistance of one ohm.
Anaerobic sealer A substance used to prevent bolts and screws from loosening. Anaerobic means that it does not require oxygen for activation. The Loctite brand is widely used.
Antifreeze A substance (usually ethylene glycol) mixed with water, and added to a vehicle's cooling system, to prevent freezing of the coolant in winter. Antifreeze also contains chemicals to inhibit corrosion and the formation of rust and other deposits that would tend to clog the radiator and coolant passages and reduce cooling efficiency.
Anti-seize compound A coating that reduces the risk of seizing on fasteners that are subjected to high temperatures, such as exhaust manifold bolts and nuts.
Asbestos A natural fibrous mineral with great heat resistance, commonly used in the composition of brake friction materials. Asbestos is a health hazard and the dust created by brake systems should never be inhaled or ingested.
Axle A shaft on which a wheel revolves, or which revolves with a wheel. Also, a solid beam that connects the two wheels at one end of the vehicle. An axle which also transmits power to the wheels is known as a live axle.
Axleshaft A single rotating shaft, on either side of the differential, which delivers power from the final drive assembly to the drive wheels. Also called a driveshaft or a halfshaft.

B

Ball bearing An anti-friction bearing consisting of a hardened inner and outer race with hardened steel balls between two races.
Bearing The curved surface on a shaft or in a bore, or the part assembled into either, that permits relative motion between them with minimum wear and friction.

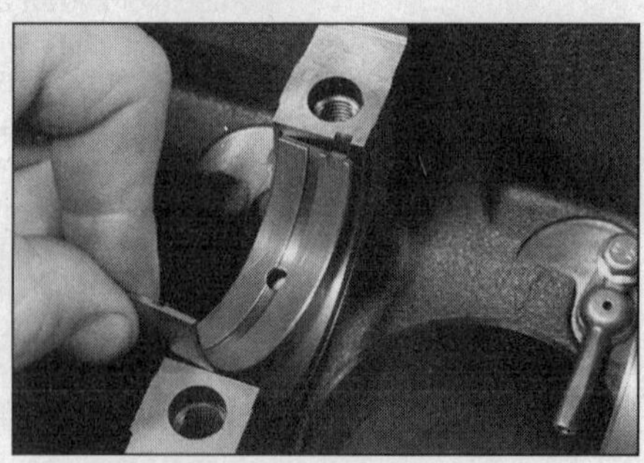

Bearing

Big-end bearing The bearing in the end of the connecting rod that's attached to the crankshaft.
Bleed nipple A valve on a brake wheel cylinder, caliper or other hydraulic component that is opened to purge the hydraulic system of air. Also called a bleed screw.
Brake bleeding Procedure for removing air from lines of a hydraulic brake system.

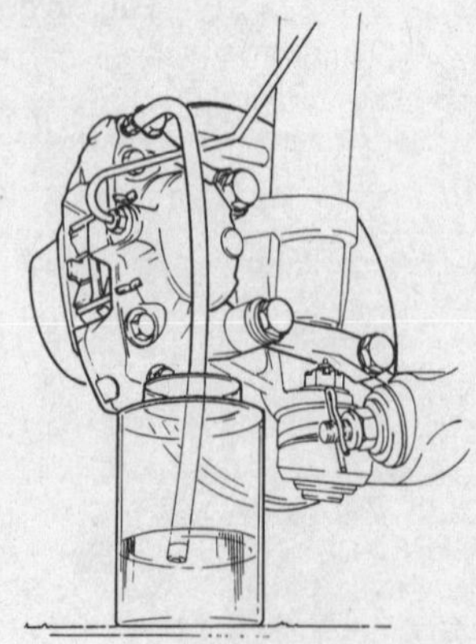

Brake bleeding

Brake disc The component of a disc brake that rotates with the wheels.
Brake drum The component of a drum brake that rotates with the wheels.
Brake linings The friction material which contacts the brake disc or drum to retard the vehicle's speed. The linings are bonded or riveted to the brake pads or shoes.
Brake pads The replaceable friction pads that pinch the brake disc when the brakes are applied. Brake pads consist of a friction material bonded or riveted to a rigid backing plate.
Brake shoe The crescent-shaped carrier to which the brake linings are mounted and which forces the lining against the rotating drum during braking.
Braking systems For more information on braking systems, consult the *Haynes Automotive Brake Manual*.
Breaker bar A long socket wrench handle providing greater leverage.
Bulkhead The insulated partition between the engine and the passenger compartment.

C

Caliper The non-rotating part of a disc-brake assembly that straddles the disc and carries the brake pads. The caliper also contains the hydraulic components that cause the pads to pinch the disc when the brakes are applied. A caliper is also a measuring tool that can be set to measure inside or outside dimensions of an object.
Camshaft A rotating shaft on which a series of cam lobes operate the valve mechanisms. The camshaft may be driven by gears, by sprockets and chain or by sprockets and a belt.
Canister A container in an evaporative emission control system; contains activated charcoal granules to trap vapours from the fuel system.

Canister

Carburettor A device which mixes fuel with air in the proper proportions to provide a desired power output from a spark ignition internal combustion engine.
Castellated Resembling the parapets along the top of a castle wall. For example, a castellated balljoint stud nut.
Castor In wheel alignment, the backward or forward tilt of the steering axis. Castor is positive when the steering axis is inclined rearward at the top.

Catalytic converter A silencer-like device in the exhaust system which converts certain pollutants in the exhaust gases into less harmful substances.

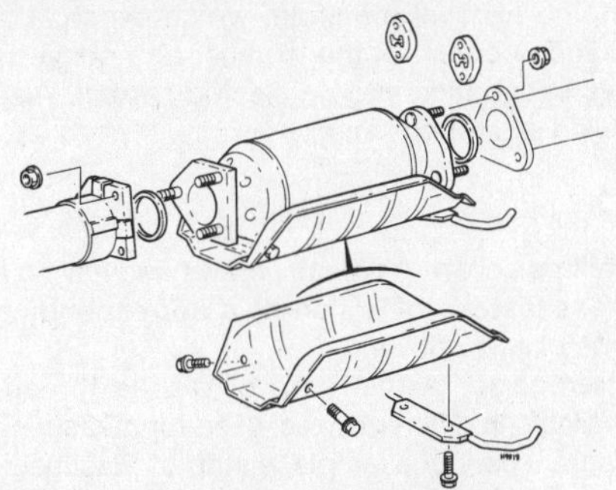

Catalytic converter

Circlip A ring-shaped clip used to prevent endwise movement of cylindrical parts and shafts. An internal circlip is installed in a groove in a housing; an external circlip fits into a groove on the outside of a cylindrical piece such as a shaft.

Clearance The amount of space between two parts. For example, between a piston and a cylinder, between a bearing and a journal, etc.

Coil spring A spiral of elastic steel found in various sizes throughout a vehicle, for example as a springing medium in the suspension and in the valve train.

Compression Reduction in volume, and increase in pressure and temperature, of a gas, caused by squeezing it into a smaller space.

Compression ratio The relationship between cylinder volume when the piston is at top dead centre and cylinder volume when the piston is at bottom dead centre.

Constant velocity (CV) joint A type of universal joint that cancels out vibrations caused by driving power being transmitted through an angle.

Core plug A disc or cup-shaped metal device inserted in a hole in a casting through which core was removed when the casting was formed. Also known as a freeze plug or expansion plug.

Crankcase The lower part of the engine block in which the crankshaft rotates.

Crankshaft The main rotating member, or shaft, running the length of the crankcase, with offset "throws" to which the connecting rods are attached.

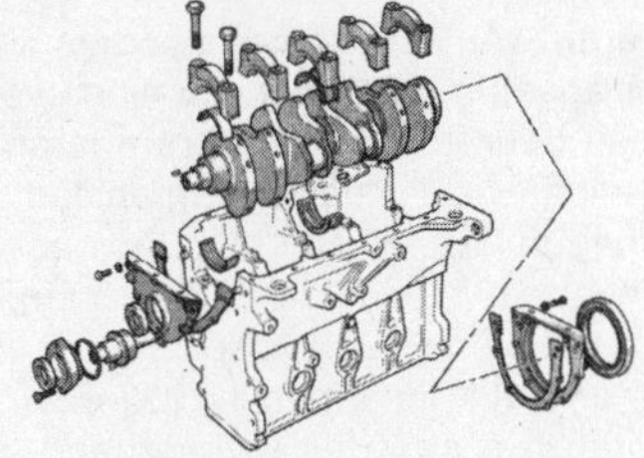

Crankshaft assembly

Crocodile clip See Alligator clip

D

Diagnostic code Code numbers obtained by accessing the diagnostic mode of an engine management computer. This code can be used to determine the area in the system where a malfunction may be located.

Disc brake A brake design incorporating a rotating disc onto which brake pads are squeezed. The resulting friction converts the energy of a moving vehicle into heat.

Double-overhead cam (DOHC) An engine that uses two overhead camshafts, usually one for the intake valves and one for the exhaust valves.

Drivebelt(s) The belt(s) used to drive accessories such as the alternator, water pump, power steering pump, air conditioning compressor, etc. off the crankshaft pulley.

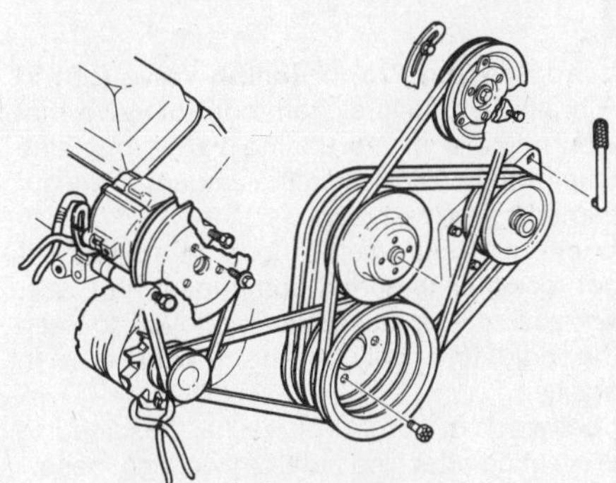

Accessory drivebelts

Driveshaft Any shaft used to transmit motion. Commonly used when referring to the axleshafts on a front wheel drive vehicle.

Drum brake A type of brake using a drum-shaped metal cylinder attached to the inner surface of the wheel. When the brake pedal is pressed, curved brake shoes with friction linings press against the inside of the drum to slow or stop the vehicle.

E

EGR valve A valve used to introduce exhaust gases into the intake air stream.

Electronic control unit (ECU) A computer which controls (for instance) ignition and fuel injection systems, or an anti-lock braking system. For more information refer to the *Haynes Automotive Electrical and Electronic Systems Manual.*

Electronic Fuel Injection (EFI) A computer controlled fuel system that distributes fuel through an injector located in each intake port of the engine.

Emergency brake A braking system, independent of the main hydraulic system, that can be used to slow or stop the vehicle if the primary brakes fail, or to hold the vehicle stationary even though the brake pedal isn't depressed. It usually consists of a hand lever that actuates either front or rear brakes mechanically through a series of cables and linkages. Also known as a handbrake or parking brake.

Endfloat The amount of lengthwise movement between two parts. As applied to a crankshaft, the distance that the crankshaft can move forward and back in the cylinder block.

Engine management system (EMS) A computer controlled system which manages the fuel injection and the ignition systems in an integrated fashion.

Exhaust manifold A part with several passages through which exhaust gases leave the engine combustion chambers and enter the exhaust pipe.

F

Fan clutch A viscous (fluid) drive coupling device which permits variable engine fan speeds in relation to engine speeds.

Feeler blade A thin strip or blade of hardened steel, ground to an exact thickness, used to check or measure clearances between parts.

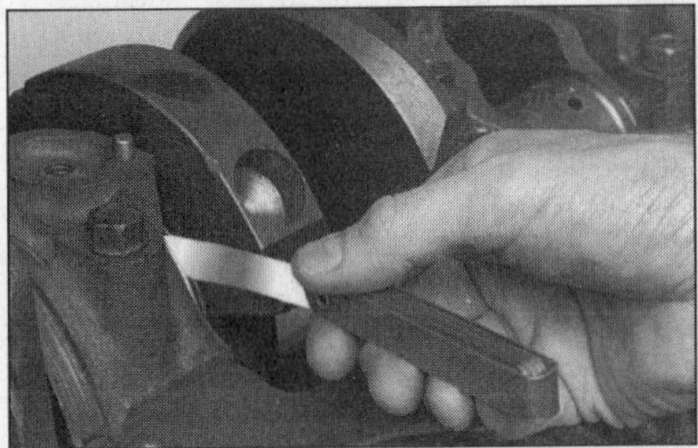

Feeler blade

Firing order The order in which the engine cylinders fire, or deliver their power strokes, beginning with the number one cylinder.

Flywheel A heavy spinning wheel in which energy is absorbed and stored by means of momentum. On cars, the flywheel is attached to the crankshaft to smooth out firing impulses.

Free play The amount of travel before any action takes place. The "looseness" in a linkage, or an assembly of parts, between the initial application of force and actual movement. For example, the distance the brake pedal moves before the pistons in the master cylinder are actuated.

Fuse An electrical device which protects a circuit against accidental overload. The typical fuse contains a soft piece of metal which is calibrated to melt at a predetermined current flow (expressed as amps) and break the circuit.

Fusible link A circuit protection device consisting of a conductor surrounded by heat-resistant insulation. The conductor is smaller than the wire it protects, so it acts as the weakest link in the circuit. Unlike a blown fuse, a failed fusible link must frequently be cut from the wire for replacement.

G

Gap The distance the spark must travel in jumping from the centre electrode to the side electrode in a spark plug. Also refers to the spacing between the points in a contact breaker assembly in a conventional points-type ignition, or to the distance between the reluctor or rotor and the pickup coil in an electronic ignition.

Adjusting spark plug gap

Gasket Any thin, soft material - usually cork, cardboard, asbestos or soft metal - installed between two metal surfaces to ensure a good seal. For instance, the cylinder head gasket seals the joint between the block and the cylinder head.

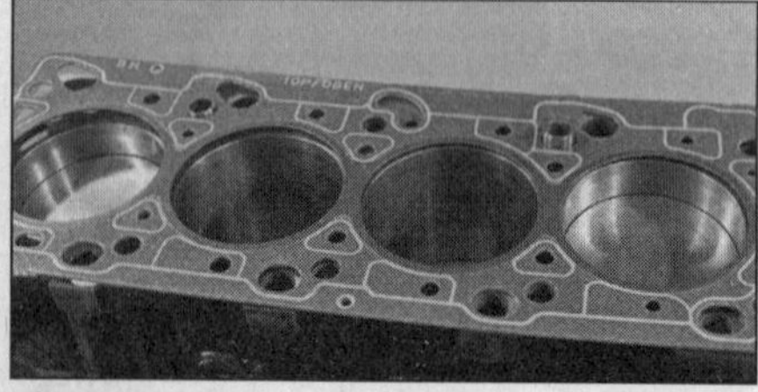

Gasket

Gauge An instrument panel display used to monitor engine conditions. A gauge with a movable pointer on a dial or a fixed scale is an analogue gauge. A gauge with a numerical readout is called a digital gauge.

H

Halfshaft A rotating shaft that transmits power from the final drive unit to a drive wheel, usually when referring to a live rear axle.

Harmonic balancer A device designed to reduce torsion or twisting vibration in the crankshaft. May be incorporated in the crankshaft pulley. Also known as a vibration damper.

Hone An abrasive tool for correcting small irregularities or differences in diameter in an engine cylinder, brake cylinder, etc.

Hydraulic tappet A tappet that utilises hydraulic pressure from the engine's lubrication system to maintain zero clearance (constant contact with both camshaft and valve stem). Automatically adjusts to variation in valve stem length. Hydraulic tappets also reduce valve noise.

I

Ignition timing The moment at which the spark plug fires, usually expressed in the number of crankshaft degrees before the piston reaches the top of its stroke.

Inlet manifold A tube or housing with passages through which flows the air-fuel mixture (carburettor vehicles and vehicles with throttle body injection) or air only (port fuel-injected vehicles) to the port openings in the cylinder head.

J

Jump start Starting the engine of a vehicle with a discharged or weak battery by attaching jump leads from the weak battery to a charged or helper battery.

L

Load Sensing Proportioning Valve (LSPV) A brake hydraulic system control valve that works like a proportioning valve, but also takes into consideration the amount of weight carried by the rear axle.

Locknut A nut used to lock an adjustment nut, or other threaded component, in place. For example, a locknut is employed to keep the adjusting nut on the rocker arm in position.

Lockwasher A form of washer designed to prevent an attaching nut from working loose.

M

MacPherson strut A type of front suspension system devised by Earle MacPherson at Ford of England. In its original form, a simple lateral link with the anti-roll bar creates the lower control arm. A long strut - an integral coil spring and shock absorber - is mounted between the body and the steering knuckle. Many modern so-called MacPherson strut systems use a conventional lower A-arm and don't rely on the anti-roll bar for location.

Multimeter An electrical test instrument with the capability to measure voltage, current and resistance.

N

NOx Oxides of Nitrogen. A common toxic pollutant emitted by petrol and diesel engines at higher temperatures.

O

Ohm The unit of electrical resistance. One volt applied to a resistance of one ohm will produce a current of one amp.

Ohmmeter An instrument for measuring electrical resistance.

O-ring A type of sealing ring made of a special rubber-like material; in use, the O-ring is compressed into a groove to provide the sealing action.

Overhead cam (ohc) engine An engine with the camshaft(s) located on top of the cylinder head(s).

Overhead valve (ohv) engine An engine with the valves located in the cylinder head, but with the camshaft located in the engine block.

Oxygen sensor A device installed in the engine exhaust manifold, which senses the oxygen content in the exhaust and converts this information into an electric current. Also called a Lambda sensor.

P

Phillips screw A type of screw head having a cross instead of a slot for a corresponding type of screwdriver.

Plastigage A thin strip of plastic thread, available in different sizes, used for measuring clearances. For example, a strip of Plastigage is laid across a bearing journal. The parts are assembled and dismantled; the width of the crushed strip indicates the clearance between journal and bearing.

Plastigage

Propeller shaft The long hollow tube with universal joints at both ends that carries power from the transmission to the differential on front-engined rear wheel drive vehicles.

Proportioning valve A hydraulic control valve which limits the amount of pressure to the rear brakes during panic stops to prevent wheel lock-up.

R

Rack-and-pinion steering A steering system with a pinion gear on the end of the steering shaft that mates with a rack (think of a geared wheel opened up and laid flat). When the steering wheel is turned, the pinion turns, moving the rack to the left or right. This movement is transmitted through the track rods to the steering arms at the wheels.

Radiator A liquid-to-air heat transfer device designed to reduce the temperature of the coolant in an internal combustion engine cooling system.

Refrigerant Any substance used as a heat transfer agent in an air-conditioning system. R-12 has been the principle refrigerant for many years; recently, however, manufacturers have begun using R-134a, a non-CFC substance that is considered less harmful to the ozone in the upper atmosphere.

Rocker arm A lever arm that rocks on a shaft or pivots on a stud. In an overhead valve engine, the rocker arm converts the upward movement of the pushrod into a downward movement to open a valve.

Rotor In a distributor, the rotating device inside the cap that connects the centre electrode and the outer terminals as it turns, distributing the high voltage from the coil secondary winding to the proper spark plug. Also, that part of an alternator which rotates inside the stator. Also, the rotating assembly of a turbocharger, including the compressor wheel, shaft and turbine wheel.
Runout The amount of wobble (in-and-out movement) of a gear or wheel as it's rotated. The amount a shaft rotates "out-of-true." The out-of-round condition of a rotating part.

S

Sealant A liquid or paste used to prevent leakage at a joint. Sometimes used in conjunction with a gasket.
Sealed beam lamp An older headlight design which integrates the reflector, lens and filaments into a hermetically-sealed one-piece unit. When a filament burns out or the lens cracks, the entire unit is simply replaced.
Serpentine drivebelt A single, long, wide accessory drivebelt that's used on some newer vehicles to drive all the accessories, instead of a series of smaller, shorter belts. Serpentine drivebelts are usually tensioned by an automatic tensioner.

Serpentine drivebelt

Shim Thin spacer, commonly used to adjust the clearance or relative positions between two parts. For example, shims inserted into or under bucket tappets control valve clearances. Clearance is adjusted by changing the thickness of the shim.
Slide hammer A special puller that screws into or hooks onto a component such as a shaft or bearing; a heavy sliding handle on the shaft bottoms against the end of the shaft to knock the component free.
Sprocket A tooth or projection on the periphery of a wheel, shaped to engage with a chain or drivebelt. Commonly used to refer to the sprocket wheel itself.
Starter inhibitor switch On vehicles with an automatic transmission, a switch that prevents starting if the vehicle is not in Neutral or Park.
Strut See MacPherson strut.

T

Tappet A cylindrical component which transmits motion from the cam to the valve stem, either directly or via a pushrod and rocker arm. Also called a cam follower.
Thermostat A heat-controlled valve that regulates the flow of coolant between the cylinder block and the radiator, so maintaining optimum engine operating temperature. A thermostat is also used in some air cleaners in which the temperature is regulated.
Thrust bearing The bearing in the clutch assembly that is moved in to the release levers by clutch pedal action to disengage the clutch. Also referred to as a release bearing.
Timing belt A toothed belt which drives the camshaft. Serious engine damage may result if it breaks in service.
Timing chain A chain which drives the camshaft.
Toe-in The amount the front wheels are closer together at the front than at the rear. On rear wheel drive vehicles, a slight amount of toe-in is usually specified to keep the front wheels running parallel on the road by offsetting other forces that tend to spread the wheels apart.
Toe-out The amount the front wheels are closer together at the rear than at the front. On front wheel drive vehicles, a slight amount of toe-out is usually specified.
Tools For full information on choosing and using tools, refer to the *Haynes Automotive Tools Manual.*
Tracer A stripe of a second colour applied to a wire insulator to distinguish that wire from another one with the same colour insulator.
Tune-up A process of accurate and careful adjustments and parts replacement to obtain the best possible engine performance.
Turbocharger A centrifugal device, driven by exhaust gases, that pressurises the intake air. Normally used to increase the power output from a given engine displacement, but can also be used primarily to reduce exhaust emissions (as on VW's "Umwelt" Diesel engine).

U

Universal joint or U-joint A double-pivoted connection for transmitting power from a driving to a driven shaft through an angle. A U-joint consists of two Y-shaped yokes and a cross-shaped member called the spider.

V

Valve A device through which the flow of liquid, gas, vacuum, or loose material in bulk may be started, stopped, or regulated by a movable part that opens, shuts, or partially obstructs one or more ports or passageways. A valve is also the movable part of such a device.
Valve clearance The clearance between the valve tip (the end of the valve stem) and the rocker arm or tappet. The valve clearance is measured when the valve is closed.
Vernier caliper A precision measuring instrument that measures inside and outside dimensions. Not quite as accurate as a micrometer, but more convenient.
Viscosity The thickness of a liquid or its resistance to flow.
Volt A unit for expressing electrical "pressure" in a circuit. One volt that will produce a current of one ampere through a resistance of one ohm.

W

Welding Various processes used to join metal items by heating the areas to be joined to a molten state and fusing them together. For more information refer to the *Haynes Automotive Welding Manual.*
Wiring diagram A drawing portraying the components and wires in a vehicle's electrical system, using standardised symbols. For more information refer to the *Haynes Automotive Electrical and Electronic Systems Manual.*

Note: *References throughout this index are in the form* **"Chapter number" • "Page number"**. *So, for example, 2•15 refers to page 15 of Chapter 2.*

Note: *References throughout this index are in the form* **"Chapter number"** • **"Page number"**. *So, for example, 2•15 refers to page 15 of Chapter 2.*

Note: *References throughout this index are in the form* **"Chapter number" • "Page number"**. *So, for example, 2•15 refers to page 15 of Chapter 2.*

Note: *References throughout this index are in the form* **"Chapter number" • "Page number"**. *So, for example, 2•15 refers to page 15 of Chapter 2.*

P

R

S

T

Note: *References throughout this index are in the form* **"Chapter number" • "Page number"**. *So, for example, 2•15 refers to page 15 of Chapter 2.*

Haynes Manuals – The Complete List

Title	Book No.
ALFA ROMEO Alfasud/Sprint (74 - 88) up to F *	**0292**
Alfa Romeo Alfetta (73 - 87) up to E *	**0531**
AUDI 80, 90 & Coupe Petrol (79 - Nov 88) up to F	**0605**
Audi 80, 90 & Coupe Petrol (Oct 86 - 90) D to H	**1491**
Audi 100 & 200 Petrol (Oct 82 - 90) up to H	**0907**
Audi 100 & A6 Petrol & Diesel (May 91 - May 97) H to P	**3504**
Audi A3 (96 - May 03) P to 03	**4253**
Audi A4 Petrol & Diesel (95 - Feb 00) M to V	**3575**
AUSTIN A35 & A40 (56 - 67) up to F *	**0118**
Austin/MG/Rover Maestro 1.3 & 1.6 Petrol (83 - 95) up to M	**0922**
Austin/MG Metro (80 - May 90) up to G	**0718**
Austin/Rover Montego 1.3 & 1.6 Petrol (84 - 94) A to L	**1066**
Austin/MG/Rover Montego 2.0 Petrol (84 - 95) A to M	**1067**
Mini (59 - 69) up to H *	**0527**
Mini (69 - 01) up to X	**0646**
Austin/Rover 2.0 litre Diesel Engine (86-93) C to L	**1857**
AUSTIN HEALEY 100/6 & 3000 (56 - 68) up to G *	**0049**
BEDFORD CF Petrol (69 - 87) up to E	**0163**
Bedford/Vauxhall Rascal & Suzuki Supercarry (86 - Oct 94) C to M	**3015**
BMW 316, 320 & 320i (4-cyl) (75 - Feb 83) up to Y *	**0276**
BMW 320, 320i, 323i & 325i (6-cyl) (Oct 77 - Sept 87) up to E	**0815**
BMW 3- & 5-Series Petrol (81 - 91) up to J	**1948**
BMW 3-Series Petrol (Apr 91 - 96) H to N	**3210**
BMW 3-Series Petrol (Sept 98 - 03) S-reg. on	**4067**
BMW 520i & 525e (Oct 81 - June 88) up to E	**1560**
BMW 525, 528 & 528i (73 - Sept 81) up to X *	**0632**
BMW 5-Series Petrol (April 96 - Aug 03) N to 03	**4151**
BMW 1500, 1502, 1600, 1602, 2000 & 2002 (59 - 77) up to S *	**0240**
CHRYSLER PT Cruiser Petrol (00 - 03) W-reg. onwards	**4058**
CITROËN 2CV, Ami & Dyane (67 - 90) up to H	**0196**
Citroën AX Petrol & Diesel (87 - 97) D to P	**3014**
Citroën BX Petrol (83 - 94) A to L	**0908**
Citroën C15 Van Petrol & Diesel (89 - Oct 98) F to S	**3509**
Citroën C3 (02 - 05) 51 to 05	**4197**
Citroën CX Petrol (75 - 88) up to F	**0528**
Citroën Saxo Petrol & Diesel (96 - 01) N to X	**3506**
Citroën Visa Petrol (79 - 88) up to F	**0620**
Citroën Xantia Petrol & Diesel (93 - 01) K to Y	**3082**
Citroën XM Petrol & Diesel (89 - 00) G to X	**3451**
Citroën Xsara Petrol & Diesel (97 - Sept 00) R to W	**3751**
Citroën Xsara Picasso Petrol & Diesel (00 - 02) W-reg. onwards	**3944**
Citroën ZX Diesel (91 - 98) J to S	**1922**
Citroën ZX Petrol (91 - 98) H to S	**1881**
Citroën 1.7 & 1.9 litre Diesel Engine (84 - 96) A to N	**1379**
FIAT 126 (73 - 87) up to E *	**0305**
Fiat 500 (57 - 73) up to M *	**0090**
Fiat Bravo & Brava Petrol (95 - 00) N to W	**3572**
Fiat Cinquecento (93 - 98) K to R	**3501**
Fiat Panda (81 - 95) up to M	**0793**
Fiat Punto Petrol & Diesel (94 - Oct 99) L to V	**3251**
Fiat Punto Petrol (Oct 99 - July 03) V-reg onwards	**4066**
Fiat Regata Petrol (84 - 88) A to F	**1167**
Fiat Tipo Petrol (88 - 91) E to J	**1625**
Fiat Uno Petrol (83 - 95) up to M	**0923**
Fiat X1/9 (74 - 89) up to G *	**0273**
FORD Anglia (59 - 68) up to G *	**0001**
Ford Capri II (& III) 1.6 & 2.0 (74 - 87) up to E *	**0283**
Ford Capri II (& III) 2.8 & 3.0 V6 (74 - 87) up to E	**1309**
Ford Cortina Mk III 1300 & 1600 (70 - 76) up to P *	**0070**
Ford Escort Mk I 1100 & 1300 (68 - 74) up to N *	**0171**
Ford Escort Mk I Mexico, RS 1600 & RS 2000 (70 - 74) up to N *	**0139**
Ford Escort Mk II Mexico, RS 1800 & RS 2000 (75 - 80) up to W *	**0735**
Ford Escort (75 - Aug 80) up to V *	**0280**
Ford Escort Petrol (Sept 80 - Sept 90) up to H	**0686**
Ford Escort & Orion Petrol (Sept 90 - 00) H to X	**1737**
Ford Escort & Orion Diesel (Sept 90 - 00) H to X	**4081**
Ford Fiesta (76 - Aug 83) up to Y	**0334**
Ford Fiesta Petrol (Aug 83 - Feb 89) A to F	**1030**
Ford Fiesta Petrol (Feb 89 - Oct 95) F to N	**1595**
Ford Fiesta Petrol & Diesel (Oct 95 - Mar 02) N to 02	**3397**
Ford Fiesta Petrol & Diesel (Apr 02 - 05) 02 to 54	**4170**
Ford Focus Petrol & Diesel (98 - 01) S to Y	**3759**
Ford Focus Petrol & Diesel (Oct 01 - 04) 51 to 54 reg.	**4167**
Ford Galaxy Petrol & Diesel (95 - Aug 00) M to W	**3984**
Ford Granada Petrol (Sept 77 - Feb 85) up to B *	**0481**
Ford Granada & Scorpio Petrol (Mar 85 - 94) B to M	**1245**
Ford Ka (96 - 02) P-reg. onwards	**3570**
Ford Mondeo Petrol (93 - Sept 00) K to X	**1923**
Ford Mondeo Petrol & Diesel (Oct 00 - Jul 03) X to 03	**3990**
Ford Mondeo Diesel (93 - 96) L to N	**3465**
Ford Orion Petrol (83 - Sept 90) up to H	**1009**
Ford Sierra 4-cyl Petrol (82 - 93) up to K	**0903**
Ford Sierra V6 Petrol (82 - 91) up to J	**0904**
Ford Transit Petrol (Mk 2) (78 - Jan 86) up to C	**0719**
Ford Transit Petrol (Mk 3) (Feb 86 - 89) C to G	**1468**
Ford Transit Diesel (Feb 86 - 99) C to T	**3019**
Ford 1.6 & 1.8 litre Diesel Engine (84 - 96) A to N	**1172**
Ford 2.1, 2.3 & 2.5 litre Diesel Engine (77 - 90) up to H	**1606**
FREIGHT ROVER Sherpa Petrol (74 - 87) up to E	**0463**
HILLMAN Avenger (70 - 82) up to Y	**0037**
Hillman Imp (63 - 76) up to R *	**0022**
HONDA Civic (Feb 84 - Oct 87) A to E	**1226**
Honda Civic (Nov 91 - 96) J to N	**3199**
Honda Civic Petrol (Mar 95 - 00) M to X	**4050**
HYUNDAI Pony (85 - 94) C to M	**3398**
JAGUAR E Type (61 - 72) up to L *	**0140**
Jaguar MkI & II, 240 & 340 (55 - 69) up to H *	**0098**
Jaguar XJ6, XJ & Sovereign; Daimler Sovereign (68 - Oct 86) up to D	**0242**
Jaguar XJ6 & Sovereign (Oct 86 - Sept 94) D to M	**3261**
Jaguar XJ12, XJS & Sovereign; Daimler Double Six (72 - 88) up to F	**0478**
JEEP Cherokee Petrol (93 - 96) K to N	**1943**
LADA 1200, 1300, 1500 & 1600 (74 - 91) up to J	**0413**
Lada Samara (87 - 91) D to J	**1610**
LAND ROVER 90, 110 & Defender Diesel (83 - 95) up to N	**3017**
Land Rover Discovery Petrol & Diesel (89 - 98) G to S	**3016**
Land Rover Freelander Petrol & Diesel (97 - 02) R-reg. onwards	**3929**
Land Rover Series IIA & III Diesel (58 - 85) up to C	**0529**
Land Rover Series II, IIA & III 4-cyl Petrol (58 - 85) up to C	**0314**
MAZDA 323 (Mar 81 - Oct 89) up to G	**1608**
Mazda 323 (Oct 89 - 98) G to R	**3455**
Mazda 626 (May 83 - Sept 87) up to E	**0929**
Mazda B1600, B1800 & B2000 Pick-up Petrol (72 - 88) up to F	**0267**
Mazda RX-7 (79 - 85) up to C *	**0460**
MERCEDES-BENZ 190, 190E & 190D Petrol & Diesel (83 - 93) A to L	**3450**
Mercedes-Benz 200D, 240D, 240TD, 300D & 300TD 123 Series Diesel (Oct 76 - 85) up to C	**1114**
Mercedes-Benz 250 & 280 (68 - 72) up to L *	**0346**
Mercedes-Benz 250 & 280 123 Series Petrol (Oct 76 - 84) up to B *	**0677**
Mercedes-Benz 124 Series Petrol & Diesel (85 - Aug 93) C to K	**3253**
Mercedes-Benz C-Class Petrol & Diesel (93 - Aug 00) L to W	**3511**
MGA (55 - 62) *	**0475**
MGB (62 - 80) up to W	**0111**
MG Midget & Austin-Healey Sprite (58 - 80) up to W *	**0265**
MITSUBISHI Shogun & L200 Pick-Ups Petrol (83 - 94) up to M	**1944**
MORRIS Ital 1.3 (80 - 84) up to B	**0705**
Morris Minor 1000 (56 - 71) up to K	**0024**
NISSAN Almera Petrol (95 - Feb 00) N to V	**4053**
Nissan Bluebird (May 84 - Mar 86) A to C	**1223**
Nissan Bluebird Petrol (Mar 86 - 90) C to H	**1473**
Nissan Cherry (Sept 82 - 86) up to D	**1031**
Nissan Micra (83 - Jan 93) up to K	**0931**
Nissan Micra (93 - 99) K to T	**3254**
Nissan Primera Petrol (90 - Aug 99) H to T	**1851**
Nissan Stanza (82 - 86) up to D	**0824**
Nissan Sunny Petrol (May 82 - Oct 86) up to D	**0895**
Nissan Sunny Petrol (Oct 86 - Mar 91) D to H	**1378**
Nissan Sunny Petrol (Apr 91 - 95) H to N	**3219**
OPEL Ascona & Manta (B Series) (Sept 75 - 88) up to F *	**0316**
Opel Ascona Petrol (81 - 88)	**3215**
Opel Astra Petrol (Oct 91 - Feb 98)	**3156**
Opel Corsa Petrol (83 - Mar 93)	**3160**
Opel Corsa Petrol (Mar 93 - 97)	**3159**
Opel Kadett Petrol (Nov 79 - Oct 84) up to B	**0634**
Opel Kadett Petrol (Oct 84 - Oct 91)	**3196**
Opel Omega & Senator Petrol (Nov 86 - 94)	**3157**
Opel Rekord Petrol (Feb 78 - Oct 86) up to D	**0543**
Opel Vectra Petrol (Oct 88 - Oct 95)	**3158**
PEUGEOT 106 Petrol & Diesel (91 - 02) J-reg. onwards	**1882**
Peugeot 205 Petrol (83 - 97) A to P	**0932**
Peugeot 206 Petrol & Diesel (98 - 01) S to X	**3757**
Peugeot 306 Petrol & Diesel (93 - 99) K to T	**3073**
Peugeot 307 Petrol & Diesel (01 - 04) Y-reg. onwards	**4147**
Peugeot 309 Petrol (86 - 93) C to K	**1266**

* Classic reprint

Title	Book No.
Peugeot 405 Petrol (88 - 97) E to P	**1559**
Peugeot 405 Diesel (88 - 97) E to P	**3198**
Peugeot 406 Petrol & Diesel (96 - Mar 99) N to T	**3394**
Peugeot 406 Petrol & Diesel (Mar 99-02) T-reg. on	**3982**
Peugeot 505 Petrol (79 - 89) up to G	**0762**
Peugeot 1.7/1.8 & 1.9 litre Diesel Engine (82 - 96) up to N	**0950**
Peugeot 2.0, 2.1, 2.3 & 2.5 litre Diesel Engines (74 - 90) up to H	**1607**
PORSCHE 911 (65 - 85) up to C	**0264**
Porsche 924 & 924 Turbo (76 - 85) up to C	**0397**
PROTON (89 - 97) F to P	**3255**
RANGE ROVER V8 Petrol (70 - Oct 92) up to K	**0606**
RELIANT Robin & Kitten (73 - 83) up to A *	**0436**
RENAULT 4 (61 - 86) up to D *	**0072**
Renault 5 Petrol (Feb 85 - 96) B to N	**1219**
Renault 9 & 11 Petrol (82 - 89) up to F	**0822**
Renault 18 Petrol (79 - 86) up to D	**0598**
Renault 19 Petrol (89 - 96) F to N	**1646**
Renault 19 Diesel (89 - 96) F to N	**1946**
Renault 21 Petrol (86 - 94) C to M	**1397**
Renault 25 Petrol & Diesel (84 - 92) B to K	**1228**
Renault Clio Petrol (91 - May 98) H to R	**1853**
Renault Clio Diesel (91 - June 96) H to N	**3031**
Renault Clio Petrol & Diesel (May 98 - May 01) R to Y	**3906**
Renault Clio Petrol & Diesel (June 01 - 04) Y-reg. onwards	**4168**
Renault Espace Petrol & Diesel (85 - 96) C to N	**3197**
Renault Laguna Petrol & Diesel (94 - 00) L to W	**3252**
Renault Mégane & Scénic Petrol & Diesel (96 - 98) N to R	**3395**
Renault Mégane & Scénic Petrol & Diesel (Apr 99 - 02) T-reg. onwards	**3916**
ROVER 213 & 216 (84 - 89) A to G	**1116**
Rover 214 & 414 Petrol (89 - 96) G to N	**1689**
Rover 216 & 416 Petrol (89 - 96) G to N	**1830**
Rover 211, 214, 216, 218 & 220 Petrol & Diesel (Dec 95 - 99) N to V	**3399**
Rover 25 & MG ZR Petrol & Diesel (Oct 99 - 04) V-reg. onwards	**4145**
Rover 414, 416 & 420 Petrol & Diesel (May 95 - 98) M to R	**3453**
Rover 618, 620 & 623 Petrol (93 - 97) K to P	**3257**
Rover 820, 825 & 827 Petrol (86 - 95) D to N	**1380**
Rover 3500 (76 - 87) up to E *	**0365**
Rover Metro, 111 & 114 Petrol (May 90 - 98) G to S	**1711**
SAAB 95 & 96 (66 - 76) up to R *	**0198**
Saab 90, 99 & 900 (79 - Oct 93) up to L	**0765**
Saab 900 (Oct 93 - 98) L to R	**3512**
Saab 9000 (4-cyl) (85 - 98) C to S	**1686**
Saab 9-5 4-cyl Petrol (97 - 04) R-reg onwards	**4156**
SEAT Ibiza & Cordoba Petrol & Diesel (Oct 93 - Oct 99) L to V	**3571**
Seat Ibiza & Malaga Petrol (85 - 92) B to K	**1609**
SKODA Estelle (77 - 89) up to G	**0604**
Skoda Favorit (89 - 96) F to N	**1801**
Skoda Felicia Petrol & Diesel (95 - 01) M to X	**3505**
SUBARU 1600 & 1800 (Nov 79 - 90) up to H *	**0995**
SUNBEAM Alpine, Rapier & H120 (67 - 74) to N *	**0051**
SUZUKI SJ Series, Samurai & Vitara (4-cyl) Petrol (82 - 97) up to P	**1942**
TALBOT Alpine, Solara, Minx & Rapier (75 - 86) up to D	**0337**

Title	Book No.
Talbot Horizon Petrol (78 - 86) up to D	**0473**
Talbot Samba (82 - 86) up to D	**0823**
TOYOTA Carina E Petrol (May 92 - 97) J to P	**3256**
Toyota Corolla (80 - 85) up to C	**0683**
Toyota Corolla (Sept 83 - Sept 87) A to E	**1024**
Toyota Corolla (Sept 87 - Aug 92) E to K	**1683**
Toyota Corolla Petrol (Aug 92 - 97) K to P	**3259**
Toyota Hi-Ace & Hi-Lux Petrol (69 - Oct 83) to A	**0304**
TRIUMPH GT6 & Vitesse (62 - 74) up to N *	**0112**
Triumph Herald (59 - 71) up to K *	**0010**
Triumph Spitfire (62 - 81) up to X	**0113**
Triumph Stag (70 - 78) up to T *	**0441**
Triumph TR2, TR3, TR3A, TR4 & TR4A (52 - 67) up to F *	**0028**
Triumph TR5 & 6 (67 - 75) up to P *	**0031**
Triumph TR7 (75 - 82) up to Y *	**0322**
VAUXHALL Astra Petrol (80 - Oct 84) up to B	**0635**
Vauxhall Astra & Belmont Petrol (Oct 84 - Oct 91) B to J	**1136**
Vauxhall Astra Petrol (Oct 91 - Feb 98) J to R	**1832**
Vauxhall/Opel Astra & Zafira Petrol (Feb 98 - Apr 04) R-reg onwards	**3758**
Vauxhall/Opel Astra & Zafira Diesel (Feb 98 - Apr 04) R-reg onwards	**3797**
Vauxhall/Opel Calibra (90 - 98) G to S	**3502**
Vauxhall Carlton Petrol (Oct 78 - Oct 86) up to D	**0480**
Vauxhall Carlton & Senator Petrol (Nov 86 - 94) D to L	**1469**
Vauxhall Cavalier Petrol (81 - Oct 88) up to F	**0812**
Vauxhall Cavalier Petrol (Oct 88 - 95) F to N	**1570**
Vauxhall Chevette (75 - 84) up to B	**0285**
Vauxhall/Opel Corsa Diesel (Mar 93 - Oct 00) K to X	**4087**
Vauxhall Corsa Petrol (Mar 93 - 97) K to R	**1985**
Vauxhall/Opel Corsa Petrol (Apr 97 - Oct 00) P to X	**3921**
Vauxhall/Opel Corsa Petrol & Diesel (Oct 00 - Sept 03) X-reg onwards	**4079**
Vauxhall/Opel Frontera Petrol & Diesel (91 - Sept 98) J to S	**3454**
Vauxhall Nova Petrol (83 - 93) up to K	**0909**
Vauxhall/Opel Omega Petrol (94 - 99) L to T	**3510**
Vauxhall/Opel Vectra Petrol & Diesel (95 - Feb 99) N to S	**3396**
Vauxhall/Opel Vectra Petrol & Diesel (Mar 99 - May 02) T-reg. onwards	**3930**
Vauxhall/Opel 1.5, 1.6 & 1.7 litre Diesel Engine (82 - 96) up to N	**1222**
VOLKSWAGEN 411 & 412 (68 - 75) up to P *	**0091**
Volkswagen Beetle 1200 (54 - 77) up to S	**0036**
Volkswagen Beetle 1300 & 1500 (65 - 75) up to P	**0039**
Volkswagen Beetle 1302 & 1302S (70 - 72) up to L *	**0110**
Volkswagen Beetle 1303, 1303S & GT (72 - 75) up to P	**0159**
Volkswagen Beetle Petrol & Diesel (Apr 99 - 01) T-reg. onwards	**3798**
Volkswagen Golf & Bora Petrol & Diesel (April 98 - 00) R to X	**3727**
Volkswagen Golf & Jetta Mk 1 Petrol 1.1 & 1.3 (74 - 84) up to A	**0716**
Volkswagen Golf, Jetta & Scirocco Mk 1 Petrol 1.5, 1.6 & 1.8 (74 - 84) up to A	**0726**
Volkswagen Golf & Jetta Mk 1 Diesel (78 - 84) up to A	**0451**

Title	Book No.
Volkswagen Golf & Jetta Mk 2 Petrol (Mar 84 - Feb 92) A to J	**1081**
Volkswagen Golf & Vento Petrol & Diesel (Feb 92 - Mar 98) J to R	**3097**
Volkswagen Golf & Bora 4-cyl Petrol & Diesel (01 - 03) X to 53	**4169**
Volkswagen LT Petrol Vans & Light Trucks (76 - 87) up to E	**0637**
Volkswagen Passat & Santana Petrol (Sept 81 - May 88) up to E	**0814**
Volkswagen Passat 4-cyl Petrol & Diesel (May 88 - 96) E to P	**3498**
Volkswagen Passat 4-cyl Petrol & Diesel (Dec 96 - Nov 00) P to X	**3917**
Volkswagen Polo & Derby (76 - Jan 82) up to X	**0335**
Volkswagen Polo (82 - Oct 90) up to H	**0813**
Volkswagen Polo Petrol (Nov 90 - Aug 94) H to L	**3245**
Volkswagen Polo Hatchback Petrol & Diesel (94 - 99) M to S	**3500**
Volkswagen Polo Hatchback Petrol (00 - Jan 02) V to 51	**4150**
Volkswagen Scirocco (82 - 90) up to H *	**1224**
Volkswagen Transporter 1600 (68 - 79) up to V	**0082**
Volkswagen Transporter 1700, 1800 & 2000 (72 - 79) up to V *	**0226**
Volkswagen Transporter (air-cooled) Petrol (79 - 82) up to Y *	**0638**
Volkswagen Transporter (water-cooled) Petrol (82 - 90) up to H	**3452**
Volkswagen Type 3 (63 - 73) up to M *	**0084**
VOLVO 120 & 130 Series (& P1800) (61 - 73) up to M *	**0203**
Volvo 142, 144 & 145 (66 - 74) up to N *	**0129**
Volvo 240 Series Petrol (74 - 93) up to K	**0270**
Volvo 262, 264 & 260/265 (75 - 85) up to C *	**0400**
Volvo 340, 343, 345 & 360 (76 - 91) up to J	**0715**
Volvo 440, 460 & 480 Petrol (87 - 97) D to P	**1691**
Volvo 740 & 760 Petrol (82 - 91) up to J	**1258**
Volvo 850 Petrol (92 - 96) J to P	**3260**
Volvo 940 Petrol (90 - 96) H to N	**3249**
Volvo S40 & V40 Petrol (96 - Mar 04) N-reg. onwards	**3569**
Volvo S70, V70 & C70 Petrol (96 - 99) P to V	**3573**

AUTOMOTIVE TECHBOOKS

Title	Book No.
Automotive Air Conditioning Systems	**3740**
Automotive Electrical and Electronic Systems	**3049**
Automotive Gearbox Overhaul Manual	**3473**
Automotive Service Summaries Manual	**3475**
Automotive Timing Belts Manual - Austin/Rover	**3549**
Automotive Timing Belts Manual - Ford	**3474**
Automotive Timing Belts Manual - Peugeot/Citroën	**3568**
Automotive Timing Belts Manual - Vauxhall/Opel	**3577**

DIY MANUAL SERIES

Title	Book No.
Haynes Manual on Bodywork	**4198**
Haynes Manual on Brakes	**4178**
Haynes Manual on Carburettors	**4177**
Haynes Manual on Diesel Engines	**4174**
Haynes Manual on Engine Management	**4199**
Haynes Manual on Fault Codes	**4175**
Haynes Manual on Practical Electrical Systems	**4267**
Haynes Manual on Small Engines	**4250**
Haynes Manual on Welding	**4176**

* Classic reprint

Preserving Our Motoring Heritage

<
The Model J Duesenberg Derham Tourster. Only eight of these magnificent cars were ever built – this is the only example to be found outside the United States of America

Almost every car you've ever loved, loathed or desired is gathered under one roof at the Haynes Motor Museum. Over 300 immaculately presented cars and motorbikes represent every aspect of our motoring heritage, from elegant reminders of bygone days, such as the superb Model J Duesenberg to curiosities like the bug-eyed BMW Isetta. There are also many old friends and flames. Perhaps you remember the 1959 Ford Popular that you did your courting in? The magnificent 'Red Collection' is a spectacle of classic sports cars including AC, Alfa Romeo, Austin Healey, Ferrari, Lamborghini, Maserati, MG, Riley, Porsche and Triumph.

A Perfect Day Out

Each and every vehicle at the Haynes Motor Museum has played its part in the history and culture of Motoring. Today, they make a wonderful spectacle and a great day out for all the family. Bring the kids, bring Mum and Dad, but above all bring your camera to capture those golden memories for ever. You will also find an impressive array of motoring memorabilia, a comfortable 70 seat video cinema and one of the most extensive transport book shops in Britain. The Pit Stop Cafe serves everything from a cup of tea to wholesome, home-made meals or, if you prefer, you can enjoy the large picnic area nestled in the beautiful rural surroundings of Somerset.

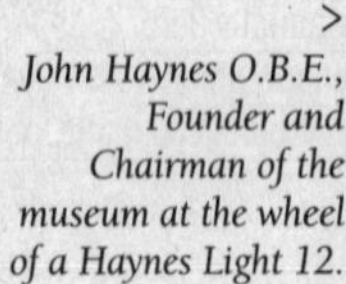

>
John Haynes O.B.E., Founder and Chairman of the museum at the wheel of a Haynes Light 12.

<
Graham Hill's Lola Cosworth Formula 1 car next to a 1934 Riley Sports.

The Museum is situated on the A359 Yeovil to Frome road at Sparkford, just off the A303 in Somerset. It is about 40 miles south of Bristol, and 25 minutes drive from the M5 intersection at Taunton.

Open 9.30am - 5.30pm (10.00am - 4.00pm Winter) 7 days a week, *except Christmas Day, Boxing Day and New Years Day*

Special rates available for schools, coach parties and outings Charitable Trust No. 292048